T0178330

Lecture Notes in Computer Science

Lecture Notes in Artificial Intelligence 13796

Founding Editor

Jörg Siekmann

Series Editors

Randy Goebel, *University of Alberta, Edmonton, Canada*
Wolfgang Wahlster, *DFKI, Berlin, Germany*
Zhi-Hua Zhou, *Nanjing University, Nanjing, China*

The series Lecture Notes in Artificial Intelligence (LNAI) was established in 1988 as a topical subseries of LNCS devoted to artificial intelligence.

The series publishes state-of-the-art research results at a high level. As with the LNCS mother series, the mission of the series is to serve the international R & D community by providing an invaluable service, mainly focused on the publication of conference and workshop proceedings and postproceedings.

Agostino Dovier · Angelo Montanari ·
Andrea Orlandini
Editors

AIxIA 2022 –
Advances in
Artificial Intelligence

XXIst International Conference
of the Italian Association for Artificial Intelligence
AIxIA 2022, Udine, Italy, November 28 – December 2, 2022
Proceedings

 Springer

Editors
Agostino Dovier [iD]
University of Udine
Udine, Italy

Angelo Montanari [iD]
University of Udine
Udine, Italy

Andrea Orlandini [iD]
National Research Council (CNR-ISTC)
Rome, Italy

ISSN 0302-9743   ISSN 1611-3349 (electronic)
Lecture Notes in Artificial Intelligence
ISBN 978-3-031-27180-9   ISBN 978-3-031-27181-6 (eBook)
https://doi.org/10.1007/978-3-031-27181-6

LNCS Sublibrary: SL7 – Artificial Intelligence

This Springer imprint is published by the registered company Springer Nature Switzerland AG
The registered company address is: Gewerbestrasse 11, 6330 Cham, Switzerland

Preface

This volume contains the proceeding of the 21st International Conference of the Italian Association for Artificial Intelligence, referred to for short as AIxIA. AIxIA is very active in organizing scientific initiatives as well as events for the dissemination of Artificial Intelligence in industry, society, and schools. Among these activities, a scientific international conference has been organized every two years since 1991 and then yearly since 2015. In the last two years, due to the Covid-19 pandemic, the conference was organized in remote mode in Torino and Milano (LNCS 13196 and 12414). Previously, it was organized as a standard conference in Rende (2019: LNCS 11946), Trento (2018: LNCS 11298), Bari (2017: LNCS 10640), Genova (2016: LNCS 10037), Ferrara (2015: LNCS 9336), Torino (2013: LNCS 8249), Palermo (2011, LNCS 6934), Reggio Emilia (2009: LNCS 5883), Roma (2007: LNCS 4733), Milano (2005: LNCS 3673), Pisa (2003: LNCS 2929), Bari (2001: LNCS 2175), Bologna (1999: LNCS 1792), Roma (1997: LNCS 1321), Firenze (1995: LNCS 992), Torino (1993: LNCS 728), Palermo (1991: LNCS 549), and Trento (1989).

The recent positive evolution of the pandemic disease allowed us to take the risk of organizing an attended conference. This seems to have been much appreciated by the community as more than 350 people attended the meeting.

As for the numbers, 54 research papers were submitted to the conference and evaluated by at least three reviewers; moreover, 29 *discussion papers* were submitted and 16 were selected for presentation at the conference. 227 authors were involved, 155 from Italy, 13 from France, 12 from USA, 8 from India, 7 from UK, and 32 from other countries. Among the regular papers, 33 papers were selected for publication in these proceedings.

The conference program included two prestigious keynote speakers, namely: Subbarao Kambhampati (Arizona State University): Symbols as a Lingua Franca for Supporting Human-AI Interaction For Explainable and Advisable AI Systems; Georg Gottlob (University of Oxford): My adventures with Datalog: Walking the thin line between theory and practice (with a paper also included in the proceedings). In addition, it offered three tutorials on hot research topics: Ferdinando Fioretto (Syracuse University): End-to-end constrained optimization learning; Antonio Lieto (University of Turin): Cognitive Design for Artificial Minds; Angelo Oddi, Riccardo Rasconi (CNR-ISTC, Rome), and Marco Baioletti (University of Perugia): Quantum computing and planning.

AIxIA 2022 also covered many aspects of theoretical and applied AI through 17 co-located workshops devoted to specific topics and bringing together the corresponding AI communities. The workshops chairs were Andrea Formisano and Alberto Finzi. Thus, in parallel to the main program, the conference features the following workshops, for a total of 175 accepted regular papers, plus a number of invited talks:

- 6th Workshop on Advances in Argumentation in Artificial Intelligence;
- 11th Workshop on Machine Learning and Data Mining;

- 4th Workshop on Artificial Intelligence and fOrmal VERification, Logic, Automata, and sYnthesis;
- 1st Workshop on Artificial Intelligence for Cultural Heritage;
- 1st Workshop on Artificial Intelligence and Creativity;
- 3rd Italian Workshop on Artificial Intelligence for an Ageing Society;
- R.i.C.e.R.c.A: RCRA Incontri E Confronti;
- 10th Italian Workshop on Planning and Scheduling;
- 9th Italian Workshop on Artificial Intelligence and Robotics;
- 1st Workshop on Artificial Intelligence for Healthcare;
- 6th Workshop on Natural Language for Artificial Intelligence;
- 3rd Workshop on Explainable Artificial Intelligence;
- 1st Workshop on Artificial Intelligence for Human Machine Interaction;
- 1st Workshop on Artificial Intelligence for Public Administration;
- 2nd Italian Workshop on Artificial Intelligence and Applications for Business and Industries;
- 1st Workshop on Bias, Ethical AI, Explainability and the role of Logic and Logic Programming;
- 1st Workshop on Strategies, Prediction, Interaction, and Reasoning in Italy.

Finally, a doctoral consortium with 20 presentations from PhD students was organized on the first day of the conference. The doctoral consortium chairs were Gabriella Cortellessa and Luca Di Gaspero.

The organization benefited from "Platinum" sponsorships from EUSTEMA, Danieli Automation, Generali, Intesa Sanpaolo, and TechEdge, "Gold" sponsorships from OverIT, Previnet, and u-blox, and "Bronze" sponsorships from BeanTech, SMC, and Confindustria Udine. The conference was kindly supported by the Artificial Intelligence Journal, and received the patronage of the European Commission, the Friuli Venezia Giulia Region, and the Municipality of Udine. A special session devoted to industry and AI was organized by Giuseppe Serra and Fabio Mercorio.

Last but not least, we would like to thank the organizing committee, in particular Andrea Brunello and Nicola Saccomanno, who did a huge amount of high-quality work. Moreover, we thank the web master Nicola Gigante, our colleagues and friends Dario Della Monica and Gabriele Puppis, and all the PhD students for their help in the practical management of the conference. Finally, we thank the board of directors of the AIxIA for their constant support, the Rector of the University of Udine for the opportunity to organize the conference in the new building of the scientific library, and the technical staff of University of Udine (in particular, Renato Spoletti, Stefano Bonomi, and Ester Orlandi) for their precious work.

December 2022

Agostino Dovier
Angelo Montanari
Andrea Orlandini

Organization

General Chair

Angelo Montanari   University of Udine, Italy

Program Committee Chairs

Agostino Dovier   University of Udine, Italy
Andrea Orlandini   National Research Council (CNR-ISTC), Italy

Program Committee

Davide Bacciu	University of Pisa, Italy
Marco Baioletti	University of Perugia, Italy
Matteo Baldoni	University of Turin, Italy
Stefania Bandini	Complex Systems & AI Research Center,Italy
Adriano Barra	University of Salento, Italy
Sebastiano Battiato	University of Catania, Italy
Stefano Bistarelli	University of Perugia, Italy
Stefano Borgo	National Research Council (CNR-ISTC), Italy
Francesco Calimeri	University of Calabria, Italy
Alberto Casagrande	University of Trieste, Italy
Antonio Chella	University of Palermo, Italy
Alessandro Cimatti	Fondazione Bruno Kessler, Italy
Gabriella Cortellessa	National Research Council (CNR-ISTC), Italy
Stefania Costantini	University of Aquila, Italy
Alessandro Dal Palù	University of Parma, Italy
Dario Della Monica	University of Udine, Italy
Stefano Ferilli	University of Bari, Italy
Alberto Finzi	University of Naples "Federico II", Italy
Fabio Fioravanti	University of Chieti-Pescara, Italy
Andrea Formisano	University of Udine, Italy

Salvatore Gaglio	University of Palermo, Italy
Chiara Ghidini	Fondazione Bruno Kessler, Italy
Gianluigi Greco	University of Calabria, Italy
Luca Iocchi	University of Rome "Sapienza", Italy
Antonio Lieto	University of Turin, Italy
Francesca A. Lisi	University of Bari, Italy
Michele Loreti	University of Camerino, Italy
Fabio Mercorio	University of Milan Bicocca, Italy
Angelo Oddi	National Research Council (CNR-ISTC), Italy
Andrea Omicini	University of Bologna "Alma Mater Studiorum", Italy
Luigi Palopoli	University of Trento, Italy
Filippo Palumbo	National Research Council (CNR-ISTI), Italy
Fabio Patrizi	University of Rome "Sapienza", Italy
Luigi Portinale	University of Piemonte Orientale, Italy
Gian Luca Pozzato	University of Turin, Italy
Luca Pulina	University of Sassari, Italy
Alessandro Raffetà	University of Venezia "Ca' Foscari", Italy
Riccardo Rasconi	National Research Council (CNR-ISTC), Italy
Francesco Ricca	University of Calabria, Italy
Fabrizio Riguzzi	University of Ferrara, Italy
Marco Roveri	University of Trento, Italy
Salvatore Ruggieri	University of Pisa, Italy
Enrico Scala	University of Brescia, Italy
Giovanni Semeraro	University of Bari, Italy
Luciano Serafini	Fondazione Bruno Kessler, Italy
Gianluca Torta	University of Turin, Italy
Mauro Vallati	University of Huddersfield, UK
Eloisa Vargiu	CETaqua Water Technology Center, Spain

Additional Reviewers

Carlo Adornetto	Pierluigi Cassotti
Damiano Azzolini	Federico Cerutti
Daniele Baccega	Riccardo De Benedictis
Patrizio Bellan	Alessandro De Paola
Gloria Beraldo	Francesco Fabiano
Luigi Bonassi	Francesco Faloci
Fabio Buttussi	Antonino Fiannaca

Federico Fogolari
Francesca Fracasso
Francesca Gasparini
Francesco Guarnera
Dario Guidotti
Eleonora Iotti
Andrea Iovine
Maria Mannone
Marta Marchiori Manerba
Claudio Masolo
Ivan Mercanti

Laura Pandolfo
Marco Polignano
Andrea Pugnana
Alessandro Quarta
Chiara Renso
Francesco Santini
Laura State
Carlo Taticchi
Alessandro Umbrico
Alberto Valese

Contents

AI Applications

Miscellany

Natural Language Processing

Keynote talk

Hybrid Approaches

The PSyKE Technology for Trustworthy Artificial Intelligence

Roberta Calegari[1] and Federico Sabbatini[2]([⊠])

[1] Alma AI – Alma Mater Research Institute for Human-Centered Artificial
Intelligence, Alma Mater Studiorum—Università di Bologna, Bologna, Italy
roberta.calegari@unibo.it
[2] Department of Pure and Applied Sciences (DiSPeA),
University of Urbino, Via S. Chiara, 27, 61029 Urbino, Italy
f.sabbatini1@campus.uniurb.it

Abstract. Transparency is one of the "Ethical Principles in the Context of AI Systems" as described in the Ethics Guidelines for Trustworthy Artificial Intelligence (TAI). It is closely linked to four other principles – respect for human autonomy, prevention of harm, traceability and explainability – and involves numerous ways in which opaqueness can have undesirable impacts, such as discrimination, inequality, segregation, marginalisation, and manipulation. The opaqueness of many AI tools and the inability to understand the underpinning black boxes contradicts these principles as well as prevents people from fully trusting them. In this paper we discuss the PSyKE technology, a platform providing general-purpose support to symbolic knowledge extraction from different sorts of black-box predictors via many extraction algorithms. The extracted knowledge results are easily injectable into existing AI assets making them meet the transparency TAI requirement.

Keywords: Trustworthy Artificial Intelligence · Transparency · Explainability · Symbolic knowledge extraction · PSyKE

1 Introduction

The innovative potential of Artificial Intelligence (AI) is clear, but AI tools can reflect, amplify, and even create untrustworthy behaviours, beliefs, decisions or results [15]. As we use AI systems to formalise, scale, and accelerate processes, we have the opportunity, as well as the duty, to revise and enhance the existing processes, avoiding perpetuating existing patterns of untrustworthiness, by detecting, diagnosing, and repairing them. To trust these systems, domain experts and stakeholders need to trust the decisions made by them. Europe's

This work has been partially supported by the EU ICT-48 2020 project TAILOR (No. 952215) and by the European Union's Horizon 2020 research and innovation programme under G.A. no. 101017142 (StairwAI project).

strategy aims to create an AI Ecosystem of Excellence and Trust where ethical and legal principles are pursued in all AI systems. Transparency is one of the "Ethical Principles in the Context of AI Systems" as described in the Ethics Guidelines for Trustworthy Artificial Intelligence (EGTAI) [9] and in the first AI regulation (the "AI Act") [8]. It is closely linked to four other principles (respect for human autonomy, prevention of harm, traceability and explainability) and involves numerous ways in which opaqueness can have undesirable impacts, such as discrimination, inequality, exclusion, segregation, marginalisation, exploitation, and manipulation.

However, the translation of ethical principles and EGTAI into practical requirements are needed to boost high quality AI innovation in Europe. Concrete methods to ensure that AI systems adhere to the transparency requirement can be borrowed from the explainability domain, since providing explanations concurs to achieve transparency. Different strategies can be exploited to meet transparency and explainability [11]. For instance, it is possible to obtain explainable data-driven solutions *only* by using *interpretable* algorithms [16]—such as decision lists, decision trees and sparse integer linear models, and algorithms based on discrete optimisation. However, this kind of technique often has repercussions on the final predictive performance, since most effective algorithms – like artificial neural networks – are not taken into account. Deriving *post-hoc* explanations [14] is an alternative strategy aimed at reverse-engineering the black-box (BB) inner behaviour to make it explicit. This is a way of combining the performance of prediction-effective (even if opaque) machine learning models with human-interpretable output predictions.

Symbolic knowledge extraction (SKE) represents one of the most promising techniques to derive *post-hoc* explanations from sub-symbolic BB models and interpret the notion of explainability under the transparency perspective, i.e. proposing a transparent model adhering to the not transparent predictor. Its main idea is to build a *symbolic* – and thus interpretable – model that mimics the behaviour of the original BB, intended as the capability to provide outputs that are as close as possible w.r.t. those of the underlying BB queried on the same inputs. Symbols may consist of comprehensible knowledge—e.g., lists or trees of *rules* that can be exploited to either derive predictions or to better understand the BB behaviour and, as a further step, as knowledge on which to perform any kind of logical reasoning. Currently, SKE techniques have been already applied in a wide variety of areas, ranging from medical diagnosis [10] to finance [1] and astrophysics [22]. Despite the wide adoption of SKE and the existence of different techniques for extracting symbolic knowledge out of a BB, a unified and general-purpose software technology supporting such methods and their comparison is currently lacking. In other words, the burden of implementing SKE algorithms, or selecting the best one from the state of the art, is currently on AI stakeholders alone, who are likely to realise custom solutions for a specific application need. Other than slowing down the adoption of SKE as an effective method for reaching transparency, such a lack of viable technologies is somewhat anachronistic in the data-driven AI era, where a plethora of libraries and frameworks are flourishing, targeting all major programming paradigms and platforms, and making state-of-the-art machine learning (ML) algorithms easily accessible to the general public—cf. SciKit-Learn[1] for Python.

Accordingly, in this paper we present a general-purpose Platform for Symbolic Knowledge Extraction – PSyKE – as a way to practicalise the TAI requirement – transparency in particular – from high-level principles to concrete methods. Moreover, one of the PSyKE goals is filling the gap between the current state of the art of SKE and the available technology as well as providing a concrete toolkit for testing, evaluating and reaching transparency in AI applications. It provides a controlled experimentation environment for transparency via SKE methods enabling the creation of different simulations/experiments for the specific application at hand. The framework comes as a toolkit in which experiments on transparency can be built and run, comparing different solutions, and selecting the best option. More precisely, PSyKE is conceived as an open library where different sorts of knowledge extraction algorithms can be realised, exploited, or compared. PSyKE supports rule extraction from both classifiers and regressors, and makes the extraction procedure as transparent as possible w.r.t. the underlying BB, depending on the particular extraction procedure at hand. The extraction of first-order logic clauses is also supported, with the twofold advantage of providing human- and machine-interpretable rules as output. These can then be used as either an explanation for the original BB or as a starting point for further symbolic computations and reasonings.

2 The PSyKE framework

PSyKE[2] [18,19] is a platform providing general-purpose support to symbolic knowledge extraction from different sorts of black-box predictors via many extraction algorithms.

2.1 Functionalities and Main Components

PSyKE comes as a software library providing general-purpose support to the extraction of logic rules out of BB′ predictors by letting users choose the most adequate SKE method for the task and data at hand. A unified API covering virtually all extraction algorithms targeting supervised learning tasks is exposed by the framework and experiments can also be run via a GUI. Currently, PSyKE grants access to state-of-the-art SKE algorithms providing the implementations of several interoperable, interchangeable, and comparable extraction SKE methods [2,6,7,13,17,20]. PSyKE is conceived as an open-ended project, exploitable to design and implement new extraction procedures behind a unique API.

Essentially, PSyKE is designed around the notion of *extractor*, whose overall design is depicted in Fig. 1. Within the scope of PSyKE, an extractor is any algorithm accepting a machine learning predictor as input (classifier or regressor), and producing a *theory* of *logic* rules as output.

---

[1] https://scikit-learn.org/stable.
[2] https://apice.unibo.it/xwiki/bin/view/PSyKE/.

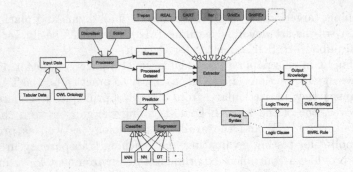

Fig. 1. PSyKE design

PSyKE extractors require additional information to complete the extraction task. Such information consists of the data set used to train the predictor and its schema. Data sets are required to allow the extraction procedure to inspect the BB behaviour – and therefore build the corresponding output rules – whereas schemas are required to allow *(i)* the extraction procedure to take decisions based on feature *types*, and *(ii)* the extracted knowledge to be more interpretable by referring to the feature *names*. Accordingly, extractors expect also the data set and its schema metadata as input. Figure 1 shows also the *discretiser* and *scaler* components. The former aims at providing some facilities for discretising (binarising) data sets including continuous (categorical) data. This is a procedure often needed for data sets involving these kinds of attributes to be given as input to extractors only accepting discrete or binary input features.

2.2   Architecture and API

As depicted in Fig. 2, a key role in the design of PSyKE is played by the `Extractor` interface, defining the general contract of any knowledge-extraction procedure. Each `Extractor` encapsulates a single machine learning `Predictor` and a particular `Discretisation` strategy. Given a set of inputs, an extractor is capable of extracting a `Theory` of logic `Rules` out of a `DataFrame`, containing the examples the `Predictor` has been trained upon.

PSyKE assumes underlying libraries to be available on the runtime adopted for implementation, from which AI facilities can be inherited. These include: a machine learning library, exposing *ad-hoc* types aimed at representing data sets, data schemas, or predictors, and a symbolic AI library, exposing *ad-hoc* types for representing and manipulating logic theories, clauses, and rules. PSyKE inherits high-level abstractions from these libraries. These include the following components:

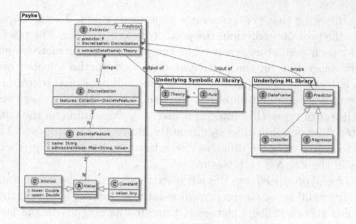

Fig. 2. PSyKE's `Extractor` interface

`DataFrame` — a container of tabular data, where rows commonly denote instances, and columns denote their features, while bulk operations are available to manipulate the table as a whole, as well as any row/column of its;

`Predictor<R>` — a computational entity which can be trained (a.k.a. fitted) against a `DataFrame` and used to draw predictions of type `R`;

`Classifier<R>` — a particular case of predictor where `R` represents a type having a finite amount of admissible values;

`Regressor<R>` — a particular case of predictor where `R` represents a type having a potentially infinite (possibly continuous) amount of admissible values;

`Rule` — a semantic, intelligible representation of the function mapping `Predictor`'s inputs into the corresponding outputs, for a portion of the input space;

`Theory` — an ordered collection of rules.

For example, PSyKE borrows ML-related abstractions – such as `DataFrame`, `Predictor`, or `Classifier` – from either Pandas or Scikit-Learn Python libraries. Similarly, it borrows high-level symbolic-AI-related abstractions – such as `Theory` or `Rule` – from 2P-KT[3] [5].

PSyKE constructs its notion of `Extractor` upon these inherited concepts—thus designing an `Extractor` as any method capable of extracting logic `Rules` out of some trained `Predictor`. PSyKE extractors are bound to the particular underpinning black-box `Predictor`, as well as to the `Discretisation` strategy exploited for the input space. `Extractors` also expose a method for extracting an explainable `Theory` from the `Predictor` – namely, `extract` – and a method to draw predictions by using the extracted rules—namely, `predict`. Any attempt to use the extracted rules to draw explainable predictions triggers extraction first—i.e., the prediction procedure implies extraction. Both extraction and prediction rely on a `DataFrame` that must be provided by the user upon invocation. Extractors, in the general case, may also be used to perform rule induction from data, without any intermediate predictor.

---

[3] https://github.com/tuProlog/2ppy.

It is worth noting that `Predictors` are parametric types. The meta-parameter R represents the type of predictions the predictor may produce. The rules possibly extracted by such predictors – as well as the predictions extracted – may differ significantly depending on the particular data and on the selected predictors. For instance, when rules are extracted from mono-dimensional regressors, R may be the type of floating point numbers, whereas, for multi-class classifiers, R may consist of the set of types (like integer, string, ...). Depending on the nature of R, the extracted rules possibly differ significantly. However, the proposed API makes it possible to switch between different extraction algorithms and predictors with no changes in the PSyKE architecture.

Output rules produced by PSyKE's extractors may be more tailored on human-interpretability or agent-/machine-interoperability [21]. In the former case, a Prolog theory of logic clauses is provided as output. In the latter case, the knowledge is extracted as an OWL ontology containing SWRL rules.

3   Examples

In this section some examples showing PSyKE working in different scenarios are reported—i.e. the Iris data set[4] as a classification task and the Combined Cycle Power Plant[5] (CCPP) data set as a regression case study.

3.1   Classification: The Iris Data Set

In the following we report the outcome of PSyKE when applying different SKE techniques to the Iris data set. All the results are resumed in Fig. 3 and Table 1. Column "Predictor" represents the ML step of the process. Column "Extractor" represents the output of PSyKE. Different extraction procedures – namely, ITER, GridEx, and CART – are applied to some selected BB classifiers. These predictors are a k-nearest neighbor with $k = 5$ (5-NN), a decision tree (DT) and a multilayer perceptron (MLP).

A numerical assessment of the aforementioned predictors and extractors is reported in Table 1 in terms of number of extracted rules and predictive performance w.r.t. data and BB predictions. The predictive performance is expressed through both classification accuracy and F_1 score metrics. Values are averaged upon 25 executions, each one with different random train/test splits, but the same test set percentage and same parameters for predictors and extractors. Table 1 also reports the underpinning BB predictor accuracy and the fidelity and accuracy of the extraction procedure.

It is worth noting that different SKE techniques can be easily compared and the best option for the scenario at hand can be selected thanks to the controlled experimentation environment provided by PSyKE.

---

4 https://archive.ics.uci.edu/ml/datasets/iris.
5 https://archive.ics.uci.edu/ml/datasets/combined+cycle+power+plant.

Extractor | Predictor

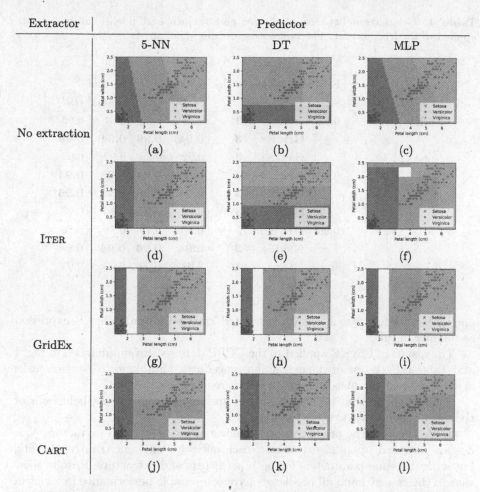

Fig. 3. Comparison between Iris data set input space partitionings performed by the algorithms implemented in PSyKE. Only the two most relevant features are reported— i.e., petal width and length.

3.2 Regression: The Combined Cycle Power Plant Data Set

In this example, PSyKE is exploited to extract rules out of different BB regressors trained upon the CCPP data set. The data set contains 9568 instances, each one composed of 4 real-valued input attributes.

Diverse regressors are trained on the CCPP data set: a 3-NN, a DT and a linear regressor (LR). Same as the previous example, PSyKE is used to extract logic rules out of the selected BB models exploring some of the SKE methods it supports—namely, ITER, GridEx, GridREx and CART. Metrics for measuring the fidelity of the extractor w.r.t. the underlying BB predictions as well as the predictive accuracy w.r.t. the data are the mean absolute error (MAE) and R^2 score. The same metrics are used to assess the predictive performance of the BBs

Table 1. Comparison between predictive performance and fidelity measurements applied to the Iris data set. The best extractors are highlighted.

Predictor			Extractor						
Type	Accuracy	F_1 score	Algorithm	Rules	Accuracy		F_1 score		
					(data)	(BB)	(data)	(BB)	
5-NN	0.96	0.96	ITER	3	0.91	0.93	0.91	0.93	
			GridEx	**3**	**0.94**	**0.96**	**0.94**	**0.96**	
			CART	3	0.92	0.93	0.92	0.93	
DT	0.96	0.96	**Iter**	**3**	**0.96**	**0.94**	**0.96**	**0.94**	
			GridEx	**3**	**0.94**	**0.96**	**0.94**	**0.96**	
			CART	3	0.89	0.93	0.89	0.93	
MLP	0.99	0.99	ITER	5	0.80	0.79	0.78	0.76	
			GridEx	**3**	**0.94**	**0.96**	**0.94**	**0.96**	
			CART	3	0.95	0.93	0.95	0.93	

and as for the Iris case study the extracted knowledge readability is expressed as number of rules.

The results of PSyKE applied to the CCPP data set are summarised in Fig. 4 and Table 2. Each one of the extraction procedures suitable for regression tasks is applied to all the aforementioned BB regressors.

Figure 4 shows that all the extractors are able to capture the behaviour of the output values w.r.t. the input variables.

Table 2 reports the predictive performance of predictors and extractors. Values are averaged upon 25 executions, each one with different train/test splits, but with the same parameters for both predictors and extractors. Results show that in the case at hand all predictors have comparable performance in terms of MAE and R^2 score. Conversely, it is possible to notice that CART, GridEx and GridREx always appear more explainable than ITER in terms of the number of extracted rules. From the Table it may be easily noticed also that GridEx and CART generally present analogous performance. This fact depends on the nature of the corresponding output rules. Indeed, they both produce rules having constant output values, introducing an undesired discretisation of the predicted variable. Both of them are able to outperform ITER also in terms of predictive performance (smaller MAE and larger R^2 score).

On the other hand, GridREx outperforms all the other algorithms, achieving higher fidelity and readability. This depends on the regressive nature of its outputs, enabling the creation of more concise output rules performing more accurate predictions. Indeed, GridREx rules have as postconditions linear combinations of the input variables.

The nature of the different predictors and extractors used in this case study may be easily noticed in Fig. 4. The boundaries identified by the 3-NN clearly follow a proximity pattern. Conversely, the DT performs variable slicing along

Extractor | Predictor

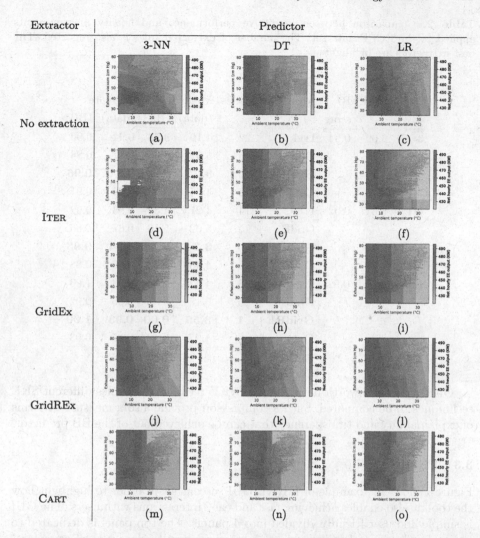

Fig. 4. Comparison between CCPP data set output predictions provided by the algorithms implemented in PSyKE. Only the two most relevant features are reported—i.e., ambient temperature and exhaust vacuum.

each input dimension and the LR produces a gradual output value decrement for growing input values. As for the extractors, for CART the same considerations made for the DT hold. The hypercubic nature of ITER and GridEx is detectable by observing the rectangular boundaries provided by them. Finally, GridREx provides local linear regressive laws for hypercubic regions, merging the advantages of both DTs and LRs.

Table 2. Comparison between predictive performance and fidelity measurements applied to the CCPP data set. The number of extracted rules is also reported. The best extractors are highlighted.

Predictor			Extractor						
Type	MAE	R^2 score	Algorithm	Rules	MAE		R^2 score	
					(data)	(BB)	(data)	(BB)
3-NN	3.09	0.94	ITER	22	4.19	3.78	0.94	0.96
			GridEx	5	5.02	4.63	0.87	0.88
			GridREx	**5**	**3.25**	**2.52**	**0.94**	**0.96**
			CART	6	4.45	3.90	0.89	0.91
DT	3.31	0.92	ITER	14	4.27	4.32	0.93	0.92
			GridEx	5	5.02	5.10	0.87	0.86
			GridREx	**5**	**3.24**	**3.38**	**0.94**	**0.93**
			CART	6	4.46	4.50	0.89	0.88
LR	3.59	0.92	ITER	43	4.42	2.74	0.93	1.00
			GridEx	5	5.15	3.80	0.86	0.92
			GridREx	**1**	**3.59**	**0.00**	**0.93**	**1.00**
			CART	6	4.97	3.49	0.87	0.93

Once again it is worth noting how PSyKE technology enables different SKE techniques to be compared. Such a comparison provide also a measure in terms of explainability and transparency that can be achieved out of the BB predictor.

3.3 PSyKE GUI

Figure 5 shows an example of PSyKE GUI screenshot in order to highlight how the toolkit also enables achieving fast and easy interactions with users. The GUI is simple and user-friendly, divided into 4 panels. The top panel is dedicated to the task selection (classification vs. regression) and to data set selection/pre-processing. Users can choose between several pre-defined data sets, as well as load a custom file. Furthermore, they can choose to discretise/scale the features and, on the right, it is possible to select among all the available features (*i*) the one to be used as output; (*ii*) those to be used as inputs; and (*iii*) those to be neglected. On the same panel it is possible to select two input features to be plotted together with the output feature. Plots appear in the right-most central panel of the GUI. The first one represents the data set instances, the second depicts the decision boundaries of the trained BB predictor and the third does the same for the selected extractor. Plots are shown after the proper button pressing, but each plot depends on the previous operations performed by the users. The predictor plot requires a BB predictor to be previously chosen and trained. This can be done by acting on the left-most central panel of the interface. Several models are available, each one with corresponding text boxes

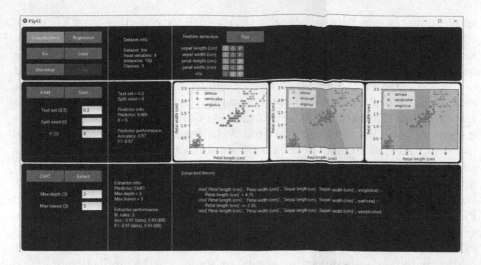

Fig. 5. PSyKE GUI

to allow users to customise the required hyper-parameters. Users can also choose the train-test splitting percentage. Each parameter has a default value, so user inputs are optional. Analogously, the bottom-most panel is dedicated to the selection, training and tuning of knowledge extractors. Training an extractor enables the visualisation of the third plot.

The knowledge extracted with PSyKE extractors is displayed below the plots, in Prolog syntax. Finally, information about the chosen data set (e.g., number of features, classes and instances), predictor (e.g., parameters and predictive performance) and extractor (e.g., parameters, predictive performance and fidelity measurements) are shown next to the corresponding selection commands (after their selection).

The example reported in Fig. 5 shows the application of PSyKE to the Iris data set. The data set has been loaded without discretisation and feature pruning, then a 5-NN has been trained on 80% of the data set. The CART extractor has finally been chosen, with maximum depth and maximum leaf amount equal to 3. Only input features about petal width and length have been selected to be plotted.

In conclusion, the framework provides the possibility to build different experiments in a controlled environment, enabling easy exploitation of the technology and offering the possibility to compare the results in a simple way.

4 Impact

The PSyKE technology may impact many research areas. It provides a well-grounded technological basis and a software engineering practice for implementing/experimenting with the transparency and explainability dimensions in AI applications. It provides an extensible framework for collecting the SKE methods and approaches proposed in the literature, creating a controlled environment for testing, evaluating and comparing transparency. PSyKE has an important role from the point of view of software engineering, providing a methodology that can be exploited for grounding all the TAI dimensions—i.e., the design and the implementation of a controlled experimentation environment that can act also as a sandbox for simulating the trustworthiness of an AI system. Accordingly, the framework provides a concrete example of the feasibility of building a practical toolkit for AI stakeholders to test the dimensions of TAI. Moreover, PSyKE has a role to play in the field of XAI [12]. Integrating symbolic and sub-symbolic AI – i.e., using them in synergy, as an ensemble – is a strategical research direction [4], and PSyKE offers a sound technological foundation for this purpose. Finally, the distributed systems community has the need for interoperable and general-purpose logic-based technologies that can be easy injectable into already existing systems [3]. There, PSyKE provides a technological layer easy injectable in distributed systems supporting agents' reasoning via the production of logical knowledge that can be exploited by agents.

Given all the potential of the described framework, there is room for several future research directions. PSyKE already enables the investigation of relevant research questions involving symbolic manipulation or automated reasoning, thanks to its modularity and interoperability. Under such a perspective, PSyKE enables exploring how to: *(i)* blend SKE with other AI techniques, and *(ii)* exploit SKE to build flexible intelligent systems.

Along these lines, future research directions will take into account the integration in the framework of a larger suite of methods for dealing with the most variety of datasets and predictors. Some preliminary experiments showed that the SKE algorithms can be exploited also for rule induction starting from data. This line is particularly interesting for all the cases in which a BB predictor is not available. Moreover, new SKE techniques are under development exploiting the combination of SKE with explainable clustering techniques increasing both performance and fidelity.

Finally, the framework is a preliminary example of how TAI dimensions can be tested and evaluated, and an interesting research line is to extend the environment in order to achieve a certification of the level of transparency – or more in general trustworthiness – for given AI applications. The challenge here is to find a way for defining effective metrics for the certification of TAI dimensions.

5   Conclusion

In this paper we discuss the PSyKE technology, a platform providing general-purpose support to symbolic knowledge extraction from different sorts of black-box predictors via many extraction algorithms, to be easily injectable into existing AI assets making them meet the transparency TAI requirement.

The framework provides a controlled experimentation environment in which transparency and explainability can be tested, assessed and compared.

Even if still in a preliminary stage, it provides a software engineering practice for grounding all the TAI dimensions, translating them from high-level principles to practical requirements.

References

1. Baesens, B., Setiono, R., De Lille, V., Viaene, S., Vanthienen, J.: Building credit-risk evaluation expert systems using neural network rule extraction and decision tables. In: Storey, V.C., Sarkar, S., DeGross, J.I. (eds.) ICIS 2001 Proceedings, pp. 159–168. Association for Information Systems (2001). http://aisel.aisnet.org/icis2001/20
2. Breiman, L., Friedman, J., Stone, C.J., Olshen, R.A.: Classification and Regression Trees. CRC Press, Boca Raton (1984)
3. Calegari, R., Ciatto, G., Mascardi, V., Omicini, A.: Logic-based technologies for multi-agent systems: a systematic literature review. Auton. Agents Multi-Agent Syst. **35**(1), 1:1–1:67 (2021). https://doi.org/10.1007/s10458-020-09478-3, http://link.springer.com/10.1007/s10458-020-09478-3. collection Current Trends in Research on Software Agents and Agent-Based Software Development
4. Calegari, R., Ciatto, G., Omicini, A.: On the integration of symbolic and sub-symbolic techniques for XAI: a survey. Intell. Artif. **14**(1), 7–32 (2020). https://doi.org/10.3233/IA-190036
5. Ciatto, G., Calegari, R., Omicini, A.: 2P-Kt: a logic-based ecosystem for symbolic AI. SoftwareX **16**(100817), 1–7 (2021). https://doi.org/10.1016/j.softx.2021.100817, https://www.sciencedirect.com/science/article/pii/S2352711021001126
6. Craven, M.W., Shavlik, J.W.: Using sampling and queries to extract rules from trained neural networks. In: Machine Learning Proceedings 1994, pp. 37–45. Elsevier (1994). https://doi.org/10.1016/B978-1-55860-335-6.50013-1
7. Craven, M.W., Shavlik, J.W.: Extracting tree-structured representations of trained networks. In: Touretzky, D.S., Mozer, M.C., Hasselmo, M.E. (eds.) Advances in Neural Information Processing Systems 8. Proceedings of the 1995 Conference, pp. 24–30. The MIT Press, June 1996. http://papers.nips.cc/paper/1152-extracting-tree-structured-representations-of-trained-networks.pdf
8. European Commission: AI Act - Proposal for a regulation of the european parliament and the council laying down harmonised rules on artificial intelligence (Artificial Intelligence Act) and amending certain union legislative acts (2021). https://eur-lex.europa.eu/legal-content/EN/TXT/?uri=CELEX:52021PC0206
9. European Commission, Directorate-General for Communications Networks, C., Technology: Ethics guidelines for trustworthy AI. Publications Office (2019). https://doi.org/10.2759/346720
10. Franco, L., Subirats, J.L., Molina, I., Alba, E., Jerez, J.M.: Early breast cancer prognosis prediction and rule extraction using a new constructive neural network algorithm. In: Sandoval, F., Prieto, A., Cabestany, J., Graña, M. (eds.) IWANN 2007. LNCS, vol. 4507, pp. 1004–1011. Springer, Heidelberg (2007). https://doi.org/10.1007/978-3-540-73007-1_121
11. Guidotti, R., Monreale, A., Ruggieri, S., Turini, F., Giannotti, F., Pedreschi, D.: A survey of methods for explaining black box models. ACM Comput. Surv. **51**(5), 1–42 (2018). https://doi.org/10.1145/3236009
12. Gunning, D., Aha, D.: DARPA's explainable artificial intelligence (XAI) program. AI Mag. **40**(2), 44–58 (2019)

13. Huysmans, J., Baesens, B., Vanthienen, J.: ITER: an algorithm for predictive regression rule extraction. In: Tjoa, A.M., Trujillo, J. (eds.) DaWaK 2006. LNCS, vol. 4081, pp. 270–279. Springer, Heidelberg (2006). https://doi.org/10.1007/11823728_26

14. Kenny, E.M., Ford, C., Quinn, M., Keane, M.T.: Explaining black-box classifiers using post-hoc explanations-by-example: the effect of explanations and error-rates in XAI user studies. Artif. Intell. **294**, 103459 (2021). https://doi.org/10.1016/j.artint.2021.103459

15. Mökander, J., Morley, J., Taddeo, M., Floridi, L.: Ethics-based auditing of automated decision-making systems: nature, scope, and limitations. Sci. Eng. Ethics **27**(4), 1–30 (2021)

16. Rudin, C.: Stop explaining black box machine learning models for high stakes decisions and use interpretable models instead. Nat. Mach. Intell. **1**(5), 206–215 (2019). https://doi.org/10.1038/s42256-019-0048-x

17. Sabbatini, F., Calegari, R.: Symbolic knowledge extraction from opaque machine learning predictors: GridREx & PEDRO. In: Kern-Isberner, G., Lakemeyer, G., Meyer, T. (eds.) Proceedings of the 19th International Conference on Principles of Knowledge Representation and Reasoning, July 31–5 August 2022, KR 2022, Haifa, Israel (2022). https://proceedings.kr.org/2022/57/

18. Sabbatini, F., Ciatto, G., Calegari, R., Omicini, A.: On the design of PSyKE: a platform for symbolic knowledge extraction. In: Calegari, R., Ciatto, G., Denti, E., Omicini, A., Sartor, G. (eds.) WOA 2021–22nd Workshop From Objects to Agents. CEUR Workshop Proceedings, vol. 2963, pp. 29–48. Sun SITE Central Europe, RWTH Aachen University (Oct 2021), 22nd Workshop From Objects to Agents (WOA 2021), Bologna, Italy, 1–3 September 2021. Proceedings (2021)

19. Sabbatini, F., Ciatto, G., Calegari, R., Omicini, A.: Symbolic knowledge extraction from opaque ML predictors in PSyKE: Platform design & experiments. Intell. Artif. **16**(1), 27–48 (2022). https://doi.org/10.3233/IA-210120

20. Sabbatini, F., Ciatto, G., Omicini, A.: GridEx: an algorithm for knowledge extraction from black-box regressors. In: Calvaresi, D., Najjar, A., Winikoff, M., Främling, K. (eds.) EXTRAAMAS 2021. LNCS (LNAI), vol. 12688, pp. 18–38. Springer, Cham (2021). https://doi.org/10.1007/978-3-030-82017-6_2

21. Sabbatini, F., Ciatto, G., Omicini, A.: Semantic web-based interoperability for intelligent agents with PSyKE. In: Calvaresi, D., Najjar, A., Winikoff, M., Främling, K. (eds.) Proceedings of the 4th International Workshop on Explainable and Transparent AI and Multi-Agent Systems. EXTRAAMAS 2022. LNCS, vol. 13283, chap. 8, pp. 124–142. Springer, Cham (2022). https://doi.org/10.1007/978-3-031-15565-9_8

22. Sabbatini, F., Grimani, C.: Symbolic knowledge extraction from opaque predictors applied to cosmic-ray data gathered with LISA pathfinder. Aeronaut. Aerosp. Open Access J. **6**(3), 90–95 (2022). https://doi.org/10.15406/aaoaj.2022.06.00145

A Declarative Approach to Contrast Pattern Mining

Francesca Alessandra Lisi[1]([⊠])[ID] and Gioacchino Sterlicchio[2][ID]

[1] Dipartimento di Informatica and CILA, University of Bari "Aldo Moro", Bari, Italy
FrancescaAlessandra.Lisi@uniba.it
[2] Department of Mechanics, Mathematics and Management,
Polytechnic University of Bari, Bari, Italy
g.sterlicchio@phd.poliba.it

Abstract. This paper proposes a declarative approach to the problem of contrast pattern mining. The approach is based on encodings of the data and the problem with Answer Set Programming (ASP), and evaluated in a novel AI application in the field of Digital Forensics.

Keywords: Contrast Pattern Mining · Answer Set Programming · Digital Forensics

1 Introduction

Pattern mining [12] is a class of data mining tasks that consist of extracting interesting structured patterns from a dataset. These tasks encompass itemset mining, sequence mining and graph mining. The interestingness measure of a pattern is, in most of the algorithms, the number of its occurrences in the dataset. Given a threshold k, interesting patterns are those that occur at least in k data instances. In this case, the task is known as *frequent pattern mining* for which many algorithms have been proposed. An interesting extension of the frequent pattern mining task is the one that aims at the discovery of so-called *contrast patterns*. Whereas frequent patterns are statistically significant regularities in a set of transactions, contrast patterns denote statistically significant differences between two or more disjoint sets of transactions [6].

Recently there has been an increasing interest in declarative approaches to pattern mining, thus giving rise to a novel stream of research known under the name of *Declarative Pattern Mining* (DPM). So far, DPM addressed tasks such as frequent itemset mining [10,13], and sequence mining [7,17]. Different declarative frameworks have been explored: SAT [13], Constraint Programming [5,10], and Answer Set Programming (ASP) [7,11]. In this paper we propose a declarative approach for contrast pattern mining which leverages the expressive and inferential power of ASP. To the best of our knowledge, this interesting class of pattern mining problems has not been addressed yet in DPM.

A. Dovier et al. (Eds.): AIxIA 2022, LNAI 13796, pp. 17–30, 2023.
https://doi.org/10.1007/978-3-031-27181-6_2

Declarative approaches are generally desirable in application domains where the requirements of transparency, verifiability and explainability of the AI techniques employed are of paramount importance. One of these cases is the field of *Digital Forensics* (DF), a branch of criminalistics that deals with the identification, acquisition, preservation, analysis and presentation of the information content of computer systems, or in general of digital devices, by means of specialized software, and according to specific regulations. A declarative approach to DF was first explored by Costantini *et al.* [2,3], and subsequently adopted by the COST Action "Digital forensics: evidence analysis via intelligent systems and practices" (DigForASP)[1]. The aim of DigForASP is to promote formal and verifiable AI methods and techniques in the analysis of evidence [4]. In this paper, we report the preliminary results obtained by applying the proposed ASP-encoded contrast pattern mining algorithm to a dataset of phone records made available within DigForASP.

The paper is organized as follows. In Sect. 2 we provide the necessary preliminaries on contrast pattern mining and ASP. In Sect. 3 we introduce the proposed ASP encoding for contrast pattern mining. In Sect. 4 we describe the application of this encoding to the analysis of phone records, and report the results of some experiments. In Sect. 5 we conclude with final remarks.

2   Preliminaries

2.1   Contrast Pattern Mining in Brief

We assume the set $I = \{1, ..., m\}$ of m items, and the set $T = \{1, ..., n\}$ of n transactions. Intuitively, a transaction $t \in T$ is a subset of items from I, which is typically associated with a transaction identifier (TID). A transactional database $\mathcal{D} \in \{0, 1\}^{n \times m}$ can be seen as a binary matrix, in which each row $\mathcal{D}_t$ represent the transaction t consisting of the items $\{i \in I | \mathcal{D}_{t,i} = 1\}$, where $\mathcal{D}_{t,i}$ denote the value on the i-th column and t-th row of $\mathcal{D}$. The subsets of I are called *itemsets* or patterns. In pattern mining we are interested in finding patterns that satisfy constraints relative to a set of transactions. In particular, given the pattern $P \subseteq I$, and a set of transactions T, the subset of T covered by P is $cover(P, T) = \{t \in T | \forall i \in P : \mathcal{D}_{t,i} = 1\}$. Then the *absolute support* of P in T is defined as:

$$supp(P, T) = |cover(P, T)| \tag{1}$$

and quantifies the number of transactions in T containing the pattern P.

Frequent pattern mining algorithms are used to discover statistically significant regularities in a set of transactions whereas the contrast pattern mining task is about detecting statistically significant differences (*contrast*) between two or more disjoint sets of transactions [6]. To this aim, we assume also a finite set L of class labels which are used by the function $\mathcal{L}(t) \in L$ to label each transaction t. In our setting, the label $\alpha \in L$ partitions T in two samples:

---

[1] https://digforasp.uca.es/.

1. $T(\alpha) = \{t \in T | \mathcal{L}(t) = \alpha\}$, i.e., the transactions labeled with α;
2. its complement $T'(\alpha) = T \setminus T(\alpha)$.

The contrast pattern P with respect to α is quantified by the so-called *absolute support difference*, which is defined as:

$$diff(P, \alpha) = supp(P, T(\alpha)) - supp(P, T'(\alpha)) \qquad (2)$$

The problem of contrast pattern mining concerns the enumeration of all frequent patterns with absolute support difference that exceeds the user-defined minimum support threshold *minDiff*. More specifically, given:

- the transaction database $\mathcal{D}$ over the set of transactions T;
- the maximum pattern length threshold *maxLength*;
- the minimum absolute support threshold $minSupp \geq 0$;
- the minimum absolute support difference threshold $minDiff \geq 0$;
- the label $\alpha \in L$.

the problem of contrast pattern mining is to find all patterns $(P, diff(P, \alpha))$ such that:

1. $|P| \leq maxLength$;
2. $supp(P, T(\alpha)) \geq minSupp$;
3. $diff(P, \alpha) \geq minDiff$.

To understand the meaning of contrast patterns, it is important to comment further the formula (2). Given a class α, a pattern P is a contrast pattern for that class if its support differs from the support of the same pattern for the complementary class. If the difference of the support is equal to 0, it means that P is present in the same way in the two classes. Therefore this pattern does not allow to find the differences between the classes. Conversely, the more the difference in support moves away from 0, the more P is to be understood as a pattern that allows to distinguish the two classes under comparison. Therefore, P is a representative pattern for the class α but not for the complementary class.

2.2 Answer Set Programming in a Nutshell

In the following we give a brief overview of the syntax and semantics of disjunctive logic programs in ASP. The reader can refer to, e.g., [1] for a more extensive introduction to ASP.

Let U be a fixed countable set of (domain) elements, also called *constants*, upon which a total order $\prec$ is defined. An *atom* α is an expression $p(t_1, \ldots, t_n)$, where p is a predicate of arity $n \geq 0$ and each t_i is either a variable or an element from U (*i.e.*, the resulting language is function-free). An atom is *ground* if it is free of variables. We denote the set of all ground atoms over U by B_U. A *(disjunctive) rule* r is of the form

$$a_1 \vee \ldots \vee a_n \leftarrow b_1, \ldots, b_k, not\ b_{k+1}, \ldots, not\ b_m$$

with $n \geq 0$, $m \geq k \geq 0$, $n + m > 0$, where $a_1, \ldots, a_n, b_1, \ldots, b_m$ are atoms, or a count expression of the form $\#count\{l : l_1, \ldots, l_i\} \bowtie u$, where l is an atom and l_j is a literal (*i.e.*, an atom which can be negated or not), $1 \geq j \geq i$, $\bowtie \in \{\leq, <, =, >, \geq\}$, and $u \in \mathbb{N}$. Moreover, "not" denotes *default negation*. The *head* of r is the set $head(r) = \{a_1, \ldots, a_n\}$ and the *body* of r is $body(r) = \{b_1, \ldots, b_k, not b_{k+1}, \ldots, not b_m\}$. Furthermore, we distinguish between $body^+(r) = \{b_1, \ldots, b_k\}$ and $body^-(r) = \{b_{k+1}, \ldots, b_m\}$. A rule r is *normal* if $n \leq 1$ and a *constraint* if $n = 0$. A rule r is *safe* if each variable in r occurs in $body^+(r)$. A rule r is *ground* if no variable occurs in r. A *fact* is a ground rule with $body(r) = \emptyset$ and $|head(r)| = 1$. An *(input) database* is a set of facts. A *program* is a finite set of rules. For a program Π and an input database D, we often write $\Pi(D)$ instead of $D \cup \Pi$. If each rule in a program is normal (resp. ground), we call the program normal (resp. ground).

Given a program Π, let U_Π be the set of all constants appearing in Π. $Gr(\Pi)$ is the set of rules $r\sigma$ obtained by applying, to each rule $r \in \Pi$, all possible substitutions σ from the variables in r to elements of U_Π. For count-expressions, $\{l : l_1, \ldots, l_n\}$ denotes the set of all ground instantiations of l, governed through $l_1, \ldots, l_n$. An interpretation $I \subseteq B_U$ satisfies a ground rule r iff $head(r) \cap I \neq \emptyset$ whenever $body^+(r) \subseteq I$, $body^-(r) \cap I = \emptyset$, and for each contained count-expression, $N \bowtie u$ holds, where $N = |\{l|l_1, \ldots, l_n\}|$, $u \in \mathbb{N}$ and $\bowtie \in \{\leq, < , =, >, \geq\}$. A ground program Π is satisfied by I, if I satisfies each $r \in \Pi$. A non-ground rule r (resp., a program Π) is satisfied by an interpretation I iff I satisfies all groundings of r (resp., $Gr(\Pi)$). A subset-minimal set $I \subseteq B_U$ satisfying the *Gelfond-Lifschitz reduct* $\Pi^I = \{head(r) \leftarrow body^+(r)|I \cap body^-(r) = \emptyset, r \in Gr(\Pi)\}$ is called an *answer set* of Π. We denote the set of answer sets for a program Π by $AS(\Pi)$.

The tools used in this work are part of the Potassco[2] collection [9]. The main tool of the collection is the *clingo* ASP solver [8].

3 Mining Contrast Patterns with ASP

Within the declarative framework of ASP, the transaction database $\mathcal{D}$ is represented by means of facts of the following two kinds: *class(t, c)*, and *db(t, f(v))*. Here, t is the TID while c represents the class, f represents a feature and v its value. In particular, we introduce the fact *db(t,f(v))* if and only if $\mathcal{D}_{t,i} = 1$. So, there is a *db*-fact for each feature.

In DPM, patterns are represented as answer sets. More precisely, a single pattern is associated with each answer set and in our approach represented by means of the *in_pattern/1* and *absolute_diff/1* predicates. The latter expresses the difference in support of the pattern between the class under consideration and the complementary class. Each pattern conveys information that allows to characterize the considered class.

---

[2] https://potassco.org/.

```
1   #const minSupp = 2.
2   #const maxLength = 3.
3   #const minDiff = 1.
4   #const class = positive.
5
6   % link facts to objects used in the encoding
7   item(I) :- db(_,I).
8   transaction(T) :- db(T,_).
9
10  % problem encoding (frequent itemset mining)
11  {in_pattern(I)} :- item(I).
12  in_support(T) :- {conflict_at(T,I) : item(I)} 0,
       transaction(T), class(T, class).
13  out_support(T) :- {conflict_out(T,I) : item(I)} 0,
       transaction(T), not class(T, class).
14  conflict_at(T,I) :- not db(T,I), in_pattern(I),
       transaction(T), class(T, class).
15  conflict_out(T,I) :- not db(T,I), in_pattern(I),
       transaction(T), not class(T, class).
16
17  % definition of absolute support difference (Dong et al.)
18  absolute_diff(D) :- N = #count{ T : in_support(T)}, M = #
       count{T : out_support(T)}, D = |N-M|.
19
20  % length constraint
21  :- maxLength+1 {in_pattern(I)}.
22  :- {in_pattern(I)} 0.
23
24  % frequency constraint
25  :- {in_support(T)} minSupp-2.
26
27  % absolute growth-rate constraint
28  :- absolute_diff(D), D < minDiff.
29
30  % print directives for an answer-set
31  #show in_pattern/1.
32  #show absolute_diff/1.
```

Listing 1.1. Full ASP encoding for contrast pattern mining.

The ASP enconding for the contrast pattern mining problem introduced in Sect. 2.1 is reported in Listing 1.1. The values for *minSupp*, *minDiff* and *maxLength* are encoded as symbolic constants. In Lines 1–4, the chosen constants are for demonstration purposes only. The predicate *in_pattern/1* (Line 11) is true for an item i if and only if i is included in a pattern P and encoding the most important part of a solution $(P, diff(P, \alpha))$. The predicate *in_support/1* (Line 12) is true for a transaction t if and only if $t \in T$. The intuition is that each t has to support each $i \in I$ in the sense that t must include i. Additionally, we use the auxiliary predicates *item/1* (Line 7, true for each item in $\mathcal{D}$), *transaction/1* (Line 8, true for each transaction in $\mathcal{D}$) and *conflict_at/2* (Line 14) which is true for *(t, i)* if and only if t does not support i, that is, we have the conflict $\mathcal{D}_{t,i} = 0$ and $i \in I$, thus violating the premises. In particular, the predicates *in_support/1* and *conflict_at/2* encode the construction of patterns for the class α. Conversely, the predicates *out_support/1* (Line 13) and *conflict_out/2* (Line 15) are used to generate patterns for the complementary class. Finally, the definition for the absolute support difference is encoded at Line 18.

After the pattern generation step, the encoding applies three constraints corresponding to the thresholds *maxLength*, *minSupp*, and *minDiff*. The first constraint is expressed by Lines 21–22 and rules out patterns having 0 items or more than *maxLength* items. The second constraint is expressed at Line 25. In fact, patterns supported by at most *minSupp-2* instances are not allowed as an answer. The third constraint, encoded at Line 28, discards patterns with absolute support difference lower than *minDiff* from the answer set. The two *#show* commands on Lines 31–32 allow, for each answer set, the display of the atoms that compose a solution $(P, diff(P, \alpha))$ to problem in hand.

The encoding and further material can be found online.[3]

4   An Application in Digital Forensics

Digital Forensics (DF) is a branch of criminalistics that deals with the identification, acquisition, preservation, analysis and presentation of the information content of computer systems, or in general of digital devices, by means of specialized software, and according to specific regulations. In particular, the phase of *Evidence Analysis* involves examining and aggregating evidence about possible crimes and crime perpetrators collected from various electronic devices in order to reconstruct events, event sequences and scenarios related to a crime. Results from this phase are then made available to law enforcement, investigators, intelligence agencies, public prosecutors, lawyers and judges.

During the investigation of a crime, it is common to analyze the communications of a particular suspect. Since nowadays mobile phones are objects owned by anyone, it can be useful for investigators to analyze the calls or messages exchanged. The telephone records are a set of data relating to the external communications of the devices. In other words, they contain all the traces of communications (calls, SMS, and all the data traffic) concerning a specific user over a certain period of time. Note that phone records do not trace sensitive data such as the audio of calls sent or received. In fact, phone records only provide a trace of the communication that has taken place but not its content.

The phone records can be requested by the Judicial Authority if deemed useful in order to carry out investigations involving the individual owner of the phone. Correctly analyzing the telephone records is essential to obtain useful hints. Depending on the analysis, different kinds of information can be extracted. The records are typically analyzed for comparing the geographical positions with

---

[3] https://github.com/mpia3/Contrast-Pattern-Mining.

respect to the declarations, and for reconstructing the network of contacts of a single user in order to trace which conversations (s)he has had with whom, where and when. In this Section we report the preliminary results obtained by applying our ASP encoding for contrast pattern mining to a dataset of phone records.

4.1   The DigForASP Dataset

For our experiments we have considered a dataset that consists of the telephone records of four users from a real-world investigative case. The dataset has been made available by Prof. David Billard (University of Applied Sciences in Geneva) under NDA to DigForASP members for academic experimentation.

Each file in the dataset has the following schema:

- *Type*: what kind of operation the user has performed (*e.g.*, incoming/outgoing call or SMS);
- *Caller*: who makes the call or sends an SMS;
- *Callee*: who receives the call or SMS;
- *Street*: where the operation has taken place;
- *Time*: when the operation has taken place (ISO format[4] HH: MM: SS);
- *Duration*: how long the operation has been (ISO format HH: MM: SS);
- *Date*: when the operation has taken place (format: day, month, year).

The type of the operation is one of the following cases: "config", "gprs", "redirect", "out_sms(SUB_TYPE)", "in_sms(SUB_TYPE)", "out_call(SUB_TYPE)", "in_call(SUB_TYPE)". Sub-types are: "simple", "ack", "foreign".

The dataset has undergone the mandatory anonymization process for reasons of privacy and confidentiality. Therefore it does not contain data that allows tracing back to the real people involved in the investigative case. For instance, there is no phone number for the caller/callee but only a fictitious name. The names and the sizes (# rows) of the four files in the dataset are the following: Eudokia Makrembolitissa (8,783), Karen Cook McNally (20,894), Laila Lalami (12,689), and Lucy Delaney (8,480).

4.2   Preprocessing and ASP Encoding of the Dataset

The DigForASP dataset in its original format cannot be considered as a set of transactions in ASP syntax. It needs to undergo a transformation into the format described in Sect. 3. In short, each row of the dataset is encoded as a collection of facts through the *class* and *db* predicates. The transformation has been done by means of a Python script.

The classes refer to the operation type, namely: "in_sms", "out_sms", "in_call", "out_call", "config", "redirect", "gprs". The features are: *caller, callee, street_a, street_b, time, weekday* and *duration*. The *weekday* feature does not appear in the original dataset. It has been added with the following values: (0 = Monday, ..., 6 = Sunday). The *duration* feature has undergone a transformation

---

[4] Format to describe dates and times: https://en.wikipedia.org/wiki/ISO_8601.

in order to obtain a value expressed in seconds. The *time* feature has been discretized into four time slots: "morning" (from 06:00:00 to 11:59:59), "afternoon" (from 12:00:00 to 17:59:59), "evening" (from 18:00:00 to 23:59:59), and "night" (from 00:00:00 to 05:59:59). Depending on the analyst's needs, it is possible to consider (and encode) only the transactions related to specific days, months or years so as to subsequently carry out a more granular analysis. The transactions are sorted by date and time, as shown in Table 1.

Table 1. ASP encoding of some transactions from Karen's phone recordings from the morning of 07/09/2040 to the night of 08/09/2040.

```
_____ 07/09/2040 morning _____        _____ 07/09/2040 evening _____
class(t1,in_sms).                             class(t93,in_call).
db(t1,caller(lauretta_ngcobo)).               db(t93,caller(lady_anne_halkett)).
db(t1,callee(karen_cook_mcnally)).            db(t93,callee(karen_cook_mcnally)).
db(t1,street_a(bowsprit_avenue)).             db(t93,street_a(bigwood_court)).
db(t1,street_b(none)).                        db(t93,street_b(none)).
db(t1,date(7,9,2040)).                        db(t93,date(7,9,2040)).
db(t1,time(morning)).                         db(t93,time(evening)).
db(t1,weekday(4)).                            db(t93,weekday(4)).
db(t1,duration(0)).                           db(t93,duration(56)).

_____ 08/09/2040 night _____
class(t113,out_sms).              db(t113,caller(karen_cook_mcnally)).
db(t113,callee(karen_platt)).     db(t113,street_a(bayhampton_court)).
db(t113,street_b(none)).          db(t113,date(8,9,2040)).
db(t113,time(night)).             db(t113,weekday(5)). db(t113,duration(0)).
```

4.3   Experiments

For the experiments here presented we have run the ASP encoding reported in Listing 1.1 over the largest file from the DigForASP dataset, namely Karen's phone records, made up of more than 20,000 rows. As regards the ASP solver, we have used the version 5.4.0 of *clingo*, with default solving parameters. The hardware and software platform used was a laptop computer with Windows 10 (with Ubuntu 20.04.4 subsystem), AMD Ryzen 5 3500U @ 2.10 GHz, 8 GB RAM without using the multi-threading mode of clingo. Multi-threading reduces the mean runtime but introduces variance due to the random allocation of tasks. Such variance is inconvenient for interpreting results with repeated executions.

Exploratory Tests. During an investigation it is useful to understand what kind of information the extracted patterns can offer, in order to guide and support law enforcement in deciding the next steps to take during the investigation.

In Listing 1.2, as an illustrative example of the potential usefulness of contrast pattern mining in the DF field, we report the results obtained on Karen's phone records for the class "out_call". Here, we have set the minimum support threshold to 10% and the maximum pattern length to 3. Overall, the nine contrast patterns returned by the algorithm provide a rich information about the habits of Karen as regards outgoing calls in contrast to other types of communication. Notably, they tell us that outgoing calls of Karen are mainly done in the morning (Line 8) or in the afternoon (Line 6). In particular, the answer at Line 4 highlights that outgoing calls are made mainly on Fridays.

```
1    in_pattern(caller(karen_cook_mcnally)) absolute_diff(430)
2    in_pattern(time(evening)) absolute_diff(24)
3    in_pattern(caller(karen_cook_mcnally)) in_pattern(time(
       evening)) absolute_diff(129)
4    in_pattern(weekday(4)) absolute_diff(14)
5    in_pattern(weekday(4)) in_pattern(caller(
       karen_cook_mcnally)) absolute_diff(126)
6    in_pattern(time(afternoon)) absolute_diff(34)
7    in_pattern(caller(karen_cook_mcnally)) in_pattern(time(
       afternoon)) absolute_diff(202)
8    in_pattern(time(morning)) absolute_diff(37)
9    in_pattern(time(morning)) in_pattern(caller(
       karen_cook_mcnally)) absolute_diff(103)
```

Listing 1.2. Contrast patterns for the "out_call" class.

Scalability Tests. With scalability tests, the goal is to assess the performance of the ASP encoding on datasets of increasing size. Once again, we have considered the file of Karen's phone records, from we have extracted 100, 1000 and 10,000 rows for the three groups of experiments. In each group, the experiments have been conducted by varying the class for the contrast and the minimum support threshold while keeping the maximum patterns length fixed to 3.

The first group of experiments considers the subset consisting of 100 rows. Observing Table 2, the class with the greatest contrast patterns concerns the "out_call" operation. With this order of magnitude, the extraction times of the patterns are less than one second for all classes. In general, the memory used for this operation is at most 25 MB.

The second group of experiments considers a subset consisting of 1,000 rows. From Table 3, we observe that the class with the greatest number of contrast patterns is again "out_call". It is worthwhile to note that, with an increase in the order of magnitude from hundreds to thousands, the execution time fluctuates in a range between 5 and 10 s with a minimum percentage variation equal to 400% (Fig. 1 B). The memory consumed in this case is much higher than the previous batch of experiments since it jumps to a minimum of more than 300 MB, and a maximum that is around 460 MB (Fig. 1 C).

The third group of experiments considers a subset consisting of 10,000 rows. Unlike the previous two groups, this group did not produce results because the amount of resources to be allocated to the RAM memory was so high

Table 2. Number of patterns, execution time (seconds), solver time (seconds) and memory consumption (MB) for 100 rows from Karen's phone records.

in_sms

Th.	#Pat.	Exec. t.	Solv. t.	Memory
10%	14	0.119	0.01	23.67
20%	0	0.087	0.00	22.11
30%	0	0.081	0.00	22.35
40%	0	0.089	0.00	22.11
50%	0	0.085	0.00	21.85

out_sms

Th.	#Pat.	Exec. t.	Solv. t.	Memory
10%	0	0.085	0.00	22.31
20%	0	0.076	0.00	21.93
30%	0	0.086	0.00	21.67
40%	0	0.086	0.00	22.31
50%	0	0.086	0.00	22.18

in_call

Th.	#Pat.	Exec. t.	Solv. t.	Memory
10%	21	0.137	0.03	24.22
20%	14	0.118	0.01	24.01
30%	7	0.120	0.01	24.01
40%	0	0.086	0.00	21.98
50%	0	0.084	0.00	21.44

out_call

Th.	#Pat.	Exec. t.	Solv. t.	Memory
10%	32	0.136	0.03	24.23
20%	14	0.122	0.02	24.23
30%	14	0.128	0.01	24.23
40%	7	0.121	0.01	24.23
50%	7	0.117	0.01	24.44

(around 8GB) that the *clingo* process was killed by the operating system. Considering the pattern generation rule at Line 11 of Listing 1.1, the number of *item* atoms that must be combined to form the *in_pattern* atoms is equal to 2010. Instead, in the case of 100 and 1,000 rows the number of items are respectively 180 and 670. Since the total number of combinations is defined by

$$C_{n,k} = \binom{n}{k} = \frac{n!}{k!(n-k)!} \tag{3}$$

and the minimum pattern length k varies from 1 to 3 in our tests, the total number of combinations for the problem in hand is given by the sum of:

– groupings of class 1: $\frac{2010!}{1!(2010-1)!}$;
– groupings of class 2: $\frac{2010!}{2!(2010-2)!}$;
– groupings of class 3: $\frac{2010!}{3!(2010-3)!}$.

It is clear that the computation required to solve the problem in hand is very heavy for a dataset size of tens of thousands rows or even more.

5   Final Remarks

DPM is a promising direction of research in AI. We do not expect DPM to be competitive with dedicated algorithms, but to take advantage of the versatility of declarative frameworks to propose pattern mining tools that could exploit background knowledge during the mining process to extract less but meaningful patterns. Such tools are particularly welcome in application domains where the requirement of transparency is particularly crucial. This motivation is at the

Table 3. Number of patterns, execution time (sec), solver time (sec) and memory consumption (MB) for 1,000 rows from Karen's phone records.

in_sms

Th.	#Pat.	Exec. t.	Solv. t.	Memory
10%	3	5.929	0.15	427.18
20%	0	5.178	0.00	345.7
30%	0	4.939	0.00	345.7
40%	0	4.843	0.00	345.7
50%	0	4.980	0.00	345.7

out_sms

Th.	#Pat.	Exec. t	Solv. t.	Memory
10%	0	4.979	0.00	336.36
20%	0	4.761	0.00	325.87
30%	0	4.715	0.00	336.36
40%	0	4.795	0.00	336.36
50%	0	4.733	0.00	323.02

in_call

Th.	#Pat.	Exec. t.	Solv. t.	Memory
10%	5	7.683	1.65	453.93
20%	1	6.834	0.71	453.92
30%	1	6.423	0.36	454.03
40%	0	4.916	0.00	346.46
50%	0	4.978	0.00	346.46

out_call

Th.	#Pat.	Exec. t.	Solv. t.	Memory
10%	9	10.155	3.87	465.07
20%	3	8.591	2.41	465.11
30%	1	7.603	1.40	464.89
40%	1	6.765	0.56	465.08
50%	0	4.945	0.00	354.01

basis of a renewed interest of the AI community in declarative approaches. In particular, the expressive power of ASP makes the definition of algorithmic variants of the basic encoding pretty easy, mainly thanks to a clever use of constraints. Also, the availability of efficient ASP solvers encourage the use in applications characterized by combinatorial problems, such as the ones in pattern mining.

Contrast Pattern Mining is an interesting class of pattern mining problems. It is somehow halfway between discrimination and characterization of a data set, due to the use of class labels to guide the search for regularities. Nevertheless, to the best of our knowledge, it has not been addressed so far in DPM research. Our declarative approach is therefore a novel contribution to pattern mining which paves the way to new exciting AI applications. In particular, due to the inherent transparency, it appears to be suitable for analysing evidence in the context of DF investigations. As a case study we have considered the analysis of a real-world dataset of anonymised phone recordings. The preliminary results are encouraging, although they highlight some weaknesses. In particular, the combinatorial explosion affects the scalability of the approach. However, when compared to sequential pattern mining on the same dataset [15,16], it is noteworthy that in contrast pattern mining the solver takes much less time. This is partially due to the fact that the labeling of transactions with classes make the search space smaller.

For the future we plan to explore several directions of improvement of the work as regards efficiency and scalability. This implies different choices for the encoding, the solver, and the computing platform. Experiments could be, for instance, replicated with other ASP solvers, such as DLV2 [14], that revealed to be scalable on large datasets. Hybrid ASP-approaches to pattern mining such as [18] could be adopted. An empirical evaluation of the approach with a more

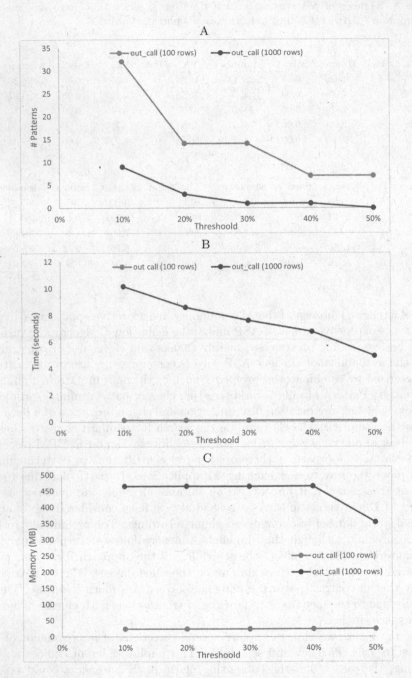

Fig. 1. Comparison w.r.t. the number of patterns extracted (A), execution time (B) and memory consumption (C) for the "out_call" class (Tables 2 and 3).

performant hardware is also planned. Besides the improvement of the current work, we intend to consider other variants of the contrast pattern mining problem. In parallel to the methodological work, we would like to benefit from a tighter interaction with DF experts in order to get their feedback as regards the validity and the usefulness of our work from DF viewpoint, and their suggestions for new interesting directions of applied research in this field.

Acknowledgments. This article is based upon work from COST Action 17124 "Digital forensics: evidence analysis via intelligent systems and practices (DigForASP)", supported by COST (European Cooperation in Science and Technology). The work is also partially funded by the Università degli Studi di Bari "Aldo Moro" under the 2017-2018 grant "Metodi di Intelligenza Artificiale per l'Informatica Forense".

References

1. Brewka, G., Eiter, T., Truszczynski, M.: Answer set programming at a glance. Commun. ACM **54**(12), 92–103 (2011). http://doi.acm.org/10.1145/2043174.2043195
2. Costantini, S., De Gasperis, G., Olivieri, R.: How answer set programming can help in digital forensic investigation. In: Ancona, D., Maratea, M., Mascardi, V. (eds.) Proceedings of the 30th Italian Conference on Computational Logic, Genova, Italy, 1–3 July 2015. CEUR Workshop Proceedings, vol. 1459, pp. 53–65. CEUR-WS.org (2015). http://ceur-ws.org/Vol-1459/paper29.pdf
3. Costantini, S., De Gasperis, G., Olivieri, R.: Digital forensics and investigations meet artificial intelligence. Ann. Math. Artif. Intell. **86**(1-3), 193–229 (2019). https://doi.org/10.1007/s10472-019-09632-y
4. Costantini, S., Lisi, F.A., Olivieri, R.: DigForASP: a european cooperation network for logic-based AI in digital forensics. In: Casagrande, A., Omodeo, E.G. (eds.) Proceedings of the 34th Italian Conference on Computational Logic, Trieste, Italy, 19–21 June 2019. CEUR Workshop Proceedings, vol. 2396, pp. 138–146. CEUR-WS.org (2019). http://ceur-ws.org/Vol-2396/paper34.pdf
5. De Raedt, L., Guns, T., Nijssen, S.: Constraint programming for data mining and machine learning. In: Twenty-Fourth AAAI Conference on Artificial Intelligence (2010)
6. Dong, G., Bailey, J.: Contrast Data Mining: Concepts, Algorithms, and Applications. CRC Press, Boca Raton (2012)
7. Gebser, M., Guyet, T., Quiniou, R., Romero, J., Schaub, T.: Knowledge-based sequence mining with ASP. In: IJCAI 2016–25th International Joint Conference on Artificial Intelligence, p. 8. AAAI (2016)
8. Gebser, M., Kaminski, R., Kaufmann, B., Schaub, T.: Clingo = ASP + control: preliminary report. arXiv preprint arXiv:1405.3694 (2014)
9. Gebser, M., Kaufmann, B., Kaminski, R., Ostrowski, M., Schaub, T., Schneider, M.: Potassco: the Potsdam answer set solving collection. AI Commun. **24**(2), 107–124 (2011)
10. Guns, T., Dries, A., Nijssen, S., Tack, G., De Raedt, L.: MiningZinc: a declarative framework for constraint-based mining. Artif. Intell. **244**, 6–29 (2017)
11. Guyet, T., Moinard, Y., Quiniou, R., Schaub, T.: Efficiency analysis of ASP encodings for sequential pattern mining tasks. In: Pinaud, B., Guillet, F., Cremilleux, B., de Runz, C. (eds.) Advances in Knowledge Discovery and Management. SCI, vol. 732, pp. 41–81. Springer, Cham (2018). https://doi.org/10.1007/978-3-319-65406-5_3

12. Han, J., Cheng, H., Xin, D., Yan, X.: Frequent pattern mining: current status and future directions. Data Min. Knowl. Discov. **15**(1), 55–86 (2007). https://doi.org/10.1007/s10618-006-0059-1

13. Jabbour, S., Sais, L., Salhi, Y.: Decomposition based SAT encodings for itemset mining problems. In: Cao, T., Lim, E.-P., Zhou, Z.-H., Ho, T.-B., Cheung, D., Motoda, H. (eds.) PAKDD 2015. LNCS (LNAI), vol. 9078, pp. 662–674. Springer, Cham (2015). https://doi.org/10.1007/978-3-319-18032-8_52

14. Leone, N., et al.: Enhancing DLV for large-scale reasoning. In: Balduccini, M., Lierler, Y., Woltran, S. (eds.) Logic Programming and Nonmonotonic Reasoning - 15th International Conference, LPNMR 2019, Philadelphia, PA, USA, 3–7 June 2019, Proceedings. LNCS, vol. 11481, pp. 312–325. Springer, Cham (2019). https://doi.org/10.1007/978-3-030-20528-7_23

15. Lisi, F.A., Sterlicchio, G.: Declarative pattern mining in digital forensics: preliminary results. In: Calegari, R., Ciatto, G., Omicini, A. (eds.) Proceedings of the 37th Italian Conference on Computational Logic, Bologna, Italy, June 29–1 July 2022. CEUR Workshop Proceedings, vol. 3204, pp. 232–246. CEUR-WS.org (2022). http://ceur-ws.org/Vol-3204/paper_23.pdf

16. Lisi, F.A., Sterlicchio, G.: Mining sequences in phone recordings with answer set programming. In: Bruno, P., Calimeri, F., Cauteruccio, F., Maratea, M., Terracina, G., Vallati, M. (eds.) HYDRA - RCRA 2022: 1st International Workshop on Hybrid Models for Coupling Deductive and Inductive Reasoning and 29th RCRA Workshop on Experimental Evaluation of Algorithms for Solving Problems with Combinatorial Explosion. CEUR Workshop Proceedings. CEUR-WS.org (2022)

17. Negrevergne, B., Guns, T.: Constraint-based sequence mining using constraint programming. In: Michel, L. (ed.) CPAIOR 2015. LNCS, vol. 9075, pp. 288–305. Springer, Cham (2015). https://doi.org/10.1007/978-3-319-18008-3_20

18. Paramonov, S., Stepanova, D., Miettinen, P.: Hybrid ASP-based approach to pattern mining. Theory Pract. Log. Program. **19**(4), 505–535 (2019). https://doi.org/10.1017/S1471068418000467

Graphs and Networks

Approximate Inference in Probabilistic Answer Set Programming for Statistical Probabilities

Damiano Azzolini[1]([✉])(iD), Elena Bellodi[2](iD), and Fabrizio Riguzzi[3](iD)

[1] Dipartimento di Scienze dell'Ambiente e della Prevenzione,
Università di Ferrara, Ferrara, Italy
damiano.azzolini@unife.it
[2] Dipartimento di Ingegneria, Università di Ferrara, Ferrara, Italy
elena.bellodi@unife.it
[3] Dipartimento di Matematica e Informatica, Università di Ferrara, Ferrara, Italy
fabrizio.riguzzi@unife.it

Abstract. "Type 1" statements were introduced by Halpern in 1990 with the goal to represent statistical information about a domain of interest. These are of the form "x% of the elements share the same property". The recently proposed language PASTA (Probabilistic Answer set programming for STAtistical probabilities) extends Probabilistic Logic Programs under the Distribution Semantics and allows the definition of this type of statements. To perform exact inference, PASTA programs are converted into probabilistic answer set programs under the Credal Semantics. However, this algorithm is infeasible for scenarios when more than a few random variables are involved. Here, we propose several algorithms to perform both conditional and unconditional approximate inference in PASTA programs and test them on different benchmarks. The results show that approximate algorithms scale to hundreds of variables and thus can manage real world domains.

Keywords: Probabilistic Answer Set Programming · Credal Semantics · Statistical statements · Approximate inference

1 Introduction

In [14] Halpern discusses the difference between "Type 1" (T1) and "Type 2" (T2) statements: the former describes a statistical property of the world of interest while the latter represents a degree of belief. "The probability that a random person smokes is 20%" is an example of "Type 1" statement while "John smokes with probability 30%", where John is a particular individual, is an example of "Type 2" statement.

Answer Set Programming (ASP) [7] is a powerful language that allows to easily encode complex domains. However, ASP does not allow uncertainty on the data. To handle this, we need to consider Probabilistic ASP (PASP) where the uncertainty is expressed through probabilistic facts, as done in Probabilistic

A. Dovier et al. (Eds.): AIxIA 2022, LNAI 13796, pp. 33–46, 2023.
https://doi.org/10.1007/978-3-031-27181-6_3

Logic Programming [10]. We focus here on PASP under the Credal Semantics [9], where each query is associated with a probability interval defined by a lower and an upper bound.

Recently, the authors of [3] introduced PASTA ("Probabilistic Answer set programming for STAtistical probabilities"), a new language (and software) where statistical statements are translated into PASP rules and inference is performed by converting the PASP program into an equivalent answer set program. However, performing exact inference is exponential in the number of probabilistic facts, and thus it is infeasible in the case of more than a few dozens of variables. In this paper, we propose four algorithms to perform approximate inference in PASTA programs: one for unconditional sampling and three for conditional sampling that adopt rejection sampling, Metropolis Hastings sampling, and Gibbs sampling. Empirical results show that our algorithms can handle programs with hundreds of variables. Moreover, we compare our algorithms with PASOCS [23], a solver able to perform approximate inference in PASP program under the Credal Semantics, showing that our algorithms reach a comparable accuracy in a lower execution time.

The paper is structured as follows: Sect. 2 discusses some related works and Sect. 3 introduces background concepts. Section 4 describes our algorithms for approximate inference in PASTA programs that are tested in Sect. 5. Section 6 concludes the paper.

2   Related Work

PASTA [3] extends Probabilistic Logic Programming [20] under the Distribution Semantics [21] by allowing the definition of Statistical statements. Statistical statements, also referred to as "Probabilistic Conditionals", are discussed in [16], where the authors give a semantics to T1 statements leveraging the maximum entropy principle. Under this interpretation, they consider the unique model that yields the maximum entropy. Differently from them, we consider all the models, thus obtaining a more general framework [3].

T1 statements are also studied in [15] and [24]: the former adopts the cross entropy principle to assign a semantics to T1 statements while the latter identifies only a specific model and a sharp probability value, rather than all the models and an interval for the probability, as we do.

We adopt the credal semantics [9] for PASP, where the probability of a query is defined by a range. To the best of our knowledge, the only work which performs inference in PASP under the Credal Semantics is PASOCS [23]. They propose both an exact solver, which relies on the generation of all the possible combinations of facts, and an approximate one, based on sampling. We compare our approach with it in Sect. 5.

Other solutions for inference in PASP consider different semantics that assign to a query a sharp probability value, such as [6,17,19,22].

3 Background

We assume that the reader is familiar with the basic concepts of Logic Programming. For a complete treatment of the field, see [18].

An Answer Set Programming (ASP) [7] rule has the form h1 ; ... ; hm :- b1, ... , bn. where each hi is an atom, each bi is a literal and :- is called the neck operator. The disjunction of the his is called the *head* while the conjunction of the bis is called the *body* of the rule. Particular configurations of the atoms/literals in the head/body identify specific types of rules: if the head is empty and the body is not, the rule is a *constraint*. Likewise, if the body is empty and the head is not, the rule is a *fact*, and the neck operator is usually omitted. We consider only rules where every variable also appears in a positive literal in the body. These rules are called *safe*. Finally, a rule is called *ground* if it does not contain variables.

In addition to atoms and literals, we also consider *aggregate atoms* of the form $\gamma_1 \omega_1 \, \#\zeta\{\epsilon_1, \ldots, \epsilon_l\} \, \omega_2 \gamma_2$ where γ_1 and γ_2 are constants or variables called *guards*, ω_1 and ω_2 are arithmetic comparison operators (such as $>$, $\geq$, $<$, and $\leq$), ζ is an aggregate function symbol, and each ϵ_i is an expression of the form $t_1, \ldots, t_i \,:\, F$ where each t_j is a term, F is a conjunction of literals, and $i > 0$. Moreover, each variable in $t_1, \ldots, t_i$ also appears in F.

We denote an answer set program with $\mathcal{P}$ and its Herbrand base, i.e., the set of atoms that can be constructed with all the symbols in it, as $B_\mathcal{P}$. An *interpretation* $I \subset B_\mathcal{P}$ satisfies a ground rule when at least one of the his is true in I when the body is true in I. A *model* is an interpretation that satisfies all the ground rules of a program $\mathcal{P}$. The *reduct* [11] of a ground program $\mathcal{P}_g$ with respect to an interpretation I is a new program $\mathcal{P}_g^r$ obtained from $\mathcal{P}_g$ by removing the rules in which a bi is false in I. Finally, an interpretation I is an *answer set* for $\mathcal{P}$ if it is a minimal model of $\mathcal{P}_g^r$. We consider minimality in terms of set inclusion and denote with $AS(\mathcal{P})$ the set of all the answer sets of $\mathcal{P}$.

Probabilistic Answer Set Programming (PASP) [8] is to Answer Set Programming what Probabilistic Logic Programming [20] is to Logic Programming: it allows the definition of uncertain data through probabilistic facts. Following the ProbLog [10] syntax, these facts can be represented with $\Pi :: f$ where f is a ground atom and Π is its probability. If we assign a truth value to every probabilistic fact (where $\top$ represents true and $\bot$ represents false) we obtain a *world*, i.e., an answer set program. There are 2^n worlds for a probabilistic answer set program, where n is the number of ground probabilistic facts. Many Probabilistic Logic Programming languages rely on the distribution semantics [21], according to which the probability of a world w is computed with the formula

$$P(w) = \prod_{i | f_i = \top} \Pi_i \cdot \prod_{i | f_i = \bot} (1 - \Pi_i)$$

while the probability of a *query* q (conjunction of ground literals), is computed with the formula

$$P(q) = \sum_{w \models q} P(w)$$

when the world has a single answer set.

For performing inference in PASP we consider the *Credal Semantics* [8], where every query q is associated with a probability range: the upper probability bound $\overline{P}(q)$ is given by the sum of the probabilities of the worlds w where there is *at least one* answer set of w where the query is present. Conversely, the lower probability bound $\underline{P}(q)$ is given by the sum of the probabilities of the worlds w where the query is present in *all* the answer sets of w, i.e.,

$$\overline{P}(q) = \sum_{w_i | \exists m \in AS(w_i),\ m \models q} P(w_i), \quad \underline{P}(q) = \sum_{w_i | |AS(w_i)| > 0\ \wedge\ \forall m \in AS(w_i),\ m \models q} P(w_i)$$

Note that the credal semantics requires that every world has at least one answer set. In the remaining part of the paper we consider only programs where this requirement is satisfied.

Example 1 (PASP Example). We consider 3 objects whose components are unknown and suppose that some of them may be made of iron with a given probability. An object made of iron may get rusty or not. We want to know the probability that a particular object is rusty. This can be modelled with:

```
1  0.2::iron(1).  0.9::iron(2).  0.6::iron(3).
2
3  rusty(X) ; not_rusty(X):- iron(X).
4  :- #count{X:rusty(X), iron(X)} = RI,
5      #count{X:iron(X)} = I, 10*RI < 6*I.
```

The constraint states that at least 60% of the object made of iron are rusty. This program has $2^3 = 8$ worlds. For example, the world where all the three probabilistic facts are true has 4 answer sets. If we consider the query q rusty(1), this world only contributes to the upper probability since the query is present only in 3 of the 4 answer sets. By considering all the worlds, we get $\underline{P}(q) = 0.092$ and $\overline{P}(q) = 0.2$, so the probability of the query lies in the range $[0.092, 0.2]$.

If we want to compute the conditional probability for a query q given evidence e, $P(q \mid e)$, we need to consider two different formulas for the lower and upper probability bounds [8]:

$$\overline{P}(q \mid e) = \frac{\overline{P}(q, e)}{\overline{P}(q, e) + \underline{P}(\neg q, e)}, \quad \underline{P}(q \mid e) = \frac{\underline{P}(q, e)}{\underline{P}(q, e) + \overline{P}(\neg q, e)} \tag{1}$$

Clearly, these are valid if the denominator is different from 0, otherwise the value is undefined. If we consider again Example 1 with query q rusty(1) and evidence e iron(2), we get $\underline{P}(q \mid e) = 0.08$ and $\overline{P}(q \mid e) = 0.2$.

Following the syntax proposed in [3], a *probabilistic conditional* is a formula of the form $(C \mid A)[\Pi_l, \Pi_u]$ stating that the fraction of As that are also Cs is between Π_l and Π_u. Both C and A are two conjunctions of literals. To perform inference, a conditional is converted into three answer set rules: i) C ; not_C :- A, ii) :- #count{X : C, A} = V0, #count{X : A} = V1, 10*V0 < 10*Π_l*V1, and iii) :- #count{X : C, A} = V0, #count{X :

A} = V1, 10*V0 > 10*Π_u*V1, where X is a vector of elements containing all the variables in C and A. If Π_l or Π_u are respectively 0 or 1, the rules ii) or iii) can be omitted. Moreover, if the probability values Π_l and Π_u have n decimal digits, the 10 in the multiplications above should be replaced with 10^n, because ASP cannot deal with floating point values.

A PASTA program [3] is composed of a set of probabilistic facts, a set of ASP rules, and a set of probabilistic conditionals.

Example 2 (Probabilistic Conditional (PASTA program)). The following program

```
1   0.2::iron(1). 0.9::iron(2). 0.6::iron(3).
2   (rusty(X) | iron(X))[0.6,1].
```

is translated into the PASP program shown in Example 1. The rule iii) is omitted since $\Pi_u = 1$.

In [3] an exact inference algorithm was proposed to perform inference with probabilistic conditionals, that basically requires the enumeration of all the worlds. This is clearly infeasible when the number of variables is greater than 20–30. To overcome this issue, in the following section we present different algorithms that compute the probability interval in an approximate way based on sampling techniques.

4 Approximate Inference for PASTA Programs

To perform approximate inference in PASTA programs, we developed four algorithms: one for unconditional sampling (Algorithm 1) and three for conditional sampling that adopt rejection sampling (Algorithm 2), Metropolis Hastings sampling (Algorithm 3), and Gibbs sampling (Algorithm 4) [4,5]. Algorithm 1 describes the basic procedure to sample a query (without evidence) in a PASTA program. First, we keep a list of sampled worlds. Then, for a given n number of times (number of samples), we sample a world id with function SAMPLEWORLD by choosing a truth value for every probabilistic fact according to its probability. For every probabilistic facts, the process is the following: we sample a random value between 0 and 1, call it r. If $r < \Pi_i$ for a given probabilistic fact f_i with associated probability Π_i, f_i is set to true, otherwise false. id is a binary string representing a world where, if the nth digit is 0, the nth probabilistic fact (in order of appearance in the program) is false, true otherwise. To clarify this, if we consider the program shown in Example 2, a possible world id could be 010, indicating that iron(1) is not selected, iron(2) is selected, and iron(3) is not selected. The probability of this world is $(1 - 0.2) \cdot 0.9 \cdot (1 - 0.6) = 0.288$. If we have already considered the currently sampled world, we look in the list of sampled worlds whether it contributes to the lower or upper counters (function GETCONTRIBUTION) and update the lower (lp) and upper (up) counters accordingly. In particular, GETCONTRIBUTION returns two values, one for the lower and one for the upper probability, each of which can be either 0 (the world id

does not contribute to the probability) or 1 (the world id contributes to the probability). If, instead, the world had never been encountered before, we assign a probability value to the probabilistic facts in the program according to the truth value (probability Π for $\top$, $1 - \Pi$ for $\bot$) that had been sampled (function SETFACTS), we compute its contribution to the lower and upper probabilities (function CHECKLOWERUPPER, with the same output as GETCONTRIBUTION), and store the results in the list of already encountered worlds (function INSERT-CONTRIBUTION). In this way, if we sample again the same world, there is no need to compute again its contribution to the two probability bounds. Once we have a number of samples equal to $Samples$, we simply return the number of samples computed for the lower and upper probability divided by $Samples$.

Algorithm 1. Function SAMPLE: computation of the unconditional probability from a PASTA program.

```
 1: function SAMPLE(Query, Samples, Program)
 2:     sampled ← {}                                              ▷ list of sampled worlds
 3:     lp ← 0, up ← 0, n ← 0
 4:     while n ≤ Samples do                        ▷ Samples is the number of samples
 5:         id ←SAMPLEWORLD(Program)
 6:         n ← n + 1
 7:         if id ∈ sampled then                         ▷ a world was already sampled
 8:             up₀, lp₀ ← GETCONTRIBUTION(sampled, id)
 9:             up ← up + up₀
10:             lp ← lp + lp₀
11:         else
12:             Programₐ ←SETFACTS(Program, id)
13:             lp₀, up₀ ← CHECKLOWERUPPER(Programₐ)
14:             lp ← lp + lp₀
15:             up ← up + up₀
16:             INSERTCONTRIBUTION(sampled, id, lp₀, up₀)
17:         end if
18:     end while
19:     return  lp/Samples ,  up/Samples
20: end function
```

When we need to account also for the evidence, other algorithms should be applied, such as rejection sampling. It is described in Algorithm 2: as in Algorithm 1, we maintain a list with the already sampled worlds. Moreover, we need 4 variables to store the joint lower and upper counters of q and e ($lpqe$ and $upqe$) and $\neg q$ and e ($lpnqe$ and $upnqe$), see Eq. 1. Then, with the same procedure as before, we sample a world. If we have already considered it, we retrieve its contribution from the $sampled$ list. If not, we set the probabilistic facts according to the sampled choices, compute the contribution to the four values, update them accordingly, and store the results. $lpqe_0$ is 1 if both the evidence and the query are present in all the answer sets of the current world, 0 otherwise. $upqe_0$ is 1 if both the evidence and the query are present in at least one answer set of the current world, 0 otherwise. $lpnqe_0$ is 1 if the evidence is present and the query is absent in all the answer sets of the current world, 0 otherwise. $upnqe_0$ is 1 if the evidence is present and the query is absent in at least one answer set of the current world, 0 otherwise. As before, we return the ratio between the number of samples combined as in Eq. 1.

Algorithm 2. Function REJECTIONSAMPLE: computation of the conditional probability from a PASTA program using Rejection sampling.

```
1: function REJECTIONSAMPLE(Query, Evidence, Samples, Program)
2:     lpqe ← 0,  upqe ← 0,  lpnqe ← 0,  upnqe ← 0,  n ← 0, sampled ← {}
3:     while n ≤ Samples do
4:         id ← SAMPLEWORLD(Program)
5:         n ← n + 1
6:         if id ∈ sampled then
7:             lpqe₀, upqe₀, lpnqe₀, upnqe₀ ← GETCONTRIBUTION(sampled, id)
8:             lpqe ← lpqe + lpqe₀,  upqe ← upqe + upqe₀
9:             lpnqe ← lpnqe + lpnqe₀,  upnqe ← upnqe + upnqe₀
10:        else
11:            Program_d ← SETFACTS(Program, id)
12:            lpqe₀, upqe₀, lpnqe₀, upnqe₀ ← CHECKLOWERUPPER(Program_d)
13:            lpqe ← lpqe + lpqe₀,  upqe ← upqe + upqe₀
14:            lpnqe ← lpnqe + lpnqe₀,  upnqe ← upnqe + upnqe₀
15:            INSERTCONTRIBUTION(sampled, id, lpqe₀, upqe₀, lpnqe₀, upnqe₀)
16:        end if
17:    end while
18:    return  lpqe/(lpqe + upnqe),  upqe/(upqe + lpnqe)
19: end function
```

In addition to rejection sampling, we developed two other algorithms that mimic Metropolis Hastings sampling (Algorithm 3) and Gibbs sampling (Algorithm 4). Algorithm 3 proceeds as follows. The overall structure is similar to Algorithm 2. However, after sampling a world, we count the number of probabilistic facts set to true (function COUNTTRUEFACTS). Then, with function CHECKCONTRIBUTION we check whether the current world has already been considered. If so, we accept it with probability $min(1, N_0/N_1)$ (line 18), where N_0 is the number of true probabilistic facts in the previous iteration and N_1 is the number of true probabilistic facts in the current iteration. If the world was never considered before, we set the truth values of the probabilistic facts in the program (function SETFACTS), compute its contribution with function CHECKLOWERUPPER, save the values (function INSERTCONTRIBUTION), and check whether the sample is accepted or not (line 27) with the same criteria just discussed. As for rejection sampling, we return the ratio between the number of samples combined as in Eq. 1.

Finally, for Gibbs sampling (Algorithm 4), we first sample a world until e is true (function TRUEEVIDENCE), saving, as before, the already encountered worlds. Once we get a world that satisfies this requirement, we switch the truth values of $Block$ random probabilistic facts (function SWITCHBLOCKVALUES, line 19) and we check the contribution of this new world as in Algorithm 2. Also there, the return value is the one described by Eq. 1.

5 Experiments

We implemented the previously described algorithms in Python 3 and we integrated them into the PASTA[1] solver [3]. We use clingo [12] to compute the answer

---

[1] Source code and datasets available at https://github.com/damianoazzolini/pasta.

Algorithm 3. Function MHSAMPLE: computation of the conditional probability from a PASTA program using Metropolis Hastings sampling.

```
 1: function MHSAMPLE(Query, Evidence, Samples, Program)
 2:     sampled ← {}
 3:     lpqe ← 0, upqe ← 0, lpnqe ← 0, upnqe ← 0, n ← 0, trueFacts₀ ← 0
 4:     while n ≤ Samples do
 5:         id ←SAMPLEWORLD(Program)
 6:         n ← n + 1
 7:         trueFacts₁ ← COUNTTRUEFACTS(id)
 8:         lpqe₀, upqe₀, lpnqe₀, upnqe₀ ←
 9:             CHECKCONTRIBUTION(Program_d, trueFacts₀, trueFacts₁, id, sampled)
10:         lpqe ← lpqe + lpqe₀,  upqe ← upqe + upqe₀
11:         lpnqe ← lpnqe + lpnqe₀,  upnqe ← upnqe + upnqe₀
12:         trueFacts₀ ← trueFacts₁
13:     end while
14:     return  lpqe/(lpqe + upnqe),  upqe/(upqe + lpnqe)
15: end function
16: function CHECKCONTRIBUTION(Program_d, N₀, N₁, id, sampled)
17:     if id ∈ sampled then
18:         if random < min(1, N₀/N₁) then          ▷ random is a random value ∈ [0, 1]
19:             return GETCONTRIBUTION(id, sampled)
20:         else
21:             return 0, 0, 0, 0
22:         end if
23:     else
24:         Program_d ← SETFACTS(Program, id)
25:         lpqe₀, upqe₀, lpnqe₀, upnqe₀ ← CHECKLOWERUPPER(Program_d)
26:         INSERTCONTRIBUTION(sampled, id, lpqe₀, upqe₀, lpnqe₀, upnqe₀)
27:         if random < min(1, N₀/N₁) then
28:             return lpqe₀, upqe₀, lpnqe₀, upnqe₀
29:         else
30:             return 0, 0, 0, 0
31:         end if
32:     end if
33: end function
```

sets. To assess the performance, we ran multiple experiments on a computer with Intel® Xeon® E5-2630v3 running at 2.40 GHz with 16 Gb of RAM. Execution times are computed with the bash command `time`. The reported values are from the `real` field.

We consider two datasets with different configurations. The first one, `iron`, contains programs with the structure shown in Example 2. In this case, the size of an instance indicates the number of probabilistic facts. The second dataset, `smoke`, describes a network where some people are connected by a probabilistic friendship relation. In this case the size of an instance is the number of involved people. Some of the people in the network smoke. A conditional states that at least 40% of the people that have a friend that smokes are smokers. An example of instance of size 5 is

```
1  0.5::friend(a,b). 0.5::friend(b,c).
2  0.5::friend(a,d). 0.5::friend(d,e).
3  0.5::friend(e,c).
4  smokes(b). smokes(d).
5  (smokes(Y) | smokes(X), friend(X,Y))[0.4,1].
```

Algorithm 4. Function GIBBSSAMPLE: computation of the conditional probability from a PASTA program using Gibbs sampling.

```
1: function GIBBSSAMPLE(Query, Evidence, Samples, Block, Program)
2:      sampledEvidence ← {}, sampledQuery ← {}
3:      lpqe ← 0, upqe ← 0, lpnqe ← 0, upnqe ← 0, n ← 0
4:      while n ≤ Samples do
5:          ev ← false, n ← n + 1
6:          while ev is false do
7:              id ←SAMPLEWORLD(Program)
8:              if id ∈ sampledEvidence then
9:                  ev ← sampledEvidence[id]
10:             else
11:                 Program_d ← SETFACTS(Program, id)
12:                 if TRUEEVIDENCE(Program_d) then
13:                     ev ← true, sampledEvidence[id] ← true
14:                 else
15:                     sampledEvidence[id] ← false
16:                 end if
17:             end if
18:         end while
19:         id_s ←SWITCHBLOCKVALUES(id, Block, Program, Evidence)
20:         if id_s ∈ sampled then
21:             lpqe_0, upqe_0, lpnqe_0, upnqe_0 ← GETCONTRIBUTION(sampled, id)
22:             lpqe ← lpqe +lpqe_0,  upqe ← upqe + upqe_0
23:             lpnqe ← lpnqe + lpnqe_0,  upnqe ← upnqe + upnqe_0
24:         else
25:             Program_d ← SETFACTS(Program, id)
26:             lpqe_0, upqe_0, lpnqe_0, upnqe_0 ← CHECKLOWERUPPER(Program_d)
27:             lpqe ← lpqe +lpqe_0,  upqe ← upqe + upqe_0
28:             lpnqe ← lpnqe + lpnqe_0,  upnqe ← upnqe + upnqe_0
29:             INSERTCONTRIBUTION(sampled, id, lpqe_0, upqe_0, lpnqe_0, upnqe_0)
30:         end if
31:     end while
32:     return (lpqe)/(lpqe + upnqe), (upqe)/(upqe + lpnqe)
33: end function
```

The number of probabilistic facts follows a Barabási-Albert preferential attachment model generated with the `networkx` [13] Python package. The initial number of nodes of the graph, n, is the size of the instance while the number of edges to connect a new node to an existing one, m, is 3.

In a first set of experiments, we fixed the number of probabilistic facts, for `iron`, and the number of people, for `smoke`, to 10 and plotted the computed lower and upper probabilities and the execution time by increasing the number of samples. All the probabilistic facts have probability 0.5. The goal of these experiments is to check how many samples are needed to converge and how the execution time varies by increasing the number of samples, with a fixed program. For the `iron` dataset, the query q is `rusty(1)` and the evidence e is `iron(2)`. Here, the exact values are $\underline{P}(q) = 0.009765625$, $\overline{P}(q) = 0.5$, $\underline{P}(q \mid e) = 0.001953125$, and $\overline{P}(q \mid e) = 0.5$. For the `smoke` dataset, the program has 21 connections (probabilistic facts): node 0 is connected to all the other nodes, node 2 with 4, 6, and 8, node 3 with 4, 5, and 7, node 4 with 5, 6, 7, and 9, and node 7 with 8 and 9. All the connections have probability 0.5. Nodes 2, 5, 6, 7, and 9 certainly smoke. The query q is `smokes(8)` and the evidence is `smokes(4)`. The targets are $\underline{P}(q) = 0.158$, $\overline{P}(q) = 0.75$, $\underline{P}(q \mid e) = 0$, and $\overline{P}(q \mid e) = 0.923$. Results for all the four algorithms are shown in Figs. 1 (`iron`) and 2 (`smoke`).

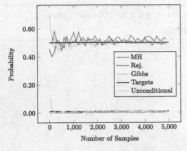
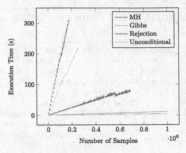

(a) Lower and upper probabilities.

(b) Execution time.

Fig. 1. Comparison of the sampling algorithms on the `iron` dataset. Straight lines are the results for PASTA while dashed lines for PASOCS.

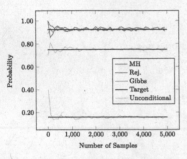
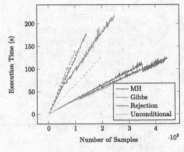

(a) Lower and upper probabilities.

(b) Execution times.

Fig. 2. Comparison of the sampling algorithms on the `smoke` dataset. Straight lines are the results for PASTA while dashed lines for PASOCS. In Fig. 2a the target line at 0.75 is for the upper unconditional probability.

For Gibbs sampling, we set the number *Block* (i.e., number of probabilistic facts to resample), to 1. All the algorithms seem to stabilize after a few thousands of samples for both datasets. For `iron`, MH seems to slightly overestimate the upper probability. Gibbs and rejection sampling require a few seconds to take 10^6 samples, while Metropolis Hastings (MH) requires almost 100 s. However, for the `smoke` dataset, MH and Rejection sampling have comparable execution times (more than 100 s for $5 \cdot 10^5$ samples) while Gibbs is the slowest among the three. This may be due to a low probability of the evidence.

We compared our results with PASOCS [23] (after translating by hand the probabilistic conditionals in PASP rules). We used the following settings: `-n_min n -n_max -1 -ut -1 -p 300 -sb 1 -b 0` where `n` is the number of considered samples, `n_min` is the minimum number of samples, `n_max` is the maximum number of samples (`-1` deactivates it), `ut` is the uncertainty threshold (`-1` deactivates it), `p` is the percentile (since they estimate values with gaussians), `sb` is the number of samples to run at once during sampling, and `b` is the burnin value for Gibbs and Metropolis Hastings sampling (0 deactivates it). We do not select parallel

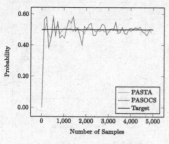

(a) Upper probability.

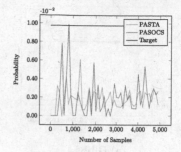

(b) Lower probability.

Fig. 3. Comparison of Gibbs sampling on the `iron` dataset.

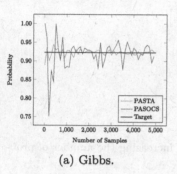

(a) Gibbs.

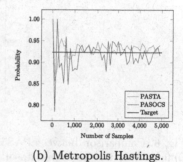

(b) Metropolis Hastings.

Fig. 4. Comparison of Gibbs sampling and MH on the `smoke` dataset.

solving, since PASTA is not parallelized yet (this may be the subject of a future work). PASOCS adopts a different approach for conditional inference: at each iteration, instead of sampling a world, it updates the probabilities of the probabilistic facts and samples a world using these values. In Fig. 1b, the execution times of PASOCS for all the tested algorithms are comparable and seem to grow exponentially with the number of samples. The lines for rejection and unconditional sampling for PASTA overlap. This also happens for the lines for MH, Gibbs, and rejection sampling for PASOCS. PASOCS seems to be slower also on the `smoke` dataset (Fig. 2b), but the difference with PASTA is smaller. We also plotted how PASTA and PASOCS perform in terms of number of samples required to converge. In Fig. 3, we compare Gibbs sampling on the `iron` dataset. Here, PASTA seems to be more stable on both lower and upper probability. However, even with 5000 samples, both still underestimate the lower probability, even if the values are considerably small. In Fig. 4 we compare PASOCS and PASTA on Gibbs sampling and Metropolis Hastings sampling on the `iron` dataset. Also here, PASTA seems more stable, but both algorithms are not completely settled on the real probability after 5000 samples. Finally, Fig. 5 compares the unconditional sampling of PASTA and PASOCS on both datasets. Here, the results are similar: after approximately 3000 samples, the computed probability

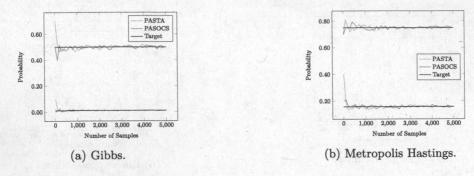

(a) Gibbs.   (b) Metropolis Hastings.

Fig. 5. Comparison of unconditional sampling on the `iron` and the `smoke` datasets.

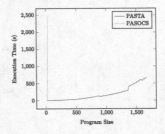

Fig. 6. Comparison between PASTA and PASOCS by increasing the number of probabilistic facts for the `iron` dataset.

seems to be stabilized. In another experiment, we fixed the number of samples to 1000, increased the size of the instances for the `iron` dataset, and plot how the execution time varies with PASTA and PASOCS. The goal is to check how the execution time varies by increasing the number of samples. The query is `rusty(1)`. Results are shown in Fig. 6. For PASOCS, we get a memory error starting from size 32. PASTA requires approximately 500 s to take 1000 samples on a program with the structure of Example 2 with 1500 probabilistic facts. Note again that, during sampling, we assume that every world has at least one answer set, since if we need to check this, all the worlds must be generated and clearly the inference will not scale.

6   Conclusions

In this paper, we propose four algorithms to perform approximate inference, both conditional and unconditional, in PASTA programs. We tested the execution time and the accuracy also against the PASOCS solver (after manually performing the conversion of probabilistic conditionals). Empirical results show that our algorithms reach a comparable accuracy in a lower execution time. As future work, we plan to better investigate the convergence of the algorithms and to develop approximate methods for abduction [1,2] in PASTA programs.

References

1. Azzolini, D., Bellodi, E., Ferilli, S., Riguzzi, F., Zese, R.: Abduction with probabilistic logic programming under the distribution semantics. Int. J. Approx. Reason. **142**, 41–63 (2022). https://doi.org/10.1016/j.ijar.2021.11.003
2. Azzolini, D., Bellodi, E., Riguzzi, F.: Abduction in (probabilistic) answer set programming. In: Calegari, R., Ciatto, G., Omicini, A. (eds.) Proceedings of the 36th Italian Conference on Computational Logic. CEUR Workshop Proceedings, vol. 3204, pp. 90–103. Sun SITE Central Europe, Aachen, Germany (2022)
3. Azzolini, D., Bellodi, E., Riguzzi, F.: Statistical statements in probabilistic logic programming. In: Gottlob, G., Inclezan, D., Maratea, M. (eds.) Logic Programming and Nonmonotonic Reasoning (LPNMR 2022), LNCS, vol. 13416, pp. 43–55. Springer, Cham (2022). https://doi.org/10.1007/978-3-031-15707-3_4
4. Azzolini, D., Riguzzi, F., Lamma, E.: An analysis of Gibbs sampling for probabilistic logic programs. In: Dodaro, C., et al. (eds.) Workshop on Probabilistic Logic Programming (PLP 2020). CEUR-WS, vol. 2678, pp. 1–13. Sun SITE Central Europe, Aachen, Germany (2020)
5. Azzolini, Damiano, Riguzzi, Fabrizio, Masotti, Franco, Lamma, Evelina: A comparison of MCMC sampling for probabilistic logic programming. In: Alviano, Mario, Greco, Gianluigi, Scarcello, Francesco (eds.) AI*IA 2019. LNCS (LNAI), vol. 11946, pp. 18–29. Springer, Cham (2019). https://doi.org/10.1007/978-3-030-35166-3_2
6. Baral, C., Gelfond, M., Rushton, N.: Probabilistic reasoning with answer sets. Theor. Pract. Log. Prog. **9**(1), 57–144 (2009). https://doi.org/10.1017/S1471068408003645
7. Brewka, G., Eiter, T., Truszczyński, M.: Answer set programming at a glance. Commun. ACM **54**(12), 92–103 (2011). https://doi.org/10.1145/2043174.2043195
8. Cozman, F.G., Mauá, D.D.: On the semantics and complexity of probabilistic logic programs. J. Artif. Intell. Res. **60**, 221–262 (2017). https://doi.org/10.1613/jair.5482
9. Cozman, F.G., Mauá, D.D.: The joy of probabilistic answer set programming: Semantics, complexity, expressivity, inference. Int. J. Approx. Reason. **125**, 218–239 (2020). https://doi.org/10.1016/j.ijar.2020.07.004
10. De Raedt, L., Kimmig, A., Toivonen, H.: ProbLog: a probabilistic Prolog and its application in link discovery. In: Veloso, M.M. (ed.) IJCAI 2007, vol. 7, pp. 2462–2467. AAAI Press/IJCAI (2007)
11. Faber, W., Pfeifer, G., Leone, N.: Semantics and complexity of recursive aggregates in answer set programming. Artif. Intell. **175**(1), 278–298 (2011). https://doi.org/10.1016/j.artint.2010.04.002
12. Gebser, M., Kaminski, R., Kaufmann, B., Schaub, T.: Multi-shot ASP solving with clingo. Theory Pract. Logic Program. **19**(1), 27–82 (2019). https://doi.org/10.1017/S1471068418000054
13. Hagberg, A.A., Schult, D.A., Swart, P.J.: Exploring network structure, dynamics, and function using NetworkX. In: Varoquaux, G., Vaught, T., Millman, J. (eds.) Proceedings of the 7th Python in Science Conference, pp. 11–15. Pasadena, CA, USA (2008)
14. Halpern, J.Y.: An analysis of first-order logics of probability. Artif. Intell. **46**(3), 311–350 (1990)
15. Jaeger, M.: Probabilistic reasoning in terminological logics. In: Doyle, J., Sandewall, E., Torasso, P. (eds.) 4th International Conference on Principles of Knowledge Representation and Reasoning, pp. 305–316. Morgan Kaufmann (1994). https://doi.org/10.1016/B978-1-4832-1452-8.50124-X

16. Kern-Isberner, G., Thimm, M.: Novel semantical approaches to relational probabilistic conditionals. In: Proceedings of the Twelfth International Conference on Principles of Knowledge Representation and Reasoning, pp. 382–392. AAAI Press (2010)

17. Lee, J., Wang, Y.: A probabilistic extension of the stable model semantics. In: AAAI Spring Symposia (2015)

18. Lloyd, J.W.: Foundations of logic programming, 2nd edn. Springer, Heidelberg (1987). https://doi.org/10.1007/978-3-642-83189-8

19. Nickles, Matthias: A tool for probabilistic reasoning based on logic programming and first-order theories under stable model semantics. In: Michael, Loizos, Kakas, Antonis (eds.) JELIA 2016. LNCS (LNAI), vol. 10021, pp. 369–384. Springer, Cham (2016). https://doi.org/10.1007/978-3-319-48758-8_24

20. Riguzzi, F.: Foundations of Probabilistic Logic Programming: Languages, Semantics, Inference and Learning. River Publishers, Gistrup, Denmark (2018)

21. Sato, T.: A statistical learning method for logic programs with distribution semantics. In: Sterling, L. (ed.) ICLP 1995, pp. 715–729. MIT Press (1995). https://doi.org/10.7551/mitpress/4298.003.0069

22. Totis, P., Kimmig, A., De Raedt, L.: SMProbLog: stable model semantics in ProbLog and its applications in argumentation. arXiv preprint arXiv:2110.01990 (2021)

23. Tuckey, D., Russo, A., Broda, K.: PASOCS: a parallel approximate solver for probabilistic logic programs under the credal semantics. arXiv preprint arXiv:2105.10908 (2021)

24. Wilhelm, M., Kern-Isberner, G., Finthammer, M., Beierle, C.: Integrating typed model counting into first-order maximum entropy computations and the connection to Markov logic networks. In: Barták, R., Brawner, K.W. (eds.) Proceedings of the Thirty-Second International Florida Artificial Intelligence Research Society Conference, pp. 494–499. AAAI Press (2019)

Decision Trees with a Modal Flavor

Dario Della Monica[1], Giovanni Pagliarini[2,3], Guido Sciavicco[3(✉)],
and Ionel Eduard Stan[2,3]

[1] University of Udine, Udine, Italy
`dario.dellamonica@uniud.it`
[2] University of Parma, Parma, Italy
`{giovanni.pagliarini,ioneleduard.stan}@unife.it`
[3] University of Ferrara, Ferrara, Italy
`guido.sciavicco@unife.it`

Abstract. Symbolic learning is the sub-field of machine learning that
deals with symbolic algorithms and models, which have been known for
decades and successfully applied to a variety of contexts, and of which
decision trees are the quintessential expression. The main limitation of
current symbolic models is the fact that they are essentially based on
classical propositional logic, which implies that data with an implicit
dimensional component, such as temporal, e.g., time series, or spatial
data, e.g., images, cannot be properly dealt with within the standard
symbolic framework. In this paper, we show how propositional logic in
decision trees can be replaced with the more expressive (propositional)
modal logics, and we lay down the formal bases of modal decision trees
by first systematically delineating interesting and well-known properties
of propositional ones and then showing how to transfer these properties
to the modal case.

Keywords: Machine learning · Decision trees · Modal logic · Learning
from dimensional data

1 Introduction

The most iconic and fundamental separation between sub-fields of machine learning is the one between *functional* and *symbolic* learning. Functional learning is the process of learning a *function* that represents the theory underlying a certain phenomenon, while symbolic learning is the process of learning a *logical description* that represents that phenomenon.

Whether one or the other approach should be preferred raised a long-standing debate among experts, which roots in the fact that functional methods tend to be more versatile and statistically accurate than symbolic ones, while symbolic methods are able to extract models that can be interpreted, explained, and then enhanced using human-expert knowledge. These characteristics of symbolic methods, both for *political* reasons (consider, for instance, the recent General Data Protection Regulation (GDPR) of the European Union [13], that highlights

A. Dovier et al. (Eds.): AIxIA 2022, LNAI 13796, pp. 47–59, 2023.
https://doi.org/10.1007/978-3-031-27181-6_4

the need for interpretable/explainable automatic learning-based decision-making processes, including those involving AI technologies) and *technical* ones (interpretable models are often easier to train, explore, integrate, and implement), are sometimes used as arguments for preferring a symbolic approach over a functional one. From a logical standpoint, canonical symbolic learning methods are all characterized by the use of propositional logic (they are, indeed, sometimes called *propositional* methods), and, among them, propositional decision trees are probably the best known.

The origin of modern decision trees dates back to the fifties [2]; a lot of work has been done since then, which includes, among others, [4,8,10,11,15–17], and decision tree models extracted using popular algorithms such as ID3, C4.5, and more recent ones, have been widely applied in the literature. Different decision tree models differ in their structure and the language on which they are based, but only slightly; from a structural point of view, it can be argued that virtually all such structures and learning algorithms stemmed, in some sense, from CART [4], which already contained all the fundamental ideas of decision trees.

Dimensional data, such as temporal or spatial data, cannot be dealt with in a proper, native way using propositional decision trees. The general to-go strategy to treat dimensional data with propositional models, such as decision trees, is to *flatten* the dimensional component, effectively hiding it. Flattening consists in massaging the dataset in such a way that dimensional attributes become scalar ones. As an example, a multivariate time series with n temporal attributes $A_1, \ldots, A_n$ can be transformed by applying one or more feature extractions function to all attributes, e.g., average, minimum, maximum, and the like, to obtain (a feature representation of) an instance $f_1(A_1), f_2(A_1), \ldots, f_1(A_2), f_2(A_2), \ldots$, which can now be treated, for example, by a standard decision tree. A more general approach consists of applying the same strategy to different *windows* along all dimensions, e.g., intervals in the temporal case, rectangles in the spatial one, and so on, obtaining several new attributes for each original one and each feature extraction function. At the limit, each temporal (spatial, ...) point may become a window. As an example, a single-variate time series A with N ordered points ends up being represented as the (unordered) collection $A(1), A(2), \ldots, A(N)$. Such a representation is called *lagged* (for temporal data) or *flattened* (for spatial ones).

In this paper, we adopt a different point of view, aiming at laying down the formal bases of *modal symbolic learning*, by means of which dimensional datasets can be dealt with in a native way. To this end, we replace propositional logic by *propositional modal logic* (*modal logic* for short) and we enhance decision trees accordingly. Modal logic [3] generalizes propositional logic by allowing one to natively express the relationships that emerge among the different *worlds*, e.g., time points, time intervals, multi-dimensional areas, that contribute to describe real-world scenarios. Since modal logic can be declined into more practical languages, such as temporal and spatial logics, and dimensional data can be seen as modal data, modal symbolic learning is immediately applicable to the dimensional case. Moreover, this is not the only possible application, as modal data emerge in a natural way also from non-dimensional data, like, for instance, in textual and graph-based data.

Here, we introduce *modal decision trees*, and we systematically study their logical properties, specifically, correctness. Standard decision trees are, indeed, correct, although the nature of their presentation, mostly driven by applications, tends to hide their theoretical aspects. While we are not interested in studying efficient implementations of learning algorithms, the driving principle of the definition of modal decision trees is the preservation of the simplicity and interpretability that characterize propositional ones. As a result, modal decision tree learning algorithms can be implemented starting from any implementation of propositional ones, and working one's way up.

The paper is organized as follows. In Sect. 2, we provide some preliminary definitions and concepts. In Sect. 3, we define modal decision trees and study their properties. Then, in Sect. 4, we briefly show how modal decision trees can be applied to learn from dimensional data, before concluding.

2   Preliminaries

Let $\mathcal{P}$ be a set of *propositional letters*. The well-formed formulas of *modal logic* (*ML*) are obtained from the following grammar:

$$\varphi ::= p \mid \neg\varphi \mid \varphi \wedge \varphi \mid \Diamond\varphi.$$

The other usual Boolean connectives can be derived from them, and, as standard, we use $\Box\varphi$ to denote $\neg\Diamond\neg\varphi$. The *modality* $\Diamond$ (resp., $\Box$) is usually referred to as *it is possible that* (resp., *it is necessary that*). Modal logic is considered as archetypical of (propositional) temporal, spatial, and spatio-temporal logics, and it is a non-conservative extension of *propositional logic* (*PL*). Its semantics is given in terms of Kripke models. A *Kripke model* $K = (W, R, V)$ *over* $\mathcal{P}$ consists of a (finite) set of *worlds* W, which contains a distinguished world w_0, called *initial world*, a binary *accessibility relation* $R \subseteq W \times W$, and a *valuation function* $V : W \to 2^{\mathcal{P}}$, which associates each world with the set of proposition letters that are true on it. The *truth* relation $K, w \Vdash \varphi$ for a model K and a world w in it is expresed by the following clauses:

$$K, w \Vdash p \qquad \text{iff } p \in V(w);$$
$$K, w \Vdash \neg\varphi \qquad \text{iff } K, w \not\Vdash \varphi;$$
$$K, w \Vdash \varphi \wedge \psi \text{ iff } K, w \Vdash \varphi \text{ and } K, w \Vdash \psi;$$
$$K, w \Vdash \Diamond\varphi \qquad \text{iff } \exists v \text{ s.t. } wRv \text{ and } K, v \Vdash \varphi.$$

We write $K \Vdash \varphi$ as an abbreviation for $K, w_0 \Vdash \varphi$.

The importance of modal logic comes from the fact that most classic temporal [5,7,14] and spatial logics [1,9] stem from (generalizations of) modal logic. Therefore, the theory of modal logic and the tools built on it can be reused to cope with more practical situations.

We now introduce the notion of modal dataset and its associated problems.

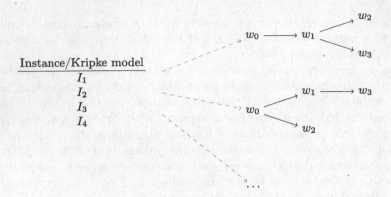

Fig. 1. An example of modal dataset with 4 instances, each described by a Kripke model.

Definition 1 (Modal dataset). *Let $\mathcal{P}$ be a set of proposition letters. A* modal dataset *$\mathcal{I} = \{I_1, \ldots, I_m\}$ over $\mathcal{P}$ is a finite collection of m instances, each of which is a Kripke model over $\mathcal{P}$, and such that I, J are not bisimilar, for each $I, J \in \mathcal{I}$ with $I \neq J$, that is, there exists at least one formula $\varphi \in ML$ with $I \Vdash \varphi$ and $J \not\Vdash \varphi$. We say that $\mathcal{I}$ is* labeled *if it is equipped with a labeling function $L : \mathcal{I} \to \mathcal{C}$ which associates every instance with a class from a finite set $\mathcal{C} = \{C_1, \ldots, C_k\}$.*

In the static case, a dataset is usually defined as a collection $\mathcal{I} = \{I_1, \ldots, I_m\}$ of m instances described, each, by the value of n distinct attributes $\mathcal{A} = \{A_1, \ldots, A_m\}$. However, since each attribute A is associated to its finite domain $dom(A)$, that is, the finite set of all values taken by A across $\mathcal{I}$, the latter naturally induces a set of propositional letters:

$$\mathcal{P} = \{A \bowtie a \mid \bowtie \in \{<, \leq, =, \geq, >\}, A \in \mathcal{A}, a \in dom(A)\}.$$

Learning-wise, therefore, we can always define a static dataset as if the corresponding set of propositional letters is fixed.

A modal dataset immediately generalizes a static one, by postulating that instances are described by Kripke frames in which attributes change value across different worlds. There are several scenarios that can be naturally modeled by modal, non-static datasets, instead; by way of example, *dimensional* datasets are characterized by each attribute in each instance being described by a d-dimensional matrix (e.g., $d = 1$ in the temporal case, and $d = 2$ in the spatial case). In such cases, fixed a set of *feature extraction function(s)* $\mathcal{F} = \{f_1, \ldots, f_k\}$, the set of induced propositional letters becomes:

$$\mathcal{P} = \{f(A) \bowtie a \mid \bowtie \in \{<, \leq, =, \geq, >\}, A \in \mathcal{A}, a \in dom(A), f \in \mathcal{F}\}.$$

Dimensional datasets are not the only source of modal datasets; in fact, our definition of modal dataset is more general, and captures a wide range of practical situations.

In the static case two instances cannot be identical, that is, there must be a propositional formula that distinguishes them; at the modal level, this requirement translates into constraining every two instances to be non-bisimilar (see, again, [3]), that is, to be distinguishable by at least one modal formula.

In machine learning, several problems are associated to a labeled dataset $\mathcal{I}$. Among them, a fundamental and ubiquitous one is the *classification* problem, that is, the problem of synthesizing an algorithm (a *classifier*) that is able to classify the instances of an unlabeled dataset $\mathcal{J}$ of the same type as $\mathcal{I}$.

In the symbolic context, learning a classifier from a dataset requires extracting from it the logical property that define each class, that is, its *characteristic* formula. Then, instances are seen as models of the considered logical formalism and the classification task is performed via model checking an instance against characteristic formulas. Although, in principle, one can be interested in learning characteristic formulas of any logic in any dataset, to modal (resp., propositional) datasets it is natural to associate modal (resp., propositional) characteristic formulas.

Binary decision trees, which are typical classifiers, are binary trees whose leaves and edges are equipped with labels. Leaf labels identify the different classes an instance can belong to; edge labels are atomic logical elements which are then composed to obtain complex formulas in the considered logical formalism (in the propositional case, edge labels edges are literals and formulas are Boolean combinations). A tree associates a formula to every class it features (i.e., every label occurring in a leaf) and it classifies an instance into a class if and only if the instance satisfies the formula corresponding to that class. As there can be exponentially many leaves in a tree, the classification process can possibly require verifying the satisfaction of an instance against exponentially many formulas.

However, decision trees provide an efficient mechanism for classifying an instance that does not explore the entire tree: for every node, starting from the root and going down towards the leaves, the truth of the formula associated with that node is checked against the instance to be classified and, depending on the outcome the instance is passed to the right or the left child and the process is repeated. When a leaf is reached, the instance is classified into the class that labels that leaf. Summing up, the desired properties for a family $\mathcal{M}$ of decision trees include: *(i)* *correctness* (every tree classifies any given instance into exactly one class); *(ii)* *completeness* (for every formula φ of the considered formalism, there is a decision tree $\tau \in \mathcal{M}$ that realizes φ); and *(iii)* *efficiency* (a decision tree τ of height h must be able to classify an instance I by checking the truth of, at most, a number of formulas polynomial in h).

In the rest of this paper we consider the problem of designing modal decision trees in such a way to be correct, complete, and efficient with respect to modal logic.

3   Modal Decision Trees

Let $\tau = (V, E)$ be a full directed finite binary tree with vertexes in V and edges in E. We denote by $root(\tau)$ the root of τ, by $V^\ell \subseteq V$ the set of its *leaves*, and by V^ι the set of its *internal nodes* (that is, non-root and non-leaf nodes). For each non-leaf node ν we denote by $\swarrow(\nu)$ (resp., $\searrow(\nu)$) its *left* (resp. *right*) *child*, and by $\wr(\nu)$ its *parent*. Similarly, for a tree τ, we denote by $\swarrow(\tau)$ (resp., $\searrow(\tau)$) its *left* (resp. *right*) *subtree*. Finally, for a node ν, the set of its *ancestors* (ν included) is denoted by $\wr^*(\nu)$, where $\wr^*$ is the transitive and reflexive closure of $\wr$; we also define $\wr^+(\nu) = \wr^*(\nu) \setminus \{\nu\}$.

A *path* $\pi^\tau = \nu_0 \rightsquigarrow \nu_h$ *in tree* τ (or, simply, π, if τ is clear form the context) of *length* $h \geq 0$ from ν_0 to ν_h is a finite sequence of $h + 1$ nodes $\nu_0, \ldots, \nu_h$ such that $\nu_i = \wr(\nu_{i+1})$, for each $i = 0, \ldots, h-1$. We denote by $\pi_1 \cdot \pi_2$ the operation of appending the path π_2 to the path π_1. We also say that a path $\nu_0 \cdot \nu_1 \rightsquigarrow \nu_h$ is *left* (resp., *right*) if $\nu_1 = \swarrow(\nu_0)$ (resp., $\nu_1 = \searrow(\nu_0)$). For a path $\pi = \nu_0 \rightsquigarrow \nu_h$, the set of its *improper prefixes* is denoted by $prefix(\pi)$, and if ν is a node in τ, π_ν^τ (or, simply, π_ν, if τ is clear from the context) denotes the unique path $root(\tau) \rightsquigarrow \nu$. Finally, a *branch* of τ is a path π_ℓ^τ (or, simply, π_ℓ, if τ is clear from the context) for some $\ell \in V^\ell$.

Definition 2 (modal decisions). *Fixed a modal dataset $\mathcal{I}$ over $\mathcal{P}$, the set of decisions is:*

$$\Lambda = \{\top, \bot, p, \neg p, \Diamond\top, \Box\bot \mid p \in \mathcal{P}\}.$$

We say that $p, \neg p$ are *propositional decisions*, while $\Diamond\top$ (resp., $\Box\bot$) are *modal existential* (resp., *modal universal*) ones, and we use the symbol $\lambda \in \Lambda$ to denote a decision. For each $\lambda \in \Lambda$, the decision that corresponds to its logical negation $\neg\lambda$ is univocally identified, so when $\lambda = \top$ (resp., $p, \Diamond\top$) we use $\neg\lambda$ to denote $\bot$ (resp., $\neg p, \Box\bot$), and vice versa.

Definition 3 (modal decision tree). *Fixed a propositional alphabet $\mathcal{P}$ and a set of classes $\mathcal{C}$, a modal decision tree τ over $\mathcal{P}$ and $\mathcal{C}$ is a structure:*

$$\tau = (V, E, b, l, s),$$

where (V, E) is a full directed finite binary tree, $l : V^\ell \to \mathcal{C}$ is the leaf-labeling *function, $b : V^\iota \to V^\iota$ is the* back-edge *function, $s : E \to \Lambda$ is the* edge-labeling *function, and the following conditions hold:*

1. $\forall \nu, \nu' \in V.(b(\nu) = \nu' \to \nu' \in \wr^*(\nu))$;
2. $\forall \nu, \nu' \in V.((b(\nu) \neq \nu \wedge b(\nu') \neq \nu') \to b(\nu) \neq b(\nu'))$;
3. $\forall \nu, \nu', \nu'' \in V.((b(\nu) = \nu' \wedge \nu' \in \wr^+(\nu'') \wedge \nu'' \in \wr^+(\nu)) \to \nu' \in \wr^+(b(\nu'')))$;
4. $\forall (\nu, \nu') \in E.((s(\nu, \nu') \in \{\bot, \Box\bot\} \wedge \nu' \notin V^\ell) \to b(\nu') \neq \nu')$;
5. $\forall (\nu, \nu'), (\nu, \nu'') \in E.(s(\nu, \nu') = \neg s(\nu, \nu''))$.

For every $c \in \mathcal{C}$, we denote by $leaves^\tau(c)$ (or, simply, $leaves(c)$, when τ is clear from the context) the set of leaves of τ labeled with c.

A propositional decision tree is a modal decision tree in which edges are labeled with propositional decisions and the back-edge function plays no role (therefore, in propositional decision trees only condition 5 is still non-trivial); thus, propositional decision trees are a particular case of modal decision trees. In the following, we denote by $\mathcal{MDT}$ the *family* of modal decision trees (or *modal decision tree classification model*), and by $\mathcal{DT}$ its propositional counterpart (that is, the sub-family of $\mathcal{MDT}$ that only contains propositional trees). From now on, we use the term decision tree to refer to an element of either $\mathcal{DT}$ or $\mathcal{MDT}$.

We now show how a modal decision tree defines a modal formula for each of its classes. This is obtained by associating a formula to each branch, and then the formula of a class is the disjunction of all the formulas associated to branches whose leaf is labeled with that class. In the propositional case, each branch is associated to the conjunction of the labels that occur on its edges; as every propositional formula can be written in disjunctive normal form, propositional decision trees are complete with respect to propositional logic. Modal logic does not have a normal form that allows one to bound the nesting of modal operators, and this makes the construction of formulas more complicated. Let us first fix the following useful concepts.

Definition 4 (contributor, node agreement). *Given a decision tree τ and a path $\pi = \nu_0 \leadsto \nu_h$, with $h > 1$, the* contributor *of π, denoted $ctr(\pi)$, is defined as the only node ν_i in π such that $\nu_i \neq \nu_1$, $0 < i < h$, and $b(\nu_i) = \nu_1$, if it exists, and as ν_1 otherwise. Moreover, given two nodes $\nu_i, \nu_j \in \pi$, with $i, j < h$, we say that they* agree *if $\nu_{i+1} = \,\searrow\!(\nu_i)$ (resp., $\nu_{i+1} = \,\swarrow\!(\nu_i)$) and $\nu_{j+1} = \,\searrow\!(\nu_j)$ (resp., $\nu_{j+1} = \,\swarrow\!(\nu_j)$), and we denote this situation by $A(\nu_i, \nu_j)$, and that they* disagree *(denoted by $D(\nu_i, \nu_j)$), otherwise.*

To our purposes, we use the following grammar to generate formulas of ML:

$$\varphi ::= \lambda \mid \lambda \wedge (\varphi \wedge \varphi) \mid \lambda \to (\varphi \to \varphi) \mid \Diamond(\varphi \wedge \varphi) \mid \Box(\varphi \to \varphi),$$

where $\lambda \in \Lambda$.

Definition 5 (implicative formulas). *We say that a modal formula φ is* implicative *if it has the form $\psi \to \xi$, or $\Box(\psi \to \xi)$, and we denote by Im the set of implicative formulas.*

As a matter of fact, in order to assign a formula to each leaf, and then to each class, we first associate a formula to every path (see Fig. 2 for an example).

Definition 6 (path-, leaf-, and class-formula). *Let τ be a decision tree. For each path $\pi = \nu_0 \leadsto \nu_h$ in τ, the* path-formula φ_π^τ *(or, simply, φ_π, when τ is clear from the context) is defined inductively as:*

- *If $h = 0$, then $\varphi_\pi = \top$.*
- *If $h = 1$, then $\varphi_\pi = s(\nu_0, \nu_1)$.*

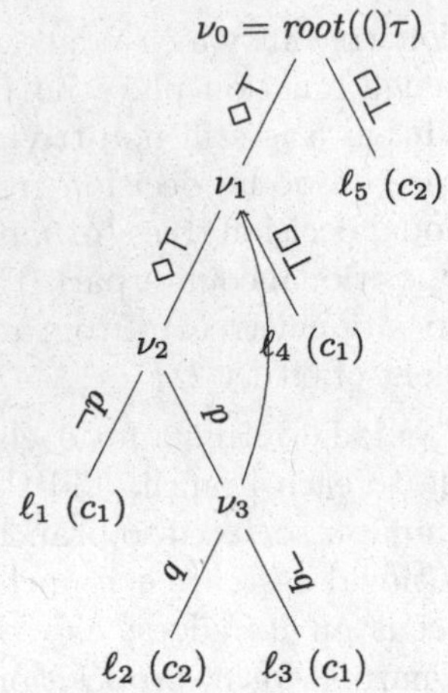

$$\nu_0 = root(()\tau)$$

$$\varphi_{\nu \rightsquigarrow \nu} = \top, \forall \nu \in V^\ell$$
$$\varphi_{\zeta(\nu)\rightsquigarrow \nu} = s(\zeta(\nu),\nu), \forall \nu \in V \setminus \{\nu_0\}$$

$$\varphi_{\nu_1 \rightsquigarrow \ell_1} = \Diamond(\top \land \neg p)$$
$$\varphi_{\nu_0 \rightsquigarrow \nu_2} = \Diamond(\top \to \Diamond\top)$$
$$\varphi_{\nu_0 \rightsquigarrow \ell_1} = \Diamond(\top \land \Diamond(\top \land \neg p)) \qquad = \varphi_{\pi_{\ell_1}}$$
$$\varphi_{\nu_1 \rightsquigarrow \nu_3} = \Box(\top \to p)$$
$$\varphi_{\nu_0 \rightsquigarrow \nu_3} = \Box(\top \to \Box(\top \to p))$$
$$\varphi_{\nu_0 \rightsquigarrow \ell_2} = \Diamond(\Box(\top \to p) \land q) \qquad = \varphi_{\pi_{\ell_2}}$$
$$\varphi_{\nu_0 \rightsquigarrow \ell_3} = \Box(\Box(\top \to p) \to \neg q) \qquad = \varphi_{\pi_{\ell_3}}$$
$$\varphi_{\nu_0 \rightsquigarrow \ell_4} = \Box(\top \to \Box\bot) \qquad\qquad = \varphi_{\pi_{\ell_4}}$$

$$\varphi_\ell = \bigwedge_{\pi \in prefix(\pi_\ell)} \varphi_\pi, \forall \ell \in V^\ell$$

$$\varphi_{c_1} = \varphi_{\ell_1} \lor \varphi_{\ell_3} \lor \varphi_{\ell_4}$$
$$\varphi_{c_2} = \varphi_{\ell_2} \lor \varphi_{\ell_5}$$

Fig. 2. On the left-hand side, an example of a modal decision tree; on the right-hand side, all relevant path-, leaf-, and class-formulas (φ_{ℓ_5} is included in the second group from the top).

- *If $h > 1$, let $\lambda = s(\nu_0, \nu_1)$, $\pi_1 = \nu_1 \rightsquigarrow ctr(\pi)$, and $\pi_2 = ctr(\pi) \rightsquigarrow \nu_h$. Then,*

$$\varphi_\pi = \begin{cases} \lambda \land (\varphi_{\pi_1} \land \varphi_{\pi_2}) & \text{if} \quad \lambda \neq \Diamond\top, A(\nu_0, ctr(\pi)), \text{ and } \varphi_{\pi_2} \notin Im, \\ & \text{or } \lambda \neq \Diamond\top, D(\nu_0, ctr(\pi)), \text{ and } \varphi_{\pi_2} \in Im; \\ \lambda \to (\varphi_{\pi_1} \to \varphi_{\pi_2}) & \text{if} \quad \lambda \neq \Diamond\top, D(\nu_0, ctr(\pi)), \text{ and } \varphi_{\pi_2} \notin Im, \\ & \text{or } \lambda \neq \Diamond\top, A(\nu_0, ctr(\pi)), \text{ and } \varphi_{\pi_2} \in Im; \\ \Diamond(\varphi_{\pi_1} \land \varphi_{\pi_2}) & \text{if} \quad \lambda = \Diamond\top, A(\nu_0, ctr(\pi)), \text{ and } \varphi_{\pi_2} \notin Im, \\ & \text{or } \lambda = \Diamond\top, D(\nu_0, ctr(\pi)), \text{ and } \varphi_{\pi_2} \in Im; \\ \Box(\varphi_{\pi_1} \to \varphi_{\pi_2}) & \text{if} \quad \lambda = \Diamond\top, D(\nu_0, ctr(\pi)), \text{ and } \varphi_{\pi_2} \notin Im, \\ & \text{or } \lambda = \Diamond\top, A(\nu_0, ctr(\pi)), \text{ and } \varphi_{\pi_2} \in Im. \end{cases}$$

Then, for each leaf $\ell \in V^\ell$, the leaf-formula φ_ℓ^τ (or, simply φ_ℓ, when τ is clear from the context) is defined as:

$$\varphi_\ell = \bigwedge_{\pi \in prefix(\pi_\ell)} \varphi_\pi.$$

Finally, for each class c, the class-formula φ_c^τ (or, simply, φ_c, when τ is clear from the context), is defined as:

$$\varphi_c = \bigvee_{\ell \in leaves(c)} \varphi_{\pi_\ell}.$$

Definition 7 (run). *Let $\tau = (V, E, b, l, s)$ be a modal decision tree, ν a node in τ, and I an instance in a modal dataset $\mathcal{I}$. Then, the run of τ on I from ν, denoted $\tau(I, \nu)$, is defined as:*

$$\tau(I,\nu) = \begin{cases} l(\nu) & \text{if } \nu \in V^{\ell} \\ \tau(I, \swarrow(\nu)) & \text{if } I \Vdash \varphi_{\pi_{\swarrow(\nu)}} \\ \tau(I, \searrow(\nu)) & \text{if } I \Vdash \varphi_{\pi_{\searrow(\nu)}}. \end{cases}$$

The run of τ on I (or the class assigned to I by τ), denoted $\tau(I)$, is defined as $\tau(I, root(\tau))$.

Following the above definition, a modal decision tree classifies an instance using its class-formulas, and does so by checking, progressively, the path-formulas that contribute to build a leaf-formula, which, in turn, is one of the disjuncts that take part in a class-formula. Observe that, inter alia, this implies that propositional decision trees can be seen as particular cases of modal decision trees even from a semantic point of view: formulas of the type $\varphi_1 \wedge \varphi_2$ behave exactly as in the propositional case, while those of the type $\varphi_1 \rightarrow \varphi_2$, are such that their the antecedent is always included as a conjunct in their corresponding leaf-formula, effectively reducing it to a conjunction, as in the propositional case.

Now, on the one side, the efficiency of classification depends on how leaf-formulas are checked, while on the other side correctness and completeness depend on their semantics. Let us start by evaluating the efficiency of modal decision trees.

Definition 8 (efficiency). *We say that a decision tree τ of height h is efficient if and only if, for every dataset $\mathcal{I}$ and every instance $I \in \mathcal{I}$, it is the case that its run $\tau(I)$ can be computed in polynomial time with respect to h and to the size of I. A family of decision trees is efficient if and only all of its decision trees are efficient.*

The following result holds due to the fact that model checking an ML formula against a Kripke structure can be done in polynomial time in the sizes of the structure and the formula [6], and the fact that the size of the formula associated to a path is linear in the length of the path itself.

Theorem 1 (efficiency of $\mathcal{MDT}$). *The family $\mathcal{MDT}$ is efficient.*

Now, we want to prove that modal decision trees are correct.

Definition 9 (correctness). *We say that a decision tree τ is correct if and only if, for every dataset $\mathcal{I}$ and every instance $I \in \mathcal{I}$, it is the case that I satisfies exactly one of its class-formulas φ_c. A family of decision trees is correct if and only all of its decision trees are correct.*

The following lemma can be proved by induction on the lengths of the paths, and the correctness of $\mathcal{MDT}$ follows.

Lemma 1. *Let τ be a modal decision tree, and let $\pi_1 = \nu_0 \rightsquigarrow \nu_{h-1} \cdot \swarrow(\nu_{h-1})$ and $\pi_2 = \nu_0 \rightsquigarrow \nu_{h-1} \cdot \searrow(\nu_{h-1})$ be two paths. Then, $\varphi_{\pi_1} \leftrightarrow \neg\varphi_{\pi_2}$ is valid.*

Theorem 2 (correctness of $\mathcal{MDT}$). *The family $\mathcal{MDT}$ is correct.*

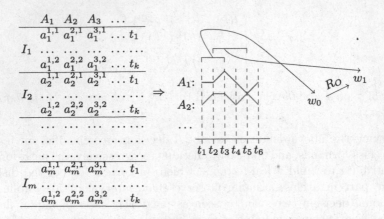

Fig. 3. Typical presentation of an implicit temporal data set.

Finally, we discuss the completeness of modal decision trees with respect to modal logic.

Definition 10 (completeness). *We say that a family of decision trees is strong- ly complete for a logical formalism if and only if, for each of its formula φ, there is a decision tree τ and a class $c \in C$ such that $\varphi_c \leftrightarrow \varphi$ is valid. We also say that a family of decision trees is weakly complete for a logical formalisms if and only if, for each of its formula φ, there is a decision tree τ and two classes $c, \bar{c} \in C$ such that $\varphi_c \rightarrow \varphi$ and $\varphi_{\bar{c}} \rightarrow \neg\varphi$ are both valid.*

Modal decision trees are strongly complete with respect to propositional logic by definition, and weakly complete with respect to modal logic.

Lemma 2. *Let $\varphi \in ML$. Then, there exists a modal decision tree τ and two leaves $\ell_c, \ell_{\bar{c}} \in V^\ell$ such that $\varphi_{\pi_{\ell_c}} \leftrightarrow \varphi$ and $\varphi_{\pi_{\ell_{\bar{c}}}} \leftrightarrow \neg\varphi$ are both valid.*

Theorem 3 (completeness of $\mathcal{MDT}$). *The family $\mathcal{MDT}$ is strongly complete for PL and weakly complete for ML.*

4   Applications

To show the potential of modal symbolic learning, in this section we consider two representative learning situations: from temporal data and from spatial data. As we have observed, spatial/temporal datasets can be seen as modal ones, and modal logic can be declined into suitable spatial/temporal logics that are able to describe such data. An example of *dimensional* dataset in the temporal case is given in Fig. 3 (left); here, m instances are described by several attributes, each one of which takes value on each of the time points that contribute to the description. Thus, this is a set of multi-variate time series; examples of real

Table 1. Test results: propositional versus modal learning from the public, 1-dimensional data set NATOPS (left), and from the public, 2-dimensional data set INDIAN PINES. Performances are reported in percentage points.

Seed	Temporal Propositional			Temporal Modal			Spatial Propositional			Spatial Modal		
	Acc.	Sen.	Spe.	Acc.	Sen.	Spe.	Acc.	Sen.	Spe.	Acc.	Sen.	Spe.
1	79.17	79.17	95.83	88.89	88.89	97.78	59.58	59.58	96.33	79.58	79.58	98.14
2	83.33	83.33	96.67	88.89	88.89	97.78	62.50	62.50	96.59	79.58	79.58	98.14
3	80.56	80.56	96.11	93.06	93.06	98.61	63.75	63.75	96.70	67.92	67.92	97.08
4	77.78	77.78	95.56	91.67	91.67	98.33	62.50	62.50	96.59	79.58	79.58	98.14
5	84.72	84.72	96.94	91.67	91.67	98.33	62.92	62.92	96.63	75.83	75.83	97.80
6	77.78	77.78	95.56	88.89	88.89	97.78	57.08	57.08	96.10	71.25	71.25	97.39
7	83.33	83.33	96.67	84.72	84.72	96.94	71.25	71.25	97.39	80.00	80.00	98.18
8	80.56	80.56	96.11	91.67	91.67	98.33	62.92	62.92	96.63	75.83	75.83	97.80
9	80.56	80.56	96.11	84.72	84.72	96.94	58.75	58.75	96.25	77.08	77.08	97.92
10	75.00	75.00	95.00	87.50	87.50	97.50	62.92	62.92	96.63	79.58	79.58	98.14
Avg.	80.27	80.27	96.05	89.16	89.16	97.83	62.42	62.42	96.58	76.62	76.62	97.87

situations that can be described by sets of multi-variate time series range from hospitalized patients that are constantly monitored, to different sport activities described by the values of wearable sensors, to industrial machines whose behaviour is recorded over time.

In many such situations, the relevant information is not necessarily visible at time points, but rather at time intervals, and in many cases the information to be extracted is concerned with prolonged events that take place at the same, or overlapping, or separate times, which is, again, a situation that is more naturally described with intervals rather than points. One way to extract such information is considering the multi-variate time series that corresponds to each instance, as in Fig. 3 (right), and each interval that can be built on it. Each such interval is regarded as a world, as in Fig. 3 (right), and worlds are connected through interval-interval relations. Taking the standard approach to do so results in having 12 interval-interval relations, excluding equality, that is *meets* (R_A), *overlaps* (R_O), *begins* (R_B), *ends* (R_E), *during* (R_D), and *later* (R_L); in turn, these give rise to a multi-modal logic which is known as HS (from the authors that first introduced it, Halpern and Shoham [7]) which we can use to extract knowledge from a single-dimensional dataset. In Fig. 3 (right), we have shown the relation *overlaps* by way of example. In the spatial case, we can generalize both the definition of world and the relations between worlds, and devise a 2-dimensional version of HS, in order to apply the same idea.

We performed a simple classification experiment on two public datasets, using a prototype, simple version of $\mathcal{MDT}$ (available at [12]); besides being publicly available, the chosen datasets have been selected taking into account their number of attributes and instances, and their representativeness for temporal and spatial problems. The first dataset is temporal, and known as NATOPS. It contains data generated by sensors on the hands, elbows, wrists and thumbs, in all three coordinates, along the temporal axis, of subjects performing several repetitions of aircraft hand signals, chosen among the 24 most often used ones; the problem consists in recognizing the specific signal. The second one is spatial, known as INDIAN PINES, and contains an hyperspectral image over a single landscape in Indiana (US) with 145×145 pixels, each represented by 220 spectral reflectance bands, and classified into one or more of sixteen types of crops; the problem is to recognize the type of cultivation in each pixel. While it would be premature to draw any conclusions from a single group of experiments, we can already see the improvement that we can expect to observe stepping from a static to a modal approach in Table 1. The results (accuracy, sensitivity, specificity) marked as *modal* are compared with those obtained with the same datasets using simple aggregating functions and propositional decision trees (*propositional*).

5   Conclusions

In this paper, we have shown how propositional decision trees can be generalized into modal decision trees. To this end, we have first highlighted the desirable properties of a family of decision trees in terms of efficiency of classification and logical properties, with respect to a given logical formalism. Then, we designed a family of efficient decision trees that is correct with respect to modal logic.

Application-wise, we have argued that, on the one side, different kinds of data are inherently non-propositional, including dimensional (temporal, spatial, spatial/temporal) data, graph-based data, and textual data, and that, on the other side, the logical formalisms that fit such cases are inherently modal. We considered two specific dimensional cases (a temporal one and a spatial one), and executed a learning experiment comparing the performances of propositional and modal decision trees on the same problem and under the same conditions. Temporal and spatial learning have been deeply studied in the machine learning literature; our purpose here is not that of comparing the performances of learning models in absolute terms, but to show the improvement that we can expect from introducing modal logic in symbolic learning schemata.

The current implementation of modal decision trees is simpler than the one presented in this paper. The problem of devising an efficient implementation of a learning algorithm that extracts full modal decision trees is still open. While the problem of extracting the optimal decision tree is knowingly NP-hard already at the propositional level, much work has been done on approximation algorithms; adapting such algorithms to this proposal, and studying their computational complexity, is an open issue as well.

Finally, decision trees are not the only symbolic learning classification method that can be generalized from the propositional to the modal case; the same can be done, at least, with rule-based systems and ensembles of trees, giving rise to what could be called *modal symbolic learning*.

References

1. Aiello, M., van Benthem, J.: A modal walk through space. J. Appl. Non-Class. Log. **12**(3–4), 319–364 (2002)
2. Belson, W.A.: A technique for studying the effects of television broadcast. J. Roy. Stat. Soc. Ser. C **5**(3), 195–202 (1956)
3. Blackburn, P., de Rijke, M., Venema, Y.: Modal Logic. Cambridge University Press, Cambridge (2001)
4. Breiman, L., Friedman, J.H., Olshen, R.A., Stone, C.J.: Classification and Regression Trees. Wadsworth Publishing Company, New York (1984)
5. Clarke, E.M., Emerson, E.A.: Design and synthesis of synchronization skeletons using branching time temporal logic. In: Kozen, D. (eds.) Logics of Programs. Logic of Programs 1981. LNCS, vol. 131, pp. 52–71. Springer, Heidelberg (1982). https://doi.org/10.1007/BFb0025774
6. Clarke, E.M., Grumberg, O., Peled, D.A.: Model Checking. MIT Press, Cambridge (2001)
7. Halpern, J.Y., Shoham, Y.: A propositional modal logic of time intervals. J. ACM **38**(4), 935–962 (1991)
8. Kass, G.V.: An exploratory technique for investigating large quantities of categorical data. J. Roy. Stat. Soc. Ser. C **29**(2), 119–127 (1980)
9. Lutz, C., Wolter, F.: Modal logics of topological relations. Log. Methods Comput. Sci. **2**(2), 1–41 (2006)
10. Messenger, R., Mandell, L.: A modal search technique for predictive nominal scale multivariate analysis. J. Am. Stat. Assoc. **67**(340), 768–772 (1972). https://doi.org/10.1080/01621459.1972.10481290
11. Morgan, J.N., Sonquist, J.A.: Problems in the analysis of survey data, and a proposal. J. Am. Stat. Assoc. **58**(302), 415–434 (1963). https://doi.org/10.2307/2283276
12. Pagliarini, G., Manzella, F., Sciavicco, G., Stan, I.E.: ModalDecisionTrees.jl: interpretable models for native time-series & image classification (v0.80) zenodo (2022). https://doi.org/10.5281/zenodo.7040420
13. Parliament and Council of the European Union: General data protection regulation (2016). https://gdpr-info.eu/
14. Pnueli, A.: The temporal logic of programs. In: 18th Annual Symposium on Foundations of Computer Science (SFCS 1977), pp. 46–57. IEEE (1977)
15. Quinlan, J.R.: Induction of decision trees. Mach. Learn. **1**, 81–106 (1986). https://doi.org/10.1007/BF00116251
16. Quinlan, J.R.: C4.5: Programs for Machine Learning. Morgan Kaufmann, Burlington (1993)
17. Quinlan, J.R.: Simplifying decision trees. Int. J. Hum. Comput. Stud. **51**(2), 497–510 (1999)

Assisted Process Knowledge Graph Building Using Pre-trained Language Models

Patrizio Bellan[1,2](✉), Mauro Dragoni[1], and Chiara Ghidini[1]

[1] Fondazione Bruno Kessler, Trento, Italy
{pbellan,dragoni,ghidini}@fbk.eu
[2] Free University of Bozen-Bolzano, Bolzano, Italy

Abstract. The automated construction of knowledge graphs from procedural documents is a challenging research area. Here, the lack of annotated data, as well as raw text repositories describing real-world procedural documents, make it extremely difficult to adopt deep learning approaches. Pre-trained language models have shown promising results concerning the knowledge extraction tasks from the models themselves. Although several works explored this strategy to build knowledge graph, the viability of knowledge base construction by using prompt-based learning strategy from such language models has not yet been investigated deeply. In this work, we present a prompt-based in-context learning strategy to extract, from natural language process descriptions, conceptual information that can be converted into their equivalent knowledge graphs. Such a strategy is performed in a multi-turn dialog fashion. We validate the accuracy of the proposed approach from both quantitative and qualitative perspectives. The results highlight the feasibility of the proposed approach within low-resource scenarios.

Keywords: Process extraction from text · In-context learning · Knowledge graph · Pre-trained language model · Business process management

1 Introduction

The automatic building of knowledge graphs (KGs) from text is a long-standing goal in the Artificial Intelligence (AI) community that opened many challenges within specific research areas, e.g. information extraction (IE), natural language processing (NLP), and knowledge representation and reasoning (KRR). KGs aim to organize raw information with an appropriate structured form by capturing the entities described within the source repositories (represented through *nodes*) and their relationships (represented through labeled edges). The availability of effective KGs may trigger reasoning tasks to infer unobserved facts from observed evidence, i.e., the nodes and the labeled edges contained within the KGs. The building of such KGs may pass through the analysis of complex and dynamic

A. Dovier et al. (Eds.): AIxIA 2022, LNAI 13796, pp. 60–74, 2023.
https://doi.org/10.1007/978-3-031-27181-6_5

textual information containing both entities and relationships that have to be included within the KG. The construction of KGs by starting from this type of information may be challenging since the relevant entities contained within these texts are common sense terms that within specific contexts can assume relevant conceptual meaning. Recent advances in NLP, like the availability of *large pre-trained language models* (PLMs) and the introduction of novel *in-context learning* approaches, enable the possibility to mimic few-shot learning techniques without changing any model parameter [6,18]. Conversational information seeking (CIS) systems can be exploited to extract conceptual information from natural language text and to represent such information in a structured form within a KG. These systems are drawing growing attention in both academia and industry. They aim at supporting search and question answering (among other tasks) using multi-turn dialogues. Given the high quality of such language models as potential representations of relational knowledge, an interesting research direction to explore is to support the automatic construction of KGs through the use of PLM to understand how much conceptual and relational knowledge they can extract, how much such knowledge differs from reality, and how it is possible to make them more effective within specific contexts.

In this paper, we explore the feasibility of using *in-context learning* to perform knowledge extraction from procedural documents in a question-and-answer multi-turn dialog fashion. To the best of our knowledge, this task is performed for the first time in the literature. An example of a multi-turn dialog is shown in Fig. 1. A user interacts with a *cognitive artificial agent* that mimics an expert of a specific domain. The agent guides the knowledge extraction task by answering a set of questions posed incrementally by the user. Then, KG is built on top of the answers generated by the PLM. As a representative scenario, we target the Business Process Management (BPM) area, and in particular the process extraction from text task [4]. This domain is characterized by a limited size of the gold-standard data available which is highly hampering its development. We use the Generative Pre-trained Transformer 3 model (GPT-3) [6] as the artificial agent. We explore different settings of the adopted PLM to perform in-context

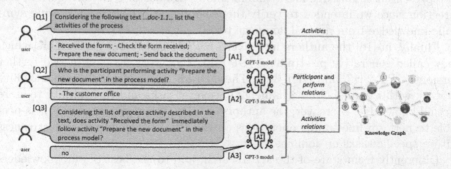

Fig. 1. In this example of multi-turn dialog, the artificial agent guides the construction of the process knowledge graph by answering the user.

learning: (i) no fine-tuning, (ii) by providing conceptual definitions, and (ii) by providing an extremely limited number of examples, i.e., to mimic the few-shot learning technique. Within our use case, we aim to extract entities and relations from procedural descriptions.

2   Related Work

The information extraction research area has been widely explored in the literature embracing many domains [14]. Specifically, on the use of PLMs, several works investigated their use aiming to understand both linguistic and semantic properties of possible word representations and also how PLMs can be exploited within specific knowledge and linguistic tasks. Compared to the aims mentioned above, our approach goes against the trend by trying to exploit PLMs to extract and store factual and common-sense knowledge with the aim of constructing KGs automatically.

However, the adoption of PLMs has been investigated from several perspectives. A systematic comparison between neural-based and count-based representations has been performed in [1]. Neural-based representations were demonstrated to be more effective with respect to the count-based ones in most of the tested tasks. Hence, given the neural-based nature of PLMs, they may be considered a suitable starting point for this work. Details about the required granularity of these representations have been investigated, instead, in [12].

The capability of PLMs concerning the understanding and, in turn, the generation of sentences grammatically correct has been investigated in [15] and [20]. The former demonstrated how ungrammatical sentences do not affect the understanding capability of PLMs. The latter investigated how PLMs are suitable for being used within different domains and tasks without particular fine-tuning activities. However, even if the flexibility of PLMs is quite high, this work highlighted how it is possible to customize them to obtain more effective PLMs addressing specific tasks or to be used in specific domains. Moreover, it provides little insight into whether these models can compete with traditional approaches to representing knowledge like symbolic knowledge bases. Our work goes in this direction since we intended to verify the feasibility of PLMs in extracting symbolic knowledge from natural language texts.

Finally, in [16] the authors introduced a PLM based on transformers which they called generative pre-training (GPT-1). This work evolved in two further versions: GPT-2 [17] and GPT-3 [6]. These PLMs demonstrated their suitability to work within zero-shot environments in several tasks and their ability to store factual knowledge. Moreover, the authors of GPT-3 demonstrated how it is possible to perform fine-tuning operations on the PLM to enhance its effectiveness within specific tasks or domains.

Differently from state-of-the-art research, and to the best of our knowledge, this is the first investigation concerning the extraction of conceptual knowledge from text using in-context learning which aims at dealing with an entire textual description without making assumptions regarding the input text. Then, it is done in an incremental and flexible conversational fashion to extract the required information via question-and-answer dialogues. Our work is the first attempt to use these models on this specific problem and therefore the results and lessons learned are likely to pave the way to future efforts, possibly involving different strategies, target entities and relations, and also other PLMs.

3   Use Case

We introduced in Sect. 1 how the strategy proposed in this paper is agnostic with respect to the domain. Indeed, the use of in-context learning techniques to extract knowledge from natural language text allows one to ask for specific types of information from a PLM without specifying a priori the domain of interest. To demonstrate the feasibility of the proposed solution, we rely on a use case related to the construction of small-size KGs by starting from natural language documents providing descriptions of procedures. This task, known as *Process information extraction from text*, can be regarded as the specific problem of finding a way to transform process descriptions into structured representations of different expressivity, up to the entire formal process model diagram [3,4]. We choose this task since it is highly hampered by data scarcity issue. We extract entities from raw texts that are relevant to populate the equivalent KG, which could then be refined or used to build graphical models. We exploited a part of the PET dataset [2] to validate our strategy. Such a dataset is the only publicly available annotated gold-standard dataset specific for process extraction from text tasks. It contains 45 texts annotated with process models elements and relations[1]. KGs are built by means of a question-answering style that mimic a multi-turn dialog with an expert. In our setup, the GPT-3 model acts as a domain expert.

4   Knowledge Extraction from Text via In-Context Learning

This section describes the approach we designed and implemented to perform the extraction of knowledge, both entities and relations, from text via in-context learning.

The starting point is a set of the conceptual elements (entities and/or relationships) we aim at extracting, and the first building block of the approach is the formulation of a series of incremental questions posed, e.g., by the user in Fig. 1 from Q1 to Q3, to the GPT-3 model in a sequential manner which enables the extraction of those specific entities and relationships. These questions become the specific entities that GPT-3 has to solve with the help of specific prompts.

---

[1] The description of the dataset, the annotation guidelines, the annotation schema, and the annotation process are out of the scope of this paper and the interested reader can find all the material at https://huggingface.co/datasets/patriziobellan/PET.

In our dialog pipeline, answers to a question *can* are used as inputs to formulate further questions. For instance, as shown in the figure, firstly we ask for the list of activities described in a text (Q1) and we use the answers (A1) to populate the KG with activity nodes. Then, for each activity, we ask who is the participants performing it (Q2). We use this information (A2) to populate the KG with the participant nodes and the perform relation. Finally, for each activity pair, we ask if they stand in a *following* relation and we use this information (A3) to complete the KG with activity-activity relations. The overall pipeline supports both options, i.e., the use of gold information to perform each step or the re-use of the output obtained from the previous step to perform the new one. In this work, we focused on the latter strategy since we intend to investigate the capability of constructing a KG from scratch and without the usage of gold information.

The second building block of the approach is the construction of the *prompt* (the input feeds to the model) to perform in-context learning. Prompts are generated starting from templates that are filled using two types of information: (i) *contextual knowledge* which enable GPT-3 to identify the specific domain at hand and the elements to be extracted for the different tasks; and (ii) few *examples* of the task at hand. Once ready the prompts are fed into the model in order to generate the answer.

The third building block of our approach is the PLM used in the conversation to mimics an expert in the field. As motivated in Sect. 2, we decided to start from GPT-3 [6] since it is one of the state-of-the-art PLM and it can be adopted without fine-tuning it toward a specific goal. Other transformer-like models such as BERT [9] or RoBERTa [13] could not be adopted to perform in-context learning since they usually require specific training (or fine-tuning) toward a down-stream task to exhibit acceptable performances. Real-world scenarios may not be often supported by transformer-like approaches due to low-resource issues. Hence, we have decided to directly start our investigation from GPT-3 and from the notion of *in-context learning* since it can overcome such an issue. We, therefore, tackle the task in a question-and-answering fashion, not as an information extraction task. We used the answers generated by the model to build the knowledge graph of the process described in a text. Needless to say, this first investigation into the usage of PLMs for process extraction from text does not aim at saying the final word on this topic but, on the contrary, it aims at opening up the possibility to better investigate and exploit this kind of approach in the future.

4.1   In-Context Learning

PLMs, such as GPT-3 [6] or BERT [9], are built by using an impressive amount of data and exploiting the advances of deep learning engineering and computational power [6,18]. PLMs are becoming a hot topic in NLP as they can be adopted and fine-tuned, to solve complex tasks in different domains, such as open question answering in prototypical common-sense reasoning [5]. While the fine-tuning of PLMs for task-specific applications has become standard practice in NLP in the last few years, the advent of GPT-3 greatly changed this paradigm. This model opens the possibility of injecting task-specific knowledge without doing a "classical" fine-tuning of the model parameters toward a specific downstream task. The model uses the knowledge provided in input to refine the reasoning capabilities toward the task to solve. This technique is called **in-context learning**, where contextual knowledge, task instruction, very few examples of how to solve the task, and the actual input data are given as input all together in a *prompt*. The prompt is then sent as input into the model.

This approach has been shown to be extremely useful to address the low-resource issue [19] and has been used to address topics ranging from medical dialogue summarization [8] to hate speech detection [11]. We illustrate the notion of prompt by showing an abstract example in Fig. 2. The prompts we used in our experiments are customization of this prompt.

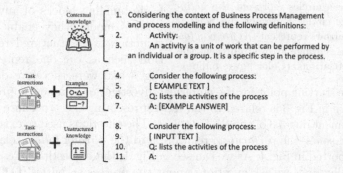

Fig. 2. Abstract example of prompt adopted in our experiment to do in-context learning.

Lines 1–3 describe the *contextual knowledge* component and provide the model with *contextual information* that is used to narrow the model's *reasoning capability* to the specific context at hand (Business Process Management, in our case). This knowledge can help the model to disambiguate the different meanings of a word (e.g., activity). In our example, they are composed of the identification of the domain (Business Process Management) and definitions of them.

Lines 4–7 describe *examples* component and provide examples of the task to be solved together with the solution. It is composed of three parts containing: (i) a textual example [line 4], (ii) the task instructions to be performed upon the text [line 6], and (iii) the correct answer(s) [line 7]. In the sample prompt, we included only one example.

Lines 8–10 describe the *task instructions* component and provide the task instructions describing the actual problem to be solved [line 10] and the *process description* in input [line 9] where the task has to be performed upon. Finally, line 11 is an *eliciting answer mark* that tells the model that the prompt is ended and to start producing an answer. At inference time, the prompt is the input feed into the model.

4.2   Implementing the Approach

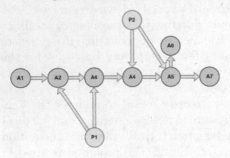

Fig. 3. The entities and relations contained in the KG of document 3.3 of the PET dataset. Green circles represent the *activities*. Orange circles represent the *participants*. Blue arrows represent the *directly follow* relations. Orange arrows represent the *performing* relations. (Color figure online)

While the overall approach presented here does not depend upon the particular process elements we extract, in this paper, we decided to use it for the extraction of *activities, participants* (that is, actors in this context), the *performing* relation between a participant and the activity(ies) it performs, and the sequence relation between activities (hereafter *directly follow* relation). We focus on these four elements as they constitute the basic building blocks of any business process model, they enable the construction of a structured representation such as the one represented in Fig. 3 and were therefore deemed an appropriate starting point for the empirical investigation of a new approach. The graph shown in Fig. 3 is related to the KG representing the procedure described in the document doc-3.3 of the PET dataset. The questions used to extract *activities, participants*, the *performing* relation, and the *directly follow* relation from text are reported in Fig. 4. As we can see in Fig. 1, these questions are performed incrementally: first, we ask questions about the process activities (**Q1**), then we enrich the activities with the participants performing them (**Q2**), and finally, we ask about the precedence relation among activities (**Q3**). Also, question **Q2** is used to retrieve both the participant and the performing relationship between activities. The incremental order of the questions is interesting because it mimics the way we often build conceptual models using follow-up questions. This first work does not aim at investigating this aspect in depth. We are aware that there is a growing literature corpus on prompt-based fine-tuning, as described, e.g. in [10]. But, an investigation into the most efficient prompt is out of scope for this first paper.

Q1: *Lists the activities of the process*;
Q2: *Who is the participant performing activity X in the process model?*
    for each activity returned by Q1;
Q3: *Considering the list of process activity described in the text, does activity X immediately follow activity Y in the process model?*,
    for each pair of different activities X and Y returned by Q1.

Fig. 4. The questions adopted as *task instructions* in prompts.

Our in-context learning approach exploits two sources of *information*: *contextual knowledge* and few *examples* related to the task at hand. For this specific paper *contextual knowledge* consists in the text in Fig. 5: (i) a preamble identifying the business process management (BPM) context and the definitions of process elements to be extracted.

Considering the context of Business Process Management and process modeling and the following definitions:

Activity: An activity is a unit of work that can be performed by an individual or a group. It is a specific step in the process.

Participant: A participant is any individual or entity that participates in a business process. This could include individuals who initiate the process, those who respond to it, or those who are affected by it.

Process Model: A process model is a model of a process in terms of process activities and their sequence flow relations.

Flow: A flow object captures the execution flow among the process activities. It is a directional connector between activities in a Process. It defines the activitieséxecution order.

Sequence Flow: A Sequence Flow object defines a fixed sequential relation between two activities. Each Flow has only one source and only one target. The direction of the flow (from source to target) determines the execution order between two Activities. A sequence relation is an ordered temporal relation between a source activity and the activity that immediately follows it in the process model.

Fig. 5. Contextual knowledge provided in prompts.

5   Empirical Assessment

We provide below the procedure adopted to evaluate the proposed approach. We start by better specifying the tasks to be solved, then by describing the experimental settings provided by the different prompts, then the dataset used for the evaluation, and finally the obtained results. Also, even if we automatically extract the target elements (activities, participants, and relations) from the GPT-3 answers, we manually validated them all. We performed the experiments by adopting the *text-davinci-001* engine and set all the other model's parameters (e.g., sampling temperature) to 0.0. We want to remark here that the comparison among different model configurations is postponed to future investigation since they are out of the scope of this paper. We performed a quantitative evaluation by applying the Graph Edit Distance (GED) [7] metric to compare the KGs created by using the gold standard annotations with the ones generated by using the information extracted from the GPT-3 PLM. Then, we provided a qualitative evaluation in which we analyze, by starting from a representative example extracted from our dataset, the main pros and cons, concerning our use case, about the usage of a PLM for automatically building a KG[2].

---

[2] The reader may find all the material of this research at https://pdi.fbk.eu/pet/aixia/ aixia2022_material.zip.

5.1   The Tasks

The overall task we are assessing is the generation of the KGs by starting from procedural documents. We designed a multi-turn dialog pipeline in which each interaction provides KG information about the nodes and the edges of the graph to obtain a process representation similar to the one proposed in Fig. 3.

In order to get the information required to build the KG, our dialog pipeline addresses two categories of sub-tasks: process elements extraction (activities and participants) and relations extraction (participant performer and activities relations). In the **Activity extraction** sub-task we customized prompt-templates *task instructions* with question **Q1**. We performed the extraction of **Process participants** together with the **Performs** relation extraction sub-task by customizing the prompt-templates *task instructions* with question **Q2**. Finally, the **Follows** relation sub-task compared pairs of activities to assess for each pair if they stand in sequential order. We customized prompt-templates *task instructions* with question **Q3**, by completing the instructions with a pair of activities at a time. We are aware that the extraction of *Participants*, and the relations *Follow* and *Performs* is influenced by the quality of the extraction of the activities. We want to remark here that we evaluated the proposed approach by comparing extracted graphs with the gold standard ones. In our experiments, we did not take into account the comparison between the accuracy of extracting such relations by using the gold annotations provided in the PET dataset. Instead, we measure the ability of the system to extract these three elements on the basis of the activities extracted by **Q1**, thus measuring the effective quality of the incremental question-answering interaction.

5.2   Experimental Setting

We evaluated the proposed approach with four experimental settings. Here we adopt the terminology described in Sect. 4 to explain our experimental settings.

In the RAW setting the GPT-3 model has been used as it is provided by the maintainers without any customization. We created this setting by providing *task instructions* and *process description text* only to the prompt template. This setting works as a baseline to observe the capability of the native model of working within complex scenarios.

We built the second experimental setting, called DEFS, on top of the RAW setting. We customized the prompt template by adding *contextual knowledge* to narrow the model's reasoning ability. The contextual knowledge we provided is composed of the *contextual information* and the definition proposed in Fig. 5. The aim was to inject domain-specific conceptual knowledge into the language model to observe the capability of the system to exploit the basic domain knowledge.

The third setting, called 2SHOTS, was built on top of the RAW setting by adding the *examples* component. In our experiments, we used the gold standard annotations provided by the documents 2.2 and 10.9 of the PET dataset. Here, for the extraction of *Activity* and *Participant* only the annotations related to activities, activity data, and participants have been provided. While, for the extraction of *Follows* and *Performs* relationships, only the annotations related to sequence flow and performing have been provided. This strategy has been adopted to avoid the injection of non-essential information that may cause noise in the model. Finally, in the DEFS+2SHOTS setting we use both strategies described above. We enhanced the DEFS setting with the *examples* component.

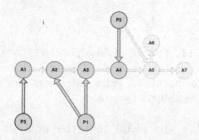

Fig. 6. The entities and relations contained in the KG of document 3.3 extracted using the RAW prompt.

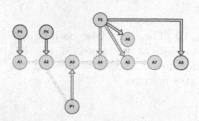

Fig. 7. The entities and relations contained in the KG of document 3.3 extracted using the DEFS prompt.

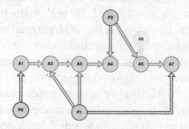

Fig. 8. The entities and relations contained in the KG of document 3.3 extracted using the 2SHOTS prompt Here, false positive *Follows* relationships have been omitted for readability purposes.

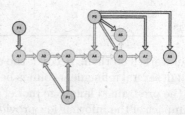

Fig. 9. The entities and relations contained in the KG of document 3.3 extracted by using the DEFS+2SHOTS prompt. Here, false positive *Follows* relationships have been omitted for readability purposes

5.3   Test Dataset

We selected 7 representative documents from the PET dataset to empirically evaluate our approach. Since the dataset is annotated with process elements and process relations, we manually constructed the gold standard graph of each test text. Table 1 reports the overall statistics of the selected documents in terms of the number of words, annotated activities, participants, and performs and follows relations.

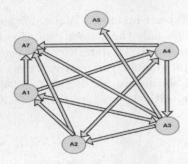

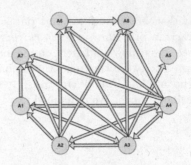

Fig. 10. The set of false positive *Follows* relations contained in the KG of document 3.3 extracted using the 2SHOTS prompt.

Fig. 11. The set of false positive *Follows* relations contained in the KG of document 3.3 extracted using the DEFS+2SHOTS prompt.

Table 1. Characteristics of test set documents.

Text	word#	activity#	participant#	follow#	perform#
doc-1.2	100	10	2	10	10
doc-1.3	162	11	5	11	12
doc-3.3	71	7	2	6	4
doc-5.2	83	7	3	6	4
doc-10.1	29	4	2	4	4
doc-10.6	30	4	2	4	4
doc-10.13	39	3	2	2	3

We are aware that the analysis of seven documents has limitations from a statistical significance perspective. However, the rationale behind this empirical evaluation is two-fold. First, since this is a first observational study of a promising groundbreaking strategy, we decided to select documents having specific characteristics in order to perform an ad-hoc analysis of how the pre-trained language model worked on them. Second, the application of the proposed approach passed through several refinement rounds before being tested since we had to understand how the pre-trained language model actually works. Hence, to better understand the impact of the information provided by us to enrich the pre-trained language model, the most suitable way was to observe such behaviors on a small but characteristic subset of documents.

5.4   Quantitative Evaluation

Table 2 provides the results of the empirical assessment performed. The table reports the GED measures obtained by comparing the gold standard graph with the graphs generated by each of the experimental settings. Such a measure represents the minimum amount of edit operations required to transform the gold standard graph into the generated one. The higher the measured value, the higher the difference between the two generated KGs. Hence, a low measure value means that the two KGs are similar.

In general, RAW and DEFS settings registered higher GED values with respect to DEFS+2SHOTS and 2SHOTS ones. Nevertheless, the results highlighted a few interesting patterns. On average, the RAW setting registered the highest GED values. This result highlights the inability of the raw PLM to extract information that is useful for the construction of the final KG. For instance, as shown in Fig. 6, when tested with the document 3.3 this prompt was able to extract only some activities, but no relations at all. For what concern participants, it was not able to address this extraction properly. Similarly, the DEFS setting suffers from the same drawback. This is proven by the same GED value in both settings obtained in several cases with the consequence of producing very similar graph representations. Indeed, considering Fig. 7, this customization was able to extract the activities described but failed completely to extract their relations. Also, it over-generated the participant elements and created many false-positive *performer* relations. An exception is given by the *doc-5.2* where the DEFS setting outperformed the other settings. Here, the conservative strategy (i.e., to not fine-tune the model with annotated procedural documents) adopted in both the RAW and DEFS settings produced slightly better results than the DEFS+2SHOTS and 2SHOTS ones. Among the DEFS+2SHOTS and 2SHOTS, the latter demonstrated to be the most effective one. Indeed, in several cases, e.g. *doc-10.6*, the 2SHOTS setting produced a KG similar to the gold standard one. Comparing these two prompts for example on document 3.3 as shown in Fig. 9 and Fig. 8, both prompts are able to detect the activities and the participants described in the text. However, the DEFS+2SHOTS prompt generated many false-positive *performer* relations.

Two interesting trends are worthy to discuss. First, the length of a text seems to be not related to the GED value obtained by each setting. This is an interesting aspect since it opens the hypothesis that the effectiveness of the model is independent of the length of a text. Future work will focus also on a deeper investigation of this aspect. Instead, the second interesting aspect is related to the impact of the few-shot strategy within the in-context learning approach. Here, we can observe the results by splitting the GED values observed with the RAW and DEFS settings and with the 2SHOTS and DEFS+2SHOTS ones. It is interesting to observe how the effectiveness of the first two settings is, generally speaking, the opposite of the other two. An example is given by the *doc-3.3* document where, unexpectedly, the few-shot strategy over-produced incorrect *Follows* relations between activities causing higher GED values a s shown in Fig. 11 and Fig. 10. Finally, we may state that the 2SHOTS and DEFS+2SHOTS settings registered an important effectiveness demonstrating the viability of a few-shot approach integrated within an in-context learning strategy. They performed well concerning the extraction of process elements from the natural language description, even if they are inclined to generate several false *Follows* relations between activities.

6   Qualitative Analysis

The quantitative analysis conducted provided some preliminary insights about the actual performance of PLMs within the adopted four experimental settings. By analyzing the GED values from a qualitative perspective, and by taking into account also the different types of process workflow described in the textual documents we considered, we can highlight some further considerations.

First, both the RAW and DEFS settings obtained very low effectiveness in the extraction of both process elements and relations. The GED values obtained were very close to their upper bounds, i.e., all extracted elements were wrong or they are not able to produce any results. Hence, we may state that these two settings are not good candidates for extracting process elements from a natural language text in a correct way. On the one side, we may conclude that, by observing the RAW strategy, in most cases, it fails concerning the extraction of all elements. This is an important point of attention because it demonstrated that PLMs per se might not be able to support the knowledge extraction task without the adoption of a fine-tuning strategy. On the other side, the DEFS setting improves the RAW one a little bit, especially concerning the identification of activities. However, it demonstrated to be inadequate concerning the detection of temporal relations among activities, i.e. the *Follows* relation.

Table 2. Graph edit distance scores results.

Text ID	RAW	DEFS	DEFS+2SHOTS	2SHOTS
doc-1.2	31.0	33.0	13.0	9.0
doc-1.3	20.0	32.0	42.0	39.0
doc-3.3	12.0	14.0	30.0	17.0
doc-5.2	30.0	12.0	22.0	21.0
doc-10.1	19.0	19.0	4.0	6.0
doc-10.6	19.0	19.0	4.0	2.0
doc-10.13	15.0	15.0	13.0	5.0
Average	21.0	18.7	11.2	7.5

Second, we have already shown how both the DEFS+2SHOTS and 2SHOTS settings demonstrated their effectiveness by demonstrating the viability of a few-shot approach integrated within an in-context learning strategy. However, some issues were highlighted concerning the extraction of relations among activities. Indeed, the DEFS+2SHOTS setting obtained good results in finding the activities themselves, but it often fails about detecting the appropriate relations between them. On the one hand, it finds the actually existing ones. On the other hand, it finds a lot of *Follows* relations that are not mentioned in the original text. The trend of obtaining many incorrect relations between activities led, obviously, to higher GED values. Overall, the 2SHOTS demonstrated to be more balanced since (i) it was able to find all the process elements described in the text; and, (ii) it did not add too many *nonexisting relations*, especially the *Follows* ones. This is an important insight because, while the use of domain-specific definitions is, anyway, useful to improve the overall effectiveness of the extraction process, it is important to dedicate effort to detecting which may be the most appropriate definitions, e.g., not overgeneralized ones. The detection of which definitions are the most appropriate ones to instruct the model is not trivial. The PLM model may provide different semantic meanings for the same words. Hence, it is crucial to support its disambiguation capability to *inject* into its correct knowledge.

Finally, by analyzing the process workflow contained within the natural language documents adopted, we may state that the detection of split points and parallel branches is challenging. Indeed, we observed that, in general, split points are difficult to be interpreted by the PLM given the necessity of taking into account a larger portion of text.

7   Conclusion

In this paper, we explored the feasibility of leveraging PLMs and in-context learning approach to automatically build KGs from textual documents in a question-answering multi-turn dialog incremental manner. The results highlighted the feasibility of the in-context learning approach when deep learning based NLP techniques are used within low-resource scenarios. The results show the feasibility of our proposed methodology. This opens the possibility to use this technique to address the construction of KGs by starting from natural language text in scenarios where it is necessary to manage the low-resources issues and by exploiting the human-in-the-loop paradigm given the role of the domain expert in processing the information provided by the model. We also reported a suite of lessons learned from this experience that will drive the development of further research.

References

1. Baroni, M., Dinu, G., Kruszewski, G.: Don't count, predict! a systematic comparison of context-counting vs. context-predicting semantic vectors. In: Proceedings of the 52nd Annual Meeting of the Association for Computational Linguistics (ACL 2014), vol. 1, pp. 238–247. The Association for Computer Linguistics (2014)
2. Bellan, P., van der Aa, H., Dragoni, M., Ghidini, C., Ponzetto, S.P.: PET: an annotated dataset for process extraction from natural language text tasks. In: Cabanillas, C., Garmann-Johnsen, N.F., Koschmider, A. (eds.) Business Process Management Workshops (BPM 2022). LNBIP, vol. 460, pp. 315–321. Springer, Cham (2023). https://doi.org/10.1007/978-3-031-25383-6_23
3. Bellan, P., Dragoni, M., Ghidini, C.: A qualitative analysis of the state of the art in process extraction from text. In: Proceedings of the AIxIA 2020 Discussion Papers Workshop Co-located with the the 19th International Conference of the Italian Association for Artificial Intelligence (AIxIA2020), Anywhere, 27th November 2020. CEUR Workshop Proceedings, vol. 2776, pp. 19–30. CEUR-WS.org (2020)
4. Bellan, P., Dragoni, M., Ghidini, C.: Process extraction from text: state of the art and challenges for the future. arXiv preprint arXiv:2110.03754 (2021)
5. Boratko, M., Li, X., O'Gorman, T., Das, R., Le, D., McCallum, A.: ProtoQA: a question answering dataset for prototypical common-sense reasoning. In: Proceedings of the 2020 Conference on Empirical Methods in Natural Language Processing (EMNLP 2020), pp. 1122–1136. ACL (2020)
6. Brown, T.B., et al.: Language models are few-shot learners. In: Annual Conference. on Neural Information Processing Systems (NeurIPS) (2020)
7. Bunke, H.: On a relation between graph edit distance and maximum common subgraph. Pattern Recognit. Lett. **18**(8), 689–694 (1997)
8. Chintagunta, B., Katariya, N., Amatriain, X., Kannan, A.: Medically aware GPT-3 as a data generator for medical dialogue summarization. In: Proceedings of the 6th Machine Learning for Healthcare Conference Proceedings of the Machine Learning Research, vol. 149, pp. 354–372. PMLR (2021)
9. Devlin, J., Chang, M., Lee, K., Toutanova, K.: BERT: pre-training of deep bidirectional transformers for language understanding. In: Proceedings of the NAACL-HLT 2019, vol. 1, pp. 4171–4186. ACL (2019)

10. Gao, T., Fisch, A., Chen, D.: Making pre-trained language models better few-shot learners. In: Proceedings of the ACL/IJCNLP 2021, pp. 3816–3830. ACL (2021). https://doi.org/10.18653/v1/2021.acl-long.295

11. Gupta, S.: Hate speech detection using OpenAI and GPT-3. Int. J. Emerging Technol. Adv. Eng. (2022)

12. Hill, F., Reichart, R., Korhonen, A.: SimLex-999: evaluating semantic models with (genuine) similarity estimation. Comput. Linguist. **41**(4), 665–695 (2015)

13. Liu, Y., et al.: RoBERTa: a robustly optimized BERT pretraining approach. arXiv preprint arXiv:1907.11692 (2019)

14. Martínez-Rodríguez, J., Hogan, A., López-Arévalo, I.: Information extraction meets the semantic web: a survey. Semantic Web **11**(2), 255–335 (2020)

15. Marvin, R., Linzen, T.: Targeted syntactic evaluation of language models. In: Proceedings of the 2018 Conference on Empirical Methods in Natural Language Processing, pp. 1192–1202. Association for Computational Linguistics (2018)

16. Radford, A., Narasimhan, K., Salimans, T., Sutskever, I.: Improving language understanding by generative pre-training. OpenAI Blog (2018)

17. Radford, A., et al.: Language models are unsupervised multitask learners. OpenAI Blog **1**(8), 9 (2019)

18. Raffel, C., et al.: Exploring the limits of transfer learning with a unified text-to-text transformer. J. Mach. Learn. Res. **21**(1), 5485–5551 (2020)

19. Scao, T.L., Rush, A.M.: How many data points is a prompt worth? In: Proceedings of the NAACL-HLT 2021, pp. 2627–2636. ACL (2021)

20. Wang, A., Singh, A., Michael, J., Hill, F., Levy, O., Bowman, S.R.: GLUE: a multi-task benchmark and analysis platform for natural language understanding. In: Linzen, T., Chrupala, G., Alishahi, A. (eds.) Proceedings of the Workshop: Analyzing and Interpreting Neural Networks for NLP, BlackboxNLP@EMNLP 2018, pp. 353–355. ACL (2018)

Neural Networks Reduction via Lumping

Dalila Ressi[1]([✉])[iD], Riccardo Romanello[1][iD], Carla Piazza[1][iD],
and Sabina Rossi[2][iD]

[1] Università di Udine, Udine, Italy
{dalila.ressi,riccardo.romanello,carla.piazza}@uniud.it
[2] Università Ca' Foscari Venezia, Venice, Italy
sabina.rossi@unive.it

Abstract. The increasing size of recently proposed Neural Networks makes it hard to implement them on embedded devices, where memory, battery and computational power are a non-trivial bottleneck. For this reason during the last years network compression literature has been thriving and a large number of solutions has been published to reduce both the number of operations and the parameters involved with the models. Unfortunately, most of these reducing techniques are actually heuristic methods and usually require at least one re-training step to recover the accuracy.

The need of procedures for model reduction is well-known also in the fields of Verification and Performances Evaluation, where large efforts have been devoted to the definition of quotients that preserve the observable underlying behaviour.

In this paper we try to bridge the gap between the most popular and very effective network reduction strategies and formal notions, such as lumpability, introduced for verification and evaluation of Markov Chains. Elaborating on lumpability we propose a pruning approach that reduces the number of neurons in a network without using any data or fine-tuning, while completely preserving the exact behaviour. Relaxing the constraints on the exact definition of the quotienting method we can give a formal explanation of some of the most common reduction techniques.

Keywords: Neural networks · Compression · Pruning · Lumpability

1 Introduction

Since 2012, when AlexNet [29] won the famous ImageNet Large Scale Visual Recognition Challenge (ILSVRC), the number of proposed *Artificial Neural Network* (*ANN* or *NN*) architectures has increased exponentially. Their intrinsic flexibility, together with the superior performance they can achieve, made neural networks the tool of choice to solve a wide variety of tasks. As these models have evolved to process large amount of data or to solve complicated tasks, their complexity has also increased at same pace [12]. Such elaborate and deep networks are the foundation of *Deep Learning* (*DL*) and they stand out both for the large number of layers they are made of and for the higher level of accuracy they can reach on difficult tasks [56].

A. Dovier et al. (Eds.): AIxIA 2022, LNAI 13796, pp. 75–90, 2023.
https://doi.org/10.1007/978-3-031-27181-6_6

While the academic community mostly focused their efforts in training large and deep models [9,28,57], being able to adopt such networks in embedded devices resulted to be a problem. Physical constraints such as battery, memory and computational power greatly limit both the number of parameters used to the define the architecture and the number of Floating Point Operations (FLOPs) required to be computed at inference time. A commonly used strategy to address this problem is called *Network Compression*. Compression literature has had a substantial growth during the last years, and for this reason there are many different ways to group together methods reducing a model in similar ways.

Methods focusing on finding the best possible structure to solve a particular tasks can be grouped together as *Architecture-related* strategies. These kind of methods usually require to train the network from scratch each time the structure is modified. In particular, *Neural Architecture Search (NAS)* techniques aim to find the best possible architecture for a certain task with minimal human intervention [14,35,44]. This is usually made possible by modelling the search as an optimization problem and applying *Reinforcement Learning (LR)*-based methods to find the best architecture [3,60]. In this group we can also find *Tensor Decomposition*, where matrix decomposition/factorization principles are applied to the d-dimensional tensors in neural networks. Tensor decomposition generalizes the widely used Principal Component Analysis (PCA) and Singular Value Decomposition (SVD) to an arbitrary number of dimensions [7,19,54]. The goal of these techniques is to reduce the rank of tensors in order to efficiently decompose them into smaller ones and drastically reduce the number of operations [12]. As the rank of a tensor is usually far from being small, the most common solutions are to either to force the network to learn filters with small rank either to use an approximated decomposition [13].

Using a similar approach *Lightweight* or *Compact Networks* focus on modifying the design of the architecture such that it performs less operations while maintaining the same capability. It is the case of the MobileNet series [23,24,46], ShuffleNet series [37,59], and EfficientNet series [52,53]. They exploit the idea of using 1×1 filters introduced by Network in Network [32] and GoogLeNet [49,50] in their inception modules. A similar concept is explored by the SqueezeNet [26] architecture in their *Fire module*, where they substitute the classical convolutional layers such that they can achieve the same accuracy of AlexNet on ImageNet dataset but with a model 510 times smaller.

A different methodology consists in training a big model from the start, and then *Pruning* superfluous parameters. In particular, *Weight Pruning* consists in zeroing connections or parameters already close to zero [30], but more elaborated methods can also take into consideration the impact of the single weights on the final results [18]. Even if weight pruning is a very powerful tool to reduce the network parameters [15], its major drawback is that it does not actually reduce the number of FLOPs at inference time.

A more effective solution consists instead in skipping completely some of the operations. It is the case of *Filter Pruning*, where whole nodes or filters (in case of convolutional layers) are removed from the architecture. Pruning usually requires some degree of re-training to recover the lost accuracy due to the reduced network capability, but an interesting phenomena that happens in the early stages of pruning is that most of the times the test accuracy actually increases, due to the regularization effect that pruning unnecessary parameters has on the network. While weight pruning allows more control on what parameters to remove, filter pruning is usually the best solution compression-wise as it allows to drastically reduce the network parameters such that the models can be actually implemented in small embedded devices [45].

Another technique often used in conjunction with pruning is called *quantization* [17]. While pruning aims to reduce the number of parameters, quantization instead targets their precision. As the weights are usually represented by floating point numbers, it is possible to reduce the bits used for the number representation down to single bits [43], without affecting the network accuracy.

In the context of performance evaluation of computer systems, stochastic models whose underlying stochastic processes are Markov chains, play a key role providing a sound high-level framework for the analysis of software and hardware architectures. Although the use of high-level modelling formalism greatly simplifies the specification of quantitative models (e.g., by exploiting the compositionality properties [21]), the stochastic process underlying even a very compact model may have a number of states that makes its analysis a difficult, sometimes computationally impossible, task. In order to study models with a large state space without using approximations or resorting to simulations, one can attempt to reduce the state space of the underlying Markov chain by aggregating states with equivalent behaviours. Lumpability is an aggregation technique used to cope with the state space explosion problem inherent to the computation of the stationary performance indices of large stochastic models. The lumpability method turns out to be useful on Markov chains exhibiting some structural regularity. Moreover, it allows one to efficiently compute the exact values of the performance indices when the model is actually lumpable. In the literature, several notions of lumping have been introduced: ordinary and weak lumping [27], exact lumping [47], and strict lumping [6].

With this paper we aim to link together the work of two different communities, the first one focusing on machine learning and network compression and the second one focusing on lumping-based aggregation techniques for performance evaluation. Even if a large number of possible efficient compression techniques has already been published, we aim instead to give a formal demonstration on how it is possible to deterministically remove some of the network parameters to obtain a smaller network with the same performance. Our method condenses many different concepts together, such as some of the ideas exploited by tensor decomposition methods, filter pruning and the lumpability used to evaluate the performance of complex systems.

The paper is structured as follows. In Sect. 2 we provide a literature review. Section 3 gives the necessary background. Section 4 formally describes our technique exploiting exact lumpability for quotienting NN. Section 5 presents some experimental results. Finally, Sect. 6 concludes the paper.

2   Related Work

To the best of our knowledge, the only paper similar to our work is [42], where the authors introduce the classical notion of equivalence between systems in Process Algebra to reduce a neural network into another one semantically equivalent. They propose a filter pruning technique based on some properties of the network that does not need any data to perform the compression. They also define an approximated version of their algorithm to relax some of the strong constraints they pose on the weights of the network.

While data free pruning algorithms are convenient when a dataset is incomplete, unbalanced or missing, they usually achieve poorer results compared to data-based compression solutions. Indeed, most pruning techniques usually require at least one stage of fine-tuning of the model. The recovery is often performed in an iterative fashion after removing a single parameter, but there are also techniques that re-train the model only after a certain level of compression has been carried out [4].

As defined in [33] filter pruning techniques can be divided according to *property importance* or *adaptive importance*. In the first group we find pruning methods that look at intrinsic properties of the networks, and do not modify the training loss, such as [8,20,25,31,42,45]. Adaptive importance pruning algorithms like [34,36] usually drastically change the loss function, requiring a heavy retrain step and to look for a new proper set of hyper-parameters, despite the fact that they often achieve better performances with respect to property importance methods. Avoiding to re-train the network at each pruning step as in [33,55] is usually faster than other solutions, but there is a higher risk to not being able to recover the performances.

Another option consists in deciding which parameters to remove according to the impact they have on the rest of the network [40,58]. Finally, while most of the already mentioned methods focus on removing whole filters or kernels from convolutional layers, some other methods actually target only fully connected layers, or are made to compress classical neural networks [2,51].

3   Preliminaries

In this section we formally introduce the notion of neural network in the style of [42]. Moreover, we recall the concept of exact lumpability as it has been defined in the context of continuous time Markov chains.

Neural Networks

A neural network is formed by a layered set of nodes or neurons, consisting of an input layer, an output layer and one or more hidden layers. Each node that does not belong to the input layer is annotated with a bias and an activation function. Moreover, there are weighted edges between nodes of adjacent layers. We use the following formal definition of neural network.

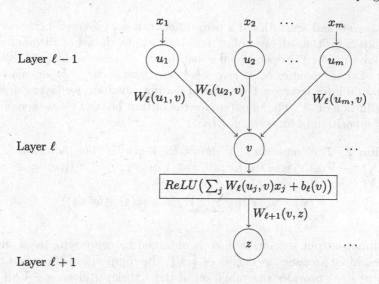

Fig. 1. Node v behaviour on input $x_1, x_2, \ldots, x_m$

For $k \in \mathbb{N}$, we denote by $[k]$ the set $\{0, 1, \ldots, k\}$, by $(k]$ the set $\{1, \ldots, k\}$, by $[k)$ the set $\{0, \ldots, k-1\}$, and by (k) the set $\{1, \ldots, k-1\}$.

Definition 1 (Neural Network). *A Neural Network (NN) is a tuple* $\mathcal{N} = (k, \mathscr{A}ct, \{\mathscr{S}_\ell\}_{\ell \in [k]}, \{W_\ell\}_{\ell \in (k]}, \{b_\ell\}_{\ell \in (k]}, \{A_\ell\}_{\ell \in (k]})$ *where:*

- *k is the number of layers (except the input layer);*
- *$\mathscr{A}ct$ is the set of activation functions;*
- *for $\ell \in [k]$, $\mathscr{S}_\ell$ is the set of nodes of layer ℓ with $\mathscr{S}_\ell \cap \mathscr{S}_{\ell'} = \emptyset$ for $\ell \neq \ell'$;*
- *for $\ell \in (k]$, $W_\ell : \mathscr{S}_{\ell-1} \times \mathscr{S}_\ell \to \mathbb{R}$ is the weight function that associates a weight with edges between nodes at layer $\ell - 1$ and ℓ;*
- *for $\ell \in (k]$, $b_\ell : \mathscr{S}_\ell \to \mathbb{R}$ is the bias function that associates a bias with nodes at layer ℓ;*
- *for $\ell \in (k]$, $A_\ell : \mathscr{S}_\ell \to \mathscr{A}ct$ is the activation association function that associates an activation function with nodes of layer ℓ.*

$\mathscr{S}_0$ and $\mathscr{S}_k$ denote the nodes in the input and output layers, respectively.

In the rest of the paper we will refer to NNs in which all the activation association function are constant, i.e., all the neurons of a layer share the same activation function. Moreover, such activation functions A_ℓ are either ReLU (Rectified Linear Unit) or LeakyReLU, i.e., they are combinations of linear functions. So, from now on we omit the set $\mathscr{A}ct$ from the definition of the NNs.

Example 1. Figure 1 shows the behaviour of node v in Layer ℓ. The input values $x_1, x_2, \ldots x_m$ are propagated by nodes $u_1, u_2, \ldots u_m$ respectively. Node v computes the *ReLU* of the weighted sum of the inputs plus the bias. The result of this application is the output of v and it is propagated to z.

The operational semantics of a neural network is as follows. Let $v : \mathscr{S}_\ell \to \mathbb{R}$ be a valuation for the ℓ-th layer of $\mathcal{N}$ and $Val(\mathscr{S}_\ell)$ be the set of all valuations for the ℓ-th layer of $\mathcal{N}$. The operational semantics of $\mathcal{N}$, denoted by $[\![\mathcal{N}]\!]$, is defined in terms of the semantics of its layers $[\![\mathcal{N}]\!]_\ell$, where each $[\![\mathcal{N}]\!]_\ell$ associates with any valuation v for layer $\ell - 1$ the corresponding valuation for layer ℓ according to the definition of $\mathcal{N}$. The valuation for the output layer of $\mathcal{N}$ is then obtained by the composition of functions $[\![\mathcal{N}]\!]_\ell$.

Definition 2. *The semantics of the ℓ-th layer is the function $[\![\mathcal{N}]\!]_\ell :$ $Val(\mathscr{S}_{\ell-1}) \to Val(\mathscr{S}_\ell)$ where for all $v \in Val(\mathscr{S}_{\ell-1})$, $[\![\mathcal{N}]\!]_\ell(v) = v'$ and for all $s' \in \mathscr{S}_\ell$,*

$$v'(s') = A_\ell(s')\Big(\sum_{s \in \mathscr{S}_{\ell-1}} W_\ell(s, s')v(s) + b_\ell(s')\Big).$$

The input-output semantics of $\mathcal{N}$ is obtained by composing these one layer semantics. More precisely, we denote by $[\![\mathcal{N}]\!]^\ell$ the composition of the first ℓ layers so that $[\![\mathcal{N}]\!]^\ell(v)$ provides the valuation of the ℓ-th layer given $v \in Val(\mathscr{S}_0)$ as input. Formally, $[\![\mathcal{N}]\!]^\ell$ is inductively defined by:

$$[\![\mathcal{N}]\!]^1 = [\![\mathcal{N}]\!]_1$$

$$[\![\mathcal{N}]\!]^\ell = [\![\mathcal{N}]\!]_\ell \circ [\![\mathcal{N}]\!]^{\ell-1} \;\; \forall \ell \in (k]$$

where $\circ$ denotes the function composition.

We are now in position to define the semantics of $\mathcal{N}$ as the input-output semantic function $[\![\mathcal{N}]\!]$ defined below.

Definition 3. *The input-output semantic function $[\![\mathcal{N}]\!] : Val(\mathscr{S}_0) \to Val(\mathscr{S}_k)$ is defined as*

$$[\![\mathcal{N}]\!] = [\![\mathcal{N}]\!]^k.$$

Lumpability

The notion of *lumpability* has been introduced in the context of performance and reliability analysis. It provides a model aggregation technique that can be used for generating a Markov chain that is smaller than the original one while allowing one to determine exact results for the original process.

The concept of lumpability can be formalized in terms of equivalence relations over the state space of the Markov chain. Any such equivalence induces a *partition* on the state space of the Markov chain and aggregation is achieved by clustering equivalent states into macro-states, reducing the overall state space.

Let $\mathscr{S}$ be a finite state space. A (time-homogeneous) Continuous-Time Markov Chain (CTMC) over $\mathscr{S}$ is defined by a function

$$Q : \mathscr{S} \times \mathscr{S} \to \mathbb{R}$$

such that for all $u, v \in \mathscr{S}$ with $u \neq v$ it holds that:

- $Q(u,v) \geq 0$ and
- $\sum_{v \in \mathscr{S}, v \neq u} Q(u,v) = -Q(u,u)$.

A CTMC defined over $\mathscr{S}$ by Q models a stochastic process where a transition from u to v can occur according to an exponential distribution with rate $Q(u,v)$.

Given an initial probability distribution p over the states of a CTMC, one can consider the problem of computing the probability distribution to which p converges when the time tends to infinity. This is the *stationary* distribution and it exists only when the chain satisfies additional constraints. The stationary distribution reveals the limit behaviour of a CTMC. Many other performance indexes and temporal logic properties can be defined for studying both the transient and limit behaviour of the chain.

Different notions of lumpability have been introduced with the aim of reducing the number of states of the chain, while preserving its behaviour [1,6,22,27,38,39,47]. In particular, we consider here the notion of *exact lumpability* [6,47].

Definition 4 (Exact Lumpability). *Let $(\mathscr{S}, Q)$ be a CTMC and $\mathscr{R}$ be an equivalence relation over $\mathscr{S}$. $\mathscr{R}$ is an* exact lumpability *if for all $S, S' \in \mathscr{R}/\mathscr{S}$, for all $v, t \in S$ it holds that:*

$$\sum_{u \in S'} Q(u,v) = \sum_{u \in S'} Q(u,t).$$

There exists always a unique maximum exact lumpability relation which allows to quotient the chain by taking one state for each equivalence class and replacing the rates of the incoming edges with the sum of the rates from equivalent states.

The notion of exact lumpability is in many applicative domains too demanding, thus providing poor reductions. This issue is well-known for all lumpability notions that do not allow any form of approximation. With the aim of obtaining smaller quotients, still avoiding rough approximations, the notion of *proportional lumpability* has been presented in [38,39,41] as a relaxation of ordinary lumpability. In this paper instead we introduce to *proportional exact lumpability* which is defined as follows.

Definition 5 (Proportional Exact Lumpability). *Let $(\mathscr{S}, Q)$ be a CTMC and $\mathscr{R}$ be an equivalence relation over $\mathscr{S}$. $\mathscr{R}$ is a proportional exact lumpability if there exists a function $\rho : \mathscr{S} \to \mathbb{R}_{>0}$ such that for all $S, S' \in \mathscr{S}/\mathscr{R}$, for all $v, t \in S$ it holds that:*

$$\rho(v) \sum_{u \in S'} Q(u,v) = \rho(t) \sum_{u \in S'} Q(u,t).$$

It can be proved that there exists a unique maximum proportional exact lumpability which can be computed in polynomial time. This is true also if $(\mathscr{S}, Q)$ is a *Labelled Graph* instead of a CTMC, i.e., no constraints are imposed on Q.

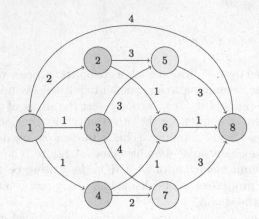

Fig. 2. Proportionally exact lumpable CTMC.

Example 2. Figure 2 shows a proportionally exact lumpable Markov chain with respect to the function ρ defined as: $\rho(1) = 1, \rho(2) = 3, \rho(3) = 1, \rho(4) = 3, \rho(5) = 1, \rho(6) = 3, \rho(7) = 1, \rho(8) = 1$ and the equivalence classes $S_1 = \{1\}, S_2 = \{2,3,4\}, S_3 = \{5,6,7\}, S_4 = \{8\}$.

4   Lumping Neural Networks

The idea of exploiting exact lumpability for quotienting NN has been proposed in [42] where a notion of pre-sum preserving backward bisimulation has been considered. It can be easily observed that such a notion coincides with that of exact lumpability. The term (probabilistic) bisimulation is standard in the area of Model Checking, where (probabilistic) temporal logical properties are used for both specifying and synthesizing systems having a desired behaviour [5,10, 11,16]. Since such logics usually formalize the behaviours in terms of forward temporal operators, the bisimulation notions tend to preserve the rates of the outgoing edges [48]. However, as proved in [42], in order to preserve the behaviour of a NN it is necessary to refer to the rates/weights of the incoming edges. This is referred to as *backward probabilistic bisimulation* and coincides with the well-known notion of *exact lumpability* used in the area of performances evaluation.

In this paper we extend the proposal of [42]. We prove that in the case of ReLU and LeakyReLU activations, proportional exact lumpability preserves the behaviour of the network allowing to obtain smaller quotients. It does not require any retraining step and it ensures the same behaviour on all possible inputs. Moreover, since the neural networks we refer to are acyclic it can be computed in linear time.

Definition 6 (Proportional Exact Lumpability over a NN). *Let $\mathcal{N}$ be a NN. Let $\mathcal{R} = \cup_{\ell \in [k)}\mathcal{R}_\ell$ be such that $\mathcal{R}_\ell$ is an equivalence relation over $\mathscr{S}_\ell$, for all $\ell \in (k)$ and $\mathcal{R}_0$ is the identity relation over $\mathscr{S}_0$. We say that $\mathcal{R}$ is a* proportional exact lumpability *over $\mathcal{N}$ if for each $\ell \in (k)$ there exists $\rho_\ell : \mathscr{S}_\ell \to \mathbb{R}_{>0}$ such that for all $S \in \mathscr{S}_\ell/\mathscr{R}_\ell$, for all $S' \in \mathscr{S}_{\ell-1}/\mathscr{R}_{\ell-1}$, for all $v, t \in S$ it holds that:*

$$\rho_\ell(v)b_\ell(v) = \rho_\ell(t)b_\ell(t),$$

$$\rho_\ell(v)\sum_{u\in S'} W_\ell(u,v) = \rho_\ell(t)\sum_{u\in S'} W_\ell(u,t).$$

There are some differences with respect to the definition of proportional exact lumpability over CTMCs. First, we impose that two equivalent neurons have to belong to the same layer. However, we could have omitted such restriction from the definition and proved that neurons from different layers are never equivalent. This is an immediate consequence of the fact that we refer to acyclic NNs. Moreover, we demand that on input and output nodes the only admissible relation is the identity. This is a substantial difference. Since the nodes in the input layer have no incoming edges the definition of proportional lumpability given over CTMCs allows to collapse them. However, the input nodes in NNs hold the input values that have to be propagated, so they cannot be collapsed. This is true also for the output nodes, since they represent the result of the computation.

It can be proved that there always exists a unique maximum proportional exact lumpability over a NN. If we use proportional exact lumpability for reducing the dimension of a NN by collapsing the equivalent neurons, we have to modify the topology and the weights of the NN as formalized below.

Definition 7 (Proportional Reduced NN). *Let $\mathcal{N} = (k, \{\mathscr{S}_\ell\}_{\ell\in[k]}, \{W_\ell\}_{\ell\in(k)}, \{b_\ell\}_{\ell\in(k)}, \{A_\ell\}_{\ell\in(k)})$ be a NN. Let $\mathscr{R}$ be a proportional exact lumpability over $\mathcal{N}$. The NN $\mathcal{N}/\mathscr{R} = (k, \{\mathscr{S}'_\ell\}_{\ell\in[k]}, \{W'_\ell\}_{\ell\in(k)}, \{b'_\ell\}_{\ell\in(k)}, \{A'_\ell\}_{\ell\in(k)})$ is defined by:*

- *$\mathscr{S}'_\ell = \{[v] \mid [v] \in \mathscr{S}_\ell/\mathscr{R}\}$, where v is an arbitrarily chosen representative for the class;*
- *$W'_\ell([u], [v]) = \rho_{\ell-1}(u)\sum_{w\in[u]} \frac{W_\ell(w,v)}{\rho_{\ell-1}(w)}$;*
- *$b'_\ell([v]) = b_\ell(v)$;*
- *$A'_\ell([v]) = A_\ell(v)$.*

Despite the arbitrary choice of the representative, we can prove that the reduced NN's behaviour coincides with that of the initial one over all the inputs.

Theorem 1. *Let $\mathcal{N}$ be a NN and $\mathscr{R}$ be a proportional exact lumpability over $\mathcal{N}$. It holds that*

$$[\![\mathcal{N}/\mathscr{R}]\!] = [\![\mathcal{N}]\!].$$

Proof. Sketch. Let us focus on two neurons v and t belonging to layer 1 that are equivalent in $\mathscr{R}_1$. Let $ReLU$ be the activation function for both of them.

On input $x_1, x_2, \ldots x_m$ for the nodes $u_1, u_2, \ldots, u_m$ of layer 0 the nodes v and t take values $Val(v) = ReLU(\sum_{j=1}^m W_1(u_j, v)x_j + b_1(v))$ and $Val(t) = ReLU(\sum_{j=1}^m W_1(u_j, t)x_j + b_1(t))$, respectively. However, since v and t are equivalent, it holds that:

$$\sum_{j=1}^m W_1(u_j, t)x_j + b_1(t) = \frac{\rho_1(v)}{\rho_1(t)} \sum_{j=1}^m W_1(u_j, v)x_j + b_1(v)$$

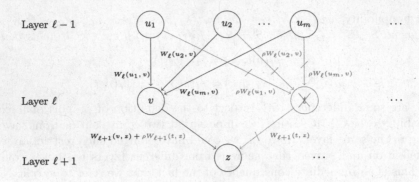

Fig. 3. Pruning one node and updating the network.

Since $\rho_1(v)$ and $\rho_1(t)$ are positive numbers, we get that:

$$Val(t) = ReLU(\textstyle\sum_{j=1}^{m} W_1(u_j, t)x_j + b_1(t))$$
$$= \frac{\rho_1(v)}{\rho_1(t)} ReLU(\textstyle\sum_{j=1}^{m} W_1(u_j, v)x_j + b_1(v)) = \frac{\rho_1(v)}{\rho_1(t)} Val(v).$$

Let now z be a neuron of layer 2. The value of z depends on

$$W_2(v, z)Val(v) + W_2(t, z)Val(t) = (W_2(v, z) + \frac{\rho_1(v)}{\rho_1(t)} W_2(t, z))Val(v)$$

So, the definition of W_2' takes care of the fact that in the reduced network v represents the equivalence class, while t has been "eliminated". Such definition ensures that the value of neuron z is unchanged.

A formal proof can be obtained generalizing the above arguments.   □

Example 3. Figure 3 shows how the pruning technique works on two nodes v, t. In particular, t input weights are proportionals to v's. The algorithm proceeds in two steps. Firstly, t is deleted together with all its input and output edges. Secondly, the weight from v to z is modified by adding $\rho W_{\ell+1}(t, z)$.

The maximum proportional exact lumpability over $\mathcal{N}$ together with the reduced network can be efficiently computed by proceeding top-down from layer 1 to $k - 1$. Since the network is acyclic, each layer is influenced only by the previous one. Hence, the computation is linear with respect to the number of edges of the network.

Theorem 2. *Let $\mathcal{N}$ be a NN. There exists a unique maximum proportional exact lumpability $\mathcal{R}$ over $\mathcal{N}$. Moreover, $\mathcal{R}$ and $\mathcal{N}/\mathcal{R}$ can be computed in linear time with respect to the size of $\mathcal{N}$, i.e., in time $\Theta(\sum_{\ell\in(k]} |\mathscr{S}_{\ell-1} \times \mathscr{S}_\ell|)$.*

Intuitively, Theorem 1 exploits the following property of ReLU (LeakyReLU):

$$\forall y \in \mathbb{R} \, \forall r \in \mathbb{R}_{>0} \ ReLU(r * y) = r * ReLU(y).$$

This allows us to remove some neurons exploiting the proportionality relation with others. In order to guarantee the correctness of the removal on all possible inputs, as stated in Theorem 1, it is not possible to exploit less restrictive relationships than proportionality. This fact can also be formally proved, under the hypothesis that the input set is sufficiently rich. However, one could ask what happens if we move from a simple proportionality relation to a linear dependence. For instance, what happens if in Definition 6 we relax the two equations by considering that t is a linear combination of v_1 and v_2, i.e.:

$$\rho_\ell(t)b_\ell(t) = \rho_\ell(v_1)b_\ell(v_1) + \rho_\ell(v_2)b_\ell(v_2),$$

$$\rho_\ell(t)\sum_{u \in S'} W_\ell(u,t) = \rho_\ell(v_1)\sum_{u \in S'} W_\ell(u,v_1) + \rho_\ell(v_2)\sum_{u \in S'} W_\ell(u,v_2).$$

In this case we could eliminate t by including its contribution on the outgoing edges of both v_1 and v_2. Unfortunately, the behaviour of the network is preserved only for those input values $x_1, x_2, \ldots, x_m$ which ensure that $\sum_{j=1}^m W_\ell(u_j, v_1)x_j + b_\ell(v_1)$ and $\sum_{j=1}^m W_\ell(u_j, v_2)x_j + b_\ell(v_2)$ have the same sign, since

$$\forall y_1, y_2 \in \mathbb{R}, \quad \forall r_1, r_2 \in \mathbb{R}_{>0},$$

$$ReLU(r_1 * y_1 + r_2 * y_2) = r_1 * ReLU(y_1) + r_2 * ReLU(y_2) \text{ iff } y_1 * y_2 \geq 0.$$

In other terms our analysis points out that reduction techniques based on linear combinations of neurons can be exploited without retraining the network only when strong hypothesis on the sign of the neurons hold.

More sophisticated methods that exploit *Principal Component Analysis* can be seen as a further shift versus approximation, since they do not only involve linear combinations of neurons, but also a base change and the elimination of the less significant dimensions.

5   Experimental Results

To assess the robustness of our method we set up some simple experiments where we implemented the neural network pruning by lumping. In particular, we want to show how the accuracy is affected when the weights of the node to prune are not simply proportional to the weights of another node in the same layer, but they are instead a linear combination of the weights of two or more other nodes.

We designed and trained a simple *Convolutional Neural Network (CNN)* made of two convolutional blocks (32 3 × 3 filters each, both followed by a maxpooling layer) and after a simple flatten we add three fully connected layers (fc), with 16, 128 and 10 nodes each, where the last one is the softmax layer. As required by our method, we use only ReLU activations, except for the output layer. We used the benchmark MNIST dataset, consisting of 7000 28 × 28 greyscale images of handwritten digits divided into 10 classes.

After a fast training of the model we focused on the second last fully connected layer for our pruning method. We randomly selected a subset of nodes in this layer and then manually overwrote the weights of the rest of the nodes in the same layer as linear combinations of the fixed ones. We then froze this synthetic layer and retrained the network to recover the lost accuracy. The resulting model presents a fully connected layer with 2176 (2048 weight + 128 bias) parameters that can be the target of our pruning method.

During the first round of experiments we confirmed that if the weights in the fixed subset have all the same sign, then our method prunes the linearly dependant vectors and the updating step does not introduce any performance loss. Differently, as illustrated in Fig. 4, when the weights in the subset have different sign, the updating step can introduce some loss. This happens only in the case that the weights are a linear combination of two or more of the weights incoming to the other nodes in the synthetic layer. In particular, the accuracy drops faster as the number of nodes involved in the linear combination increases.

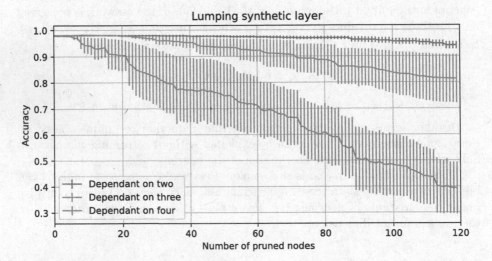

Fig. 4. Accuracy loss when pruning nodes which incoming weights are linear combination of two, three and four other nodes' weights in the same layer.

6   Conclusion

In this paper we present a data free filter pruning compression method based on the notion of lumpability. Even though we impose rigid constraints on the weights in order to obtain a reduced network, in doing so we also demonstrate how the resulting model exhibits the same exact behaviour. Regardless the limitations of our method, this work opens the door to a new research field where the aggregation techniques typical of performance evaluation are adopted in network compression, usually explored only by the machine learning community. In the future, we would like to further analyze how our algorithm works for different study cases, and in particular to test how an approximation of the linear dependence would affect the accuracy under different conditions. Another interesting experiment would be to use SVD on the fully connected layers to estimate how many vectors are linearly independent and therefore compute the reduction potentially achieved by our method, especially for quantized networks.

Acknowledgements. This work has been partially supported by the Project PRIN 2020 "Nirvana - Noninterference and Reversibility Analysis in Private Blockchains" and by the Project GNCS 2022 "Proprietà qualitative e quantitative di sistemi reversibili".

References

1. Alzetta, G., Marin, A., Piazza, C., Rossi, S.: Lumping-based equivalences in Markovian automata: algorithms and applications to product-form analyses. Inf. Comput. **260**, 99–125 (2018)
2. Ashiquzzaman, A., Van Ma, L., Kim, S., Lee, D., Um, T.W., Kim, J.: Compacting deep neural networks for light weight IoT & SCADA based applications with node pruning. In: 2019 International Conference on Artificial Intelligence in Information and Communication (ICAIIC), pp. 082–085. IEEE (2019)
3. Baker, B., Gupta, O., Naik, N., Raskar, R.: Designing neural network architectures using reinforcement learning. arXiv preprint arXiv:1611.02167 (2016)
4. Blalock, D., Gonzalez Ortiz, J.J., Frankle, J., Guttag, J.: What is the state of neural network pruning? Proc. Mach. Learn. Syst. **2**, 129–146 (2020)
5. Bossi, A., Focardi, R., Macedonio, D., Piazza, C., Rossi, S.: Unwinding in information flow security. Electron. Notes Theor. Comput. Sci. **99**, 127–154 (2004)
6. Buchholz, P.: Exact and ordinary lumpability in finite Markov chains. J. Appl. Probab. **31**, 59–75 (1994)
7. Carroll, J.D., Chang, J.J.: Analysis of individual differences in multidimensional scaling via an n-way generalization of "Eckart-Young" decomposition. Psychometrika **35**(3), 283–319 (1970). https://doi.org/10.1007/BF02310791
8. Castellano, G., Fanelli, A.M., Pelillo, M.: An iterative pruning algorithm for feedforward neural networks. IEEE Trans. Neural Netw. **8**(3), 519–531 (1997)
9. Dai, Z., Liu, H., Le, Q.V., Tan, M.: CoAtNet: Marrying convolution and attention for all data sizes. In: Advances in Neural Information Processing Systems, vol. 34, pp. 3965–3977 (2021)
10. Dang, T., Dreossi, T., Piazza, C.: Parameter synthesis using parallelotopic enclosure and applications to epidemic models. In: Maler, O., Halász, Á., Dang, T., Piazza, C. (eds.) HSB 2014. LNCS, vol. 7699, pp. 67–82. Springer, Cham (2015). https://doi.org/10.1007/978-3-319-27656-4_4
11. Dang, T., Dreossi, T., Piazza, C.: Parameter synthesis through temporal logic specifications. In: Bjørner, N., de Boer, F. (eds.) FM 2015. LNCS, vol. 9109, pp. 213–230. Springer, Cham (2015). https://doi.org/10.1007/978-3-319-19249-9_14
12. Deng, L., Li, G., Han, S., Shi, L., Xie, Y.: Model compression and hardware acceleration for neural networks: a comprehensive survey. Proc. IEEE **108**(4), 485–532 (2020)
13. Denton, E.L., Zaremba, W., Bruna, J., LeCun, Y., Fergus, R.: Exploiting linear structure within convolutional networks for efficient evaluation. In: Advances in Neural Information Processing Systems, pp. 1269–1277 (2014)
14. Elsken, T., Metzen, J.H., Hutter, F.: Neural architecture search: a survey. J. Mach. Learn. Res. **20**(1), 1997–2017 (2019)

15. Frankle, J., Carbin, M.: The lottery ticket hypothesis: finding sparse, trainable neural networks. arXiv preprint arXiv:1803.03635 (2018)
16. Gallina, L., Hamadou, S., Marin, A., Rossi, S.: A probabilistic energy-aware model for mobile ad-hoc networks. In: Al-Begain, K., Balsamo, S., Fiems, D., Marin, A. (eds.) ASMTA 2011. LNCS, vol. 6751, pp. 316–330. Springer, Heidelberg (2011). https://doi.org/10.1007/978-3-642-21713-5_23
17. Han, S., Mao, H., Dally, W.J.: Deep compression: compressing deep neural networks with pruning, trained quantization and Huffman coding. arXiv preprint arXiv:1510.00149 (2015)
18. Han, S., Pool, J., Tran, J., Dally, W.J.: Learning both weights and connections for efficient neural networks. arXiv preprint arXiv:1506.02626 (2015)
19. Harshman, R.A., et al.: Foundations of the PARAFAC procedure: models and conditions for an "explanatory" multimodal factor analysis (1970)
20. He, Y., Liu, P., Wang, Z., Hu, Z., Yang, Y.: Filter pruning via geometric median for deep convolutional neural networks acceleration. In: Proceedings of the IEEE/CVF Conference on Computer Vision and Pattern Recognition, pp. 4340–4349 (2019)
21. Hillston, J.: A compositional approach to performance modelling. Ph.D. thesis, Department of Computer Science, University of Edinburgh (1994)
22. Hillston, J., Marin, A., Piazza, C., Rossi, S.: Contextual lumpability. In: Proceedings of ValueTools 2013 Conference, pp. 194–203. ACM Press (2013)
23. Howard, A., et al.: Searching for MobileNetV3. In: Proceedings of the IEEE/CVF International Conference on Computer Vision, pp. 1314–1324 (2019)
24. Howard, A.G., et al.: MobileNets: efficient convolutional neural networks for mobile vision applications. arXiv preprint arXiv:1704.04861 (2017)
25. Hu, H., Peng, R., Tai, Y.W., Tang, C.K.: Network trimming: a data-driven neuron pruning approach towards efficient deep architectures. arXiv preprint arXiv:1607.03250 (2016)
26. Iandola, F.N., Han, S., Moskewicz, M.W., Ashraf, K., Dally, W.J., Keutzer, K.: SqueezeNet: AlexNet-level accuracy with 50x fewer parameters and < 0.5 mb model size. arXiv preprint arXiv:1602.07360 (2016)
27. Kemeny, J.G., Snell, J.L.: Finite Markov Chains. Springer, New York (1976)
28. Kolesnikov, A., et al.: Big Transfer (BiT): general visual representation learning. In: Vedaldi, A., Bischof, H., Brox, T., Frahm, J.-M. (eds.) ECCV 2020. LNCS, vol. 12350, pp. 491–507. Springer, Cham (2020). https://doi.org/10.1007/978-3-030-58558-7_29
29. Krizhevsky, A., Sutskever, I., Hinton, G.E.: ImageNet classification with deep convolutional neural networks. In: Advances in Neural Information Processing Systems, vol. 25 (2012)
30. LeCun, Y., Denker, J.S., Solla, S.A.: Optimal brain damage. In: Advances in Neural Information Processing Systems, pp. 598–605 (1990)
31. Li, H., Kadav, A., Durdanovic, I., Samet, H., Graf, H.P.: Pruning filters for efficient convnets. arXiv preprint arXiv:1608.08710 (2016)
32. Lin, M., Chen, Q., Yan, S.: Network in network. arXiv preprint arXiv:1312.4400 (2013)
33. Lin, M., et al.: HRank: filter pruning using high-rank feature map. In: Proceedings of the IEEE/CVF Conference on Computer Vision and Pattern Recognition, pp. 1529–1538 (2020)
34. Lin, S., et al.: Towards optimal structured CNN pruning via generative adversarial learning. In: Proceedings of the IEEE/CVF Conference on Computer Vision and Pattern Recognition, pp. 2790–2799 (2019)

35. Liu, Y., Sun, Y., Xue, B., Zhang, M., Yen, G.G., Tan, K.C.: A survey on evolutionary neural architecture search. IEEE Trans. Neural Netw. Learn. Syst. **34**(2), 550–570 (2023)

36. Liu, Z., Li, J., Shen, Z., Huang, G., Yan, S., Zhang, C.: Learning efficient convolutional networks through network slimming. In: Proceedings of the IEEE International Conference on Computer Vision, pp. 2736–2744 (2017)

37. Ma, N., Zhang, X., Zheng, H.-T., Sun, J.: ShuffleNet V2: practical guidelines for efficient CNN architecture design. In: Ferrari, V., Hebert, M., Sminchisescu, C., Weiss, Y. (eds.) Computer Vision – ECCV 2018. LNCS, vol. 11218, pp. 122–138. Springer, Cham (2018). https://doi.org/10.1007/978-3-030-01264-9_8

38. Marin, A., Piazza, C., Rossi, S.: Proportional lumpability. In: André, É., Stoelinga, M. (eds.) FORMATS 2019. LNCS, vol. 11750, pp. 265–281. Springer, Cham (2019). https://doi.org/10.1007/978-3-030-29662-9_16

39. Marin, A., Piazza, C., Rossi, S.: Proportional lumpability and proportional bisimilarity. Acta Informatica **59**(2), 211–244 (2022). https://doi.org/10.1007/s00236-021-00404-y

40. Molchanov, P., Mallya, A., Tyree, S., Frosio, I., Kautz, J.: Importance estimation for neural network pruning. In: Proceedings of the IEEE/CVF Conference on Computer Vision and Pattern Recognition, pp. 11264–11272 (2019)

41. Piazza, C., Rossi, S.: Reasoning about proportional lumpability. In: Abate, A., Marin, A. (eds.) QEST 2021. LNCS, vol. 12846, pp. 372–390. Springer, Cham (2021). https://doi.org/10.1007/978-3-030-85172-9_20

42. Prabhakar, P.: Bisimulations for neural network reduction. In: Finkbeiner, B., Wies, T. (eds.) VMCAI 2022. LNCS, vol. 13182, pp. 285–300. Springer, Cham (2022). https://doi.org/10.1007/978-3-030-94583-1_14

43. Rastegari, M., Ordonez, V., Redmon, J., Farhadi, A.: XNOR-Net: ImageNet classification using binary convolutional neural networks. In: Leibe, B., Matas, J., Sebe, N., Welling, M. (eds.) ECCV 2016. LNCS, vol. 9908, pp. 525–542. Springer, Cham (2016). https://doi.org/10.1007/978-3-319-46493-0_32

44. Ren, P., et al.: A comprehensive survey of neural architecture search: challenges and solutions. ACM Comput. Surv. (CSUR) **54**(4), 1–34 (2021)

45. Ressi, D., Pistellato, M., Albarelli, A., Bergamasco, F.: A relevance-based CNN trimming method for low-resources embedded vision. In: Bandini, S., Gasparini, F., Mascardi, V., Palmonari, M., Vizzari, G. (eds.) AIxIA 2021 – Advances in Artificial Intelligence, AIxIA 2021. Lecture Notes in Computer Science, vol. 13196, pp. 297–309. Springer, Cham (2022). https://doi.org/10.1007/978-3-031-08421-8_20

46. Sandler, M., Howard, A., Zhu, M., Zhmoginov, A., Chen, L.C.: MobileNetV2: inverted residuals and linear bottlenecks. In: Proceedings of the IEEE Conference on Computer Vision and Pattern Recognition, pp. 4510–4520 (2018)

47. Schweitzer, P.: Aggregation methods for large Markov chains. In: Procedings of the International Workshop on Computer Performance and Reliability, pp. 275–286. North Holland (1984)

48. Sproston, J., Donatelli, S.: Backward stochastic bisimulation in CSL model checking. In: 2004 First International Conference on the Quantitative Evaluation of Systems, QEST 2004. Proceedings, pp. 220–229. IEEE (2004)

49. Szegedy, C., et al.: Going deeper with convolutions. In: Proceedings of the IEEE Conference on Computer Vision and Pattern Recognition, pp. 1–9 (2015)

50. Szegedy, C., Vanhoucke, V., Ioffe, S., Shlens, J., Wojna, Z.: Rethinking the inception architecture for computer vision. In: Proceedings of the IEEE Conference On Computer Vision and Pattern Recognition, pp. 2818–2826 (2016)

51. Tan, C.M.J., Motani, M.: DropNet: reducing neural network complexity via iterative pruning. In: International Conference on Machine Learning, pp. 9356–9366. PMLR (2020)

52. Tan, M., Le, Q.: EfficientNet: rethinking model scaling for convolutional neural networks. In: International Conference on Machine Learning, pp. 6105–6114. PMLR (2019)

53. Tan, M., Le, Q.V.: EfficientNetV2: smaller models and faster training. arXiv preprint arXiv:2104.00298 (2021)

54. Tucker, L.R.: Some mathematical notes on three-mode factor analysis. Psychometrika **31**(3), 279–311 (1966). https://doi.org/10.1007/BF02289464

55. Wang, Z., Xie, X., Shi, G.: RFPruning: a retraining-free pruning method for accelerating convolutional neural networks. Appl. Soft Comput. **113**, 107860 (2021)

56. Xiao, L., Bahri, Y., Sohl-Dickstein, J., Schoenholz, S., Pennington, J.: Dynamical isometry and a mean field theory of CNNs: how to train 10,000-layer vanilla convolutional neural networks. In: International Conference on Machine Learning, pp. 5393–5402. PMLR (2018)

57. Yu, J., Wang, Z., Vasudevan, V., Yeung, L., Seyedhosseini, M., Wu, Y.: CoCa: contrastive captioners are image-text foundation models. arXiv preprint arXiv:2205.01917 (2022)

58. Yu, R., et al.: NISP: pruning networks using neuron importance score propagation. In: Proceedings of the IEEE Conference on Computer Vision and Pattern Recognition, pp. 9194–9203 (2018)

59. Zhang, X., Zhou, X., Lin, M., Sun, J.: ShuffleNet: an extremely efficient convolutional neural network for mobile devices. In: Proceedings of the IEEE Conference on Computer Vision and Pattern Recognition, pp. 6848–6856 (2018)

60. Zoph, B., Le, Q.V.: Neural architecture search with reinforcement learning. arXiv preprint arXiv:1611.01578 (2016)

Knowledge Enhanced Neural Networks
for Relational Domains

Alessandro Daniele[✉] and Luciano Serafini

Data and Knowledge Management Research Unit, Fondazione Bruno Kessler,
Trento, Italy
{daniele,serafini}@fbk.eu

Abstract. In the recent past, there has been a growing interest in
Neural-Symbolic Integration frameworks, i.e., hybrid systems that integrate connectionist and symbolic approaches to obtain the best of both
worlds. In this work we focus on a specific method, KENN (Knowledge
Enhanced Neural Networks), a Neural-Symbolic architecture that injects
prior logical knowledge into a neural network by adding on its top a residual layer that modifies the initial predictions accordingly to the knowledge. Among the advantages of this strategy, there is the inclusion of
clause weights, learnable parameters that represent the strength of the
clauses, meaning that the model can learn the impact of each rule on
the final predictions. As a special case, if the training data contradicts
a constraint, KENN learns to ignore it, making the system robust to
the presence of wrong knowledge. In this paper, we propose an extension of KENN for relational data. One of the main advantages of KENN
resides in its scalability, thanks to a flexible treatment of dependencies
between the rules obtained by stacking multiple logical layers. We show
experimentally the efficacy of this strategy. The results show that KENN
is capable of increasing the performances of the underlying neural network, obtaining better or comparable accuracies in respect to other two
related methods that combine learning with logic, requiring significantly
less time for learning.

1 Introduction

In the last decade, deep learning approaches gained a lot of interest in the
AI community, becoming the state of the art on many fields, such as Computer Vision [17], Machine Translation [2], Speech Recognition [14], etc. Indeed,
Neural networks (NNs) are suited for pattern recognition, even in the presence
of noisy data. They are particularly good at mapping low-level perceptions to
more abstract concepts (for instance, going from images to classes). However,
it is hard for a NN to reason with these high-level abstractions. Furthermore,
NNs are demanding in terms of training data. On the other hand, pure logical
approaches are not suited for learning from low-level features and they struggle in the presence of noise. Nevertheless, they perform well in reasoning with
highly abstract concepts and learning from a small number of samples. Given
these opposite strengths and weaknesses, it is not a surprise that a lot of interest

© The Author(s), under exclusive license to Springer Nature Switzerland AG 2023
A. Dovier et al. (Eds.): AIxIA 2022, LNAI 13796, pp. 91–109, 2023.
https://doi.org/10.1007/978-3-031-27181-6_7

has been drawn toward Neural-Symbolic (NeSy) systems. Indeed, the goal is to combine these two paradigms to obtain the best of the two worlds.

Among NeSy methods there is KENN (*Knowledge Enhanced Neural Network*) [6], a model composed of a Neural Network enhanced with additional layers which codify logical knowledge. KENN has multiple advantages over other NeSy methods, such as its capacity to learn *clause weights* and the ability to impose the knowledge not only during training but even at inference time. In particular, KENN showed remarkable results on the Predicate Detection task of Visual Relationship Detection Dataset (VRD Dataset) [19] using a manually curated prior knowledge proposed by [9], outperforming the previous state of the art results, with really good performances on the *Zero Shot Learning* subtask [6]. Moreover, it outperformed Logic Tensor Networks [29], one of its major competitors, using the same knowledge.

Despite its good empirical results, KENN has been applied only on multilabel classification tasks with no relational data. Indeed, a limitation of KENN resides in its inability to take into account binary predicates. This is because KENN expects the NN's predictions to be stored in a matrix format, where the columns represent different unary predicates and the rows their possible groundings (i.e., substitutions of the free variable for such predicates). For this reason, it is not straightforward to apply KENN to relational data, where binary predicates are available.

In this paper, we propose an updated version of KENN which can deal with relational data. Particular attention was paid to defining a scalable strategy to deal with binary predicates, obtaining good performances in terms of execution time. Indeed, KENN assumes independence between the logical rules, allowing for scalable inclusion of the underlying knowledge. However, the assumption is often violated in real scenarios, in particular in the contexts of relational domains. To deal with this problem, we propose a strategy that consists of adding multiple logical layers inside the model. We provide proof of the efficacy of this strategy in a simple scenario with two logical rules. Additionally, we tested this idea on Citeseer, a dataset for Collective Classification [28], showing that the additional layers improve the performance of the model. Moreover, the experiments on this dataset provide a comparison between KENN and two other approaches: Semantic Based Regularization (SBR) [8] and Relational Neural Machines (RNM) [22].

2   Related Works

Many previous works attempt to combine learning models with logical knowledge. Among them there is Statistical Relational Learning (SRL), a subfield of Machine Learning that aims at applying statistical methods in domains that exhibit both uncertainty and relational structure [16]. Generally speaking, SRL deals with the knowledge either by combining logic rules with probabilistic graphical models (e.g., Markov Logic Networks [25], and *Probabilistic Soft Logic* (PSL) [1]) or by extending logic programming languages to handle uncertainty (e.g., ProbLog [7]).

The recent achievements of deep learning methods lead to a renewed interest in another line of research, called Neural-Symbolic Integration, which focuses on combining neural network architectures with logical knowledge [3]. This can be achieved in multiple ways depending on the role of the knowledge. For instance, works like TensorLog [5], Neural Theorem Prover (NTP) [26,27], Deep-ProbLog [21], Neural Logic Machines [10], and NeuralLog [13] focus on the development of differentiable approaches for reasoning, which can be used in combination with neural networks. Another line of research comes from methods like ∂ILP [4,11], and Neural Logic Rule Layer (NLRL) [24]. In these cases, the goal is to learn general knowledge from the data, either from scratch or by refining an initial knowledge. Finally, more related to our purposes, some methods focus on learning in the presence of prior knowledge, which acts as additional supervision. In this section, we are going to focus on these types of methods, since KENN falls in this category.

There are mainly two approaches for learning in the presence of prior knowledge: the first consists of treating logical rules as constraints on the predictions of the neural network. The problem is reduced to maximize the satisfiability of the constraints and can be efficiently tackled by adding a regularization term in the Loss function. The second approach is to modify the neural network by injecting the knowledge into its structure.

Two notable examples of regularization approaches are *Logic Tensor Network* (LTN) [29] and *Semantic Based Regularization* (SBR) [8]. Both methods maximize the satisfaction of the constraints, expressed as FOL formulas, under a fuzzy logic semantic. A similar strategy is employed also by *Semantic Loss Function* [30], but instead of relying on fuzzy logic, it optimizes the probability of the rules being true. Nevertheless, this approach is restricted to propositional logic. [12] introduces DL2. Nonetheless, it can be used only in the context of regression tasks, where the predicates correspond to comparison constraints (e.g. $=$, $\neq$, $\leq$). [23] also proposes a method that regularizes the Loss, but they focus on a specific task of Natural Language Processing. Their approach differs from the others because it makes use of adversarial examples to calculate the regularization term. Finally, in [15], a distillation mechanism is used to inject FOL rules: here a teacher network (which encodes the rules) is used to regularize the Loss applied to a student network.

Approaches based on regularization force the constraints satisfaction solely at training time. As a consequence, there are no guarantees that they will be satisfied at inference time as well. Instead, model-based methods inject knowledge directly into the model structure, and they are naturally capable of enforcing the knowledge at inference time. Another advantage is the possibility to learn a weight that codifies the importance of a logical rule directly from the data. This is no possible at all with methods based on regularization, since the logical formulas are directly codified inside the Loss function.

Among the model-based approaches there is KENN, a framework that injects knowledge on top of the NN model through an additional layer which increases the satisfaction of the constraints in a fuzzy logic semantic. Another approach is provided by Li and Srikumar who recently proposed a method that codifies the logical constraints directly into the neural network model [18]. However, they restrict the rules to implications with exactly one consequent and they do not provide the possibility to learn clause weights, which in their system are added as hyper-parameters. Going in the same direction, [22] proposed Relational Neural Networks (RNM). RNM can be also inserted in the set of approaches that add the logic directly into the model and, as the best of our knowledge, it is the only method other than KENN which is capable of integrating logical knowledge with a neural network while learning the clause weights. RNM integrates a neural network model with a FOL reasoner. This is done in two stages: in the first one, the NN is used to calculate initial predictions for the atomic formulas; in the second stage a graphical model is used to represent a probability distribution over the set of atomic formulas. To obtain the final predictions a Maximum a Posteriori (MAP) estimation is performed, finding the most probable assignment to the grounded atoms given the output of the NN and the set of constraints. At a high-level RNM approach is similar to KENN, since in both cases a NN makes initial predictions and a post elaboration step is applied to such predictions to provide the final classification. However, RNM requires to solve an optimization problem at inference time and after each training step. This has the advantage of considering all the logical rules together at the same time at the expense of an increased computational effort. Contrary, in KENN each rule is considered separately from the others, and the second stage is directly integrated inside the model as a differentiable function that can be trained end-to-end with the NN. However, with this strategy there could be some contradictory changes when combining multiple clauses with the same predicates. We will further analyze this aspect in Sect. 3.4, proposing a strategy to handle this limitation. Moreover, in Sect. 4, we analyze this strategy empirically.

3   Knowledge Enhanced Neural Networks

We define the prior knowledge in terms of formulas of a function-free first order language $\mathcal{L}$. Its signature is defined with a set of domain constants $\mathcal{C} \triangleq \{a_1, a_2, ...a_m\}$ and a set of predicates $\mathcal{P} \triangleq \{P_1, P_2...P_q\}$. In our setting, predicates can be unary or binary/Binary predicates can express relations among pairs of objects in the domain, e.g. $Friends(a, b)$ states that person a is a friend of b. The prior knowledge is defined as a set of clauses: $\mathcal{K} \triangleq \{c_1, c_2, ...c_r\}$. A clause is a disjunction of literals, each of which is a possibly negated atom: $c \triangleq \bigvee_{i=1}^{k} l_i$, where k is the number of literals in c and l_i is the ith literal. We assume that there are no repeated literals. Since we are interested in representing only general knowledge, the literals do not contain any constant, only variables that are assumed to be universally quantified. If the predicate is binary, the two variables are x and y, otherwise only x. When an entire clause contains only variable x (i.e., only unary predicates), we call it *unary*. Similarly, if it contains both x and y we call it *binary*[1].

---

[1] We restrict to the case where clauses contain at most two variables.

As an example, the clause $\neg Smoker(x) \vee Cancer(x)$ is unary and states that all smokers have also cancer (notice that the clauses are not assumed to be hard constraints). Instead, the clause

$$\neg Smoker(x) \vee \neg Friends(x, y) \vee Smoker(y) \tag{1}$$

is binary. It states that if a person x is a smoker and he is a friend of another person y, then y is also a smoker. We will use extensively this clause in the remaining of the paper, referring to it as c_{SF}.

We define the grounding of a unary clause c, denoted by $c[a]$, as the clause obtained by substituting the x variable with constant a. Similarly, if c is binary, its grounding $c[a, b]$ is obtained by substituting x and y with a and b respectively. For instance, the grounding $c_{SF}[a, b]$ of the clause defined in Eq. 1 correspond to $\neg Smoker(a) \vee \neg Friends(a, b) \vee Smoker(b)$.

3.1 KENN Architecture

Suppose we have a NN for a classification task which takes as input a matrix $\mathbf{x} \in \mathbb{R}^{d \times n}$ containing n features for d samples, and returns an output $\mathbf{y} \in [0, 1]^{d \times q}$ which contains the predictions for q classes corresponding to the q predicates. A prior knowledge $\mathcal{K}$ is also provided. It can be used by KENN to improve the predictions of the NN.

Figure 1(left) shows a high-level overview of KENN where a residual layer, called *Knowledge Enhancer* (KE), is inserted between the NN and the final activation function. The role of KE is to revise the final predictions returned by the NN in order to increase the truth value of each clause $c \in \mathcal{K}$. It does so by calculating a residue $\boldsymbol{\delta}$, a matrix that is added to the predictions of the NN.

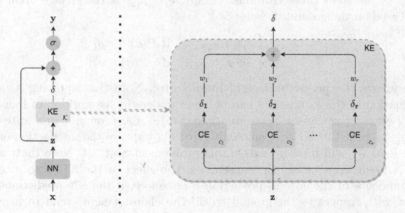

Fig. 1. Model architecture. Left: KENN model overview. Right: Knowledge Enhancer.

The KE works in the pre-activations space, i.e. on $\mathbf{z}$, and the activation function (σ) is called later. In order for KENN to work, the activation function must be monotonic and return values in the range $[0, 1]^2$. Since both NN and KE are

---

[2] For more details on why the KE is applied on pre-activations, please refer to [6].

differentiable, the entire architecture is differentiable end-to-end, making it possible to apply back-propagation algorithm on the whole model. Figure 1(right) shows the architecture of KE, which calculates the residual matrix δ.

More in details, for each clause $c \in \mathcal{K}$, the KE contains a submodule, the *Clause Enhancer* (CE), which proposes the changes δ_c to be applied on the NN's preactivations in order to increase the satisfaction of c. Indeed, the CE computes a soft differentiable approximation of a function called *t-conorm boost function* (TBF). Intuitively, a TBF is a function $\phi : \mathbb{R}^k \to \mathbb{R}_+^k$ that proposes the changes to be applied on the pre-activations $\mathbf{z}$ of k truth values, such that $\perp(\sigma(\mathbf{z} + \phi(\mathbf{z}))) \geq \perp(\sigma(\mathbf{z}))$, where $\perp : [0,1]^k \to [0,1]$ is a t-conorm function, used in fuzzy logic to represent the semantics of the disjunction operator[3]. In [6] it has been defined the function

$$\phi(\mathbf{z})_i = \begin{cases} 1 & \text{if } i = \text{argmax}_{j=1}^n z_j \\ 0 & \text{otherwise} \end{cases} \tag{2}$$

and proved that such a function is the optimal TBF for the Gödel t-conorm. KENN employs the softmax function as a continuous and differentiable approximation of ϕ.

The δ_c matrices are combined linearly inside the KE to obtain the final change δ to be applied on the NN's predictions, and finally the δ is summed to the initial pre-activations $\mathbf{z}$ and passed to the activation function:

$$y_{P(a)} = \sigma\left(z_{P(a)} + \sum_{\substack{c \in \mathcal{K} \\ P(x) \in c}} w_c \cdot \delta_{c[a], P(a)}\right) \tag{3}$$

where w_c is the *clause weight*, $P(a)$ a grounded atom, $y_{P(a)}$ its final prediction, and $z_{P(a)}$ the NN's pre-activations. Finally, $\delta_{c[a], P(a)}$ is the change applied to $P(a)$ based on the grounded clause $c[a]$:

$$\delta_{c[a], P(a)} = \begin{cases} \phi(\mathbf{z}_c)_{P(a)} & \text{if } P(a) \in c[a] \\ -\phi(\mathbf{z}_c)_{\neg P(a)} & \text{if } \neg P(a) \in c[a] \end{cases} \tag{4}$$

where $\mathbf{z}_c$ are the pre-activations of literals of c. Note that applying a linear combination of the δ_c matrices can be done under the assumption of independence between the clauses. When multiple clauses share common predicates the changes proposed by KENN could only partially improve the satisfaction of the knowledge. We will further analyze this problem in Sect. 3.4. Note that, when the NN predictions satisfy the constraints, the effect of the KE is to increase the confidence of the current predictions. Therefore, if the NN predictions are correct with respect to the ground truth, the clause weights tend to increase during learning.

3.2 Extending KENN for Relational Domains

In the architecture defined so far, the groundings involve a single object and $\mathbf{z}$ is defined as a matrix, where columns represent predicates and rows constants.

---

[3] In [6], function ϕ is called δ. Here we changed the name to avoid confusions with its output which is also referred as δ.

Figure 2(left) introduces the representation of $\mathbf{z}$: it is defined as a matrix such that the element z_{ij} contains the pre-activation of $P_j(a_i)$, with P_j the jth predicate and a_i the ith constant. Note that this kind of representation is common when working with neural networks since the columns (predicates) correspond to the labels and the rows (groundings) to the samples. An important aspect of this representation lies in the fact that each grounded atom can be found in the matrix exactly one time. This allows to parallelize computations of Eq. 3 since a grounded clause involves only atoms in the same row, and each row can be managed in parallel inside a GPU. This can be done only if the same atom does not appear in multiple rows, since the changes are applied independently to each row and are not aggregated together. This property always holds with unary clauses.

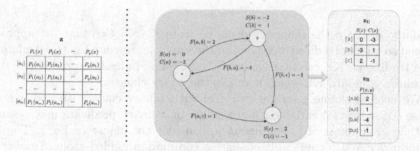

Fig. 2. The representation of NN's final pre-activations. Left: unary case. Right: representation of relational data. Pre-activations are represented as integers instead of reals to simplify the figure. (Color figure online)

To represent relational data, we extend KENN with an extra matrix $\mathbf{z}_B$, which contains the binary predicates' pre-activations. For uniformity of notation we use $\mathbf{z}_U$ to denote the unary matrix $\mathbf{z}$ of the not relational KENN. Matrix $\mathbf{z}_B$ contains one row for every pair of objects we are interested in and a column for each binary predicate. Figure 2(right) shows this representation using the classical Smoker-Friends-Cancer example, where the domain is composed of three constants (persons) $\mathcal{C} = \{a, b, c\}$, the unary predicates are S and C (for *Smoker* and *Cancer*), and a binary predicate F (for *Friends*). The blue box shows the graph representation with nodes and edges labelled with pre-activation of unary and binary predicates respectively. The grey box shows the corresponding matrix representation used by KENN. Notice that it is not required that the entire graph is computed by the NN. For instance, in the experiments on Citeseer, the *Cite* predicate is provided directly as a feature (see Sect. 4).

The architecture of KENN for relational domains is very similar to the architecture of traditional KENN of Fig. 1, with KE substituted by a *Relational KE* (RKE). From a high level perspective, the RKE differs from the traditional KE on the amount of inputs and outputs. As seen before, in the relational case the pre-activations are divided in two different matrices ($\mathbf{z}_U$ and $\mathbf{z}_B$) and, as a consequence, also the δ matrix and predictions $\mathbf{y}$ are now splitted in unary and binary matrices (δ_U and δ_B for the residues, $\mathbf{y}_U$ and $\mathbf{y}_D$ for the final predictions).

The RKE has the same role as the KE in the unary case. However, it is capable to consider also binary predicates. When binary knowledge is available, additional steps are required since the independence between object can not be assumed anymore.

Let $\mathcal{K}_U$ be the set of unary clauses and $\mathcal{K}_B$ the set of binary clauses. The prior knowledge is now defined as $\mathcal{K} = \mathcal{K}_U \cup \mathcal{K}_B$. The idea is to apply the KE to these two sets separately. Equation 3 can be decomposed using the new defined partition of the knowledge: $y_A = \sigma\left(z_A + \sum_{c\in\mathcal{K}_U[\mathcal{C}]} w_c \cdot \delta_{c,A} + \sum_{c\in\mathcal{K}_B[\mathcal{C}]} w_c \cdot \delta_{c,A}\right)$, where A is a grounded atom (i.e. $P(a)$ or $P(a,b)$, depending on the arity of P). We define $\delta_{\mathcal{K}_U}$ as the changes deriving from unary clauses:

$$\delta_{\mathcal{K}_U,P(a)} = \sum_{\substack{c\in\mathcal{K}_U \\ P(x)\in c}} w_c \cdot \delta_{c[a],P(a)} \qquad (5)$$

Similarly, $\delta_{\mathcal{K}_B}$ are the changes calculated from $\mathcal{K}_B$. Notice that the approach defined so far can be directly applied to the unary knowledge $\mathcal{K}_U$ to calculate δ_U since traditional KE can manage unary knowledge. Indeed, internally the RKE contains a standard KE which manages the unary clauses.

We need to define a strategy to deal with binary clauses. Indeed, when a clause c contain two variables, a grounding of a unary predicate may occur in multiple groundings of c. For instance, consider the clause of Eq. 1. The two groundings $c_{SF}[a, b]$ and $c_{SF}[b, c]$ share a common grounded atom: $Smoker(b)$. For this reason, when dealing with the predictions of a unary predicate in a relational domain, we need to account for such repetitions:

$$\delta_{\mathcal{K}_B,P(a)} = \sum_{b\neq a}\left(\sum_{\substack{c\in\mathcal{K}_B \\ P(x)\in c}} w_c \cdot \delta_{c[a,b],P(a)} + \sum_{\substack{c\in\mathcal{K}_B \\ P(y)\in c}} w_c \cdot \delta_{c[b,a],P(a)}\right) \qquad (6)$$

Putting all together, the predictions $y_{P(a)}$ for a grounded unary predicate P are:

$$y_{P(a)} = \sigma(z_{P(a)} + \delta_{\mathcal{K}_U,P(a)} + \delta_{\mathcal{K}_B,P(a)}) \qquad (7)$$

The predictions for a binary predicate R can be found only in binary clauses and any possible grounding of R can be found in only one corresponding grounding of each clause $y_{R(a,b)} = \sigma(z_{R(a,b)} + \delta_{\mathcal{K}_B,R(a,b)})$, with

$$\delta_{\mathcal{K}_B,R(a,b)} = \sum_{\substack{c\in\mathcal{K}_B \\ R(x,y)\in c}} w_c \cdot \delta_{c[a,b],R(a,b)} \qquad (8)$$

3.3   Time Complexity

Here we analyze the time complexity of an RKE layer with respect to domain size m, number of predicates $|\mathcal{P}|$, and number of rules $|\mathcal{K}|$. We also assume the maximum number L of literals in a clause to be a small constant.

Let us first analyze the time complexity for calculating the $\delta_{c[a]}$ used in Eqs. 5, and 6. Each $\delta_{c[a],P(a)}$ can be calculated in time $O(1)$ (see Eq. 4). Computing $\delta_{c[a]}$

also requires constant time. The sum of Eq. 5 require time $O(|\mathcal{K}|)$, which is the time necessary to compute $\delta_{\mathcal{K}_U, P(a)}$. Note that neural networks are usually run on GPUs, where the computations can be parallelized. Assuming enough parallel processes ($|\mathcal{K}|$ in this case), a sum can be performed in a time logarithmic with respect to the number of addends, and complexity for $\delta_{\mathcal{K}_U, P(a)}$ becomes $O(log(|\mathcal{K}|))$. Finally, Eq. 5 needs to be calculated for all the grounded unary predicates $P(a)$, for a total time of $O(m \cdot |\mathcal{P}| \cdot |\mathcal{K}|)$ in a single process, and $O(log(|\mathcal{K}|))$ with multiple parallel processes (each of the grounded atom can be considered independently from the others). With a similar reasoning, we found the time complexity of Eqs. 6 and 8 to be $O(m^2 \cdot |\mathcal{P}| \cdot |\mathcal{K}|)$. Note that with enough parallel processes we can compute all the deltas in $O(log(m) + log(|\mathcal{K}|))$.

3.4 Treatment of Dependencies Among the Rules

In the previous section we showed the efficacy of the method in terms of execution time, which can be achieved thanks to the assumption of independence. However, when this assumption is violated, KENN does not provide any guarantees on the satisfaction of the knowledge. As an example, suppose that we have two grounded clauses $c_1 : \neg A \vee B$ and $c_2 : \neg B \vee C$ with their respective clause enhancers CE_1 and CE_2, where A, B and C are grounded unary or binary predicates. The atom B appears in both clauses with opposite signs. Since the CE increase the highest literal value (see Eq. 2), if $A < B^4$ and $C < \neg B$, then CE_1 increases B and CE_2 decreases it. As a consequence, the satisfaction of only one between c_1 and c_2 is increased. The satisfaction of the entailed clause $\neg A \vee C$ is also not improved.

For any grounded atom G, lets define $G^{(0)}$ as its initial prediction and $G^{(i)}$ as the prediction of the ith KE layer. Moreover, suppose that all KEs share the same clause weights w_1 and w_2 (for c_1 and c_2 respectively). From Eqs. 3 and 4 we can derive $B^{(1)} = B^{(0)} + w_1 - w_2$, and $\neg B^{(1)} = \neg B^{(0)} + w_2 - w_1$. If $w_1 \geq w_2$, then $A^{(1)} = A^{(0)} < B^{(0)} \leq B^{(1)}$. As a consequence, the first rule will increase again B even at the next KE layer. On the other hand, the value of $\neg B$ is reduced, which means that there is an increased chance for $C^{(1)} > \neg B^{(1)}$, which would solve the problem since CE_2 would increase C instead of $\neg B$. Notice that, since the weights are the same at each level, it is always true that $\neg B^{(i+1)} \leq \neg B^{(i)}$, meaning that with enough KE layers both clauses' satisfaction will be increased (and as a consequence, also their entailments).

The problem analyzed in this section becomes even more relevant in relational domains since in these contexts an atom can be shared not only by multiple clauses but also by different groundings of the same clause (for instance, in $c_{SF}[a, b]$ and $c_{SF}[b, c]$). For this reason, in these contexts stacking multiple RKEs is recommended (more details in Sect. 4.2).

4   Evaluation of the Model

In this section, the relational extension of KENN is tested on the task of Collective Classification: given a graph, we are interested in finding a classification

---

[4] With an abuse of notation, we use atoms symbols to refer also to their truth value.

for its nodes using both features of the nodes (the objects) and the information coming from the edges of the graph (relations between objects) [28].

In Collective Classification, there are two different learning tasks: inductive and transductive learning. In inductive learning, there are two separate graphs, one for training and the other for testing. On the contrary, in transductive learning, there is only one graph that contains nodes both for training and testing. In other words, in inductive learning, there are no edges between nodes for training and testing, while in transductive learning there are. The tests have been performed on both tasks to analyze the behavior of KENN in the contexts of relational domains. In particular, we tested KENN with a varying number of KEs layers to validate the proposal of Sect. 3.4[5].

4.1   Experimental Setup

We followed the evaluation methodology of [22], where the experiments have been carried out on Citeseer dataset [20] using SBR and RNM. The Citeseer dataset used in the evaluation is a citation network: the graph's nodes represent documents and the edges represent citations. The nodes' features are bag-of-words vectors, where an entry is zero if the corresponding word of the dictionary is absent in the document, and one if it is present. The classes to be predicted represent possible topics for a document. The dataset contains 3312 nodes that must be classified in 6 different classes: AG, AI, DB, IR, ML, and HCI. The classification is obtained from the 3703 features of the nodes, with the addition of the information coming from the citations (4732 edges).

We use the same NN and knowledge as in [22], allowing for the comparison with SBR and RNM. The NN is a dense network with 3 hidden layers, each with 50 hidden nodes and ReLU activation function. The knowledge consists of six rules obtained by substituting the topic T in $\neg T(x) \vee \neg Cite(x, y) \vee T(y)$ with all the classes, codifying the idea that papers cite works of the same topic. Tests have been conducted by selecting 10%, 25%, 50%, 75%, and 90% of nodes for training to evaluate the efficacy of the three methods on the varying of the training set dimension. For each of these values, the training and evaluation were performed 100 times, each with a different split of the dataset. At each run the training set is created by selecting random nodes of the graph, with the constraints that the dataset must be balanced.

4.2   Results

Figure 3 shows the test accuracies obtained by KENN while increasing the number of KEs layers, starting from 0 (corresponding to the NN accuracy) up to 6. Note that, for each line in the figure, there is a surrounding border corresponding to a 99% confidence interval. To calculate the intervals, we assumed the distribution of improvements obtained by the injection of the logical rules to

---

[5] Source code of the experiments are available on https://github.com/rmazzier/ KENN-Citeseer-Experiments.

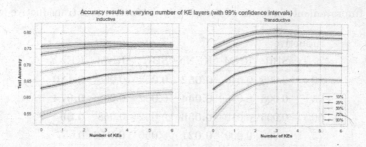

Fig. 3. Accuracies of KENN at the varying of KEs layers. (Color figure online)

be a normal distribution (see figures in Appendix B and C). We also computed the p-values for each setting, assuming as null Hypothesis that the distribution of accuracies of the NN is the same as KENN. Since the number of runs are quite high, the resulting p-values are very small. For this reason, we can safely reject the null Hypothesis, and we are very confident that the improvements given by KENN do not depend on the random initialization of the models' parameters or the specific choices of the splits of the dataset. More in detail, we found p-values in the range from 8.2e−42 to 1.6e−09 in the inductive case, and from 53e−72 to 2.1e−23 for the transductive one. The only exception is with 90% of the samples in the inductive scenario where the p-value is 0.35. This is because the improvements over the NN are very small. Indeed, in both learning paradigms, the effect of the knowledge is reduced when the amount of available data is larger. This behavior is consistent with the simple intuition that, when the training data is scarce, the usage of knowledge should bring higher benefits.

A more important result coming from these experiments is the fact that in all cases adding a new KE layer does not reduce the test accuracy. On the contrary, most of the time the metric is increased until a certain number of layers is reached, and after that, the accuracy stabilizes. This behavior is in line with the discussion of Sect. 3.4 and confirms the efficacy of the proposed strategy to deal with the violation of independence assumption.

Finally, Fig. 3 provide also a measure of the amount of information carried out by the knowledge. For instance, consider blue and yellow lines, corresponding to a training set with 25% and 50% of the samples, respectively. In the inductive scenario, the accuracy obtained with 25% with the addition of the knowledge is almost the same as the standard NN with 50% of the data (even higher in the transductive scenario). In this case, adding the knowledge has the same effect of doubling up the training data! Indeed, one of the main motivations behind Neural-Symbolic Integration consists in reducing the required amount of training samples since collecting labeled data is costly in practice.

Table 1. Improvements in terms of accuracy on inductive and transductive learning.

Inductive				Transductive		
% Tr	SBR	RNM	KENN	SBR	RNM	KENN
10	0.005	0.040	**0.052**	0.063	0.068	**0.110**
25	0.008	0.035	**0.044**	0.062	0.068	**0.074**
50	0.005	0.019	**0.036**	0.052	0.058	**0.064**
75	0.002	0.009	**0.021**	0.056	**0.058**	0.057
90	0.003	**0.009**	0.001	**0.054**	**0.054**	0.043

4.3   Comparison with Other NeSy Frameworks

Table 1 shows a comparison of KENN with SBR and RNM. We used the results of KENN with 3 KEs since more layers do not provide a significant advantage (see Sect. 4.2). As we can see from the table, in the inductive case SBR produces much lower improvements compared to the other two methods. Note that these results are in line with previous results obtained on VRD dataset, where another regularization approach (LTN) was compared with KENN [6]. Indeed, the results obtained in both VRD and Citeseer suggest better performances of model-based approaches as compared to the ones based on regularization. Note that methods based on regularization of the loss do not impose the knowledge at inference time. In the transductive scenario, the situation is different and SBR behaves similarly to the other two. Indeed, in this case, citations between training and test nodes are available and there is no distinction between training and inference.

Finally, the results suggest that KENN is particularly useful when the training data available is scarce. On the contrary, when data is abundant, our results tend to degrade faster than RNM and SBR. However, the greatest advantage of KENN over other architectures is its scalability. This is confirmed by the comparison of the execution times of the three methods: we found KENN to be very fast as compared to the other two methods with an average of 7.96 s required for a single run, as compared to the NN which requires 2.46 s (on average of 1.83 s for each KE layer). A run of SBR cost 87.36 s (almost 11 times slower than KENN), while RNM required 215.69 s per run (27 times slower)[6].

---

[6] All the experiments have been run on the same architecture, an NVIDIA Tesla v100.

5   Conclusions

KENN is a NeSy architecture that injects prior logical knowledge inside a neural network by stacking a residual layer on its top. In [6], it proved to be able to effectively inject knowledge in the context of multi-label classification tasks. In this work, we extended KENN for relational domains, where the presence of both unary and binary predicates doesn't allow for the usage of the simple tabular representation of the data used in the previous version of the framework. Moreover, we propose a strategy to deal with the violation of the independence assumption made by KENN. The experiments on Citeseer show the effectiveness of this strategy, obtaining statistically relevant improvements over the NN performances, meaning that KENN can successfully inject knowledge even in the presence of relational data. Finally, KENN provided quality results also in comparison with other two NeSy frameworks. In particular, the large difference in performances between KENN/RNM and SBR provides additional evidence in support of model-based approaches in comparison to regularization ones, with KENN the best option in terms of scalability. However, the scalability of KENN largely depends on the fixed structure of the knowledge, with only universally quantified formulas allowed. This is a limitation of KENN in comparison with other frameworks, like LTN, which support the usage of existential quantifiers.

Appendix

A   Relational KENN Architecture

See Fig. 4.

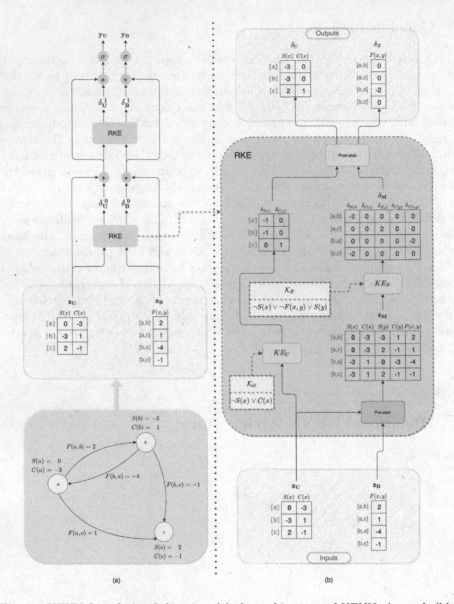

Fig. 4. KENN for relational domains: (a) the architecture of KENN. A graph (blue box) is represented in terms of the two matrices $\mathbf{z}_U$ and $\mathbf{z}_B$ and given as input to the Relational KE (RKE). Multiple RKEs are stacked together and the activation function is called; (b) the architecture of the RKE module: the unary knowledge is enforced directly by the KE_U; the binary knowledge is enforced by the KE_B on matrix $\mathbf{z}_M$, which is created by joining $\mathbf{z}_U$ with $\mathbf{z}_B$ on the pre-elab step. $\mathbf{z}_M$ contains multiple instances of the same atoms, for instance $S[a]$ (red cells). As a consequence, multiple residues are returned for a single atom, and such values are summed in the post-elab (blue cells). Pre and post elaboration steps are efficiently implemented using TensorFlow *gather* and *scatter_nd* functions. (Color figure online)

B   Results Distribution - Inductive Learning

See Fig. 5.

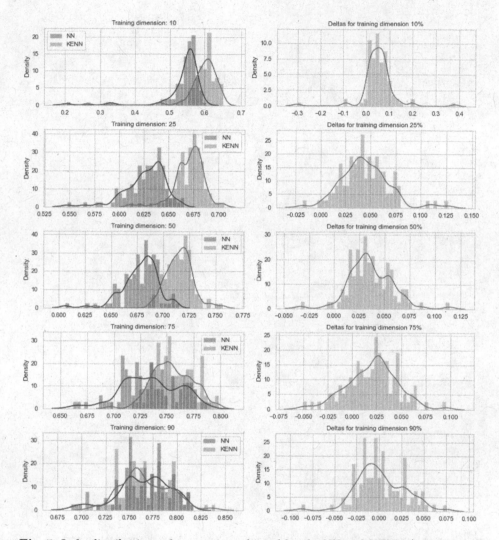

Fig. 5. Left: distributions of accuracies achieved by the NN and KENN (3 KE layers) on 100 runs of Inductive Learning; Right: distributions of the improvements in accuracy obtained by the injection of the logical rules.

C   Results Distribution - Transductive Learning

See Fig. 6.

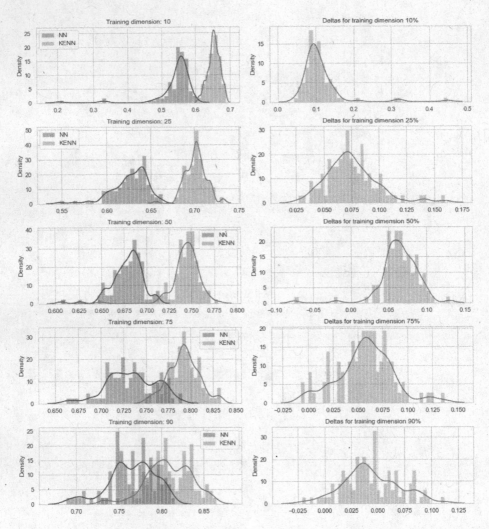

Fig. 6. Left: distributions of accuracies achieved by the NN and KENN (3 KE layers) on 100 runs of Transductive Learning; Right: distributions of the improvements in accuracy obtained by the injection of the logical rules.

D   Comparison with SBR and RNM

Test Accuracy

See Fig. 7.

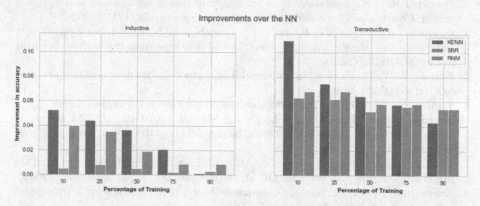

Fig. 7. Comparison between KENN (3 KE layers), SBR and RNM in terms of accuracy improvements over the NN.

Execution Time

See Fig. 8.

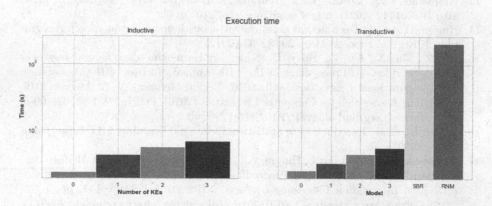

Fig. 8. Execution time in logarithmic scale of the different methods. A bar labelled with number i corresponds to KENN with i KEs layers (0 represents the NN without logic).

References

1. Bach, S.H., Broecheler, M., Huang, B., Getoor, L.: Hinge-loss Markov random fields and probabilistic soft logic. J. Mach. Learn. Res. **18**(109), 1–67 (2017)
2. Bahdanau, D., Cho, K., Bengio, K.: Neural machine translation by jointly learning to align and translate. arXiv preprint arXiv:1409.0473 (2014)
3. Besold, T.R. et al.: Neural-symbolic learning and reasoning: a survey and interpretation. CoRR, abs/1711.03902 (2017). http://arxiv.org/abs/1711.03902
4. Campero, A., Pareja, A., Klinger, T., Tenenbaum, J., Riedel, S.: Logical rule induction and theory learning using neural theorem proving. arXiv preprint arXiv:1809.02193 (2018)
5. Cohen, W.W.: TensorLog: a differentiable deductive database. arXiv preprint arXiv:1605.06523 (2016)
6. Daniele, A., Serafini, L.: Knowledge enhanced neural networks. In: Nayak, A.C., Sharma, A. (eds.) PRICAI 2019. LNCS (LNAI), vol. 11670, pp. 542–554. Springer, Cham (2019). ISBN: 978-3-030-29908-8. https://doi.org/10.1007/978-3-030-29908-8_43
7. De Raedt, L., Kimmig, A., Toivonen, A.: ProbLog: a probabilistic prolog and its application in link discovery. In: IJCAI, Hyderabad, vol. 7, pp. 2462–2467 (2007)
8. Diligenti, M., Gori, M., Saccà, C.: Semantic-based regularization for learning and inference. Artif. Intell. **244**, 143–165 (2017)
9. Donadello, I.: Semantic image interpretation - integration of numerical data and logical knowledge for cognitive vision. Ph.D. thesis, Trento Univ., Italy (2018)
10. Dong, H., Mao, J., Lin, T., Wang, C., Li, L., Zhou, D.: Neural logic machines. arXiv preprint arXiv:1904.11694 (2019)
11. Evans, R., Grefenstette, E.: Learning explanatory rules from noisy data. J. Artif. Intell. Res. **61**, 1–64 (2018)
12. Fischer, M., Balunovic, M., Drachsler-Cohen, D., Gehr, T., Zhang, C., Vechev, M.: DL2: training and querying neural networks with logic. In: International Conference on Machine Learning, pp. 1931–1941 (2019)
13. Guimarães, V., Costa, V.S.: NeuralLog: a neural logic language. CoRR, abs/2105.01442 (2021). http://arxiv.org/abs/2105.01442
14. Hinton, G., et al.: Deep neural networks for acoustic modeling in speech recognition. IEEE Sig. Process. Mag. **29**, 82–97 (2012)
15. Hu, Z., Ma, X., Liu, Z., Hovy, E., Xing, E.: Harnessing deep neural networks with logic rules. In: Proceedings of the 54th Annual Meeting of the Association for Computational Linguistics, ACL 2016, Berlin, Germany, 7–12 August 2016, vol. 1. The Association for Computer Linguistics (2016). ISBN: 978-1-945626-00-5. http://aclweb.org/anthology/P/P16/P16-1228.pdf
16. Koller, D., et al.: Introduction to Statistical Relational Learning. MIT Press, Cambridge (2007)
17. Krizhevsky, A., Sutskever, I., Hinton, G.E.: ImageNet classification with deep convolutional neural networks. In: Proceedings of the 25th International Conference on Neural Information Processing Systems, NIPS 2012, USA, vol. 1, pp. 1097–1105. Curran Associates Inc. (2012). http://dl.acm.org/citation.cfm?id=2999134.2999257
18. Li, T., Srikumar, V.: Augmenting neural networks with first-order logic. In: Proceedings of the 57th Annual Meeting of the Association for Computational Linguistics, Florence, Italy, pp. 292–302. Association for Computational Linguistics, July 2019. https://doi.org/10.18653/v1/P19-1028. https://www.aclweb.org/anthology/P19-1028

19. Lu, C., Krishna, R., Bernstein, M., Fei-Fei, L.: Visual relationship detection with language priors. In: Leibe, B., Matas, J., Sebe, N., Welling, M. (eds.) ECCV 2016. LNCS, vol. 9905, pp. 852–869. Springer, Cham (2016). https://doi.org/10.1007/978-3-319-46448-0_51

20. Lu, Q., Getoor, L.: Link-based classification. In: Proceedings of the Twentieth International Conference on International Conference on Machine Learning, ICML 2003, pp. 496–503. AAAI Press (2003). ISBN: 1577351894

21. Manhaeve, R., Dumancic, S., Kimmig, A., Demeester, T., De Raedt, L.: Deep-ProbLog: neural probabilistic logic programming. In: Advances in Neural Information Processing Systems, pp. 3749–3759 (2018)

22. Marra, G., Diligenti, M., Giannini, F., Gori, M., Maggini, M.: Relational neural machines. arXiv preprint arXiv:2002.02193 (2020)

23. Minervini, P., Riedel, S.: Adversarially regularising neural NLI models to integrate logical background knowledge. arXiv preprint arXiv:1808.08609 (2018)

24. Reimann, J.N., Schwung, A.: Neural logic rule layers. arXiv preprint arXiv:1907.00878 (2019)

25. Richardson, M., Domingos, P.: Markov logic networks. Mach. Learn. **62**(1–2), 107–136 (2006). ISSN: 0885-6125. https://doi.org/10.1007/s10994-006-5833-1

26. Rocktäschel, T., Riedel, S.: Learning knowledge base inference with neural theorem provers. In: Proceedings of the 5th Workshop on Automated Knowledge Base Construction, pp. 45–50 (2016)

27. Rocktäschel, T., Riedel, S.: End-to-end differentiable proving. In: Advances in Neural Information Processing Systems, pp. 3788–3800 (2017)

28. Sen, P., Namata, G.M., Bilgic, M., Getoor, L., Gallagher, B., Eliassi-Rad, T.: Collective classification in network data. AI Mag. **29**(3), 93–106 (2008)

29. Serafini, L., d'Avila Garcez, A.: Logic tensor networks: deep learning and logical reasoning from data and knowledge. CoRR, abs/1606.04422 (2016)

30. Xu, J., Zhang, Z., Friedman, T., Liang, Y., Van den Broeck, G.: A semantic loss function for deep learning with symbolic knowledge. In: Dy, J., Krause, A. (eds.) Proceedings of the 35th International Conference on Machine Learning, Volume 80 of Proceedings of Machine Learning Research, Stockholmsmässan, Stockholm, Sweden, 10–15 July 2018, pp. 5502–5511. PMLR (2018). http://proceedings.mlr.press/v80/xu18h.html

Logic Tensor Networks for Top-N Recommendation

Tommaso Carraro[1,2]([⊠]) [iD], Alessandro Daniele[2] [iD], Fabio Aiolli[1] [iD], and Luciano Serafini[2] [iD]

[1] Department of Mathematics, University of Padova, Padova, Italy
tommaso.carraro@studenti.unipd.it
[2] Data and Knowledge Management Research Unit,
Fondazione Bruno Kessler (FBK), Trento, Italy

Abstract. Despite being studied for more than twenty years, state-of-the-art recommendation systems still suffer from important drawbacks which limit their usage in real-world scenarios. Among the well-known issues of recommender systems, there are data sparsity and the cold-start problem. These limitations can be addressed by providing some background knowledge to the model to compensate for the scarcity of data. Following this intuition, we propose to use Logic Tensor Networks (LTN) to tackle the top-n item recommendation problem. In particular, we show how LTN can be used to easily and effectively inject commonsense recommendation knowledge inside a recommender system. We evaluate our method on MindReader, a knowledge graph-based movie recommendation dataset containing plentiful side information. In particular, we perform an experiment to show how the benefits of the knowledge increase with the sparsity of the dataset. Eventually, a comparison with a standard Matrix Factorization approach reveals that our model is able to reach and, in many cases, outperform state-of-the-art performance.

Keywords: Recommender systems · top-n recommendation · Logic tensor networks · Neural-symbolic integration

1 Introduction

Recommender system (RS) technologies are nowadays an essential component for e-services (e.g., Amazon, Netflix, Spotify). Generally speaking, an RS aims at providing suggestions for items (e.g., movies, songs, news) that are most likely of interest to a particular user [25]. Since the first appearance of RSs in early 2000, Collaborative Filtering (CF) [1,16,28] has affirmed of being the standard recommendation approach. In particular, Latent Factor models, and especially Matrix Factorization (MF), have dominated the CF scene [14,20,22] for years, and this has been further emphasized with the deep learning rise [7,13,19,26,27]. Despite their success, state-of-the-art models still suffer from important drawbacks, which limit their applicability in real-world scenarios. Among the most

A. Dovier et al. (Eds.): AIxIA 2022, LNAI 13796, pp. 110–123, 2023.
https://doi.org/10.1007/978-3-031-27181-6_8

crucial problems, there are data sparsity and the cold-start problem [21,25]. Data sparsity leads to datasets where the density of ratings is usually less than 1%, while cold-start makes the recommendation challenging for new users and items. One way to address these limitations is to provide additional information to the models to compensate for the scarcity of data. Following this intuition, methods based on Tensor Factorization [4] and Factorization Machines [24,30] have been proposed recently. These models allow to effectively extend the user-item matrix by adding new dimensions containing content (e.g., movie genres, demographic information) and/or contextual side information (e.g., location, time). Though these techniques have been shown to improve the recommendation performance, they are usually specifically designed for one type of side information (e.g., the user or item content) and lack explainability [6,31]. Novel recommendation datasets (e.g., [5]) provide manifold side information (e.g., ratings on movie genres, actors, directors), and hence models which can exploit all the available information are required.

Neural-Symbolic Integration (NeSy) [3] and Statistical Relational Learning (SRL) [23] represent good candidates to incorporate knowledge with learning. These two branches of Artificial Intelligence study approaches for the integration of some form of prior knowledge, usually expressed through First-Order Logic (FOL), with statistical models. The integration has been shown beneficial to address data scarcity [11].

In this paper, we propose to use a Logic Tensor Network (LTN) [2] to inject commonsense knowledge into a standard Matrix Factorization model for the top-n item recommendation task. LTN is a NeSy framework that allows using logical formulas to instruct the learning of a neural model. We propose to use the MindReader dataset [5] to test our model. This dataset includes a variety of information, such as users' tastes across movie genres, actors, and directors. In this work, we show how LTN can naturally and effectively exploit all this various information to improve the generalization capabilities of the MF model. In addition, an experiment that drastically reduces the density of the training ratings reveals that our model can effectively mitigate the sparsity of data, outperforming the standard MF model, especially in the most challenging scenarios.

2   Related Works

The integration of logical reasoning and learning in RSs is still in its early stages. Among the NeSy approaches for RSs, the most prominent is Neural Collaborative Reasoning (NCR) [10]. In this work, the recommendation problem is formalized into a logical reasoning problem. In particular, the user's ratings are represented using logical variables, then, logical operators are used to construct formulas that express facts about them. Afterward, NCR maps the variables to *logical* embeddings and the operators to neural networks which act on those embeddings. By doing so, each logical expression can be equivalently organized as a neural network, so that logical reasoning and prediction can be conducted in a continuous space. In [9], the idea of NCR is applied to knowledge graphs for RSs, while [29] uses a NeSy approach to tackle the explainability of RSs.

The seminal approach that successfully applied SRL to RSs has been HyPER [17], which is based on Probabilistic Soft Logic (PSL) [15]. In particular, HyPER exploits the expressiveness of FOL to encode knowledge from a wide range of information sources, such as multiple user and item similarity measures, content, and social information. Then, Hinge-Loss Markov Random Fields are used to learn how to balance the different information types. HyPER is highly related to our work since the logical formulas that we use resemble the ones used in HyPER. After HyPER, other SRL approaches have been proposed for RSs [8,12].

3   Background

This section provides useful notation and terminology used in the remainder of the paper.

3.1   Notation

Bold notation is used to differentiate between vectors, e.g., $\mathbf{x} = [3.2, 2.1]$, and scalars, e.g., $x = 5$. Matrices and tensors are denoted with upper case bold notation, e.g., $\mathbf{X}$. Then, $\mathbf{X}_i$ is used to denote the i-th row of $\mathbf{X}$, while $\mathbf{X}_{i,j}$ to denote the position at row i and column j. We refer to the set of users of a RS with $\mathcal{U}$, where $|\mathcal{U}| = n$. Similarly, the set of items is referred to as $\mathcal{I}$ such that $|\mathcal{I}| = m$. We use $\mathcal{D}$ to denote a dataset. $\mathcal{D}$ is defined as a set of N triples $\mathcal{D} = \{(u, i, r)^{(j)}\}_{j=1}^{N}$, where $u \in \mathcal{U}$, $i \in \mathcal{I}$, and $r \in \mathbb{N}$ is a rating. We assume that a user u cannot give more than one rating to an item i, namely $\not\exists r_1, r_2 \in \mathbb{N}, r_1 \neq r_2 : \{(u, i, r_1)\} \cup \{(u, i, r_2)\} \subseteq \mathcal{D}$. $\mathcal{D}$ can be reorganized in the so-called user-item matrix $\mathbf{R} \in \mathbb{N}^{n \times m}$, where users are on the rows and items on the columns, such that $\mathbf{R}_{u,i} = r$ if $(u, i, r) \in \mathcal{D}$, 0 otherwise.

3.2   Matrix Factorization

Matrix Factorization (MF) is a Latent Factor Model that aims at factorizing the user-item matrix $\mathbf{R}$ into the product of two lower-dimensional rectangular matrices, denoted as $\mathbf{U}$ and $\mathbf{I}$. $\mathbf{U} \in \mathbb{R}^{n \times k}$ and $\mathbf{I} \in \mathbb{R}^{m \times k}$ are matrices containing the users' and items' latent factors, respectively, where k is the number of latent factors. The objective of MF is to find $\mathbf{U}$ and $\mathbf{I}$ such that $\mathbf{R} \approx \mathbf{U} \cdot \mathbf{I}^\top$. An effective way to learn the latent factors is by using gradient-descent optimization. Given the dataset $\mathcal{D}$, a MF model seeks to minimize the following loss function:

$$L(\boldsymbol{\theta}) = \frac{1}{N} \sum_{(u,i,r) \in \mathcal{D}} ||\tilde{r} - r||^2 + \lambda ||\boldsymbol{\theta}||^2 \tag{1}$$

where $\tilde{r} = \mathbf{U}_u \cdot \mathbf{I}_i^\top$ and $\boldsymbol{\theta} = \{\mathbf{U}, \mathbf{I}\}$. The first term of Eq. (1) is the Mean Squared Error (MSE) between the predicted and target ratings, while the second one is an $L2$ regularization term. λ is an hyper-parameter to set strength of the regularization.

3.3   Logic Tensor Networks

Logic Tensor Networks [2] (LTN) is a Neural-Symbolic framework that enables effective integration of deep learning and logical reasoning. It allows to define a knowledge base composed of a set of logical axioms and to use them as the objective of a neural model. To define the knowledge base, LTN uses a specific first-order language, called Real Logic, which forms the basis of the framework. It is fully differentiable and has a concrete semantics that allows mapping every symbolic expression into the domain of real numbers. Thanks to Real Logic, LTN can convert logical formulas into computational graphs that enable gradient-based optimization based on fuzzy logic semantics.

Real Logic is defined on a first-order language $\mathcal{L}$ with a signature that contains a set $\mathcal{C}$ of constant symbols, a set $\mathcal{X}$ of variable symbols, a set $\mathcal{F}$ of functional symbols, and a set $\mathcal{P}$ of predicate symbols. A term is constructed recursively from constants, variables, and functional symbols. An expression formed by applying a predicate symbol to some term(s) is called an atomic formula. Complex formulas are constructed recursively using connectives (i.e., $\neg, \wedge, \vee, \implies, \leftrightarrow$) and quantifiers (i.e., $\forall, \exists$).

To emphasize the fact that symbols are mapped onto real-valued features, we use the term *grounding*[1], denoted by $\mathcal{G}$. In particular, each individual (e.g., a user) is grounded as a tensor of real features (e.g., user's demographic information), functions as real functions, and predicates as real functions that specifically project onto a value in the interval $[0,1]$. A variable x is grounded to a *sequence* of n_x individuals from a domain, with $n_x \in \mathbb{N}^+, n_x > 0$. As a consequence, a term $t(x)$ or a formula $P(x)$, constructed recursively with a free variable x, will be grounded to a sequence of n_x values too. Afterward, connectives are grounded using fuzzy semantics, while quantifiers using special aggregation functions. In this paper, we use the *product configuration*, which is better suited for gradient-based optimization [18]. Specifically, conjunctions are grounded using the product t-norm T_{prod}, negations using the standard fuzzy negation N_S, implications using the Reichenbach implication I_R, and the universal quantifier using the generalized mean w.r.t. the error values ME_p. The other connectives and quantifiers are not used in this paper, hence not reported.

$$T_{prod}(u,v) = u * v, \ u,v \in [0,1]$$
$$I_R(u,v) = 1 - u + u * v, \ u,v \in [0,1]$$
$$N_S(u) = 1 - u, \ u \in [0,1]$$
$$ME_p(u_1,\ldots,u_n) = 1 - (\frac{1}{n}\sum_{i=1}^{n}(1-u_i)^p)^{\frac{1}{p}}, p \geq 1, u_1,\ldots,u_n \in [0,1]$$

Connective operators are applied element-wise to the tensors in input, while aggregators aggregate the dimension of the tensor in input that corresponds to

---

[1] Notice that this is different from the common use of the term *grounding* in logic, which indicates the operation of replacing the variables of a term or formula with constants or terms containing no variables.

the quantified variable. Real Logic provides also a special type of quantification, called diagonal quantification, denoted as $\text{Diag}(x_1, \ldots, x_n)$. It applies only to variables that have the same number of individuals (i.e., $n_{x_1} = n_{x_2} = \cdots = n_{x_n}$) and allows to quantify over specific tuples of individuals, such that the i-th tuple contains the i-th individual of each of the variables in the argument of Diag. An intuition about how these operations work in practice is given in Sect. 3.4.

Given a Real Logic knowledge base $\mathcal{K} = \{\phi_1, \ldots, \phi_n\}$, where $\phi_1, \ldots, \phi_n$ are closed formulas, LTN allows to learn the grounding of constants, functions, and predicates appearing in them. In particular, if constants are grounded as embeddings, and functions/predicates onto neural networks, their grounding $\mathcal{G}$ depends on some learnable parameters $\boldsymbol{\theta}$. We denote a parametric grounding as $\mathcal{G}(\cdot|\boldsymbol{\theta})$. In LTN, the learning of parametric groundings is obtained by finding parameters $\boldsymbol{\theta}^*$ that maximize the satisfaction of $\mathcal{K}$:

$$\boldsymbol{\theta}^* = \operatorname{argmax}_{\boldsymbol{\theta}} \text{SatAgg}_{\phi \in \mathcal{K}} \mathcal{G}(\phi|\boldsymbol{\theta}) \tag{2}$$

where, $\text{SatAgg} : [0,1]^* \mapsto [0,1]$ is a formula aggregating operator, often defined using ME_p.

Because Real Logic grounds expressions in real and continuous domains, LTN attaches gradients to every sub-expression and consequently learns through gradient-descent optimization.

3.4   Intuition of Real Logic Grounding

In Real Logic, differently from first-order logic, a variable x is grounded as a *sequence* of n_x individuals (i.e., tensors) from a domain, with $n_x \in \mathbb{N}^+, n_x > 0$. As a direct consequence, a term $t(x)$ or a formula $P(x)$, with a free variable x, is grounded to a sequence of n_x values too. For example, $P(x)$ returns a vector in $[0,1]^{n_x}$, namely $\langle P(x_i)\rangle_{i=1}^{n_x}$, where x_i is the i-th individual of x. Similarly, $t(y)$ returns a matrix in $\mathbb{R}^{n_y \times z}$, assuming that t maps to individuals in $\mathbb{R}^z$. This formalization is intuitively extended to terms and formulas with arity greater than one. In such cases, Real Logic organizes the output tensor in such a way that it has a dimension for each free variable involved in the expression. For instance, $t_2(x, y)$ returns a tensor in $\mathbb{R}^{n_x \times n_y \times z}$, assuming that t_2 maps to individuals in $\mathbb{R}^z$. In particular, at position (i, j) there is the evaluation of $t_2(x_i, y_j)$, where x_i denotes the i-th individual of x and y_j the j-th individual of y. Similarly, $P_2(x, y)$ returns a tensor in $[0,1]^{n_x \times n_y}$, where at position (i, j) there is the evaluation of $P(x_i, y_j)$.

The connective operators are applied element-wise to the tensors in input. For instance, $\neg P_2(x, y)$ returns a tensor in $[0,1]^{n_x \times n_y}$, where at position (i, j) there is the evaluation of $\neg P_2(x_i, y_j)$, namely N_S (i.e., $\neg$) is applied to each truth value in the tensor $P_2(x, y) \in [0,1]^{n_x \times n_y}$. For binary connectives, the behavior is similar. For instance, let Q be a predicate symbol and u a variable. Then, $P_2(x, y) \wedge Q(x, u)$ returns a tensor in $[0,1]^{n_x \times n_y \times n_u}$, where at position (i, j, k) there is the evaluation of the formula on the i-th individual of x, j-th individual of y, and k-th individual of u.

The quantifiers aggregate the dimension that corresponds to the quantified variable. For instance, $\forall x P_2(x, y)$ returns a tensor in $[0, 1]^{n_y}$, namely the aggregation is performed across the dimension of x. Since y is the only free variable remaining in the expression, the output has one single dimension, corresponding to the dimension of y. Specifically, the framework computes $P_2(x, y) \in [0, 1]^{n_x \times n_y}$ first, then it aggregates the dimension corresponding to x. Similarly, $\forall (x, y) P_2(x, y)$ returns a scalar in $[0, 1]$, namely the aggregation is performed across the dimensions of both variables x and y.

In the case of diagonal quantification, the framework behaves differently. For instance, $\forall \mathrm{Diag}(w, v) P_2(w, v)$, where w and v are two variables with the same number of individuals $n_w = n_v$, returns a scalar in $[0, 1]$, which is the result of the aggregation of n_w truth values, namely $P_2(w_1, v_1), P_2(w_2, v_2), \ldots, P_2(w_{n_w}, v_{n_v})$. Without diagonal quantification (i.e., $\forall (w, v) P_2(w, v)$), the framework performs an aggregation across the dimensions of both variables, involving n_w^2 values, namely $P_2(w_1, v_1), P_2(w_1, v_2), \ldots, P_2(w_{n_w}, v_{n_v-1}), P_2(w_{n_w}, v_{n_v})$. Intuitively, $\forall (w, v)$ aggregates all the values in $[0, 1]^{n_w \times n_v}$, while $\forall \mathrm{Diag}(w, v)$ aggregates only the values in the diagonal.

4 Method

Our approach uses a Logic Tensor Network to train a basic Matrix Factorization (MF) model for the top-n item recommendation task. The LTN is trained using a Real Logic knowledge base containing commonsense knowledge facts about the movie recommendation domain. This section formalizes the knowledge base used by our model, how the symbols appearing in it are grounded in the real field, and how the learning of the LTN takes place.

4.1 Knowledge Base

The Real Logic knowledge base that our model seeks to maximally satisfy is composed of the following axioms.

$$\phi_1 : \forall \mathrm{Diag}(user, movie, rating)(\mathrm{Sim}(\mathrm{Likes}(user, movie), rating)) \tag{3}$$

$$\phi_2 : \forall (user, movie, genre)(\neg \mathrm{LikesGenre}(user, genre) \wedge \mathrm{HasGenre}(movie, genre) \\ \implies \mathrm{Sim}(\mathrm{Likes}(user, movie), rating_-)) \tag{4}$$

where $user$, $movie$, $rating$, and $genre$ are variable symbols to denote the users of the system, the items of the system, the ratings given by the users to the items, and the genres of the movies, respectively. $rating_-$ is a constant symbol denoting the negative rating. $\mathrm{Likes}(u, m)$ is a functional symbol returning the prediction for the rating given by user u to movie m. $\mathrm{Sim}(r_1, r_2)$ is a predicate symbol measuring the similarity between two ratings, r_1 and r_2. $\mathrm{LikesGenre}(u, g)$ is a predicate symbol denoting whether the user u likes the genre g. HasGenre(m, g) is a predicate symbol denoting whether the movie m belongs to the genre g.

Notice the use of the diagonal quantification on Axiom (3). When $user$, $movie$, and $rating$ are grounded with three sequences of values, the i-th value of each variable matches with the values of the other variables. This is useful in this case since the dataset $\mathcal{D}$ comes as a set of triples. Diagonal quantification allows forcing the satisfaction of Axiom (3) for these triples only, rather than any combination of users, items, and ratings in $\mathcal{D}$.

4.2   Grounding of the Knowledge Base

The grounding allows to define how the symbols of the language are mapped onto the real field, and hence how they can be used to construct the architecture of the LTN. In particular, given $\mathcal{D} = \{(u, m, r)\}_{j=1}^{N}$, $\mathcal{G}(user) = \langle u^{(j)} \rangle_{j=1}^{N}$, namely $user$ is grounded as a sequence of the N user indexes in $\mathcal{D}$. $\mathcal{G}(movie) = \langle m^{(j)} \rangle_{j=1}^{N}$, namely $movie$ is grounded as a sequence of the N movie indexes in $\mathcal{D}$. $\mathcal{G}(rating) = \langle r^{(j)} \rangle_{j=1}^{N}$ with $r^{(j)} \in \{0, 1\}$ $\forall j$, namely $rating$ is grounded as a sequence of the N ratings in $\mathcal{D}$, where 0 denotes a negative rating and 1 a positive one. $\mathcal{G}(rating_-) = 0$, namely $rating_-$ is grounded as the negative rating. $\mathcal{G}(genre) = \langle 1, \ldots, N_g \rangle$, namely $genre$ is grounded as a sequence of N_g genre indexes, where N_g is the number of genres appearing in the movies of $\mathcal{D}$. $\mathcal{G}(\text{Likes}|\mathbf{U}, \mathbf{I}) : u, m \mapsto \mathbf{U}_u \cdot \mathbf{I}_m^{\top}$, namely Likes is grounded onto a function that takes as input a user index u and a movie index m and returns the prediction of the MF model for user at index u and movie at index m, where $\mathbf{U} \in \mathbb{R}^{n \times k}$ and $\mathbf{I}^{m \times k}$ are the matrices of the users' and items' latent factors, respectively. $\mathcal{G}(\text{LikesGenre}) : u, g \mapsto \{0, 1\}$, namely LikesGenre is grounded onto a function that takes as input a user index u and a genre index g and returns 1 if the user u likes the genre g in the dataset, 0 otherwise. Similarly, $\mathcal{G}(HasGenre) : m, g \mapsto \{0, 1\}$, namely HasGenre is grounded onto a function that takes as input a movie index m and a genre index g and returns 1 if the movie m belongs to genre g in the dataset, 0 otherwise. Finally, $\mathcal{G}(\text{Sim}) : \tilde{r}, r \mapsto \exp(-\alpha||\tilde{r} - r||^2)$, namely Sim is grounded onto a function that computes the similarity between a predicted rating $\tilde{r}$ and a target rating r. The use of the exponential allows to treat Sim as a predicate since the output is restricted in the interval $[0, 1]$. The squared is used to give more penalty to larger errors in the optimization. α is an hyper-parameter to change the smoothness of the function.

Intuitively, Axiom (3) states that for each user-movie-rating triple in the dataset $\mathcal{D} = \{(u, m, r)^{(j)}\}_{j=1}^{N}$, the prediction computed by the MF model for the user u and movie m should be similar to the target rating r provided by the user u for the movie m. Instead, Axiom (4) states that for each possible combination of users, movies, and genres, taken from the dataset, if the user u does not like a genre of the movie m, then the prediction computed by the MF model for the user u and movie m should be similar to the negative rating $rating_-$, namely the user should not like the movie m. By forcing the satisfaction of Axiom (3), the model learns to factorize the user-item matrix using the ground truth, while Axiom (4) acts as a kind of regularization for the latent factors of the MF model.

4.3   Learning of the LTN

The objective of our LTN is to learn the latent factors in $\mathbf{U}$ and $\mathbf{I}$ such that the axioms in the knowledge base $\mathcal{K} = \{\phi_1, \phi_2\}$ are maximally satisfied, namely $\text{argmax}_{\theta}\,\text{SatAgg}_{\phi \in \mathcal{K}}\mathcal{G}_{(user,movie,rating) \leftarrow \mathcal{D}}(\phi|\boldsymbol{\theta})$, where $\boldsymbol{\theta} = \{\mathbf{U}, \mathbf{I}\}$. The notation $(user, movie, rating) \leftarrow \mathcal{D}$ means that variables $user$, $movie$, and $rating$ are grounded with the triples taken from the dataset $\mathcal{D}$, namely $user$ takes the sequence of user indexes, $movie$ the sequence of movie indexes, and $rating$ the sequence of ratings. In practice, this objective corresponds to the following loss function:

$$L(\boldsymbol{\theta}) = (1 - \text{SatAgg}_{\phi \in \mathcal{K}}\mathcal{G}_{(user,movie,rating) \leftarrow \mathcal{B}}(\phi|\boldsymbol{\theta})) + \lambda||\boldsymbol{\theta}||^2 \qquad (5)$$

where $\mathcal{B}$ denotes a batch of training triples randomly sampled from $\mathcal{D}$. An $L2$ regularization term has been added to the loss to prevent overfitting. Hyperparameter λ is used to define the strength of the regularization. Notice that the loss does not specify how the variable $genre$ is grounded. Its grounding depends on the sampled batch $\mathcal{B}$. In our experiments, we grounded it with the sequence of genres of the movies in the batch.

It is worth highlighting that the loss function depends on the semantics used to approximate the logical connectives, quantifiers, and formula aggregating operator. In our experiments, we used the *stable product configuration*, a stable version of the product configuration introduced in [2]. Then, we selected ME_p as formula aggregating operator, with $p = 2$.

5   Experiments

This section presents the experiments we have performed with our method. They have been executed on an Apple MacBook Pro (2019) with a 2,6 GHz 6-Core Intel Core i7. The model has been implemented in Python using PyTorch. In particular, we used the LTNtorch[2] library. Our source code is freely available[3].

5.1   Dataset

In our experiments, we used the MindReader [5] dataset. It contains 102,160 explicit ratings collected from 1,174 real users on 10,030 entities (e.g., movies, actors, movie genres) taken from a knowledge graph in the movie domain. The explicit ratings in the dataset can be of three types: *like* (1), *dislike* (-1), or *unknown* (0). The dataset is subdivided in 10 splits. In our experiments, we used split 0. Each split has a training set, a validation set, and a test set. The

---

[2] https://github.com/logictensornetworks/LTNtorch.
[3] https://github.com/tommasocarraro/LTNrec.

training set contains both ratings given on movies and on the other entities, while validation and test sets contain only ratings given on movies. The validation and test sets are built in such a way to perform a *leave-one-out* evaluation. In particular, for each user of the training set, one random positive movie rating is held out for the validation set, and one for the test set. The validation/test example of the user is completed by adding 100 randomly sampled negative movie ratings from the dataset. To improve the quality of the dataset, we removed the unknown ratings. Moreover, we removed the top 2% of popular movies from the test set to reduce the popularity bias and hence see how the model performs on non-trivial recommendations, as suggested in [5]. Afterward, we considered only the training ratings given on movies and movie genres since our model uses only this information. After these steps, we converted the negative ratings from -1 to 0. Our final dataset contains 962 users, 3,034 movies, 164 genres, 16,351 ratings on movies, and 10,889 ratings on movie genres. The density of the user-movie ratings is 0.37%.

5.2   Experimental Setting

In our experiments, we compared the performance of three models: (1) a standard MF model trained on the movie ratings of MindReader using Eq. (1), denoted as MF, (2) a LTN model trained on the movie ratings of MindReader using Eq. (5) with $\mathcal{K} = \{\phi_1\}$, denoted as LTN, and (3) a LTN model trained on the movie and genre ratings of MindReader using Eq. (5) with $\mathcal{K} = \{\phi_1, \phi_2\}$, denoted as LTN$_{genres}$. To compare the performance of the models, we used two widely used ranking-based metrics, namely `hit@k` and `ndcg@k`, explained in Sect. 5.3. In our experiments, we used the following procedure: (1) we generated additional training sets by randomly sampling the 80%, 60%, 40%, and 20% of the movie ratings of each user from the entire training set, referred to as 100%. Then, (2) for each training set $Tr \in \{100\%, 80\%, 60\%, 40\%, 20\%\}$ and for each model $m \in \{MF, LTN, LTN_{genres}\}$: (2a) we performed a grid search of model m on training set Tr to find the best hyper-parameters on the validation set using `hit@10` as validation metric; then, (2b) we tested the performance of the best model on the test set in terms of `hit@10` and `ndcg@10`. We repeated this procedure 30 times using seeds from 0 to 29. The test metrics have been averaged across these runs and reported in Table 1. Due to computational time, the grid search has been computed only for the first run. Starting from the second run, step (2a) is replaced with the training of model m on the training set Tr with the best hyper-parameters found during the first run. A description of the hyper-parameters tested in the grid searches as well as the training details of the models is explained in Sect. 5.4.

5.3   Evaluation Metrics

The selected ranking-based metrics are defined as follows:

- `hit@k`: Hit Ratio measures whether a testing item is placed in the top-k positions of the ranking, considering the presence of an item as a hit;

– `ndcg@k`: Normalized Discounted Cumulative Gain measures the quality of the recommendation based on the position of the target item in the ranking. In particular, it uses a monotonically increasing discount to emphasize the importance of higher ranks versus lower ones.

Formally, let us define $\omega(r)$ as the item at rank r, $\mathbb{I}[\cdot]$ as the indicator function, and I_u as the set of held-out items for user u. `hit@k` for user u is defined as

$$\text{hit@}k(u, \omega) := \mathbb{I}\left[\left(\sum_{r=1}^{k} \mathbb{I}\left[\omega(r) \in I_u\right]\right) \geq 1\right].$$

Truncated discounted cumulative gain (`dcg@k`) for user u is defined as

$$\text{dcg@}k(u, \omega) := \sum_{r=1}^{k} \frac{2^{\mathbb{I}[\omega(r) \in I_u]} - 1}{\log(r + 1)}.$$

`ndcg@k` is the `dcg@k` linearly normalized to $[0, 1]$ after dividing by the best possible `dcg@k`, where all the held-out items are ranked at the top. Notice that in this paper $|I_u| = 1$.

Specifically, for each validation/test example, the scores for the positive movie and the 100 randomly sampled negative movies are computed using the Likes(u, m) function (i.e., the dot product between user and movie latent factors). Then, a ranking is created based on these scores. The metrics evaluate the recommendation based on the position of the positive movie in the produced ranking.

5.4 Training Details

The hyper-parameters tested during the grid searches explained in Sect. 5.2 vary depending on the model. For all the models, we tried a number of latent factors $k \in \{1, 5, 10, 25\}$, regularization coefficient $\lambda \in \{0.001, 0.0001\}$, batch size in $\{32, 64\}$, and whether it was better to add users' and items' biases to the model. For LTN and LTN$_{genres}$, we tried $\alpha \in \{0.05, 0.1, 0.2\}$ for the predicate Sim and used $p = 2$ for the aggregator ME$_p$ of Axiom (3). For LTN$_{genres}$, we tried $p \in \{2, 5\}$ for the aggregator ME$_p$ of Axiom (4). Notice that $\lim_{p \to \infty} \text{ME}_p(u_1, \ldots, u_n) = \min\{u_1, \ldots, u_n\}$. Intuitively, p offers flexibility to account for outliers in the data. The higher the p, the more focus the model will have on the outliers.

For all the models, the latent factors **U** and **I**, for users and items, respectively, have been randomly initialized using the *Glorot* initialization, while the biases with values sampled from a normal distribution with 0 mean and unitary variance. All the models have been trained for 200 epochs by using the Adam optimizer with a learning rate of 0.001. For each training, we used early stopping to stop the learning if after 20 epochs no improvements were found on the validation metric (i.e., `hit@10`).

6   Results

A comparison between MF, LTN, and LTN$_{genres}$ is reported in Table 1. The table reports the performance of the three models on a variety of tasks with different sparsity.

Table 1. Test `hit@10` and `ndcg@10` averaged across 30 runs. Standard deviations are between brackets.

% of training ratings	Metric	MF	LTN	LTN$_{genres}$
100%	`hit@10`	$0.4499_{(0.0067)}$	$0.4636_{(0.0040)}$	$\mathbf{0.4642}_{(0.0054)}$
	`ndcg@10`	$0.1884_{(0.0028)}$	$0.1899_{(0.0014)}$	$\mathbf{0.1905}_{(0.0022)}$
80%	`hit@10`	$0.4459_{(0.0057)}$	$0.4585_{(0.0066)}$	$\mathbf{0.4616}_{(0.0069)}$
	`ndcg@10`	$0.1864_{(0.0023)}$	$0.1881_{(0.0023)}$	$\mathbf{0.1894}_{(0.0025)}$
60%	`hit@10`	$0.4274_{(0.0107)}$	$0.4475_{(0.0087)}$	$\mathbf{0.4487}_{(0.0080)}$
	`ndcg@10`	$0.1798_{(0.0039)}$	$0.1853_{(0.0034)}$	$\mathbf{0.1862}_{(0.0031)}$
40%	`hit@10`	$0.3983_{(0.0105)}$	$0.4087_{(0.0117)}$	$\mathbf{0.4322}_{(0.0102)}$
	`ndcg@10`	$0.1692_{(0.0047)}$	$0.1726_{(0.0052)}$	$\mathbf{0.1807}_{(0.0049)}$
20%	`hit@10`	$0.2956_{(0.0196)}$	$\mathbf{0.3764}_{(0.0170)}$	$0.3761_{(0.0160)}$
	`ndcg@10`	$0.1367_{(0.0093)}$	$0.1594_{(0.0069)}$	$\mathbf{0.1598}_{(0.0068)}$

By looking at the table, it is possible to observe that LTN outperforms MF in all the five tasks. In particular, for the dataset with 20% of training ratings, the improvement is drastic, with a 27.33% increase on `hit@10`. We want to emphasize that the two models only differ in the loss function. This demonstrates that the loss based on fuzzy logic semantics of LTN is beneficial to deal with the sparsity of data. Then, with the addition of knowledge regarding the users' tastes across the movie genres, it is possible to further improve the results, as shown in the last column of the table. LTN$_{genres}$ outperforms the other models on almost all the tasks. For the dataset with the 20% of the ratings, the `hit@10` of LTN$_{genres}$ is slightly worse compared to LTN. This could be related to the quality of the training ratings sampled from the original dataset. This is also suggested by the higher standard deviation associated with the datasets with higher sparsity.

6.1   Training Time

A comparison of the training times required by the models on the different datasets is presented in Table 2. The models have been trained for 200 epochs with a learning rate of 0.001, batch size of 64, one latent factor (i.e., $k = 1$), without bias terms, and without early stopping. The other hyper-parameters do not affect training time. In particular, LTN$_{genres}$ increases the time complexity considerably. This is due to Axiom 4, which has to be evaluated for each possible combination of users, items, and genres. This drawback can limit the applicability of LTN$_{genres}$ in datasets with a higher number of users and items since more groundings of the formula have to be evaluated. Generally, when the number of groundings becomes huge, Logic Tensor Networks have scalability issues. However, it is possible to mitigate this problem by designing logical axioms which make use of diagonal quantification. This special quantification allows to considerably reduce the number of evaluated groundings by explicitly specifying them. Eventually, by looking at the results in Sect. 6, it is possible to observe that the improvements of LTN_{genres} w.r.t. LTN are marginal. This proves that LTN can implicitly learn user preferences among movie genres without direct supervision. This finding suggests avoiding using LTN_{genres} in this particular scenario since the underlying MF model is powerful enough while being also more efficient. We believe that LTN_{genres} is best suited for extremely sparse datasets and cold-start scenarios. We leave this investigation for future work.

Table 2. Training time in seconds.

% of training ratings	MF	LTN	LTN_{genres}
100%	26.99	50.87	247.30
80%	22.52	37.79	213.62
60%	18.31	28.97	145.86
40%	15.60	20.09	97.43
20%	8.12	10.68	50.85

7 Conclusions

In this paper, we proposed to use Logic Tensor Networks to tackle the top-n recommendation task. We showed how, by design, LTN permits to easily integrate side information inside a recommendation model. We compared our LTN models with a standard MF model, in a variety of tasks with different sparsity, showing the benefits provided by the background knowledge, especially when the task is challenging due to data scarcity.

References

1. Aiolli, F.: Efficient top-n recommendation for very large scale binary rated datasets. In: Proceedings of the 7th ACM Conference on Recommender Systems, RecSys 2013, pp. 273–280. Association for Computing Machinery, New York (2013). https://doi.org/10.1145/2507157.2507189
2. Badreddine, S., d'Avila Garcez, A., Serafini, L., Spranger, M.: Logic tensor networks. Artif. Intell. **303**, 103649 (2022). https://doi.org/10.1016/j.artint.2021.103649
3. Besold, T.R., et al.: Neural-symbolic learning and reasoning: a survey and interpretation (2017). https://doi.org/10.48550/ARXIV.1711.03902
4. Bhargava, P., Phan, T., Zhou, J., Lee, J.: Who, what, when, and where: multidimensional collaborative recommendations using tensor factorization on sparse user-generated data. In: Proceedings of the 24th International Conference on World Wide Web, WWW 2015, pp. 130–140. International World Wide Web Conferences Steering Committee, Republic and Canton of Geneva, CHE (2015). https://doi.org/10.1145/2736277.2741077

5. Brams, A.H., Jakobsen, A.L., Jendal, T.E., Lissandrini, M., Dolog, P., Hose, K.: MindReader: recommendation over knowledge graph entities with explicit user ratings. In: CIKM 2020, pp. 2975–2982. Association for Computing Machinery, New York (2020). https://doi.org/10.1145/3340531.3412759
6. Carraro, T., Polato, M., Aiolli, F.: A look inside the black-box: towards the interpretability of conditioned variational autoencoder for collaborative filtering. In: Adjunct Publication of the 28th ACM Conference on User Modeling, Adaptation and Personalization, UMAP 2020 Adjunct, pp. 233–236. Association for Computing Machinery, New York (2020). https://doi.org/10.1145/3386392.3399305
7. Carraro, T., Polato, M., Bergamin, L., Aiolli, F.: Conditioned variational autoencoder for top-n item recommendation. In: Pimenidis, E., Angelov, P., Jayne, C., Papaleonidas, A., Aydin, M. (eds.) ICANN 2022. LNCS, vol. 13530, pp. 785–796. Springer, Cham (2022). https://doi.org/10.1007/978-3-031-15931-2_64
8. Catherine, R., Cohen, W.: Personalized recommendations using knowledge graphs: a probabilistic logic programming approach. In: Proceedings of the 10th ACM Conference on Recommender Systems, RecSys 2016, pp. 325–332. Association for Computing Machinery, New York (2016). https://doi.org/10.1145/2959100.2959131
9. Chen, H., Li, Y., Shi, S., Liu, S., Zhu, H., Zhang, Y.: Graph collaborative reasoning. In: Proceedings of the Fifteenth ACM International Conference on Web Search and Data Mining, WSDM 2022, pp. 75–84. Association for Computing Machinery, New York (2022). https://doi.org/10.1145/3488560.3498410
10. Chen, H., Shi, S., Li, Y., Zhang, Y.: Neural collaborative reasoning. In: Proceedings of the Web Conference 2021. ACM, April 2021. https://doi.org/10.1145/3442381.3449973
11. Daniele, A., Serafini, L.: Neural networks enhancement with logical knowledge (2020). https://doi.org/10.48550/ARXIV.2009.06087
12. Gridach, M.: Hybrid deep neural networks for recommender systems. Neurocomputing **413**, 23–30 (2020). https://doi.org/10.1016/j.neucom.2020.06.025. https://www.sciencedirect.com/science/article/pii/S0925231220309966
13. He, X., Liao, L., Zhang, H., Nie, L., Hu, X., Chua, T.S.: Neural collaborative filtering. In: Proceedings of the 26th International Conference on World Wide Web, WWW 2017, pp. 173–182. International World Wide Web Conferences Steering Committee, Republic and Canton of Geneva, CHE (2017). https://doi.org/10.1145/3038912.3052569
14. Hu, Y., Koren, Y., Volinsky, C.: Collaborative filtering for implicit feedback datasets. In: 2008 Eighth IEEE International Conference on Data Mining, pp. 263–272 (2008). https://doi.org/10.1109/ICDM.2008.22
15. Kimmig, A., Bach, S., Broecheler, M., Huang, B., Getoor, L., Mansinghka, V.: A short introduction to probabilistic soft logic, pp. 1–4 (2012). https://lirias.kuleuven.be/retrieve/204697
16. Koren, Y., Bell, R.: Advances in collaborative filtering. In: Ricci, F., Rokach, L., Shapira, B., Kantor, P. (eds.) Recommender Systems Handbook, pp. 145–186. Springer, Boston (2011). https://doi.org/10.1007/978-0-387-85820-3_5
17. Kouki, P., Fakhraei, S., Foulds, J., Eirinaki, M., Getoor, L.: HyPER: a flexible and extensible probabilistic framework for hybrid recommender systems. In: RecSys 2015, pp. 99–106. Association for Computing Machinery, New York (2015). https://doi.org/10.1145/2792838.2800175
18. van Krieken, E., Acar, E., van Harmelen, F.: Analyzing differentiable fuzzy logic operators. Artif. Intell. **302**, 103602 (2022). https://doi.org/10.1016/j.artint.2021.103602

19. Liang, D., Krishnan, R.G., Hoffman, M.D., Jebara, T.: Variational autoencoders for collaborative filtering. In: Proceedings of the 2018 World Wide Web Conference, WWW 2018, pp. 689–698. International World Wide Web Conferences Steering Committee, Republic and Canton of Geneva, CHE (2018). https://doi.org/10.1145/3178876.3186150

20. Ning, X., Karypis, G.: SLIM: sparse linear methods for top-n recommender systems. In: 2011 IEEE 11th International Conference on Data Mining, pp. 497–506 (2011). https://doi.org/10.1109/ICDM.2011.134

21. Polato, M., Aiolli, F.: Exploiting sparsity to build efficient kernel based collaborative filtering for top-n item recommendation. Neurocomputing **268**, 17–26 (2017). Advances in Artificial Neural Networks, Machine Learning and Computational Intelligence. https://doi.org/10.1016/j.neucom.2016.12.090. https://www.sciencedirect.com/science/article/pii/S0925231217307592

22. Polato, M., Aiolli, F.: Boolean kernels for collaborative filtering in top-n item recommendation. Neurocomput. **286**(C), 214–225 (2018). https://doi.org/10.1016/j.neucom.2018.01.057

23. Raedt, L.D., Kersting, K.: Statistical relational learning. In: Sammut, C., Webb, G.I. (eds.) Encyclopedia of Machine Learning, pp. 916–924. Springer, Boston (2010). https://doi.org/10.1007/978-0-387-30164-8_786

24. Rendle, S.: Factorization machines. In: 2010 IEEE International Conference on Data Mining, pp. 995–1000 (2010). https://doi.org/10.1109/ICDM.2010.127

25. Ricci, F., Rokach, L., Shapira, B.: Recommender systems: introduction and challenges. In: Ricci, F., Rokach, L., Shapira, B. (eds.) Recommender Systems Handbook, pp. 1–34. Springer, Boston (2015). https://doi.org/10.1007/978-1-4899-7637-6_1

26. Shenbin, I., Alekseev, A., Tutubalina, E., Malykh, V., Nikolenko, S.I.: RecVAE: a new variational autoencoder for top-n recommendations with implicit feedback. In: Proceedings of the 13th International Conference on Web Search and Data Mining. ACM, January 2020. https://doi.org/10.1145/3336191.3371831

27. Steck, H.: Embarrassingly shallow autoencoders for sparse data. In: The World Wide Web Conference, WWW 2019, pp. 3251–3257. Association for Computing Machinery, New York (2019). https://doi.org/10.1145/3308558.3313710

28. Su, X., Khoshgoftaar, T.M.: A survey of collaborative filtering techniques. Adv. Artif. Intell. (2009). https://doi.org/10.1155/2009/421425

29. Xian, Y., et al.: CAFE: coarse-to-fine neural symbolic reasoning for explainable recommendation. In: Proceedings of the 29th ACM International Conference on Information & Knowledge Management, CIKM 2020, pp. 1645–1654. Association for Computing Machinery, New York (2020). https://doi.org/10.1145/3340531.3412038

30. Xin, X., Chen, B., He, X., Wang, D., Ding, Y., Jose, J.: CFM: convolutional factorization machines for context-aware recommendation. In: Proceedings of the Twenty-Eighth International Joint Conference on Artificial Intelligence, IJCAI-2019, pp. 3926–3932. International Joint Conferences on Artificial Intelligence Organization, July 2019. https://doi.org/10.24963/ijcai.2019/545

31. Zhang, Y., Chen, X.: Explainable recommendation: a survey and new perspectives. Found. Trends® Inf. Retrieval **14**(1), 1–101 (2020). https://doi.org/10.1561/1500000066

Multiagent Systems

A Review of the Muddy Children Problem

Yusuf Izmirlioglu$^{(\boxtimes)}$, Loc Pham, Tran Cao Son, and Enrico Pontelli

New Mexico State University, Las Cruces, NM 88003, USA
{yizmir,locpham}@nmsu.edu, {tson,epontell}@cs.nmsu.edu

Abstract. The "Muddy Children" puzzle is a well known problem in
the multi-agent epistemic reasoning literature, however it has not been
studied in other fields of Artificial Intelligence. In this paper, we present
the "Muddy Children" problem as a challenge to the Artificial Intelligence and Computer Science community. The interesting aspect of this
problem is that agents have asymmetric and incomplete information; and
each agent needs to reason about his own knowledge as well as knowledge
of other agents. The existing solutions use Kripke structure and possible
world semantics which are not scalable for large problem sizes. Hence we
stimulate for alternative solution methodologies and discover its relation
to the other problems in the applied sciences. We go over several variations of the Muddy Children puzzle and discuss the challenges for future
research.

Keywords: Muddy children · Multi-agent systems · Epistemic
reasoning · Analytical puzzles

1 Introduction

In this paper, we present the *"Muddy Children"* problem as a challenge to the
general Artificial Intelligence and Computer Science community. The Muddy
Children is a well-known puzzle in the multi-agent epistemic reasoning literature,
however it has not been studied in other fields of Artificial Intelligence. This
problem has been originally introduced by [2]; it also appears in the literature
under different names, such as *"Three Wise Men"* [12] and *"Coloured Hat"* [14].

The interesting aspect of this problem is that agents have asymmetric and
incomplete information and they cannot directly disclose their knowledge to the
other agents. Rather, an agent can only learn partial knowledge of others through
their actions. Thus agents need to perform sophisticated reasoning of available
information to reach the actual state. In particular, this puzzle requires not only
reasoning of an agent about himself, but also reasoning about other agents. That
is, an agent need to put himself "in the shoes of others" to infer their knowledge
about the world.

There are several existing solutions to this puzzle using possible world semantics and epistemic reasoning. These solutions employ Kripke structures as representation of agents' knowledge, which has exponential number of worlds in the

A. Dovier et al. (Eds.): AIxIA 2022, LNAI 13796, pp. 127–139, 2023.
https://doi.org/10.1007/978-3-031-27181-6_9

number of agents. As such, they are not scalable for larger problem sizes. Furthermore, the existing methods cannot offer complete solutions to the variations of the problem which we present in this paper.

Our objective in introducing the Muddy Children problem is to suggest research challenges and inspire new solution methodologies. We believe that the Muddy Children puzzle may have alternative or more efficient solutions using methodologies in Game Theory, Dynamic Programming, Constraint Programming or other fields.

In the rest of the paper, we first explain the problem, its formal definition, followed by possible variations and then briefly go over the existing solutions.

2   The Muddy Children Problem

For understandability, let us first illustrate a particular instance of the Muddy Children problem with 3 children. We assume that all agents are truthful and they are perfect reasoners. Each child can hear the announcements and observe the actions of other agents. The children have played outside and then returned to home together. Their father looks at the children and tells them that at least one of them has mud on his forehead. Each child can see the forehead of other children but not his own. Consequently a child can observe whether the other children are muddy or not, but cannot identify his own status. The father asks the following question to the children: *"Those of you who know whether he has mud on his own head or not, please raise your hand"*. But no children raises their hands. The father asks the same question the second time, again no children raises their hands. However, when the father asks the same question the third time, all children raise their hands. How is this outcome possible and how did the children understand their status at the third time?

The resolution of the puzzle with 3 children is as follows: After the father's initial announcement, it is common knowledge that the number of muddy children is 1 or more. Similarly, at each round, raising or not raising hand of a child is also a public announcement action which reveals his knowledge to the other agents. After child i executes (not) raising hand action, it is common knowledge that i does (not) know whether he is muddy or not.

At round 1, child 1 does not raise his hand, so it must be the case that at least one of child 2 or child 3 is muddy. Otherwise child 1 would infer that he is muddy since there is at least one muddy child. Child 2 and 3 do not raise their hand hence at least one of child 1 or child 3 must be muddy and at least one of child 1 or child 2 must be muddy. In sum, at the end of round 1, we understand that at least two children are muddy. Still, no children knows whether he is muddy or not since none of them raised their hands at round 2. Now suppose that exactly two children are muddy, say children 1 and 2. If this was the case, the two muddy children would raise their hands at round 2. The reasoning is as follows: At the end of round 1, child 1 would realize that he is muddy. Child 1 can observe that child 2 is muddy and child 3 is not muddy. He will think that *"If I were not muddy, then child 2 would raise his hand at round 1. Therefore I must be muddy"*. The situation is symmetric for the other muddy child 2, so he would also understand that he is muddy at the end of round 1. Therefore the number of muddy children cannot be two and hence all children must be muddy.

Until now, we have made an analysis as an outsider who only reads the narrative but does not know the status of the children beforehand. Let us look at the puzzle from the viewpoint of the individual children. We first examine the case of child 1. At the beginning of round 0, child 1 can observe that child 2 and 3 are muddy hence the announcement action of his father does not change his beliefs. At the beginning of round 1, child 1 does not know whether he is muddy or not, and does not raise his hand. Child 1 also knows that child 2 observes that child 3 is muddy and vice versa, so the other children did not raise their hand in the first round as he expected.

After round 1, child 1 still does not know whether he is muddy or not, so he does not raise his hand in round 2. The other children did not raise their hands either. Then after the actions in round 2, child 1 performs the following reasoning: *"If I were not muddy, then child 2 and 3 would raise their hand in round 2; because in round 1 no one raised their hands. Assuming that I am not muddy, at the beginning of round 2, child 2 would think that if he were not muddy child 3 would have raised his hand in round 1. Hence child 2 would understand that he is muddy and raise his hand at round 2. Since this did not happen, I must be muddy!"*

Therefore at the beginning of round 3, child 1 realizes that he is muddy and he raises his hand at this round. Since all children are muddy and their actions are the same at every round, the analysis is symmetric for children 2 and 3.

3   Properties

In the previous section, we have made an analysis for a specific instance of the problem with 3 children and all of them muddy. What would be the outcome if the number of children or muddy children were different? We now provide some results about the game with different parameters.

Theorem 1. *In the muddy children problem, suppose that there are n children and ℓ of them are muddy, $1 \leq \ell \leq n$. At round 0, the father announces that at least one child is muddy and in the consecutive rounds he asks every child whether he knows whether he is muddy or not. Then, at round ℓ, all muddy children will raise their hands and at round $\ell + 1$ all non-muddy children (if any) will raise their hands.*

Theorem 1 and its proof have been developed by [1,5]. Using a similar induction technique, we can establish the next theorem.

Theorem 2. *In the muddy children problem, suppose that there are n children and ℓ of them are muddy, $1 \leq \ell \leq n$. If the father announces that at least q children are muddy at round 0, then all muddy children will raise their hands at round $\ell - q + 1$ and all non-muddy children (if any) will raise their hands at round $\ell - q + 2$.*

4 Possible Worlds Semantics

This section provides background information about possible world semantics. A *Kripke structure* represents the agents' own beliefs and their beliefs about other agents using possible worlds. Properties of the world are represented by binary-valued atomic propositions called *fluents*. A world is a complete interpretation of the fluents. Beliefs of the agents are encoded by accessibility relations between possible worlds. Let us now provide the formal definition of the Kripke structure and the semantics of belief formulae.

A *multi-agent* domain $\langle \mathcal{AG}, \mathcal{F} \rangle$ includes a finite and non-empty set of agents $\mathcal{AG}$ and a finite set of fluents $\mathcal{F}$ encoding the properties of the world. *Belief formulae* over $\langle \mathcal{AG}, \mathcal{F} \rangle$ are defined by the BNF:

$$\varphi ::= p \mid \neg\varphi \mid (\varphi \wedge \varphi) \mid (\varphi \vee \varphi) \mid \mathbf{B}_i\varphi \mid \mathbf{E}_\alpha\varphi \mid \mathbf{C}_\alpha\varphi$$

where $p \in \mathcal{F}$ is a fluent, $i \in \mathcal{AG}$ and $\emptyset \neq \alpha \subseteq \mathcal{AG}$. $\mathbf{B}_i$ is the belief operator and $\mathbf{B}_i\varphi$ stands for *"agent i believes in formula φ"*. $\mathbf{E}_\alpha\varphi$, $\mathbf{C}_\alpha\varphi$ denote Group Belief formulae and their semantics are defined below; intuitively, $\mathbf{E}_\alpha\varphi$ indicates that all agents in α believe φ, while $\mathbf{C}_\alpha\varphi$ indicates that φ is common belief among α. We refer to a belief formula which does not contain any occurrences of $\mathbf{B}_i$, $\mathbf{E}_\alpha$, $\mathbf{C}_\alpha$ as a *a fluent formula*. Let $\mathcal{L}_{\mathcal{AG}}$ denote the set of belief formulae over $\langle \mathcal{AG}, \mathcal{F} \rangle$. To exemplify, in the muddy children domain, the fluents $\mathcal{F} = \{m_1, ..., m_n\}$ denote whether each child is muddy. The fluent formula $m_1 \vee m_2 \vee ... \vee m_n$ states that at least one child is muddy, the belief formula $\neg\mathbf{B}_2\, m_1 \wedge \neg\mathbf{B}_2\,\neg m_1$ states that agent 2 does not know whether agent 1 is muddy or not.

A Kripke structure M is a tuple $\langle S, \pi, \mathcal{B}_1, \ldots, \mathcal{B}_n \rangle$, where S is a set of worlds (denoted by $M[S]$), $\pi : S \mapsto 2^{\mathcal{F}}$ is a function that associates an interpretation of $\mathcal{F}$ to each element of S (denoted by $M[\pi]$), and for $i \in \mathcal{AG}$, $\mathcal{B}_i \subseteq S \times S$ is a binary relation over S (denoted by $M[i]$). For convenience, we will often draw a Kripke structure M as a directed labeled graph, whose set of labeled nodes represent S and whose set of labeled edges contains $s \xrightarrow{i} t$ iff $(s, t) \in \mathcal{B}_i$. The label of each node has two parts: the name of the world followed by the associated interpretation. For $u \in S$ and a fluent formula φ, $M[\pi](u)$ and $M[\pi](u)(\varphi)$ denote the interpretation associated to u via π and the truth value of φ with respect to $M[\pi](u)$. For a world $u \in M[S]$, (M, u) is a *pointed Kripke structure*, also called *state* hereafter.

Accessibility relations of an agent in the Kripke structure show uncertainity in his beliefs. That is, if the agent considers multiple worlds with different valuations, then his beliefs involve uncertainity.

Satisfaction of belief formulae is defined over *pointed Kripke structures* [7]. Given a belief formula φ, a Kripke structure $M = \langle S, \pi, \mathcal{B}_1, \ldots, \mathcal{B}_n \rangle$ and a possible state $u \in S$:

(i) $(M, u) \vDash p$ if $p \in \mathcal{F}$ and $M[\pi](u) \vDash p$;

(ii) $(M, u) \vDash \neg\varphi$ if $(M, u) \nvDash \varphi$;

(iii) $(M, u) \vDash \varphi_1 \vee \varphi_2$ if $(M, u) \vDash \varphi_1$ or $(M, u) \vDash \varphi_2$;

(iv) $(M, u) \vDash \varphi_1 \wedge \varphi_2$ if $(M, u) \vDash \varphi_1$ and $(M, u) \vDash \varphi_2$;

(v) $(M, u) \vDash \mathbf{B}_i \varphi$ if $(M, t) \vDash \varphi$ for every t such that $(u, t) \in \mathcal{B}_i$;

(vi) $(M, u) \vDash \mathbf{E}_\alpha \varphi$ if $(M, u) \vDash \mathbf{B}_i \varphi$ for every $i \in \alpha$;

(vii) $(M, u) \vDash \mathbf{C}_\alpha \varphi$ if $(M, u) \vDash \mathbf{E}_\alpha^k \varphi$ for every $k \geq 0$, where $\mathbf{E}_\alpha^0 \varphi = \varphi$ and $\mathbf{E}_\alpha^{k+1} = \mathbf{E}_\alpha(\mathbf{E}_\alpha^k \varphi)$.

5   Formal Definition of the Muddy Children Problem

We describe the Muddy Children problem as $\langle \mathcal{AG}, \mathcal{I}, \mathcal{A} \rangle$ where $\mathcal{AG} = \{f, 1, .., n\}$ is the set of agents, I is the set of children who are muddy and $\mathcal{A} = \{announce\_atleast\_one, raise\_hand\langle i \rangle, not\_raise\_hand\langle i \rangle\}$ is the set of possible actions, $i \in \{1, .., n\}$. Here n is the number of children and $l = |I|$ is the number of muddy children. The action $announce\_atleast\_one$ denotes the announcement of the father that at least one child is muddy. $raise\_hand\langle i \rangle$ denotes the raising hand action of child i, and $not\_raise\_hand\langle i \rangle$ action denotes child i not raising his hand. For the particular problem instance in the introduction, $n = 3$ and $I = \{1, 2, 3\}$.

The game proceeds as follows: At round 0, the father executes the action $announce\_atleast\_one$. Then, at round $j \geq 1$, every child i executes exactly one of $raise\_hand\langle i \rangle$ or $not\_raise\_hand\langle i \rangle$ action, $i \in \{1, .., n\}$. The actions of children are simultaneous. We assume that all agents announce truthfully. At each round, all agents observe the actions of other agents and update their beliefs accordingly. The game ends at round k when all children raise their hand.

6   Related Literature and Existing Solutions

The existing solutions to the Muddy Children puzzle employ possible world semantics and epistemic reasoning methods. The state of the world is represented by a Kripke structure with an external view. Namely, the Kripke structure shows the unique actual world and the agents' beliefs by accessibility relations to other possible worlds. The Kripke structure is updated by a state transition function upon an action. If the actions of children are simultaneous, the state transition function treats them as a single action and updates the Kripke structure once. We now provide the details of the solutions in the literature.

6.1   Eliminating Possible Worlds

Let $D = \langle \mathcal{AG}, \mathcal{I}, \mathcal{A}, \mathcal{F} \rangle$ be the Muddy Children domain. We illustrate the solution of [5,10] with $n = 3$ children of which $l = 2$ of them are muddy, and the father announces that at least $q = 1$ child is muddy. But their method also works for other values of n, l, q. For this instance, $\mathcal{AG} = \{f, 1, 2, 3\}$, $\mathcal{I} = \{1, 2\}$, $\mathcal{F} = \{m_1, m_2, m_3\}$, $\mathcal{A} = \{atleast\_one\_muddy, know\_muddy\langle i \rangle, not\_know\_muddy\langle i \rangle\}$ for $i \in \{1, 2, 3\}$. The actions are modelled as epistemic actions, i.e., announcements of belief formulae. For example, the action $know\_muddy\langle i \rangle$ announces the belief formula $\mathbf{B}_i m_i \vee \mathbf{B}_i \neg m_i$.

Formal definition of the transition function is as follows. Suppose that the initial state and the agents' beliefs are represented by a pointed Kripke structure (M, s), where s is the actual world (i.e., the "real" state of affairs). Consider the occurrence of an action a which announces the belief formula γ to all agents, and an agent i observes the action occurrence. At the next state (M', s), the set of worlds, their valuations, and the actual world remains the same but agent i revises his accessibility relations such that $(u, v) \in M'[i]$ if $(u, v) \in M[i]$ and $(M, v) \vDash \gamma$.

The Kripke structure showing the actual world and the beliefs of the agents at the beginning of the problem is depicted in Fig. 1(a). There are $2^3 = 8$ possible worlds encoding different combinations of m_1, m_2, m_3. To make the figure easy to read, each world is represented by its valuation of fluents—e.g., in the world 100, child 1 is muddy (i.e., m_1 is true) but children 2 and 3 are not (i.e., m_2, m_3 are false). In the actual world, only children 1 and 2 are muddy (denoted by a double circle in the figure). The accessibility relations of the agents show the worlds that they consider, and the uncertainty in their belief. In the actual world, child 1 considers both 110 and 010 possible since he cannot distinguish these two worlds based on his knowledge. Child 2 considers the worlds 110 and 100 possible. As another example, in the world 100, child 3 considers 100 and 101 possible. By the nature of the Kripke structure, the accessibility relations form the belief/knowledge of an agent about the beliefs of other agents (higher order beliefs). According to the semantics of entailment explained in Sect. 4, in the actual world 110, child 1 believes that child 2 believes that child 3 is not muddy, child 1 believes that child 2 does not know whether he is muddy or not, and child 1 believes that child 2 knows whether child 1 is muddy or not. In reality, child 1 does not know his own status but he knows that child 2 knows the status of child 1.

(a)   **(b)**

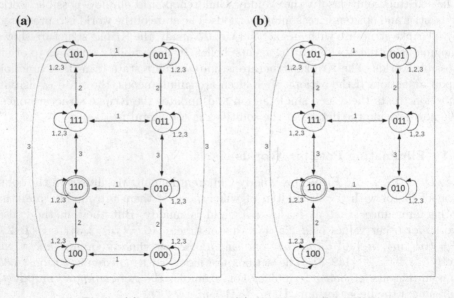

Fig. 1. (a) The initial state (b) At the end of round 0

The method of [5,10] uses elimination of accessibility relations to those worlds which do not satisfy the announced belief formula. After the father's announcement, the children update their beliefs by removing their accessibility relations to the world 000 which does not satisfy the announced belief formula $\gamma_1 = m_1 \vee m_2 \vee m_3$. Namely, since all children hear the announcement, they stop considering this world possible. The updated Kripke structure representing the agents' beliefs at the end of round 0 is in Fig. 1(b).

After round 0, in the actual world, none of the children knows whether they are muddy or not, i.e., $(M, 110)$ entails the belief formulae $\neg \mathbf{B}_1 m_1 \wedge \neg \mathbf{B}_1 \neg m_1$, $\neg \mathbf{B}_2 m_2 \wedge \neg \mathbf{B}_2 \neg m_2$, $\neg \mathbf{B}_3 m_3 \wedge \neg \mathbf{B}_3 \neg m_3$. Thus, at round 1, the children do not raise their hands. The children's actions are simultaneous and all of them can observe each other's actions. We can consider the three simultaneous actions as a *single epistemic action* announcing the belief formula $\gamma_2 = (\neg \mathbf{B}_1 m_1 \wedge \neg \mathbf{B}_1 \neg m_1) \wedge (\neg \mathbf{B}_2 m_2 \wedge \neg \mathbf{B}_2 \neg m_2) \wedge (\neg \mathbf{B}_3 m_3 \wedge \neg \mathbf{B}_3 \neg m_3)$. Upon this action, the agents update their beliefs of Fig. 1(b), by removing their accessibility relations to the worlds which do not satisfy γ_2. Note that the world 100 does not satisfy child 1 not knowing his status, the world 010 does not satisfy child 2 not knowing his status and the world 001 does not satisfy child 3 not knowing his status. Hence agents remove their accessibility relations to the worlds 100, 010, 001. The new Kripke structure at the end of round 1 is depicted in Fig. 2(a). In the actual world of the updated structure, children 1 and 2 now know that they are muddy, while child 3 does not know whether he is muddy or not.

In round 2, children 1 and 2 raise their hands but child 3 does not. Similar to round 1, we can consider this as a single epistemic action which announces the belief formula $\gamma_3 = (\mathbf{B}_1 m_1 \vee \mathbf{B}_1 \neg m_1) \wedge (\mathbf{B}_2 m_2 \vee \mathbf{B}_2 \neg m_2) \wedge (\neg \mathbf{B}_3 m_3 \wedge \neg \mathbf{B}_3 \neg m_3)$. Since all children observe this action, each of them removes the edges to the worlds which do not satisfy γ_3. The worlds 011, 111, 101 in Fig. 2(a) do not satisfy γ_3, because in 011, 111 child 1 does not know whether he is muddy or not, and in 101 child 2 does not know whether he is muddy or not. Consequently the agents remove the edges to the worlds 011, 111, 101. The updated Kripke structure at the end of round 2 is shown in Fig. 2(b). Now child 3 also knows his status: he is not muddy. In fact, all children know the actual state of the world at the end of round 2. Therefore all children raise their hands at round 3 and the game ends.

6.2 Logic Programming

Baral et al. [1] use Answer Set Programming (ASP) to solve the Muddy Children problem. They develop an ASP program, i.e. a set of logical rules, to encode the beliefs, actions and the state transition. The advantage of Answer Set Programming is that the state transition and the entailment of belief formulae can be computed by simple logical rules. In the ASP formulation, the possible worlds and the accessibility relations in the Kripke structure are represented by propositional atoms. The initial beliefs of the agents are given as an input to the ASP program and the initial state and the initial accessibility

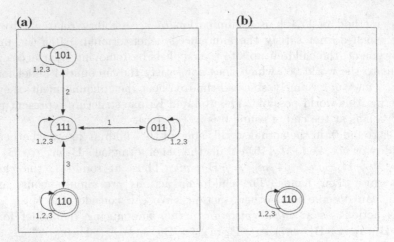

Fig. 2. (a) At the end of round 1 (b) At the end of round 2

relations are nondeterministically generated to satisfy the given beliefs. In their model, the father tells the children that at least one of them is muddy at step 0. This action is encoded as an epistemic action which announces a belief formula. In step 1, and odd-indexed steps, the father executes the *ask* action. In step 2, and in even-indexed steps, the children reply "Yes" or "No" simultaneously. Occurrence of an *ask*, *Reply Yes*, *Reply No* actions are represented by logical atoms $occ(ask,T)$, $occ(announce\_k(A,true),T)$, $occ(announce\_k(A,false),T)$ atoms respectively, where A is the agent and T is the time step.

The *ask* action does not change beliefs of agents hence the same Kripke structure carries over to the next step. However announcement actions alter agents' beliefs and change the Kripke structure. Their state transition works as follows. At every step, the entailment of belief formulae at each world is computed by a set of ASP rules. After the father or children announce a belief formula, the worlds which do not satisfy the announced formula are identified and the accessibility relations of agents to these worlds are removed from the structure. Hence children commonly observe the effect of every action and update their beliefs. The game continues until all children answer *Yes*. The authors give an example with 3 children (child 1, 2 are muddy) and show that the ASP program yields an answer set in which all children respond *Yes* at step 6, as expected. They also prove a general proposition which states that if there are l muddy children, then the father must ask l questions before all children answer *Yes*.

6.3   Other Potential Solutions

Alternative solutions to the Muddy Children may be developed in the future by using Game Theory, Mathematical Programming or other fields. One potential solution may be modeling it as an incomplete information game. Agents' strategies depend on the history of actions and they update their beliefs accordingly. Another solution to the puzzle can be Mathematical Programming. By constraint programming, we can impose constraints on the number of muddy children and possible configurations of the children. Constraint rules can eliminate some configurations based on the actions in the previous rounds. Dynamic programming can be used to memoize the possible configurations that agents consider at every round. Then the children's actions are computed from their beliefs and some configurations can be eliminated at the next state.

7   Variations of the Muddy Children Puzzle

There are several variations of the muddy children puzzle with respect to the father's announcement, the order of the children's announcement, abilities of the children and the mistake factor.

Father's Announcement: In one variation, also discussed in [8], the father can make an announcement of the form: *"Q of you have mud on their foreheads."*, where Q can be substituted by the quantifiers such as *"At least q"*, *"At most q"*, *"Exactly q"*, *"An even number"* etc. We assume that the father can see the foreheads of all children and always tells the truth.

Order of Children: In the original formulation, at every round, the actions of the children are simultaneous. In another situation, the children can take actions in a sequential manner. This situation is equivalent to a single child taking an action at every round. The children can take action in a predetermined fixed order (i.e., a permutation of $(1, ..., n)$) or in a random order. When child i makes his announcement action, the other children update their beliefs and this process goes on with the next child in the sequence. We represent the order of children by $\mathcal{O}$. If the actions of children are sequential, $\mathcal{O}$ is a permutation of $(1, 2, ..., n)$; if their actions are simultaneous, $\mathcal{O} = \emptyset$.

Agent Abilities: We can also imagine an alternative scenario where some children lack a subset of sensing or action abilities. For example, some children cannot see the foreheads of other children and/or cannot observe when other children raise their hands. Moreover some of children may not be able to raise their own hands. Let $\mathcal{W} = (X, Y, Z)$ denotes the abilities of children, where X, Y, Z are the sets which include the indices of children who cannot see the forehead of others, the children who cannot observe the actions of other children, and the children who cannot raise their hands, respectively. Note that a child may lack multiple abilities (i.e., the three sets may not be disjoint). We assume that sensing or action abilities of children are common knowledge among all agents. The children who cannot see the foreheads of other children will consider the actions of other children to update their beliefs and reach the actual state. The children who cannot observe the actions of other children still know the number of rounds of the problem from the father's announcements, and hence may infer the number of muddy children. Consequently, each child needs to take into account the abilities of others while reasoning and updating his beliefs.

Rationazibility and Mistake: Another feasible case is that not all children are perfect reasoners. Some of them are boundedly rational and can sometimes make mistakes in their reasoning. These agents are not able to process all available information and therefore their beliefs might be different from a perfectly reasoning agent. Hence the announcement action of these children might be incorrect. If the identities of the boundedly rational children are common knowledge, this case can be handled simply by disregarding the actions of boundedly rational children. Another case is that the perfectly rational children commonly know there are exactly b (or at least $\underline{b}$, at most $\overline{b}$) number of boundedly rational children but do not know their identities. Then the children need to make more sophisticated reasoning to resolve this case. We denote the information about boundedly rational children by $\mathcal{U}$. In the former case, $\mathcal{U}$ is a set which includes the index of boundedly rational children, in the latter case $\mathcal{U} = [\underline{b}, \overline{b}]$.

Considering all the above variations, we describe the general Muddy Children problem by $D = \langle \mathcal{AG}, \mathcal{I}, \mathcal{A}, \mathcal{O}, \mathcal{W}, \mathcal{U} \rangle$. The set of actions $\mathcal{A}$ includes the father's various announcement actions with different cardinality Q. Namely, $\mathcal{A} = \{ number\_muddy \langle Q \rangle,\ know\_muddy \langle i \rangle,\ not\_know\_muddy \langle i \rangle \}$, where $i \in \{1, .., n\}$ and Q is an identifier like "at least q", "odd", "prime".

The Active Muddy Child Problem: The Active Muddy Child [10] is another version of the Muddy Children problem in which a particular child, with index k, needs to find out whether he is muddy or not by asking questions. There are n children and ℓ of them are non-muddy. The father makes an announcement action at round 0, as before. The active child asks an individual child at each round whether he is muddy or not. The requested child answers the question truthfully and all agents listen to his response. The problem is to find the optimal strategy for the active child to achieve his goal in the smallest number of time steps. Note that a strategy is a conditional plan which specifies the index of the next child to ask depending on a history of children responses.

8 Challenges

Now we describe the current challenges in the Muddy Children problem and its variations, which need to be addressed for future research.

Representation of the State: The initial state H of an epistemic problem is generally given as a set of the literals for the actual world and the agents' beliefs (including their beliefs about other agents). For the muddy children instance in Sect. 2, the initial state is[1] $H = \{m_1,\ m_2,\ m_3,\ \mathbf{C}(\neg \mathbf{B}_1 m_1 \wedge \neg \mathbf{B}_1 \neg m_1),\ \mathbf{C}\mathbf{B}_1 m_2, \mathbf{C}\mathbf{B}_1 m_3, ...,\ \mathbf{C}\mathbf{B}_3 m_1, \mathbf{C}\mathbf{B}_3 m_2,\ \mathbf{C}(\neg \mathbf{B}_3 m_3 \wedge \neg \mathbf{B}_3 \neg m_3)\}$. However, in epistemic reasoning, state transition functions and entailment of belief formulae are defined over pointed Kripke structures. Thus, we need to determine the Kripke structure(s) which corresponds to the initial state of the epistemic problem; unfortunately, in general, the resulting Kripke structure may not be unique [13]. This is indeed the issue in epistemic reasoning and planning

---

[1] When we omit the set of agents in the formulae C_α, we assume $\alpha = \mathcal{AG}$.

methods. The state should be represented as a set of belief formulae B, but it is represented by a Kripke structure (M_t, s_t) where t is the time point and s_t is the actual world. Then the state transition function Φ applies to the current Kripke structure to obtain the next structure i.e. $(M_{t+1}, s_{t+1}) = \Phi((M_t, s_t), a)$. Some authors [9,11] have developed transition functions which operate on the set of beliefs. The belief set is revised in order to incorporate the incoming belief formulae. However [9] allows only propositional common knowledge, and the method of [11] requires prespecification of agents' beliefs at the next time step for each possible belief formula in the current time step, in the action description. Ideally, agents' beliefs at the next time step should arise endogenously as an outcome of the model, instead of being given as an input.

Individual View: The existing solutions look at the problem from an external view. However, in reality, agents observe the world from their own private individual perspective. Each child has his own Kripke structure representing his beliefs and does not know the actual world. An example of an individual Kripke structure of child 2 is shown in Fig. 3(a). The actual world is 100 but child 2 considers two worlds 100 and 110 possible.

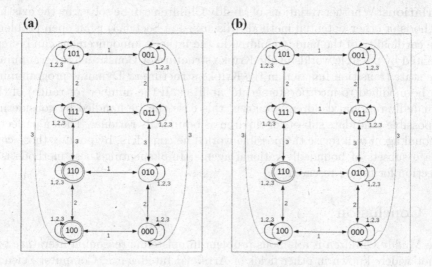

Fig. 3. (a) A private view (b) A contingency

As in external view, removing accessibility relations to the worlds which do not satisfy announced formula also works for the individual view of the Muddy Children problem. However this edge removal method is found to be problematic for other epistemic problems which involve multiple possible worlds [3,4]. The reason is that after removing edges, an agent might end up considering no world possible. As an alternative approach, researchers apply the action sequence to each possible world in the initial structure as a contingency [3,4,6]. The intuition is that the agent considers each of those worlds as if it is the actual world and examines the outcome upon a sequence of actions. Then the state transition function yields branching on contingencies. But this method might produce counter-intuitive results for the Muddy Children problem as in the following example: In the Kripke structure in Fig. 3(b), child 2 considers as if world 110 is the actual world. He updates the structure upon every action using the same edge removal method and obtains its final form in Fig. 4. However this Kripke structure is not realistic for the individual view of child 2: He believes that the actual world is 110 but he believes in another world 100! Thus how to solve the Muddy Children problem using a distributed setting and how to make the state transition for an individual agent is a challenge for future research.

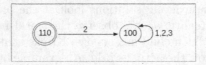

Fig. 4. The outcome if the actual world is 110

Variations: Whether variations of Muddy Children can be solved by the existing methods or other potential methods (discussed in Sect. 6.3) is an open problem. The cardinality of the muddy children in the father's announcement can be represented by possible worlds in the Kripke structure or Constraint Programming. The state transition function in the Kripke structure or Dynamic programming can be modified to incorporate agents' abilities. If the number (or range) of the boundedly rational children is known, this case can be handled by considering all possible candidate subsets of children as boundedly rational. Then a perfectly rational agent will revise the possible worlds he considers, by pooling those candidate subsets of boundedly rational agents. Implementing these methods is a direction for future research.

9   Conclusion

The Muddy Children is a famous problem in epistemic reasoning literature but is not widely known in other fields of Artificial Intelligence, Computer Science, Game Theory. The challenge of this problem is that it is a repeated game and requires sophisticated reasoning about other agents' beliefs at every round. Besides, the agents cannot directly reveal their knowledge to other agents but they need to infer other agents' knowledge from their actions. This paper have introduced the Muddy Children puzzle and variations to the general AI and Computer Science community. We have provided some theorems about the outcome for some variations of the problem. We have illustrated the existing solutions of the puzzle which use epistemic reasoning methods and stressed that they are not scalable and cannot solve all variations. In our opinion, the Muddy Children problem may be related to other problems in AI and Game Theory, and may stimulate further research ideas and solution methodologies in other fields.

References

1. Baral, C., Gelfond, G., Son, T.C., Pontelli, E.: Using answer set programming to model multi-agent scenarios involving agents' knowledge about other's knowledge. In: Proceedings of the 9th International Conference on Autonomous Agents and Multiagent Systems, vol. 1, pp. 259–266 (2010)
2. Barwise, J.: Scenes and other situations. J. Philos. **78**(7), 369–397 (1981)
3. Bolander, T., Andersen, M.: Epistemic planning for single and multi-agent systems. J. Appl. Non-Classical Logics **21**(1) (2011)
4. Bolander, T.: A gentle introduction to epistemic planning: the del approach. arXiv preprint arXiv:1703.02192 (2017)
5. Van Ditmarsch, H., van der Hoek, W., Kooi, B.: Dynamic Epistemic Logic, 1st edn. Springer, Heidelberg (2007)
6. Engesser, T., Bolander, T., Mattmüller, R., Nebel, B.: Cooperative epistemic multi-agent planning for implicit coordination. In: Ghosh, S., Ramanujam, R. (eds.) Proceedings of the Ninth Workshop on Methods for Modalities, M4M@ICLA 2017, Indian Institute of Technology, Kanpur, India, 8th to 10th January 2017. EPTCS, vol. 243, pp. 75–90 (2017)
7. Fagin, R., Halpern, J., Moses, Y., Vardi, M.: Reasoning About Knowledge. MIT Press, Cambridge (1995)
8. Gierasimczuk, N., Szymanik, J.: A note on a generalization of the muddy children puzzle. In: Proceedings of the 13th Conference on Theoretical Aspects of Rationality and Knowledge, pp. 257–264 (2011)
9. Huang, X., Fang, B., Wan, H., Liu, Y.: A general multi-agent epistemic planner based on higher-order belief change. In: Proceedings of the Twenty-Sixth International Joint Conference on Artificial Intelligence (IJCAI 2017) (2017)
10. Kominis, F., Geffner, H.: Beliefs in multiagent planning: from one agent to many. In: Proceedings of the Twenty-Fifth International Conference on Automated Planning and Scheduling, ICAPS 2015, Jerusalem, Israel, 7–11 June 2015, pp. 147–155 (2015)
11. Liu, Q., Liu, Y.: Multi-agent epistemic planning with common knowledge. In: Lang, J. (ed.) Proceedings of the Twenty-Seventh International Joint Conference on Artificial Intelligence, IJCAI 2018, Stockholm, Sweden, 13–19 July 2018, pp. 1912–1920. ijcai.org (2018)
12. McCarthy, J.: Formalization of two puzzles involving knowledge. Formalizing Common Sense: Papers by John McCarthy, pp. 158–166 (1990)
13. Son, T.C., Pontelli, E., Baral, C., Gelfond, G.: Finitary S5-theories. In: Fermé, E., Leite, J. (eds.) JELIA 2014. LNCS (LNAI), vol. 8761, pp. 239–252. Springer, Cham (2014). https://doi.org/10.1007/978-3-319-11558-0_17
14. van Tilburg, G.: Doe wel en zie niet om (do well and don't look back). Katholieke Illustratie (Catholic Illustrated Journal) **90**(32), 47 (1956)

Multi-agent Cooperative Argumentation
in Arg2P

Giuseppe Pisano[1]([✉]) [ID], Roberta Calegari[2] [ID], and Andrea Omicini[2] [ID]

[1] Alma AI – Alma Mater Research Institute for Human-Centered Artificial
Intelligence, Alma Mater Studiorum, Università di Bologna, Bologna, Italy
g.pisano@unibo.it
[2] Dipartimento di Informatica – Scienza e Ingegneria (DISI), Alma Mater Studiorum,
Università di Bologna, Bologna, Italy
{roberta.calegari,andrea.omicini}@unibo.it,
http://giuseppepisano.apice.unibo.it,
http://robertacalegari.apice.unibo.it,
http://andreaomicini.apice.unibo.it

Abstract. This work focuses on cooperative argumentation and conversation in multi-agent systems by introducing an extension of the Arg2P technology that enables parallelisation and distribution of the argumentation process. The computational model and the implementation underpinning the Arg2P technology are presented and discussed.

Keywords: Argumentation · Arg2P · Cooperative argumentation ·
Multi-agent systems · Cooperative reasoning

1 Introduction

Human-centred intelligent systems are densely populated by agents (either software or human) capable of understanding, arguing about, and reporting, via factual assertions and arguments, what is happening and what they could make happen [19]. A multi-agent system (MAS) based on argumentation, dialogue, and conversation can then work as the basis for designing human-centred intelligent systems: through argumentation, dialogue, and adherence to social justice, the behaviour of the intelligent system can be reached, shaped, and controlled [1, 25], and conflict can be resolved by adopting a *cooperative argumentation* approach [10].

There, the purpose of multi-agent argumentative dialogues is to let agents reach an agreement on *(i)* the evaluation of goals and corresponding actions (or plans), and *(ii)* the adoption of a decentralised strategy for reaching a goal, by allowing agents to refine or revise other agents' goals and defend one's proposals. In this scenario, intelligent behaviours are likely to become associated with the capability of arguing about situations as well as the current state and circumstances, by reaching a consensus on what is happening around and what is

A. Dovier et al. (Eds.): AIxIA 2022, LNAI 13796, pp. 140–153, 2023.
https://doi.org/10.1007/978-3-031-27181-6_10

needed, and by triggering and orchestrating proper decentralised semantic conversations so as to determine how to collectively act in order to reach a future desirable state [8]. Thus, argumentation [14] and related technologies become a fundamental building block for the design of these systems, thanks to their potential to be an effective communication medium for heterogeneous intelligent agents while enabling a natural form of interaction between users and computational systems, towards explainability features.

However, for argumentation tools to be able to meet the aforementioned expectations, a huge effort is required from a software engineering perspective. The last decades' continuous improvement in the design and development of technologies for human-centred intelligent systems has not been matched by an analogous improvement of argumentation technologies, where the technological landscape is nowadays populated by very few systems—and most of them are mere prototypes [6]. A key problem in existing argumentation technology is that a widely-acknowledged well-founded computational model for argumentation is currently missing: this makes it difficult to investigate convergence and scalability of argumentation techniques in highly-distributed environments [10,18]. At the same time, the field has seen a constant flow of theoretical contributions [17,20].

Arg2P [9] is a logic-based technology, offering a thorough instantiation of the ASPIC$^+$ framework [21] for structured argumentation. The purpose of this paper is to effectively distribute the argumentation process (evaluation of arguments) so as to enable the exploitation of Arg2P in the context of cooperative argumentation, according to the aforementioned perspective. Accordingly, the work is structured as follows. Section 2 contains a brief introduction to structured argumentation. Section 3 presents the core contribution of this work, i.e., the distribution of the argumentation process and its implementation. Finally, Sect. 4 concludes the work.

2 Background Notion: Structured Argumentation

Let us start by defining a generic structured argumentation framework. This introduction has two purposes: *(i)* to give the reader with no specific knowledge in the formal argumentation field an idea of its main concepts and notions, (ii) to serve as a basis for the analysis contained in subsequent sections. For a more complete introduction we invite the reader to consult the vast amount of available literature on the topic [3,4].

We first introduce the notion of *argumentation language*. In the argumentation language, a literal is either an atomic proposition or its negation.

Notation 1. *For any literal ϕ, its complement is denoted as $\overline{\phi}$. That is, if ϕ is a proposition p, then $\overline{\phi} = \neg p$, while if ϕ is $\neg p$, then $\overline{\phi}$ is p.*

Literals are brought into relation through rules.

Definition 1 (Rules). *A **defeasible rule** r has the form: $\rho : \phi_1, ..., \phi_n \Rightarrow \psi$ with $0 \leq n$, and where*

 – ρ is the unique identifier for r;
 – each $\phi_1, \ldots \phi_n, \psi$ is a literal;
 – the set $\{\phi_1, \ldots \phi_n\}$ is denoted by $Antecedent(r)$ and ψ by $Consequent(r)$.

Defeasible rules – denoted by DefRules – are rules that can be defeated by contrary evidence. Pragmatically, a defeasible rule is used to represent defeasible knowledge, i.e., tentative information that may be used if nothing could be posed against it. For the sake of simplicity, we define non-axiom premises via defeasible rules with empty *Antecedent*. A theory consists of a set of rules.

Definition 2 (Theory). *A **defeasible theory** is a set* Rules $\subseteq$ DefRules.

Arguments are built from defeasible rules. Given a defeasible theory, arguments can be constructed by chaining rules from the theory, as specified in the definition below—*cf.* [21].

Definition 3 (Argument). *An **argument** A constructed from a defeasible theory* $\langle$Rules$\rangle$ *is a finite construct of the form:*

$$A : A_1, \ldots A_n \Rightarrow_r \phi$$

with $0 \leq n$, where

 – *r is the top rule of A, denoted by* TopRule(A);
 – *A is the argument's unique identifier;*
 – *Sub(A) denotes the entire set of subarguments of A, i.e., Sub(A) = Sub(A_1)$\cup$ \ldots $\cup$ Sub(A_n) $\cup$ {A};*
 – *ϕ is the* conclusion *of the argument, denoted by* Conc(A);

Arguments can be in conflict, accordingly to two kinds of attack: rebuts and undercutting, here defined as in [21].

Definition 4 (Attack). *An argument A **attacks** an argument B (i.e., A is an **attacker** of B) at $B' \in$ Sub(B) iff A undercuts or rebuts B (at B'), where:*

 – *A undercuts B (at B') iff Conc(A) = $\overline{TopRule(B')}$*
 – *A rebuts B (at B') iff Conc(A) = $\bar{\phi}$ and Conc(B') = ϕ*

Then, an abstract argumentation framework can be defined by exploiting arguments and attacks.

Definition 5 (Argumentation Framework). *An **argumentation framework** constructed from a defeasible theory T is a tuple $\langle \mathcal{A}, \rightsquigarrow \rangle$, where $\mathcal{A}$ is the set of all arguments constructed from T, and $\rightsquigarrow$ is the attack relation over $\mathcal{A}$. The corresponding **argumentation graph** is a directed graph whose arcs are attacks and nodes are arguments.*

Notation 2. *Given an argumentation framework $G = \langle \mathcal{A}, \rightsquigarrow \rangle$, we write $\mathcal{A}_G$ and $\rightsquigarrow_G$ to denote the framework's arguments and attacks, respectively.*

Given an argumentation framework, we leverage on labelling semantics [2,14] to compute the sets of arguments that are accepted or rejected. Accordingly, each argument is associated with one label which is either IN, OUT, or UND—respectively meaning that the argument is either accepted, rejected, or undecided. Given a labelling for a framework, a IN, OUT, UND labelling for the statements claimed by the arguments in the graph can be also derived.

3   Distributed Argumentation in Arg2P

Arg2P is a logic-based technology, an easily-deployable argumentation tool built to meet the requirements of intelligent software systems.[1] It is built upon 2P-KT—a reboot of the tuProlog [11,13] project offering a general, extensible, and interoperable ecosystem for logic programming and symbolic AI. Whereas a complete overview of the features of this specific implementation is out of the scope of this paper, we refer the reader to [7,9,24] for more details. In this section we focus on how to effectively distribute its argumentation process (evaluation of arguments).

A first version of a message-based distributed argumentation algorithm is here discussed as the basic pillar of a computational model for cooperative argumentation in MAS. We ignore issues such as agent autonomy and MAS coordination artefacts [22,23], and focus instead on the distribution issues of cooperative argumentation, which enables agent dialogue and defeasible reasoning in MAS.

The first issue when facing computational issues of cooperative argumentation is the parallelisation of the argumentation process. Parallelisation needs to be tackled under two distinct perspectives: *(i)* the algorithmic perspective and *(ii)* the data perspective. Under the algorithmic perspective, we divide the argument evaluation (w.r.t. a given semantics) into smaller sub-tasks to be executed in parallel. Under the data perspective, instead, we split the data used by the algorithm—i.e., the argumentation defeasible theory. Action here is therefore at the data level, looking for possible data partitioning on which the argumentation process can be run in parallel. As a premise, we first introduce the algorithm that served as a starting point in the parallelisation of the argumentation process.

Among the available libraries, Arg2P includes a *query-based* mode, which allows for single-query evaluation according to the selected semantics.[2] The feature is accessible in the default instance of the Arg2P framework through the predicate

<code>answerQuery(+Goal, -Yes, -No, -Und)</code>

which requests the evaluation of the given *Goal*, and gets the set of facts matching the goal distributed in the three sets IN, OUT, and UND as a result.

The algorithm used to evaluate a single claim (or query) according to grounded semantics is inspired by the DeLP dialectical trees evaluation [15]. Listing 1.1 shows the pseudo-code – `AnswerQuery(Goal)` – for the `answerQuery/4` predicate: given a claim (`Goal`) as input, the function first builds all the arguments sustaining that claim (`buildSustainingArguments(Goal)`), and then requires their evaluation via the `Evaluate(A, Chain)` function.

In order to assess the $A_1, ..., A_n$ status (acceptability or rejection), three conditions are evaluated:

(Cond1) if a conflicting argument labelled as IN exists, then A_1 is OUT;
(Cond2) if a cycle in the route from the root to the leaves (`Chain`) exists, then
    A_1 argument is UND;

---

[1] http://arg2p.apice.unibo.it.
[2] At the time of writing, only grounded semantics is fully implemented.

Listing 1.1. Structured argumentation, Arg2P answer query algorithm for grounded semantic (pseudo-code).

```
AnswerQuery(Goal):
  A₁,...,Aₙ = buildSustainingArguments(Goal)
  Res = ∅
  for A in A₁,...,Aₙ:
    Res = Res ∪ Evaluate(A, ∅)
  return Res.

Evaluate(A, Chain):
  if(∃ B ∈ Attacker(A): Evaluate(B, A ∪ Chain) = IN)
    return OUT
  if(∃ B ∈ Attacker(A): B ∈ Chain)
    return UND
  if(∃ B ∈ Attacker(A): Evaluate(B, A ∪ Chain) = UND)
    return UND
  return IN.
```

(Cond3) if a conflicting argument labelled as UND exists, then also the A_1 argument is UND.

If none of the above conditions is met, then the argument can be accepted.

Example 1. Let us consider the following theory and the corresponding arguments (depicted in Fig. 1).

r1 : $\Rightarrow a$	A0 : $\Rightarrow_{r1} a$
r2 : $a \Rightarrow b$	A1 : A0 $\Rightarrow_{r2} b$
r3 : $\Rightarrow \neg b$	A2 : $\Rightarrow_{r3} \neg b$
r4 : $b \Rightarrow c$	A3 : A1 $\Rightarrow_{r4} c$

According to grounded semantic $A0$ is IN – there are no arguments contending its claim or undercutting its inferences – whereas $A1$, $A2$ and $A3$ are UND—$A1$ and $A2$ have opposite conclusions and thus attack each other; the conflict is then propagated to the derived argument $A3$.

Let us suppose we require the evaluation of claim b via the `AnswerQuery(Goal)` function in Listing 1.1. First, the arguments sustaining b are created, in this case only $A1$. Then the evaluation conditions on $A1$ attackers – only $A2$ in this case – are assessed. However, $A2$ admissibility depends, in turn, on $A1$—as you can see in Fig. 1 also $A1$ attacks $A2$. There is a cycle in the graph (Cond2), and no other attackers matching (Cond1). As a consequence, $A2$ is UND and thus $A1$ (Cond3). Accordingly, claim b is labelled UND as expected.

Let us now consider the algorithm in Listing 1.1 to analyse the requirements and implications of its parallelisation. The algorithm structure is simple: the argument evaluation leverages the evaluation obtained from its attackers—i.e., the attackers are recursively evaluated using the same algorithm and the result is exploited to determine the state of the target argument. Intuitively, a first point

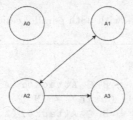

Fig. 1. Argumentation graph for arguments from Example 1, in which nodes are arguments and edges are attacks between arguments.

of parallelisation can be found in the search and evaluation of the `Attackers`. Indeed, every condition exploited by the algorithm – (Cond1), (Cond2), and (Cond3) – to evaluate an argument requires one and only one attacker to match the constraint. Those conditions directly suggest a parallelisation in the search and evaluation of the attackers. We could evaluate the arguments simultaneously under different branches, and the success in one of the branches would lead to the success of the entire search.

However, the algorithm exposes another point of parallalisation. The order in the evaluation of the conditions is essential for the soundness of the algorithm—as illustrated by the following example.

Example 2. Let us consider argument A and its two attackers B and C. Let it be the case in which we know B and C's labelling, IN for the former and UND for the latter. If we do not respect the order dictated by the algorithm, A's labelling is either UND (Cond3) or OUT (Cond1). Of course, the first result would be in contrast with the original grounded semantic requirements for which every argument having an IN attacker should be definitively OUT. Conversely, if we respect the evaluation order, A's labelling would be OUT in every scenario.

Although the evaluation order is strict, we can evaluate all the conditions simultaneously and consider the ordering only while providing the labelling for the target argument. In other words, the three conditions are evaluated in parallel, but the result is given accordingly to the defined priorities. If (Cond1) is met, the argument is labelled as OUT. Conversely, even if (Cond2) or (Cond3) are met, one should first verify that (Cond1) does not hold. Only then the argument can be labelled as UND.

Listing 1.2 contains the version of the algorithm taking into account both points of parallelisation. The three conditions – (Cond1), (Cond2) and (Cond3) – are evaluated at the same time. Then the results of the three sub-tasks are combined to provide the final solution according to the conditions' priority. Of course, if we consider a scenario where only the first condition (Cond1) is required to determine the status of the argument in input, the parallel evaluation of all three conditions would lead to a waste of computational resources. However, this problem is easily mitigated by evaluating the sub-task results as soon as they are individually available—i.e. in the case we receive a positive result from a

Listing 1.2. `Evaluate` predicate with both parallel conditions evaluation and parallel attackers

```
Evaluate(A, Chain):
  PARALLEL {
    Cond1 = PARALLEL { ∃ B ∈ Attacker(A):
        Evaluate(B, A ∪ Chain) = IN }
    Cond2 = PARALLEL { ∃ B ∈ Attacker(A): B ∈ Chain }
    Cond3 = PARALLEL { ∃ B ∈ Attacker(A):
        Evaluate(B, A ∪ Chain) = UND }
  }
  if(Cond1) return OUT
  if(Cond2 AND NOT Cond1) return UND
  if(Cond3 AND NOT Cond1) return UND
  if(NOT Cond1 AND NOT Cond2 AND NOT Cond3) return IN
```

single sub-task, and it is enough to compute the argument status, we can cut the superfluous computational branches and return the final solution.

In the first part of our analysis we focused on the parallelisation problem from a pure computational perspective, by discussing whether the evaluation task could be split into a group of sub-task to be executed simultaneously. However, there is another perspective to take into account when parallelising: the one concerning the data.

Example 3. For instance, let us consider a job computing the sum and the product of a set of numbers. Using the sub-task approach, we could have two subroutines running in parallel, one computing the sum and the other computing the product of the numbers. However, leveraging the associative property of addition and multiplication, we can split the problem into a series of tasks computing both sum and product on a subset of the original data. Then the final result would be the sum and the multiplication of the tasks' results.

Let us suppose to apply the same principle to the argumentation task. We build arguments from a base theory according to the relations illustrated in Sect. 2. The logic theory is, for all intents, the input data of our algorithm (argumentation task). Now, the question is whether we can effectively split the data into sub-portions to be evaluated in parallel without affecting the global soundness of the original algorithm. Let us consider a splitting principle based on rules dependency – i.e., if two rules can be chained, they must stay together –, and the algorithm in Listing 1.2. According to the algorithm, the search and evaluation of the attackers are performed in a distinct subtask (concurrent evaluation). Then, we can split the knowledge concerning attacked and attackers into separate sets, since the subtasks evaluating an attacker require only the knowledge to infer such an attacker—i.e., the *Dependency* principle must be respected. Indeed, there is no task that needs to know how to build both an argument and its attackers, since the search is delegated to another process. In other words, a single subprocess in charge of evaluating an argument needs only the portion of the theory needed to infer the argument itself—i.e., the chainable rules concluding the target claim.

3.1   Computational Model: The Master-Slave Actor Model

We can now provide a complete and sound mechanism for the admissibility task in a fully-concurrent way, exploiting the insights from Sect. 3 and applying them to an actor-based model [16].

In short, the actor model is based on a set of computational entities – the actors – communicating with each other through messages. The interaction between actors is the key to computation. Actors are pure reactive entities that, only in response to a message, can:

- create new actors;
- send messages to other actors;
- change their internal state through a predefined behaviour.

Actors work in a fully-concurrent way – asynchronous communication and message passing are fundamental to this end – making the actor model suited to concurrent applications and scenarios. We choose this model for its simplicity: it presents very few abstractions making it easy to study both how to model a concurrent system and its properties. The final goal is to provide a sound model for agents' cooperative argumentation in MAS, enabling concurrent evaluation of the argumentation algorithms (focusing on distribution). The actor paradigm is a straightforward choice for an analysis of this sort.

Since the actor model focuses on actors and their communication, the following design will review the structure and behaviour of the actors involved. Although a fully-distributed version of the model is possible, we choose to adopt a master-slave approach in order to simplify the functioning of the system as much as possible. Accordingly, two main sorts of actors are conceived in the system: *master* and *worker*. Master actors coordinate the knowledge-base distribution phase, while the workers hold a portion of the theory, concurring with the evaluation of a claim through their interaction.

Let us start with the knowledge distribution. Since actors are reactive entities, in order to completely adhere to the actor model the master knowledge base can be changed from outside the actor system. If the master receives the order to add a new element to the theory, three possible scenarios can be configured:

1. none of the workers contains a compatible knowledge base (kb) – i.e., it is not possible to chain the new rule to the knowledge base – and consequently, the master creates a new worker containing the portion of the theory;
2. one or more workers have a compatible knowledge base, and they add the element to their kb;
3. a set of workers possess overlapping knowledge bases – i.e. the union set of workers' knowledge bases can be used to create a unique inference chain –, and, as a consequence, we merge their knowledge bases and destroy the extra workers;

Iterating this procedure for all the elements of an input knowledge base, as a result, we should obtain a set of workers each of them containing a portion of the theory in accordance with the *dependency* splitting principle.

Once the knowledge has been correctly split between workers, we can proceed with the actor-based evaluation of an argument. Each actor is responsible for evaluating those arguments that can be built using his portion of the theory. When the actor receives an evaluation request, it first checks if attackers exist, w.r.t. its portion of the knowledge base. Then, the actor can: *(i)* register the impossibility to evaluate the argument – only if a cycle through the evaluation chain is detected –, *(ii)* require the attacker arguments evaluation to all the other actors. In the latter case, the actor shall answer the original evaluation request only after receiving a response from others actors. The conditions to match while evaluating an argument are the same as the original algorithm in Listing 1.1:

- if one counterargument is admissible, we evaluate the argument as OUT;
- if any number of actors decide for the argument undecidability with none advancing its rejection, we mark the argument as UND;
- if all the actors agree that no counterarguments can be provided as acceptable, we evaluate the argument as IN;

Actors provide their suggestions on the state of the requested argument according to all the labels of their counterarguments.

We can describe the interactions between the system's actors as a sequence diagram (Fig. 2) of messages exchanged between masters and workers, where:

- **Add**, sent from the master to a worker, through which the master sends the new theory member to be stored in the workers' kb; the decision on which is the right worker to send the data to is the responsibility of the master that knows the entire state of the system and how data has been divided;
- **RequireEvaluation**, sent from outside the system to the master to require the evaluation of a claim;
- **Eval**, sent from the master to all workers to require the evaluation of a claim
- **FindAttacker**, sent from a worker to master to require the broadcasting of a request for counterarguments to all the available workers;
- **ExpectedResponses**, sent from master to a worker to communicate the number of expected responses to a request for counterarguments;
- **AttackerResponse**, sent from a worker to a worker in response to a request for counterarguments; the message contains the state of the counterargument obtained through a new **FindAttacker** evaluation;
- **EvalResponse**, sent from workers to the master to communicate their decision on a claim; the decision is taken after all the **AttackerResponse** containing the state of possible counterarguments have been received;
- **EvaluationResponse**, message sent from master containing the system decision on the state of a claim.

Note that the **Add** and **RequireEvaluation** messages come from outside the actor system and start the distribution and evaluation process. This interaction

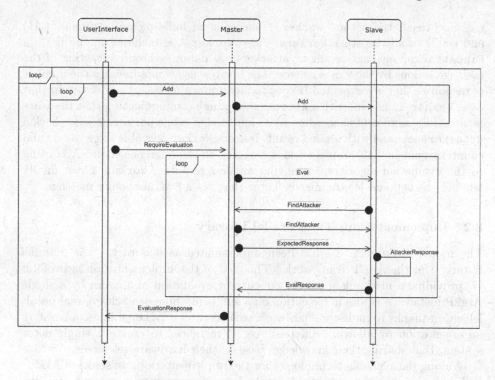

Fig. 2. Master-slave interaction for argument evaluation.

model implements both the parallelisation strategies described in Listing 1.2: the search for counterarguments is executed concurrently by all the worker nodes, as also the evaluation of the admissibility of arguments.

Example 4. Let us consider again the theory in Example 1. Let us assume a single `MasterActor` and the following order in the inclusion of the rules in the system: $r1$, $r3$, $r4$, $r2$.[3] As for the first three rules, the behaviour is the same. Since the rules are not chainable, it creates three distinct workers and sends a single rule to every one of them via the `Add` message. We now have `Worker 1`, `Worker 2`, and `Worker 3` with respectively $r1$, $r3$, and $r4$ in their knowledge bases. Then the inclusion of rule $r2$ is required, and both workers 1 and 3 results in having a chainable knowledge base. Rule $r2$ is, in fact, the missing link in the inference chain of $r1$ and $r4$. As a consequence, the `Master` stops the two workers, creates a new one, and then requires to it the inclusion of rules $r1$, $r4$, $r2$ via three `Add` messages. At the end of the distribution phase, we have two workers, one containing $r1$, $r2$, $r4$, and the other just $r3$. The dependency principle is thus respected. Going on with the example, we require the evaluation of claim b via the `RequireEvaluation` message: so, the `Master` sends an `Eval`

---

[3] The order of inclusion affects the steps required to converge, not the final state of the system.

message to all the actors. Worker 1 succeeds in building an argument ($A1$) and sends to all the other Workers – also Worker 1 is included in the list – a FindAttacker message requiring attackers evaluation—the broadcasting of the message is done by the Master actor. The master also communicates the number of responses that are expected (ExpectedResponses message)—only two in that case. Worker 1 answers with a AttackerResponse communicating that there are no attacking arguments according to its knowledge, while Worker 2 sends back a AttackerResponse with an Und result. Indeed, Worker 2 is able to create a valid counterargument ($A2$), but a cycle is detected in the inference chain. According to the evaluation algorithm, receiving an Und response, Worker 1 can finally label $A1$ as UND and let the master know that via a EvalResponse message.

3.2 Implementation: The Parallel Library

The model in Subsect. 3.1 has been implemented as a library – the *Parallel* library – for the Arg2P framework.[4] The goal of the implementation is twofold: (*i*) providing a mechanism for the concurrent evaluation of a claim by a single Arg2P instance – actors in execution on a single machine can achieve real parallelisation thanks to multicore hardware architectures – (*ii*) enabling cooperative argumentation by allowing different Arg2P instances to create a single actor system, thus sharing their knowledge base or their hardware resources.

Among the available technologies for the implementation, we selected Akka.[5] [12] Akka is an open source middleware for programming concurrent and distributed actor systems based on the original Actor model by Hewitt [16]. Built upon the JVM platform, the framework offers an easy way of deploying network distributed systems observant of the original actor principles—e.g. reactivity, asynchronous communications, and absence of states of shared memory between actors. All these features made the Akka framework one of the reference technologies in the distributed landscape.

The final implementation makes use of the *Akka Clustering* features to enable the collaboration of different Arg2P instances. In particular, we rely on *Cluster Singletons*[6] to handle the Master actor lifecycle, and *Cluster Sharding*[7] for Worker nodes. The *Parallel* library makes available five directives:

- join(Port), requesting the creation of an actor system on the local machine exposed on port Port;
- join(Port, Address), to join an actor system on the machine at the given Address, exposed on port Port;
- load, requesting the distribution of the rules contained in the knowledge base of the local instance between all the members of the actor systems;
- reset, requesting the deletion of the data previously distributed in the actor system via the load directive;

---

[4] Sources available at https://github.com/tuProlog/arg2p-kt.
[5] https://akka.io/.
[6] https://doc.akka.io/docs/akka/current/typed/cluster-singleton.html.
[7] https://doc.akka.io/docs/akka/current/typed/cluster-sharding.html.

- `solve(Goal, In, Out, Und)`, requesting the evaluation of the `Goal` claim to the actor system according to the procedure in Fig. 2. Results are the set of facts matching the goal distributed in the three sets IN, OUT, and UND.

All the application scenarios can be modelled by using the directives above. We achieve a parallel evaluation of a claim on a single Arg2P instance in three steps: *(i)* creating a local actor system (`join(Port)`), *(ii)* distributing the theory between local actors (`load`), *(iii)* requiring the evaluation of a statement through the `solve(Goal, In, Out, Und)` directive. At the same time we could have others Arg2P instances offering their hardware resources (`join(Port, Address)`) or also participating in the resolution if they share their own knowledge (`load`).

4   Conclusion

In this work, given the relevance of issues such as pervasiveness and interconnection in the current technological landscape, we address the problem of distribution of the argumentation workload. We follow some insights from [5] and [22,23]. In [5] the first proposal of a tuProlog-based is presented that exploits a dialogical argumentation mechanism—i.e., argumentation is performed across multiple processes proposing arguments and counterarguments. However, the argumentation algorithm distribution has not been addressed there. Conversely, in [22,23] authors directly address the problem of enabling argumentation techniques in MAS. Nonetheless, their approach just depicts a general-purpose architectural solution for the multi-party argumentation problem in the MAS context, providing for neither an actual technology nor a precise model for the distribution and parallelisation of the argumentation process.

Overall, we believe that our approach is a step forward in the direction of a full argumentation-based MAS, and more in general of the diffusion of argumentation theories as a solid foundation for the engineering of complex intelligent systems. Yet, many issues are still to be considered. We should provide a complete analysis of the computational properties of the presented model – e.g., correctness, completeness, termination –, and also consider its relation with alternative distribution schemes (e.g., peer-to-peer). Moreover, an empirical evaluation of the performance of the system compared to traditional solvers should also be provided. Another topic of future investigations is the extension to different argumentation semantics. The main difference would be in the labelling conditions used to classify the arguments according to the different semantics. Moreover, a branching mechanism to allow the coexistence of multiple labellings should be devised in order to support the semantics with multiple extensions. However, most of the ideas behind the presented model should still remain applicable.

Acknowledgements. This work was supported by the H2020 ERC Project "CompuLaw" (G.A. 833647).

References

1. Andrighetto, G., Governatori, G., Noriega, P., van der Torre, L.W.: Normative multi-agent systems, Dagstuhl Follow-Ups, vol. 4. Schloss Dagstuhl-Leibniz-Zentrum fuer Informatik (2013). http://www.dagstuhl.de/dagpub/978-3-939897-51-4
2. Baroni, P., Caminada, M., Giacomin, M.: An introduction to argumentation semantics. Knowl. Eng. Rev. **26**(4), 365–410 (2011). https://doi.org/10.1017/S0269888911000166
3. Baroni, P., Gabbay, D., Giacomin, M., van der Torre, L.: Handbook of Formal Argumentation. College Publications, London (2018). https://www.collegepublications.co.uk/handbooks/?00003
4. Besnard, P., et al.: Introduction to structured argumentation. Argument Comput. **5**(1), 1–4 (2014). https://doi.org/10.1080/19462166.2013.869764
5. Bryant, D., Krause, P.J., Vreeswijk, G.: Argue tuProlog: a lightweight argumentation engine for agent applications. In: Computational Models of Argument. Frontiers in Artificial Intelligence and Applications, vol. 144, pp. 27–32. IOS Press (2006). https://ebooks.iospress.nl/publication/2929
6. Calegari, R., Contissa, G., Lagioia, F., Omicini, A., Sartor, G.: Defeasible systems in legal reasoning: a comparative assessment. In: Araszkiewicz, M., Rodríguez-Doncel, V. (eds.) Legal Knowledge and Information Systems, JURIX 2019: The Thirty-second Annual Conference, Frontiers in Artificial Intelligence and Applications, vol. 322, pp. 169–174. IOS Press (2019). https://doi.org/10.3233/FAIA190320
7. Calegari, R., Contissa, G., Pisano, G., Sartor, G., Sartor, G.: Arg-tuProlog: a modular logic argumentation tool for PIL. In: Villata, S., Harašta, J., Křemen, P. (eds.) Legal Knowledge and Information Systems, JURIX 2020: The Thirty-third Annual Conference. Frontiers in Artificial Intelligence and Applications, vol. 334, pp. 265–268 (2020). https://doi.org/10.3233/FAIA200880
8. Calegari, R., Omicini, A., Sartor, G.: Computable law as argumentation-based MAS. In: Calegari, R., Ciatto, G., Denti, E., Omicini, A., Sartor, G. (eds.) WOA 2020–21st Workshop "From Objects to Agents". CEUR Workshop Proceedings, vol. 2706, pp. 54–68. Sun SITE Central Europe, RWTH Aachen University, Aachen, Germany (2020). http://ceur-ws.org/Vol-2706/paper10.pdf, 21st Workshop "From Objects to Agents" (WOA 2020), Bologna, Italy, 14–16 September 2020. Proceedings
9. Calegari, R., Pisano, G., Omicini, A., Sartor, G.: Arg2P: an argumentation framework for explainable intelligent systems. J. Logic Comput. **32**(2), 369–401 (2022). https://doi.org/10.1093/logcom/exab089, Special Issue from the 35th Italian Conference on Computational Logic (CILC 2020)
10. Carrera, Á., Iglesias, C.A.: A systematic review of argumentation techniques for multi-agent systems research. Artif. Intell. Rev. **44**(4), 509–535 (2015). https://doi.org/10.1007/s10462-015-9435-9
11. Ciatto, G., Calegari, R., Omicini, A.: 2P- KT: a logic-based ecosystem for symbolic AI. SoftwareX **16**(100817), 1–7 (2021). https://doi.org/10.1016/j.softx.2021.100817
12. Cossentino, M., Lopes, S., Nuzzo, A., Renda, G., Sabatucci, L.: A comparison of the basic principles and behavioural aspects of Akka, JaCaMo and Jade development frameworks. In: Proceedings of the 19th Workshop "From Objects to Agents". CEUR Workshop Proceedings, vol. 2215, pp. 133–141. CEUR-WS.org (2018). http://ceur-ws.org/Vol-2215/paper_21.pdf

13. Denti, E., Omicini, A., Ricci, A.: Multi-paradigm Java-Prolog integration in tuProlog. Sci. Comput. Program. **57**(2), 217–250 (2005). https://doi.org/10.1016/j.scico.2005.02.001

14. Dung, P.M.: On the acceptability of arguments and its fundamental role in nonmonotonic reasoning, logic programming and n-person games. Artif. Intell. **77**(2), 321–358 (1995). https://doi.org/10.1016/0004-3702(94)00041-X

15. García, A.J., Simari, G.R.: Defeasible logic programming: an argumentative approach. Theory Pract. Logic Program. **4**(1–2), 95–138 (2004). https://doi.org/10.1017/S1471068403001674

16. Hewitt, C., Bishop, P.B., Steiger, R.: A universal modular ACTOR formalism for artificial intelligence. In: 3rd International Joint Conference on Artificial Intelligence, pp. 235–245. William Kaufmann (1973). http://ijcai.org/Proceedings/73/Papers/027B.pdf

17. Hulstijn, J., van der Torre, L.W.: Combining goal generation and planning in an argumentation framework. In: International Workshop on Non-monotonic Reasoning (NMR 2004), pp. 212–218 (2004). https://www.pims.math.ca/science/2004/NMR/papers/paper28.pdf

18. Jung, H., Tambe, M., Kulkarni, S.: Argumentation as distributed constraint satisfaction: applications and results. In: 5th International Conference on Autonomous Agents (Agents 2001), pp. 324–331 (2001). https://doi.org/10.1145/375735.376322

19. Krippendorff, K.: Intrinsic motivation and human-centred design. Theor. Issues Ergon. Sci. **5**(1), 43–72 (2004). https://doi.org/10.1080/1463922031000086717

20. Modgil, S., Caminada, M.: Proof theories and algorithms for abstract argumentation frameworks. In: Simari, G., Rahwan, I. (eds.) Argumentation in Artificial Intelligence, pp. 105–129. Springer, Heidelberg (2009). https://doi.org/10.1007/978-0-387-98197-0_6

21. Modgil, S., Prakken, H.: The ASPIC$^+$ framework for structured argumentation: a tutorial. Argument Comput. **5**(1), 31–62 (2014). https://doi.org/10.1080/19462166.2013.869766

22. Oliva, E., McBurney, P., Omicini, A.: Co-argumentation artifact for agent societies. In: Rahwan, I., Parsons, S., Reed, C. (eds.) ArgMAS 2007. LNCS (LNAI), vol. 4946, pp. 31–46. Springer, Heidelberg (2008). https://doi.org/10.1007/978-3-540-78915-4_3

23. Oliva, E., Viroli, M., Omicini, A., McBurney, P.: Argumentation and artifact for dialogue support. In: Rahwan, I., Moraitis, P. (eds.) ArgMAS 2008. LNCS (LNAI), vol. 5384, pp. 107–121. Springer, Heidelberg (2009). https://doi.org/10.1007/978-3-642-00207-6_7

24. Pisano, G., Calegari, R., Omicini, A., Sartor, G.: A mechanism for reasoning over defeasible preferences in Arg2P. In: Monica, S., Bergenti, F. (eds.) CILC 2021 - Italian Conference on Computational Logic. Proceedings of the 36th Italian Conference on Computational Logic. CEUR Workshop Proceedings, Parma, Italy, vol. 3002, pp. 16–30. CEUR-WS (2021). http://ceur-ws.org/Vol-3002/paper10.pdf

25. Vasconcelos, W.W., Sabater, J., Sierra, C., Querol, J.: Skeleton-based agent development for electronic institutions. In: 1st International Joint Conference on Autonomous Agents and Multiagent Systems: Part 2 (AAMAS 2002), pp. 696–703. ACM, New York (2002). https://doi.org/10.1145/544862.544911

Ethics by Design for Intelligent and Sustainable Adaptive Systems

Luca Squadrone, Danilo Croce[(✉)], and Roberto Basili[(✉)]

Department of Enterprise Engineering, University of Roma, Tor Vergata,
Via del Politecnico 1, 00133 Rome, Italy
{croce,basili}@info.uniroma2.it

Abstract. AI systems are increasingly dependent on the data and information sources they are developed with. In particular, learning machines are highly exposed to undesirable problems due to biased and incomplete coverage of training data. The autonomy exhibited by machines trained on low-quality data raises an ethical concern, as it may infringe on social rules and security constraints.

In this paper, we extensively experiment with a learning framework, called *Ethics by Design*, which aims to ensure a supervised learning policy that can pursue both the satisfaction of ethical constraints and the optimization of task (i.e., business) accuracy. The results obtained on tasks and datasets confirm the positive impact of the method in ensuring ethical compliance. This paves the way for a large set of industrial applications, whose ethical dimension is critical to increasing the trustworthiness with respect to this technology.

Keywords: Ethical issues of AI · Ethics by design in machine learning · Bias in deep learning · Empirical evaluation of ethical AI systems

1 Introduction

Machine learning applications are experiencing exponential growth and are now being implemented in high-risk ethical scenarios, such as lending, hiring, or legal decision support [22]. The clear advantages of using machine learning algorithms include the ability to quickly and accurately analyze large amounts of data.

However, this paves the way for algorithms to generate discriminatory predictions against individuals or social groups [1,2,6,23][1], as per the bias inherent in the way historical data are collected.

Consider, for example, COMPAS, a system used as a support tool by judges to predict a defendant's risk of recidivism. African American defendants have

---

[1] The articles for [2] and [23] can be found respectively at https://www.propublica.org/article/machine-bias-risk-assessments-in-criminal-sentencing and https://www.aclu.org/blog/privacy-technology/surveillance-technologies/amazons-face-recognition-falsely-matched-28.

A. Dovier et al. (Eds.): AIxIA 2022, LNAI 13796, pp. 154–167, 2023.
https://doi.org/10.1007/978-3-031-27181-6_11

been found to be exposed to a higher risk of recidivism than Caucasian defendants due to unbalanced representation in historical data. This is further evidenced by recent studies [1, 2, 6, 12, 16, 23][2] which have shown how machine learning algorithms may emphasize human factors such as prejudices, cliches, and errors of assessment.

Since the algorithms are based on mathematical and statistical principles, they cannot independently recognize the ethical values related to the fair treatment of races or genders. This negatively impacts the trust with respect to this class of methods, especially in critical scenarios. Therefore, it becomes critically important that machines are somehow able to make data-driven decisions aligned with human values and expectations, in order to avoid the risk of dangerous drifts in terms of ethics and human values.

The framework proposed in [21], while extending the generic applications of AI, focuses primarily on learning ethical behavior by numerical optimization, that is, through a deep neural model. The core idea is to model ethics as automated reasoning over formal descriptions of fair decisions, e.g., ontologies, but making it available *during the learning stage*. Note that this approach does *not* induce a set of ethical rules from a set of observable behaviors, but rather does the opposite. This approach takes for granted an explicit formulation of ethical principles (as done, for example, in earlier work [5, 24]) and focuses on a form of ethical learning as external alignment (learning from others, [15]).

It uses evidence inferred from an ethical ontology to guide model selection during the training process.

The resulting deep neural network jointly models the functional and ethical conditions that characterize the underlying decision-making process. In this way, the discovery of latent ethical knowledge (that is, information hidden in the data that is meaningful from an ethical perspective) is enabled and made available to the learning process. Instead of relying on simulation to proceed in ethical decisions [24], the adopted framework integrates the acquisition of high-quality inference abilities that *simultaneously* reflect ethical expectations. In other words, the learning machine is expected to select the "best decision" among those that are also ethically sustainable.

In this work, we test the beneficial impact of the above *Ethics by Design* technology[3] on five well-known datasets by (1) adopting ethical principles, that allow the ethical encoding of original instances into a space corresponding to ethical properties, and (2) by reformulating the learning function to favor decisions that better balance operational (i.e., business) efficiency and ethical compliance. The proposed experiments adopt ethical principles in form of task-specific ethical rules that constrain the learning algorithm through the definition of dedicated preferences, the so-called *truth-makers*, as in [21].

We measured the impact of the *Ethics by Design* approach by showing the effectiveness of parameterization and "tweaking" of ethical constraint weights.

---

[2] The study referred by [12] is available at: https://www.bloomberg.com/graphics/2016-amazon-same-day/.

[3] The code is made available at: https://github.com/crux82/nn-ebd.

As a result, we show that in all data sets, i.e., tasks, ethical conditions, and domains, a large improvement in ethical behavior (lower ethical risks) can be achieved at the cost of a small reduction in accuracy.

In the remainder of the article, ethical issues in example-based machine learning approaches are first presented in Sect. 2. Section 3 summarizes the *Ethics by Design* approach, as a neural architecture that applies ethical constraints during the training process. In Sect. 4, experimental results are reported. Finally, in Sect. 5 the conclusions are drawn.

2   Ethics in Inductive Decision Systems

2.1   Ethics in Different Application Scenarios

Regardless of their effectiveness, ethical concerns are raised about the autonomy exhibited by machines trained on (possibly limited) data and their potential to violate social rules and security constraints.

A first example involves Amazon's recruitment algorithm, which is used to automatically screen candidates' curricula during the selection process. As indicated by the Business Insider report[4], this algorithm was found discriminatory against women, particularly in professions requiring technological skills. This bias was introduced by the data (i.e., real curricula) used in training: these were mostly related to male candidates, so the algorithm overweighted the contribution of candidate gender-related characteristics.

In [6], the output of facial recognition algorithms released to the market by three major tech companies showed a significant racial and gender bias: these methods had very low error rates (never more than 0.8%) in determining the sex of light-skinned men, but when applied to dark-skinned women this increased to ranges of 20% and 34%. In automatic recommendation, the analysis presented in [1] suggests that the algorithm adopted by Facebook for recommendation also applies racial and gender biases when offering ads to more than two billion users, based on their demographic information. Similar issues are surveyed in [23].

As a consequence, growing attention is paid to the analysis of "sensitive features" (e.g., gender, ethnicity, and age) to identify and limit undesirable effects of bias, discrimination, or prejudice, as surveyed in [8]. Several studies have shown that the definition and acquisition of a dataset affected by (any kind of) bias significantly affect the quality of a data-driven method trained on it, as discussed below.

The *COMPAS*[5] (*Correctional Offender Management Profiling for Alternative Sanctions*) dataset discussed in [20] was released by ProPublica in 2016 based on the Broward County data. It assigns people a recidivism risk score that is computed using the defendant's responses to the COMPAS screening survey. This dataset is generally used to train machine learning algorithms that predict

---

[4] www.businessinsider.com/amazon-built-ai-to-hire-people-discriminated-against-women-2018-10.

[5] https://github.com/propublica/compas-analysis.

if an individual will be arrested again within two years after the first arrest. According to ProPublica's analysis [2], African Americans are more likely than Caucasians to be mislabeled as being at higher risk.

The *German credit dataset*[6] is defined to represent bank account holders and it is used in automatic risk assessment prediction, that is, to determine whether or not it is risky to extend credit to a person. The potential ethical risk of deriving a data-driven model that makes it difficult to lend to women, youth, or foreign workers is generally discussed, as in [20].

The *Adult dataset*[7] was derived from U.S. Census data in 1994. It includes attributes describing social information about registered citizens (in terms of age, race, sex, or marital status) and is generally used to determine whether a person's annual income exceeds 50,000 US dollars. As discussed in [20], this dataset is subject to bias, as automatic classifiers generally overweight information about the sex and race of the individuals being considered.

The *Default Credit Card Clients*[8] dataset investigated the customers' default payments and contains payment information, demographics, credit data, and payment history. The goal is to predict whether or not a client will default in the next month. However, as suggested by [20], women are penalized compared to men.

The *Law School Dataset*[9] is defined after the survey conducted by the Law School Admission Council (LSAC) across 163 law schools in the United States. The dataset contains the law school admission records and it is generally used to predict whether a candidate would pass the bar exam or to predict a student's first-year average grade (FYA). As discussed in [20], this prediction is generally biased by features like the `gender` or the `race` of the candidates.

2.2   Computational Methods for Fair Inductive Systems

When training machine learning methods over potentially unfair datasets, much of the discussion focuses on various solutions to reduce "bias" in algorithms, such as modifying training data or diversifying data sources to reduce disparities between groups [10,11]. However, research such as [17][10] suggests that such approaches may fail when it is difficult to isolate protected attributes from data. As extensively discussed in [8,19] and [18], methods to reduce bias effects fall under three categories: *pre-processing*, *in-processing*, and *post-processing* algorithms.

Pre-processing methods manipulate the training dataset *before* training a model, under the assumption that changing input data can prevent the insurgence of undesirable effects. In-processing methods modify the learning machine

---

[6] https://archive.ics.uci.edu/ml/datasets/statlog+(german+credit+data).

[7] https://archive.ics.uci.edu/ml/datasets/adult.

[8] https://archive.ics.uci.edu/ml/datasets/default+of+credit+card+clients.

[9] https://storage.googleapis.com/lawschool_dataset/bar_pass_prediction.csv.

[10] The study referred by [17] can be found at: https://hai.stanford.edu/sites/default/files/2021-12/Policy%20Brief%20-%20Risks%20of%20AI%20Race%20Detection%20in%20the%20Medical%20System.pdf.

itself, while post-processing techniques modify the decisions made by a given machine.

An example of a pre-processing approach is presented in [13], where a classification model is learned on biased training data but works impartially for future data: a ranking function is learned to detect biased data that must be "sanitized", to learn a non-discriminatory model. In [10] a different approach is defined to modify each attribute, so that the marginal distributions based on subsets of that attribute characterized by a given sensitive value are all the same, without changing the target training labels.

On the other hand, [7] and [11] present post-processing methods. Rather than changing a training pipeline, they propose post-processing frameworks for measuring and removing discrimination based on "protected" attributes.

In-processing methods do not directly process input/output data, but instead, extend a machine learning algorithm so that (in addition to the originally targeted task) they also consider one or more additional tasks reflecting some sort of ethical principles. Such an extension is generally based on regularization, constraint optimization, or adversarial learning techniques. In [3, 4, 9, 14], authors outline a general framework for empirical risk minimization under fairness constraints, such as the introduction of specific regularizers.

Regardless of the type of approach used among those discussed so far, the goal is always to minimize the negative effect of sensitive variables during the training process. In practice, adding constraints generally results in a trade-off: a fairer algorithm at the cost of small drops in accuracy in the original problem.

Inspired by [21] and [13], we are interested here in methods that allow controlling this trade-off between system performance (in terms of accuracy on the target task) and ethics. We extensively investigate the method in [21], a neural framework that allows us (i) to directly control the trade-off between accuracy and ethical principles and (ii) to explicitly define these principles in terms of truth-makers, described hereafter.

2.3   Ethics, Principles and *Truth-Makers*

Ethical approaches to data-driven applications aim at minimizing the undesirable effects that learning processes may introduce on the acceptability of the resulting decisions. This "ethical acceptability" is often related to principles that establish norms over the decisions. Violations of principles correspond to an imbalance in the treatment of equal rights among individuals, i.e., ethical *risks*, or missed opportunities for individuals or social groups, i.e., reduced *benefits*. The idea in [21] is to introduce the notion of a *truth-maker* as a model for representing ethical risks and benefits and exploiting them during the training process of a learning algorithm. We promote an ethical approach by assuming that reasoning over ethical ontologies is carried out through principles that apply as truth-makers.

As an example, the application of an ethical principle such as "*All minorities must be protected and ensured by equal rights*" to an inductive classification method C is based on training datasets where some social groups, e.g., women, are somehow disadvantaged. Women might be discriminated against by C, such as when they take out a loan: an ethical constraint might be in this case to assume an ethical advantage when the loan is given to a woman. From a computational perspective determining such an advantage requires some explicit "rules", that work as a constraint for the learning process without any manipulation of the training data. In this way, two aspects are optimized: on the one side, the quality of future decisions should reflect the past ones (as we usually do by optimizing accuracy), and, on the other end, they should also satisfy ethical compliance, i.e., work on minimizing ethical risks and maximizing any potential ethical benefit.

In the ProPublica case, as the COMPAS dataset suggests, African Americans are more often mislabeled as being at higher risk than Caucasians. An ethical principle that may be used against this potentially unfair situation could be expressed as *"Safeguard the minority of African Americans from discriminatory classification can be achieved by avoiding severe decisions when identifying them as repeat offenders."* This principle suggests a constraint favoring situations in which it is particularly *beneficial* to protect a minority, such as African Americans.

At the same time, decisions about African Americans being repeat offenders are also risky, because of the community's potential social characterization. In fact, the COMPAS dataset contains the variable `race` (expressing if the individual is African American or Caucasian), which seems to suggest that African Americans are positively correlated with the `repeat offender class` on average: however, race should not be linked to such bias and the following principle can be used to counterbalance this trend: *"We expect there is a **substantial benefit** and **low risk** in classifying an African American as a non-repeat offender"*.

Rules used to summarize the above principles sentences can be derived for "NON-REPEAT OFFENDER" decisions:

- the BENEFIT in categorizing an African American as a NON-REPEAT OFFENDER is *high*;
- the RISK in classifying an African American as a NON-REPEAT OFFENDER is *low*;

as well as "REPEAT OFFENDER" decisions:

- the BENEFIT in classifying an African American as a repeat offender is *very low*;
- the RISK in classifying an African American as a repeat offender is *very high*.

The above rules are typical examples of truth-makers, as constraints on the decisions about recidivism based on the `race` feature. Notice that the adjective *low, very high* or *high* are vague but can be easily translated into fuzzy sets, as subjective models of the two meta-variables expressing the RISK and BENEFIT of any individual decision, as formalized in [21].

3   Formalizing Principles, Rules and Truth-Makers

The core of the adopted approach [21] is to model ethics via automated reasoning over formal descriptions, e.g., ontologies, but by making it available *during the learning stage.* We suggest the explicit formulation of ethical principles through truth-makers and let the resulting ethical evidence to guide the model selection of deep learning architecture. This network will jointly model causal as well as ethical conditions that characterize optimal decision-making. In this way, rules (i.e., truth-makers) are used to estimate risks and benefits connected to training cases; then the discovery of latent ethical knowledge, i.e., hidden information in the data that is meaningful under the ethical perspective, is carried out; finally, the latter evidence is made available when learning the target decision function. This framework results in a learning machine able to select the best decisions among those that are also ethically sustainable.

As already exemplified, abstract ethical principles can be enforced through *Ethical Rules* that constrain individual features (e.g., gender or race) and determine the degree of the ethicality of decisions. Ethical Rules usually depend on one or more features and assign values (or better, establish some probability distributions) over the domains of some features. These rules are termed as *truth-makers* ($\mathcal{TM}$), as they account for the possibly uncertain ethical state of the world determined by decisions over individual instances.

Truth-makers are thus rules of an ethical ontology $\mathcal{EO}$ that actively determine the ethical profile of a decision $d(i)$ over an input instance i, e.g., an individual associated to the **repeat offender class** in the COMPAS dataset. In particular, given a pair $(i, d(i))$, a truth-maker tm will determine a probability distribution to the set of ethical benefit and ethical risk dimensions. For every tm, ethical dimension $e_j(i)$ and possible ethical value $v_k \in V$, e.g. *low* or *high* risk[11], the following probability is defined:

$$P\Big(e_j(i) = v_k \mid (\vec{i}, d(i)), tm\Big) \qquad \forall j, \forall k = 1, \ldots, 5$$

which expresses the evaluation of the truth-maker tm onto the representation $\vec{i}$ of an instance i. Here $d(i)$ denotes the decision over the i-th instance and k-th is the value of the j-th ethical dimensions (constrained by the truth-maker). A truth-maker thus assigns probabilities to the ethical signature of an individual i for all possible combinations of business characteristics $\vec{i}$ and decisions $d(i)$; if no truth-maker is triggered by an instance the uniform probability distribution u is used, i.e., $P\Big(e_j(i) = v_k | (\vec{i}, d(i)), tm\Big) = \frac{1}{m}$, over the values v_k and different ethical features, i.e., $\forall j, k$. Multiple truth-makers can contribute to a given ethical feature $e_j(i)$ by individually biasing their overall probability $P(e_j(i))$. When all truth-makers are fired, the resulting *ethical signature* $\vec{es}(i)$ over an instance $\vec{i}$ and its decision $d(i)$ consists $\forall j, k$:

$$es_j(i) = \prod_{tm} P\Big(tm | \mathcal{EO}\Big) P\Big(e_j(i) = v_k \mid (\vec{i}, d(i)), tm\Big)$$

---

[11] Consistently with [21] for both benefits and risks, we fixed $m = 5$ and limit values in the $[0, 1]$ range. The following five labels can be adopted $\{$ *"very_low"*, *"low"*, *"mild"*, *"high"*, *"very_high"* $\}$ corresponding to the numerical values $v_1 = 0.1, v_2 = 0.25, v_3 = 0.5, v_4 = 0.75$ and $v_5 = 0.9$.

The Deep Network Architecture. The network consists of several components, each trained under different constraints expressed by specific loss functions (Fig. 1). In the first component, an Ethics Encoding network is defined, as responsible for learning the combinations of input features that capture possible relationships between business observations and (desired or undesired) ethical consequences: the network acts as an encoder of ethical consequences (i.e., further features) for each instance i. A second component includes two networks: a Business Expert and an Ethics Expert, whose roles are respectively to *independently* estimate the distributions of suitable business decisions, on the one side, and predict as well their ethical consequences. In the final component, an Ethical-aware Deep Neural Network (DNN) is responsible for estimating the joint probability of possible triplets (decision, benefit, risk), which determines the risks and benefits associated with individual decisions for each instance.

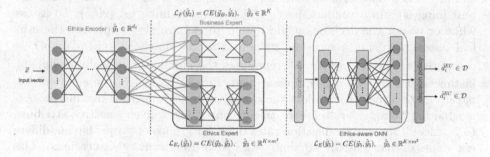

Fig. 1. Network architecture proposed in [21]

This last component produces the *final business decision* of the network by applying a certain decision policy over risks and opportunities. Different policies are possible: from rejecting all decisions that are not ethically adequate (above thresholds imposed to the probability of risks and benefits) to selecting other specific trade-offs between business accuracy and ethical compliance. Policies are designed as different loss functions used to train the specialized sub-networks, i.e., the Business Expert and the Ethics Expert. This architecture formulation allows thus to emphasize the contribution of each triple in the probability estimation through a factor β (the exponential Tweaking factor in [21]): in this way, we can train the overall network by balancing business accuracy and ethical compliance. Emphasis on ethical consequences can be achieved by amplifying the ethics constraints, i.e., by tweaking β toward larger values.

Notice that training data usually provide discrete (i.e., crisp) business decisions, that do not give rise to any uncertainty. However, these are not guaranteed to be ethical decisions. Introducing probability distributions for all possible outcomes and smoothing them towards the non-gold decisions allows us to disregard unethical cases and reserve some probability to decisions d_i different from the gold standard ones.

Several policies exist to derive the final decisions: in this work, this is derived only from the probability triplets that respect the ethical constraints. For more details, refer to the paper [21].

4   Evaluating Ethical Compliance in Inductive Learning

The effectiveness of the investigated method is evaluated using five well-known datasets, always preserving the architecture across them, while defining task-specific truth-makers reflecting different ethical principles. To verify the effectiveness of the "tweaking" parameter in controlling the trade-off between the task-specific accuracy and the sensitivity to ethical principles, we systematically measure the system in a range with $\beta \in \{0.001, 0.03, 0.05, 0.07, 0.1, 0.12, 0.14\}$, where higher values for β correspond to more influential ethical losses during training. Each dataset is divided into three parts: a test set (10%), and the remaining 90% in a validation set (10%), and a training set (90%). To assess whether or not the decisions made by our model are also respecting the ethical ontology in use, a measure, namely *Ethical Compliance* (*EthCompl*), is computed as $\frac{D^+}{D^+ + D^-}$, where D^+ represents the number of ethically compliant instances and D^- the non-compliant ones. Finally, as in [25], we adopted disparate mistreatment to measure the change in bias. A decision-making process is suffering from disparate mistreatment concerning a given sensitive attribute (e.g., race) if the misclassification rates differ for groups of people having different values of that sensitive attribute (e.g., Afro-Americans vs. Caucasians). The following equation

$$D_{FPR} = P(\hat{y} \neq y \mid z = 0, y = -1)$$
$$- P(\hat{y} \neq y \mid z = 1, y = -1)$$
$$D_{FNR} = P(\hat{y} \neq y \mid z = 0, y = 1)$$
$$- P(\hat{y} \neq y \mid z = 1, y = 1)$$

quantifies the disparate mistreatment incurred by a classifier, whereas the closer the values of D_{FPR} and D_{FNR} to 0, the lower the degree of disparate mistreatment.

4.1   Use Cases

We now describe the different investigated datasets, emphasizing the targeted sensitive features and adopted truth-makers.

The *COMPAS* Use Case. We selected the subset of instances completely defined in COMPAS, obtaining a subset of 6,908 samples. The target variable is_recid indicates whether a defendant committed a crime in the two years after he was scored. The definition of the truth-maker focused on the sensitive attribute race, so that it assigns a high benefit in classifying African Americans as not recidivists, a high risk in classifying them as recidivists while not acting on the other subpopulations, such as Caucasians (no benefit and risks assigned to the other subpopulations).

The *German Credit* Use Case. This dataset contains 1, 000 examples, each described by 21 attributes, where the target variable *default* indicates good or bad customers. The truth-maker focused on the `sex` attribute (derived from `personal-status-and-sex`) assigning high benefit in classifying females as good customers, a high risk in classifying them as bad customers while not acting on males.

The *Adult* Use Case. The Adult dataset consists of 48, 842 instances, each described via 15 attributes. The target boolean variable y indicates whether the annual income of a person exceeds 50, 000 US dollars. The truth-maker focused on the `sex` attribute, by assigning low benefits in classifying females as "under 50, 000 US dollars", and low risk in classifying them as "over 50, 000 US dollars" while not acting on males.

The *Default Credit Card* Use Case. The dataset includes 30,000 customers described by 24 attributes. The target variable `default` indicates whether a customer will suffer the default payment situation in the next month (1) or not (0). The truth-maker focused on the `sex` attribute, by assigning high benefits in classifying males as "NOT default", a high risk in classifying them as "default" while not acting on females.

The *Law School* Use Case. The Law school dataset has 26, 553 instances, where the target variable `pass_bar` indicates that a person passes the bar exam. The truth-maker focused on the *race* attribute, by assigning low benefits in classifying *other races* as "NOT passed the exam", low risk in classifying them as "passed" while not acting on *white*.

4.2 Discussion of the Results

Table 1 reports the experimental results. Cross-validation has been applied to study the behavior of *Accuracy* and *EthCompl* scores according to different values of β. The first line for each dataset in the table shows the performance of a Multi-Layer Perceptron (MLP) whose loss does not depend on any ethical dimension of the problem. This is compared with the proposed ethical networks achieved with different settings of the β parameters, whose role is to increase the impact of ethical constraints.

The overall experimental outcome strongly confirms the ability of the network to learn ethical constraints. In fact, in any of the targeted datasets, the measure of ethical compliance *EthCompl* grows as long as β (which emphasizes the impact of the ethical component of the network on the loss) increases. At the same time, disparate mistreatment also seems to be reduced: this is shown by the last pairs of columns in Table 1 (namely Disp. mistr.) and by the false positive rates on protected groups that are comparable to the corresponding rate on non-protected groups (e.g., African Americans vs. other races in COM-PAS). This is exactly the impact of unfair decisions we expect. The fact that

Table 1. Results by varying the parameter β on the COMPAS, German Credit, Adult, Default and Law school datasets. Values express the average over 5 different runs.

COMPAS

β	Accuracy	Eth.Compl.	Afr. Americans		Others		Disp. mistr.	
			FPR	FNR	FPR	FNR	DFPR	DFNR
(MLP)	0.681	0.682	0.433	0.233	0.183	0.506	0.250	−0.273
0.001	0.676	0.681	0.442	0.237	0.168	0.539	0.274	−0.302
0.030	0.668	0.723	0.359	0.318	0.146	0.584	0.212	−0.267
0.050	0.666	0.742	0.317	0.353	0.140	0.595	0.177	−0.242
0.070	0.664	0.761	0.279	0.391	0.133	0.603	0.146	−0.212
0.100	0.653	0.782	0.246	0.435	0.108	0.664	0.138	−0.228
0.120	0.645	0.802	0.213	0.480	0.092	0.697	0.121	−0.216
0.140	0.640	0.814	0.196	0.507	0.089	0.705	0.107	−0.198

German Credit

β	Accuracy	Eth.Compl.	Male		Female		Disp. mistr.	
			FPR	FNR	FPR	FNR	DFPR	DFNR
(MLP)	0.704	0.490	0.542	0.185	0.413	0.275	0.130	−0.090
0.001	0.688	0.522	0.489	0.229	0.316	0.347	0.173	−0.118
0.030	0.671	0.558	0.436	0.282	0.310	0.357	0.126	−0.075
0.050	0.645	0.611	0.361	0.359	0.319	0.359	0.042	0.000
0.070	0.637	0.603	0.382	0.351	0.286	0.416	0.096	−0.065
0.100	0.625	0.640	0.328	0.403	0.266	0.410	0.062	−0.007
0.120	0.613	0.668	0.288	0.445	0.235	0.418	0.053	0.027
0.140	0.598	0.695	0.242	0.482	0.235	0.448	0.007	0.034

Adult

β	Accuracy	Eth.Compl.	Male		Female		Disp. mistr.	
			FPR	FNR	FPR	FNR	DFPR	DFNR
(MLP)	0.852	0.822	0.106	0.364	0.029	0.459	0.076	−0.095
0.001	0.853	0.831	0.094	0.385	0.023	0.499	0.072	−0.114
0.030	0.852	0.847	0.078	0.427	0.020	0.520	0.058	−0.092
0.050	0.849	0.859	0.068	0.462	0.018	0.554	0.050	−0.092
0.070	0.847	0.871	0.058	0.498	0.015	0.570	0.042	−0.073
0.100	0.841	0.893	0.040	0.564	0.012	0.618	0.028	−0.053
0.150	0.824	0.924	0.022	0.676	0.008	0.712	0.014	−0.036

Default

β	Accuracy	Eth.Compl.	Male		Female		Disp. mistr.	
			FPR	FNR	FPR	FNR	DFPR	DFNR
(MLP)	0.818	0.945	0.063	0.620	0.049	0.640	0.015	−0.020
0.001	0.818	0.947	0.060	0.632	0.045	0.649	0.014	−0.017
0.030	0.818	0.951	0.053	0.654	0.044	0.653	0.009	0.001
0.050	0.819	0.954	0.049	0.669	0.043	0.655	0.006	0.014
0.070	0.818	0.957	0.045	0.687	0.043	0.657	0.002	0.030
0.100	0.817	0.962	0.038	0.718	0.040	0.668	−0.002	0.050

Law school

β	Accuracy	Eth.Compl.	White		Others		Disp. mistr.	
			FPR	FNR	FPR	FNR	DFPR	DFNR
(MLP)	0.829	0.964	0.869	0.009	0.547	0.089	0.322	−0.081
0.001	0.827	0.964	0.873	0.010	0.556	0.091	0.318	−0.081
0.030	0.827	0.971	0.885	0.007	0.617	0.060	0.269	−0.053
0.050	0.827	0.975	0.893	0.006	0.656	0.045	0.237	−0.039
0.070	0.824	0.978	0.909	0.004	0.691	0.037	0.218	−0.032
0.100	0.823	0.983	0.921	0.003	0.740	0.022	0.181	−0.020

this effect is systematic across all the analyzed datasets is a strong evidence of the proposed method as an effective and reliable *in-process* approach to fairness. These datasets in fact represent quite different tasks and domains characterized by different sensible features as well as by different data distributions.

As already noticed, the proposed Ethics by Design inevitably faces some drop-in (business) accuracy, to adjust unfair training data (i.e., gold decisions to be neglected for sake of fairness). However, such a small loss in accuracy corresponds to more balanced (i.e., ethical) decisions: for example, a 0.682 vs. 0.814 increase in ethical compliance in the COMPAS dataset corresponds to a small accuracy loss, 0.681 vs. 0.640.

It seems that tweaking the ethical sensitivity of the method is thus effective. It allows identifying the optimal balance, as an operationally cost-effective compromise, between the business and the ethical performance of the system.

The injection of ethical rules within neural learning seems to be effective in balancing biases that arise within datasets. Biased human judgments are the main cause of errors as statistical surveys suggest. The ethical rules we have defined have reduced this distortion, leading to more ethically effective outcomes. Although not conclusive, this approach results in an improvement.

The suggested framework allows the management of incoming data based on an ethical perspective. When operational decisions are monitored across time, further adjustments through training are possible and incremental ethical optimization is enabled.

5   Conclusions

In this work, we experimented with the Ethics by Design framework, discussed by [21], against quite different biased datasets, such as COMPAS. The tests confirm the method's ability to strongly foster fairness, in order to ensure responsibility and accountability of AI systems' behavior. For example in COMPAS, the results are much better decisions over African Americans, without costs, i.e., with basically no change on any other social group.

This result is systematically achieved in the different datasets adopted at the expense of a more than acceptable loss of (business) performance, which in our view is a very significant result. This confirms the large applicability of the Ethics-by-Design framework [21].

As a future extension, the automatic identification of sensible features and strategies adopted by the model to propose truth-makers against the corresponding "unfair" decisions is under investigation. The possibility of cross-validating the role of different features through quantitative assessment (i.e., the fairness measures proposed) makes it possible to assume an autonomous behavior for auditing the system in search of ethical balancing between social groups.

References

1. Ali, M., Sapiezynski, P., Bogen, M., Korolova, A., Mislove, A., Rieke, A.: Discrimination through optimization: how Facebook's ad delivery can lead to biased outcomes. Proc. ACM Hum.-Comput. Interact. **3**(CSCW), 1–30 (2019)
2. Angwin, J., et al.: Machine bias (2016)
3. Bechavod, Y., Ligett, K.: Penalizing unfairness in binary classification. arXiv preprint arXiv:1707.00044 (2017)
4. Berk, R., et al.: A convex framework for fair regression. arXiv preprint arXiv:1706.02409 (2017)
5. Bonnemains, V., Saurel, C., Tessier, C.: Embedded ethics: some technical and ethical challenges. Ethics Inf. Technol. **20**(1), 41–58 (2018). https://doi.org/10.1007/s10676-018-9444-x
6. Buolamwini, J., Gebru, T.: Gender shades: intersectional accuracy disparities in commercial gender classification. In: Conference on Fairness, Accountability and Transparency, pp. 77–91. PMLR (2018)
7. Calders, T., Verwer, S.: Three Naive Bayes approaches for discrimination-free classification. Data Min. Knowl. Disc. **21**(2), 277–292 (2010)
8. Caton, S., Haas, C.: Fairness in machine learning: a survey. arXiv preprint arXiv:2010.04053 (2020)
9. Donini, M., Oneto, L., Ben-David, S., Shawe-Taylor, J., Pontil, M.: Empirical risk minimization under fairness constraints. arXiv preprint arXiv:1802.08626 (2018)
10. Feldman, M., Friedler, S.A., Moeller, J., Scheidegger, C., Venkatasubramanian, S.: Certifying and removing disparate impact. In: Proceedings of the KDD 2015, pp. 259–268 (2015)
11. Hardt, M., Price, E., Srebro, N.: Equality of opportunity in supervised learning. In: Advances in Neural Information Processing Systems, vol. 29, pp. 3315–3323 (2016)
12. Ingold, D., Soper, S.: Amazon doesn't consider the race of its customers. Should it? (2016)
13. Kamiran, F., Calders, T.: Classifying without discriminating. In: 2009 2nd International Conference on Computer, Control and Communication, pp. 1–6. IEEE (2009)
14. Kamishima, T., Akaho, S., Asoh, H., Sakuma, J.: Fairness-aware classifier with prejudice remover regularizer. In: Flach, P.A., De Bie, T., Cristianini, N. (eds.) ECML PKDD 2012. LNCS (LNAI), vol. 7524, pp. 35–50. Springer, Heidelberg (2012). https://doi.org/10.1007/978-3-642-33486-3_3
15. Kleiman-Weiner, M., Saxe, R., Tenenbaum, J.B.: Learning a commonsense moral theory. Cognition **167**, 107–123 (2017). Moral Learning
16. Lambrecht, A., Tucker, C.: Algorithmic bias? An empirical study of apparent gender-based discrimination in the display of stem career ads. Manag. Sci. **65**(7), 2966–2981 (2019)
17. Lungren, M.: Risks of AI race detection in the medical system (2021)
18. Mehrabi, N., Morstatter, F., Saxena, N., Lerman, K., Galstyan, A.: A survey on bias and fairness in machine learning. ACM Comput. Surv. (CSUR) **54**(6), 1–35 (2021)
19. Pessach, D., Shmueli, E.: Algorithmic fairness. arXiv preprint arXiv:2001.09784 (2020)
20. Quy, T.L., Roy, A., Iosifidis, V., Ntoutsi, E.: A survey on datasets for fairness-aware machine learning. arXiv preprint arXiv:2110.00530 (2021)

21. Rossini, D., Croce, D., Mancini, S., Pellegrino, M., Basili, R.: Actionable ethics through neural learning. In: Proceedings of the AAAI Conference on Artificial Intelligence, vol. 34, pp. 5537–5544 (2020)

22. Savani, Y., White, C., Govindarajulu, N.S.: Intra-processing methods for debiasing neural networks. arXiv preprint arXiv:2006.08564, vol. 33, pp. 2798–2810 (2020)

23. Snow, J.: Amazon's face recognition falsely matched 28 members of congress with mugshots (2018)

24. Vanderelst, D., Winfield, A.: An architecture for ethical robots inspired by the simulation theory of cognition. Cogn. Syst. Res. **48**, 56–66 (2018). Cognitive Architectures for Artificial Minds

25. Zafar, M.B., Valera, I., Gomez Rodriguez, M., Gummadi, K.P.: Fairness beyond disparate treatment & disparate impact: learning classification without disparate mistreatment. In: Proceedings of the 26th International Conference on World Wide Web, pp. 1171–1180 (2017)

Automated Planning and Scheduling

Verification of Numeric Planning Problems Through Domain Dynamic Consistency

Enrico Scala[1] , Thomas L. McCluskey[2] , and Mauro Vallati[2(✉)]

[1] Università degli Studi di Brescia, Brescia, Italy
[2] University of Huddersfield, Huddersfield, UK
m.vallati@hud.ac.uk

Abstract. Verification of the development of complex problem models is an open problem in real-world applications of automated planning. To facilitate the verification task, this paper introduces the notion of Domain Dynamic Consistency for planning problems expressed in PDDL. This notion is aimed at signalling suspicious inputs arising at the intersection between the abstract description of the model and its concrete instantiation. Together with the notion we present an approximation based approach that is devoted to automatically solve the problem of deciding when a PDDL numeric planning problem is not Domain Dynamic Consistent. The paper terminates with an example of application of this notion and its related technique within a Urban Traffic Control scenario.

Keywords: Automated planning · Numeric planning · Verification

1 Introduction

AI Planning is an important research area of Artificial Intelligence that deals with the problem of finding a sequence of actions whose application in an initial state of the environment leads to a desired goal state [12]. Automated planning is exploited in many real-world applications as it is a common capability requirement for intelligent autonomous agents [18]. Example application domains include drilling [11], smart grid [28], machine tool calibration [20], and mining [16].

Modelling AI planning problems is a challenging and error-prone tasks, as even small mistakes can compromise the validity of a representation. In real-world planning applications, where knowledge is acquired from different sources, the verification of the problem model is crucial. This may be caused both by some erroneous input done by the user, or by some automatic tool that does not work properly. For instance, one can simply forget to mention the initial value of a variable and this may indirectly cause some other variable to be not changeable anymore. Syntactic errors are easily recognised, whilst more profound interactions among the variables are difficult to intercept.

A. Dovier et al. (Eds.): AIxIA 2022, LNAI 13796, pp. 171–183, 2023.
https://doi.org/10.1007/978-3-031-27181-6_12

Verification of a problem model means demonstrating that it is a correct implementation of the abstract or conceptual model. One important aspect of this is checking that the implementation does not introduce errors or behaviours inconsistent with the conceptual model. To help address this problem, we propose the notion of Domain Dynamic Consistency (DDC) of a planning problem, and illustrate its use in problems expressed in the Planning Domain Definition Language (PDDL), the standard de-facto language used by the AI Planning community. Intuitively, we say that a planning problem is DDC if each variable that is present in the initial state is fluent in the same way in which it is fluent in the model of domain dynamics. Consider the problem involving a robot that can move in a metric uni-dimensional space. Assume that variable x is used to model its position, and that the movement of such a robot is modelled through a single move-right PDDL action, whose precondition requires the fuel to be at least of one unit. Further assume that the effects simply state that the position of the robot is increased by 1 unit anytime the action is applied. Now consider a state where the position of the robot is such that $x = 1$, and the fuel is equal to 1. The initial state, and therefore the planning problem, is DDC in that the only fluent variable that we are modelling can indeed be increased by 1 unit. Let us consider another situation. This time, assume a state has variable x set to 1 (as before) but the fuel is instead equal to 0. According to our definition, this state is not DDC in that the variable can never be increased. Although this does not represent an issue from a semantics perspective in that it is perfectly possible given the domain and the problem instance, this is somewhat a suspicious situation for an initial state; why would a state like this one make any sense at all if we cannot even model the movement of the robot? Why did we bother modelling its position and its modification, if this position cannot actually be changed? Though the illustration above is simple, in reality, when initial states are complex and/or auto-generated, this property helps to uncover errors in the verification and validation process.

Other works have looked into the problem of verification and validation of planning problems, e.g., [3,8,22,27]. Yet, to the best of our knowledge, none has investigated the problem through the lens of planning *with* numeric information [9] and *without* the need to express some additional explicit knowledge (e.g., through Linear Temporal Logic [6,21]).

In this study we formally characterise the notion of DDC focusing on PDDL 2.1, the extension of PDDL that lets the user explicitly express numeric conditions and numeric changes. First, we discuss the general difficulty of the apparently simple problem of checking problems for DDC, observing that in general terms deciding when an initial state is DDC is as hard as solving a planning problem. To overcome this barrier we present an approximation schema and show how this can be used to verify whether a planning problem is not DDC. Finally, we show an example of the use of the DDC in strategy generation for Urban Traffic Control.

The remainder of this paper is organised as follows. Section 2 provides the necessary background. Then, the Domain Dynamic Consistency notion is intro-

duced, and Sect. 4 presents an approach to test the DDC property. The usefulness of the notion is then assessed using a case study, that is presented in Sect. 5.
Finally, conclusions are given.

2 Background

This section provides the necessary background on numeric planning, the corresponding definition of a numeric planning problem, and on the additive interval-
based relaxation.

2.1 Numeric Planning

We consider planning problems [12] as those that can be expressed in PDDL2.1
level 2 [9]. These problems are called numeric planning problems [25], but we
will in the rest simply refer to planning problems. Without loss of generality, we
restrict our attention to the case with untyped objects, and with only numeric
fluents[1] (see below). A full treatment of the syntax and semantics of the language
is beyond the scope of this work; the full details can be found in [9]. Next, we
provide only those aspects necessary to understand our proposal.

A planning problem consists of two elements: a domain model and a problem model. Following the PDDL terminology, the domain model contains the
definition of the predicates, the numeric fluents, and a set of actions. In particular, numeric fluents indicate properties of lists of objects; mathematically, they
define mappings between lists of objects to numeric values. The domain model
defines them in an abstract way: it specifies a name, a string label for each such
mapping, and a list of variables. Variables specify the order and the number of
objects to be mapped.

An action a is defined by means of a name (which we will often omit
in the interest of space), a list of variables (called the parameters of the
actions), a precondition formula (i.e., $pre(a)$) and a set of effects (i.e., $eff(a)$).
The precondition formula is a first-order logic proposition having equalities or
inequalities involving numeric fluents as terms (e.g., (> (battery ?r1) 4) $\land$
(> (battery ?r2) 5)). Each formula can make use of the standard logical connectives from propositional logic, i.e., $\land, \lor, \neg$, together with arbitrary nesting
of universal ($\forall$) and existential ($\exists$) quantifier over the objects of the problem.
Effects are triplets of the form $\langle\{inc, dec, ass\}, x, \xi\rangle$, where the first term is the
modifier, and can either be an increase (i.e., inc), a decrease (i.e., dec) or an
assignment (i.e., ass), the second term is a numeric fluent, and the third term
is a numeric expression that together with the modifier determines the state of
the numeric fluent if the action is applied.

Each numeric fluent in the action structure can have its parameters expressed
as concrete objects (i.e., actual objects of the problem to be solved) or variables.
When all parameters are concrete objects, a numeric fluent is said to be ground.

---

[1] A Boolean fluent can be mapped into a $\{0, 1\}$ numeric fluent.

Similarly, an action with all parameters and free variables substituted with concrete objects is said to be ground. This also requires to eliminate all quantifiers in the preconditions using standard quantifier elimination techniques. In this work we focus on actions whose effects can increase, decrease or assign the value to a numeric fluent by means of a constant (e.g., (increase (battery ?r1) 5.4)).

A domain model is a tuple $\langle \mathcal{X}, A \rangle$ where $\mathcal{X}$ is the numeric fluents set as above, and A the set of actions. Let $\mathcal{O}$ be a set of objects and x a numeric fluent from $\mathcal{X}$. The grounding of x is the set of numeric fluents each having the same name of x but the list of variables replaced with concrete objects from some subset of $\mathcal{O}$. The set of ground numeric fluents given $\mathcal{O}$ is denoted by $\mathcal{X}[\mathcal{O}]$. Finally, we use $abs(x)$ to denote the abstraction of an object x into a variable, i.e., the ungrounded version of the numeric fluent.

A state s gives a value to each numeric fluent in $\mathcal{X}[\mathcal{O}]$. The domain of each numeric fluent is the set of rational number plus the special term $\perp$; $\perp$ is used to state that a given numeric fluent is undefined. Let $x \in \mathcal{X}$ and s be a state, we denote with $[x]_s$ the value of numeric fluent x in state s. Then, we use $succ(s)$ for the set of states reachable by s through actions from A. For more information on what a ground action is, and how actions can be grounded automatically, look at [14] and [26].

A ground action is applicable in state s iff its precondition is satisfied in s. A precondition is satisfied iff, by assigning all numeric fluents their values as for state s, the evaluation of the formula returns true. The application of a ground action in a state s generates a new state $s' = s[a]$ such that all numeric fluents conform with the effects of the action. For instance, if an action features a numeric effect $\langle inc, x, 1 \rangle$ and the state is such that $x = 1$, then the successor state will be such that $x = 2$.

A problem model is given by a set of objects, a state, called the initial state, and a goal. The goal is structured as the precondition of an action, with the difference that any component which is not quantified only involves ground numeric fluents. A problem model is formally expressed as a tuple $\langle \mathcal{O}, I, G \rangle$. The combination of a domain and a problem instance is a planning problem $\mathcal{P} = \langle D, P \rangle$. A plan for a planning problem is a sequence of actions τ such that τ can be iteratively applied starting from the initial state I, and the last produced state is one where the goal G is satisfied.

2.2   Problem Relaxation and Heuristics

A popular technique to finding plans for planning problems is that of performing a search over the state space induced by the problem. In order to make such a search effective, planners usually employ heuristics devised directly from the description of the problem, and a very solid approach to make that happen is to extract such a heuristic from a proper relaxation of the problem itself [5]. State space planners use these two facilities during search by avoiding the exploration of dead-ends states, and by steering the search only towards the most promising paths. Heuristics that well approximate the cost to reach the goal can lead the search to only explore a linear number of states on the length of the optimal path.

The Additive Interval-Based Relaxation (AIBR) of a numeric planning problem is a relaxation specifically designed to support problems involving complex numeric expressions. As many other relaxations (e.g., [5,7,25]), the AIBR serves two purposes in state-space planners: the former is to prune states and the latter is providing the basis for computing heuristic estimates [2,15,24]. Pruning is given by the ability of the AIBR to correctly identify when a state does not allow the planner to reach the goal. Heuristic estimates can be computed by finding concrete relaxed plan, that is, plans that solve the problem at a relaxation level. As hinted at above, the additive interval-based relaxation belongs to the family of frameworks that tries to exploit as much as possible the structure of the problem expressed in some language, in our case PDDL. This means that the user can take advantage of induced heuristics without the need of providing them manually.

The relaxation at the basis of the AIBR grounds on a reinterpretation of the semantics of the numeric planning problem. Such a reinterpretation guarantees to over-approximate whether some goal or subgoal is reachable. Indeed AIBR is able to correctly identify unsolvable problems with an algorithm that is polynomial on the size of the problem. It does so with the following expedients. First, under AIBR, a planning state is not a single valuation for each numeric fluent. Rather, each numeric fluent x is mapped into an interval (x^-, x^+) defining the minimum (i.e., x^-) and the maximum (i.e., x^+) value for x; this way, a AIBR planning relaxed state approximates a concrete state with a number of intervals. Each such interval approximates all values that can ever be attained by a single numeric fluent. Second, the AIBR changes the way satisfiability of a formula is evaluated. Instead of operating using standard arithmetic operations, it uses interval analysis [19]. That is, let s be some state, an inequality in some formula is evaluated using interval enclosures of the possible evaluation of the numeric fluents it encompasses. Then a generic propositional formula is evaluated by combining the evaluated terms recursively navigating a tree-shaped formula up to the root. Finally, whenever an action is applied in the AIBR, the result is given by the convex union of the interval for each variable associated with the state in which the action is applied, and the interval associated to the state obtained by applying the effects of the action. This way, the successor state monotonically accepts the values of the state in which the action is applied, and the new values that can be obtained by the execution of the action. Because of this, all formulas that are satisfied before the execution of the action are also satisfied after its application. To make this process run for a finite number of times, the AIBR makes use of the notion of asymptotic supporters. Intuitively, each asymptotic supporter makes the effect of an action idempotent, therefore limiting the number of iterations needed to estimate the relaxed reachability of a condition.

The AIBR is not the only heuristic seen in the literature. For instance, [25] defines subgoaling-based relaxations that work with a different principle. Albeit such relaxations can provide more guidance, they are focused more on improving on the performances of state-space planners. The AIBR on the other hand aims at handling general numeric planning problems, which is what we target in this paper.

3   Domain Dynamic Consistency

Modelling planning problems using abstract, parametrized actions (also known as lifted actions) is very convenient. Indeed, one may encode compactly several actual transitions by just declaring the types of the variables the actions depend on. However, the plans that are going to be executed are composed by ground actions only. That is, actions where all variables are substituted with concrete objects from some particular problem model. While the modelling of abstract actions make things much more elegant, it may introduce some false expectations too. We argue that when one model an action at an abstract level, it is very likely that if some set of objects compatible with that action have most but not all object relevant conditions in the action preconditions satisfiable, some modelling bug may have occurred at the level of the problem formulation. And this may be related to the fact that one condition that we were expecting to be satisfiable at some point, it is actually not satisfiable because it does not follow the dynamics that we were expecting at an abstract level.

To capture situations as this one, we formalise the notion of Dynamic Domain Consistency. Roughly speaking we say that a problem is dynamic domain consistent if and only if, whenever we have some object fluent that is expected to be dynamic at an abstract level, this object is dynamic at a ground level too. Though, we focus our attention on numeric fluents only, as we expect these can be the main source of domain inconsistencies.

In what follows we formalise the notion of Domain Dynamic Consistency (DDC). DDC is a property that is desired by some particular state. Such a notion makes sense when the state is evaluated in a planning problem context.

Definition 1 (Domain Dynamic Consistency). *Let* $\mathcal{P} = \langle D, P \rangle$ *be a planning problem such that* $D = \langle \mathcal{X}, A \rangle$ *and* $P = \langle \mathcal{O}, I, G \rangle$. *We say that* $\mathcal{P}$ *is Domain Dynamic Consistent (DDC) iff* $\forall x \in \mathcal{X}[\mathcal{O}]$ *it holds that*

- *if* $\exists \langle inc, y, k \rangle \in \mathit{eff}(a)$ *for some* $a \in A$ *with* $k > 0$ *s.t.* $y = x$ *or* $y = abs(x)$ *then* $\exists s' \in succ(I)$ *s.t.* $[x]_I < [x]_{s'}$
- *if* $\exists \langle dec, y, k \rangle \in \mathit{eff}(a)$ *for some* $a \in A$ *with* $k > 0$ *s.t.* $y = x$ *or* $y = abs(x)$ *then* $\exists s' \in succ(I)$ *s.t.* $[x]_I > [x]_{s'}$
- *if* $\exists \langle ass, y, k \rangle \in \mathit{eff}(a)$ *for some* $a \in A$ *with* $k \neq [x]_I$ *s.t.* $y = x$ *or* $y = abs(x)$ *then* $\exists s' \in succ(I)$ *s.t.* $[x]_{s'} = k$

Intuitively, the notion establishes that a planning problem is DDC if each numeric fluent mentioned in the initial state is dynamic, i.e. if actions in the domain model enable the numeric fluent to dynamically change, at an abstract level. We are interested in determining if that is the case. To understand whether this property is generally true for well formed and operational planning problems, we considered a range of well known numeric benchmark instances [23]. The set includes the following domains: Counters, Plant-watering, Block-grouping, Sailing, and Farmland. We manually checked all the instances of the benchmarks, and observed that all of them are DDC. In all the considered instances, all the numeric fluents that can be modified via actions are indeed initially set to be modifiable. This empirical evidence gives a solid ground to support our intuition, and suggests that it can provide a meaningful way to verify initial states. Of course, the considered instances are very easy to be checked, given their simple structure. Yet, and that is also where the DDC notion can be helpful, real-world planning applications can lead to problem models that are complex and large. An example will be given in Sect. 5. It can be proven that, in general, checking the DDC is indeed much more involved.

Proposition 1. *Deciding whether a planning problem is DDC is undecidable.*

Proof (Sketch). Observe that deciding whether a planning problem is DDC is as hard as finding a solution plan for it. Indeed, we can emulate a planning problem by encoding the goal into the precondition of a dummy action having a single numeric effect. Then we make sure that this action is necessary to solve the problem. To do so we introduce a fresh numeric fluent initially set to a random number, say 0, and model a numeric effect for this action to set the fresh numeric variable to 1. Checking whether this problem is DDC necessitates making sure that the precondition of this action is achievable. Therefore, this is possible iff the original problem admits a solution. As numeric planning is undecidable [13], so is the problem of verifying whether a planning problem is DDC.

4 Approximating Domain Dynamic Consistency

To overcome the complexity of determining if a planning problem $\mathcal{P}$ is DDC, we approximate the DDC checking through the additive interval-based relaxation [1,24].

We make use of the AIBR for a different purpose than that employed in state-space planners (e.g., [15,24]). Our objective is not to provide a heuristic estimate or doing pruning. Instead, we aim at evaluating the DDC of a problem. As a very first step, we run the AIBR up to fix point – note that such a fix point does exist and can be computed efficiently because of the use of asymptotic supporters. This gives us an interval for each associated variable. Then we use such intervals to predict whether the conditions of Definition 1 are satisfied. More precisely, for each variable for which we know that there exists an action that can change its value abstractly, we see whether this may happen also at the ground level. We do so for each of the conditions that we want to evaluate.

Algorithm 1 reports the AIBR reachability algorithm [24], slightly modified to return the last relaxed state obtained after fix-point computation. Algorithm 2 describes how to use Algorithm 1 to approximate the DDC of a problem w.r.t. a

---

Algorithm 1: AIBR (slightly revisited from Scala et al. 2016)

Input: $\mathcal{P}^{++}$
Output: The set of intervals at the asymptotic fix-point
1 $\Omega = $ supporters of A.
2 $s^+ = s_0^+$.
3 $S = \{a \in \Omega : s^+ \models pre(a)\}$
4 **while** $S \neq \emptyset$ **do**
5 $\quad\quad s^+ = \text{succ}^+(s^+, S)$
6 $\quad\quad \Omega = \Omega \backslash S$
7 $\quad\quad S = \{a \in \Omega : s^+ \models pre(a)\}$
8 **return** s^+

Algorithm 2: DDC Approximation

Input: $\mathcal{P} = \langle D, P \rangle$
Output: Is $\mathcal{P}$ Domain Dynamic Consistent?
1 $\mathcal{P}_g = \text{grounding}(\mathcal{P})$
2 $s^+ = AIBR(\mathcal{P}_g^{++})$
3 **foreach** $x \in X_P$ **do**
4 $\quad\quad$ **foreach** $a \in A_D$ such that $\exists \langle x', +=, k \rangle \in \textit{eff}(a).x' = abs(x) \wedge k > 0$ **do**
5 $\quad\quad\quad$ **if** $up([x]_{s^+}) = [x]_{P_I}$ **then**
6 $\quad\quad\quad\quad$ **return** *False*
7 $\quad\quad$ **foreach** $a \in A_D$ such that $\exists \langle x', -=, k \rangle \in \textit{eff}(a).x' = abs(x) \wedge k > 0$ **do**
8 $\quad\quad\quad$ **if** $lo([x]_{s^+}) = [x]_{P_I}$ **then**
9 $\quad\quad\quad\quad$ **return** *False*
10 $\quad\quad$ **foreach** $a \in A_D$ such that $\exists \langle x', =, k \rangle \in \textit{eff}(a).x' = abs(x) \wedge k \neq [x]_{P_I}$ **do**
11 $\quad\quad\quad$ **if** $k \notin [x]_{s^+}$ **then**
12 $\quad\quad\quad\quad$ **return** *False*
13 **return** *True*

---

domain. For any fluent x, $[x]_{s^+}$ is used to denote the interval of values for x in s^+. $lo([x]_{s^+})$ and $up([x]_{s^+})$ denote the minimum and maximum value, respectively.

Algorithm 2 works as follows. First, it grounds the planning problem, obtaining $\mathcal{P}_g$; AIBR indeed is defined for fully grounded problems only. Then it calls the AIBR specified by Algorithm 1. This algorithm returns the fix point AIBR planning state. Then, we iterate over all the variables that are expressed in the initial state of P. This set is denoted by X_P. For each action that abstractly modifies the variable under iteration, we distinguish the three possible effects of an action on the variable: an increase, a decrease and an assignment. If the action abstractly increases (decreases) the value of a numeric fluent x, then we check whether the interval for x at the fix point s^+ has increased (decreased) the variable. This is done by inspecting the lower and the upper bound of the interval (function lo and up in the code), and determining whether the fix-point value admits an increase, a decrease, or the foreseen assignment; for the assignment it suffices to check whether the interval at fix point does not include the value k. For instance, if we have a variable x with an initial value of 0, an effect $\langle inx, x', 5 \rangle$ where x' is the abstracted version of x, a fixpoint $[x]_{s+} = [-\inf, 0]$ will imply that x is never going to be increased, even if it was supposed to do so at an abstract level. If at least one of these cases is not satisfied, the algorithm returns that the problem is not DDC. Otherwise it carries on and explores the next variable from X_p.

Algorithm 2 correctly identifies whether a problem is not DDC and can thus be used to signal suspicious situations.

Proposition 2. *If Algorithm 2 returns False for a problem $\mathcal{P}$, then $\mathcal{P}$ is not DDC.*

Proof (Sketch). Observe that the algorithm terminates with True only for those cases where the relaxation proves that one variable violates Definition 1. AIBR overestimates all values that can ever be obtained. If some value is not reached under AIBR, it is not reachable in real semantics either.

5   The Case of Urban Traffic Control

Urban traffic control (UTC) aims at optimising traffic flows in urban areas by reducing travel time delays and avoiding congestion of road links. One possibility, which is usually considered by traffic authorities, is configuring traffic lights on the intersections [17,29]. A *traffic signal configuration* of an intersection is defined by a sequence of green light phases, each with its specified duration, that, in consequence, affects the traffic movement through the intersection. Traffic movements are described in terms of Passenger Car Units (PCUs) that on average can move from incoming to outgoing links of the intersection. Traffic signal configurations operate in cycles, i.e. the sequences of green phases they define are being repeated (until the configuration changes). When specifying a configuration, we need to keep in mind any rules governing minimum and maximum green phase length. In addition, we also need to respect the constraints on minimum and maximum duration of entire cycles as well. Intergreens typically have specified durations which we are not allowed to change.

This section shows an UTC instance where the notion of DDC can be used to capture when the PDDL encoding of the UTC is faulty because of some erroneous input in defining the problem.

A UTC problem includes the definition of two actions modelling extension and reduction of the length of the default green time for a *stage s* in a *junction j*. The PDDL abstract model for such two actions is reported in Fig. 1.

To change the default green time for a phase, several conditions have to be satisfied; focusing on numeric conditions, time needs to be less than the maximum green time or higher than the minimum green time. It is important, therefore, that both the minimum green time and the maximum green time are

```
(:action extendStage
    :parameters (?p1 - stage ?i - junction)
    :precondition (and (controllable ?i)
        (contains ?i ?p1)
        (active ?p1)
        (< (defaultgreentime ?p1)
        (maxgreentime ?p1))
        (< (cycletime ?i) (maxcycletime ?i)))
    :effect (and
        (increase (defaultgreentime ?p1) (granularity))
        (increase (cycletime ?i) (granularity))))
(:action reduceStage
    :parameters (?p1 - stage ?i - junction)
    :precondition (and (controllable ?i)
        (contains ?i ?p1)
        (active ?p1)
        (> (defaultgreentime ?p1) (mingreentime ?p1))
        (> (cycletime ?i) (mincycletime ?i)))
    :effect (and
        (decrease (defaultgreentime ?p1) (granularity))
        (decrease (cycletime ?i) (granularity))))
```

Fig. 1. Snippet of PDDL UTC model. All blocks find a direct correspondence to the more mathematical formalisation provided in Sect. 2.

properly set in order to give room to the planner to modify the value of the default green time if necessary.

Figure 2 shows an excerpt of a problem specification. Notably, UTC problem specifications include knowledge pulled from a range of different data sources, that may therefore be inconsistent or noisy and need to be carefully verified [4]. Further, the models are large, composed by thousands of lines, making manual verification unfeasible. Run over the problem of Fig. 2, Algorithm 2 yields a fix-point interval state where (defaultgreentime wrac1_stage1) is any value between $-\infty$ and ∞. Instead, in the considered excerpt, the value of (defaultgreentime wrac1_ stage2) will never change through time. Indeed, neither reduceStage nor extendStage can be applied. The default green time is not within the minimum and maximum green time. Although this is not a problem modelling wise, the notion of DDC detects this as a suspicious situation. The abstract version of default green time is non static due to the actions of Fig. 1. Yet, there is a concrete specialisation, (defaultgreentime wrac1_stage2) that is static, and this makes the problem to be non consistent w.r.t. the domain. Because such a problem is deemed as non Domain Dynamic Consistent, the user can be alarmed and fix the problem accordingly, i.e., modifying the minimum green time variable for wrac1_stage2 to a consistent value.

Using a prototype implementation of the presented algorithm on real-world data, we were able to quickly identify a dozen of issues and inconsistencies on automatically generated UTC initial states, effectively addressing the issues rais-

```
(:objects
    wrac1 - junction
    ...
    wrac1_stage1 wrac1_stage2 - stage)
(:init
    (= (granularity) 10.0)
    (active wrac1_stage1)
    (active wrac1_stage2)
    (= (cycletime wrac1) 100)
    (= (maxcycletime wrac1) 200)
    (= (mincycletime wrac1) 50)
    (= (defaultgreentime wrac1_stage1) 45)
    (= (defaultgreentime wrac1_stage2) 14)
    (controllable wrac1)
    (contains wrac1 wrac1_stage1)
    (contains wrac1 wrac1_stage2)
    (= (mingreentime wrac1_stage1 ) 10 )
    (= (maxgreentime wrac1_stage1 ) 120 )
    (= (mingreentime wrac1_stage2 ) 15 )
    (= (maxgreentime wrac1_stage2 ) 120 )
    ...
```

Fig. 2. Snippet of a UTC problem, presenting some elements of a single junction with two stages. In PDDL syntax, the block ":init" is the initial state; ":objects" define the universe of objects.

ing from pulling data from different sources. The use of DDC also allowed to identify unforeseen failure points of the knowledge acquisition process. For instance, we identified a case where one junction went offline and did not communicate its status (missing `defaultgreentime` value).

6   Conclusion

The use of automated planning in real-world applications, particularly when instances are generating by including data pulled together from a range of sources, comes with the challenge of verifying that the resulting instances are consistent. In this paper, to address the above-mentioned challenge, we introduced the notion of Domain Dynamic Consistency (DDC) to identify instances that may not behave as expected. The notion of DDC can be used as a means to verify the knowledge acquisition process of a planning problem initial state, and the fact that pulled data provide a consistent overall figure.

The DDC notion has been captured in PDDL, a well known formalism used by the planning community. This notion can be useful in contexts where one wants to have an automatic mechanism to inspect suspicious input. The idea being that DDC does not necessarily identify mistakes, but can flag aspects that are suspicious and deserve in-depth investigation. We then presented a sound technique to prove when a problem is not DDC, that leverages on existing numeric relaxation-based heuristics. Finally, we provided an example application where the use of DDC helped in catching a number of issues in large PDDL models.

We see several avenues for future work. First, we are interested in extending the DDC notion to more complex planning formalisms, for instance PDDL+ [10]. Second, we plan to develop a suitable interface to allow non-planning experts to take advantage of this technique. Finally, we are interested in exploiting the DDC notion also to suggest potential issues of the domain models, to provide a tool that can also help in revising and improving the planning models used.

Acknowledgements. Mauro Vallati was supported by a UKRI Future Leaders Fellowship [grant number MR/T041196/1]. Enrico Scala has been partially supported by AIPlan4EU, a project funded by EU Horizon 2020 research and innovation programme under GA n. 101016442, and by the Italian MUR programme PRIN 2020, Prot.20203FFYLK (RIPER – Resilient AI-Based Self-Programming and Strategic Reasoning).

References

1. Aldinger, J., Mattmüller, R., Göbelbecker, M.: Complexity of interval relaxed numeric planning. In: Hölldobler, S., Krötzsch, M., Peñaloza, R., Rudolph, S. (eds.) KI 2015. LNCS (LNAI), vol. 9324, pp. 19–31. Springer, Cham (2015). https://doi.org/10.1007/978-3-319-24489-1_2

2. Aldinger, J., Nebel, B.: Interval based relaxation heuristics for numeric planning with action costs. In: Kern-Isberner, G., Fürnkranz, J., Thimm, M. (eds.) KI 2017. LNCS (LNAI), vol. 10505, pp. 15–28. Springer, Cham (2017). https://doi.org/10.1007/978-3-319-67190-1_2

3. Bensalem, S., Havelund, K., Orlandini, A.: Verification and validation meet planning and scheduling. Int. J. Softw. Tools Technol. Transf. **16**(1), 1–12 (2014)

4. Bhatnagar, S., Mund, S., Scala, E., McCabe, K., McCluskey, L., Vallati, M.: On the challenges of on-the-fly knowledge acquisition for automated planning applications. In: 14th International Conference on Agents and Artificial Intelligence (2022)

5. Bonet, B., Geffner, H.: Planning as heuristic search. Artif. Intell. **129**(1–2), 5–33 (2001)

6. De Giacomo, G., Vardi, M.: Synthesis for LTL and LDL on finite traces. In: Proceedings of the International Joint Conference on Artificial Intelligence (IJCAI), pp. 1558–1564. AAAI Press (2015)

7. Edelkamp, S., Kissmann, P.: Partial symbolic pattern databases for optimal sequential planning. In: Dengel, A.R., Berns, K., Breuel, T.M., Bomarius, F., Roth-Berghofer, T.R. (eds.) KI 2008. LNCS (LNAI), vol. 5243, pp. 193–200. Springer, Heidelberg (2008). https://doi.org/10.1007/978-3-540-85845-4_24

8. Fourati, F., Bhiri, M.T., Robbana, R.: Verification and validation of PDDL descriptions using Event-B formal method. In: Proceedings of the 5th International Conference on Multimedia Computing and Systems (ICMCS), pp. 770–776 (2016)

9. Fox, M., Long, D.: PDDL2.1: an extension to PDDL for expressing temporal planning domains. J. Artif. Intell. Res. **20**, 61–124 (2003)

10. Fox, M., Long, D.: Modelling mixed discrete-continuous domains for planning. CoRR abs/1110.2200 (2011)

11. Fox, M., Long, D., Tamboise, G., Isangulov, R.: Creating and executing a well construction/operation plan. uS Patent App. 15/541,381 (2018)
12. Ghallab, M., Nau, D.S., Traverso, P.: Automated Planning and Acting. Cambridge University Press, Cambridge (2016)
13. Helmert, M.: Decidability and undecidability results for planning with numerical state variables. In: Proceedings of the Sixth International Conference on Artificial Intelligence Planning Systems (AIPS), pp. 44–53. AAAI (2002)
14. Helmert, M.: Concise finite-domain representations for PDDL planning tasks. Artif. Intell. **173**(5–6), 503–535 (2009)
15. Hoffmann, J.: The Metric-FF planning system: translating "ignoring delete lists" to numeric state variables. J. Artif. Intell. Res. **20**, 291–341 (2003)
16. Lipovetzky, N., Burt, C.N., Pearce, A.R., Stuckey, P.J.: Planning for mining operations with time and resource constraints. In: Proceedings of the International Conference on Automated Planning and Scheduling (2014)
17. McCluskey, T.L., Vallati, M., Franco, S.: Automated planning for urban traffic management. In: Proceedings of the International Joint Conference on Artificial Intelligence (IJCAI), pp. 5238–5240 (2017)
18. McCluskey, T.L., Vaquero, T.S., Vallati, M.: Engineering knowledge for automated planning: towards a notion of quality. In: Proceedings of the Knowledge Capture Conference, K-CAP, pp. 14:1–14:8 (2017)
19. Moore, R.E., Kearfott, R.B., Cloud, M.J.: Introduction to Interval Analysis. SIAM (2009)
20. Parkinson, S., Longstaff, A., Fletcher, S.: Automated planning to minimise uncertainty of machine tool calibration. Eng. Appl. Artif. Intell. **30**, 63–72 (2014)
21. Pnueli, A.: The temporal semantics of concurrent programs. In: Proceedings of Semantics of Concurrent Computation, pp. 1–20 (1979)
22. Raimondi, F., Pecheur, C., Brat, G.: PDVer, a tool to verify PDDL planning domains. In: Proceedings of Workshop on Verification and Validation of Planning and Scheduling Systems, ICAPS (2009)
23. Scala, E., Haslum, P., Thiébaux, S.: Heuristics for numeric planning via subgoaling. In: Proceedings of the International Joint Conference on Artificial Intelligence (IJCAI), pp. 3228–3234. IJCAI/AAAI Press (2016)
24. Scala, E., Haslum, P., Thiébaux, S., Ramírez, M.: Interval-based relaxation for general numeric planning. In: Proceedings of the 22nd European Conference on Artificial Intelligence (ECAI), pp. 655–663 (2016)
25. Scala, E., Haslum, P., Thiébaux, S., Ramírez, M.: Subgoaling techniques for satisficing and optimal numeric planning. J. Artif. Intell. Res. **68**, 691–752 (2020)
26. Scala, E., Vallati, M.: Exploiting classical planning grounding in hybrid PDDL+ planning engines. In: Proceedings of the 32nd IEEE International Conference on Tools with Artificial Intelligence (ICTAI), pp. 85–92 (2020)
27. Shrinah, A., Eder, K.: Goal-constrained planning domain model verification of safety properties. In: STAIRS@ECAI (2020)
28. Thiébaux, S., Coffrin, C., Hijazi, H., Slaney, J.: Planning with MIP for supply restoration in power distribution systems. In: Proceedings of the International Joint Conference on Artificial Intelligence (2013)
29. Vallati, M., Magazzeni, D., Schutter, B.D., Chrpa, L., McCluskey, T.L.: Efficient macroscopic urban traffic models for reducing congestion: a PDDL+ planning approach. In: Proceedings of the Thirtieth AAAI Conference on Artificial Intelligence, pp. 3188–3194 (2016)

Comparing Multi-Agent Path Finding Algorithms in a Real Industrial Scenario

Enrico Saccon$^{(\boxtimes)}$, Luigi Palopoli , and Marco Roveri

University of Trento, Trento, Italy
{enrico.saccon,luigi.palopoli,marco.roveri}@unitn.it

Abstract. There is an increasing trend for automating warehouses and factories leveraging on teams of autonomous agents. The orchestration problem for a fleet of autonomous robotic cooperating agents has been tackled in the literature as Multi-Agent Path Finding (MAPF), for which several algorithms have been proposed. However, these algorithms have been only applied to synthetic randomly generated scenarios. The application in real scenarios demands scalability (being able to deal with realistic size warehouses) and efficiency (being able to quickly adapt to changes in the problems, e.g., new orders or change in their priorities).
In this work we perform an analysis of the MAPF literature, we selected the most effective algorithms, we implemented them and we carried out an experimental analysis on a real scalable warehouse of a large distribution company to evaluate their applicability in such scenarios.
The results show that a) no algorithm prevails on the others; b) there are difficult (realistic) cases out of the scope of all the algorithms.

1 Introduction

Robots are becoming a familiar presence in the daily life of people, helping them in different application domains: industry, warehouse, healthcare, search and rescue, and office automation. Despite this, industry is the domain in which automated machines have had the most successful applications. Indeed, the 4.0 industrial revolution meant for many workers an increased level of interaction with the machines present in the factory [4], with a significant impact on productivity [29]. Indeed, robotics proves to enhance and solve more easily logistics and manufacturing problems allowing for a better use of the industrial space [12]. Since the last decade, robots have been used with great profit in the healthcare sector. For example, they have been successfully used in precise surgical procedures to help surgeons reach difficult anatomical compartments and doing operations that would otherwise be impossible [5]. Also, robotics has been applied to help elderly and impaired people move more freely, besides being used to assist during rehabilitation [10]. Robots have been also successfully utilized is

M. Roveri—The work of M. Roveri was partially funded by the Italian MUR programme PRIN 2020, Prot.20203FFYLK (RIPER – Resilient AI-Based Self-Programming and Strategic Reasoning).

search and rescue missions in challenging environments [1]. Finally, robots can be used to help in the day-to-day life of an office allowing affairs to be sped up and simplifying the general workday [27]. The majority of the above applications, involve multiple robots that need to cooperate while moving in a shared environment (e.g. a warehouse) without interfering with each other in order to complete one or multiple tasks in the most efficient way possible, and requiring prompt response to contingencies (e.g., arrival of a new task). This can be achieved by an automatic synthesis of a plan (i.e., a sequence of movements for each agent) to fulfill the full set of tasks. The automatic synthesis to be applied in real industrial scenarios requires that i) the solution plan will be generated for real-size industrial scenarios; ii) the solution plan will be generated quickly (e.g., in at most 1 minute) to quickly adapt to contingencies (E.g., new order, change of priority, order cancellation).

The problem of finding a plan for coordinating a fleet of autonomous robotic cooperating agents aiming to complete assigned tasks has been tackled in the literature as Multi-Agent Path Finding (MAPF). Several algorithms have been proposed to solve the MAPF problem like e.g., the Kornhauser's algorithm [13], the Extended A* [11], the Increasing Cost Tree Search (ICTS) [22], several variants of the Constraint Based Search (CBS) [21], and the Constraint Programming (CP) and Mixed Integer Linear Programming (MILP) approaches. However, as far as our knowledge is concerned, these algorithms have been only applied to synthetic randomly generated graphs, and their application in real scenarios has not been studied.

In this work we make the following contributions. First, we perform a detailed analysis of the MAPF literature, from which we selected the most effective algorithms, and we implemented them as efficiently as possible. Second, we carry out an experimental analysis on a real warehouse of a large distribution company. To evaluate the performance and applicability of the considered algorithms we decomposed the whole warehouse in sub-areas of increasing size (from a smaller area to the whole warehouse). For each scenario we considered different number of agents and several randomly generated tasks for each agent. The results show that the CP approach is able to solve very small cases and does not scale to large real-size scenarios, although it generates optimal solutions and is able to solve also small critical hard problems. The algorithms that performs better are the two variants of the CBS, although none of them is able to solve many cases. This work also contributed to identify some situations for which none of the considered algorithms is able to find a solution in a set amount of time. These results contribute to pave the way for investigating new heuristics to solve these hard problems that appear in real scenarios.

This paper is organized as follows. In Sect. 2, we revise the literature about MAPF. In Sect. 3, we formally define the problem we aim to, and we provide an high-level description of the most relevant approaches studied in the literature. In Sect. 4, we describe the most relevant implementation details, the considered warehouse, and we critically discuss the results. Finally, in Sect. 5, we draw the conclusions and we outline future works.

2   Related Works

In this work, we focus on the aspect of motion planning considering the equally important problem of mission planning as completed before starting the motion planning task. While the former focuses on the best path to follow starting from a position, executing the intermediate objectives and reaching the final destination [14], the latter focuses on the best way of organizing the goals for each robots in the environment [6]. The reason why mission planning is not considered is due to the fact that usually warehouses use specialized software to handle their internal structures, and such software is usually responsible for the generation of an ordered set of goals. The aspect of motion planning is particularly important in a populated environment because it needs to guarantee people safety.

2.1   Single-Agent Path Finding

The Single-Agent Path Finding (SAPF) problem is the problem of finding the best path on a graph between two given nodes or vertexes. Such problem is of great importance in various scenarios. Indeed, one of the main algorithms used to solve the SAPF problem, A*, has been successfully applied to GPS localization in order to improve the way-points accuracy for remote controlled agents [15]. Nevertheless, the field in which single-agent path finding has found the most importance is the field of robot routing and planning, as the problem name also suggests. SAPF algorithms have been successfully implemented in robot routing, where they have been used to search a graph constructed by environmental data in order to avoid obstacles and to explore possible routes [2].

This thesis focuses on the path planning problem that can be defined as follows:

Definition 1 (Single-Agent Path Finding). *Given an undirected graph $G = (V, E)$, where V is the set of the vertexes (that correspond to possible locations for the agent) and E the set of edges joining two vertexes (representing the possible transitions between two locations), the Single-Agent Path Finding (SAPF) problem consists in finding the shortest feasible plan π between a starting vertex $v_S \in V$ and a final one $v_F \in V$.*

A plan π is the sequence of N actions $\alpha_i, i \in \{1, \ldots N\}$ that take the agent from the starting position $v_S \in V$ to the final position v_F in N steps by following the graph edges:

$$\pi = [\alpha_1, ..., a_N] : \pi(v_S) = \alpha_N(...\alpha_2(\alpha_1(v_S))...) = v_F$$

where with $\alpha_i(v_s)$ we denote the movement to the vertex $v_e \in V$ from $v_s \in V$, such that $\langle v_s, v_e \rangle \in E$. We denote with $\pi[h], h \leq N$ the h-th action of the plan $\pi = [\alpha_1, ..., \alpha_N]$, i.e. $\pi[h] = \alpha_h$. We also denote with $|\pi| = N$ the length of the plan $\pi = [\alpha_1, ..., \alpha_N]$.

Due to its definition, the SAPF problem can be reduced to the problem of finding the shortest path on a graph. What follows is a brief description of the main algorithms that can be applied to single-agent path finding which can be divided in deterministic algorithms (e.g. Dijkstra's) and heuristic ones (e.g. A*).

Dijkstra's Algorithm. Dijkstra's algorithm [9] aims to find the shortest path between two nodes on a graph whose edges have only positive values. Note that the graph needs to be strongly connected, i.e., there must be at least one path between any two nodes. While this seems quite a strong limitation, industrial scenarios usually provide such graph: no node can be a sink since it must be possible for an agent to come back from each location, that is, usually graphs modeled on warehouses are either undirected, and hence strongly connected, or directed but no node can be a sink. The work of Dijkstra published in 1959 [9] presents two possible algorithms, one to find the shortest path from one node to another and one to find a tree of minimum length starting from a node and reaching all the other nodes. We focus on the second aspect. The complexity of the algorithm depends on the number of vertexes and edges. Moreover, different and improved versions of the algorithm have different worst-case performance, but the initial one proposed by Dijkstra runs in time $O((|V| + |E|) \log |V|)$. Finally, the algorithm has been successfully used in robot path planning [7,16,28].

A* Algorithm. A* is an heuristic best-first search algorithm for finding the shortest path on a graph [25]. It is also an admissible algorithm, that is, it is guaranteed to find an optimal from the starting node to the arrival one [11]. The idea of A* is to direct the search over the nodes towards the arrival node without having to necessarily examine all the vertexes. To do so, A* keeps a set of nodes to be visited, which is initialized with only the starting node, but then it is enlarged with the neighbors that the algorithm deems worthy to be expanded. A node is said to be expanded when it is added to the set to be analyzed later on. The choice of which nodes should be expanded and which not, is given by the heuristic function. Indeed, when examining the neighbors $u \in \texttt{neigh(n)}$ of the considered node, A* uses a heuristic $h(u)$ to estimate the distance to the arrival vertex. Let $h * (u)$ be the perfect heuristic, that is, a function that returns the correct distance from the node u to the arrival vertex, then if $h * (u)$ is known for all the nodes, the best path is obtained just by choosing to go to the neighbor with the lower heuristic distance between neighbors. It has been proved that if $h(n) \leq h * (n)$, then the heuristic is admissible and A* is optimal [11].

3 Problem Statement

The Single-Agent Path Finding (SAPF) problem is the problem of planning feasible movements for multiple agents [18] such that each one can reach its final location from a respective initial.

Definition 2 (Multi-Agent Path Finding). *Given a finite set $A = \{a_1, ..., a_k\}$ of k agents, given an undirected graph $G = (V, E)$, where V is the set of the vertexes (that correspond to possible locations for the agents) and E the set of edges joining two vertexes (representing the possible transitions between two locations), given an initial start location $v_S^{a_i} \in V$ and final location $v_F^{a_i}$ for each agent a_i, the Single-Agent Path Finding (SAPF) problem consists in finding*

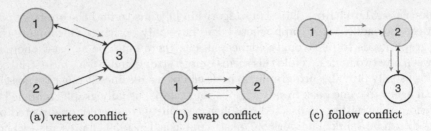

(a) vertex conflict   (b) swap conflict   (c) follow conflict

Fig. 1. The different kinds of conflicts.

a joint feasible plan $\Pi = \{\pi_{a_1}, ..., \pi_{a_k}\}$ such that for each π_{a_i}, $\pi_{a_i}(v_S^{a_i}) = v_F^{a_i}$, and it minimizes a given cost function $C(\Pi)$.

In this work, we focus on edges with unitary cost (i.e. all edges have cost 1, whereas extensions for which edges have non-unitary costs will be left for future work). We say that a joint plan Π is *feasible* if no conflict happens between any two different agents. In the literature, the most widely used notions of conflicts are the following [18]:

- *Vertex conflict*: when two agents $a_i, a_j \in A$ with $i \neq j$ are not occupying the same vertex at the same time. We say that the two agents have a vertex conflict iff $\exists 1 \leq h \leq N$ such that $\pi_{a_i}[h](v_S^{a_i}) = \pi_{a_j}[h](v_S^{a_j})$.
- *Edge conflict*: when two agents $a_i, a_j \in A$ with $i \neq j$ are aiming to use the same edge on the same direction at the same time. We say that the two agents have an edge conflict iff $\exists 1 \leq h < N$ such that $\pi_{a_i}[h](v_S^{a_i}) = \pi_{a_j}[h](v_S^{a_j}) \land \pi_{a_i}[h+1](v_S^{a_i}) = \pi_{a_j}[h+1](v_S^{a_j})$.
- *Swap conflict*: when two agents $a_i, a_j \in A$ with $i \neq j$ are aiming to use the same edge but on opposite direction at the same time. We say that the two agents have a swap conflict iff $\exists 1 \leq h < N$ such that $\pi_{a_i}[h](v_S^{a_i}) = \pi_{a_j}[h+1](v_S^{a_j}) \land \pi_{a_i}[h+1](v_S^{a_i}) = \pi_{a_j}[h](v_S^{a_j})$.
- *Follow conflict*: when two agents $a_i, a_j \in A$ with $i \neq j$ are such that agent a_i want to occupy a position at a given time h that was occupied by agent a_j at time $h - 1$. We say that the two agents have a follow conflict iff $\exists 1 < h \leq N$ such that $\pi_{a_i}[h](v_S^{a_i}) = \pi_{a_j}[h-1](v_S^{a_j})$.

In Fig. 1, we provide a pictorial representation for the vertex, swap, and follow conflicts. The edge conflict is pictorially similar to the swap conflict where the two agents are in the same location and want to take the same edge. It should be noted that avoiding vertex conflicts will avoid edge conflicts by definition.

In the literature, two different kinds of cost function $C(\Pi)$ have been considered: the *makespan* and the *sum of costs* (we refer to [18] for a more thorough discussion).

- The *makespan* is a function that returns the length of the longest plan $\pi_{a_j} \in \Pi$: I.e. $C(\Pi) = \mathrm{MKS}(\Pi) = \max_{\pi_{a_i} \in \Pi} |\pi_{a_i}|$. Thus, minimizing the makespan means finding the plan that contains the shortest path among the possible longest paths.

- The *sum of costs* is a function that returns the sum of the individual cost of the different plan $\pi_{a_j} \in \Pi$: I.e. $C(\Pi) = \text{SIC}(\Pi) = \sum_{\pi_{a_i} \in \Pi} |\pi_{a_i}|$. Here we assume that each action costs 1. If a cost c_e for $e_i \in E$ is associated to each edge, then instead of the length of the plan, one has to consider the sum of the cost of each action in the plan.

The classical multi-agent path finding problem has been proved to be NP-hard, i.e., it is not possible to find an optimal solution in polynomial time [17, 26,30]. Notice that the problem is NP-hard when finding an optimal solution, i.e., a solution that minimize the objective function, may it be the makespan or the sum of individual costs.

3.1 Solutions

In the literature, several algorithms to solve the MAPF problem have been proposed. These algorithms can be *correct* and *complete* (i.e. if they terminate with a solution, then the computed solution is a solution to the given MAPF problem, and if the problem admits no solution the algorithm says that no solution exists); and can compute an *optimal* solution if it minimizes the given cost function, or a *bounded optimal* one if the computed solution minimizes the cost function within a given bound (i.e. there is some degree of freedom), or a *non optimal* one if there is no guarantee of optimality for the computed solution.

In the following description, we consider the these approaches with the corresponding algorithms: the Kornhauser's algorithm [13], the Extended A* [24], the Increasing Cost Tree Search (ICTS) [22], the Constraint Based Search (CBS) [21], and the Constraint Programming (CP) and Mixed Integer Linear Programming (MILP) approaches.

The Kornhauser's algorithm [13] is a complete but not optimal algorithm that solves the MAPF problem in $O(|V|^3)$. This algorithm considers all the agents in their position, and it tries to move one single agent to a neighbor free location one at a time with the aim to find a way to move all the agents from one arrangement to another. The solution is obtained by decomposing the problem in sub-problems each one composed by the agents that can reach the same set of nodes and the sub-graph made of these nodes [19]. This algorithm has been considered very hard to be implemented efficiently [25].

The extended A algorithm* considers moving all possible agents from one location to a free neighbor one at the same time. This results in a search space of $|V|^k$ and a branching factor of $\left(\frac{|E|}{|V|}\right)^k$, which are both exponential in the number of agents and hence intractable [25]. Two extensions were proposed to solve the MAPF problem [24]: Operator Decomposition (OD) and Independence Detection (ID). The first aims at reducing the exponential branching factor while the other tries to decouple the problem of k agents to smaller problems with less agents. The two extensions can also be combined. This algorithm is correct, complete and optimal.

The Increasing Cost Tree Search (ICTS) algorithm is a two-stage search in which a high-level search aims at finding the lengths of the paths for the different agents, while the low-level search carries out the creation of the path for the various agents with the *cost constraints* given by the high-level search [22, 25]. This algorithm creates a tree called Increasing Cost Tree (ICT) in which each node contains a vector of the costs C_i of the individual path of each agent a_i. The total cost of the node C is given by the result of the objective function applied to the joint plan and all the nodes at the same level in the tree have the same total cost. The root of the tree is initialized with the costs of the individual paths of the agents as if they were considered in a SAPF problem. If there are no conflicts, then the solution is fine as it is and the algorithm stops. If instead a conflict was found, then k new nodes are going to be created, one for each agent: the i-th node is composed of the solution of the parent and by only increasing the cost solution for the i-th agent by one unit than before. The idea is the following: if with a given solution it was not possible to find a solution without conflicts, then it may be possible to find a solution by increasing the path of an agent by one. The algorithm continues until a solution is found. The ICT nodes not containing conflicts are called *goal nodes*. The low-level search is instead the part of the algorithm that has to find a path for the i-th agent of cost C_i and such that it reaches its final destination. There may be different implementations for this part of the algorithm: the most trivial would be to start from the initial node and enumerate all the possible path of length C_i and check which are reaching the final node. This though may become very expensive as the number of possible paths of cost C_i may be exponential. The solution proposed [22] uses an Multi-value Decision Diagram (MDD) [23] which are a generalization of the binary decision diagrams in the sense that they allow for more than two choices for every node. Basically, the MDD has a single source node which corresponds to the starting node of the agent. Then, it keeps track of all the neighbors of the source node adding them only if the path going through them can lead to the final node with cost C_i. This implies also that the MDD has a single sink and that it is the final goal of the agent. The problem is then how to choose which path is best to return to the high-level search since a path may produce more conflicts than another leading to a bigger and sub-optimal ICT. This is done by doing the cross-product, i.e., merging, the different MDDs and removing those branches that contains conflicts. We remark that, given the structures of the ICT and of the cross-product of the MDDs, the optimization problem can be reduced to a satisfaction problem: the first ICT node that satisfy the constraint of not having any conflict is also going to be optimal, and the same is true for the paths found in the combination of the MDDs.

The Constraint Based Search (CBS) algorithm uses two distinct search processes similarly to ICTS, a high-level and a low-level one, and a tree to solve the MAPF problem. Differently from ICTS, the CBS algorithm builds a Constraint Tree (CT) composed of nodes tracking three elements: i) the joint plan; ii) the cost of the joint plan; iii) a set of *constraints* associated with the joint plan. The idea is that whenever a joint plan contains a conflict, it is resolved by creating two new nodes with different constraints, which are limitations of an agent movement. In particular, the original CBS [21] defines constraint as a negative restriction tuple (a_i, n, t), meaning that the agent a_i is not allowed to be on node n at time t. The protocol works in the following way: the root is built by considering the paths of the agents as in a single-agent path finding (SAPF) problem. Then, the high-level search checks for possible conflicts. Let π_i and π_j be the plans for agents a_i and a_j respectively, and suppose that they have a vertex conflict at time t on node n. Then, the high-level search creates two new CT nodes from the parent, one in which agent a_i *cannot* be on node n at time t, and the other CT node in which agent a_j *cannot* be on node n at time t. An improvement to CBS [3] suggests that using two positive constraints and a negative one may produce better results since the set of paths that complies with the constraints is disjoint [25]. This means that, instead of having two children from a node, the high-level search creates three children, one in which agent a_i must be on node n at time t, one in which agent a_j must be on node n at time t and one in which neither of them is allowed to be on node n at time t. The process of expanding nodes, i.e., creating new children, stops when there are no more conflicts to be solved. Whenever a new node is added, the low-level search is called to find a solution to the problem with the new added constraints. If a feasible solution can be found, then the node is added to the set of nodes to be further explored. To pick the next node to examine, CBS uses the cost function of the joint plan. Finally, as it regards the low-level search, it can be any SAPF algorithm, although it needs to be properly modified to support the presence of constraints.

The Constraint Programming (CP) approach leverages a mathematical modeling paradigm in which the problem is encoded as a set of constraints among two kind of variables: state variable and decision variables. This approach is usually divided in two parts: a modeling part that addresses the shaping of the aspects of the problem introducing variables over specific domains and constraints over such variables; a solving part that aims at choosing the value of the decision variables that minimize a given cost function and that make the constraints satisfiable. If the constraints are well-formed, i.e., they correctly cover the variables and their domains, than constraint programming is both optimal and correct. Typical modeling considers Boolean variables for each agent for each vertex for each time point, and a constraint that enforces that each agent can occupy only one vertex in each time step (thus ensuring no vertex conflict). Agents are positioned on their initial position at the first time step, and must be on their arrival position at the last time step. Agents move along edges towards neighbors of the node on which they are: this is to ensure the validity of the solution since an agent cannot jump from one node to another. Once the constraints are fixed, the model can be solved with any off-the-shelf constraint solver, which tries to look at all the possible combinations without infringing any constraint.

4 Experimental Evaluation

In this section, we first provide the high level details of the implementation of the considered algorithms, and the information about the software and hardware infrastructure used for the experiments. Then we describe the considered industrial scenarios, we report and critically discuss the results of the experiments.

4.1 Implementation

For the implementation we have considered only three of the approaches discussed in Sect. 3. We implemented the CP approach and two variants of the CBS family of algorithms, in particular the Spanning Tree (ST) and the Time-Dependant Shortest Path (TDSP). The CBS ST and the CBS TDSP differs in the low-level search used to build the constraint tree. The CBS ST in the local search builds a spanning tree as to allow the high-level search to choose among the possible different paths that have the same length. The CBS TDSP in the local search uses a variant of the Dijkstra [9] algorithm to compute shortest paths where the costs of the edges depends on the time the edge is considered. We do not report here the pseudo-code of the considered algorithms for lack of space, and we refer to [20] for further details. We decided not to implement the Kornhauser's algorithm since this algorithm has been considered very hard to be implemented efficiently from the research community [25], and it produces non-optimal solutions. We did not implement the extended A* algorithm because of its large branching factor that will make it not applicable in large industrial scenarios. Finally, we also did not implement the ICTS approach since it requires to know possible bounds for the costs of the searched solutions a priori (an impractical information to get for realistic scenarios).

All the algorithms have been implemented in C++ using the standard template libraries. For the CP algorithm we have leveraged the latest release of the C++ API of the CPLEX commercial constraint solver [8]. The source code with the implementation of all the algorithms is available at our open repository[1].

We run all the experiments on an AMD Ryzen 3700X equipped with an 8 core CPU at 3.6 GHz base clock, and 32 GB of RAM running Linux. We considered as run-time timeouts 1 s, 10 s, and 60 s to mimic the time response expectations requested in industrial realistic scenarios.

4.2 Industrial Scenarios

For the experiments we considered a real warehouse taken from a collaboration with a company operating in the field of robotic assisted warehouses. The entire warehouse and its graph representation is depicted in Fig. 2. The topological graph obtained from the map consists of 414 nodes with undirected edges. For the experiments we decomposed the warehouse into sub-problems as follows: i) WH1 that corresponds to the gold rectangle in the top right corner of Fig. 2; ii)

---

[1] https://www.bitbucket.org/chaff800/maof.

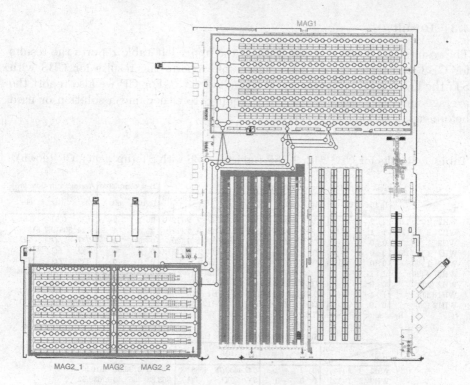

Fig. 2. The schema of the real warehouse considered for the experiments.

WH2 that corresponds to the blue rectangle in the bottom left corner of Fig. 2; iii) WH2_1 that corresponds to the red rectangle in the bottom left corner of Fig. 2; iv) WH2_2 that corresponds to the green rectangle in the bottom left corner of Fig. 2; v) WH2_1_1 that corresponds to the top 4 rows of red rectangle in the bottom left corner of Fig. 2; vi) WH2_1_2 that corresponds to the bottom 4 rows of red rectangle in the bottom left corner of Fig. 2; vii) WH2_2_1 that corresponds to the top 4 rows of green rectangle in the bottom left corner of Fig. 2; viii) WH2_2_2 that corresponds to the bottom 4 rows of green rectangle in the bottom left corner of Fig. 2. For each scenario, we considered problems with increasing number of robotic agents taken from {2, 5, 10, 20} and increasing number of goals taken from {1, 2, 5, 10, 20}. These numbers are the results of the discussion with the company owner of the reference warehouse we considered. The goals have been generated to resemble typical goals taken from the logistic activities carried out in the considered warehouse. In the results, we only report the name of the scenario followed by the number of problems considered in that scenario in parenthesis (E.g., WH2_2_2 (10) means the scenario WH2_2_2 with ten problems). For each experiment, we report the number of problems solved among the one considered, and the average search time in milliseconds (ms) required for the solved problems. We use TO to indicate that the algorithm was not able to find a solution within the given time budget for any of the problem in the scenario.

4.3   Results

The results are reported in the Table 1: the upper left table reports the results for CBS with TDSP; the upper right table reports the results for CBS with ST; the lower down table reports the results for CP. For CP we also report the average memory in megabytes (MB) required to either find a solution or used before ending in timeout.

Table 1. Results for CBS with TDSP (up left), CBS with ST (up right), CP (down).

Test \ Timeout	Test completed 1s	10s	60s	Average run time [ms] 1s	10s	60s
WH2_2_2 (12)	2	2	2	5.58	9.96	5.53
WH2_2_1 (12)	1	1	1	5.29	4.88	4.84
WH2_1_1 (20)	0	0	0	TO	TO	TO
WH2_1_2 (15)	0	0	0	TO	TO	TO
WH2_1 (20)	0	0	0	TO	TO	TO
WH2_2 (20)	1	1	1	1.93	1.94	3.64
WH2 (20)	0	0	0	TO	TO	TO
WH1 (20)	1	1	1	159.91	159.05	158.77
WH12 (25)	0	0	0	TO	TO	TO

Results for CBS with TDSP.

Test \ Timeout	Test completed 1s	10s	60s	Average run time [ms] 1s	10s	60s
WH2_2_2 (12)	2	2	2	0.70	0.61	0.64
WH2_2_1 (12)	2	3	4	6.14	3051.67	6130.67
WH2_1_1 (20)	0	0	0	TO	TO	TO
WH2_1_2 (15)	0	0	0	TO	TO	TO
WH2_1 (20)	0	0	0	TO	TO	TO
WH2_2 (20)	2	2	2	31.86	31.96	34.04
WH2 (20)	0	0	0	TO	TO	TO
WH1 (20)	0	0	0	TO	TO	TO
WH12 (25)	0	0	0	TO	TO	TO

Results for CBS with ST

Test \ Timeout	Test completed 1s	10s	60s	Average run time [ms] 1s	10s	60s	Average memory [MB] 1s	10s	60s
WH2_2_2 (12)	0	2	2	TO	4459.78	4688.98	714.33	3195.38	9310.51
WH2_2_1 (12)	0	0	0	TO	TO	TO	863.83	3653.43	12630.42
WH2_1_1 (20)	0	0	0	TO	TO	TO	973.95	7311.85	19306.53
WH2_1_2 (15)	0	0	0	TO	TO	TO	951.51	4719.59	14422.11
WH2_1 (20)	0	0	0	TO	TO	TO	776.29	9682.30	24465.94
WH2_2 (20)	0	0	1	TO	TO	45942.20	896.01	7629.73	20344.22
WH2 (20)	0	0	0	TO	TO	TO	733.01	8299.46	25802.48
WH1 (20)	0	0	0	TO	TO	TO	1071.18	6575.35	29965.53
WH12 (25)	0	0	0	TO	TO	TO	1438.79	7072.68	29261.20

Results for CP

The results clearly show that none of the considered algorithm was able to solve all the problems in the considered budget constraints but only very few cases (e.g. in the WH2_2, WH2_2_2, WH1). In particular, the results show that the CBS algorithms are able to solve slightly more scenarios than CP (which solves only 3 cases in the 60s time boundaries with the best run-time completed in 1.1s). More specifically, the results show that the CBS algorithms are complementary. Indeed, for WH2_2_2 CBS TDSP is slower than the CBS ST, whereas for WH1 CBS TDSP is able to solve one instance while CBS ST none ending always in TO. CP is always worse in performance than the CBS algorithms. As the table with the results for CP reports, it is clear that this approach consumes a larger amount of memory w.r.t. the other approaches. Indeed, each time it does not finds a solution, it tries to increase the time steps by 1 unit thus resulting in a much larger complexity due to the used variables matrix structure.

These results clearly show that although these algorithms have been thoroughly studied in the literature, and experimented on random graphs with random goals, when applied to realistic scenarios, they fail to find solutions in typical industrial budget of resources. A more thorough analysis of the cases where no solution was found (even with larger resource budgets) are cases where two robotic agents need to follow the same shortest path but in opposite direction thus requiring to swap places in one edge (see Fig. 3). In this cases, a simple strat-

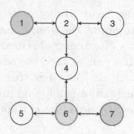

Fig. 3. A simple scenario not solvable by CBS.

egy would move one of the two agents into a lateral position (if available) to allow the other to pass, and then go back to the previous location (thus taking a longer path that visit the same node more than once). The problem in solving such a situation stands in the difficulty to differentiate between a waiting action, which can be done on the node on which the agent currently is, or the action of exploring the neighbors of the node. Algorithms such as TDSP and ST are not meant to visit multiple times the same node. To solve this problem, both the high-level and low-level searches of CBS should be modified, the former to consider multiple possible nodes for a given time step h on the plan of an agent, and the latter to allow moving over the same node multiple times. Both changes are already planned for future works.

5   Conclusions

In this paper, we studied the performance of the state-of-the-art MAPF algorithms on a set of scalable industrial scenarios all derived from a real warehouse of a large distribution company. The results show that the CP approach find optimal solutions, but it is applicable to only very small scenarios. The CBS approaches scale better and allows to solve in the given resource budgets more problems. However, these approaches fail to find a solution in cases where it was requested some agent to move to other locations and then go back to the same location to continue the motion to allow other agents to exit from conflicting cases. This particular case is really likely to happen by construction of the graph: the aisles are long and they can basically be occupied by just one agent at a time without having to solve many swap conflicts.

The results show that there is not a clear winner, but all the approaches have pros and cons. This work paves the way for several future works that go from investigating new heuristics to solve hard problems that appear in real scenarios, to new algorithms that combine the pros of each approach, or that consider the use of divide-et-impera approaches to leverage different low-level search strategies. Moreover, we aim also to extend the work so that each agent does not only consider a set of tasks, but also other information such as batteries level and the possibility to recharge. Also, while in this work we have given the mission planning for granted, integrating mission planning in the MAPF problem may lead to more effective ways of allocating tasks to the different agents to minimize the overall cost of the computed solution.

The final goal is an open source framework containing different MAPF solvers that can be used to tackle the problem and that may be integrated in platforms such as ROS. For this same reason, the algorithms have been re-implemented instead of employing pre-existing code. Moreover, any existing code would have had to be adapted to our use-case, leading to a loss in performance.

References

1. Arnold, R.D., Yamaguchi, H., Tanaka, T.: Search and rescue with autonomous flying robots through behavior-based cooperative intelligence. J. Int. Humanit. Action **3**(1), 1–18 (2018). https://doi.org/10.1186/s41018-018-0045-4
2. Bhattacharya, S., Likhachev, M., Kumar, V.: Topological constraints in search-based robot path planning. Auton. Robots **33**, 273–290 (2012). https://doi.org/10.1007/s10514-012-9304-1
3. Boyarski, E., et al.: ICBS: the improved conflict-based search algorithm for multi-agent pathfinding (2015)
4. BraganÃ§a, S., Costa, E., Castellucci, I., Arezes, P.M.: A brief overview of the use of collaborative robots in industry 4.0: human role and safety (2019). https://doi.org/10.1007/978-3-030-14730-3_68
5. Brett, P., Taylor, R., Proops, D., Coulson, C., Reid, A., Griffiths, M.: A surgical robot for cochleostomy, pp. 1229–1232. IEEE (2007). https://doi.org/10.1109/IEMBS.2007.4352519
6. Brumitt, B., Stentz, A.: Dynamic mission planning for multiple mobile robots, pp. 2396–2401. IEEE (1996). https://doi.org/10.1109/ROBOT.1996.506522
7. Chen, Y.Z., Shen, S.F., Chen, T., Yang, R.: Path optimization study for vehicles evacuation based on Dijkstra algorithm. Procedia Eng. **71**, 159–165 (2014). https://doi.org/10.1016/j.proeng.2014.04.023
8. Corportation, I.: Ibm ilog cplex optimization studio
9. Dijkstra, E.W.: A note on two problems in connexion with graphs. Numer. Math. **1**, 269–271 (1959). https://doi.org/10.1007/BF01386390
10. Ferrari, F., et al.: Human–robot interaction analysis for a smart walker for elderly: the ACANTO interactive guidance system. Int. J. Soc. Robot. **12**(2), 479–492 (2019). https://doi.org/10.1007/s12369-019-00572-5
11. Hart, P.E., Nilsson, N.J., Raphael, B.: A formal basis for the heuristic determination of minimum cost paths. IEEE Trans. Syst. Sci. Cybern. **4**, 100–107 (1968). https://doi.org/10.1109/TSSC.1968.300136
12. Javaid, M., Haleem, A., Singh, R.P., Suman, R.: Substantial capabilities of robotics in enhancing industry 4.0 implementation. Cogn. Robot. **1**, 58–75 (2021). https://doi.org/10.1016/j.cogr.2021.06.001
13. Kornhauser, D., Miller, G., Spirakis, P.: Coordinating pebble motion on graphs, the diameter of permutation groups, and applications, pp. 241–250. IEEE (1984). https://doi.org/10.1109/SFCS.1984.715921
14. Latombe, J.C.: Robot Motion Planning, vol. 124. Springer Science & Business Media, Berlin, Heidelberg (2012). https://doi.org/10.1007/978-1-4615-4022-9
15. Pouke, M.: Using GPS data to control an agent in a realistic 3D environment, pp. 87–92. IEEE, September 2013. https://doi.org/10.1109/NGMAST.2013.24

16. Qing, G., Zheng, Z., Yue, X.: Path-planning of automated guided vehicle based on improved Dijkstra algorithm, pp. 7138–7143. IEEE, May 2017. https://doi.org/10.1109/CCDC.2017.7978471
17. Ratner, D., Warmuth, M.K.: Finding a shortest solution for the n × n extension of the 15-puzzle is intractable (1986)
18. Roni, S., et al.: Multi-agent pathfinding: definitions, variants, and benchmarks. CoRR abs/1906.08291 (2019)
19. Röger, G., Helmert, M.: Non-optimal multi-agent pathfinding is solved (since 1984) (2012)
20. Saccon, E.: Comparison of Multi-Agent Path Finding Algorithms in an Industrial Scenario. Master's thesis, Department of Information Engineering and Computer Science - University of Trento, July 2022. https://www5.unitn.it/Biblioteca/en/Web/RichiestaConsultazioneTesi
21. Sharon, G., Stern, R., Felner, A., Sturtevant, N.R.: Conflict-based search for optimal multi-agent pathfinding. Artif. Intell. **219**, 40–66 (2015). https://doi.org/10.1016/j.artint.2014.11.006
22. Sharon, G., Stern, R., Goldenberg, M., Felner, A.: The increasing cost tree search for optimal multi-agent pathfinding. Artif. Intell. **195**, 470–495 (2013). https://doi.org/10.1016/j.artint.2012.11.006
23. Srinivasan, A., Ham, T., Malik, S., Brayton, R.: Algorithms for discrete function manipulation, pp. 92–95. IEEE Computer Society Press. https://doi.org/10.1109/ICCAD.1990.129849
24. Standley, T.: Finding optimal solutions to cooperative pathfinding problems, vol. 24, pp. 173–178 (2010)
25. Stern, R.: Multi-agent path finding - an overview (2019). https://doi.org/10.1007/978-3-030-33274-7_6
26. Surynek, P.: An optimization variant of multi-robot path planning is intractable, vol. 2, July 2010
27. Veloso, M.M., Biswas, J., Coltin, B., Rosenthal, S.: CoBots: robust symbiotic autonomous mobile service robots, pp. 4423–4429, July 2015
28. Wang, H., Yu, Y., Yuan, Q.: Application of Dijkstra algorithm in robot path-planning, pp. 1067–1069. IEEE (2011). https://doi.org/10.1109/MACE.2011.5987118
29. Wurman, P.R., D'Andrea, R., Mountz, M.: Coordinating hundreds of cooperative, autonomous vehicles in warehouses. AI Mag. **29**, 9 (2008). https://doi.org/10.1609/aimag.v29i1.2082, https://ojs.aaai.org/index.php/aimagazine/article/view/2082
30. Yu, J., LaValle, S.M.: Structure and intractability of optimal multi-robot path planning on graphs, pp. 1443–1449. AAAI Press (2013)

Logic-Based Ethical Planning

Umberto Grandi[1], Emiliano Lorini[1], Timothy Parker[1(✉)], and Rachid Alami[2]

[1] IRIT, CNRS, Toulouse University, Toulouse, France
`timothy.parker@irit.fr`
[2] LAAS, CNRS, Toulouse, France

Abstract. In this paper we propose a framework for ethical decision-making in the context of planning, with intended application to robotics. We put forward a compact but highly expressive language for ethical planning that combines linear temporal logic with lexicographic preference modelling. This original combination allows us to assess plans both with respect to an agent's values and its desires, introducing the novel concept of the morality level of an agent and moving towards multi-goal, multi-value planning. We initiate the study of computational complexity of planning tasks in our setting, and we discuss potential applications to robotics.

1 Introduction

In ethical planning the planning agent has to find a plan for promoting a certain number of ethical values. The latter include both abstract values such as justice, fairness, reciprocity, equity, respect for human integrity and more concrete ones such as "greenhouse gas emissions are reduced". Unlike classical planning in which the goal to be achieved is unique, in ethical planning the agent can have multiple and possibly conflicting values, that is, values that cannot be concomitantly satisfied. It is typical of ethical planning the problem of facing a moral struggle which is "...provoked by inconsistencies between value commitments and information concerning the kinds of decision problems which arise..." [18, p. 8]. Consequently, in ethical planning the agent needs to evaluate and compare the ideality (or goodness) of different plans depending on how many and which values are promoted by each of them.

In this paper our intended application field is that of robotics. Including ethical considerations in robotics planning requires (at least) three steps. First, identify ethically sensitive situations in the robotics realm, and how are these situations represented. Planning seems to be the first candidate in which to include ethical considerations, thus we assume that values or ethical judgments are expressed about the results of plans. Second, design a language to express such values, bearing in mind that they can be, and often are, potentially conflicting in multiple ways: among values, between a value and a goal, or between a value and good practices. Such a value representation language needs to be compact and computationally tractable. Third, complete the picture of ethical planning by designing algorithms that compare plans based on the ethical values.

© The Author(s), under exclusive license to Springer Nature Switzerland AG 2023
A. Dovier et al. (Eds.): AIxIA 2022, LNAI 13796, pp. 198–211, 2023.
https://doi.org/10.1007/978-3-031-27181-6_14

In this paper we put forward a framework for ethical planning based on a simple temporal logic language to express both an agent's values and goals. For ease of exposition we focus on single-agent planning with deterministic sequential actions in a known environment. Our model borrows from the existing literature on planning and combines it in an original way with research in compact representation languages for preferences. The latter is a widely studied topic in knowledge representation, where logical and graphical languages are proposed to represent compactly the preferences of an agent over a combinatorial space of alternatives, often described by means of variables. In particular, we commit to a prioritised or lexicographic approach to solve the possible arising inconsistencies among goals, desires, and good practices in a unified planning model.

2   Related Work

There is considerable research in the field of ethics and AI, see Müller [25] for a general overview. Popular ethical theories for application are consequentialism, deontology, and virtue ethics.[1] Our approach should be able to work with any notion of "good actions" but is probably a most natural fit for pluralistic consequentialism [30].

While there is a lot of work at the theoretical/abstract level, there is comparatively less that examines how ethical reasoning in artificial agents could actually be done in practice. There are approaches both in terms of formal models [12] and allowing agents to learn ethical values [2]. Yu et al. [33] provides a recent survey of this research area. The closest approaches to ours are the recent work on (*i*) logics for ethical reasoning and (*ii*) the combination of a compact representation language, such as conditional preference networks, with decision-making in an ethically sensitive domain. The former are based on different methodologies including event calculus (ASP) [6], epistemic logic and preference logic [22,24], BDI (belief, desire, intention) agent language [11], classical higher-order logic (HOL) [5]. The latter was presented in "blue sky" papers [21,28] complemented with a technical study of distances between CP-nets [20] and, more recently, with an empirical study on human ethical decision-making [4]. CP-nets are a compact formalism to order states of the world described by variables.

We take inspiration from these lines of work, but depart from them under two aspects. First, robotics applications are dynamic ones, and ethical principles must be expressed over time. Hence, unlike existing logics for ethical reasoning, our focus is on a specification language for values based on linear temporal logic. Second, ethical decision-making in robotic applications requires mixing potentially conflicting values with desires of the agent and to express the notion of plan, and CP-nets alone are not sufficient.

In the field of robotics, there are approaches to enabling artificial agents to compute ethical plans. The evaluative component, which consists in assessing the "goodness" of an action or a plan in relation to the robot's values, is made explicit

---

[1] See Copp [9] for a philosophical introduction, and Jenkins et al. [15], Powers [27], and Vallor [31] for a discussion of these three theories in robotics.

by Arkin et al. [3] and Vanderelst and Winfield [32]. Evans et al. [13] focuses on a collision scenario involving an autonomous vehicle, proposing to prioritise the ethical claims depending on the situation, e.g. by giving more priorities to the claims of the more endangered agents. Related work explores the design of planning algorithms designed to help robots produce socially acceptable plans by assigning weights to social rules [1].

In preference-based planning by Bienvenu et al. [7] plans are compared relative to a *single* (possibly lexicographic) preference formula about temporal properties. Similarly, Lindner et al. [19] evaluate the permissibility of plans according to a *specific* ethical principle such as the deontological principle, the utilitarian principle, the do-no-harm or the double effect principle. In our approach plans are compared relative to *sets* of values. Comparison of alternatives (e.g., plans, states, histories) relative to a set of values is an essential aspect of ethics which is not considered in these two works. As we will show in Sect. 3.5, it opens up the possibility of formalizing the notion of moral conflict.

3   Model

In this section, we present the formal model of ethical evaluation and planning which consist, respectively, in comparing the goodness of plans and in finding the best plan relative to a given base of ethical values.

3.1   LTL Language

Let *Prop* be a countable set of atomic propositions and let *Act* be a finite nonempty set of action names. Elements of *Prop* are noted $p, q, \ldots$, while elements of *Act* are noted $a, b, \ldots$. We assume the existence of a special action skip. The set of states is $S = 2^{Prop}$ with elements $s, s', \ldots$

In order to represent the agent's values, we introduce the language of LTL_f (Linear Temporal Logic over Finite Traces) [10,26], noted $\mathcal{L}_{\mathsf{LTL}_f}(Prop)$ (or $\mathcal{L}_{\mathsf{LTL}_f}$), defined by the following grammar:

$$\varphi ::= p \mid \neg \varphi \mid \varphi_1 \wedge \varphi_2 \mid \mathsf{X}\varphi \mid \varphi_1 \mathsf{U} \varphi_2,$$

with p ranging over *Prop*. X and U are the operators "next" and "until" of LTL_f. Operators "henceforth" (G) and "eventually" (F) are defined in the usual way: $\mathsf{G}\varphi \stackrel{\text{def}}{=} \neg(\top \mathsf{U} \varphi)$ and $\mathsf{F}\varphi \stackrel{\text{def}}{=} \neg\mathsf{G}\neg\varphi$. The propositional logic fragment of $\mathcal{L}_{\mathsf{LTL}_f}$ is noted $\mathcal{L}_{\mathsf{PL}}$ and is defined in the usual way. We will use $\mathcal{L}_{\mathsf{PL}}$ to describe the effect preconditions of the agent's actions.

3.2   Histories

The notion of history is needed for interpreting formulas in $\mathcal{L}_{\mathsf{LTL}_f}$. We define a k-history to be a pair $H = (H_{st}, H_{act})$ with

$$H_{st} : [0, k] \longrightarrow S \text{ and } H_{act} : [1, k] \longrightarrow Act.$$

A history specifies the actual configuration of the environment at a certain time point and the action executed by the agent that leads to the next state. The set of k-histories is noted $Hist_k$. The set of histories is $Hist = \bigcup_{k \in \mathbb{N}} Hist_k$. Semantic interpretation of formulas in $\mathcal{L}_{\mathsf{LTL}_f}$ relative to a k-history $H \in Hist$ and a time point $t \in [0, k]$ goes as follows (we omit boolean cases which are defined as usual):

$$H, t \models p \iff p \in H_{st}(t),$$
$$H, t \models \mathsf{X}\varphi \iff t < k \text{ AND } H, t+1 \models \varphi,$$
$$H, t \models \varphi_1 \cup \varphi_2 \iff \exists t' \geq t : t' \leq k \text{ AND } H, t' \models \varphi_2 \text{ AND }$$
$$\forall t'' \geq t : \text{ IF } t'' < t' \text{ THEN } H, t'' \models \varphi_1.$$

3.3 Action Theory

We suppose actions in Act are described by an action theory $\gamma = (\gamma^+, \gamma^-)$, where γ^+ and γ^- are, respectively, the positive and negative effect precondition function $\gamma^+ : Act \times Prop \longrightarrow \mathcal{L}_{\mathsf{PL}}$ and $\gamma^- : Act \times Prop \longrightarrow \mathcal{L}_{\mathsf{PL}}$.

The fact $\gamma^+(a, p)$ guarantees that proposition p will be *true* in the next state when action a is executed, while $\gamma^-(a, p)$ guarantees that proposition p will be *false* in the next state when action a is executed. We stipulate that if $\gamma^+(a, p)$ and $\gamma^-(a, p)$ are concomitantly true at a given state and action a is executed, then the truth value of p will not change in the next state. The latter captures an inertial principle for fluents.

Definition 1 (Action-compatible histories). *Let $\gamma = (\gamma^+, \gamma^-)$ be an action theory and let $H = (H_{st}, H_{act})$ be a k-history. We say H is compatible with γ if the following condition holds, for every $t \in [1, k]$ and for every $a \in Act$:*

$$\text{IF } H_{act}(t) = a \text{ THEN}$$
$$H_{st}(t) = \Big(H_{st}(t-1) \setminus \{p \in Prop : H, t-1 \models \neg\gamma^+(a, p) \wedge$$
$$\gamma^-(a, p)\}\Big) \cup \{p \in Prop : H, t-1 \models \gamma^+(a, p) \wedge$$
$$\neg\gamma^-(a, p)\}.$$

The set of γ-compatible histories is noted $Hist(\gamma)$.

3.4 Plans

Let us now move from the notion of action to the notion of plan. Given $k \in \mathbb{N}$, a k-plan is a function

$$\pi : \{1, \ldots, k\} \longrightarrow Act.$$

The set of k-plans is noted $Plan_k$. The set of plans is $Plan = \bigcup_{k \in \mathbb{N}} Plan_k$. The following definition introduces the notion of history generated by a k-plan π at an initial state s_0. It is the action-compatible k-history along which the agent executes the plan π starting at state s_0.

Definition 2 (History generated by a k-plan). *Let $\gamma = (\gamma^+, \gamma^-)$ be an action theory, $s_0 \in S$ and $\pi \in Plan_k$. Then, the history generated by plan π from state s_0 in conformity with the action theory γ is the k-history $H^{\pi,s_0,\gamma} = (H_{st}^{\pi,s_0,\gamma}, H_{act}^{\pi,s_0,\gamma})$ such that:*

    (i) $H^{\pi,s_0,\gamma} \in Hist(\gamma)$,

    (ii) $H_{st}^{\pi,s_0,\gamma}(0) = s_0$,

    (iii) $\forall k'$ s.t. $1 \leq k' \leq k : H_{act}^{\pi,s_0,\gamma}(k') = \pi(k')$,

Given a set of LTL_f-formulas Σ, we define $Sat(\Sigma, \pi, s_0, \gamma)$ to be the set of formulas from Σ that are guaranteed to be true by the execution of plan π at state s_0 under the action theory γ. That is,

$$Sat(\Sigma, \pi, s_0, \gamma) = \left\{ \varphi \in \Sigma : H^{\pi,s_0,\gamma}, 0 \models \varphi \right\}.$$

3.5 Moral Conflicts

An ethical planning agent is likely to have multiple values that it wishes to satisfy when making plans. Some of these values will be ethical in nature ("do not harm humans"), and some may not be ("do not leave doors open"). However, the more values the robot has the more likely it is to experience scenarios where it cannot satisfy all of its values with any given plan, and must violate some of them. In such a scenario, the agent must first work out which subsets of its value base are jointly satisfiable, and then which of those subsets it should choose to satisfy.

To this end we define a notion of a moral conflict (note that in line with Levi [18] we refer to any conflict between an agent's values as a "moral conflict" even if some or all of those values are not strictly moral/ethical in nature).

Definition 3 (Moral problem). *A moral problem is a tuple $M = (\Omega, \gamma, s_0)$ where:*

- *$\Omega \subseteq \mathcal{L}_{\mathsf{LTL}_f}$ is a set of values (which may or may not be strictly moral in nature);*
- *$\gamma = (\gamma^+, \gamma^-)$ is an action theory and s_0 is an initial state, as described above.*

Definition 4 (Moral conflict). *A moral problem $M = (\Omega, \gamma, s_0)$ is a moral conflict if:*

- *$\forall k \in \mathbb{N}$, there is no k-plan π such that $Sat(\Omega, \pi, s_0, \gamma) = \Omega$.*

In other words, a moral conflict occurs when it is not possible to satisfy all of our values with any given plan. In some cases, a moral conlict may not depend on any particular feature of the start state, but may result simply from the value base and action theory, or even the value base alone. This allows us to define two further notions of moral problem.

Definition 5 (Physical moral problem). *A physical moral problem is a pair* (Ω, γ) *where:*

- $\Omega \subseteq \mathcal{L}_{\mathsf{LTL}_f}$ *is a set of values;*
- γ *is an action theory.*

Definition 6 (Logical moral problem). *A logical moral problem is a set of values* $\Omega \subseteq \mathcal{L}_{\mathsf{LTL}_f}$.

We can also define moral conflict for these moral problems. A physical (logical) moral problem is a physical (logical) value conflict if for every possible start state s_0 (and every possible action theory γ), the resultant moral value problem $M = (\Omega, \gamma, s_0)$ is a moral conflict. By our definition, conflict mirrors the concept of necessity. Necessity would imply that *every* possible plan satisfies all the values in Ω, whereas conflict implies that *no* plan satisfies all values. Thus it is interesting to note that our definitions of conflict have mirrors in philosophical literature [16]. A physical moral conflict mirrors the notion of nomic necessity (necessary given the laws of nature) (at least from the perspective of the robot, for whom the action theory comprises the laws of nature) whereas a logical moral conflict mirrors the notion of logical necessity (necessary given the nature of logic).

If an agent is experiencing a moral conflict, one response would be to "temporarily forget" values until it has a satisfiable set.

Definition 7 (Contraction). *If* $M = (\Omega, \gamma, s_0)$ *is a moral problem and* $M' = (\Omega', \gamma, s_0)$ *is a moral problem, we say that* M' *is a contraction of* M *if:*

- $\Omega' \subseteq \Omega$
- M' *is not a moral conflict.*

Note that if $M = (\Omega, \gamma, s_0)$ is a moral problem, π is a plan, and $\Omega' = Sat(\Omega, \pi, s_0, \gamma)$ then $M' = (\Omega', \gamma, s_0)$ must be a contraction of M.

In this case, we refer to M' as the contraction generated by π. This also illustrates that the current notion of contraction is unhelpful for an agent attempting to select a plan in a moral conflict, as all plans generate contractions. What would be helpful is some notion of a "minimal" or "ideal" contraction that sacrifices as few values as possible.

Definition 8 (Minimal contraction). *If* $M = (\Omega, \gamma, s_0)$ *is a moral problem and* $M' = (\Omega', \gamma, s_0)$ *is a contraction of* M, M *is:*

- *A qual-minimal contraction if there is no contraction* $M'' = (\Omega'', \gamma, s_0)$ *such that* $\Omega' \subset \Omega''$;
- *A quant-minimal contraction if there is no contraction* M'' *such that* $|\Omega'| < |\Omega''|$

Proposition 1. *If* $M = (\Omega, \gamma, s_0)$ *is a moral problem and is not a moral conflict, then the only qual-minimal and quant-minimal contraction of* M *is* M.

For either notion of minimality, we will have cases where there are multiple minimal contractions of a given moral conflict. This can produce unintuitive results, as if there is some moral conflict with $\Omega = \{$"do not kill humans", "do not leave the door open"$\}$ with contractions $\{$"do not kill humans"$\}$ and $\{$"do not leave the door open"$\}$ then either notion of minimality will tell you that both contractions are ideal. On the other hand, it does seem that any stronger notion of minimality should at least respect qualitative minimality, since (intuitively), if plan π_1 fulfills all of the values fulfilled by π_2, and fulfills more values, then π_1 should be preferred to π_2.

Proposition 2. *Given a moral conflict M, a contraction M' is quant-minimal only if it is qual-minimal.*

One way to recognise this is to recognise, in line with Levi [18], that some of our values are only used as tiebreakers to separate otherwise-equivalent plans, and should not be considered directly alongside our more important values. To model this, our values exist in lexicographically ordered sets, where each set is examined only if the sets above cannot deliver a verdict.

3.6   Lexicographic Value Base

Together with an action theory and an initial state, an agent's value base constitutes an ethical planning domain.

Definition 9 (Ethical planning domain). *An ethical planning domain is a tuple $\Delta = (\gamma, s_0, \overline{\Omega})$ where:*

- *$\gamma = (\gamma^+, \gamma^-)$ is an action theory and s_0 is an initial state, as specified above;*
- *$\overline{\Omega} = (\Omega_1, \ldots, \Omega_m)$ is the agent's value base with $\Omega_k \subseteq \mathcal{L}_{\mathsf{LTL}_f}$ for every $1 \leq k \leq m$.*

Ω_1 is the agent's set of values with priority 1, Ω_2 is the agent's set of values with priority 2, and so on. For notational convenience, given a value base $\overline{\Omega} = (\Omega_1, \ldots, \Omega_m)$, we note $dg(\overline{\Omega})$ its degree (or arity).

Agent's values are used to compute the *relative ideality* of plans, namely, whether a plan π_2 is at least as ideal as another plan π_1. Following [24], we call *evaluation* the operation of computing an ideality ordering over plans from a value base. Building on classical preference representation languages [17], we define the following qualitative criterion of evaluation, noted $\preceq_\Delta^{qual}$, which compares two plans lexicographically on the basis of inclusion between sets of values.

Definition 10 (Qualitative ordering of plans). *Let $\Delta = (\gamma, s_0, \overline{\Omega})$ be an ethical planning domain with $\overline{\Omega} = (\Omega_1, \ldots, \Omega_m)$ and $\pi_1, \pi_2 \in Plan$. Then, $\pi_1 \preceq_\Delta^{qual} \pi_2$ if and only if:*

> *(i) $\exists 1 \leq k \leq m$ s.t. $Sat(\Omega_k, \pi_1, s_0, \gamma) \subset Sat(\Omega_k, \pi_2, s_0, \gamma)$, and*
> $\forall 1 \leq k' < k, Sat(\Omega_{k'}, \pi_1, s_0, \gamma) = Sat(\Omega_{k'}, \pi_2, s_0, \gamma)$; or*
> *(ii) $\forall 1 \leq k \leq m, Sat(\Omega_k, \pi_1, s_0, \gamma) = Sat(\Omega_k, \pi_2, s_0, \gamma)$.*

Note that a quantitative criterion could also be defined by counting the number of satisfied values in each level and, in line with the previous definition, compare these values lexicographically.

The quantitative criterion, noted $\preceq_\Delta^{quant}$, compares two plans lexicographically on the basis of comparative cardinality between sets of values.

Definition 11 (Quantitative ordering of plans). *Let $\Delta = (\gamma, s_0, \overline{\Omega})$ be an ethical planning domain with $\overline{\Omega} = (\Omega_1, \ldots, \Omega_m)$ and $\pi_1, \pi_2 \in Plan$. Then, $\pi_1 \preceq_\Delta^{quant} \pi_2$ if and only if:*

(i) $\exists 1 \leq k \leq m$ *s.t.* $|Sat(\Omega_k, \pi_1, s_0, \gamma)| < |Sat(\Omega_k, \pi_2, s_0, \gamma)|$, *and*
$\forall 1 \leq k' < k, |Sat(\Omega_{k'}, \pi_1, s_0, \gamma)| = |Sat(\Omega_{k'}, \pi_2, s_0, \gamma)|$; *or*
(ii) $\forall 1 \leq k \leq m, |Sat(\Omega_k, \pi_1, s_0, \gamma)| = |Sat(\Omega_k, \pi_2, s_0, \gamma)|$.

This allows us to define another notion of minimal contraction for a moral conflict, namely a minimal contraction with respect to a lexicographic value base.

Definition 12 (Lexicographic-minimal contraction). *If $M = (\Omega, \gamma, s_0)$ is a moral problem, and $\overline{\Omega} = (\Omega_1, \ldots, \Omega_m)$ is a value base such that $\cup \overline{\Omega} = \Omega$ then $M' = (\Omega', \gamma, s_0)$ is a $\overline{\Omega}$-qual-minimal contraction of M if and only if:*

(i) $\Omega' \subseteq \Omega$;
(ii) M' *is not a moral conflict;*
(iii) *If $M'' = (\Omega'', \gamma, s_0)$ is also a contraction of M,*
$\nexists k : (a)$ $1 \leq k \leq m$ *and* $\Omega' \cap \Omega_k \subset \Omega'' \cap \Omega_k$, *and*
(b) $\forall 1 \leq i < k, \Omega' \cap \Omega_i = \Omega'' \cap \Omega_i$.

Note that by combining definitions 11 and 12 we can define a notion of $\overline{\Omega}$-quant-minimal contraction.

Proposition 3. *Given a moral conflict M, a contraction M' is $\overline{\Omega}$-qual-minimal or $\overline{\Omega}$-quant-minimal only if it is qual-minimal.*

3.7 Adding Desires

The behavior of autonomous ethical agents is driven not only by ethical values aimed at promoting the good for society but also by their endogenous motivations, also called *desires* or *goals*. Following existing theories of ethical preferences in philosophy, economics and logic [14,23,29], we assume that (i) desires and values are competing motivational attitudes, and (ii) the agent's degree of morality is a function of its disposition to promote the fulfilment of its values at the expense of the satisfaction of its desires. The following definition extends the notion of ethical planning domain by the notions of desire and introduces the novel concept of degree of morality.

Definition 13 (Mixed-motive planning domain). *A mixed-motive planning domain is a tuple $\Gamma = (\gamma, s_0, \overline{\Omega}, \Omega_D, \mu)$ where*

– $(\gamma, s_0, \overline{\Omega})$ is an ethical planning domain (Definition 9);
– $\Omega_D \subseteq \mathcal{L}_{\mathsf{LTL}_f}$ is the agent's set of desires or goals;
– $\mu \in \{1, \ldots, dg(\overline{\Omega}) + 1\}$ is the agent's degree of morality.

A mixed-motive planning domain induces an ethical planning domain whereby the agent's set of desires is treated as a set of values whose priority level depends on the agent's degree of morality. Specifically, the lower the agent's degree of morality, the higher the priority of the agent's set of desires in the induced ethical planning domain. In many practical applications it is likely to be desirable to restrict the range of values that μ can take, in order to prevent (for example) the robot's goal from overriding its safety values.

Definition 14 (Induced ethical planning domain). *Let* $\Gamma = (\gamma, s_0, \overline{\Omega}, \Omega_D, \mu)$ *be a mixed-motive planning domain. The ethical planning domain induced by* Γ *is the tuple* $\Delta = (\gamma, s_0, \overline{\Omega}')$ *such that* $dg(\overline{\Omega}') = dg(\overline{\Omega}) + 1$ *with:*

(i) $\Omega'_\mu = \Omega_D$;

(ii) $\Omega'_k = \Omega_k$ for $1 \le k < \mu$;

(iii) $\Omega'_k = \Omega_{k-1}$ for $\mu < k \le dg(\overline{\Omega}) + 1$.

4   An Example

Consider a blood delivery robot in a hospital. The robot mostly makes deliveries between different storage areas, and sometimes delivers blood to surgeries. The robot may have to deal with various kinds of obstacles to complete its deliveries, but we will consider only one: people blocking the robot. The robot has two methods to resolve this obstacle, it can ask for them to move and then wait for them to move (ask), or it can use a loud air-horn to "force" them to move (horn). Once the person has moved, the robot can reach its destination (move). We suppose that the robot can tell some things about its environment, it knows if it is blocked (blocked), if it is near the operating theatre (theatre) and if it has reached its destination (destination). We can then define the action model as follows:

$$\gamma^+(\mathsf{move}, \mathsf{destination}) = \neg\mathsf{blocked}$$
$$\gamma^-(\mathsf{ask}, \mathsf{blocked}) = \mathsf{blocked}$$
$$\gamma^+(\mathsf{ask}, \mathsf{delayed}) = \top$$
$$\gamma^-(\mathsf{horn}, \mathsf{blocked}) = \mathsf{blocked}$$
$$\gamma^+(\mathsf{horn}, \mathsf{annoyed}) = \top$$
$$\gamma^+(\mathsf{horn}, \mathsf{dangerous}) = \mathsf{theatre}$$
$$\text{otherwise,}\ \gamma^\pm(a, p) = \bot$$

The propositions delayed, annoyed and dangerous are used to keep track of the robot's actions, we suppose that using the horn near the operating theatre is dangerous. The values and desires of the robot can be presented as follows:

$$\overline{\Omega} = \{\Omega_1, \Omega_2\}$$
$$\Omega_1 = \{\text{G}\neg\text{dangerous}\}$$
$$\Omega_2 = \{\text{G}\neg\text{annoyed}\}$$
$$\Omega_D = \{\text{Fdestination}, \text{F(destination} \wedge \neg\text{delayed)}\}$$

In words, the robot's goal is to reach its destination without delays, with the primary value to never do anything dangerous, and the secondary value to never be annoying. Let $\overline{\Omega}'$ be the value base induced by $\overline{\Omega}$, Ω_D and $\mu = 3$.

Now we can compare the following 2-plans $\pi_1 = (\text{ask}, \text{move})$ and $\pi_2 = (\text{horn}, \text{move})$. If we assume that in the initial state the robot is blocked but far from an operating theatre, we can represent the histories generated from these plans as follows (each block contains exactly the propositions that are true in that state):

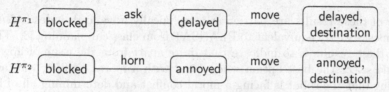

In this case $Sat(\overline{\Omega}', \pi_1, s_0, \gamma) = \{\text{G}\neg\text{dangerous}, \text{G}\neg\text{annoyed}, \text{Fdestination}\} = A \supseteq \Omega_1 \cup \Omega_2$ whereas $Sat(\overline{\Omega}', \pi_2, s_0, \gamma) = \{\text{G}\neg\text{dangerous}, \text{Fdestination}, \text{F(destination} \wedge \neg\text{delayed)}\} = B \supseteq \Omega_1 \cup \Omega_D$. Therefore π_1 will be preferred to π_2. However, if we change the morality level to 2, perhaps to represent an urgent delivery to an ongoing surgery, then we see that the robot will choose plan π_2 rather than π_1. This illustrates how we can adjust the morality level of the robot to reflect the urgency of its goals. If we move the example to the operating theatre (so now theatre $\in s_0$ instead of $\neg$theatre $\in s_0$), then the robot would not sound its horn even if the delivery was urgent, as Ω_1 still overrides Ω_D. This also means that for this robot we should restrict μ to 2 or 3 to ensure that being safe is always prioritised over goals. Furthermore, notice that for any lexicographic value structure containing exactly these values and goals, the set of non-dominated plan will always contain either π_1, π_2 or both, since A and B are exactly the qual-minimal contractions of $\cup\overline{\Omega}'$ given an initial state where the robot is blocked.

5   Computational Complexity

In this section we initiate the study of the computational complexity of ethical planning in our setting. We borrow our terminology from the work of Lang [17] on compact preference representation, but the problems we study have obvious counterparts in the planning literature, as should be clear from the proofs. In the interest of space all proofs can be found in the appendix.

We begin by studying the problem CONFLICT, which determines if a moral problem is also a moral conflict.

CONFLICT
Input: Moral problem $M = (\Omega, \gamma, s_0)$
Question: Is there some $k \in \mathbb{N}$ such that there is a k-plan π' such that $Sat(\Omega, \pi, s_0, \gamma) = \Omega$?

Theorem 1. CONFLICT *is PSPACE-complete.*

We then study the case of contractions, in particular, determining if a given moral problem is a qual-minimal contraction.

MINIMAL-CONTRACTION
Input: Moral problem $M = (\Omega, \gamma, s_0)$, moral problem $M' = (\Omega', \gamma, s_0)$
Question: Is M' a qual-minimal contraction of M?

Theorem 2. MINIMAL-CONTRACTION *is PSPACE-complete.*

Neither of these results are particularly technically advanced, indeed CON-FLICT is almost exactly equivalent to PLANSAT from classical planning [8]. The purpose of these results is to indicate that quite apart from the issue of how a robot should select the best option when faced with a moral conflict, the task of identifying that the robot is facing a moral conflict and determining all of its options is extremely computationally difficult.

On the subject of planning, we begin by studying the problem COMPARISON, which given two k-plans π_1 and π_2, asks whether $\pi_1 \preceq^{qual}_\Delta \pi_2$. Despite the apparent complexity of our setting this problem can be solved efficiently:

COMPARISON
Input: Ethical planning domain $\Delta = (\gamma, s_0, \overline{\Omega})$, $k \in \mathbb{N}$, k-plans π_1, π_2
Question: is it the case that $\pi_1 \preceq^{qual}_\Delta \pi_2$?

Theorem 3. COMPARISON *is in* P.

We then move to the problem of non-dominance, i.e., the problem of determining if given a g-plan π_1 there exists a better k-plan wrt. $\preceq^{qual}_\Delta$ (where $g \leq k$).

NON-DOMINANCE
Input: Ethical planning domain $\Delta = (\gamma, s_0, \overline{\Omega})$, $k \in \mathbb{N}$, g-plan π for $g \leq k$
Question: is there a k-plan π' such that $\pi \preceq^{qual}_\Delta \pi'$ and $\pi' \npreceq^{qual}_\Delta \pi$?

We show that this problem, as most instances of classical planning satisfaction, is PSPACE-complete:

Theorem 4. NON-DOMINANCE *is PSPACE-complete.*

Proposition 4. *Given an ethical planning domain* $\Delta = (\gamma, s_0, \overline{\Omega})$, *a k-plan* π *and* $S = Sat(\cup\overline{\Omega}, \pi, s_0, \gamma)$ π *is non-dominated for* Δ *if and only if* $M = (S, \gamma, s_0)$ *is a* $\overline{\Omega}$-*qual-minimal contraction for* $(\cup\overline{\Omega}, \gamma, s_0)$.

Theorems 3 and 4 are to be interpreted as baseline results showing the computational feasibility of our setting for ethical planning with LTL_f. One clear direction for future work would expand on the computational complexity analysis, identifying tractable fragments and exploring their expressivity in ethical applications.

An important property for an ethical planner is *explainability*. While explaining why a particular plan was chosen is difficult to do succinctly (even for humans), a simpler problem is to explain why the chosen plan was better than another proposed alternative. Our approach enables this in a way that is both computationally straightforward and intuitively understandable to humans, since by the lexicographic ordering of plans there always exists a single value or set of values that decides between two plans.

6 Conclusion

We put forward a novel setting for ethical planning obtained by combining a simple logical temporal language with lexicographic preference modelling. Our setting applies to planning situations with a single agent who has deterministic and instantaneous actions to be performed sequentially in a static and known environment. Aside from the addition of values, our framework differs from classical planning in two aspects, by having multiple goals and by allowing temporal goals. In particular, the expressiveness of LTL means that we can express a wide variety of goals and values, including complex temporal values such as "if the weather is cold, close external doors immediately after opening them", with a computational complexity equivalent to that of standard planners. As a limitation, the system is less able to express values that tend to be satisfied by degree rather than absolutely or not at all. Among the multiple directions for future work that our definitions open, we plan to study the multi-agent extension with possibly conflicting values among agents, moving from plans to strategies (functions from states or histories to actions), from complete to incomplete information, and, most importantly, test our model by implementing it in simple robotics scenarios. Furthermore, given the computational complexity of CONFLICT, MININAL-CONTRACTION and NON-DOMINANCE, it may often be the case that in practical applications we cannot guarantee finding a non-dominated plan. Therefore, it would be valuable to find more tractable algorithms that at least guarantee some degree of approximation of a non-dominated plan, or restrictions (likely to the language or action theory) that improve tractability of the problem.

Acknowledgements. This work is supported by the CNRS project LEXIA ("The Logic of Explanation: From Explainable to Explaining Legal Knowledge-based Systems").

References

1. Alili, S., Alami, R., Montreuil, V.: A task planner for an autonomous social robot. In: Asama, H., Kurokawa, H., Ota, J., Sekiyama, K. (eds.) Distributed Autonomous Robotic Systems 8. Springer, Berlin, Heidelberg (2009). https://doi.org/10.1007/978-3-642-00644-9_30

2. Anderson, M., Anderson, S.L.: Geneth: a general ethical dilemma analyzer. Paladyn (Warsaw) **9**(1), 337–357 (2018)

3. Arkin, R.C., Ulam, P., Wagner, A.R.: Moral decision making in autonomous systems: enforcement, moral emotions, dignity, trust, and deception. Proc. IEEE **100**(3), 571–589 (2012)

4. Awad, E., et al.: When is it acceptable to break the rules? Knowledge representation of moral judgement based on empirical data. CoRR abs/2201.07763 (2022)

5. Benzmüller, C., Parent, X., van der Torre, L.W.N.: Designing normative theories for ethical and legal reasoning: logiKEy framework, methodology, and tool support. Artif. Intell. **287**, 103–348 (2020)

6. Berreby, F., Bourgne, G., Ganascia, J.: A declarative modular framework for representing and applying ethical principles. In: Proceedings of the 16th Conference on Autonomous Agents and MultiAgent Systems (AAMAS) (2017)

7. Bienvenu, M., Fritz, C., McIlraith, S.A.: Planning with qualitative temporal preferences. In: Doherty, P., Mylopoulos, J., Welty, C.A. (eds.) Proceedings of the 10th International Conference on Principles of Knowledge Representation and Reasoning (KR), pp. 134–144. AAAI Press (2006)

8. Bylander, T.: The computational complexity of propositional STRIPS planning. Artif. Intell. **69**(1–2), 165–204 (1994)

9. Copp, D.: The Oxford Handbook of Ethical Theory. Oxford University Press, Oxford (2007)

10. De Giacomo, G., Vardi, M.Y.: Linear temporal logic and linear dynamic logic on finite traces. In: Rossi, F. (ed.) Proceedings of the 23rd International Joint Conference on Artificial Intelligence (IJCAI), pp. 854–860. IJCAI/AAAI (2013)

11. Dennis, L.A., Fisher, M., Slavkovik, M., Webster, M.: Formal verification of ethical choices in autonomous systems. Robot. Auton. Syst. **77**, 1–14 (2016)

12. Dennis, L.A., del Olmo, C.P.: A defeasible logic implementation of ethical reasoning. In:1st International Workshop on Computational Machine Ethics (CME) (2021)

13. Evans, K., de Moura, N., Chauvier, S., Chatila, R., Dogan, E.: Ethical decision making in autonomous vehicles: The AV ethics project. Sci. Eng. Ethics **26**(6), 3285–3312 (2020)

14. Harsanyi, J.: Utilitarianism and beyond. In: Sen, A.K., Williams, B. (eds.) Morality and the Theory of Rational Behaviour. Cambridge University Press, Cambridge (1982)

15. Jenkins, R., Talbot, B., Purves, D.: When robots should do the wrong thing. In: Robot Ethics 2.0. Oxford University Press, New York (2017)

16. Kment, B.: Varieties of Modality. In: Zalta, E.N. (ed.) The Stanford Encyclopedia of Philosophy. Spring (2021)

17. Lang, J.: Logical preference representation and combinatorial vote. Ann. Math. Artif. Intell. **42**(1–3), 37–71 (2004)

18. Levi, I.: Hard Choices: Decision Making Under Unresolved Conflict. Cambridge University Press, Cambridge (1990)

19. Lindner, F., Mattmüller, R., Nebel, B.: Moral permissibility of action plans. In: Proceedings of the 33rd AAAI Conference on Artificial Intelligence (AAAI), pp. 7635–7642. AAAI Press (2019)
20. Loreggia, A., Mattei, N., Rossi, F., Venable, K.B.: On the distance between cp-nets. In: Proceedings of the 17th International Conference on Autonomous Agents and MultiAgent Systems (AAMAS) (2018)
21. Loreggia, A., Rossi, F., Venable, K.B.: Modelling ethical theories compactly. In: The Workshops of the 31st AAAI Conference on Artificial Intelligence (2017)
22. Lorini, E.: A logic for reasoning about moral agents. Logique Analyse **58**(230), 177–218 (2015)
23. Lorini, E.: Logics for games, emotions and institutions. FLAP **4**(9), 3075–3113 (2017)
24. Lorini, E.: A logic of evaluation. In: Proceedings of the 20th International Conference on Autonomous Agents and Multiagent Systems (AAMAS), pp. 827–835. ACM (2021)
25. Müller, V.C.: Ethics of artificial intelligence and robotics. In: Zalta, E.N. (ed.) The Stanford Encyclopedia of Philosophy. Summer 2021 (2021)
26. Pnueli, A.: The temporal logic of programs. In: Proceedings of the 18th Annual Symposium on Foundations of Computer Science (FOCS) (1977)
27. Powers, T.M.: Deontological machine ethics. In: Anderson, M., Anderson, S.L., Armen, C. (eds.) Association for the Advancement of Artificial Intelligence Fall Symposium Technical Report (2005)
28. Rossi, F., Mattei, N.: Building ethically bounded AI. In: The 33rd AAAI Conference on Artificial Intelligence (AAAI) (2019)
29. Searle, J.: Rationality in Action. Cambridge University Press, MIT Press (2001)
30. Sen, A.: On Ethics and Economics. Basil Blackwell, Oxford (1987)
31. Vallor, S.: Technology and the Virtues: A Philosophical Guide to a Future Worth Wanting. Oxford University Press, New York (2016)
32. Vanderelst, D., Winfield, A.F.T.: An architecture for ethical robots inspired by the simulation theory of cognition. Cogn. Syst. Res. **48**, 56–66 (2018)
33. Yu, H., Shen, Z., Miao, C., Leung, C., Lesser, V.R., Yang, Q.: Building ethics into artificial intelligence. In: Proceedings of the 27th International Joint Conference on Artificial Intelligence (IJCAI) (2018)

A Hybrid Recommender System
with Implicit Feedbacks in Fashion Retail

Ilaria Cestari[1,2], Luigi Portinale[2,3(✉)], and Pier Luigi Riva[1]

[1] ORS Group, Roddi, Italy
{ilaria.cestari,pierluigi.riva}@ors.it
[2] Computer Science Institute, DiSIT, Univ. Piemonte Orientale, Alessandria, Italy
luigi.portinale@uniupo.it
[3] Inferendo srl, Alessandria, Italy

Abstract. In the present paper we propose a hybrid recommender system dealing with implicit feedbacks in the domain of fashion retail. The proposed architecture is based on a collaborative-filtering module taking into account the fact that users feedbacks are not explicit scores about the items, but are obtained through user interactions with the products in terms of number of purchases; moreover, a second module provides a knowledge-based contextual post-filtering, based on both customer-oriented and business-oriented objectives. We finally present a case study where "look-oriented" recommendations have been implemented for a specific fashion retail brand.

Keywords: Recommender systems · Implicit feedbacks · Hybrid architecture · Fashion retail

1 Introduction

Recommender Systems (RS) are software products based on machine learning having the goal of learning user preferences for specific items or services in very different contexts, particularly e-commerce and on-line retail. They can employ various methods such as collaborative filtering, content-based, hybrid, and knowledge-based approaches [13]. The most widely adopted approaches are those based on collaborative filtering; the idea is that user preferences about specific items can be captured by looking at the interactions such users have on the set of available items.

In general, one can think to the user-item interaction as a "feedback" the user provides with respect to the item. Formally, given a set of m users U, a set of n items I and a set of possible feedbacks F, we can define a feedback matrix $R_{(m \times n)} = \{r_{ij} = f | i \in U, j \in I, f \in F\}$. In the most general case, values in set F are ranked preferences expressed in natural numbers (e.g., from 1 stars up to 5 stars). In this situation we talk about explicit feedbacks, and a special case is that of binary feedbacks, where $F = \{0, 1\}$ (i.e., like, dislike). However, very often users are not able or willing to leave explicit feedbacks, and what

A. Dovier et al. (Eds.): AIxIA 2022, LNAI 13796, pp. 212–224, 2023.
https://doi.org/10.1007/978-3-031-27181-6_15

can be done is to "count" the interactions between users and items. In this case $r_{ij} \geq 0$ is just the number of times user i has interacted with item j. Interactions must be defined as specific actions such as item search, item view, item purchase or others. Of course, different kind of interactions can have different meaning, leading to different information concerning the user preferences. For instance, some actions can be considered as positive (purchase, addition to cart), while others are actually negative (removal from cart). Positive and negative actions should be treated according to their meaning (for example adding 1 to r_{ij} if the action is positive and subtracting 1 when it is negative). Moreover, even if all the actions are positive, they may have different relevance (e.g., a search is usually less indicative of a preference than a purchase); the different role of the different actions can be taken into account directly into the collaborative filtering process [6, Chapter 4], or by resorting to some hybrid form of recommendation taking into account multiple kinds of knowledge [2,9].

In the present paper we consider implicit feedbacks in the form of positive interactions, counting the number of purchases of an item by a given user. We addresses the problem of implicit feedbacks by resorting to the confidence model proposed in [8], and by adopting a hybrid architecture where collaborative filtering is complemented with a knowledge-based subsystem taking into account specific business rules. The considered domain is that of fashion retail.

The paper is organized as follows: in Sect. 2, the main concepts about the collaborative filtering and the approach proposed to deal with implicit feedbacks are discussed; Sect. 3 illustrates the proposed hybrid architecture, focusing on each module, explaining how they have been developed, and in Sect. 4 a case study illustrating the different steps of the recommendation process implemented for an important fashion retailer is discussed. Section 5 finally reports the conclusions and some comparisons with related works.

2   Collaborative Filtering with Implicit Feedbacks

Collaborative Filtering (CF) produces user specific recommendations based on patterns of user actions such us ratings or item usage, without the need of explicit user or item meta information. One of the most popular CF approach is the latent factor model, a model based technique based on the low-rank factorization of the feedback matrix [14]. It addresses the sparsity problem by projecting users and items into a reduced latent space containing the most salient features about their interactions. Given the feedback matrix $R_{(m \times n)}$, the idea is to decompose it into two matrices $U_{(m \times k)}$ and $V_{(n \times k)}$ such that

$$R_{(m \times n)} \approx U_{(m \times k)} V_{(k \times n)}^T$$

where $k \ll n$ and $k \ll m$ is the size of the latent space and U, V are the latent feature matrices for users and items respectively.

Once this factorization is obtained, if u_i represents the i-th row of matrix U and v_j the j-th row of matrix V, we can predict the feedback of each pair (i, j) of users and items as

$$\hat{r}_{ij} = u_i \cdot v_j^T = \sum_{h=1}^{k} u_{ih} v_{hj}^T$$

that is computable for each user-item pair, even for those having a missing entry in the original matrix R. Let the set of all user-item pairs (i,j), which are observed in R, be denoted by S: $S = \{(i,j) : r_{ij} \text{ is observed}\}$. A typical way of solving this factorization problem involves an optimization procedure (e.g., stochastic gradient descent) on the following objective function

$$J(U, V) = \frac{1}{2}\left(\sum_{(i,j) \in S} (r_{ij} - \hat{r}_{ij})^2 + \lambda(\|u_i\|^2 + \|v_j\|^2) \right)$$

where λ is a regularization hyper-parameter.

The above characterization is suitable when the entries encoded into the feedback matrix are explicit, such as precise ratings provided by the users. In case of implicit feedbacks, which are those that interest us in the present work, some modifications to the framework must be considered. First of all, we must notice that in our case only positive interactions are considered, leading to the fact that when the feedback is not null, then there is an interest of the user for the corresponding item. We then introduce an auxiliary indicator variable p_{ij} representing the generic interest of user i for item j and simply defined as

$$p_{ij} = \begin{cases} 1 & \text{if } r_{ij} > 0 \\ 0 & \text{otherwise} \end{cases}$$

Following the approach suggested in [8], we also consider a confidence level for the indicator p_{ij}, depending on the actual number of interactions a user had on a given item and defined as follows:

$$c_{ij} = 1 + \alpha r_{ij}$$

Given this characterization we have to find a user matrix U and an item matrix V minimizing the following cost function:

$$J(U, V) = \frac{1}{2}\left(\sum_{i,j} c_{ij}(p_{ij} - u_i \cdot v_j^T)^2 + \lambda(\sum_i \|u_i\|^2 + \sum_j \|v_j\|^2)\right) \quad (1)$$

In other words, we need to find a vector u_i for each user and a vector v_j for each item factorizing in the best possible way the user preferences. Preferences are represented by p_{ij} and must be computed as the inner product $u_i \cdot v_j^T$.

The main differences with the explicit feedback framework is that we need to take into account confidence levels c_{ij}, but mostly the fact that we need to consider every possible user-item pair (i,j) and not only those pairs for which we have an explicit interaction. This makes standard optimization procedures such as stochastic gradient descent impractical. A possible solution is to adopt Alternating Least Squares (ALS) optimization. The idea is conceptually simple: fix the user matrix U and find the optimal item matrix V; then fix the item matrix V and find the optimal user matrix U; keep alternating the previous steps until convergence. However, the implicit feedback framework requires a careful strategy to deal with a dense cost function (all possible user-item pairs must be considered) and to integrate the confidence levels.

In [8], Hu et al. proposes the following procedure. First we compute user factors from item factors contained in $V_{(n \times k)}$.

- Compute the $(k \times k)$ matrix $V^T V$ in time $O(k^2 n)$
- For each user i, let $C^i_{(n \times n)}$ be a diagonal matrix with $C^i_{jj} = c_{ij}$ (the diagonal contains the confidence in the preferences of the given user with respect to all n possible items); let also $p(i) \in \mathbb{R}^n$ be the vector containing preferences p_{ij} of user i.
- the following expression[1] minimizes the cost function in (1):

$$u_i = (V^T C^i V + \lambda I)^{-1} V^T C^i p(i)$$

In a similar fashion, once the user matrix U has been obtained we can re-compute[2] the entries of the item matrix as

$$v_j = (U^T C^j U + \lambda I)^{-1} U^T C^j p(j)$$

where $C^j_{(m \times m)}$ is the diagonal matrix with $C^j_{ii} = c_{ij}$ (the diagonal contains the confidence in the preferences of the given item with respect to all m possible users), and $p(j) \in \mathbb{R}^m$ be the vector containing preferences p_{ij} for item j of every possible user.

The procedure alternates the above user factors and item factors computation until convergence. Once the final matrices U and V have been computed, the K available items with the largest score $\hat{p}_{ij} = u_i \cdot v_j^T$ are recommended to user i.

3   System Architecture

The main goal of the present work is to define an architecture for the recommendation of products in the fashion domain. Recommender systems in fashion retail are usually integrated into e-commerce platforms or in digital marketing campaigns, as personalized recommendations generators [15]; in this setting it is really hard that users are able to release explicit "scores" on the products, thus the designed system must deal with the availability of feedbacks which are implicit by nature (i.e., user-item interactions such as purchases).

Moreover, such a system also needs to fulfill specific objectives that can be divided into "customer-oriented" and "business-oriented". Regarding customers, an important aspect of fashion recommendations is the ability to propose an

---

[1]   In [8] the authors shows that the corresponding computation can be performed in time $O(k^2 \mathcal{N} + k^3 m)$ where $\mathcal{N}$ is the total number of non-zero entries in the feedback matrix.

[2]   Similarly to previous step we can show that the computation takes $O(k^2 \mathcal{N} + k^3 n)$ time steps.

overall look composed by different type of products that may fit well together and tailor to the user individual preferences. Indeed, fashion products belonging to different technical categories are commonly bought together, in order to obtain a given look which can fit the customer style; thus the level of accuracy may be reduced with the goal of achieving higher levels of diversity and novelty, and to prevent overspecialization over the customer past purchases. On the business point of view, the user satisfaction after buying the recommended products can improve the customer loyalty, while the goal of recommending products belonging to various categories can be helpful also to increase the cross-selling and, in a more general way, to let the user explore, and ideally buy, as more products as possible.

For these reasons, we propose a hybrid architecture based on two main modules (see Fig. 1):

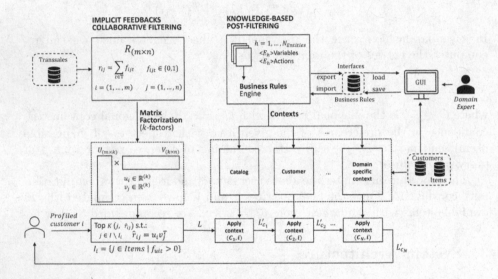

Fig. 1. Hybrid system architecture.

– a collaborative filtering module with implicit feedbacks
– a knowledge-based post-filtering module

3.1   Collaborative Filtering Module

We know that entities involved in the recommendation process are the customers (the set of users U) and the products (the set of items I); in the considered domain, the interactions between them can be collected from the purchases history in various distribution channels (retail, outlet, web) and from any available system capable of tracking user activities, such as visiting products pages or searching for keywords, or ideally giving an explicit rating to purchased products.

In the absence of such systems, purchases can be considered a good starting point to learn customers preferences and how they are distributed.

Usually, transactions (S) are stored in relational databases as receipt rows represented with tuples:

$$s = \langle t, p, i, j, a \rangle$$

where t is the transaction date, p, i, and j are the point of sale, customer and item identifier respectively, and a is the activity or transaction type. Rows may be decorated with other data about the transaction, e.g. whether the customer used a coupon, the actual purchase value or the chosen payment method; all of these can be used as further analysis to better characterize the customers. In the present work, we only consider transactions corresponding to purchases, e.g., $a = 1$; in addition, in the following discussion we are only interested in tracking which user has purchased a given item, in a given set of stores and in a particular time interval. We then define an indicator

$$f_{ijt} = \begin{cases} 1 & \text{if } \exists s = \langle t, \_, i, j, 1 \rangle \\ 0 & \text{otherwise} \end{cases}$$

with symbol $\_$ meaning "don't care" (and last element of s equal to 1 meaning purchase). Hence, by projecting S on users and items, and by considering a given time interval T, the transaction table can be reduced to tuples having the following structure:

$$\langle i, j, r_{ij} \rangle \text{ with } r_{ij} = \sum_{t \in T} f_{ijt}$$

Finally, the (sparse) feedback matrix is defined a $R_{m \times n} = [r_{ij}]$ where $m = |U|$ and $n = |I|$. As described in Sect. 2, the feedback matrix is then used as the basis for the implementation of the collaborative filtering module: we first produce the factorization $R_{m \times n} = U_{m \times k} V_{k \times n}^T$, then compute the predicted feedback $\hat{r}_{ij} = u_i \cdot v_j^T$, and finally for a given user $i \in U$, we return the top k items $j \in I$ with respect to $\hat{r}_{i,j}$.

3.2 Knowledge-Based Post-filtering Module

The second module executes a knowledge-based post-filtering on the results list produced by the CF model. It allows the filter of the results by adding constraints based on product features or contextual data, such as location, time, or other domain-specific elements. In our case, constraints are defined by domain experts as *business rules*, which describe known relationships between the domain entities (users or items), and used to adjust the model results by either filtering out or replace some items, or by adding gain and penalties on the scores, in order to change the ranking. Such rules are defined using a GUI (Fig. 2).

For each entity, a set of variables is defined representing its characteristics (e.g., the product description, the customer age or the estimated annual income). In addition, a set of actions available on specific instances is also defined; the main action, especially for item entities $j \in I$, is to select the instance and add

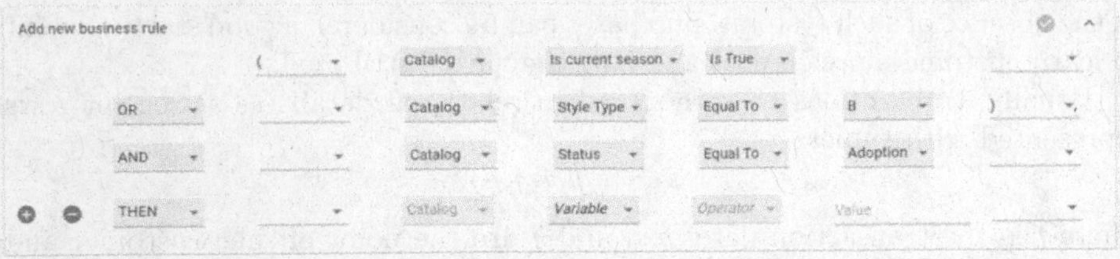

Fig. 2. An example of rule definition using the developed GUI: experts can choose the target entity and define multiple conditions with logical operators over their variables.

it to an output list to proceed with the post-filtering operations. This is also the main goal of the rules in this architecture: they can be considered as queries targeting the selection of some recommended products on which to execute a specific filtering function.

A rule is composed of a condition over some entity variables, and a consequence which determines the action the system must perform on the instances satisfying the constraint. Actions select instances whose values meet a given conditions or, in more complex cases, they link the status of one instance to that of the instances of another entity, in order to create an explicit correlation between them. For example, lets consider some features of the entities I ("Status", "IsCurrentSeason" and "ConsumerGroup") and U ("Age" and "Gender"). A rule representing a constraint on items is reported in (2), and a more complex rule that links the two entities in (3):

$$I.\texttt{Status} = \text{``}Adoption\text{''} \wedge I.\texttt{IsCurrentSeason} = \texttt{True} \tag{2}$$

$$U.\texttt{Gender} = \text{``}F\text{''} \wedge U.\texttt{Age} \geq 18 \Rightarrow I.\texttt{ConsumerGroup} = \text{``}Misses\text{''} \tag{3}$$

The first rule selects every item in the "Adoption" production status and available for the current season; the second one is used to define a constraint on the entity I on the basis of the instance of U (i.e., the target user).

Such rules can be applied in a modular way over the model results, by introducing the idea of "context", which is an aspect of the domain a group of rules refers to. Following the framework proposed in [1], the aim is to implement a type of context-aware recommender system, with contextual post-filtering. For each context, the domain expert defines the filtering operations to perform on the instances selected by the context's rules. The number of contexts may vary depending on the number of entities involved, or the different objectives that the system must achieve. In fashion retail, one usually consider almost two main contexts: the "catalog context", containing constraints about products availability, which can change depending on the temporal context of the recommendation or other external causes; the "customer context", that allows the retailers to define correlations between the features of products and customers. Next section describes how they can be applied in a specific case study.

4   Case Study and Experimental Results

In a fashion store or e-commerce platform, item features are usually organized hierarchically. The actual hierarchy can vary from one brand to another; in this paper we refer to a case study concerning an important fashion brand, where a given product belongs to a *merchandise group* characterized by the department store (outlet or retail), the technical category (such as trousers, shirts or skirts), and the "lifecycle" (fashion or basic). Inside a given merchandise group we identify different *models*; the model identifies a series of technical features like the garment materials, fitting and other specific characteristics that help to distinguish the product style. Finally for a given model we can specify "low-level" features such as color or size of the garment (see Table 1).

Table 1. Hierarchy of products features with an example case of a men's dress shirt.

Hierarchy level	Description	Example
Merchandise Group	Indicates the product's department, technical category and lifecycle	Retail, Dress Shirt, Fashion
Group Type	The target customer group	Men
Model	Id that identifies the stylistic features of the product	Regular Point Collar
Color (Style)	Color shade	Blue Navy
Size	Stock Keeping Unit (SKU), unit sold and registered in the receipts	S

Customers buy products at the lowest hierarchy level: the so called Stock Keeping Unit (SKU). Each SKU represents a specific garment as an instance of a merchandise group (store type, technical category and lifecycle) with a specific model, size and color. Typically, all these features are categorical and may have a broad range of values. The CF model discussed in Sect. 2 does not use the explicit features of users and products to learn their latent factors, so it is crucial to decide over which items the preferences should be determined. By considering the feedbacks as purchases at the SKU level, the user-item preference is implicitly computed over all the product characteristics, thus the model will propose the most preferable SKUs for the users. Depending on the recommender's final objectives, it may be useful to consider a more abstract level of attributes (i.e., to get rid of some details such as size and color for instance) or to group the values of some features. In this way, we can learn preferences over more abstract aspects, such as the style, instead of specific characteristics such as the size or the shade of color. Furthermore, this can help to reduce the number of user-item pairs and so the dimensionality of the feedback matrix.

In the present case study, we are targeting look-oriented recommendations; in this situation, the size is too specific, related more to the user's need to find clothes suitable for her/his body, rather than to an actual preference, thus it should be excluded. On the other hand, color is a fundamental feature of fashion products, very representative of the user's preferences, but with a huge number of "nuances"; this could led to recommendations which are too biased by a specific color shade. Hence, shades have been grouped into their main color (e.g., "blue" instead of "light blue", "dark blue" or "navy blue") to keep the recommendation more generic as possible, and to easily recommend different colors as well. We have taken into account the retail transactions history of the last two years, containing purchases from both stores and web distribution channels of the considered brand, and by selecting customers with at least 3 purchases; the final (sparse) feedback matrix $R_{m \times n}$ contained $5,200,649$ positive interactions between $m = 662,964$ loyal customers and $n = 26,185$ model-color items. In the following, in order to provide a recommendation example, we consider a specific user case: a 30 years old man, for which some purchases are listed in the first column of Table 2.

Table 2. Some of the customer purchases and the top 5 recommendations of the model with $k = 500$ factors. In the description of the recommended items are reported also their seasonality and production status.

Purchased	Recommended	$\hat{r}_{ij}$	Item id
Ribbed Crew Socks Beige Men	Ribbed Crew Socks Black Men (Ongoing, Design)	0.749	46943
Leather Belt Brown Men	Casual Trousers Relaxed Plain Blue Men (Ongoing, Adoption)	0.710	99337
Supima Cotton Crewneck Sweater Stripe Blue Men	Dress Shirt Blue Men (Fall, Adoption)	0.688	126718
Dress Shirt Stretch White Summer Men	Ribbed Crew Socks Blue Men (Ongoing, Design)	0.686	46945
Dress Shirt Purple Fall Men	Set Shorts Bermuda Dyed Beige Men (Fall, Adoption)	0.657	71958

The model has been fitted in two versions: one with $k > 1$ factors, which is the main model, and one benchmark with 1 factor (equivalent to recommend the most popular items in terms of purchases); the model's parameters have been tuned with a 10-fold cross-validation and the best results have been obtained with $k = 500$ factors, achieving an AUC score of 0.73 on the test set against the 0.56 of the benchmark model. If we indicate as I_i the set of items already purchased by user i, the output for the user i will be a list L of pairs $(j, \hat{r}_{ij})$ with $j \in (I \setminus I_i)$ and ranked by $\hat{r}_{ij}$ (see Sect. 2). Table 2 reports (last three columns) the top 5 items recommended by the model for the customer described above, together with the corresponding $\hat{r}_{ij}$ score.

For the post-filtering module, three contexts have been defined: "catalog", "customer", and "look". As described in Sect. 3.2, the catalog context determines which items are available at the time of the recommendation; it identifies two subsets I_{out} and I_v of unavailable and valid items respectively. The post-filtering operation consists in removing from the output list L any pair $(j, \hat{r}_{ij})$ for $j \in I_{out}$, by replacing it with the pair $(j', \hat{r}_{ij'})$ where $j' \in I_v$ is the most similar (available) item to j (in case such a j' exists). In the present case study, the similarity score between two items j_1, j_2 has been computed as $s_{j_1 j_2} = v_{j_1} v_{j_2}^T$, reusing the latent factors V learned by the CF model (see Sect. 2). The score of the new replacing item j' is again computed from latent factors as $\hat{r}_{ij'} = u_i v_{j'}^T$ (see again Sect. 2). The catalog context has the higher priority, and thus the strongest effect on the recommended items. For instance, considering rule (2) as the only rule in the catalog context, Table 4 reports the new top 5 items (first column), in which only product with ItemID=99337 is kept and the others have been replaced. Score s_1 in Table 4 refers to the usual item relevance score $\hat{r}_{ij}$ (i being the current user and j the considered item).

Customer context rules are applied after catalog rules and link customer and item characteristics with respect to known statistical correlations, such as relationships between age (or genre) and particular garment categories, relationships between an item price and how much the customer usually spends, and so on. However, the descriptive characteristics of loyal customers are not necessarily representative of their normal buying behaviour or style preferences: a common case is when registered customer buy products for family members or other people. Thus, the application of this context shouldn't be too disruptive to the model's output and consists in increasing the score of the current recommended items j as follows:

$$s_2 = s_1(1 + P(j, C_i)) \tag{4}$$

where s_1 is the old item relevance score, C_i is the set of customer context rules whose antecedent is satisfied by features of user i, and $P(j, C_i)$ is a term computed as:

$$P(j, C_i) = \frac{t(j, C_i)}{|C_i|}$$

where $t(j, C_i)$ is the number of the customer context rules in C_i whose consequent is satisfied by features of item j. The idea is to increment the score by a quantity proportional to the number of rules that are satisfied. In Table 3 some examples of customer context rules are shown. The item listed in Table 4 are those items resulting from first applying catalog rule (2), then by replacing items different than ItemId = 99337 (the only one satisfying the rule) with their most similar available items. Score s_2 is the result of selecting the customer context rule 1 of Table 3 (the only one satisfied by the current user) and applying formula (4).

Finally, the look context has been added to introduce more diversity between the recommended product categories, in order to increase the cross-selling. In this phase, items present in the current recommended list are penalized with a term $c(T_j)$, which represents how many times the technical category T_j of item

Table 3. Rules available in the customer context. Given the target customer's profile, since his parental status is unknown, rule 1 his the only that can be added to the customer's specific context C_i, and thus $|C_i| = 1$.

Rule	Definition
0	$Gender = \text{``}F\text{''} \wedge Age \geq 18 \Rightarrow ConsumerGroup = \text{``}Misses\text{''}$
1	$Gender = \text{``}M\text{''} \wedge Age \geq 18 \Rightarrow ConsumerGroup = \text{``}Men\text{''}$
2	$Children = \text{``}Yes\text{''} \Rightarrow ConsumerGroup = (\text{``}Boys\text{''} \vee \text{``}Girls\text{''})$

Table 4. Changes in scores after applying the catalog and the customer contexts. Here, listed items are available in the current season and in adoption status (L'_{c_1}) and all have had an increase by the customer context, since all the visible items belong to the "Men" consumer group.

Item	Score s_1	Score s_2	Description
99337	0.710	1.420	Casual Trousers Relaxed Plain Blue Men
99341	0.489	0.976	Pants Lightweight Stretch Chino Gray Men
74393	0.437	0.874	Shoes Leather Boat Blue Men
57871	0.436	0.871	Boots Field Chukka Brown Men
99302	0.421	0.842	Casual Trousers Relaxed Plain Blue

j has already appeared in higher rank positions in the list. The new score for each item is computed as:

$$s'_{ij} = \frac{s_{ij}}{c(T_j)}$$

Table 5 shows the results of applying this penalty score to the items of Table 4. Here it is not necessary to define explicit rules, because the post-filtering operation is performed on every item without any selection; notice that in principle, one could also integrate business rules to replace the penalized items with others "compatible" with those in the list.

Table 5. Penalties assigned by the look context and the final score of each recommended item

Item	Score	Tech. category	Penalty	New score
99337	1.420	CASUAL TROUSERS	1	1.420
99341	0.976	CASUAL TROUSERS	2	0.488
74393	0.874	SHOES	1	0.874
57871	0.871	SHOES	2	0.436
99302	0.842	CASUAL TROUSERS	3	0.281

5   Conclusions and Related Works

As reported in [5], fashion and apparel industries have grown tremendously over the last years, especially because of the availability of a great amount of products in online stores, coupled with the support provided by recommender systems. One specific challenge is the large vocabulary of distinct fashion items, leading to very sparse user-item interaction matrices, often represented with a given overspecification level (as we discussed above). Other issues in fashion recommendation, are related to the suggestion of a suitable "look" or outfit [4,10], as well as the evolution of a fashion trend across time and location [11].

The vocabulary problem is often tackled through computer vision techniques for the determination of item category and attributes [3,7], while the other issues can be addressed by learning suitable models via massive amount of social data [16], or customer reported information [12], as well as customer reviews [17].

In the present work, we have dealt with the above issues by resorting to a hybrid architecture, where collaborative filtering is complemented with specific contextual knowledge-based rules. The cons is that expert knowledge must be elicited, in order to build the contextual rules; however, as we have outlined in the case study, the fashion domain provides precise contextual situations where such rules can be obtained from experts without a huge effort. The experience gained in this application suggests that the approach is feasible and beneficial.

References

1. Adomavicius, G., Mobasher, B., Ricci, F., Tuzhilin, A.: Context-aware recommender systems. AI Mag. 67–80 (2011)
2. Burke, R.: Hybrid recommender systems: survey and experiments. User Model. User-Adap. Int. **12**(4), 31–370 (2002)
3. Chen, H., Gallagher, A., Girod, B.: Describing clothing by semantic attributes. In: Fitzgibbon, A., Lazebnik, S., Perona, P., Sato, Y., Schmid, C. (eds.) ECCV 2012. LNCS, vol. 7574, pp. 609–623. Springer, Heidelberg (2012). https://doi.org/10.1007/978-3-642-33712-3_44
4. Chen, W., et al.: POG: personalized outfit generation for fashion recommendation at Alibaba iFashion. In: Proceedings of 25th ACM SIGKDD International Conference on Knowledge Discovery and Data Mining, pp. 2662–2670 (2019)
5. Deldjoo, Y., et al.: A review of modern fashion recommender systems. ACM Comput. Surv. **37**(4), 111:1–111:35 (2021)
6. Dunning, T., Friedman, E.: Practical Machine Learning: Innovations in Recommendation. O'Reilly, Sebastopol (2014)
7. Ferreira, B., Costeira, J., Sousa, R., Gui, L.Y., Gomes, J.: Pose guided attention for multi-label fashion image classification. In: Proceedings of IEEE/CVF International Conference on Computer Vision (ICCVW 2019), pp. 3125–3128 (2019)
8. Hu, Y., Koren, Y., Volinsky, C.: Collaborative filtering for implicit feedbacks datasets. In: Proceedings of 8th IEEE International Conference on Data Mining (ICDM), pp. 263–272 (2008)
9. Koren, Y., Bell, R.: Advances in collaborative filtering. In: Ricci, F., Rokach, L., Shapira, B. (eds.) Recommender Systems Handbook, pp. 77–118. Springer, Boston (2015). https://doi.org/10.1007/978-1-4899-7637-6_3

10. Lin, Y.L., Tran, S., Davis, L.: Fashion outfit complementary item retrieval. In: Proceedings of IEEE/CVF Conference on Computer Vision and Pattern Recognition (CVPR 2020), pp. 3311–3319 (2020)
11. Matzen, K., Bala, K., Snavely, N.: Streetstyle: exploring world-wide clothing styles from millions of photos. CoRR abs/1706.01869 (2017). http://arxiv.org/abs/1706.01869
12. Parr, J., Pookulangara, S.: The impact of true fit technology on consumer confidence in their online clothing purchase. In: Proceedings of Annual Conference on International Textile and Apparel Association. Iowa State University Press (2017)
13. Ricci, F., Rokach, L., Shapira, B.: Recommender Systems Handbook, 2nd edn. Springer, New York (2015). https://doi.org/10.1007/978-1-4899-7637-6
14. Takacs, G., Pilaszy, I., Nemeth, B., Tikk, D.: Scalable collaborative filtering approaches for large recommender systems. J. Mach. Learn. Res. **10**, 623–656 (2009)
15. Walter, F., Battiston, S., Yildirim, M., Schweitzer, F.: Moving recommender systems from on-line commerce to retail stores. Inf. Syst. e-Bus. Manag. **10**, 367–393 (2012)
16. Wen, Y., Liu, X., Xu, B.: Personalized clothing recommendation based on knowledge graph. In: Proceedings of International Conference on Audio, Language and Image Processing (ICALIP 2018), pp. 1–5 (2018)
17. Zhao, K., Hu, X., Bu, J., Wang, C.: Deep style match for complementary recommendation. CoRR abs/1708.07938 (2017). http://arxiv.org/abs/1708.07938

Incremental Timeline-Based Planning for Efficient Plan Execution and Adaptation

Riccardo De Benedictis[✉][ID], Gloria Beraldo[ID], Amedeo Cesta[ID], and Gabriella Cortellessa[ID]

CNR - Italian National Research Council, ISTC,
Via S. Martino della Battaglia 44, 00185 Rome, RM, Italy
{riccardo.debenedictis,gloria.beraldo,amedeo.cesta,
gabriella.cortellessa}@istc.cnr.it
https://istc.cnr.it

Abstract. The increasing deployment, in real environments, of intelligent and distributed systems like robotic platforms, wearable sensors and AI-based devices, requires robust solutions that allow planned activities to converge with the emerging dynamic reality. Once a planning problem has been solved, indeed, it needs to be executed and, in the real world, things might not go as expected. While planned activities may be carried out by some underlying reactive modules, in fact, the adaptation to the surrounding environment provided by such components may not be sufficient to achieve the planned goals. Planned activities, for example, can be delayed or last longer than expected. The execution of other activities could fail threatening the achievement of the desired goals. Finally, new objectives may emerge during execution thus requiring changes to ongoing plans. This paper presents a timeline-based framework for efficiently adapting plans in order to cope with possible complications which might emerge during execution. By exploiting the information gathered during the finding solution process, the proposed framework allows, efficiently and without overturning it, to adapt the generated plan in case of unexpected events during its execution. Empirical results show that, compared to re-planning from scratch, plan adaptations can be obtained more efficiently, reducing computational costs and consequently enhancing the ability of the whole system to react quickly to unexpected events.

Keywords: Automated planning · Plan execution · Plan adaptation · Timeline-based planning

1 Introduction

Automated planning has been defined as *"the reasoning side of acting"* [24]. Planning, in particular, represents an abstract, explicit deliberation process that

This work is partially supported by "SI-ROBOTICS: SocIal ROBOTICS for active and healthy ageing" project (Italian M.I.U.R., PON – Ricerca e Innovazione 2014–2020 – G.A. ARS01_01120).

chooses and organizes actions by anticipating their expected outcomes. Although automated planning constitutes a rich technical field, however, most of the literature on domain-independent planning is biased towards that "reasoning" side [36]. Whether due to a partial knowledge of the world, or to the impossibility of predicting the actions of other agents that autonomously act in the same environment, a large part of any agent's behavior can be traced back to its ability to *react* to dynamic changes occurring, or predicted, in the world. Unlike other approaches that propose integration of planning systems into the executives of the autonomous ones [6,31,38], this paper has the twofold objective of: a) concentrating on a specific form of planning, called timeline-based [34]; and b) proposing a new framework which, by exploiting the knowledge acquired during the previous reasoning processes, is able to adapt plans more efficiently than by adopting from scratch re-planning.

The reasons for concentrating on timeline-based planning are mainly due to the fact that the constraints, introduced among the different elements of the plan during the reasoning process, produce a partial plan [47] which, compared to total order plans usually generated by more classical approaches, often result more suitable for adaptations during plan execution. Despite its ability to adapt dynamically, however, this type of formalism is particularly expressive and, consequently, is associated with a high computational complexity which makes the reasoning process significantly onerous, with consequent long computation times. While in [13] it has been demonstrated that the computation time could be effectively reduced, thanks to the introduction of some domain-independent heuristics, herein we focus on showing how the introduction of some of the data structures necessary for the computation of the above heuristics, as will be detailed further on, allows as well to efficiently manage the dynamic adaptation of the plans during their execution.

2   Related Works

The problem of the dynamic adaptation of plans has already been tackled from various points of view. Some approaches, such as those relying on simple temporal networks with uncertainty [32,33,50] or those based on model-checking [2,3], aim to generate robust solutions that don't require (or, in any case, that minimize) the need for adaptations at runtime. Although desirable in those contexts in which certain safety conditions in interacting with people are required (such as, for example, in industrial contexts), these approaches prove to be unattractive in situations with fairly free interactions (e.g., navigation or dialogues) between the user and the machine.

Unlike in standard planning problems, solving a contingency planning problem, as described in [39,48], does not generate a plan, but a decision tree with different contingent branches that could arise at execution time, whose execution allows the agent to achieve the planned objectives. These approaches allow for practically immediate adaptation at runtime and therefore, once the solution is found, they are probably the best possible choice. Nonetheless, these approaches require to consider, in the problem solving phase, all the possible events that may occur during the execution, making the reasoning process particularly burdensome even for relatively simple problems. Furthermore, the approaches adopted in contingency planning rarely manage forms of numerical and/or temporal reasoning.

Nebel et al. compare the advantages of re-planning from scratch and of reusing information from the old plan to generate a new one, showing that, from a theoretical point of view, the two approaches have, not surprisingly, the same computational complexity [37]. By relying on such theoretical results, approaches like ROSPlan [6] generate a new planning problem all over again whenever an exogenous event, incompatible with the current solution, occurs. These approaches have the great advantage of being able to use any existing planner as a black-box. However, it has the obvious disadvantage of potentially taking a lot of computational time whenever some exogenous event requiring adaptation occurs. Despite the theoretical results, indeed, further studies, such as [16,22,28,40,41], show that plan adaptation can be, in practice, more effective than re-planning. Such repair approaches, furthermore, help to maintain the plan stability, that is, how close the newly generated plan is to the one that it must replace. The approach proposed in this document is situated within the latter context. Unlike the cited approaches, however, we focus on a particular class of automated planning which, in addition to explicitly allowing forms of temporal and numerical reasoning, relies on partial order planning and, hence, produces solutions that usually require a smaller number of causal adaptations when unexpected events occur at execution time.

Particularly relevant to our approach, the Flexible Acting and Planning Environment (FAPE), introduced by [15], combines plan-space planning with simple temporal networks and hierarchical decomposition rules. A dispatcher calls for each planned action a set of skills and keeps track of their evolution over time allowing plan repair, extension, and re-planning, while being able to check and keep up to date the temporal relations and the causal constrains. Compared to FAPE, our architecture assigns a more central role to the acting component, giving it the ability to determine when and how to generate plans, execute them, adapt them or, if no longer needed as a consequence of a drastic change in the environment, destroy them and generate new ones. More than on architectural aspects, however, we focus, in this document, on the possibility of dynamically and efficiently adapting plans in the event of failures. When dealing with failures, indeed, FAPE is limited to the removal of just the one failing action, without considering cascades of other potential failures. Thanks to the adaptation of classical planning heuristics, as we will see, and similarly to what is done in the previously cited works applied to classical planning, we are able to overcome this limitation.

3   Technical Background

Timeline-based planning constitutes a form of deliberative reasoning which, in an integrated way, allows to carry out different forms of semantic and causal reasoning. Although this approach to planning has mostly been relegated to forms of causal reasoning in the space domain, many solvers have been proposed over the time like, for example, I_xT_eT [23], EUROPA [26], ASPEN [11], the TRF [8,19] on which the APSI framework [20] relies and, more recently, PLATINUm [45]. Some theoretical works on timeline-based planning like [18,26] were mostly dedicated to identifying connections with classical planning a-la PDDL [17]. The work on I_xT_eT and TRF has tried to clarify some keys underlying principles but mostly succeeded in underscoring the role of time and resource reasoning [9,29]. The planner CHIMP [44] follows a Meta-CSP approach having meta-Constraints which havely resembles timelines. The already mentioned FAPE [4,15] tightly integrates structures similar to timelines with acting. The Action Notation Modeling Language (ANML) [42] is an interesting development which combines the Hierarchical Task Network (HTN) [7,35,49] decomposition methods with the expressiveness of the timeline representation. Finally, it is worth mentioning that the timeline-based approaches have been often associated to resource managing capabilities. By leveraging on constraint-based approaches, most of the above approaches like I_xT_eT [10,29,30,43] or [46] integrate planning and scheduling capabilities. Finally, [12] proposes a recent formalization of timeline-based planning.

Given the mentioned link with the heuristics we will refer, in this paper, to the timeline-based planning formalization as defined in [13]. According to this formalization, specifically, the basic building block of timeline-based planning is the *token* which, intuitively, is used to represent the single unit of information. Through their introduction and their constraining during the planning process, in particular, tokens allow to represent the different components of the high-level plans. In its most general form, a token is formally described by an expression like $n(x_0, \ldots, x_i)_\chi$. In particular, n is a *predicate* symbol, $x_0, \ldots, x_i$ are its *parameters* (i.e., constants, numeric variables or object variables) and $\chi \in \{f, g\}$ is a constant representing the class of the token (i.e., either a *fact* or a *goal*).

The token's parameters are constituted, in general, by the variables of a *constraint network* $\mathcal{N}$ (refer to [14] for further details) and can be used, among other things, to represent temporal information such as the start or the end of some tasks. The semantics of the χ constant, on the contrary, is borrowed from Constraint Logic Programming (CLP) [1]. Specifically, while the facts are considered inherently true, the goals must be achieved as defined by a set of *rules*. Rules, in particular, are expressions of the form $n(x_0, \ldots, x_k) \leftarrow \mathbf{r}$ where $n(x_0, \ldots, x_k)$ is the *head* of the rule and $\mathbf{r}$ is the *body* of the rule. In particular, $\mathbf{r}$ represents the *requirement* for achieving any goal having the "form" of the head of the rule. Such requirements can be either a token, a *constraint* among tokens (possibly including the $x_0, \ldots, x_k$ variables), a *conjunction* of requirements or a *disjunction* of requirements. It is worth noting the recursive definition of requirement, which allows the definition of the body of a rule as any logical combination of tokens and constraints.

Similarly to CLP, through the application of the rules it is hence possible to establish and generate relationships among tokens. Compared to CLP, however, timelines introduce an added value: some tokens may be equipped with a special

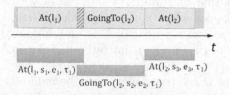

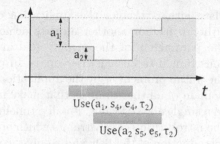

(a) An *inconsistent* state-variable time-line. The first *At* token and the *GoingTo* token are temporally overlapping. The inconsistency can be removed, for example, by introducing a $e_1 \leq s_2$ constraint.

(b) A *consistent* reusable-resource time-line. The overlap of tokens is allowed as long as the simultaneous use of the resource is less than its capacity.

Fig. 1. Different timelines extracted by their associated tokens.

object variable τ that identifies the *timeline* affected by the token. Different tokens with the same value for the τ parameter, in particular, affect the same timeline and, depending on the nature of the timeline, might interact with each other. There can, indeed, be different types of timelines. In case of *state-variable* timelines (see Fig. 1a), for example, different tokens on the same state-variable cannot temporally overlap. In case of *reusable-resource* timelines (see Fig. 1b), on the contrary, tokens represent resource usages and can, hence, overlap as long as the concurrent uses remain below the resource's capacity.

Given the ingredients mentioned above we can now formally introduce the addressed planning problem. A *timeline-based planning problem*, specifically, is a triple $\mathcal{P} = (\mathbf{O}, \mathcal{R}, \mathbf{r})$, where $\mathbf{O}$ is a set of typed objects, needed for instantiating the initial domains of the constraint network variables and, consequently, the tokens' parameters, $\mathcal{R}$ is a set of rules and $\mathbf{r}$ is a requirement. Intuitively, a solution to such a problem should be described by a set of tokens whose parameters assume values so as to guarantee the satisfaction of all the constraints imposed by the problem's requirement, by the application of the rules, as well as by the cumulative constraints imposed by the timelines. Unfortunately, the previous definition, although intuitive, is not easily translatable into a reasoning process which guarantees its achievement starting from the definition of the planning problem. For this reason, just like common partial-order planners, timeline-based planners often rely on the concepts of *flaw* and *resolver*. The planner, in particular, internally maintains a data structure, called *token network*, which represents a partial plan $\pi = (\mathcal{T}, \mathcal{N})$, where $\mathcal{T}$ is a set of tokens whose parameters are constrained by the constraint network $\mathcal{N}$. During the resolution process, the reasoner incrementally refines the current token network π by identifying its flaws and by solving them through the application of resolvers, while maintaining consistent the constraints of $\mathcal{N}$.

There can be, in general, different types of flaws, each resolvable by applying the corresponding resolvers. The achievement of a goal, for example, can take place either through the application of a rule or through a *unification* with either a fact or another already achieved goal with the same predicate (i.e., the parameters of the current goal and the token with which is unifying are constrained to be pairwise equal). In case of disjunctions, introduced either in the initial problem or by the application of a rule, a disjunct must be chosen. The domain of all the variables that make up the token parameters must be reduced to a single allowed value. Finally, timelines must be consistent, possibly requiring the introduction of constraints which prevent not allowed overlaps. Thanks to the introduction of the flaw and resolver concepts, it is therefore possible to provide an implementable definition of solution. Specifically, a *solution* to a timeline-based planning problem is a flawless token network whose constraint network is consistent.

3.1   A Lifted Heuristic for Timeline-Based Planning

Finding a solution to a timeline-based planning problem is far from simple. Choosing the *right* flaw and the *right* resolver, in particular, constitutes a crucial aspect for coping with the computational complexity and hence efficiently generating solutions. Taking a cue from classical planning heuristics, [13] describes how, by building a *causal graph* and by analyzing its topology, it is possible to estimate the costs for the resolution of the flaws and for the application of the resolvers. Flaws and resolvers, in particular, are seen as if they are, respectively, classical planning propositions and actions. The effect of applying a resolver is, intuitively, the resolution of a flaw (the sole positive effect of the corresponding classical action). In the case of the application of a rule or the choice of a disjunct in a disjunction, however, further flaws (the preconditions for the corresponding classical action) can be introduced. Starting from the initial facts, with a zero estimated resolution cost, the cost of applying a resolver can be estimated as an intrinsic cost of the resolver plus the maximum cost (h^{max} heuristic). The cost of resolving a flaw, on the other hand, is given by the minimum cost of its resolvers. Starting from the top-level goals present in the planning problem, initially estimated with infinite cost, a graph is constructed by proceeding backwards, considering all the possible resolvers for all the possible flaws. The estimated costs are updated every time a unification is found or in those cases in which the resolver does not introduce further flaws. Finally, the graph building procedure proceeds until a finite estimate cost for the top-level goals is reached.

Compared to other state-of-the-art timeline-based solvers, the above heuristics allow solving problems up to one order of magnitude faster [13]. The most interesting aspect for the current topic, however, concerns the management of the causal constraints in the causal graph. Similar to planning models based on satisfiability [27], indeed, a set of propositional variables is assigned to flaws and to resolvers. For the sake of brevity we will use subscripts to indicate flaws (e.g., φ_0, φ_1, etc.), resolvers (e.g., ρ_0, ρ_1, etc.) as well as their associated propositional variables. Additionally, given a flaw φ, we refer to the set of its possible resolvers by means of $res(\varphi)$ and, by means of $cause(\varphi)$, to the set of resolvers (possibly empty, in case of the flaws of the problem's requirement) which are responsible for introducing it. Moreover, given a resolver ρ, we refer to the set of its preconditions (e.g., the set of tokens introduced by the application of a rule) by means of $precs\,(\rho)$ and to the flaw solved through its application by means of $eff\,(\rho)$.

The introduction of such variables allows to constrain them so as to guarantee the satisfaction of the causal relations. Specifically, for each flaw φ_i, we guarantee that the preconditions of all the applied resolvers are satisfied $(\varphi_i = \bigwedge_{\rho_k \in cause(\varphi_i)} \rho_k \ (1))$ and that at least one resolver is active whenever the flaw becomes active $(\varphi_i \Rightarrow \bigvee_{\rho_l \in res(\varphi_i)} \rho_l \ (2))$. Additionally, we need a gimmick to link the presence of the tokens with the causality constraint. A further variable $\sigma \in \{inactive, active, unified\}$, in this regard, is associated to each token. A partial solution will hence consist solely of those tokens of the token network which are *active*. Moreover, in case such tokens are goals, the bodies of the associated rules must also be present within the solution. Later on, we refer to tokens by means of the σ variables (we will use subscripts to describe specific tokens, e.g., σ_0, σ_1, etc.) and to the flaws introduced by tokens by means of the $\varphi\,(\sigma)$ function.

The last aspect to consider concerns the update of such variables as a consequence of the activation of a rule application resolver and of a unification resolver. Specifically, each rule application resolver ρ_a binds the σ_a variable of the goal token, whose rule has been applied, to assume the *active* value (formally, $\rho_a = [\varphi\,(\sigma_a) = active]$). Finally, for each unification resolver ρ_u representing the unification of a token σ_u with a target token σ_t, the constraints $\rho_u = [\sigma_u = unified]$ and $\rho_u \Rightarrow [\sigma_t = active]$ guarantee the update of the σ variables while adding $\varphi\,(\sigma_t)$ to the preconditions of ρ_u guarantees the operation of the heuristic.

3.2   An Explanatory Example

In order to better understand how the heuristics and the causality constraints work, we introduce in this section a very simple example of planning problem, whose objective is to plan a physical rehabilitation session for an hypothetical user. Figure 2 shows the causal graph which is generated for the problem, whose problem requirement is constituted by the sole goal σ_0. Estimated costs for flaws (boxes) and resolvers (circles) are on their upper right. The propositional

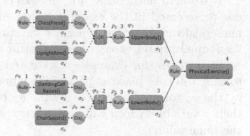

Fig. 2. An example of causal graph for the planning of a physical rehabilitation session. Tokens' parameters are omitted to avoid burdening the notation.

variables that participate in the causal constraints are on their upper left. Solid (TRUE) and dashed (UNASSIGNED) contour lines are used to distinguish flaws' and resolvers' associated propositional variables' values. In the figure, in particular, the φ_0 variable, representing a flaw which is present in the problem requirement and therefore must necessarily be solved, assumes the TRUE value.

It is worth noting that, in the example, the φ_0 flaw, for achieving the σ_0 goal, can only be solved through the ρ_0 resolver, which is hence directly applied (notice the solid line) as a consequence of the propagation of the causal constraints. Since $res\,(\varphi_0) = \{\rho_0\}$, indeed, the expression (2) translates into $\varphi_0 \Rightarrow \rho_0$. This, in turn, forces the σ_0 goal to assume the *active* value as a consequence of $\rho_0 = [\varphi\,(\sigma_0) = active]$. The ρ_0 resolver, furthermore, represents the application of a rule having a *PhysicalExercise* () in the head and, in the body, a conjunction of the two σ_1 and σ_2 goals. The application of this resolver, in particular, introduces the $\varphi_1 = \varphi\,(\sigma_1)$ and the $\varphi_2 = \varphi\,(\sigma_2)$ flaws, each of which must necessarily be resolved as a consequence of the $\varphi_1 = \rho_0$ and $\varphi_2 = \rho_0$ causal constraints, from the expression (1). These flaws, in turn, can be solved through the application of the ρ_1 and of the ρ_2 resolvers which introduce, respectively, the disjunctions represented by the φ_3 and φ_4 flaws.

Proceeding backwards, the propagation of the causal constraints no longer allows to infer what is present in the current partial plan (notice the dashed lines). The resolution of the φ_3 and φ_4 flaws, in particular, constitute two choices that the planner must make during the resolution process. The φ_3 flaw, for example, can be solved either by applying the $Disj_0$ disjunct, represented by the ρ_3 resolver, or by applying the $Disj_1$ disjunct, represented by the ρ_4 resolver. The graph construction process, however, which proceeds following a breadth-first approach, has identified, in the example, a possible solution for the φ_3 flaw by applying first the ρ_3 resolver and then the ρ_7 resolver (the latter corresponding, in this simple example, to a rule with an empty body). The heuristics' estimated costs propagation procedure, hence, makes the ρ_3 resolver, with an estimated cost of 2, much more attractive than the ρ_4 resolver, with an estimated cost of ∞. For a similar reason, the ρ_5 resolver will be preferred over the ρ_6 resolver, leading to a (possible) solution of the planning problem.

It is worth noting that, for the sake of simplicity, the tokens' parameters are not represented in the example figure. All tokens, however, are endowed with numerical variables that represent the start and the end of the associated activities, appropriately constrained according to common sense. Upper and lower body exercises, for example, represented respectively by the σ_1 and by the σ_2 tokens, will take place as part of the more general physical exercise represented by the σ_0 token. The σ_3 and by the σ_5 tokens, additionally, are endowed with their τ variables which will avoid their temporal overlapping if they will assume the same value.

4   An Architecture for Deliberative and Reactive Reasoning

In order to integrate the deliberative and reactive capabilities we have adopted an architecture that, from a high-level perspective, is depicted in Fig. 3. Taking inspiration from classical robotics architectures [21], specifically, our system consists of a *deliberative* tier responsible for the generation, the execution and the dynamic adaptation of the plans; a *sequencing* tier which, through the application of a policy (out of the scope of this paper), executes a sequence of actions according to the current state of the system; and a *sensing* and a *controlling* tier, which respectively interprets data produced by sensors and translates the sequencer's actions into lower level commands for the actuators. Particularly interesting from an execution perspective, it is worth noting that the state, according to which actions are selected from the sequencer tier policy, is described by the combination of three distinct states:

- the s_s state, generated by the sensing tier and characterized as a consequence of the interpretation of sensory data, is able to represent, for example, the intentions of the users, the estimation of their current pose, the users' emotions perceived from the camera, as well as situations which might be dangerous for both the users and for the robot;
- the s_c state, generated by the control tier, representing the state of the controllers such as whether the robot is navigating or not, or whether the robot is talking to or listening to the user;
- the s_d state, generated by the deliberative tier, representing the high-level commands generated as a result of the execution of the planned plans

Similarly, the actions executed by the sequencer tier can be of three distinct types:

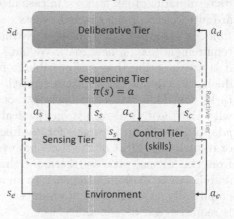

Fig. 3. The three-layer architecture.

- the a_s actions, towards the sensors, responsible, for example, for their activation or for their shutdown;
- the a_c actions, towards the controllers, responsible, for example, for activating contextual navigation commands as well as conversational interactions with the users;
- the a_d actions, towards the deliberative tier, responsible, for example, for the creation and for the adaptation of the generated plans.

It is worth noting that, through the application of the $\pi(s)$ policy, the sequencing tier can act both indirectly on the environment, through the a_c actions, and, through the a_d actions, introspectively on other higher-level forms of reasoning adopted by the agent itself. The high-level actions generated by the deliberative tier while executing the plans, moreover, constituting only one component among those that determine the choice of the actions by the policy, are not mandatory for the autonomy of the robot and represent a sort of "suggestions", for the agent, on the things to do.

5   Plan Execution and Possible Adaptations

Once the graph has been built, the heuristics introduced in the previous section guide the resolution process by providing an indication of the flaws to be solved (those with the most expensive estimate) through the application of their best resolvers (those with the least expensive estimate)[1]. After a flawless partial plan has been found, it is time to execute it. An internal *current-time* variable, in particular, is incremented at each execution step (e.g., every second) and whenever its value is greater than or equal to the beginning (end) of unexecuted (executing) tasks, these are started (ended). The generated plan, however, must deal with the evolving reality of all the (often, unpredictable) events that can happen in the real world. More than simply dispatching the planned activities, indeed, the main challenge of executing a plan consists in modifying it to make it fit the current reality. The introduction of the causal graph, in particular, can also be useful during the execution of the plan whenever should it be necessary to update it. Coherently with what described in [25], the possible adaptations that a plan can undergo during its execution, specifically, represented by the a_d actions of Fig. 3, can be of four types: temporal *delays*, in case tasks are not ready to start/end; variable *freezes*, to freeze, for example, a start variable of a task and prevent the violation of a duration constraint in case of delays on its termination; task *failures*, in case inconsistent constraints related to the task are introduced or unexpected events decrees its failure; and requirement *additions*, in case the underlying reactive module requires the introduction of a new requirement (e.g., a new goal). We have no theoretical results in this regard but it is worth noting that it is possible to build a new plan by incrementally introducing new requirements from scratch. Additionally, adding delays and failing tasks can bring the solver back to root level. These considerations, coherently with the theoretical results on classical planning, suggest that the cost of the adaptations, exception made for the freezes, is equal, asymptotically, to the cost of re-planning. Most of the time, however, an adapted plan has little difference from the original plan. Furthermore, the information gathered during the initial search can be exploited to generate an adapted plan. For this reason we aim to empirically show that adaptation, especially in those contexts where reactivity is required, can be advantageous.

The pursued approach consists of introducing a new propositional variable, called ξ, that will be used, before starting the execution, to force the propagation of the execution constraints (i.e., delays and freezes). Additional propositional variables, called σ_i^ξ and associated to each token σ_i, will be used as the "reason" for the propagation of the execution constraints. Finally, these variables must be causally linked to the planned activities, so as to allow, as a consequence of the introduction of an inconsistent constraint, the removal from the plan of the corresponding activity. We obtain this result by introducing, for each token σ_i, the clause $\left(\neg\xi, \neg\left[\sigma_i = active\right], \sigma_i^\xi\right)$. Once the planning problem has been solved, the assignment of the true value to the ξ variable will cause, through propagation, the assignment of the true value to the σ_i^ξ variables corresponding to those

---

[1] There is, intuitively, no guarantee that the built graph contains a solution. Similarly to what happens in Graphplan [5], indeed, it might be required the addition of a "layer" to the graph.

tokens σ_i which are in the current plan. Since variables σ_i^ξ are assigned at the last search level, they can be safely used as the "reason" for the propagation of the execution constraints. The introduction of an inconsistent constraint will first lead to the analysis of the introduced conflict, allowing to carry out a more targeted backtracking (a.k.a, backjumping [14]). Whenever possible, the tokens incompatible with the execution are eliminated and, subsequently, the resolution process is invoked to guarantee the satisfaction of the causal constraints. Finally, in case some delaying constraints cannot be added or, in the absence of alternative plans, some tokens cannot be removed, the false value is assigned to the ξ variable, decreeing the unexecutability of the plan and, consequently, the need to re-plan.

6   Experimental Results

(a) A comparison between adaptation and re-planning from scratch in the event that activities fail.

(b) A comparison between adaptation and re-planning from scratch in the event that new requirements dynamically arise.

Fig. 4. Adaptation vs re-planning from scratch in case of failures and new requirements.

We have conducted some experiments to demonstrate the effectiveness of the proposed approach. Given the project needs, in particular, we focused on planning problems similar to those described in Sect. 3.2, in which the user has to carry out some physical and cognitive rehabilitation exercises to keep active and prolong his/her health well-being. In particular, series of physical exercises chosen from 14 different types (e.g., Chest press, Biceps curl, etc.) are planned in order to guarantee the training of all parts of the body. The exercises are repeated several times and with different characteristics depending on the profile of user.

The interesting aspect regarding the current experimentation is that the user may refuse to perform these exercises, or he/she may have problems at doing them. For this reason, the planner must be ready to provide alternatives that still achieve the desired rehabilitative goals (i.e., training all the parts of the body). Whenever the user is particularly confident in carrying out the exercises, on the contrary, the system could add new tasks through the addition of new goals to the planning problem, hence requesting the adaptation of the plan for taking into account the new requirements dynamically introduced. We have left out the temporal adaptations as they are less interesting and already managed by several existing frameworks.

Figure 4a shows a comparison between adaptation and re-planning in 5 different generated plans. To demonstrate the effectiveness of the proposed approach, in particular, we artificially made the first, the second and the third activity fail during execution. This allows us to compare the adaptation times with the times required by the solver to generate a new plan from scratch without failing the task. It is worth noting how, often, the time required for subsequent adaptations takes less and less time. This is because the information collected during the previous searches (the topology of the causal graph and the no-goods learned during the search) are exploited to make the adaptation more effective. Figure 4b, on the contrary, compares the adaptation times with the re-planning times in the case of adding one and two new goals. Also in this case the information collected during the previous searches are exploited, reducing the calculation time necessary for the addition of new goals. In the event new plans have to be generated from scratch, on the contrary, these would have an increasing number of goals and would therefore require more and more calculation times.

Although the reasoning times are relatively small, for this type of planning problems, we are talking about robots that interact with people. Reducing the computation times allows such robots to behave more fluidly in a dynamic environment, in which the activities fail easily and where new goals can emerge during the execution of the planned tasks. Whether it's a failure or the addition of a new requirement, the sum of the reasoning times of the adaptations is significantly less than the sum of the reasoning times of the re-plannings. Furthermore, as the number of adaptation increases, there is an ever greater divergence between adaptive and re-planning behaviors, showing that the more dynamic the environment, the more advantageous the adaptive approach is.

7   Conclusions

The word *agent* comes from the Latin word *agere* which means, in English, "to do". Much of the literature on automated planning, however, focuses on those forms of reasoning that lead to the definition of a plan, rather than its actual application to the real world, hence neglecting much of that *agere*. Acting in the real world requires an agent to be able to adapt to the agent's perception which might not necessarily be consistent with the expected plans, either because the agent's knowledge is partial, or because of the impossibility to predict the behavior of other agents acting in the same environment. Much of an agent's behavior in the real world is therefore related to reacting to its dynamical evolution, taking advantage, from time to time, of higher-level information coming from more deliberative forms of reasoning which in turn require high adaptability skills.

In this paper we have presented some techniques that allow to realize these adaptation skills. An underlying reactive tier, in particular, continuously reacts to the environment's dynamic changes. When perceiving particular situations, this module triggers adjustments to the planned tasks, which can range from introducing delays to the removal of some tasks till to the generation of (part of) new plans. Adapting a plan, in general, can be as complex as generating a new plan from scratch. Since an adapted plan is typically similar to the original plan, however, it is possible to exploit part of the information learned in the initial search to make the adaptation more efficient. Empirical results show that some of the data structures introduced to make the reasoning process more efficient can be exploited also to improve the dynamic adaptation of the plan to the emerging reality.

References

1. Apt, K.R., Wallace, M.G.: Constraint Logic Programming Using ECL^{i}PS^e. Cambridge University Press, New York (2007)
2. Bensalem, S., Havelund, K., Orlandini, A.: Verification and validation meet planning and scheduling. Int. J. Softw. Tools Technol. Transfer **16**(1), 1–12 (2014)
3. Bertoli, P., Cimatti, A., Roveri, M., Traverso, P.: Strong planning under partial observability. Artif. Intell. **170**(4), 337–384 (2006). https://doi.org/10.1016/j.artint.2006.01.004. https://www.sciencedirect.com/science/article/pii/S0004370206000075
4. Bit-Monnot, A., Ghallab, M., Ingrand, F., Smith, D.E.: FAPE: a Constraint-based Planner for Generative and Hierarchical Temporal Planning. arXiv preprint arXiv:2010.13121 (2020)
5. Blum, A.L., Furst, M.L.: Fast planning through planning graph analysis. Artif. Intell. **90**(1–2), 281–300 (1997)
6. Cashmore, M., et al.: ROSPlan: planning in the robot operating system. In: Proceedings of the Twenty-Fifth International Conference on International Conference on Automated Planning and Scheduling, ICAPS 2015, pp. 333–341. AAAI Press (2015)
7. Castillo, L., Fdez-Olivares, J., García-Pérez, O., Palao, F.: Efficiently handling temporal knowledge in an HTN planner. In: Proceedings of the Sixteenth International Conference on International Conference on Automated Planning and Scheduling, ICAPS 2006, pp. 63–72. AAAI Press (2006)
8. Cesta, A., Cortellessa, G., Fratini, S., Oddi, A.: Developing an end-to-end planning application from a timeline representation framework. In: IAAI 2009, Proceedings of the 21st Innovative Applications of Artificial Intelligence Conference, Pasadena, CA, USA, pp. 66–71 (2009)
9. Cesta, A., Oddi, A.: Gaining efficiency and flexibility in the simple temporal problem. In: Chittaro, L., Goodwin, S., Hamilton, H., Montanari, A. (eds.) Proceedings of the Third International Workshop on Temporal Representation and Reasoning (TIME 1996), pp. 45–50. IEEE Computer Society Press, Los Alamitos (1996)
10. Cesta, A., Oddi, A., Smith, S.F.: A constraint-based method for project scheduling with time windows. J. Heuristics **8**(1), 109–136 (2002). https://doi.org/10.1023/A:1013617802515
11. Chien, S., Tran, D., Rabideau, G., Schaffer, S., Mandl, D., Frye, S.: Timeline-based space operations scheduling with external constraints. In: ICAPS 2010, Proceedings of the 20th International Conference on Automated Planning and Scheduling, pp. 34–41 (2010)

12. Cialdea Mayer, M., Orlandini, A., Umbrico, A.: Planning and execution with flexible timelines: a formal account. Acta Informatica **53**(6), 649–680 (2016). https://doi.org/10.1007/s00236-015-0252-z

13. De Benedictis, R., Cesta, A.: Lifted heuristics for timeline-based planning. In: ECAI-2020, 24th European Conference on Artificial Intelligence, pp. 498–2337. Santiago de Compostela, Spain (2020)

14. Dechter, R.: Constraint Processing. Elsevier Morgan Kaufmann, Cambridge (2003)

15. Dvořák, F., Bit-Monnot, A., Ingrand, F., Ghallab, M.: Plan-space hierarchical planning with the action notation modeling language. In: IEEE International Conference on Tools with Artificial Intelligence (ICTAI), Limassol, Cyprus (2014). https://hal.archives-ouvertes.fr/hal-01138105

16. Fox, M., Gerevini, A., Long, D., Serina, I.: Plan stability: replanning versus plan repair. In: Long, D., Smith, S.F., Borrajo, D., McCluskey, L. (eds.) Proceedings of the Sixteenth International Conference on Automated Planning and Scheduling, ICAPS 2006, Cumbria, UK, 6–10 June 2006, pp. 212–221. AAAI (2006). http://www.aaai.org/Library/ICAPS/2006/icaps06-022.php

17. Fox, M., Long, D.: PDDL2.1: an extension to PDDL for expressing temporal planning domains. J. Artif. Intell. Res. **20**, 61–124 (2003)

18. Frank, J., Jónsson, A.K.: Constraint-based attribute and interval planning. Constraints **8**(4), 339–364 (2003)

19. Fratini, S., Pecora, F., Cesta, A.: Unifying planning and scheduling as timelines in a component-based perspective. Arch. Control Sci. **18**(2), 231–271 (2008)

20. Fratini, S., Cesta, A., De Benedictis, R., Orlandini, A., Rasconi, R.: APSI-based deliberation in goal oriented autonomous controllers. In: ASTRA 2011 (2011)

21. Gat, E.: On three-layer architectures. In: Artificial Intelligence and Mobile Robots, pp. 195–210. AAAI Press (1997)

22. Gerevini, A., Serina, I.: Fast plan adaptation through planning graphs: local and systematic search techniques. In: Chien, S.A., Kambhampati, S., Knoblock, C.A. (eds.) Proceedings of the Fifth International Conference on Artificial Intelligence Planning Systems, Breckenridge, CO, USA, 14–17 April 2000, pp. 112–121. AAAI (2000). http://www.aaai.org/Library/AIPS/2000/aips00-012.php

23. Ghallab, M., Laruelle, H.: Representation and control in IxTeT, a temporal planner. In: AIPS 1994, Proceedings of the 2nd International Conference on AI Planning and Scheduling, pp. 61–67 (1994)

24. Ghallab, M., Nau, D., Traverso, P.: Automated Planning: Theory and Practice. Morgan Kaufmann Publishers Inc., Burlington (2004)

25. Ingrand, F., Ghallab, M.: Robotics and artificial intelligence: a perspective on deliberation functions. AI Commun. **27**(1), 63–80 (2014). https://doi.org/10.3233/AIC-130578. https://hal.archives-ouvertes.fr/hal-01138117

26. Jonsson, A., Morris, P., Muscettola, N., Rajan, K., Smith, B.: Planning in interplanetary space: theory and practice. In: AIPS 2000, Proceedings of the Fifth International Conference on AI Planning and Scheduling, pp. 177–186 (2000)

27. Kautz, H., Selman, B.: Planning as satisfiability. In: ECAI, vol. 92, pp. 359–363 (1992)

28. van der Krogt, R., de Weerdt, M.: Plan repair as an extension of planning. In: Biundo, S., Myers, K.L., Rajan, K. (eds.) Proceedings of the Fifteenth International Conference on Automated Planning and Scheduling (ICAPS 2005), 5–10 June 2005, Monterey, California, USA, pp. 161–170. AAAI (2005). http://www.aaai.org/Library/ICAPS/2005/icaps05-017.php

29. Laborie, P.: Algorithms for propagating resource constraints in AI planning and scheduling: existing approaches and new results. Artif. Intell. **143**, 151–188 (2003)

30. Laborie, P., Ghallab, M.: Planning with sharable resource constraints. In: Proceedings of the 14th International Joint Conference on Artificial Intelligence - Volume 2, IJCAI 1995, pp. 1643–1649. Morgan Kaufmann Publishers Inc. (1995)

31. McGann, C., Py, F., Rajan, K., Thomas, H., Henthorn, R., Mcewen, R.: A deliberative architecture for AUV control. In: 2008 IEEE International Conference on Robotics and Automation, pp. 1049–1054. IEEE (2008)

32. Morris, P., Muscettola, N., Vidal, T.: Dynamic control of plans with temporal uncertainty. In: Proceedings of the 17th International Joint Conference on Artificial Intelligence - Volume 1, IJCAI 2001, pp. 494–499. Morgan Kaufmann Publishers Inc., San Francisco (2001)

33. Morris, P.H., Muscettola, N.: Temporal dynamic controllability revisited. In: Veloso, M.M., Kambhampati, S. (eds.) Proceedings, The Twentieth National Conference on Artificial Intelligence and the Seventeenth Innovative Applications of Artificial Intelligence Conference, 9–13 July 2005, Pittsburgh, Pennsylvania, USA, pp. 1193–1198. AAAI Press/The MIT Press (2005). http://www.aaai.org/Library/AAAI/2005/aaai05-189.php

34. Muscettola, N.: HSTS: integrating planning and scheduling. In: Zweben, M., Fox, M.S. (ed.) Intelligent Scheduling. Morgan Kauffmann (1994)

35. Nau, D.S., et al.: SHOP2: an HTN planning system. J. Artif. Intell. Res. **20**, 379–404 (2003)

36. Nau, D.S., Ghallab, M., Traverso, P.: Blended planning and acting: Preliminary approach, research challenges. In: Bonet, B., Koenig, S. (eds.) Proceedings of the Twenty-Ninth AAAI Conference on Artificial Intelligence, 25–30 January 2015, Austin, Texas, USA, pp. 4047–4051. AAAI Press (2015)

37. Nebel, B., Koehler, J.: Plan reuse versus plan generation: a theoretical and empirical analysis. Artif. Intell. **76**(1–2), 427–454 (1995)

38. Niemueller, T., Hofmann, T., Lakemeyer, G.: Goal reasoning in the CLIPS executive for integrated planning and execution. In: Proceedings of the International Conference on Automated Planning and Scheduling, vol. 29, no. 1, pp. 754–763 (2021)

39. Peot, M.A., Smith, D.E.: Conditional nonlinear planning. In: Proceedings of the First International Conference on Artificial Intelligence Planning Systems, pp. 189–197. Morgan Kaufmann Publishers Inc., San Francisco (1992)

40. Saetti, A., Scala, E.: Optimising the stability in plan repair via compilation. In: Kumar, A., Thiébaux, S., Varakantham, P., Yeoh, W. (eds.) Proceedings of the Thirty-Second International Conference on Automated Planning and Scheduling, ICAPS 2022, Singapore (virtual), 13–24 June 2022, pp. 316–320. AAAI Press (2022)

41. Scala, E., Torasso, P.: Deordering and numeric macro actions for plan repair. In: Yang, Q., Wooldridge, M.J. (eds.) Proceedings of the Twenty-Fourth International Joint Conference on Artificial Intelligence, IJCAI 2015, Buenos Aires, Argentina, 25–31 July 2015, pp. 1673–1681. AAAI Press (2015)

42. Smith, D.E., Frank, J., Cushing, W.: The ANML language. In: ICAPS Workshop on Knowledge Engineering for Planning and Scheduling (KEPS) (2008)

43. Smith, D.E., Frank, J., Jónsson, A.K.: Bridging the gap between planning and scheduling. Knowl. Eng. Rev. **15**(1), 47–83 (2000)

44. Stock, S., Mansouri, M., Pecora, F., Hertzberg, J.: Hierarchical hybrid planning in a mobile service robot. In: KI 2015 Proceedings, pp. 309–315 (2015)

45. Umbrico, A., Cesta, A., Cialdea Mayer, M., Orlandini, A.: Platinum: a new framework for planning and acting. In: AI*IA 2017 Proceedings, pp. 498–512 (2017)

46. Verfaillie, G., Pralet, C., Lemaître, M.: How to model planning and scheduling problems using constraint networks on timelines. Knowl. Eng. Rev. **25**(3), 319–336 (2010)

47. Weld, D.S.: An introduction to least commitment planning. AI Mag. **15**(4), 27–61 (1994)

48. Weld, D.S., Anderson, C.R., Smith, D.E.: Extending graphplan to handle uncertainty and sensing actions. In: Proceedings of the Fifteenth National/Tenth Conference on Artificial Intelligence/Innovative Applications of Artificial Intelligence, AAAI 1998/IAAI 1998, pp. 897–904. American Association for Artificial Intelligence, USA (1998)

49. Wilkins, D.E.: Practical Planning: Extending the Classical AI Planning Paradigm. Morgan Kaufmann Publishers, San Mateo (1988)

50. Zavatteri, M., Viganò, L.: Conditional simple temporal networks with uncertainty and decisions. Theor. Comput. Sci. **797**, 77–101 (2019). https://doi.org/10.1016/j.tcs.2018.09.023. https://www.sciencedirect.com/science/article/pii/S0304397518305942. Temporal Representation and Reasoning (TIME 2017)

Knowledge Acquisition and Completion for Long-Term Human-Robot Interactions Using Knowledge Graph Embedding

Ermanno Bartoli[2], Francesco Argenziano[1](✉), Vincenzo Suriani[1]📷,
and Daniele Nardi[1]📷

[1] Department of Computer, Control, and Management Engineering,
Sapienza University of Rome, Rome, Italy
{argenziano,suriani,nardi}@diag.uniroma1.it
[2] Division of RPL (Robotics, Perception and Learning),
KTH Royal Institute of Technology, Stockholm, Sweden
bartoli@kth.se

Abstract. In Human-Robot Interaction (HRI) systems, a challenging task is sharing the representation of the operational environment, fusing symbolic knowledge and perceptions, between users and robots. With the existing HRI pipelines, users can teach the robots some concepts to increase their knowledge base. Unfortunately, the data coming from the users are usually not enough dense for building a consistent representation. Furthermore, the existing approaches are not able to incrementally build up their knowledge base, which is very important when robots have to deal with dynamic contexts. To this end, we propose an architecture to gather data from users and environments in long-runs of continual learning. We adopt Knowledge Graph Embedding techniques to generalize the acquired information with the goal of incrementally extending the robot's inner representation of the environment. We evaluate the performance of the overall continual learning architecture by measuring the capabilities of the robot of learning entities and relations coming from unknown contexts through a series of incremental learning sessions.

Keywords: Human-robot interaction · Knowledge graphs ·
Knowledge graphs embeddings · Continual learning · Robots ·
Knowledge base · Knowledge representation

1 Introduction

In the last years, robots started leaving laboratories to enter our daily environments where they are asked to autonomously operate, often sharing the working area with humans. To be effective in this goal, representing and storing information in a suitable way is fundamental regardless of the specific robotic applications. In particular, this problem acquires more relevance when designing Human-Robot Interaction (HRI) systems, since there is the intrinsic need to

---

E. Bartoli and F. Argenziano—These two authors contributed equally.

A. Dovier et al. (Eds.): AIxIA 2022, LNAI 13796, pp. 241–253, 2023.
https://doi.org/10.1007/978-3-031-27181-6_17

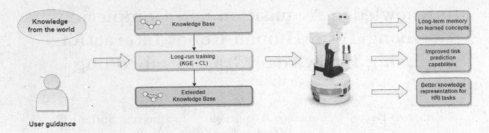

Fig. 1. Complete architecture of the system: from the interaction with the user to the deployment of learned knowledge and capabilities after long-run training.

make the human and the robot participants interact with each other. In order to make this interaction successful, the robot and the human not only must be able to communicate and understand each other, but also they should have a mutual understanding of the world they both operate in. Therefore, a shared semantic of the environment is needed in order to make the interaction successful. In many HRI applications, this knowledge (that is the building block on which the whole system is built) is often embedded in the agent's behaviour and changes from one episode to another. A way to improve it can be through a generalization of the knowledge that is transferred and acquired by the robot. In fact, usually, it is very domain-dependent for the specific application of the system (Fig. 1).

In this paper, we propose a novel architecture for acquiring knowledge from sparse data acquisition from environments. The acquired knowledge is represented and organized to improve the completeness of the previous knowledge base of the robot. This process leads to the creation of a resulting more extensive knowledge base that is built up incrementally. The nature of the architecture is meant to be robust to any change in the context so that it can be suitable in several HRI applications, even if very different from each other. A major advantage of the proposed approach is that, differently from previous HRI systems, it is not necessary to modify the software architecture when the context of the interaction changes, but it is only needed to start a new learning session that shapes the existing learning skills of the robot. The acquisition of the data is human-driven, and the human who collaborates with the robot is not required to know anything about the software of the agent, nor how the knowledge is represented, but the user just needs to share his knowledge of the world with the robot. This process needs to take into account some aspects. First of all, this kind of interaction is not defined over a short period of time, long-runs are necessary to achieve good results. However, long-runs are not that common in the HRI field, since the interactions between humans and robots happen quite fast, and therefore this problem must be treated. Moreover, because of these long-runs, the robot will face information that needs to be stored and effectively processed, without forgetting acquired knowledge as the run goes on. To solve these problems, the methodology we propose relies on Continual Learning (CL) and Knowledge Graph Embeddings (KGEs): the former is used to deal with the catastrophic forgetting phenomenon during incremental knowledge acquisition sessions, while the latter is used to efficiently use the information, stored in a

Fig. 2. Interaction with the robot before the long-run training and knowledge acquisition. The robot still has difficulties in carrying on a correct interaction.

Fig. 3. Interaction with the robot after the long-run training and knowledge acquisition. The robot has improved its capabilities, can correctly carry on the interaction, and exploits it to learn new relations.

Knowledge Graph (KG) database, to perform the knowledge completion. In the end, the knowledge of the system spans from grounded facts about the environment to more general concepts on which the system can make predictions. This knowledge allows for several reasoning processes, based on the kind of query that the human operator may ask: if the query is very specific (namely the human asks for a particular object in a particular location), the robot can answer by exploiting its *experience*, that is what it has detected in the past explorations; for more general queries (namely, general objects or concepts), the robot can answer by making predictions depending on what it has learned, so by using an *ontological scheme* of the environment that it has slowly built in the past days.

2   Related Work

In order to have robots working and acting in human-shaped environments, semantic mapping approaches have been studied, aiming at constructing a common representation of the world between robots and humans [11]. To this end, there was a growing need of representing the knowledge of the robot with appropriate techniques in order to allow for faster and more precise reasoning about the environment the agents lived in. One particular way of knowledge representation that is demonstrated to be very effective is through triples [12], in which objects of the worlds are linked together by some sort of relation. This way of memorizing facts enabled the usage of a particular kind of data structure, the Knowledge Graphs (KGs) [4], in which is it possible to represent collections of triples as directed graphs. In those graphs, objects and entities are represented as nodes, and relations between entities are represented as directed edges. This representation allows for better data integration, unification, and reuse of information since it is also easier to represent ontological structures by the use of them. However, one of the biggest problems of KGs is that they do not scale well with size: the bigger the graph, the harder is to navigate through it and the harder is to make any sort of inference from it. For this reason, instead of working directly with KGs, through the years techniques of Knowledge Graph Embeddings (KGEs) [15] have been developed, in which KGs are transformed into lower-dimensional representation in order to reduce the number of parameters of the system while also preserving the information of the graph. Another problem in representing information with KGs is that when knowledge comes from multiple sources, there is often the possibility of incorporating contradictory pieces of information that will eventually compromise the quality of the system (in particular during the training of the embedding). For this reason, it is important to introduce in the process of knowledge acquisition some sort of validation procedure, and this validation can be done by interacting with humans. In recent years, the human participant in the interaction has acquired a bigger and bigger role in the robot's acquisition of knowledge from the world [3,13], and this is because through the filtering process of a human we are able to transfer to the robot only useful information, that can significantly improve further reasoning processes down the interaction pipeline. Although the human can get rid of useless information, a human-drive acquisition of knowledge needs much time to be robust and efficient, because the data that the robot acquires through the human can be sparse and not cohesive. For that purpose, the development of systems capable to handle long-runs of one single experiment has become more popular [8]. This kind of experiment allows the robot to build up robust and dense knowledge. An interesting way to build up the robot's knowledge is doing it incrementally through human-robot interaction. Such a class of problems has been addressed in applications focused on learning without forgetting [7]. These approaches typically operate in a task-based sequential learning setup. This formulation, which is rarely encountered in practical applications under this assumption, has been also studied in a task-free scenario [1].

3   Methodology

The proposed approach aims at making the robot able to address the multi-relational embedding problem while incrementally building up the robot's knowledge base in a unique long-run. The goal mentioned can be subdivided into three subtasks which are addressed at the same time: acquiring data in collaboration with the human, incorporating the acquired data in the infrastructure designed for semantic mapping, improving the accuracy of the robot's predictions by training the model on the new data (Fig. 4).

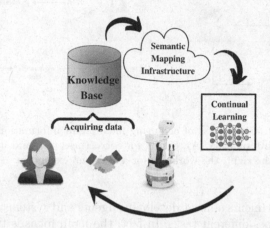

Fig. 4. The final task is the composition of three sub-tasks.

3.1 Acquiring and Extending the Knowledge Base

To properly build a knowledge base (KB) for the purpose of this work, we chose to have a basic predicate represented by a *triple*, (h, r, t), where h is the head entity, t is the tail entity, and r is the relation that connects the head to the tail. A set of those triples can be suitable for Continual Learning on Knowledge Graph Embedding. In fact, a dataset of triples can be easily split into learning sessions, each of them comprising a portion of the data. This can be used to simulate the fact that data are not all available at once, so in the training session n, only the $n - th$ portion of the dataset is given to the model, and it trains itself only on those data. This procedure is valid, but it is assumed that even if the dataset is not given to the model entirely, it must be known in advance in order to be able to divide it. This is a huge constraint when dealing with real robots and real environments for two main reasons. The first is that, when the robot is put into an environment, the number and the type of the object in the environment are unknown. This means that the number of predicates that the robot collects when evolving in the environment, so the number of entities and relations of the robot's knowledge base, can vary. The second reason is that also the number of tasks can vary. In fact, when the robot detects an unknown object, the system has to take care of a new entity but also a new task. The architecture will assign an embedding to the new entity and the next training will include also such an entity. From a conceptual point of view, the interaction between the robot and the human that cooperate in order to enlarge the knowledge base is shown in Fig. 5, on the left. In the context of Interactive Task Learning (ITL) [6], the

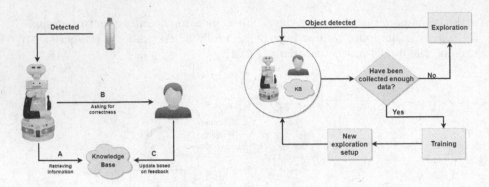

Fig. 5. On the left, the process of acquiring meaningful information, composed by 3 phases: retrieving information (A), asking for correctness (B), and updating based on feedback (C). On the right, the workflow for a long-run execution.

setup of our experiments aims at developing agents and systems that are focused on generality across different tasks. In fact, the main focus is the ability of the system to abstract concepts from different domains on a more general level. Our work, which exploits embedding algorithms on the triples of a KG, adopts these principles.

The knowledge acquisition procedure consists of three different phases, that are chronologically consecutive. First, the objects detected using the YOLO Neural Network [14] come into the robot as simple labels, and the **phase A** starts. The robot queries its KB in order to retrieve the semantic meaning of the object detected. The semantic meaning could be also inaccurate: in fact, the more that entity appears in the KB, the more the embedding of that entity will be precise and, the predictions on that entity, more accurate. If there are not enough data that grant an accurate embedding of the entity, the predictions will be incorrect. The predictions are represented by the predicates (h, r, t) where the head entity is the detected object, the relation is chosen randomly among all the known relations, and the tail entity is the result of the prediction. After the generation of the predicates, the **phase B** starts. Here the robot asks the human for the correctness of the predicates by asking questions for each predicate. Communication is very important and it needs to be well-defined because misunderstanding could provoke incorrect answers that lead to the addition of wrong data to the KB. Since the data of the KB are not always human interpretable ("objInLoc" stands for "object is in Location"), according to the relation of the predicates, the question is generated so that it is human-understandable. As soon as the robot asks the question to the user, it waits for the user's answer, and **phase C** starts. In this phase, the user can answer positively or negatively. If the user answers positively, it means that the robot's prediction was correct, and the predicate (h, r, t) is a true fact, so it can be added to the KB. If the prediction is judged as false, the robot asks the user for the correct tail of the predicate $(h, r, ?)$, where h and r are the same head entity and relation as before. Once the user answers the robot with the correct tail entity, a new predicate is created, and it is added to the KB. In the end, both a correct prediction and an incorrect prediction lead to an addition of a true predicate in the KB. Moreover, when the robot adds the predicate to its KB, it provides an implicit consensus to the user. In this way, the user is able to know which predicate is being added to the knowledge base, and if there is an error, the user can recover from it.

3.2 Knowledge Graph Embedding

In order to predict new predicates, we adopted the Knowledge Graph Embedding (KGE) technique, which uses supervised learning models capable to learn vector representations of nodes and edges. By definition, the objective of Knowledge Graph Embedding problem is to learn a continuous vector representation of a Knowledge Graph $\mathcal{G}$ which encodes vertices that represent entities $\mathcal{E}$ as a set of vectors $v_{\mathcal{E}} \in \mathbb{R}^{|\mathcal{E}| \times d_{\mathcal{E}}}$, where $d_{\mathcal{E}}$ is the dimension of the vector of entities $\mathcal{E}$, and as a set of edges which represent relations $\mathcal{R}$ as mappings between vectors $W_{\mathcal{R}} \in \mathbb{R}^{|\mathcal{R}| \times d_{\mathcal{R}}}$, where $d_{\mathcal{R}}$ is the dimension of the vector of relations. The knowledge graph $\mathcal{G}$ is composed by triples (h, r, t), where $h, t \in \mathcal{E}$ are the head and tail of the relations, while $r \in \mathcal{R}$ is the relation itself. One example of such a triple is (*bottle, hasMaterial, plastic*). In literature, there are numerous ways of embedding the knowledge in a knowledge graph: *transitional models, rotational models, gaussian models*, and many others. However, independently on what is the class of methods that are used, the embedding is learned by minimizing the loss $\mathcal{L}$ computed on a scoring function $f(h, r, t)$ over the set of triples in the knowledge graph, and over the set of negative triples that are generated by negative sampling over the same graph. For this research, the embedding model we used is ANALOGY that represents a relation as a matrix. This model can cope with asymmetrical relations and imposes the structure of the matrix to be a diagonal-block matrix, to minimize the number of parameters that need to be stored by the system.

ANALOGY. In the field of KGEs, there are many numerous ways of representing the relations into lower dimensional spaces. Usually, these techniques are grouped in families of models that describe the general principle that makes the embedding of the information possible. For instance, translational models (like TransE [2]) represent relationships as translations in the embedding space, while Gaussian embeddings model also takes the uncertainty of the information contained in a KG. Despite these models being simpler than other models, they fail to correctly represent more complex kinds of relations (like symmetrical relations), and so more advanced models are needed. For this reason, we chose ANALOGY as our KGE model. ANALOGY is an improvement of the RESCAL [9] model that is a tensor factorization approach able to perform collective training on multi-relational data. In this approach, a triple $(h.r.t)$ is represented as an entry in a three-way tensor $\mathcal{X}$. A tensor entry $\mathcal{X}_{ijk} = 1$ means that the triple composed by the i-th and the k-th entity as, respectively, head and tail, and the j-th relation is a true fact. Otherwise, unknown or non-existing facts have their entry set to 0. Each slice $\mathcal{X}_k$ of the tensor is then factorized as $\mathcal{X}_k \approx AR_kA^T$, where A is a matrix that contains the latent-component representation of the entities, while instead R_k is a matrix that models the interactions of the latent components, and both are computed by solving the minimization problem

$$\min_{A,R_k} f(A, R_k) + g(A, R_k) \tag{1}$$

where

$$f(A, R_k) = \frac{1}{2} \left(\sum_k \|\mathcal{X}_k - AR_kA^T\|_F^2 \right) \tag{2}$$

and g is a regularization term

$$g(A, R_k) = \frac{1}{2}\lambda \left(\|A\|_F^2 + \sum_k \|R_k\|_F^2 \right) \tag{3}$$

Starting from this approach, ANALOGY makes some important improvements: it constrains R to be a diagonal matrix (like DistMult), and it introduces complex-valued embeddings to cope with asymmetric relations $X = EW\bar{E}^T$ (like ComplEx does), but most importantly it imposes analogical structures among the representations by the means of a diagonal-block matrix (reducing the number of parameters needed by the model) by modifying the objective function as follows

$$\begin{aligned} \min_{v,W} \ &\mathbb{E}_{s,r,o,y \sim \mathcal{D}} \ell(\phi_{v,W}(s,r,o), y) \\ \text{s.t.} \quad &W_rW_r^\top = W_r^\top W_r \forall r \in \mathcal{R} \\ &W_rW_{r'} = W_{r'}W_r \quad \forall r, r' \in \mathcal{R} \end{aligned} \tag{4}$$

3.3   Long-Run

The process described is robust, because allows a robot that is put in a completely unknown environment, to incrementally build a robust knowledge of it. A completely unknown environment means that no entity or relation is present in the KB of the robot at the beginning. Moreover, one of the advantages of this approach is that some knowledge could be transferred to the robot. For example, it is possible to exploit existing knowledge graph databases to give some a-priori knowledge to the robot. In this way, the robot will learn to build up its KB much faster. During this process, the KB of the robot evolves in the environment, acquiring information and communicating with the human. This approach is meant for designing a single long-run, instead of multiple short runs. Figure 5, on the right, shows the block scheme of such approach.

The circular block, depicting the robot and the user, wraps all the infrastructure responsible for enlarging the KB and communicating with the human, which is shown in Fig. 5, on the left. The two blocks, i.e. *exploration* and *training*, are mutually exclusive. These 2 blocks are called whether or not a condition is verified. There are three different conditions that have been implemented. The

Table 1. HITS@10 of ANALOGY with standard settings

	sess_0	sess_1	sess_2	sess_3	sess_4	sess_5
classical_context on ai2thor_5	-	-	-	-	-	0.705
classical_context on ai2thor_4	-	-	-	-	0.238	0.764
classical_context on ai2thor_3	-	-	-	0.346	0.336	0.676
classical_context on ai2thor_2	-	-	0.382	0.371	0.389	0.647
classical_context on ai2thor_1	-	0.402	0.385	0.361	0.380	0.558
classical_context on ai2thor_0	0.339	0.355	0.343	0.343	0.336	0.500

Table 2. MRR of ANALOGY with standard settings

	sess_0	sess_1	sess_2	sess_3	sess_4	sess_5
classical_context on ai2thor_5	-	-	-	-	-	0.569
classical_context on ai2thor_4	-	-	-	-	0.104	0.385
classical_context on ai2thor_3	-	-	-	0.129	0.128	0.338
classical_context on ai2thor_2	-	-	0.136	0.127	0.130	0.322
classical_context on ai2thor_1	-	0.153	0.146	0.141	0.146	0.270
classical_context on ai2thor_0	0.151	0.134	0.134	0.130	0.130	0.198

first (shown in Fig. 5, on the right) deals with the amount of data collected by the robot during the exploring phase. This kind of condition makes it possible that at each learning session the robot collects the same amount of data, so the dataset will always be balanced. The second condition deals with the battery level of the robot. With this condition, the robot is free to explore the environment until the battery goes under a certain threshold, so the robot comes back to its docking station and, while recharging, it performs a training session. The final condition only includes time. Two periods, namely *day* and *night*, are defined. In the first one, the robot is in exploration, while in the latter, the robot is in training.

4   Results

In the evaluation of the presented work, we would like to capture the capability of the robot to exploits its knowledge during the process of learning whatever the human teaches to it.

The learning procedure is built so as to recognize the entities in a certain environment, also to learn the relations between these entities, and predict them even when they are not explicitly mentioned by the human. The first thing that we want to prove is that models based on the standard learning process tend to forget what they have learned when new things to learn come. In order to prove this, we have simulated with the TIAGo robot a situation in which it

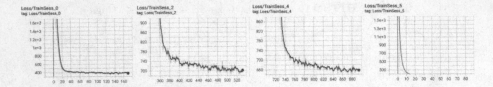

Fig. 6. The *Loss* during the learning sessions: 0, 2, 4, 5. (The last one, in blue, represents the training considering the last subset of the data acquired through the proposed methodology). This shows that the trend is constantly decreasing. (Color figure online)

learns from the human some information belonging to a certain context, and then it is asked to learn other information from a different context. From a technical point of view, this experiment consists of training the robot over 6 learning sessions, using a dataset structure that is inspired by AI2THOR [5]. In the first one, the dataset sess_5_ai2thor has been taken as input. Instead, for the subsequent 5 learning sessions, the dataset *sess_i_ai2thor* with $i \in \{0, 1, 2, 3, 4\}$ has been used. In particular, the dataset sess_5_ai2thor has been created by the robot through the methodology described. Moreover, the model used for this experiment is **ANALOGY**, and it has been developed in "classical_context" which means that it has not been made suitable for continual learning, but it is such as the standard model for KGEs.

The results of this experiment are showed in Tables 1 and 2. The two tables show the performances of the model in terms of **HITS@10** (Hits at 10) and **MRR** (Mean Reciprocal Rank). The 2 metrics **HITS@10** and **MRR** are defined as follows:

$$MRR = \frac{1}{|Q|} \sum_{i=1}^{|Q|} \frac{1}{\text{rank}_{(s,p,o)_i}} \tag{5}$$

$$Hits@N = \sum_{i=1}^{|Q|} 1 \text{ if } \text{rank}_{(s,p,o)_i} \leq 10 \tag{6}$$

Each table must be read from the top to the bottom because the order is chronological. In each row, there is the performance of the model (trained on the subset i of the dataset) with respect to the other subsets. The first row of Table 1 for instance, shows the HITS@10 of ANALOGY which has been trained on sess_5_ai2thor. Since it has only been trained on that subset of the dataset, it has been evaluated only on sess_5_ai2thor. The row "classical_context on 2_ai2thor", shows the HITS@10 of ANALOGY which has been trained on sess_5_ai2thor, sess_4_ai2thor, sess_3_ai2thor (**previously**), and sess_2_ai2thor (**currently**). It means that can be evaluated on the subset *sess_i_ai2thor* where $i \in \{2, 3, 4, 5\}$. The model comes across the catastrophic forgetting phenomenon because, the more it trains on subsets *sess_i_ai2thor* where $i \in \{4, 3, 2, 1, 0\}$ which contain the same entities and relations, the less it is precise on HITS@10 on sess_5_ai2thor whose data are unseen for all the subsequent learning sessions.

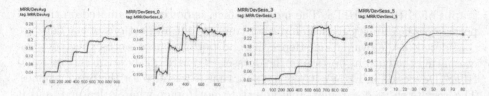

Fig. 7. The *MRR* during the learning sessions: 0, 3, 5 (the last one, in blue, represents the training considering the last subset of the data acquired through the proposed methodology). The graph on the left compare the MRR of last learning session with the average MRR among all the previous learning sessions. (Color figure online)

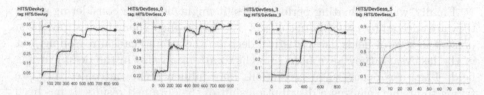

Fig. 8. The HITS@10 function during the learning sessions: 0, 3, 5 (the last one, depicted in blue, represents the training considering the last subset of the data acquired through the proposed methodology). The graph on the left compares the HITS@10 of the last learning session with the average MRR among all the previous learning sessions. (Color figure online)

For the next experiment, the model ANALOGY is considered only with continuous_context, because it proves efficient for the problem of catastrophic forgetting. The same dataset considered previously has been used, i.e. *sess_5_ai2thor* with $i \in \{0, 1, 2, 3, 4, 5\}$, where the partitions $i \in \{0, 1, 2, 3, 4\}$ are composed by the same types of entities, while the partition $i = 5$ consists mostly of new entities.

In Fig. 6 are shown 5 different graphs, representing the trend of the loss function for each learning session. By only looking at these graphs, there are some elements that are very important. First, the trend of the loss is always decreasing. The most decreasing shape is reached in the first forty epochs of each learning session. Since in each learning session there is a limited amount of data, after some epochs the trend is quite stable, and the model is no longer improving. Here comes the "early stopping", which is set with a patience = 50, that stops the training for that learning session and starts the next learning session. Although the entities are almost the same in each learning session, the predicates are different, and for this reason, at the beginning of each learning session the loss is pretty high, but then it decreases. The overall trend of the loss decreases learning session by learning session.

The loss function is an important metric for checking if the model is learning or not, but is not significant if considered alone, in fact Fig. 7 and Fig. 8 show the graphs of the two metrics considered for the evaluation of the models, which are *MRR* and *HITS@10*. The increasing learning skills are confirmed by the graphs of MRR and HITS. The model, in fact, is not only evaluated on the nth portion of the dataset given in input for training but all portions of the data are considered in the evaluation. Hence, if good performances were expected when evaluating the current portion of the dataset (see MRR/DevSess_5 in Fig. 7 and HITS/DevSess_5 in Fig. 8), it was not sure that it was also for the previous ones. The results showed a remarkable ability to not forget what is learned, and it is visible in MRR/DevSess_i with $i \in \{0, 1, 2, 3, 4\}$ and HITS/DevSess_i with $i \in \{0, 1, 2, 3, 4\}$. In these graphs, the performance of the last learning session is marked with the color blue. Both for MRR and for HITS the performances of the last learning session (represented in blue color) are not worse than the performance of the model at the previous learning session (depicted in red).

Finally, when evaluating performances, it might be worth considering also if they are affected by *performative effects* [10]. These phenomena have always been present in several fields like statistical decision theory and causal reasoning, but in the last years, they have been brought to attention also in the deep learning field. They can occur when predictions may influence the outcomes they are trying to predict, causing a distribution shift of the obtained results. It has been observed that these effects are reduced if multiple re-training procedures are performed. In the present work, we proposed a re-training procedure at the end of each learning session. This operation would reduce such distribution shifts.

A video representing a key result of this work can be found in the following link: https://www.youtube.com/watch?v=vQbyn7hs8_4. It shows, through some snapshots of the video, the process of enlarging the knowledge base of the robot, thanks to the interaction with the human. With this procedure, entities that were first unknown, become part of the knowledge of the robot.

5   Conclusions and Future Directions

In this work, we show (as in Fig. 2 and 3) the ability of the robot to learn from unknown environments, relying on the answers of the human. Thanks to the proposed architecture, the robot uses Knowledge Graph Embedding techniques to generalize the acquired information with the goal of incrementally extending its inner representation of the environment. We evaluate the performance of the overall architecture by measuring the capabilities of the robot of learning entities and relations coming from unknown contexts through a series of incremental learning sessions, demonstrating the ability of the presented architecture to cope with the catastrophic forgetting phenomenon. For example, at the beginning of the experiments, the robot is unable to find any meaningful information of an unknown detected object, if it has been never encountered before. After some learning sessions, it has become able to retrieve accurate information about it. The learning process of the robot is human-driven, and the human is no more required to be an expert. This allows the application of the system in many dynamic scenarios when a robot needs to learn information about the operating environment. Despite the data that drive the learning being sparse and unbalanced, the designed architecture allows the learning curve to converge quickly.

The whole architecture, in addition to these improvements, would make the interactions between humans and robots more natural, making a further step toward the creation of systems that can handle long interactions with humans in an environment whose knowledge of it is incrementally built during the interaction, and it is not needed to give it in advance to the robot.

References

1. Aljundi, R., Kelchtermans, K., Tuytelaars, T.: Task-free continual learning. In: Proceedings of the IEEE/CVF Conference on Computer Vision and Pattern Recognition, pp. 11254–11263 (2019)
2. Bordes, A., Usunier, N., Garcia-Duran, A., Weston, J., Yakhnenko, O.: Translating embeddings for modeling multi-relational data. In: Advances in Neural Information Processing Systems, vol. 26 (2013)
3. Gemignani, G., Capobianco, R., Bastianelli, E., Bloisi, D.D., Iocchi, L., Nardi, D.: Living with robots: interactive environmental knowledge acquisition. Robot. Auton. Syst. **78**, 1–16 (2016)
4. Ji, S., Pan, S., Cambria, E., Marttinen, P., Philip, S.Y.: A survey on knowledge graphs: representation, acquisition, and applications. IEEE Trans. Neural Netw. Learn. Syst. **33**(2), 494–514 (2021)
5. Kolve, E., et al.: AI2-THOR: an interactive 3D environment for visual AI. arXiv preprint arXiv:1712.05474 (2017)
6. Laird, J.E., et al.: Interactive task learning. IEEE Intell. Syst. **32**(4), 6–21 (2017)
7. Li, Z., Hoiem, D.: Learning without forgetting. IEEE Trans. Pattern Anal. Mach. Intell. **40**(12), 2935–2947 (2018). https://doi.org/10.1109/TPAMI.2017.2773081
8. Lindblom, J., Andreasson, R.: Current challenges for UX evaluation of human-robot interaction. In: Schlick, C., Trzcieliński, S. (eds.) Advances in Ergonomics of Manufacturing: Managing the Enterprise of the Future, pp. 267–277. Springer, Cham (2016). https://doi.org/10.1007/978-3-319-41697-7_24
9. Nickel, M., Tresp, V., Kriegel, H.P.: A three-way model for collective learning on multi-relational data. In: ICML (2011)
10. Perdomo, J., Zrnic, T., Mendler-Dünner, C., Hardt, M.: Performative prediction. In: International Conference on Machine Learning, pp. 7599–7609. PMLR (2020)
11. Pronobis, A.: Semantic mapping with mobile robots. Ph.D. thesis, KTH Royal Institute of Technology (2011)
12. Pronobis, A., Jensfelt, P.: Large-scale semantic mapping and reasoning with heterogeneous modalities. In: 2012 IEEE International Conference on Robotics and Automation, pp. 3515–3522. IEEE (2012)
13. Randelli, G., Bonanni, T.M., Iocchi, L., Nardi, D.: Knowledge acquisition through human-robot multimodal interaction. Intel. Serv. Robot. **6**(1), 19–31 (2013)
14. Redmon, J., Farhadi, A.: Yolov3: an incremental improvement. arXiv preprint arXiv:1804.02767 (2018)
15. Wang, Q., Mao, Z., Wang, B., Guo, L.: Knowledge graph embedding: a survey of approaches and applications. IEEE Trans. Knowl. Data Eng. **29**(12), 2724–2743 (2017)

Construct, Merge, Solve and Adapt Applied to a Bus Driver Scheduling Problem with Complex Break Constraints

Roberto Maria Rosati[1]([✉]), Lucas Kletzander[2], Christian Blum[3],
Nysret Musliu[2], and Andrea Schaerf[1]

[1] DPIA, University of Udine, via delle Scienze 206, 33100 Udine, Italy
{robertomaria.rosati,andrea.schaerf}@uniud.it
[2] Christian Doppler Laboratory for Artificial Intelligence and Optimization for
Planning and Scheduling, DBAI, TU Wien, Vienna, Austria
{lucas.kletzander,nysret.musliu}@tuwien.ac.at
[3] Artificial Intelligence Research Institute (IIIA-CSIC),
Campus of the UAB, Bellaterra, Spain
christian.blum@iiia.csic.es

Abstract. Bus Driver Scheduling (BDS) is a combinatorial optimization problem that consists in assigning atomic driving duties (legs) belonging to predetermined routes to bus drivers. We consider the highly-constrained, real-world version of the problem proposed by Kletzander and Musliu (2020), with complex break rules specified by a collective agreement and public regulation. We propose a Construct, Merge, Solve and Adapt (CMSA) algorithm, which is a recent metaheuristic proposed by Blum et al. (2016) based on the idea of problem instance reduction. At each iteration of the algorithm, sub-instances of the original instance are solved by an exact solver. These sub-instances are obtained by merging the components of the solutions generated by a probabilistic greedy algorithm. We compare our method with the state-of-the-art approaches on the benchmark instances. The results show that CMSA compares favourably with other metaheuristics on most instances and with exact techniques on large ones.

Keywords: Bus driver scheduling · Metaheuristics · Optimization · CMSA

1 Introduction

Driver scheduling problems are complex combinatorial problems that integrate the scheduling part with routing issues, due to the fact that drivers and vehicles get moved to different locations by their duties. Different driver scheduling problems have been proposed in the literature, differing among themselves mainly depending on the type of vehicles that are involved and constraints.

© The Author(s), under exclusive license to Springer Nature Switzerland AG 2023
A. Dovier et al. (Eds.): AIxIA 2022, LNAI 13796, pp. 254–267, 2023.
https://doi.org/10.1007/978-3-031-27181-6_18

We consider here a Bus Driver Scheduling (BDS) problem, which is characterized by the fact that the atomic driving duties (called *legs*) are short compared to other vehicles (e.g., planes or trains). Therefore, the daily shift of a driver is composed of a relatively large number of independent legs, which must be assembled in a working shift respecting various regulations mainly connected to safety issues.

We focus on the specific BDS formulation proposed by [13], which arises from a public transportation setting in Austria and is subject to many constraints related to rest time (breaks) regulated by legal requirements and collective agreements. This formulation comes with a challenging dataset composed of many realistic instances, which has already been used in the experimental analysis of a few exact and metaheuristic techniques [12,13,15].

We propose for this problem a Construct, Merge, Solve and Adapt (CMSA) approach, which is a metaheuristic technique recently proposed by [3], and applied to a variety of combinatorial problems [9,16,22].

Additionally, we have been able to reuse a greedy algorithm developed in a previous work [13], that we suitably randomized in order to employ it for the generation of solutions within the CMSA algorithm.

For our CMSA solver, we performed a principled tuning procedure in order to obtain the best configuration of the parameters and we compared our tuned solver with the best results from the literature. The outcome is that our solver is able to improve the state-of-the-art results for a range of problem instances, in particular for the large ones.

2 Problem Description

The investigated Bus Driver Scheduling problem deals with the assignment of bus drivers to vehicles that already have a predetermined route for one day of operation, according to the rules specified by an Austrian collective agreement. We use the same specification as presented in previous work [13], where the reader can find a more detailed description of the problem.

2.1 Problem Input

The bus routes are given as a set $\mathcal{L}$ of individual bus legs, each leg $\ell \in \mathcal{L}$ is associated with a tour $tour_\ell$ (corresponding to a particular vehicle), a start time $start_\ell$, an end time end_ℓ, a starting position $startPos_\ell$, and an end position $endPos_\ell$. The actual driving time for the leg is denoted by $drive_\ell$. The benchmark instances use $drive_\ell = length_\ell = end_\ell - start_\ell$.

Table 1 shows a short example of one particular bus tour. The vehicle starts at time 360 (6:00 am) at position 0, does multiple legs with stops including waiting time at positions 1 and 2 and finally returns to position 0. A valid tour never has overlapping bus legs and consecutive bus legs satisfy $endPos_i = startPos_{i+1}$. A tour change occurs when a driver has an assignment of two consecutive bus legs i and j with $tour_i \neq tour_j$.

Table 1. A bus tour example

ℓ	$tour_\ell$	$start_\ell$	end_ℓ	$startPos_\ell$	$endPos_\ell$
1	1	360	395	0	1
2	1	410	455	1	2
3	1	460	502	2	1
4	1	508	540	1	0

A distance matrix specifies, for each pair of positions p and q, the time $d_{p,q}$ a driver takes to get from p to q when not actively driving a bus. If no transfer is possible, then $d_{p,q} = \infty$. $d_{p,q}$ with $p \neq q$ is called the *passive ride time*. $d_{p,p}$ represents the time it takes to switch tour at the same position, but is not considered passive ride time.

Finally, each position p is associated with an amount of working time for starting a shift ($startWork_p$) and ending a shift ($endWork_p$) at that position. The instances in this paper use $startWork_p = 15$ and $endWork_p = 10$ at the depot ($p = 0$), to take into account the time needed to enter and exit the depot. These values are 0 for other positions, given that the bus is already on the street.

2.2 Solution

A solution to the problem is an assignment of exactly one driver to each bus leg. Criteria for feasibility are:

- No overlapping bus legs are assigned to any driver.
- Changing tour or position between consecutive assignments i and j requires $start_j \geq end_i + d_{endPos_i, startPos_j}$.
- Each shift respects all hard constraints regarding work regulations as specified in the next section.

2.3 Work and Break Regulations

Valid shifts for drivers are constrained by work regulations and require frequent breaks. First, different measures of time related to a shift s containing the set of bus legs $\mathcal{L}_s$ need to be distinguished, as visualized in Fig. 1:

- The total amount of driving time: $D_s = \sum_{i \in \mathcal{L}_s} drive_i$
- The span from the start of work until the end of work T_s with a maximum of $T_{max} = 14$ h.
- The working time $W_s = T_s - unpaid_s$, not including certain unpaid breaks.

Driving Time Regulations. The maximum driving time is restricted to $D_{max} = 9$ h. The whole distance $start_j - end_i$ between consecutive bus legs i and j qualifies as a driving break, including passive ride time. Breaks from driving need to be taken repeatedly after at most 4 h of driving time. In case a

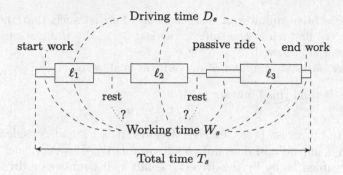

Fig. 1. Example shift

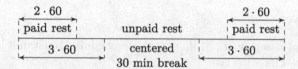

Fig. 2. Rest break positioning

driving break is split in several parts, all parts must occur before a driving block exceeds the 4-h limit. Once the required amount of break time is reached, a new driving block starts. The following options are possible:

- One break of at least 30 min
- Two breaks of at least 20 min each
- Three breaks of at least 15 min each

Working Time Regulations. The working time W_s has a hard maximum of $W_{max} = 10$ h and a soft minimum of $W_{min} = 6.5$ h. If the employee is working for a shorter period of time, the difference has to be paid anyway. The actual paid working time is $W'_s = \max\{W_s; \ 390\}$.

A minimum rest break is required according to the following options:

- $W_s < 6$ h: no rest break
- 6 h $\leq W_s \leq 9$ h: at least 30 min
- $W_s > 9$ h: at least 45 min

The rest break may be split into one part of at least 30 min and one or more parts of at least 15 min. The first part has to occur after at most 6 h of work. Note that a break can be a rest break and driving break simultaneously or just qualify as one of the two types.

Whether rest breaks are paid or unpaid depends on break positions according to Fig. 2. Every period of at least 15 min of consecutive rest break is unpaid as long as it does not intersect the first 2 or the last 2 h of the shift (a longer rest break might be partially paid and partially unpaid). The maximum amount of unpaid rest is limited:

– If 30 consecutive minutes of rest break are located such that they do not intersect the first 3 h of the shift or the last 3 h of the shift, at most 1.5 h of unpaid rest are allowed.
– Otherwise, at most one hour of unpaid rest is allowed.

Rest breaks beyond this limit are paid.

Shift Splits. If a rest break exceeds 3 hours, it is instead considered a shift split, which is unpaid and does not count towards W_s. However, such splits are typically regarded badly by the drivers. A shift split counts as a driving break, but does not contribute to rest breaks.

2.4   Objectives

As argued in previous work [13], practical schedules must not consider only operating costs. The objective

$$cost_s = 2 \cdot W'_s + T_s + ride_s + 30 \cdot ch_s + 180 \cdot split_s \tag{1}$$

represents a linear combination of several criteria for shift s. The paid working time W'_s is the main objective and it is combined with the total time T_s to reduce long unpaid periods for employees. The next sub-objectives reduce the passive ride time $ride_s$ and the number of tour changes ch_s, which is beneficial for both employees and efficient schedules. The last objective aims to reduce the number of shift splits $split_s$ as they are very unpopular.

3   Related Work

Different variants of BDS have been studied from the early 60's [27]. The BDS is often modelled as a Set Partitioning Problem and exact methods have been used in many publications to solve various variants of this problem [8,15,18, 23,25]. To solve very large real-world problems in a reasonable time, several metaheuristic methods have been studied for BDS. Such methods include Greedy approaches [20], Tabu Search [12,24], Simulated Annealing [13], GRASP [7], and Genetic Algorithms [17,19].

   The problem definition of BDS is highly dependent on the country's labour regulations, therefore, algorithms for other BDS variants cannot be used directly for the Austrian rules, which are more complex than most found in the literature. Previous work mostly focuses on cost only, sometimes including minimizing idle times and vehicle changes [6,11], but without considering the additional objectives for shift ergonomics that are considered for the BDS problem in this paper. Our problem variant has been introduced recently in the literature, and, to the best of our knowledge, the recently introduced exact approach based on branch and price [15], the metaheuristic approaches simulated annealing [13] and tabu search [12], as well as the application of problem-independent hyper-heuristics in combination with a set of problem-dependent low-level heuristics [14], represent the current state of the art for this problem. Although these approaches give very good results, the optimal solutions are still not known for most instances. Therefore, the investigation of new approaches is important for this problem.

4   The CMSA Approach to the BDS Problem

Construct, Merge, Solve and Adapt (CMSA) is a metaheuristic that was proposed recently in [3] and it is based on the idea of problem instance reduction [4]. At each iteration, the algorithm generates a number of solutions in a probabilistic way (Construct). The solution components found in these solutions are added to an initially empty sub-instance of the tackled problem instance (Merge). Then, an independent algorithm—typically an exact solver—is applied to the current sub-instance, in order to find the best, or possibly best, solution to the original problem instance that only contains solution components currently present in the sub-instance (Solve). Finally, the sub-instance is adapted according to the result of the independent algorithm, in such a way that those solution components that are frequently chosen by the independent algorithm are kept and those that are never used along a certain number of iterations are discarded (Adapt). The four phases are repeated in a loop until a certain stop criterion is met, where CPU running time is the most commonly employed. When the independent algorithm is a MIP solver like CPLEX or Gurobi, and this is the typical case for CMSA, the procedure can be said to be a matheuristic, because it envelopes an exact solver inside a metaheuristic procedure.

4.1   The CMSA Algorithm

Our CMSA algorithm for the BDS Problem is based on the following main idea. Given the set of legs $\mathcal{L} = \{\ell_1...\ell_n\}$, let $\mathcal{S}$ be the collection of all possible feasible bus shifts, where each shift $s \in \mathcal{S}$ is a sequence of legs that does not violate any of the constraints of the problem. A feasible solution is any collection of shifts $\phi \subset \mathcal{S}$ such that every leg $\ell \in \mathcal{L}$ belongs to one and only one shift $s \in \phi$. Solution ϕ is a valid solution for the set partitioning problem on $\mathcal{S}$. Let then $t_{\ell s} \in \{0, 1\}$ be 1 if leg ℓ forms part of shift s, and 0 otherwise. Moreover, let c_s be the cost of shift s, calculated according to the objectives explained in Sect. 2. If we were able to enumerate all shifts in $\mathcal{S}$, the optimal solution of the BDS problem could be found by solving the following ILP model of the set partitioning problem to optimality.

$$\min \sum_{s \in \mathcal{S}} c_s x_s \tag{2}$$

$$\text{s.t.} \sum_{s \in \mathcal{S}} x_s t_{\ell s} = 1 \qquad \forall\, \ell \in \mathcal{L} \tag{3}$$

$$x_s \in \{0, 1\} \qquad \forall\, s \in \mathcal{S} \tag{4}$$

Algorithm 1. CMSA for the BDS Problem

1: **input:** a set of legs $\mathcal{L}$, values for n_{sols}, d_{rate}, age_{limit}
2: $\Phi_{bsf} \leftarrow \emptyset$; $\mathcal{S}' \leftarrow \emptyset$
3: **while** CPU time limit not reached **do**
4:     **for** $i \leftarrow 1,...,n_{sols}$ **do**
5:         $\Phi_{cur} \leftarrow$ ProbabilisticGenerateSolution($\mathcal{L}$, d_{rate})
6:         **if** Φ_{cur} is better than Φ_{bsf} **then** $\Phi_{bsf} \leftarrow \Phi_{cur}$ **end if**
7:         **for** all $s \in \Phi_{cur}$ such that $s \notin \mathcal{S}'$ **do**
8:             $\mathcal{S}' \leftarrow \mathcal{S}' \cup s$
9:             $age[s] \leftarrow 0$
10:        **end for**
11:    **end for**
12:    $\Phi_{opt} \leftarrow$ ApplyExactSolver($\mathcal{S}'$)
13:    **if** Φ_{opt} is better than Φ_{bsf} **then** $\Phi_{bsf} \leftarrow \Phi_{opt}$ **end if**
14:    **for** all $s \in \mathcal{S}'$ **do**
15:        **if** $s \in \Phi_{opt}$ **then** $age[s] \leftarrow 0$ **else** $age[s] \leftarrow age[s] + 1$ **end if**
16:        **if** $age[s] > age_{limit}$ **then** $\mathcal{S}' \leftarrow \mathcal{S}' \setminus s$ **end if**
17:    **end for**
18: **end while**
19: **output:** Φ_{bsf}

This ILP model is based on a binary variable x_s for each bus shift $s \in \mathcal{S}$, whereby a value of $x_s = 1$ means that shift s is chosen to be part of the solution. Moreover, constraints (3) ensure that each leg ℓ in $\mathcal{L}$ is present exactly once among the chosen bus shifts. In this way, all bus legs will be assigned to exactly one bus driver and no legs will be left uncovered. The objective (2) is to minimize the total cost, which is the sum of the costs c_s of the shifts that belong to the solution.

Nonetheless, in real-world instances, and in most instances proposed for this formulation, the cardinality of set $\mathcal{S}$ is too big for making the enumeration of the shifts a practical solution, and even the application of some efficient generation procedures, such as backtracking, would lead to ILP models that are too large to be solved in reasonable time with the current availability of memory and computational resources. However, we can use the above ILP model for solving reduced sub-instances $\mathcal{S}' \subset \mathcal{S}$, as required by the solve phase of CMSA.

Algorithm 1 provides the pseudo-code of our CMSA algorithm for the BDS problem. The CMSA takes as input the values for the following three parameters:

- n_{sols}, which fixes the number of solutions to be probabilistically generated by the construction procedure at each CMSA iteration.
- d_{rate}, which guides the determinism rate in the solution construction procedure.
- age_{limit}, which limits the number of iterations a solution component (shift) s can remain in the sub-instance $\mathcal{S}'$ without being chosen by the exact solver. Note that the age of a solution component s is maintained in a variable $age[s]$.

CMSA starts with the initialization of the best solution found so far, Φ_{bsf}, to an empty solution. Moreover, the sub-instance $\mathcal{S}'$ is initialized to an empty set. The main loop of CMSA starts in line 3 of Algorithm 1. The four phases of CMSA take place, respectively: *construct* at line 5, *merge* at lines 7–10, *solve* at line 12 and *adapt* at lines 14–17. At each CMSA iteration, the construct and merge steps are repeated until n_{sols} are generated and merged into $\mathcal{S}'$. The construction procedure, specifically, is called at line 5, and it consists in a probabilistic greedy heuristic for generating a solution Φ_{cur} to the original set $\mathcal{L}$. The construction procedure uses a parameter d_{rate} to decide whether certain internal choices are performed in a deterministic or probabilistic way. Details on the heuristic procedure are given in Sect. 4.2. After the construction of every new solution, the corresponding merge step is performed in lines 7–10, that is, all those shifts $s \in \Phi_{cur}$ that are not yet present in sub-instance $\mathcal{S}'$ are added to $\mathcal{S}'$, and their age values $age[s]$ are initialized to zero. After generating and merging n_{sols} solutions, the CMSA algorithm enters into the solve phase, which takes place at line 12. In our case, the ILP solver CPLEX 20.1 is applied in function ApplyExactSolver($\mathcal{S}'$). This is done by solving the ILP model stated at the beginning of this section after replacing all occurrences of $\mathcal{S}$ with $\mathcal{S}'$. We do not make use of a time limit for CPLEX, and the time limit for the solve phase is equal to the remaining CPU time budget. This implies that, apart from the last iteration of CMSA, when CPLEX may be capped by the time limit, the solution Φ_{opt} found in the solve phase is always the optimal one for the sub-instance $\mathcal{S}'$. Finally, in lines 14–17, the sub-instance is adapted. This adaptation comprises the following steps. First, the ages of shifts in Φ_{opt} are re-set to zero. Secondly, the age values of all remaining shifts from $\mathcal{S}'$ are incremented by one. Finally, all shifts $s \in \mathcal{S}'$ with $age[s] > age_{limit}$ are removed from $\mathcal{S}'$.

4.2 Greedy Heuristic

The greedy heuristic employed in the construction step of our CMSA, which is called at line 5 of Algorithm 1, is described in Algorithm 2. It is a revisited and randomized version of the greedy algorithm proposed in [13]. The procedure takes as input a value for parameter d_{rate}. The algorithm starts by sorting the legs, which is done at line 3 of Algorithm 2 in function ApplySorting. This sub-procedure adds the legs—one by one—into a sorted sequence $\mathcal{L}_{sorted}$, initially empty, choosing among those legs that have not been added to $\mathcal{L}_{sorted}$ yet. Every new entry is chosen according to the following criterion: with probability d_{rate}, the leg with the earliest start time is added to $\mathcal{L}_{sorted}$. Otherwise—that is, with probability $1 - d_{rate}$—a random leg is chosen. If d_{rate} is set to 1.0, legs in $\mathcal{L}_{sorted}$ are sorted according to their start time, as done in the original algorithm [13]. Then, beginning at line 4, the main loop of the algorithm takes place. The legs are explored in the order defined by $\mathcal{L}_{sorted}$ and each leg ℓ is inserted either in the shift that produces the least cost increase or a new shift is created, if the cost of the new shift containing solely ℓ is less than the least cost increase plus a certain threshold τ. Function SetThreshold chooses the value of τ as follows: with probability d_{rate}, τ is set to a fixed value of 500, while with probability $1 - d_{rate}$,

Algorithm 2. Probabilistic greedy procedure

1: **input:** a set of legs $\mathcal{L}$, value for d_{rate}
2: $\Phi_{cur} \leftarrow \emptyset$
3: $\mathcal{L}_{sorted} = \mathsf{ApplySorting}(\mathcal{L}, d_{rate})$
4: **for all** ℓ in $\mathcal{L}_{sorted}$ **do**
5:    $s_{best} = \mathrm{argmin}_{s \in \Phi_{cur}}(c_{s \cup \{\ell\}} - c_s)$
6:    $\tau = \mathsf{SetThreshold}(d_{rate})$
7:    **if** $c_{\{\ell\}} < c_{s_{best} \cup \{\ell\}} - c_{s_{best}} + \tau$ **then**
8:      Add new shift $\{\ell\}$ to Φ_{cur}
9:    **else**
10:      Add leg ℓ to shift s_{best} in Φ_{cur}
11:    **end if**
12:    **for all** $\ell' \neq \ell$ in $\mathcal{L}_{sorted}$ such that $tour(\ell') = tour(\ell)$ **do**
13:      Add leg ℓ' to shift s_{best} in Φ_{cur} if $s_{best} \cup \{\ell'\}$ is feasible
14:    **end for**
15:    Remove from $\mathcal{L}_{sorted}$ all legs added to shifts in Φ_{cur} at current iteration.
16: **end for**
17: **output:** Φ_{cur}

a random number between 500 and 1000 is chosen uniformly. These bounds (500, respectively 1000) were selected according to problem-specific knowledge. After inserting a leg ℓ in an existing or in a new shift, the algorithm tries to perform all feasible additions of other legs ℓ' that belong to the same tour of ℓ to that shift. This sub-procedure explores the legs by increasing start time, and it terminates at the first infeasible insertion or where no other legs with the same tours are left. The procedure ends when all legs from $\mathcal{L}_{sorted}$ have been added to the shifts in the solution Φ_{cur}.

5   Experimental Results

We tested the CMSA algorithm on the wide set of realistic instances available in the literature. Instances sizes range from 10 tours (about 70 legs) to 250 tours (at most 2500 legs). The instances with sizes 10–100 were released in [13], while the larger instances with sizes 150–250 were introduced later in [12].

We compare our CMSA with the state-of-the-art algorithms previously presented in the literature: Simulated Annealing (SA) and Hill Climbing (HC) [13], Tabu Search (TS) [12], and three hyper-heuristics using low-level heuristics proposed in [14]: Chuang-Pruning (CH-PR) [5], a combination of adaptive mechanisms to manage a set of active low-level heuristics (GIHH) [21], and a streamlined (lean) version of GIHH (L-GIHH) [1]. We compare the results also with the Branch and Price (B&P) developed by [15].

Table 2. CMSA parameters, the considered domains for parameter tuning, and the finally determined parameter values.

Parameter	10–100 tours		150 − 250 tours	
	Domain	Value	Domain	Value
n_{sols}	$\{2, 3, ..., 500\}$	300	$\{2, 3, ..., 200\}$	66
d_{rate}	$[0.50, 1.00]$	0.77	$[0.80, 1.00]$	0.96
age_{limit}	$\{2, 3, ..., 50\}$	4	$\{2, 3, ..., 30\}$	4

We implemented the CMSA in C++ and compiled with GNU g++, version 9.4.0, on Ubuntu 20.04.4 LTS. The experiments were run on a machine equipped with an AMD Ryzen Threadripper PRO 3975WX processor with 32 cores, with a base clock frequency of 3.5 GHz, 64 GB of RAM. We allowed one core per experiment. The experiments for other algorithms were run on a different and slower machine, with a base clock frequency of 2.20 GHz and max frequency of 2.90 GHz.

Although a completely fair comparison is not possible, for the above-mentioned reasons and because the algorithms were not all implemented in the same programming language, experimental data presented in Sect. 5.2 clearly shows that CMSA is able to outperform other metaheuristics on most instance classes, even if the time limit for CMSA is kept much shorter than for other methods.

5.1 Parameters Tuning

We tuned the values for parameters n_{sols}, d_{rate} and c_{list} through the automatic algorithm configuration tool json2run [26], which implements the F-RACE procedure [2]. The parameter space was sampled using a Hammersley point set [10]. We independently tuned the parameters for the instances with sizes from 10 to 100 tours and for the new larger instances, with sizes spread from 150 to 250 tours. Indeed, we had to allow smaller domains for the larger instances because combinations of high values of age_{limit} and n_{sols} together with small d_{rate} are very likely to give birth to ILP models that are too large and that may saturate the memory during the solve phase. Parameters n_{sols} and age_{limit} have domains of natural numbers, while d_{rate} takes real numbers with a precision of two decimal places. Table 2 shows the domains that we applied to the parameters and the different outcomes of the tuning procedures.

5.2 Analysis of the Results

Table 3 shows the average results grouped by instance sizes for different methods. Each instance size class contains five distinct instances and we executed 10 independent runs on each instance, so that each value is calculated over 50 runs. The values for SA and HC are also taken over 10 runs per instance, while for

Table 3. Average results (costs) for classes of instances (sizes expressed by number of tours) and methods.

Size	CMSA	SA	HC	TS	CH-PR	GIHH	L-GIHH	B&P
10	14879.7	**14739.6**	14988.4	15036.4	14956.2	14847.4	14810.6	<u>14709.2</u>
20	**30745.9**	30971.0	31275.6	31248.4	30896.7	30892.2	30810.8	<u>30294.8</u>
30	**50817.2**	51258.0	51917.4	51483.0	51331.4	51059.4	51037.6	<u>49846.4</u>
40	**68499.9**	69379.8	71337.6	69941.2	69182.9	68988.4	69022.2	<u>67000.4</u>
50	**86389.2**	87557.4	87262.4	87850.6	87394.3	87184.4	87145.2	<u>84341.0</u>
60	**102822.9**	104333.0	104296.4	104926.2	103921.5	103491.6	103467.3	<u>99727.0</u>
70	**121141.9**	123225.6	123304.0	123632.2	122502.9	122198.6	122321.8	<u>118524.2</u>
80	**138760.3**	140914.0	140508.0	140482.4	139931.8	139648.2	139551.9	<u>134513.8</u>
90	**155078.3**	157426.0	156862.4	156296.4	155520.8	155560.8	155649.6	<u>150370.8</u>
100	<u>**171786.7**</u>	174501.8	172909.0	172916.0	171901.0	171879.8	172763.7	172582.2
150	<u>**263387.7**</u>	266705.5	265492.3	265654.8	–	–	–	–
200	<u>**349017.0**</u>	354408.4	353494.9	350747.2	–	–	–	–
250	<u>**439234.5**</u>	446525.0	446000.9	443845.8	–	–	–	–

the hyper-heuristics 5 runs per instance were executed. TS and B&P are deterministic, so runs are not repeated. All algorithms worked with time limits of 1 h, except for B&P, which was allowed up to 2 h. Values in bold report best results within metaheuristics, while underlined values are the best values including also the exact approach. We can observe that CMSA outperforms other metaheuristics on all instance groups but the smallest one, sized 10. In general, the best results for instances up to size 90 remain the one set by the B&P, whilst, for larger instances, CMSA gets the new best results. For larger instances sized 150, 200 and 250 tours, only data for SA, HC and TS are available for comparison.

Table 4 shows mean values of the objective function collected from the same CMSA experiments as those presented in Table 3 after 15 min (900 s) and 30 min (1800 s). We compare them with the state-of-the-art metaheuristic, which is specified in the column *benchmark*. We report also the results of the B&P, which has a time limit of 2 h, but it may stop before, if an optimal solution is found, so actual B&P execution time is specified as well. Results that improve or equal the current state-of-the-art within metaheuristics are marked in bold.

Data show that CMSA converges very quickly toward good solutions. After 15 min it already shows better results than other metaheuristics for 10 out of 13 instance classes, and for 11 out of 13 after 30 min. For instances sized 100, CMSA after 15 or 30 min is already capable to perform better also than the exact method in 2 h, but not better than the hyper-heuristic L-GIHH. Data suggest also that CMSA is not likely to get stuck on early local minima, as we can see always a consistent decrease of the cost function value over time.

Finally, the fact that CMSA is able to provide good solutions quickly may be interesting for real-world applications, where human decision makers are likely to prefer to wait short times to have in hand the results of the automated scheduling.

Table 4. CMSA results (costs) measured after 15, 30, and 60 min (900, 1800 and 3600 s), and comparison with state-of-the-art metaheuristics and B&P. Best values among metaheuristic methods are in bold.

Instances sizes	CMSA - average			Benchmark		B&P	
	900 s	1800 s	3600 s	Method	3600 s	Time	Best
10	14899.0	14886.4	14879.7	SA	**14739.6**	7.2	14709.2
20	**30805.1**	**30770.3**	**30745.9**	L-GIHH	30810.8	1201.4	30294.8
30	**50911.6**	**50863.0**	**50817.2**	L-GIHH	51037.6	3610.6	49846.4
40	**68711.3**	**68600.2**	**68499.9**	GIHH	68988.4	3605.8	67000.4
50	**86674.3**	**86517.0**	**86389.2**	L-GIHH	87145.2	3674.4	84341.0
60	**103206.0**	**102998.3**	**102822.9**	L-GIHH	103467.3	4373.2	99727.0
70	**121734.6**	**121410.7**	**121141.9**	GIHH	122198.6	6460.4	118524.2
80	**139397.4**	**139073.7**	**138760.3**	L-GIHH	139551.9	5912.4	134513.8
90	155674.5	**155387.4**	**155078.3**	CH-PR	155520.8	7390.4	150370.8
100	172447.3	172086.9	**171786.7**	L-GIHH	171833.5	7395.8	172582.2
150	**264261.6**	**263803.9**	**263387.7**	HC	265492.3	-	-
200	**350638.9**	**349707.2**	**349017.0**	TS	350747.2	-	-
250	**441917.3**	**440364.5**	**439234.5**	TS	443845.8	-	-

6   Conclusions

We applied the CMSA metaheuristic to BDS, a complex and challenging real-world problem that integrates scheduling and routing issues. CMSA turned out to compare favourably with the state-of-the-art metaheuristics for this problem. In particular, it showed good performances on the large instances, which are in general the most critical ones.

In the future, we plan to investigate the use of feature-based tuning mechanisms, in which the parameters are not fixed to specific values, but are computed by functions of the features of instance. Indeed, our analysis highlighted that the best parameter configuration depends on some of the features, in particular those related to the size of the instance.

We would like to study also the option of performing an online tuning of the CMSA parameters, so that the parameters are adjusted during the single execution of the algorithm, using some learning mechanism.

Finally, we will investigate the use of different techniques for the building blocks of the CMSA technique, in particular for the construct phase. To this aim, we plan to test both other greedy techniques and some form of backtracking procedure to generate shifts with suitable characteristics.

Acknowledgements. We thank Tommaso Mannelli Mazzoli for helpful discussions about the BDS problem and for sharing the code of the problem validator with us.

Roberto Maria Rosati acknowledges support by TAILOR, a project funded by EU Horizon 2020 research and innovation programme under GA No 952215, which facilitated his research stay at the IIIA-CSIC.

The financial support by the Austrian Federal Ministry for Digital and Economic Affairs, the National Foundation for Research, Technology and Development and the Christian Doppler Research Association is gratefully acknowledged by Lucas Kletzander and Nysret Musliu.

Finally, Christian Blum acknowledges support by grant PID2019-104156GB-I00 funded by MCIN/AEI/10.13039/501100011033.

References

1. Adriaensen, S., Nowé, A.: Case study: an analysis of accidental complexity in a state-of-the-art hyper-heuristic for HyFlex. In: 2016 IEEE Congress on Evolutionary Computation (CEC), pp. 1485–1492. IEEE (2016)
2. Birattari, M., Yuan, Z., Balaprakash, P., Stützle, T.: F-race and iterated F-race: an overview. In: Experimental Methods for the Analysis of Optimization Algorithms, pp. 311–336 (2010)
3. Blum, C., Pinacho, P., López-Ibáñez, M., Lozano, J.A.: Construct, merge, solve & adapt a new general algorithm for combinatorial optimization. Comput. Oper. Res. **68**, 75–88 (2016)
4. Blum, C., Raidl, G.R.: Hybridization based on problem instance reduction. In: Blum, C., Raidl, G.R. (eds.) Hybrid Metaheuristics. AIFTA, pp. 45–62. Springer, Cham (2016). https://doi.org/10.1007/978-3-319-30883-8_3
5. Chuang, C.Y.: Combining multiple heuristics: studies on neighborhood-base heuristics and sampling-based heuristics. Ph.D. thesis, Carnegie Mellon University (2020)
6. Constantino, A.A., de Mendonça Neto, C.F.X., de Araujo, S.A., Landa-Silva, D., Calvi, R., dos Santos, A.F.: Solving a large real-world bus driver scheduling problem with a multi-assignment based heuristic algorithm. J. Univ. Comput. Sci. **23**(5), 479–504 (2017)
7. De Leone, R., Festa, P., Marchitto, E.: Solving a bus driver scheduling problem with randomized multistart heuristics. Int. Trans. Oper. Res. **18**(6), 707–727 (2011)
8. Desrochers, M., Soumis, F.: A column generation approach to the urban transit crew scheduling problem. Transp. Sci. **23**(1), 1–13 (1989)
9. Ferrer, J., Chicano, F., Ortega-Toro, J.A.: CMSA algorithm for solving the prioritized pairwise test data generation problem in software product lines. J. Heuristics **27**(1), 229–249 (2021)
10. Hammersley, J.M., Handscomb, D.C.: Monte Carlo Methods. Chapman and Hall, London (1964)
11. Ibarra-Rojas, O., Delgado, F., Giesen, R., Muñoz, J.: Planning, operation, and control of bus transport systems: a literature review. Transp. Res. Part B Methodol. **77**, 38–75 (2015)
12. Kletzander, L., Mazzoli, T.M., Musliu, N.: Metaheuristic algorithms for the bus driver scheduling problem with complex break constraints. In: Proceedings of the Genetic and Evolutionary Computation Conference, pp. 232–240 (2022)
13. Kletzander, L., Musliu, N.: Solving large real-life bus driver scheduling problems with complex break constraints. In: Proceedings of the International Conference on Automated Planning and Scheduling, vol. 30, pp. 421–429 (2020)

14. Kletzander, L., Musliu, N.: Hyper-heuristics for personnel scheduling domains. In: Proceedings of the International Conference on Automated Planning and Scheduling, vol. 32, pp. 462–470 (2022)
15. Kletzander, L., Musliu, N., Van Hentenryck, P.: Branch and price for bus driver scheduling with complex break constraints. In: Proceedings of the AAAI Conference on Artificial Intelligence, vol. 35, pp. 11853–11861 (2021)
16. Lewis, R., Thiruvady, D., Morgan, K.: Finding happiness: an analysis of the maximum happy vertices problem. Comput. Oper. Res. **103**, 265–276 (2019)
17. Li, J., Kwan, R.S.: A fuzzy genetic algorithm for driver scheduling. Eur. J. Oper. Res. **147**(2), 334–344 (2003)
18. Lin, D.Y., Hsu, C.L.: A column generation algorithm for the bus driver scheduling problem. J. Adv. Transp. **50**(8), 1598–1615 (2016)
19. Lourenço, H.R., Paixão, J.P., Portugal, R.: Multiobjective metaheuristics for the bus driver scheduling problem. Transp. Sci. **35**(3), 331–343 (2001)
20. Martello, S., Toth, P.: A heuristic approach to the bus driver scheduling problem. Eur. J. Oper. Res. **24**(1), 106–117 (1986)
21. Misir, M., De Causmaecker, P., Vanden Berghe, G., Verbeeck, K.: An adaptive hyper-heuristic for CHeSC 2011. In: OR53 Annual Conference, Date: 2011/09/06–2011/09/08, Location: Nottingham, UK (2011)
22. Pinacho-Davidson, P., Bouamama, S., Blum, C.: Application of CMSA to the minimum capacitated dominating set problem. In: Proceedings of the Genetic and Evolutionary Computation Conference, pp. 321–328 (2019)
23. Portugal, R., Lourenço, H.R., Paixão, J.P.: Driver scheduling problem modelling. Public Transp. **1**(2), 103–120 (2008)
24. Shen, Y., Kwan, R.S.K.: Tabu search for driver scheduling. In: Fandel, G., Trockel, W., Aliprantis, C.D., Kovenock, D., Voß, S., Daduna, J.R. (eds.) Computer-Aided Scheduling of Public Transport, vol. 505, pp. 121–135. Springer, Heidelberg (2001). https://doi.org/10.1007/978-3-642-56423-9_7
25. Smith, B.M., Wren, A.: A bus crew scheduling system using a set covering formulation. Transp. Res. Part A General **22**(2), 97–108 (1988)
26. Urli, T.: json2run: a tool for experiment design & analysis. CoRR abs/1305.1112 (2013)
27. Wren, A.: Scheduling vehicles and their drivers-forty years' experience. University of Leed, Technical report (2004)

Topic Modelling and Frame Identification for Political Arguments

Shohreh Haddadan[1], Elena Cabrio[2], Axel J. Soto[3,4], and Serena Villata[2(✉)]

[1] University of Luxembourg, Esch-sur-Alzette, Luxembourg
shohreh.haddadan@gmail.com
[2] Université Côte d'Azur, CNRS, Inria, I3S, Nice, France
{elena.cabrio,serena.villata}@univ-cotedazur.fr
[3] Universidad Nacional del Sur, Bahía Blanca, Argentina
[4] Institute for Computer Science and Engineering (CONICET–UNS),
Bahía Blanca, Argentina
axel.soto@cs.uns.edu.ar

Abstract. Presidential debates are one of the most salient moments of a presidential campaign, where candidates are challenged to discuss the main contemporary and historical issues in a country. These debates represent a natural ground for argumentative analysis, which has been always employed to investigate political discourse structure in philosophy and linguistics. In this paper, we take the challenge to analyse these debates from the topic modeling and framing perspective, to enrich the investigation of these data. Our contribution is threefold: first, we apply transformer-based language models (i.e., BERT and RoBERTa) to the classification of generic frames showing that these models improve the results presented in the literature for frame identification; second, we investigate the task of topic modelling in political arguments from the U.S. presidential campaign debates, applying an unsupervised machine learning approach; and finally, we discuss various visualisations of the identified topics and frames from these U.S. presidential election debates to allow a further interpretation of such data.

Keywords: Argument mining · Framing · Political debates

1 Introduction

Argumentation is a rhetoric means used by politicians to put forward their own arguments in front of their audience. As highlighted by Boydstun *et al.* [3], candidates strive to focus the debate on a topic that advantages them and/or their party. A candidate whose party's or administration's economy was thriving would either prefer to discuss topics related to economy or try as much as she can to portray her arguments on other topics from the perspective of economics. The later strategy is referred to as *framing* in rhetoric. Entman [10] defines framing as follows: "*To frame is to select some aspects of a perceived reality and make them more salient in a communicating text, in such a way as*

*to promote a particular problem definition, casual interpretation, moral evalua-
tion and/or treatment recommendation.*" In the U.S. presidential debates, topics
are customarily demanded by the audience either explicitly (i.e., through questions by moderators), e.g., the Iraq war which dominates debates in 2004, or
implicitly, i.e., as an important issue which the audience might crave hearing
about like the Watergate scandal in 1976.

Topics and frames cover two different viewpoints on the arguments put forward in the debate. On the one hand, topics are identified by the keywords that
make them distinct from the other topics. The language or the set of keywords
describing the topic of an argument are the same regardless of the stance the
debater is taking towards this topic, e.g., Iraq, war, military, Saddam Hossein.
On the other hand, framing is how an argument by a debater is put forward
through selected words to react to the discussion about the topics in debate.
Lakoff [11] highlights the importance of *framing* in political speeches and debates
by giving an example from the United States politics. He points out that the
term "tax relief" introduced by George W. Bush's administration puts the topic
of "taxation" in a frame which implies that the party who is advocating taxation is a villain, while the (Republican) party against it is relieving people from
this affliction. In the example below, about the topic of "death penalty", from
the 1988 U.S. presidential elections, the candidate from the Democratic party
Micheal Dukakis chooses words such as *education* and *prevention* in his premises
against death penalty, whilst the Republican candidate George H.W Bush uses
words like *inhibiting, rape* and *brutalization.* Dukakis's choice of words portrays
his argument on death penalty in a different framing dimension than Bush's
one, and this is how their stance for and against death penalty is formed. Both
arguments are on the *topic* of "death penalty". Thus, framing can be a determining factor in the recognition of the stance for or against a topic in a debate, as
framing defines the aspects about which a topic can be discussed.

1. **Bush-Dukakis, September 25, 1988:**
   DUKAKIS: "I'm opposed to the death penalty. I think everybody knows that.
   I'm also very tough on violent crime. And that's one of the reasons why my state
   has cut crime by more than any other industrial state in America. It's one of the
   reasons why we have the lowest murder rate of any industrial state in the country.
   It's one of the reasons why we have a drug **education** and **prevention** program
   that is reaching out and helping youngsters all over our state, the kind of thing I
   want to do as president of the United States... "

   LEHRER: "Response, Mr. Vice President."

   BUSH: "... And I favor the death penalty. I know it's tough and honest people can
   disagree. But when a narcotics wrapped up guy goes in and murders a police officer,
   I think they ought to pay with their life. And I do believe it would be **inhibiting**.
   And so I am not going to furlough men like Willie Horton, and I would meet with
   their, the victims of his last escapade, the **rape** and the **brutalization** of the family
   down there in Maryland. Maryland would not extradite Willie Horton, the man who
   was furloughed, the murderer, because they didn't want him to be furloughed again.
   And so we have a fundamental difference on this one."

The automatic identification of topics and frames in political argumentation is therefore of main importance to enrich argument-based information like the claims put forward in the debate, the supporting evidence, and the relations between the identified arguments. In this paper, we address this issue on the ElecDeb60To16 dataset[1] of U.S. political presidential debates [12,14]. More precisely, the three main contributions of this paper are the following: first, we apply transformer-based language models (i.e., BERT and RoBERTA) to classify generic frames on the "Media Frame Corpus" dataset with five topics, showing that these models improve the results achieved in the literature for the task of frame identification; second, we apply an unsupervised machine learning approach for topic modeling which takes advantage of sentence embeddings to represent the debates. This approach integrates the argument components in the debates as a source to extract issue-specific frames from the ElecDeb60To16 dataset; finally, we provide some visualisations of the identified topics and frames from different debates which allow for insightful interpretations. Such visualisations are also meant to be consumed by lay people, hence enabling the use of NLP methods by non-technical persons.

2   Related Work

In this section, we discuss the related literature focusing on Argument Mining (AM) with topic modeling and frame identification in the political domain.

In computational studies of rhetoric in the political domain, two main definitions of frames have been discussed. In the first one, frames are defined in a certain predefined dimension space as in Boydstun et al. [4]: this definition is referred to as *generic frames* [20]. The other approach considers frames as an extra topic dimension to a speech which is defined by the choice of words in a statement [1,25]. This is referred to as *issue-specific frames*. The "Policy Frames Codebook" [4] considers the following 15 frames to be comprehensive enough to cover most issue-specific frames in most topics: economic frames, capacity and resources frames, morality frames, fairness and equality frames, constitutionality and jurisprudence frames, policy prescription and evaluation frames, law, order, crime and justice frames, security and defense frames, health and safety frames, quality of life frames, cultural identity frames, public opinion frames, political frames, external regulations and reputation frames and other frames. Boydstun et al. [4] discuss that issue-specific frames such as "right of life for a fetus" in the argument against the topic of "abortion" can be interpreted to fall into one of such generic framing dimensions, i.e., "Morality".

From the computational point of view, some approaches address the issue of automatically identifying topics and classifying frames in text. Nguyen et al. [21] introduce the concept of Hierarchical Ideal Point Topic Model (HIPTM) to identify Ideal Points from the bill speeches and voting patterns of Republican legislators in the U.S. Congress. Using the hierarchy of topics, they identify the issue-specific frames politicians used in their arguments. Tsur et al. [25]

---

[1] https://github.com/pierpaologoffredo/disputool2.0/tree/main/Dataset/ElecDeb60 To16.

analyse framing strategies in an unsupervised setting using topic models fitted on time series through regression methods. The authors use this framework to identify temporal topic relations, and expressed agendas and analysis of framing dynamics known as "political spin". They use lagged dependency between two time series to uncover framing patterns or attention shifts in the campaigns. The data they use consists of 134000 statements made by 641 representatives (i.e., members of Congress) between two Congressional Elections in 2010 and 2012.

In alignment with the growth of attention towards applying computational methods in identifying frames in the social/political domains, Card et al. [5] build the Media Frame Corpus of news articles annotated with the above mentioned generic frames and the tone of the article (i.e., pro, anti, neutral). We describe this dataset in detail in Sect. 3. Hartmann et al. [15] also introduce a dataset of online fora discussions extracted from the Argument Extraction Corpus [24] annotated with a subset of generic frames from the Policy Frame Cookbook. Finally, Naderi and Hirst [20] compare several baselines with neural network based methods on multi-class classification and one-against-others classification to identify the generic frames on the Media Frame Corpus. They achieve highest accuracy using GRUs with pre-trained GloVe embeddings as features.

Ajjour et al. [1] also leverage the concept of framing in arguments. They define frames to be non-overlapping aspects of arguments on the same subject while concealing other aspects. In this context, frames are aspects taken for/against a controversial issue. They build a dataset of premise-conclusion pairs from Debatepedia[2], and annotate each pair with a few key-phrases, that are then lemmatised and unified. As an example of unification, the terms *unhealthy*, *non-smoker*, and *US business* are transformed to health, smoker and business, respectively. Counting the number of labels for each pair, frames are considered as generic when the label is used for more than one argument, and as topic-specific when the label is in one argument pair only. The final dataset includes 7052 generic frame arguments (i.e., economics, public opinion, environment, feasibility, rights, democracy, crime, politics, security and safety), and 5274 specific frame arguments. They first cluster the documents into topics using TF-IDF features of the debate and argument components with *k-means*, then they remove the topic from these clusters by using the prominent terms for each topic extracted by C-TF-IDF[3] and again cluster the results into frames. Analogously, Dumani et al. [9] consider the classification of stances and frames as a preliminary stage of argument clustering for the argument retrieval task.

Also reframing, i.e., controllable text generation, has recently attracted attention in similar studies. The aim of reframing is to change the perspective of the argument with respect to its target audience and the aspects that might be more appealing to it. Chen et al. [7] train neural models to reframe sentences on the Media Frame Corpus. They apply a sentence-level blank filling method. Chakrabarty et al. [6] create a parallel dataset of arguments with mutual purpose but different framings. Then, they apply a text generation method along with textual entailment to reframe the arguments.

---

[2] http://www.debates.org.
[3] C stands for cluster.

3   Datasets

In this section, we present the datasets we used in this paper for our experiments.

– **Media Frame Corpus:** It consists of English news articles on 5 controversial topics (gun control, death penalty, same sex marriage, immigration
and smoking) annotated with general frames using the 15 framing dimensions introduced in [4], on three different levels: 1) headline frame, 2) primary
frame, and 3) span level [5]. The following example from Card et al. [5] depicts
a piece of a news article from the 2006 editorial in the *Denver Post* on the
topic of immigration annotated with headline and span frames.

> • **[WHERE THE JOBS ARE]**Economic
> [Critics of illegal immigration can make many cogent arguments to support
> the position that the U.S. Congress and the Colorado legislature must develop
> effective and well-enforced immigration policies that will restrict the number of
> people who migrate here legally and illegally.]Public opinion
> [It's true that all forms of immigration exert influence over our economic
> and [cultural make-up.]Cultural identity In some ways, immigration improves our
> economy by adding laborers, taxpayers and consumers, and in other ways
> [immigration detracts from our economy by increasing the number of students,
> health care recipients and other beneficiaries of public services.]Capacity]Economic
> [Some economists say that immigrants, legal and illegal, produce a net economic
> gain, while others say that they create a net loss.]Economic There are rational
> arguments to support both sides of this debate, and it's useful and educational
> to hear the varying positions.

The Inter-Annotator Agreement (IAA) of primary frames in three stages of
annotation is reported between 0.4 and 0.6 based on Krippendorf's α, which
is considered as moderate agreement [2]. However, due to the complexity of
overlapping span-level annotation, IAA on this task is at highest 0.23 on one
of the topics, which is in any case higher than chance agreement.[4]

– **ElecDeb60To16:** This dataset contains the transcripts of the speeches from
the candidates during final stages of the US presidential debates between
the two major parties (in 1980 and 1992 independent candidates were also
included in the final debates). The dataset contains 6666 speech turns from
41 different debates through these years (1960–2016). No annotation on
Frames/Topics is available for this dataset. However, each debate has been
segmented in sections where the moderator asks a new question. There are
467 sections in all debates, in average each debate contains approximately 12
sections. This dataset is annotated with argument components and relations,
which we will profit from in the methodology adopted in this paper [14].

---

[4] For more details, see https://github.com/dallascard/media_frames_corpus.

4   Topic Modeling and Frame Classification for Arguments

In this section, we describe the two tasks we focus on to enrich the analysis of political argumentation. The first task consists in uncovering the topics discussed in political debates data. Following the work of Ajjour et al. [1] for unsupervised issue-specific frame identification, we also apply a hierarchical topic modeling approach using sentence-based transformer language models to discover the framing of the arguments by the presidential candidates in the ElecDeb60To16 .dataset. This experimental setting is discussed in Sect. 4.1.

Secondly, we focus on identifying frames in arguments occurred in the same dataset of presidential debates. We adopt a frame identification approach by training a supervised model using transformer-based language models on the "Media Frame Corpus" to classify generic frame spans and primary frames. We later use this model to classify frames in the ElecDeb60To16 dataset. This experimental setting is discussed in Sect. 4.2.

4.1   Generic Frame Classification

Naderi and Hirst [20] applied different approaches on the Media Frame Corpus data to classify frames at sentence level, and achieved best results with LSTM-based neural networks. In this paper, we employ transformer-based models like BERT [8] and RoBERTa [16] to address the task of generic frame classification and compare our results with those obtained by Naderi and Hirst [20]. It is noteworthy that their experiments were done on version v1.0 of the Media Frame Corpus, whilst we run ours on v2.0. To address a fair comparison, we implemented the experiments of Naderi and Hirst [20] and ran them on v2.0 of the dataset, applying the same data pre-processing. We use the pre-trained embeddings of BERT (uncased) and RoBERTa, and used a softmax function for the labels of sequence classification. The fine-tuning process is done in 4 epochs using an Adam optimiser with learning rate of 2^{-e5} and epsilon parameter of 1^{e-8}. The Media Frame Corpus contains frame annotations at article level (primary frame) and span level. We perform our experiments on both levels. Furthermore, we perform a cross-topic experiment to evaluate to what extent the fine-tuned model is able to predict the frame on a topic which has not seen before on the training data (albeit from the same dataset). This experiment has been conducted on both primary frames of the news article and the span-level frames.

4.2   Topic Modeling and Issue-Specific Frame Identification

In this second experimental setting, we address the topic modeling task on the ElecDeb60To16 dataset, taking advantage of the debate features like questions of the debates, speeches and sections identified in this dataset. Furthermore, we employ this topic modeling approach and the annotated argument components in this dataset to identify issue-specific frames used in candidates' arguments on various topics. More precisely, this experimental setting includes:

- **Topics from questions:** We assume that the questions asked by the moderators, panelists and audiences set the theme and determine the topic for the arguments made by candidates. The theme set for the debate is then discussed by the candidates using various frames to structure their arguments concerning the issue/topic/theme. For instance, in Example 2 below, the moderator explicitly sets the topic of the debate to "gun control laws".

  2. **Clinton-Trump, October 19, 2016:**
     WALLACE: [...] I want to focus on two issues that, in fact, by the justices that you name could end up changing the existing law of the land. First is one that you mentioned, Mr. Trump, and that is guns.

- **Topics from Speeches:** Occasionally candidates digress from topics set by moderators and set another topic for the rest of the debate. This argumentative technique is called *agenda setting* [3]. In order to retrieve topics initiated through this rhetorical technique, we also consider extracting topics from the speeches made by candidates during the debates.

- **Frames from argument components:** Frames are provided as a contextual setting for taking a stance for or against an argument. For instance, the topic of "tax laws" can be argued in different frames such as "middle class famililes", "small business owners". The two argument components annotated on the debate of September 26th, 2008 in Example 3 below indicate two different frames provided by the two candidates (belonging to different parties) on the topic of "taxation law". Based on this evidence, we assume that extracting more detailed topics from the argument components may help retrieve the frames about the discussed topics.

  3. **Maccin-Obama, September 26, 2016:**
     Obama: And I think that the fundamentals of the economy have to be measured by whether or not the middle class is getting a fair shake.
     Maccian: Senator Obama's secret that you don't know is that his tax increases will increase taxes on 50 percent of small business revenue.

Topic modeling [26] has been used for a long time along with bag of words features and Latent Dirichlet Allocation (LDA) or other matrix factorisation models. Recently, with the advancement of Language Models, topic modeling has also been adapted to the use of transformer-based models such as BERT [8], and later on sentence embeddings [22]. In order to obtain these sentence embeddings, Reimers and Gurevych [22] add a pooling layer (MEAN pooling as a default) on top of the pre-trained BERT output layer to get a fixed size vector. Then they rely on siamese and triplet neural networks, previously used in machine vision [23], to fine-tune the model. They use different objective functions (Classification, Regression, Triplet) depending on the task. The sentence embeddings resulting from this model are shown to improve the results of many semantic textual similarity tasks and clustering algorithms.

We apply some pre-processing steps on the text inputs (i.e., questions, speeches and argument components) before encoding them using the sentence embedding model proposed by Reimers and Gurevych [22]. This pre-processing

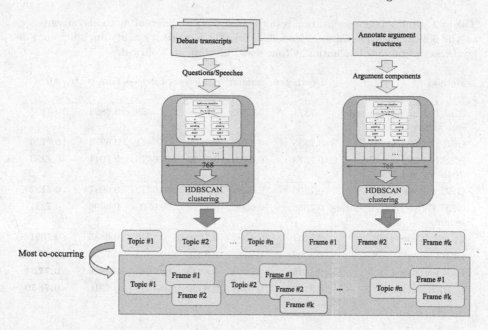

Fig. 1. Overall architecture of the clustering system implemented for topic modeling and issue-specific frame identification.

includes replacing the name of candidates in the debates by "candidate" or "other candidate" depending on the speaker. Speeches shorter than 16 tokens (word tokeniser function from the `nltk` library [17]) have been removed, as well as interruptions and cut-off speeches, such as "Can I respond?", "Thank you". Applying this pre-processing - based on the assumption that these speeches do not contribute to the topic distribution in the debates-, ~25% of the speeches are set aside from the clustering data input.

We then apply a topic modeling approach on the input, which is implemented with a density based clustering method called HDBSCAN [18]. In this way, we cluster documents based on their encoded representations using sentence-embeddings, based on the implementation of Grootendorst and Reimers [13]. They reduce the dimensions of the input encoded by the sentence embeddings with UMAP [19], and they implement c-tf-idf to automatically extract the prominent terms characterising each cluster. We adopt this architecture on the different levels to extract the topics and frames in the debates, employing the annotated argument structure. Our architecture is visualized in Fig. 1.

5   Results

In this section, we report the obtained results for the two tasks presented in Sect. 4, and we discuss some visualisations that helps to get a better understanding of the identified topics and frames.

Table 1. Multi-class classification results (accuracy) of different methods on sentences on the 5 most common frames: Economic, Legality Constitutionality Jurisdiction, Policy Prescription and Evaluation, Crime and Punishment, Political.

Method	Death pen.	Immigr.	Same sex marriage	Tobacco	Gun contr.	All
BiLSTM no pre-trained embeddings	0.7371	0.6270	0.7618	0.6369	0.6892	0.7131
BiLSTM Glove emb.	0.7535	0.6207	0.7699	0.6441	0.6974	0.7120
BiLSTM Glove emb. updating weights	0.7573	0.6310	0.7856	0.6419	0.7041	0.7236
GRU (Glove emb.)	0.7406	0.6238	0.7687	0.6412	0.6967	0.7132
GRU Glove Emb. updating weights	0.7555	0.6366	0.7776	0.6505	0.6996	0.7231
LSTM (Glove emb.)	0.7521	0.6105	0.7786	0.6346	0.6885	0.7091
BERT-cased	0.8097	0.7316	0.8276	0.7562	0.7730	**0.7737**
BERT-uncased	0.8115	0.7450	0.8349	0.7641	0.7826	**0.7764**
RoBERTa	0.8117	0.7395	0.8320	0.7578	0.7916	**0.7859**

Naderi and Hirst [20] provide the results for generic frame classification both for all classes of generic frames and also the results of multi-class classification for the most occurring 5 frames, which cover more than 60% of the data, namely: Economic, Legality constitutionality and jurisprudence, Policy prescription and evaluation, Crime and punishment, and Politics. We also run our experiments on all these classes. Table 1 compares the results of the multi-class classification on the 5 most common frames using the methods applied by Naderi and Hirst [20] with the fine-tuning of pre-trained transformer-based models BERT and RoBERTa. It is worth noticing that results improve by at least 0.7% when applying frame classification on all topics. The results of the multi-class classification of news articles from the Media Frame Corpus on all frames are reported in Table 2. Table 3 shows the results of the primary frame classification task using the same methods. Results in all experiments shows an improvement using the fine-tuning of pre-trained BERT and RoBERTa.

Table 4 shows the results of span-level frame identification, when the articles of a particular topic is left out from the training data and used only in the test set. Results indicate that span-level identification does not change drastically whilst the primary frame identification seems to be very correlated with the topic being used in the train data, leading to a substantial impairment in the results which are therefore not reported. Due to the highly imbalanced number of frame classes, we report the weighted measures for F-score in all results.

We illustrate the results of topic modeling and issue-specific frame identification using some visualisations techniques to get a better understanding of the obtained results. In Fig. 2, the size of each bubble represents the topic frequency while the colour is given by the party that uses that topic the most. The figure on the left shows how prominent the topic of "Iraq and Afghanistan war" is in

Table 2. Multi-class classification results (in terms of accuracy) of different methods on sentences on all 15 frames, plus the irrelevant class.

Method	Death pen.	Immigr.	Same sex marriage	Tobacco	Gun contr.	All
BiLSTM Glove emb. upd. weights	0.6027	0.4840	0.5856	0.5320	0.5660	0.5761
GRU (Glove emb. upd. weights)	0.6065	0.5034	0.5942	0.5454	0.5858	0.5805
LSTM (Glove emb.) upd. weights	0.6109	0.4879	0.5876	0.5368	0.5685	0.5718
BERT-uncas.-base	0.70	0.6217	0.6869	0.6715	0.6657	**0.6514**
RoBERTa-base	0.7040	0.6234	0.6845	0.6721	0.6732	**0.6672**

Table 3. Multi-class classification results of primary frames of articles.

Method	Death penalty			Immigration			Same sex marriage		
	P	R	F1	P	R	F1	P	R	F1
LSTM	0.7064	0.7042	0.6890	0.6444	0.6469	0.6309	0.7086	0.7129	0.6880
BiLSTM	0.7077	0.7061	0.7068	0.6482	0.6423	0.6349	0.7376	0.7371	0.7363
GRU	0.7208	0.7167	0.7070	0.6981	0.6906	0.6827	0.7742	0.7678	0.7575
BERT-uncased-base	0.7071	0.7081	0.6964	0.8284	0.8262	0.8088	0.7491	0.7167	0.7070
RoBERTa-base	0.7240	0.7343	0.7256	0.8248	0.8404	0.8286	0.7160	0.7167	0.7126
	Tobacco			Gun control			ALL		
	P	R	F1	P	R	F1	P	R	F1
LSTM	0.6715	0.6589	.0.6440	0.9139	0.9118	0.9106	0.5514	0.5604	0.5417
BILSTM	0.6100	0.5845	0.5970	0.9084	0.9057	0.9046	0.5635	0.5761	0.5661
GRU	0.7046	0.7013	0.6950	0.9225	0.8348	0.8627	0.7506	0.7531	0.7495
BERT-base-uncased	0.7389	0.7652	0.7387	0.9413	0.9416	0.9377	0.8540	0.8547	0.8540
RoBERTa-base	0.7409	0.7591	0.7307	0.9238	0.9260	0.9208	0.8086	0.8114	0.8093

2004, while the figure on the right shows that the topic of "schools and education" is twice as much discussed by the Democratic candidate than by his opponent in 1960. This visualisation also reveals the participation of each candidate in each topic (e.g., in the second figure, on the 16%·of the speeches on "school and education", 10.71% were from Kennedy and only 4.11% from Nixon).

Figure 3 shows the distribution of frames on the topic of abortion in 1984. Two of the highest occurrence of frames in the topic of abortion represented by topic words "abortion, women, life, child" are "church, faith, religion, religious, catholic, prayer, separation, practice, state" and "abortion, abortions, life, pro-life, unborn, rape, birth, child, reduce, incest" from argument components.

Figure 4 also illustrates the highest ranking frames on the topic of energy in 1980 to be "oil, drilling, gas, offshore, gasoline, dependence, pipeline, production, natural" ,"environment, clean, environmental, water, air, pollution, toxic, waste, standards" and "energy, solar, independence, wind, coal, policy, alternative, gas, independent". The keywords dependence and independence refer to the energy production in the U.S. being dependant on other countries.

Table 4. Multi-class classification results of sentences of articles taking one set of articles as test set after fine-tuning.

Test set	Precision	Recall	F-score	Size of test set
Death penalty	0.6270	0.6084	0.5958	38590
Immigration	0.5476	0.5413	0.5251	45959
Tobacco	0.6119	0.5901	0.5919	30773
Gun control	0.6207	0.6027	0.6070	45544
Same sex marriage	0.6546	0.6521	0.6486	35774

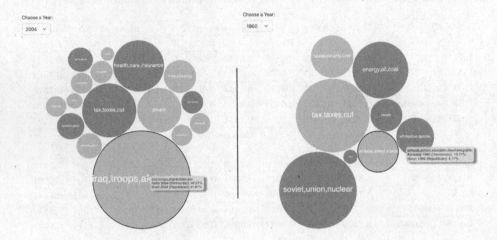

Fig. 2. Visualisation of the distribution of topics in 2004 and 1960.

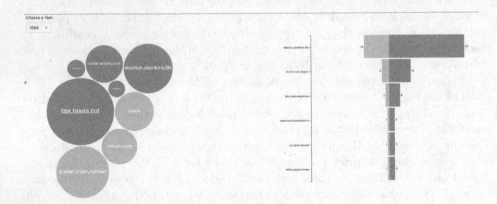

Fig. 3. Distribution of frames over the topic of Abortion in 1984.

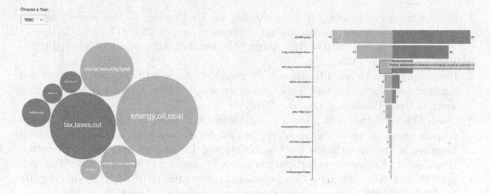

Fig. 4. Distribution of frames over the topic of Energy in 1980.

6 Concluding Remarks

In this paper, we presented a new architecture to automatically identify and classify the topics and frames in political debates, namely the debates of the US presidential campaigns from 1960 to 2016. Our extensive empirical evaluation shows good results, outperforming standard baselines and similar approaches [20]. Finally, we proposed some intuitive visualisations of the extracted topics and frames which allow to get a better understanding about the nuances of the argumentation. Future work perspectives include, in addition to an improvement in the obtained results, a time-guided analysis of the evolution of the topics and frames in the U.S. presidential debates, with the goal to highlight how the way politicians discuss these topics has changed over time.

Acknowledgments. This work was partly supported by the French government, through the 3IA Côte d'Azur Investments in the Future project managed by the National Research Agency (ANR) with the reference number ANR-19-P3IA-0002. This work was partly supported also by EU Horizon 2020 project AI4Media, under contract no. 951911 (https://ai4media.eu/), and MIREL (http://www.mirelproject.eu/), under contract no. 690974. Shohreh Haddadan hereby acknowledges that this research is supported by the Luxembourg National Research Fund (FNR) (10929115).

References

1. Ajjour, Y., Alshomary, M., Wachsmuth, H., Stein, B.: Modeling frames in argumentation. In: Proceedings of the 2019 Conference on Empirical Methods in Natural Language Processing and the 9th International Joint Conference on Natural Language Processing (EMNLP-IJCNLP), pp. 2922–2932. Association for Computational Linguistics (2019). https://doi.org/10.18653/v1/D19-1290, https://www.aclweb.org/anthology/D19-1290
2. Artstein, R., Poesio, M.: Inter-coder agreement for computational linguistics. Comput. Linguist. **34**(4), 555–596 (2008). https://doi.org/10.1162/coli.07-034-R2, https://direct.mit.edu/coli/article/34/4/555-596/1999

3. Boydstun, A.E., Glazier, R.A., Pietryka, M.T.: Playing to the crowd: agenda control in presidential debates. Polit. Commun. **30**(2), 254–277 (2013). https://doi.org/10.1162/coli.07-034-R2, https://www.tandfonline.com/doi/abs/10.1080/10584609.2012.737423

4. Boydstun, A.E., Gross, J.H., Resnik, P., Smith, N.A.: Identifying media frames and frame dynamics within and across policy issues. In: New Directions in Analyzing Text as Data Workshop, London (2013)

5. Card, D., Boydstun, A.E., Gross, J.H., Resnik, P., Smith, N.A.: The media frames corpus: annotations of frames across issues. In: Proceedings of the 53rd Annual Meeting of the Association for Computational Linguistics and the 7th International Joint Conference on Natural Language Processing (Volume 2: Short Papers), pp. 438–444. Association for Computational Linguistics (2015). https://doi.org/10.3115/v1/P15-2072, https://www.aclweb.org/anthology/P15-2072

6. Chakrabarty, T., Hidey, C., Muresan, S.: ENTRUST: argument reframing with language models and entailment. In: Proceedings of the 2021 Conference of the North American Chapter of the Association for Computational Linguistics: Human Language Technologies, pp. 4958–4971. Association for Computational Linguistics (2021). https://doi.org/10.18653/v1/2021.naacl-main.394, https://aclanthology.org/2021.naacl-main.394

7. Chen, W.F., Al Khatib, K., Stein, B., Wachsmuth, H.: Controlled neural sentence-level reframing of news articles. In: Findings of the Association for Computational Linguistics: EMNLP 2021, pp. 2683–2693. Association for Computational Linguistics (2021). https://aclanthology.org/2021.findings-emnlp.228

8. Devlin, J., Chang, M., Lee, K., Toutanova, K.: BERT: pre-training of deep bidirectional transformers for language understanding. In: Proceedings of NAACL-HLT 2019, pp. 4171–4186 (2019). https://doi.org/10.18653/v1/n19-1423

9. Dumani, L., Wiesenfeldt, T., Schenkel, R.: Fine and coarse granular argument classification before clustering. In: Proceedings of the 30th ACM International Conference on Information & Knowledge Management, CIKM 2021, pp. 422–432. Association for Computing Machinery (2021). https://doi.org/10.1145/3459637.3482431

10. Entman, R.M.: Framing: toward clarification of a fractured paradigm. J. Commun. **43**(4), 51–58 (1993). https://doi.org/10.1111/j.1460-2466.1993.tb01304.x, https://academic.oup.com/joc/article/43/4/51-58/4160153

11. George Lakoff: The ALL NEW Don't Think of an Elephant!: Know Your Values and Frame the Debate. Chelsea Green Publishing (2014). google-Books-ID: FSqP-BAAAQBAJ

12. Goffredo, P., Haddadan, S., Vorakitphan, V., Cabrio, E., Villata, S.: Fallacious argument classification in political debates. In: Raedt, L.D. (ed.) Proceedings of the Thirty-First International Joint Conference on Artificial Intelligence, IJCAI 2022, Vienna, Austria, 23–29 July 2022, pp. 4143–4149. ijcai.org (2022). https://doi.org/10.24963/ijcai.2022/575

13. Grootendorst, M., Reimers, N.: MaartenGr/BERTopic: v0.9.3 - quickfix. Zenodo (2021). https://doi.org/10.5281/zenodo.5574296

14. Haddadan, S., Cabrio, E., Villata, S.: Yes, we can! mining arguments in 50 years of US presidential campaign debates. In: Proceedings of the 57th Annual Meeting of the Association for Computational Linguistics, pp. 4684–4690. Association for Computational Linguistics (2019). https://doi.org/10.18653/v1/P19-1463, https://www.aclweb.org/anthology/P19-1463

15. Hartmann, M., Jansen, T., Augenstein, I., Søgaard, A.: Issue framing in online discussion fora. In: Proceedings of the 2019 Conference of the North American Chapter

of the Association for Computational Linguistics: Human Language Technologies, Volume 1 (Long and Short Papers), pp. 1401–1407. Association for Computational Linguistics (2019). https://doi.org/10.18653/v1/N19-1142, https://aclanthology.org/N19-1142

16. Liu, Y., et al.: Roberta: a robustly optimized bert pretraining approach. CoRR abs/1907.11692 (2019). https://arxiv.org/abs/1907.11692

17. Loper, E., Bird, S.: NLTK: the natural language toolkit (2002). arXiv:cs/0205028, https://arxiv.org/abs/cs/0205028

18. McInnes, L., Healy, J., Astels, S.: HDBSCAN: hierarchical density based clustering. J. Open Source Softw. **2**(11), 205 (2017). https://doi.org/10.21105/joss.00205, https://joss.theoj.org/papers/10.21105/joss.00205

19. McInnes, L., Healy, J., Melville, J.: UMAP: uniform manifold approximation and projection for dimension reduction (2020). arXiv:1802.03426 [cs, stat], https://arxiv.org/abs/1802.03426

20. Naderi, N., Hirst, G.: Classifying frames at the sentence level in news articles. In: Proceedings of the International Conference Recent Advances in Natural Language Processing, RANLP 2017, pp. 536–542. INCOMA Ltd. (2017-09). https://doi.org/10.26615/978-954-452-049-6_070

21. Nguyen, V.A., Boyd-Graber, J., Resnik, P., Miler, K.: Tea party in the house: a hierarchical ideal point topic model and its application to republican legislators in the 112th congress. In: Proceedings of the 53rd Annual Meeting of the Association for Computational Linguistics and the 7th International Joint Conference on Natural Language Processing (Volume 1: Long Papers), pp. 1438–1448. Association for Computational Linguistics (2015). https://doi.org/10.3115/v1/P15-1139, https://aclweb.org/anthology/P15-1139

22. Reimers, N., Gurevych, I.: Sentence-BERT: sentence embeddings using Siamese BERT-networks. In: Proceedings of the 2019 Conference on Empirical Methods in Natural Language Processing and the 9th International Joint Conference on Natural Language Processing (EMNLP-IJCNLP), pp. 3982–3992. Association for Computational Linguistics (2019). https://doi.org/10.18653/v1/D19-1410, https://www.aclweb.org/anthology/D19-1410

23. Schroff, F., Kalenichenko, D., Philbin, J.: FaceNet: a unified embedding for face recognition and clustering. In: 2015 IEEE Conference on Computer Vision and Pattern Recognition (CVPR), pp. 815–823. IEEE (2015). https://doi.org/10.1109/CVPR.2015.7298682, https://ieeexplore.ieee.org/document/7298682/

24. Swanson, R., Ecker, B., Walker, M.: Argument mining: extracting arguments from online dialogue. In: Proceedings of the 16th Annual Meeting of the Special Interest Group on Discourse and Dialogue, pp. 217–226. Association for Computational Linguistics (2015). https://doi.org/10.18653/v1/W15-4631, https://aclanthology.org/W15-4631

25. Tsur, O., Calacci, D., Lazer, D.: A frame of mind: using statistical models for detection of framing and agenda setting campaigns. In: Proceedings of the 53rd Annual Meeting of the Association for Computational Linguistics and the 7th International Joint Conference on Natural Language Processing (Volume 1: Long Papers), pp. 1629–1638. Association for Computational Linguistics (2015). https://doi.org/10.3115/v1/P15-1157, https://aclweb.org/anthology/P15-1157

26. Xia, L., Luo, D., Zhang, C., Wu, Z.: A survey of topic models in text classification. In: 2019 2nd International Conference on Artificial Intelligence and Big Data (ICAIBD), pp. 244–250 (2019). https://doi.org/10.1109/ICAIBD.2019.8836970

Substitute Plastic Film with Kraft Paper in Automatic Pallet Wrapping: An AI Pipeline

Eleonora Iotti[1]([✉])(iD), Alessandro Dal Palù[1](iD), Gianluca Contesso[2],
and Francesco Bertinelli[2]

[1] Department of Mathematical, Physical and Computer Sciences,
University of Parma, Parco Area delle Scienze 53/A, 43124 Parma, Italy
{eleonora.iotti,alessandro.dalpalu}@unipr.it
[2] ACMI S.p.A., Via G. Di Vittorio, 60, 43045 Fornovo di Taro, Parma, Italy
{gianluca.contesso,francesco.bertinelli}@acmispa.com

Abstract. This paper presents and discuss an overview of an AI pipeline to analyze the effects of substituting plastic film with Kraft paper in the tertiary packaging, i.e., in the external envelope of a pallet. Since there is no prior knowledge about *paper* wrapping yet, the goal is to understand the physics of the load unit—wrapped in paper—when subject to horizontal accelerations. This permits to study and analyze its rigidity and robustness to permanent deformations and/or excessive shifting during road or rail freight, to avoid damages and ripping of the envelope. The idea behind our AI pipeline is to virtually *simulate* such a situation, to precisely identify critical use cases, and eventually suggest a correction in the wrapping format. The first gain in using such an approach is to drastically reduce the number of physical tests needed to build a solid base knowledge about the behavior of Kraft paper enveloping the pallet during motion. The proposed pipeline consists of three phases: *(i)* data collection from real tests, *(ii)* modeling of the simulation, fitting relevant parameters between the actual test and the simulated one, and *(iii)* performing of virtual experiments on different settings, to suggest the best format. Computer vision and machine learning techniques are employed to accomplish these tasks, and preliminary results show encouraging performances of the proposed idea.

Keywords: Multi-physics simulation · Machine learning · Multiple objects tracking · Automatic pallet wrapping

1 Motivations

For some years now, we have witnessed the rise of a global movement pointing towards a more sustainable future. Such campaign caused a renewed interest

Project entitled "*Machine learning to substitute LLDPE plastic film with Kraft paper in automatic pallet wrapping,*" supported by ACMI S.p.A. and funded with D.M. 10.08.2021 n.1062 on FSE REACT-EU, by Ministero dell'Università e della Ricerca (MUR), under the Programma Operativo Nazionale (PON) "Ricerca e Innovazione" 2014–2020–Azione Green.

from companies and institutions, that resulted in the search for novel technologies to reduce pollution and plastic usage, and in the advance of strategic actions to change their course. Regarding the public institutions, this translates into long-term objectives and into the development of resolutions and plans like, for example, the European Strategy for Plastics in a Circular Economy [9]. In particular, such a strategy was put in place in January 2018, and still applies in the broader context of the European Green Deal [10] which consists of a set of proposals, actions, and funding during the five-year term 2019–2024.

The EU strategy for plastics imposed a crucial challenge to companies and industries working in the field of packaging, especially for food and beverages. As a matter of fact, the majority of primary and secondary packaging (respectively the single product actual container and their grouping into a larger set for handling purposes) for food and beverages consists of multi-layered plastic, which is not recyclable, but still plays an important role in food safety compared to other available materials. A recent survey on the effects of the EU plastic resolution pointed out these issues, and definitely stated that there are currently "no viable alternatives" that could ensure the same level of safety and avoidance of food waste [31], and at the same time those conditions, lack of safety and risk to waste food, are sufficient to produce bad environmental impacts. However, there are also evidences of virtuous examples of plastic elimination or at least reduction and recycling in the primary packaging of food [19].

Despite these discussions, attempts, and efforts on primary and secondary packaging, nowadays the LLDPE (Linear Low Density Polyethylene) stretch film and the heat-shrink wrap are still the best available choices for tertiary packaging of food and beverages (the enclosure or wrapping of stacked secondary packaging onto a pallet for safe transportation and logistics). During years, the amount of plastic material and its thickness were constantly decreased, and the use of recyclable plastic for wrapping made possible in some cases to comply with EU requirements. Managing plastic materials and adapting them to shrink around the loaded pallet is a well-known automation task that is currently efficiently performed by end-of-line packaging machines. Nevertheless, due to this know-how and due to some of LLDPE main properties, like resistance to water and UV rays, to the best of our knowledge, there were no attempts worldwide to automatic pallet wrapping with sustainable materials.

ACMI S.p.A.[1] is an Italian manufacturer of high-tech bottling and packaging lines, specialized for beverages and food. ACMI has international relevance, serving both national companies and large multinational groups, such as Coca-Cola Company[TM]. The recent work of ACMI is significant in the open discussion about plastic, since their novel "green" approach to the end-of-line proposed to replace the external wrapping material from LLDPE to Kraft paper (a recyclable and biodegradable paper with specific elastic strength). This represents the first attempt in substituting plastic tertiary packaging for food and beverages industry. A completely plastic-free end-of-line opens up to a series of engineering and automation challenges which have yet to be explored.

---

[1] https://www.acmispa.it/en/.

One of these challenges is to ensure that the wrapped envelope could withstand to road or rail freight, thus guaranteeing safety for truck workers and avoiding loss of product. This aspect is of key importance in the plastic-paper transition of tertiary packaging and it requires a thorough understanding of the paper behavior in relation to safety aspects, such as, e.g., how many layers of paper are needed for wrapping and how they should be stratified, how much pulling tension has to be applied to paper while wrapping, what is the optimal pallet loading packaging schema for better stability, and so on. Such knowledge should, in turn, give back to engineers some hints for the actual development of the automatic wrapping machine and its controlling software.

1.1   A Note on Methodology and Purposes of This Work

The growth and increasing impact of Artificial Intelligence (AI) technologies [24], in almost every aspect of human development opens up also to the challenges posed by the field of automation [37, 42]. The research question posed by ACMI's innovative idea (to wrap pallets of food or beverages products within Kraft paper instead of plastic) requires rethinking the design of so-called wrapping formats, i.e., those series of parameters and indications given to the pallet stretch wrapper to perform the actual wrapping of products. Therefore, the long-term goal of the research project is to develop an intelligent automatic recommendations system that is able to suggest the safer, robust, and most reliable wrapping format to the paper wrapping machine. To pursue such an objective, preliminary studies have to be done with the help of other machinery. In our case, we make use of an in-house special testing bench, which is able to reproduce the actual horizontal acceleration of the transport with the load unit carried on, to control the dynamics parameters and to record a video of the test. This paper focuses on the short-term goal of using such raw data to incrementally build enough knowledge to virtually simulate the behavior of any physical setup, while minimizing the number of actual experiments needed to gain useful information.

In summary, the proposed AI pipeline consists of a low-level computer vision system to extract raw data, a realistic multi-body simulation enhanced with a machine learning method to fit the concrete behavior of the pallet during the test, and the use of such a simulation to perform virtual tests and give feedback on a possible improvement of the wrapping format. The approach allows to estimate and simulate any wrapping, from plastic to paper and even to simulate an arbitrary number of wrapping overlapping. Input of the first phase are raw video recordings of load units subject to horizontal accelerations. Those videos are analyzed with standard computer vision techniques. The goal of such techniques is to extract the centers of gravity of the wooden pallet and of the bundles (secondary packages) over the pallet. Moreover, we also extract rotations of each package, in order to detect instability and deformations. The second phase is about the development of a simulation of the test case, by using a multi-physics engine that models the testing machine, its acceleration, and the load unit. At the beginning of this phase, the simulation cannot be realistic, due to the lack of physical parameters related to secondary/tertiary packaging (i.e., static and dynamic friction forces at work). We aim at *learning* those parameters, and, in turn, the global behavior of the pallet during acceleration, by matching the ideal conditions of the simulation to the actual measurements of the centers of gravity obtained from the vision system. Such a task employs machine learning algorithms to match the actual behavior. Once the physical parameters are accurate enough, the third phase proceeds to identifying critical issues of a specific wrapping, e.g. points with a high risk of ripping of the paper, and suggest corrections. This paper overviews the whole pipeline, covering in particular the implementation details of the first and second phases of the project.

2 Background

Pallets wrapped with paper, as those with plastic envelope, must comply with the European Road Worthiness Directive in order to guarantee the security during rail or road freight. In such a field, safety and reliability are expressed in terms of the European Standard EUMOS 40509 [3], that aims at quantifying the rigidity of the pallet when it is subject to a force (due to an acceleration) along a direction. The situation that aims to be simulated and investigated by such a standard is the motion dynamic of a truck loaded with one or more EUR pallets. The rigidity of the load, in fact, impacts the transport effectiveness, and measuring such quantity is needed to prevent permanent deformations or excessive shifting of the load during transportation, in other words, the stability of the load unit [41]. Moreover, such rigidity and robustness directly impact on the holding strength of the external wrapping, which in turn could be deformed or ripped during motion. Excessive deformations and/or shifting of the loaded units result in a lack of stability of the overall truck and in an unsafe transportation.

In detail, the Acceleration Bench Test, in line with EUMOS 40509, defines a test load unit which is typically a pallet with a number of layers of products on it and wrapped with plastic film (or Kraft paper, in our case), and that can be oriented in the LP-direction, i.e., the long side of the pallet is parallel to acceleration direction, or in the BP-direction, i.e., the short side of the pallet is parallel to acceleration direction. Such a test unit with its orientation is then subject, using a special testing machinery detailed later, to an acceleration impulse that immediately stops and gives rise to a constant deceleration, until the load unit stops. In a real setting, the acceleration impulse is modeled as a constant acceleration that lasts for half a second. Typical tests are performed with constant accelerations from 0.2 g up to 0.5 g, which is the acceleration to be supported, as stated by EUMOS 40509. The acceleration may cause permanent deformations and elastic deformations, which are respectively the residual deformations of the load unit after the test and the deformation of the load unit during the test. In the latter case, the tilting of the entire load unit during test is not considered as an elastic deformation, since the wooden pallet is taken as reference for the coordinate system to measure such deformations.

Acceleration Bench Test of EUMOS 40509 defines the test setup and some test acceptance criteria, as follows: (i) the permanent displacement of all parts of

Fig. 1. The ESTL Machine in the R&D Department of ACMI S.p.A. The acceleration bench holds on a sleight where a wooden pallet is loaded with two layers.

Fig. 2. Centers of gravity of pallet and packages, returned by MOSSE tracker

the test load unit (after the test) must not exceed 5% of the total height of load unit; (ii) permanent displacement in the lowest 20 cm of the test load unit is to be less than 4 cm on the wooden pallet; (iii) the elastic displacement of all parts of the test load unit (during the test) must not exceed 10% of the total height of load unit; (iv) there must be no visible structural damage and/or leakage of products at the end of the test. The development new wrapping technologies must cope with the compliance of such criteria.

2.1   The ESTL Machine

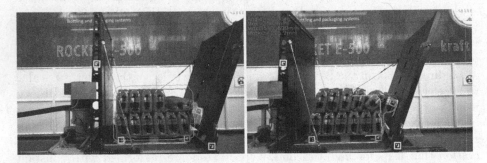

Fig. 3. Example of static (on the left) and dynamic (on the right) deformations, recorded by ESTL vision system after the test and during the test.

Tests are performed with a special testing machine, called here *ESTL Machine* from the name of the manufacturer company [2].

The pallets are loaded on a movable platform, called sleight, on an acceleration bench. An example is illustrated in Fig. 1. Once the pallet is loaded, the acceleration bench can generate a constant horizontal acceleration impulse, which moves the sleight with the load unit on. The acceleration can be set between $0\,m/s^2$ and $10\,m/s^2$ in steps of $0.5\,m/s^2$. The duration of the acceleration is at least $500\,ms$. These parameters permit to simulate road transport events such as diverting maneuvers and/or emergency stops. Usually the pallets are tested at different acceleration levels: tests start at a low acceleration level of $0.2\,g$ or $0.3\,g$ (about $1.962\,m/s^s$ and $2.943\,m/s^2$, respectively). Then, if the result is successful (w.r.t. EUMOS 40509), the constant acceleration impulse is increased by a value of $0.1\,g$, heading for the legal requirement of $0.5\,g$ for load safety.

While testing the acceleration impulse, high speed recordings are made. Three markers are attached to the load unit and two markers on the sleight, as in Fig. 1, so that the ESTL Machine vision system can detect fluctuations of the pallet. In fact, to detect the plastic (or static) deformation of the load unit after the test, measurements are taken at three different points. Those measurements are made before and after the test. The difference between them gives an indication of the plastic deformation. The elastic (or dynamic) deformation, instead, is measured at a height of approximately $1\,m$, with an ultrasonic sensor. Then, video recordings are annotated by ESTL vision system with the detected boundaries of the load over the wooden pallet, the value (in mm) of the current and maximum deformation and its angle. Figure 3 shows an example of the annotations of the ESTL system on the video recording, denoting the static and dynamic deformations happened during and after the test.

The actual acceleration and displacement of the sleight is known, since the ESTL machine employs also an X-Y accelerometer, and the acceleration profile data are recorded and plotted as well, as shown in Fig. 4. The plot shows the detected acceleration and deceleration along the x and y axes in a $0.3\,g$ test, respectively in orange and black colors (it is worth noting that acceleration in the y direction is almost zero for the whole duration of the tests). Theoretical values of speeds (magenta) and displacements (blue) are also plotted.

3   Multiple Tracking of Bundles

The first goal of this work is to extract relevant information regarding the behavior of the pallet and bundles during motion. This phase is necessary to understand the dynamic of the sleight-pallet-load system of the ESTL machine in terms of visible displacements of each part of such a system. We want to identify the actual displacement of the load unit, i.e. the wooden pallet and the layers of product, w.r.t. the sleight, and the relative displacements between each couple of elements of the load unit. Each unit of product is called a bundle, and the traceable bundles are only those in front of the camera. In general, the displacement of the pallet and the traceable bundles could vary according to the type of pallet, its orientation, the type of product, and also the primary and secondary packaging make their contribution on the dynamic of the system. Moreover, the possible presence of paper/plastic interlayer between the layers of bundles also impacts the amount of displacement. It can be noticed that the motion of the

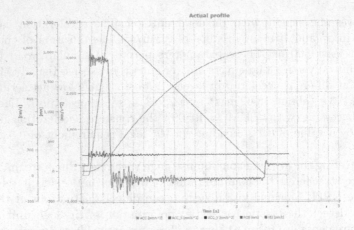

Fig. 4. Examples of acceleration profiles measured by ESTL machine, with a 0.3 g acceleration impulse setting. (Color figure online)

entire load unit is delayed w.r.t. the motion of the sleight, because of friction between the two objects. With the sleight displacement that serves as reference, we can compute the difference between such a displacement and the one of the load unit. The same reasoning could be made to obtain the relative differences of pallet and bundles displacements, and of each layer of bundles. Such differences are strongly related to friction coefficients (static and dynamic) of the pallet over the sleight, of each bundle over the pallet, and of bundles with each other. To the best of our knowledge, we are not aware of similar approaches in the context of estimating friction constants and parameters for simulation of pallet dynamics.

In literature there are plenty of AI approaches to process video raw data, in order to detect objects and their positions. Such approaches could be roughly divided into standard computer vision ones and deep learning approaches. Deep neural networks and learning algorithm outperform standard techniques in almost any mainstream recognition/segmentation/detection task, like recognition of common objects [20,21,27,34,35], segmentation of a typical external scene [36], tracking of pedestrians from surveillance camera [17], human pose estimation [38], recognition of handwritten text [28]. Unfortunately, except for some notable examples [33], yet not mature enough for video processing, deep learning methods usually require a huge amount of homogeneous data, that have to be carefully annotated in case of supervised learning. This is one of the reasons why, by deviating from mainstream applications, deep neural networks are difficult to train and not always successful at generalizing information.

Moreover, recent criticism pointed out that such networks are often treated as black boxes full of parameters which do not have a intelligible semantics, thus a deep network could not explain its decisions [30]. There are cutting-edge works that try to achieve a natural language explanation from such systems, but those results are still subject of discussion in the field of eXplainable Artificial Intelligence (XAI) [14]. Explainability is of course an appreciable feature of an

AI system, but in particular it is crucial for those high risk safety systems. The topic of XAI in critical systems is being addressed by the European Commission, which developed an AI strategy to rule the trustworthiness of AI systems and enhance the excellence in such field [11, 12].

In our case, the first phase of the AI pipeline does not require to produce transparent processes or explain its outputs, but those features will be useful in the last phase of the project, where suggestions and recommendations to correct the wrapping format have to be delivered to the final user. Despite this, following a deep learning plan for the development of the computer vision system remains unfeasible due to the requirement of a vast amount of data. Our raw data, in fact, are produced by physical experiment with the acceleration testing machine, and each experiment has a high cost in terms of time and power consumption. Moreover, even if we would like to use pre-trained networks, mainstream datasets on which those networks are trained are too general, and making efforts to switch from their to our domain could result in a global lowering of the network performances (multi-domain methods are still subject of investigations).

Therefore, our system was crafted for the specific task, with the aid of standard computer vision algorithms and techniques. Our computer vision system consists of a program which processes the video frame by frame. We employ (i) automatic methods to identify a region of interest (ROI), based on the prediction of the position of the load unit given by the acceleration profile data of the test; (ii) a template matching technique on the ROI to detect bundles; (iii) a set of multi-tracking algorithms tailored on the specific task, with the goal to follow the bundles during motion; (iv) optical flow detection methods to measure the actual displacements and rotations of packages.

In order to help the detection of bundles in raw videos we input the system some general template images to be matched to the pallet and to the visible bundles. These templates are subject to standard augmentation by stretching, rotating, cutting the reference image. Given the dimensions of the pallet template and of a bundle template, together with the number of layers loaded on the pallet, the ROI is obtained. In fact, in the few first frames of the video, the load unit is approximately in the center of the visual. Displacement data from ESTL machine, that were obtained from the acceleration profile depicted in Fig. 4, are used to slightly move the ROI frame by frame. This process is correct only at the very beginning of video processing, since the perspective is not much noticeable. The ROI is maintained until the template matching algorithm (a normalized cross-correlation between templates and pixels of the ROI) recognizes all bundles, and the tracking is ready to start. To prevent the explosion of computational times, a Non-Maximum Suppression (NMS) algorithm [32] follows the template matching.

We used several state-of-the-art methods for multi-object tracking: from basic Discriminative Correlation Filter with Channel and Spatial Reliability (CSRT) [29] and Kernelized Correlation Filter (KCF) [23], to the AdaBoost-based Boosting tracker [22], and Multiple Instance Learning (MIL) algorithm [15], but also TLD (Tracking-learning-detection) [26], Median-Flow [25], and Minimum Output Sum of Squared Error (MOSSE) [16] trackers have been tested. When tracking starts, the ROI detaches from the acceleration profile models (which in the meantime became more and more incorrect), and takes the center of the tracked bundles as a reference. We consider 1 frame every 3, to reduce the computation burden. If the tracking loses a bundle for some frames, the template matching phase is repeated (inside the new ROI).

Finally, a dense optical flow is computed using an algorithm based on [18], for all points in the frame. Then the vector field of the optical flow is converted in polar coordinates to trace rays and rotations of groups of pixels, for each bundle and the wooden pallet. Optical flow thus retrieves information about bundles displacements and their bounces/tilting/turning. For each bundle and the wooden pallet, an approximation of the center of gravity is computed, by taking a weighted mean of all displacements centered in the center of the bounding box of the tracked object. Figure 2 shows an example of results, where colored dots are the computed centers of gravity of bundles and the wooden pallet.

4   Developing the Simulation

The second phase of the AI pipeline consists of the development of a simulation of acceleration tests and tuning of such a simulation on 'real' data from video recordings. Those simulations are called multi-(rigid)-body dynamics simulations, and there are many commercial and free software capable of more or less accurate reproduction of rigid bodies motion, such as AutoDesk AutoCAD [1], MathWorks Simscape Multibody [8], NVIDIA PhysX [6], and so on. Each of them differs from the others by the way it manages frictions, velocity, particles motion, using specific formulations. For our purposes we need an engine that allows the user to model wrapping envelopes, and that it is flexible enough to shape the parameters of such an envelope. Kraft paper, and in general, paper dynamics are still an open challenge for those types of engines. On the other hand, our preliminary work, aims at reproducing the dynamics of un-wrapped load units (wooden pallet and bundles) first. A closed envelope is a complex system, thus the understanding of the global system dynamics is subject to what is happening to single packages under the cover.

The choice fell on an open-source multi-physics simulation engine called Project Chrono [13,40], developed by University of Wisconsin (Madison) and University of Parma, allows the positioning of some rigid bodies on a scene, along with various types of links between them. Each body can be a simple shape (e.g. a box, a sphere) and/or a user defined 3D model. Each body has a center of gravity, a mass, a moment of inertia and a collision model. Masses of pallets and bundles are easily obtainable from real measurements. Initial centers of gravity of objects depend on their shape and their initial position in the simulation. We choose to approximate bundles with boxes, so the center of gravity could be easily calculated. Then, a linear motor engine is initialized to model the sleight. Chrono has a facility to create functions for vertical and/or horizontal motion, and in our case a constant x acceleration could be modeled by imposing the ramp length and height (of the speed function), the ending time of the acceleration and the starting time of the deceleration. All such parameters could be easily obtained from the acceleration profile provided by the ESTL machine.

In Chrono engine, each body has its own material properties. The ESTL machine, the wooden pallet, and each of the bundles are composed of different materials. For each object/material a value of static friction and a value of kinetic friction must be set. Since these values are unknown, we employ a machine learning method to approximate them. Input data are the extracted positions (centers of gravity) $p_i(t) = (x_{p_i}^{(t)}, y_{p_i}^{(t)})$ of each relevant object i visible in the video recordings of ESTL machine at time t. The predicted outputs are the computed positions $c_j(t) = (x_{c_j}^{(t)}, y_{c_j}^{(t)}, z_{c_j}^{(t)})$ of all the objects in the simulation at time t. Let us note that a computed position also depends on static and kinetic friction coefficient of its material, $c_j(t) = c_j(t, \mu_s, \mu_k)$. Of the latter, only the visible ones should be compared to extracted data, i.e. the line of bundles in front of the camera. Being a constant position on the z axis, we consider only $c_i(t) = (x_{c_i}^{(t)}, y_{c_i}^{(t)})$. The objective is to minimize the distance between real position and simulated positions, for each time instant t, with a L_2 loss:

$$L_2(p_i, c_i) = \sum_{t=0}^{T} \|p_i(t) - c_i(t, \mu_s, \mu_k)\|^2 \tag{1}$$

where T is the final time instant, i.e. the last frame of the video. The idea is to apply the gradient descent algorithm with (1) cost function to find μ_s and μ_k. However, input data frames are few (~ 50 positions for each bundle) and also very noisy due to previous calculations (matching, tracking, optical flow detection). A statistical method to denoise data is Exponential Moving Average (EMA), that defines a novel sequence from raw data depending on the value of a parameter $\beta \in (0, 1)$. Larger (close to 1) values of β produce smoother sequences. The machine learning method is a variation of the gradient descent algorithm, which uses EMA on gradient sequence.

$$\begin{cases} v_0 = \nabla_0 L_2(p_i, c_i) \\ v_k = \beta v_{k-1} + (1 - \beta)\nabla_k L_2(p_i, c_i) \end{cases} \tag{2}$$

where $\nabla_k L_2(p_i, c_i)$ is the loss gradient at step k of gradient descent. Each step moves the values of μ_s and μ_k toward the minimum of the loss function, as follows.

$$\begin{cases} \mu_*^{(0)} \text{ is randomly initialized} \\ \mu_*^{(k)} = \mu_*^{(k-1)} - \eta v_k \end{cases} \tag{3}$$

where η is the learning rate of gradient descent method. In deep learning field, such a method is known as gradient descent with momentum [39].

5   Experiments

The computer vision system and the virtual simulation are developed in Python 3.8.12. We used the Python versions of OpenCV [5] open-source library and of the Project Chrono, PyChrono [7]. IRRLicht [4] engine renders the simulation. Both programs run on an Anaconda environment on a laptop with a 6-cores 10th gen. i7 CPU, base speed 1.61 GHz up to 3.60 GHz, and 16 GB of RAM.

We choose bundles of six Coca-Cola Zero^{TM} and maintained the same product for all the experiments. Different products would have different shapes and dynamics, thus making it impossible to compare experiments among each other. In the future, nevertheless, we plan to extend our test to different types of products. We performed 3 single-layer tests, with accelerations 0.2 g, 0.3 g, and 0.4 g. The orientation of the load unit was LP, and the layout of products over the pallet is the first layer of a columnar one. At a later time, double-layers experiments were made. First three tests use a columnar layout. In detail, the first test has no interlayer between layers, the second includes a paper one, and the third a plastic one. Then, we tested two types of symmetric cross layouts, the first one including a deliberate fracture line that impacts negatively on load stability. Plastic and paper interlayers were also considered in combination with cross layouts, resulting in six more experiments. All double-layers experiments were performed with acceleration 0.3 g. Recordings of experiments last 8–10 s, at a rate of 20 frames per second, with 1920×1200 frames size.

Table 1. CPU execution times of tracking algorithms on the whole video, for tests in absence of interlayers, columnar layouts and 0.3 g constant acceleration.

Tracker name	CPU execution time [seconds]	
	Single-layer	Double-layer
Boosting	91.671	122.828
CSRT	112.531	176.094
KCF	62.734	63.641
MedianFlow	81.750	118.187
MIL	184.953	295.0312
MOSSE	**46.719**	**56.484**
TLD	263.781	453.312

Table 1 shows CPU execution times of the computer vision system with the different tracking algorithms, and Fig. 5 shows visual results of some of these elaborations (the faster ones). Using Boosting tracker, the retrieved centers of gravity were then passed to the machine learning algorithm to tune the simulation. Figure 6 shows two different time instants of a simulation that reproduces the behavior of a single-layer unit and LP orientation. From initial $\mu_s = 0.5$ and $\mu_k = 0.5$ for bundles, and $\mu_s = 0.5$ and $\mu_k = 0.06$ for the pallet, final values decrease to $\mu_s = 0.1$, $\mu_k = 0.001$ for bundles and $\mu_s = 0.15$, $\mu_k = 0.04$ for pallet. Figure 6 shows how the lack of z axis in parameters fitting results in a uncontrolled expansion of the columnar layer also in the z direction.

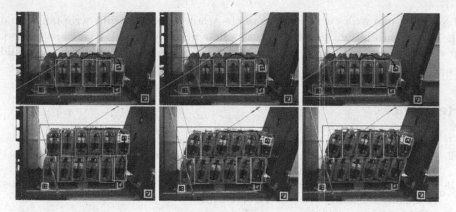

Fig. 5. Example results of elaborations on video recordings, where the first column refers to Boosting, the second to KFC, and the third to MOSSE trackers.

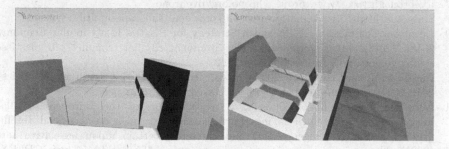

Fig. 6. Example frames of a simulation with only one layer of products, at 0.4 g acceleration. On the left, the rotation of the rightmost bundles, and on the right the expansion of the columnar layout in z direction.

6   Conclusions and Future Works

This paper proposes an AI pipeline to tackle the challenge of substituting LLDPE stretch film with Kraft paper in automatic pallet wrapping. The design of the pipeline strongly relies on the EUMOS 40509 requirements of safety for rail and road transport of packages. The key idea is to simulate acceleration tests bench according to such a regulation, to produce an automatic recommendation system for the development of wrapping formats. The first important step of the pipeline is to fit the simulation on real tests. A computer vision approach, with mixed methods, serves as an input to retain measurements of products displacements during acceleration tests with ESTL machine. Attempts with single- and double-layers settings showed good results. Handling of noisy data was addressed by using a momentum version of gradient descent, which aims at tuning the parameters of the virtual simulation. Results are promising, even if further investigations are needed, and future work will be devoted to the identification of critical points of tension which could impact the paper wrapping, the developing of a realistic simulation of the whole envelope (with wrapping), and the use of such insight to tell final users how many wrapping layers are needed, at which heights, with what tension, and so on. Moreover, XAI techniques would be of primarily relevance in this last phase of the pipeline.

References

1. Autocad: https://www.autodesk.it/solutions/simulation/overview
2. Engineering & solutions for transport & logistic nv (estl nv, https://www.estl.be). Wafelstraat 46, 8540 Deerlijk, Belgium
3. EUMOS, the European safe logistics association. quality standards. https://eumos.eu/quality-standards/. Accessed 5 Aug 2022
4. Irrlicht: https://irrlicht.sourceforge.io/
5. Opencv: https://opencv.org/
6. Physx: https://github.com/NVIDIAGameWorks/PhysX
7. Pychrono: https://www.projectchrono.org/pychrono/
8. Simscape: https://www.mathworks.com/products/simscape-multibody.html
9. European Commission: A European Strategy for Plastics in a Circular Economy 2018a (2018). https://ec.europa.eu/environment/circular-economy/pdf/plastics-strategy-annex.pdf. Accessed 5 Aug 2022
10. European Green Deal (2019–2024). https://ec.europa.eu/info/strategy/priorities-2019-2024/european-green-deal_en. Accessed 5 Aug 2022
11. European Commission. Proposal for a regulation of the European Parliament and of the council laying down harmonised rules on Artificial Intelligence (Artificial Intelligence act) and amending certain union legislative acts (2021). https://eur-lex.europa.eu/legal-content/EN/TXT/HTML/?uri=CELEX:52021PC0206&from=EN. Accessed 5 Aug 2022
12. European Commission. A European approach to artificial intelligence (2022). https://digital-strategy.ec.europa.eu/en/policies/european-approach-artificial-intelligence. Accessed 5 Aug 2022
13. Anitescu, M., Tasora, A.: An iterative approach for cone complementarity problems for nonsmooth dynamics. Comput. Optim. Appl. **47**(2), 207–235 (2010). https://doi.org/10.1007/s10589-008-9223-4
14. Arrieta, A.B., et al.: Explainable artificial intelligence (XAI): concepts, taxonomies, opportunities and challenges toward responsible AI. Inf. Fusion **58**, 82–115 (2020)
15. Babenko, B., Yang, M.H., Belongie, S.: Visual tracking with online multiple instance learning. In: 2009 IEEE Conference on Computer Vision and Pattern Recognition, pp. 983–990. IEEE (2009)
16. Bolme, D.S., Beveridge, J.R., Draper, B.A., Lui, Y.M.: Visual object tracking using adaptive correlation filters. In: 2010 IEEE Computer Society Conference on Computer Vision and Pattern Recognition, pp. 2544–2550. IEEE (2010)
17. Brunetti, A., Buongiorno, D., Trotta, G.F., Bevilacqua, V.: Computer vision and deep learning techniques for pedestrian detection and tracking: a survey. Neurocomputing **300**, 17–33 (2018)
18. Farnebäck, G.: Two-frame motion estimation based on polynomial expansion. In: Bigun, J., Gustavsson, T. (eds.) SCIA 2003. LNCS, vol. 2749, pp. 363–370. Springer, Heidelberg (2003). https://doi.org/10.1007/3-540-45103-X_50
19. Foschi, E., Bonoli, A.: The commitment of packaging industry in the framework of the European strategy for plastics in a circular economy. Adm. Sci. **9**(1), 18 (2019)

20. Girshick, R.: Fast R-CNN. In: Proceedings of the IEEE International Conference on Computer Vision, pp. 1440–1448 (2015)
21. Girshick, R., Donahue, J., Darrell, T., Malik, J.: Rich feature hierarchies for accurate object detection and semantic segmentation. In: Proceedings of the IEEE Conference on Computer Vision and Pattern Recognition, pp. 580–587 (2014)
22. Grabner, H., Grabner, M., Bischof, H.: Real-time tracking via on-line boosting. In: Bmvc. vol. 1, p. 6. Citeseer (2006)
23. Henriques, J.F., Caseiro, R., Martins, P., Batista, J.: High-speed tracking with kernelized correlation filters. IEEE Trans. Pattern Anal. Mach. Intell. **37**(3), 583–596 (2014)
24. Iman, M., Arabnia, H.R., Branchinst, R.M.: Pathways to artificial general intelligence: a brief overview of developments and ethical issues via artificial intelligence, machine learning, deep learning, and data science. In: Arabnia, H.R., Ferens, K., de la Fuente, D., Kozerenko, E.B., Olivas Varela, J.A., Tinetti, F.G. (eds.) Advances in Artificial Intelligence and Applied Cognitive Computing. TCSCI, pp. 73–87. Springer, Cham (2021). https://doi.org/10.1007/978-3-030-70296-0_6
25. Kalal, Z., Mikolajczyk, K., Matas, J.: Forward-backward error: automatic detection of tracking failures. In: 2010 20th International Conference on Pattern Recognition, pp. 2756–2759. IEEE (2010)
26. Kalal, Z., Mikolajczyk, K., Matas, J.: Tracking-learning-detection. IEEE Trans. Pattern Anal. Mach. Intell. **34**(7), 1409–1422 (2011)
27. Krizhevsky, A., Sutskever, I., Hinton, G.E.: ImageNet classification with deep convolutional neural networks. In: Advances in neural Information Processing Systems, vol. 25 (2012)
28. LeCun, Y., Bottou, L., Bengio, Y., Haffner, P.: Gradient-based learning applied to document recognition. Proc. IEEE **86**(11), 2278–2324 (1998)
29. Lukezic, A., Vojir, T., Zajc, L.C., Matas, J., Kristan, M.: Discriminative correlation filter with channel and spatial reliability. In: Proceedings of the IEEE Conference on Computer Vision and Pattern Recognition, pp. 6309–6318 (2017)
30. Marcus, G.: Deep learning: A critical appraisal. arXiv preprint arXiv:1801.00631 (2018)
31. Matthews, C., Moran, F., Jaiswal, A.K.: A review on European union's strategy for plastics in a circular economy and its impact on food safety. J. Clean. Prod. **283**, 125263 (2021)
32. Neubeck, A., Van Gool, L.: Efficient non-maximum suppression. In: 18th International Conference on Pattern Recognition (ICPR'06), vol. 3, pp. 850–855. IEEE (2006)
33. Nichol, A., Achiam, J., Schulman, J.: On first-order meta-learning algorithms. arXiv preprint arXiv:1803.02999 (2018)
34. Redmon, J., Divvala, S., Girshick, R., Farhadi, A.: You only look once: unified, real-time object detection. In: Proceedings of the IEEE Conference on Computer Vision and Pattern Recognition, pp. 779–788 (2016)
35. Ren, S., He, K., Girshick, R., Sun, J.: Faster R-CNN: towards real-time object detection with region proposal networks. In: Advances in Neural Information Processing Systems, vol. 28 (2015)
36. Ronneberger, O., Fischer, P., Brox, T.: U-Net: convolutional networks for biomedical image segmentation. In: Navab, N., Hornegger, J., Wells, W.M., Frangi, A.F. (eds.) MICCAI 2015. LNCS, vol. 9351, pp. 234–241. Springer, Cham (2015). https://doi.org/10.1007/978-3-319-24574-4_28
37. Shekhar, S.S.: Artificial intelligence in automation. Artif. Intell. **3085**(06), 14–17 (2019)

38. Sun, K., Xiao, B., Liu, D., Wang, J.: Deep high-resolution representation learning for human pose estimation. In: Proceedings of the IEEE/CVF Conference on Computer Vision and Pattern Recognition, pp. 5693–5703 (2019)
39. Sutskever, I., Martens, J., Dahl, G., Hinton, G.: On the importance of initialization and momentum in deep learning. In: International Conference on Machine Learning, pp. 1139–1147. PMLR (2013)
40. Tasora, A., et al.: Chrono: an open source multi-physics dynamics engine. In: Kozubek, T., Blaheta, R., Šístek, J., Rozložník, M., Čermák, M. (eds.) HPCSE 2015. LNCS, vol. 9611, pp. 19–49. Springer, Cham (2016). https://doi.org/10.1007/978-3-319-40361-8_2
41. Tkaczyk, S., Drozd, M., Kędzierski, Ł, Santarek, K.: Study of the stability of palletized cargo by dynamic test method performed on laboratory test bench. Sensors **21**(15), 5129 (2021)
42. Wan, J., Li, X., Dai, H.N., Kusiak, A., Martínez-García, M., Li, D.: Artificial-intelligence-driven customized manufacturing factory: key technologies, applications, and challenges. Proc. IEEE **109**(4), 377–398 (2021). https://doi.org/10.1109/JPROC.2020.3034808

AI Applications

Transformer Based Motion In-Betweening

Pavithra Sridhar(✉), V. Aananth, Madhav Aggarwal, and R. Leela Velusamy

National Institute of Technology - Tiruchirappalli, Tiruchirappalli 620015, TN, India
pavisri99@gmail.com, leela@nitt.edu

Abstract. In-betweening is the process of drawing transition frames between temporally-sparse keyframes to create a smooth animation sequence. This work presents a novel transformer-based in-betweening technique that serves as a tool for 3D animators. We first show that this problem can be represented as a sequence-to-sequence problem and introduce Tween Transformers - a model that synthesizes high-quality animations using temporally-sparse keyframes as input constraints.

We evaluate the model's performance via two complementary methods - quantitative and qualitative evaluation. The model is compared quantitatively with the state-of-the-art models using LaFAN1, a high-quality animation dataset. Mean-squared metrics like L2P, L2Q, and NPSS are used for evaluation. Qualitatively, we provide two straightforward methods to assess the model's output. First, we implement a custom ThreeJs-based motion visualizer to render the ground truth, input, and output sequences side by side for comparison. The visualizer renders custom sequences by specifying skeletal positions at temporally-sparse keyframes in JSON format. Second, we build a motion generator to generate custom motion sequences using the model.

Keywords: Motion in-betweening · Kinematics · Transformer · LAFAN1

1 Introduction

Realistic and accurate animation generation is an important but challenging problem with many applications, including animating 3D characters in films, real-time character motion synthesis in Video Games, and Educational applications. One widely used method to generate animations is motion in-betweening, commonly known as tweening. It generates intermediate frames called in-betweens between two temporally sparse keyframes to deliver an illusion of movement by smoothly transitioning from one position to another.

In traditional animation pipelines, animators manually draw motion frames between a set of still keyframes indicative of the most critical positions the body must be at during its motion sequence. Recent improvements include Motion Capture (MOCAP) technologies [9] and query-based methods [15, 19] to generate animations. However, MOCAP technology is expensive, and human-drawn animations are preferred. With the rise of computer-aided animation, deep learning-based algorithms have enabled the smooth generation of keyframes from sparse

A. Dovier et al. (Eds.): AIxIA 2022, LNAI 13796, pp. 299–312, 2023.
https://doi.org/10.1007/978-3-031-27181-6_21

frames by learning from large-scale motion capture data. Existing models currently use Recurrent Neural Networks (RNNs) [7,10], Long Short Term Memory Networks (LSTMs) [8], and BERT-based models [3,4].

The complexity of generating character animations includes

1. Replicating complex human behavior to create realistic characters
2. Predominantly used transition generation methods are either expensive or inefficient
3. RNNs/LSTMs, though they can capture long-term dependencies, cannot be parallelized due to the sequential processing of input, resulting in longer training times
4. RNNs/LSTMs do not support transfer learning making it hard to use pretrained models

Inspired by the concept of self-attention to capture long-term dependencies, this paper proposes a transformer-based model to generate realistic animation sequences. Model generalization constitutes the main effort this framework puts into improving the performance of machine learning predictions. This would be analogous to large text transformer models like GPT-3 [2]. This work not only eases the effort put in by the animators but also helps researchers by unblocking transfer learning for the task of in-betweening, thus introducing a level of generalization into the model.

Overall, the contributions in this paper can be summarized as follows:[1]

1. Represent motion in-betweening as a sequence to sequence problem where the input sequence consists of keyframes and the output sequence represents the complete and smoothed motion sequence.
2. Set a baseline for the input sequence by filling the frames between the keyframes with interpolated values.
3. Experiment with the efficiency and viability of using transformers to achieve sequence to sequence translation for human motion and compare them with the existing results.
4. Evaluate the model against other state-of-the-art models [4,8,16] for the same task using L2P, L2Q, and NPSS metrics.
5. Build a visualizer and a motion generator that qualitatively evaluates the output of the model in comparison to the ground truth and input sequences.

2   Related Work

The problem is analogous to machine translation, where sequence-to-sequence (seq2seq) architectures are prevalent [1,18,21]. "Encoder-only" models like BERT [3] are designed to learn the context of a word based on all its surroundings (left and right of the word), making them suitable for feature extraction, sentiment classification, or span prediction tasks but not for generative tasks like

---

[1] Code can be found in https://github.com/Pavi114/motion-completion-using-transformers.

translation or sequence completion. The pre-training objectives used by encoder-decoder transformers like T5 [17] include a fill-in-the-blank task where the model predicts missing words within a corrupted piece of text that is analogous to in-betweening when motion sequences replace sentences.

Early works in human motion prediction include using Conditional Restricted Boltzmann Machines (RBMs) [20] to encode the sequence information in latent variables and predict using decoders. More recently, many RNN-based approaches like Encoder-Recurrent-Decoder (ERD) networks [5] propose separating spatial encoding and decoding from the temporal dependencies. Other recent approaches investigate new architectures like transformers [13] and loss functions to improve human motion prediction further [6,12].

Initial approaches in motion in-betweening focused on generating missing frames by integrating keyframe information with spacetime models [23]. The following widely successful method for in-betweening adopted a probabilistic approach, framing it as a Maximum A posterior Optimization problem (MAP) [14], dynamical Gaussian process model [22], or Markov models with dynamic auto-regressive forests [11]. The latest deep learning approaches include works by Holden et al. [10], and Harvey et al. [7] and helped RNNs dominate this field. The latest work using RNN focuses on augmenting a Long Short Term Memory(LSTM) based architecture with time-to-arrival embeddings and a scheduled target noise vector, allowing the system to be robust to target distortions [8]. Some recent work includes BERT-based encoder-only models [3,4] that predict the entire sequence in one pass and deep learning approaches for interpolation [16]. However, BERT-based models will be less effective than encoder-decoder models for generative tasks.

3   Methodology

The following sections detail the model architecture, **Tween Transformers**, to perform motion frame completion similar to sentence completion.

3.1   Tween Transformers (TWTR)

The architecture of Tween Transformers (TWTR) consists of four main components:

1. Input masking module
2. Input encoding neural network that encodes each motion sequence and converts the input to a set of sequential tokens
3. Transition generation network that includes a standard transformer comprising encoder and decoder modules with feed-forward and multi-head attention networks.
4. Output decoding neural network that computes a sequence of character motion.

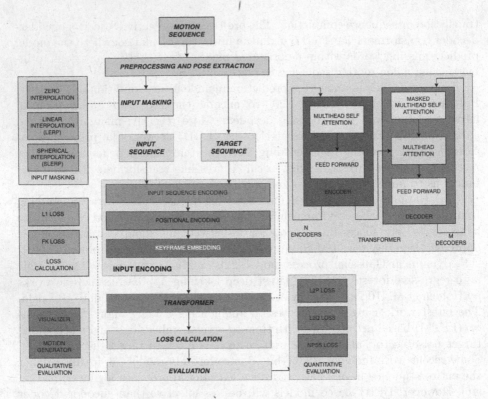

Fig. 1. Model architecture of TWTR

While the transition generation module learns the temporal dependencies, the input and output encoding networks aim to learn spatial dependencies between the different body joints for encoding and decoding motion sequences. Finally, the model also uses multiple losses, including forward kinematics loss, to improve the realism of the generated sequences. It is assumed that the input has both position (x, y, z) and orientation (q0, q1, q2, q3) variables. Therefore, a single pose can be defined with a root position coordinate $P \in R^3$ and a quaternion matrix $Q \in R^{J \times 4}$, where J represents the joint number of the input pose (here, 22). The following sections discuss the model's architecture in detail, as indicated in Fig. 1.

Input Masking. There are multiple keyframe gaps k specified in the model configuration. The frames belonging to the keyframe gap are filled with interpolated values derived from the frames constituting the two ends of the keyframe gap. Two kinds of interpolations are carried out and compared. They are implemented in the following ways:

- positions and rotations are linearly interpolated
- positions are linearly interpolated while rotations are spherically interpolated

Input Encoding. As seen in Fig. 1, model encoding has three modules - Input Sequence Encoding, Positional Encoding, and Keyframe Embedding.

1. Input Sequence Encoding:
   The input sequence encoder network is a set of three Linear encoders fully connected to two-layer Feed-Forward Networks (FFN) with ReLU activations. The input sequence encoder takes in the global root position $root\_p$, local quaternions q, and global root velocity $root\_v$ and outputs a set of "sequential tokens". The hidden sizes of the FFNs are 16, 8, and 8 for q, $root\_p$, and $root\_v$, respectively. The *embedding* hyperparameter defines the output sizes of the FFNs. The outputs from the FFNs are concatenated to form the output of the input sequence encoding network. Equation (1) describes the Linear Encoder, and Eq. (2) describes the Input Sequence Encoder.

$$L(x) = \text{Linear}(\text{ReLU}(\text{Linear}(x))) \tag{1}$$

$$I(root\_p, root\_v, q) = L_p(root\_p) \parallel L_v(root\_v) \\ \parallel L_q(q_1) \parallel ... \parallel L_q(q_J) \tag{2}$$

   where $root\_p \in R^3$, $root\_v \in R^3$, $q_i \in R^4$, I denotes the Input Sequence Encoder, and L denotes the Linear Encoder.
2. Positional Encoding: Positional encoding, a popular method introduced by Vaswani et al. [21], involves adding a set of predefined sinusoidal and cosine signals to introduce temporal knowledge to the transformer model. The positional encoding for source $Z_s = [z_{tta,2i}]$ and target $Z_t = [z_{tta,2i}]$ is computed using Eq. (3)

$$z_{tta,2i} = \sin(\frac{tta}{basis^{2i/d}})$$
$$z_{tta,2i+1} = \cos(\frac{tta}{basis^{2i/d}}) \tag{3}$$

   where tta is the number of timesteps until arrival and the *basis* component influences the rate of change in frequencies along the embedding dimension d. A basis of 10,000 is used.
3. Keyframe Embedding: Following previous works [4], the model incorporates additive keyframe embeddings. The keyframe embeddings E_{kf} classify the frames in the sequence into keyframes, unknown frames, and ignored frames. They're represented by learnable embedding vectors $\{\hat{e}_0, \hat{e}_1, \hat{e}_2\}$ respectively. The keyframe embeddings are represented by Eq. (4), where $e_{kf}^t \in \{\hat{e}_0, \hat{e}_1, \hat{e}_2\}$ and T is the sequence length. The embeddings are added to the input sequence, similar to positional encodings.

$$E_{kf} = [e_{kf}^1, e_{kf}^2, ..., e_{kf}^T] \tag{4}$$

Transformer. A transformer consists of multiple encoder and decoder layers. Each encoder includes a multi-head self-attention layer (MHSA) and a feed-forward network (FFN), and each decoder consists of a masked multi-head self-attention layer (MMHSA), multi-head attention layer (MHA) and a feed-forward network. The attention function leveraged in the transformer maps a query and a set of key-value pairs - all vectors - to an output. The processing of a single attention head can be represented as follows:

$$Attention(Q, K, V) = Softmax(\frac{QK^T}{\sqrt{d_k}})V \qquad (5)$$

where $Q = W_q A$ represents a query matrix, $K = W_k A$ represents a key matrix, and $V = W_v A$ represents a value matrix. W_q, W_k, and W_v are the corresponding weight matrices, and d_k represents the dimension of the key matrix. The Query matrix can be interpreted as the keyframe for which Attention is calculated. The Key and Value matrices represent the keyframes that are "attended to", i.e., how relevant that keyframe is to the query keyframe. In MMHSA, the target is masked before applying the attention mechanism. All the attention outputs are concatenated and sent to the FFN.

Output Decoding. The decoder takes in the concatenated "sequential tokens" outputted by the Input Sequence Encoder and outputs the global root position $root\_p$, local quaternions q, and global root velocity $root\_v$. To reverse engineer the spatial dependencies, each of the three FFNs, one for each output, comprises two linear layers with ReLU activation. The hidden sizes of the FFNs are the same as in the Input Sequence Encoder, and the output sizes are defined by the original dimensions of the three parameters. Equation (6) describes the Output Decoder.

$$O(x) = (L_p(x[: d_p]), L_v(x[d_p : d_p + d_v]), Q) \qquad (6)$$

$$Q = \begin{bmatrix} L_q(x\,[\,d_p + d_v : d_p + d_v + d_q]) \\ L_q(x\,[\,d_p + d_v + d_q : d_p + d_v + 2 \times d_q] \\ ... \\ L_q(x\,[\,d_p + d_v + (J-1) \times d_q : d_p + d_v + J \times d_q]) \end{bmatrix}$$

where d_p, d_v, and d_q are embedding dimensions for p, v, and q. $x\,[i : j]$ represents a tensor containing the values in x from the ith index to the $(j-1)^{th}$ index. J denotes the number of joints in the skeleton, $Q \in R^{J \times 4}$ denotes the tensor of stacked quaternions, O denotes the Output Decoder, and L denotes the Linear Encoder.

3.2   Loss Computation

Given a collection of predicted motion sequences and the ground truth, in-betweening loss is computed as the scaled sum of two individual losses - Reconstruction loss and Forward Kinematics (FK) loss.

$$L = \alpha_r L_R + \alpha_{fk} L_{FK} \tag{7}$$

where α_r and α_{FK} are constants to balance the disparity of individual losses. For training we use $\alpha_r = 100$ and $\alpha_{FK} = 1$.

Reconstruction Loss L_R. Reconstruction loss evaluates the ability of the model to "reconstruct" the target sequence from the input sequence. Reconstruction loss accounts for the difference in output and target quaternions values and is computed using an L1 norm. While Harvey et al. [8] compute and sum reconstruction losses for q, x, and *contacts*, they acknowledge that the most important component is q. Reconstruction loss is computed using Eq. (8).

$$L_R = \frac{1}{NT} \sum_{n=0}^{N-1} \sum_{t=0}^{T-1} \hat{q}_n^t - q_n^t \tag{8}$$

where $\hat{q}_n^t$ is the rotational quaternion of the predicted motion sequence n at time t. q refers to the ground truth quaternion. N refers to the number of sequences, and T refers to the length of each motion sequence.

Forward Kinematics Loss L_{FK}. Forward Kinematics loss compares the difference in the global positions of joints between the ground truth and the model's output. Forward Kinematics loss evaluates the ability of the model to "understand" the relationships between relative angles and global positions. Although the offsets of various joints in the skeleton are not provided to the model, it learns to respect human geometry and maintain correct posture by minimizing the Forward Kinematics loss. The Forward Kinematics loss is computed using Eq. (9).

$$L_{FK} = ||\hat{p}_{global} - p_{global}||_1 + ||\hat{q}_{global} - q_{global}||_1 \tag{9}$$

where $\hat{p}_{global}$ and $\hat{q}_{global}$ can be derived from the local coordinates using Forward Kinematics $FK(\hat{p}_{local}, \hat{q}_{local})$ and, similarly p_{global} and q_{global} can be derived from the local coordinates using Forward Kinematics $FK(p_{local}, q_{local})$.

3.3 Training

Following previous works [8,16], the entire dataset was split into windows of maximum length $T_{max} = 65$. To construct each batch, the number of start keyframes are set to 10 and the number of end keyframes to 1. The number of in-between frames is sampled from the range [5, 44] without replacement.

The weight associated with the number of in-between frames n_{in} is set to be inversely proportional to it, $w_{n_{in}} = \frac{1}{n_{in}}$. This prevents overfitting on the windows with a large number of in-between frames. Shorter windows are sampled more often as they are more abundant and hence harder to overfit. Therefore, the number of unique non-overlapping sequences of a given total length $10 + 1 + n_{in}$ is approximately inversely proportional to n_{in}. Finally, given the total sampled sequence length, the sequence start index is sampled uniformly at random in the range $[0, T_{max} - (1 + 10 + n_{in})]$.

Fig. 2. Stills from the Ground Truth, LERP, Model Output, and Smoothed Output sequences at different timestamps for the action "Aiming2" performed by subject "Subject5". Considering the frames at $t = 20$, it is clear that the output produced by our model resembles the ground truth more than the interpolated sequence.

4   Setup and Experimental Results

4.1   Dataset

The publicly available Ubisoft La Forge Animation (LaFAN1) Dataset was used for all the experiments. Introduced by Harvey et al. [8] in Ubisoft, LaFAN1 consists of general motion capture clips in high definition. The motion sequences are in BVH format. The LaFAN1 dataset comprises five subjects, 77 sequences, and 496,672 motion frames at 30 fps for a total of 4.6 h. There are around 15 themes, from everyday actions like walking, sprinting, and falling to uncommon actions like crawling, aiming, and a few sports movements. Similar to other works [4,8,16], all sequences of subject five were used for testing and benchmarking, with the remaining used for training.

4.2   Evaluation Metrics

The model is evaluated against the L2P, L2Q, and NPSS metrics used in previous studies on the subject five sequences of the LAFAN1 dataset. The L2P defines the average L2 distances of the positions between the predicted motion sequence and the ground truth sequence. Equation 10 shows the L2P calculation. Similarly, the L2Q defines the average L2 distances of the global quaternions. A combination of local quaternions, positions, and motion sequence properties is used to compute these metrics. Equation 11 shows the L2Q calculation.

$$L2P = \frac{1}{NT} \sum_{n=0}^{N-1} \sum_{t=0}^{T-1} \hat{p}_n^t - {p_n}^t \qquad (10)$$

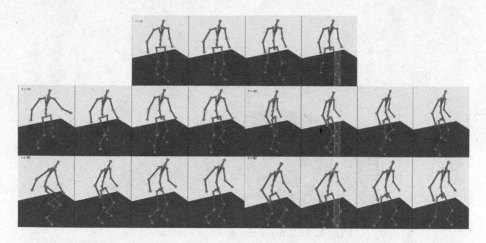

Fig. 3. Stills from the Ground Truth, LERP, Model Output, and Smoothed Output sequences at different timestamps for the action "Dance2" performed by subject "Subject5". The dance action is unconventional and full of seemingly random movements. Considering the frames at $t = 10$, $t = 20$, and $t = 30$, the output produced by the model is better at $t = 10$, the output produced by interpolation is better at $t = 20$, and neither come close at $t = 30$.

$$L2Q = \frac{1}{NT} \sum_{n=0}^{N-1} \sum_{t=0}^{T-1} \hat{q}_n^t - q_n^t \tag{11}$$

where $\hat{q}$ is the rotational quaternion of the predicted motion sequence n at time t. q refers to the ground truth quaternion. Similarly, $\hat{p}$ refers to the position of the predicted motion sequence p refers to the ground truth position. N refers to the number of sequences, and T refers to the length of each motion sequence.

Normalized Power Spectrum Similarity (NPSS) is an approach comparing angular frequencies with the ground truth. It is an Earth Mover Distance (EMD) based metric over the power spectrum, which uses the squared magnitude spectrum values of the Discrete Fourier Transform coefficients. Equation (12) computes the NPSS metric.

$$NPSS = \frac{\sum_{i=0}^{N-1} \sum_{j=0}^{T-1} w_{i,j} * emd_{i,j}}{\sum_{i=0}^{N-1} \sum_{j=0}^{T-1} w_{i,j}} \tag{12}$$

where $emd_{i,j}$ refers to the EMD distance, and $w_{i,j}$ refers to the weights.

Harvey et al. [8] state that the L2P metric is a better metric than any angular loss for assessing the visual quality of transitions with global displacements as it helps us weigh the positions of the bones and joints. Hence, they argue that L2P is a much more critical metric than L2Q and NPSS.

Fig. 4. Still from the motion generator

4.3   Data Preprocessing

First, the local position and orientation values from the BVH files provided in the LaFAN1 dataset [7] are extracted. Twenty-two joints are considered for the skeleton model. Forward Kinematics was used to compute the absolute positions of each joint from the relative positions (relative to hip) given in the dataset. Positions are modeled as standard matrices, and orientations are modeled using quaternions. Further, global position and root velocity are computed from local positions using Forward kinematics.

4.4   Hyperparameters

Most hyperparameters from previous baselines are retained to show the relative improvement in performance using Transformers. This study presents a novel hyperparameter comparison using different interpolation techniques - Linear and Spherical, to compare the performance of several baseline studies. A batch size of 64 for 100 epochs was used. Adam optimizer with a learning rate of 10^{-4} along with a constant dropout of 0.2 was utilized. Keyframe gaps of 5, 15, and 30 were tested to compare the performance of the transformer over higher frame gaps.

4.5   Visualizer and Motion Generator

To qualitatively evaluate the model, a visualizer was built using Node and ThreeJs that juxtaposed the ground truth, interpolated sequence, output sequence, and a smoothed output sequence of the transformer model. The model's output is stored in JSON format and rendered using a custom web-based visualizer. The visualizer was built from scratch using Typescript, NodeJs, Express, and ThreeJs. Figures 2 and 3 show a sample output of the model generated using the visualizer. Further, the motion generator was built using Python,

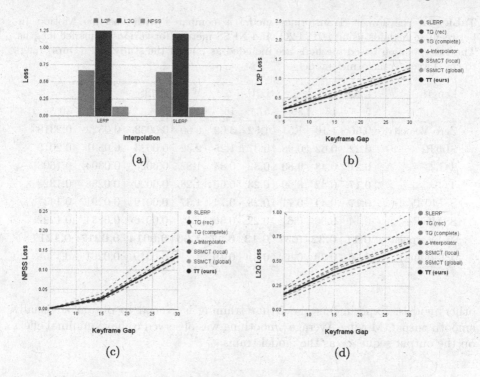

Fig. 5. (a) Comparision of model performance at keyframe gap = 30 with three commonly used metrics - L2P, L2Q, and NPSS, (b) Comparison of L2P losses at various keyframe gaps of the motion in-betweening methods included in this study, (c) Comparison of NPSS losses at various keyframe gaps of the motion in-betweening methods included in this study, (d) Comparison of L2Q losses at various keyframe gaps of the motion in-betweening methods included in this study.

Flask, Node, and ThreeJs using the visualizer module as a base. The motion generator allows a user to modify keyframes in a given motion sequence and generate in-between frames for the same. The plugin consists of a backend Flask server that uses an instance of our model to generate the in-between frames. Figure 4 shows a still from the motion generator where the stick model is animating a generated custom motion sequence.

4.6 Inferences

As expected, SLERP performs better than LERP. However, it is observed that the performance at 30 fps is almost comparable, as seen in Fig. 5a. This is because the spherical motion becomes almost linear for very short timescales. As seen in Table 1, it is inferred that the Tween Transformer model outperforms the interpolation model and performs closely with the baseline models. Figures 5b, 5d, and 5c confirm that Tween Transformers follow a similar trend to that of

Table 1. The Tween Transformer model is compared with baseline Motion In-betweening methods using L2P, L2Q, and NPSS metrics for various sequence lengths. The Interpolation based methods are included as part of the study. TT (Ours) refers to the Tween Transformer model.

Length	L2Q			L2P			NPSS		
	5	15	30	5	15	30	5	15	30
Zero Velocity	0.56	1.10	1.51	1.52	3.69	6.60	0.0053	0.0522	0.2318
SLERP	0.22	0.62	0.98	0.37	1.25	2.32	0.0023	0.0391	0.2013
TG_{rec}	0.21	0.48	0.83	0.32	0.85	1.82	0.0025	0.0304	0.1608
$TG_{complete}$	0.17	0.42	0.69	0.23	0.65	1.28	0.0020	0.0258	0.1328
$SSMCT_{local}$	0.17	0.44	0.71	0.23	0.74	1.37	0.0019	0.0291	0.143
$SSMCT_{Global}$	0.14	0.36	0.61	0.22	0.56	1.1	0.0016	0.0234	0.1222
Δ-Interpolator	**0.11**	**0.32**	**0.57**	**0.13**	**0.47**	**1.00**	**0.0014**	**0.0217**	**0.1217**
TT (Ours)	0.16	0.39	0.65	0.21	0.59	1.21	0.0019	0.0261	0.1358

other models. Experiments show that training is crucial to obtain a visually smooth output. Moving Average Smoothing was observed to have minimal effect on the output sequence as the model trains.

5   Conclusion

This work presents the Tween Transformer, a novel, robust, transformer-based motion in-betweening technique that serves as a tool for 3D animators and overcomes the challenges faced by existing RNN-based models [8,16], including sequential training, capturing long-term dependencies, and transfer learning. The generic model treats the application of in-betweening as a sequence-to-sequence problem and solves it using a transformer-based encoder-decoder architecture. It unboxes the potential of robust Transformer-based models for motion in-betweening applications. To conclude, the results encourage the application of low-resource cost-efficient models and enable further developments with the scope of transfer learning on the generalized implementation.

References

1. Bahdanau, D., Cho, K., Bengio, Y.: Neural machine translation by jointly learning to align and translate. In: Bengio, Y., LeCun, Y. (eds.) 3rd International Conference on Learning Representations, ICLR 2015, San Diego, CA, USA, 7–9 May 2015, Conference Track Proceedings (2015). https://arxiv.org/abs/1409.0473
2. Brown, T., et al.: Language models are few-shot learners. In: Larochelle, H., Ranzato, M., Hadsell, R., Balcan, M.F., Lin, H. (eds.) Advances in Neural Information Processing Systems, vol. 33, pp. 1877–1901. Curran Associates, Inc. (2020). https://proceedings.neurips.cc/paper/2020/file/1457c0d6bfcb4967418bfb8ac142f6 4a-Paper.pdf

3. Devlin, J., Chang, M.W., Lee, K., Toutanova, K.: BERT: pre-training of deep bidirectional transformers for language understanding. In: Proceedings of the 2019 Conference of the North American Chapter of the Association for Computational Linguistics: Human Language Technologies, Volume 1 (Long and Short Papers), pp. 4171–4186. Association for Computational Linguistics, Minneapolis, Minnesota (2019). https://doi.org/10.18653/v1/N19-1423, https://aclanthology.org/N19-1423

4. Duan, Y., et al.: Single-shot motion completion with transformer. arXiv preprint arXiv:2103.00776 (2021)

5. Fragkiadaki, K., Levine, S., Malik, J.: Recurrent network models for kinematic tracking. CoRR abs/1508.00271 (2015). https://arxiv.org/abs/1508.00271

6. Gopalakrishnan, A., Mali, A.A., Kifer, D., Giles, C.L., II, A.G.O.: A neural temporal model for human motion prediction. CoRR abs/1809.03036 (2018). https://arxiv.org/abs/1809.03036

7. Harvey, F.G., Pal, C.: Recurrent transition networks for character locomotion. In: SIGGRAPH Asia 2018 Technical Briefs. SA 2018, Association for Computing Machinery, New York, NY, USA (2018). https://doi.org/10.1145/3283254.3283277

8. Harvey, F.G., Yurick, M., Nowrouzezahrai, D., Pal, C.: Robust motion inbetweening. ACM Trans. Graph. **39**(4), 1–12 (2020). https://doi.org/10.1145/3386569.3392480

9. Holden, D.: Robust solving of optical motion capture data by denoising. ACM Trans. Graph. **37**(4), 1–12 (2018). https://doi.org/10.1145/3197517.3201302

10. Holden, D., Saito, J., Komura, T.: A deep learning framework for character motion synthesis and editing. ACM Trans. Graph. **35**(4), 1–11 (2016). https://doi.org/10.1145/2897824.2925975

11. Lehrmann, A.M., Gehler, P.V., Nowozin, S.: Efficient nonlinear Markov models for human motion. In: Proceedings of the IEEE Conference on Computer Vision and Pattern Recognition (CVPR) (2014)

12. Liu, Z., et al.: Towards natural and accurate future motion prediction of humans and animals. In: 2019 IEEE/CVF Conference on Computer Vision and Pattern Recognition (CVPR), pp. 9996–10004 (2019). https://doi.org/10.1109/CVPR.2019.01024

13. Martínez-González, Á., Villamizar, M., Odobez, J.: Pose transformers (POTR): human motion prediction with non-autoregressive transformers. CoRR abs/2109.07531 (2021). https://arxiv.org/abs/2109.07531

14. Min, J., Chen, Y.L., Chai, J.: Interactive generation of human animation with deformable motion models. ACM Trans. Graph. **29**(1), 1–12 (2009). https://doi.org/10.1145/1640443.1640452

15. Müller, M., Röder, T., Clausen, M.: Efficient content-based retrieval of motion capture data. ACM Trans. Graph. **24**(3), 677–685 (2005). https://doi.org/10.1145/1073204.1073247

16. Oreshkin, B.N., Valkanas, A., Harvey, F.G., Ménard, L.S., Bocquelet, F., Coates, M.J.: Motion Inbetweening via Deep Δ-Interpolator. arXiv e-prints arXiv:2201.06701 (2022)

17. Dhariwal, P., Sastry, G., McCandlish, S.: Enct5: Fine-tuning t5 encoder for discriminative tasks (2021)

18. Ren, M., Kiros, R., Zemel, R.S.: Exploring models and data for image question answering. In: Proceedings of the 28th International Conference on Neural Information Processing Systems, vol. 2, pp. 2953–2961. NIPS 2015, MIT Press, Cambridge, MA, USA (2015)

19. Tanuwijaya, S., Ohno, Y.: TF-DF indexing for mocap data segments in measuring relevance based on textual search queries. Vis. Comput. **26**(6–8), 1091–1100 (2010). https://doi.org/10.1007/s00371-010-0463-9
20. Taylor, G.W., Hinton, G.E.: Factored conditional restricted Boltzmann machines for modeling motion style. In: Proceedings of the 26th Annual International Conference on Machine Learning ICML 2009, pp. 1025–1032. Association for Computing Machinery, New York, NY, USA (2009). https://doi.org/10.1145/1553374.1553505
21. Vaswani, A., et al.: Attention is all you need. In: Proceedings of the 31st International Conference on Neural Information Processing Systems NIPS 2017, pp. 6000–6010. Curran Associates Inc., Red Hook, NY, USA (2017)
22. Wang, J.M., Fleet, D.J., Hertzmann, A.: Gaussian process dynamical models for human motion. IEEE Trans. Pattern Anal. Mach. Intell. **30**(2), 283–298 (2008). https://doi.org/10.1109/TPAMI.2007.1167
23. Witkin, A., Kass, M.: Spacetime constraints. In: Proceedings of the 15th Annual Conference on Computer Graphics and Interactive Techniques SIGGRAPH 1988, pp. 159–168. Association for Computing Machinery, New York, NY, USA (1988). https://doi.org/10.1145/54852.378507

A Logic-Based Tool for Dynamic Generation and Classification of Musical Content

Antonio Lieto[✉][iD], Gian Luca Pozzato[✉][iD], Alberto Valese, and Mattia Zito

Dipartimento di Informatica, Università di Torino, Turin, Italy
{antonio.lieto,gianluca.pozzato,alberto.valese}@unito.it,
mattia.zito@edu.unito.it

Abstract. In this work we present NERVOUS, an intelligent recommender system exploiting a probabilistic extension of a Description Logic of typicality to dynamically generate novel contents in AllMusic, a comprehensive and in-depth resource about music, providing data about albums, bands, musicians and songs (https://www.allmusic.com). The tool can be used for both the generation of novel music genres and styles, described by a set of typical properties characterizing them, and the reclassification of the available songs within such new genres.

1 Introduction

The ability of generating new knowledge via conceptual combination concerns high-level capacities associated to creative thinking and problem solving, and it represents an open challenge for artificial intelligence [2]. Indeed, dealing with this problem requires, from an AI perspective, the harmonization of two conflicting requirements: on the one hand, the need of a syntactic and semantic compositionality; on the other hand, the need of capturing typicality effects. However, such requirements can be hardly accommodated in standard symbolic systems, including formal ontologies [4]. According to a well-known argument [18], prototypes, namely commonsense conceptual representations based on typical properties, are not compositional. Consider a concept like *pet fish*: it results from the composition of the concept *pet* and of the concept *fish*, however, the prototype of *pet fish* cannot result from the composition of the prototypes of a pet and a fish. For instance, a typical pet is furry, whereas a typical fish is grayish, but a typical pet fish is neither furry nor grayish (typically, it is red). This is a paradigmatic example of the difficulty to address when building formalisms and systems trying to imitate this combinatorial human ability. Examples of such difficulties concern handling exceptions to attribute inheritance and handling the possible inconsistencies arising between conflicting properties of the concepts to be combined.

In this work we continue our activity started in [9, 10] with the definition of a Typicality Description Logic for concept combination ($\mathbf{T}^{CL}$, typicality-based compositional logic), that we have exploited in order to build a goal-oriented framework for knowledge invention in the cognitive architecture of SOAR [8, 11, 12], as well as for the generation and the suggestion of novel editorial content in multimedia broadcasting [3] and in the artistic domain of paintings, poetic content [15], and museum items [13]. In the Description Logic $\mathbf{T}^{CL}$, "typical" properties can be directly specified by means of

A. Dovier et al. (Eds.): AIxIA 2022, LNAI 13796, pp. 313–326, 2023.
https://doi.org/10.1007/978-3-031-27181-6_22

a "typicality" operator $\mathbf{T}$ enriching the underlying DL, and a TBox can contain inclusions of the form $\mathbf{T}(C) \sqsubseteq D$ to represent that "typical Cs are also Ds". As a difference with standard DLs, in the logic $\mathbf{T}^{CL}$ one can consistently express exceptions and reason about defeasible inheritance as well. Typicality inclusions are also equipped by a real number $p \in (0.5, 1]$ representing the probability/degree of belief in such a typical property: this allows us to define a semantics inspired to the DISPONTE semantics [20] characterizing probabilistic extensions of DLs, which in turn is used in order to describe different *scenarios* where only some typicality properties are considered. Given a KB containing the description of two concepts C_H and C_M occurring in it, we then consider only *some* scenarios in order to define a revised knowledge base, enriched by typical properties of the combined concept $C \sqsubseteq C_H \sqcap C_M$ by also implementing a HEAD/MODIFIER heuristics coming from the cognitive semantics.

In this work we exploit the logic $\mathbf{T}^{CL}$ in order to dynamically generate novel knowledge by means of a mechanism for commonsense combination, that we apply to data extracted from AllMusic (https://www.allmusic.com), a comprehensive and in-depth resource about music. In particular, we introduce NERVOUS (dyNamic gEneratoR of noVel cOntent in mUSic), a tool which is able to compute the following activities:

- it builds the prototypical description of 18 basic musical genres (Blues, Classical, Country, Easy Listening, Holiday and so on), by extracting data about musical genres and songs in AllMusic by means of a crawler. Such prototypes are formalized by means of a $\mathbf{T}^{CL}$ knowledge base, whose TBox contains both *rigid* inclusions of the form

$$BasicGenre \sqsubseteq Concept$$

in order to express essential desiderata but also constraints, for instance *Childrens* $\sqsubseteq$ $\neg Sex$ (due to law restrictions, sexual contents for kids are forbidden), as well as *prototypical* properties of the form

$$p :: \mathbf{T}(BasicGenre) \sqsubseteq TypicalConcept,$$

representing typical concepts of a given genre, where p is a real number in the range $(0.5, 1]$, expressing the degree of belief of such a concept in items belonging to that genre: for instance, $0.84 :: \mathbf{T}(AvantGarde) \sqsubseteq Cerebral$ is used to express that typical songs belonging to the Avant-garde genre are Cerebral (in some sense) with a probability/degree of belief of the 84%, and such a degree is automatically extracted by NERVOUS from the data available on AllMusic for that genre;
- it allows the generation of new musical genres by exploiting the reasoning capabilities of the logic $\mathbf{T}^{CL}$ in order to generate new *derived* genres as the result of the creative combination of two basic or derived ones;
- it implements a mechanism of reclassification of the available songs of AllMusic within new genres generated in the previous phase. Intuitively, a song is classified as belonging to the new genre if its moods and themes match the typical properties of the prototype of such a genre, obtaining a *score of compatibility* higher than 0. A positive matching, namely the same property has a high score in the song and is a typical property in the genre, provides a positive score, whereas a negative one, e.g. the song has a high score for a property which is negated in the prototype of

the genre, produces a negative score. Songs having at least one positive match and having no negative ones has an overall positive score and is then recommended by NERVOUS for that genre.

We have tested NERVOUS by reclassifying the available songs in the highlights of AllMusic with respect to the new generated genres, as well as with an evaluation, in the form of a controlled user study experiment, of the feasibility of using the obtained reclassifications as recommended contents. The obtained results are encouraging and pave the way to many possible further improvements and research directions.

2 Combining Concepts: The Description Logic $\mathbf{T}^{\mathsf{CL}}$

The tool NERVOUS exploits the Description Logic $\mathbf{T}^{\mathsf{CL}}$ [9,10] for the generation of new genres as the combination of two existing ones. The language of $\mathbf{T}^{\mathsf{CL}}$ extends the basic DL $\mathcal{ALC}$ by *typicality inclusions* of the form

$$p :: \mathbf{T}(C) \sqsubseteq D$$

where $p \in (0.5, 1]$ is a real number representing its degree of belief, whose meaning is that "we believe with degree p that, normally, Cs are also Ds". We avoid degrees $p \leq 0.5$ since it would be misleading for typicality inclusions, since typical knowledge is known to come with a low degree of uncertainty.

We define a knowledge base $\mathcal{K} = \langle \mathcal{R}, \mathcal{T}, \mathcal{A} \rangle$ where $\mathcal{R}$ is a finite set of rigid properties of the form $C \sqsubseteq D$, $\mathcal{T}$ is a finite set of typicality properties of the form $p :: \mathbf{T}(C) \sqsubseteq D$ where $p \in (0.5, 1] \subseteq \mathbb{R}$ is the degree of belief of the typicality inclusion, and $\mathcal{A}$ is the ABox, i.e. a finite set of formulas of the form either $C(a)$ or $R(a, b)$, where $a, b \in \mathsf{O}$ and $R \in \mathsf{R}$.

The Description Logic $\mathbf{T}^{\mathsf{CL}}$ relies on the DL of typicality $\mathcal{ALC} + \mathbf{T}_{\mathbf{R}}$ introduced in [5], which allows one to describe the *prototype* of a concept, in this case a musical genre. As a difference with standard DLs, in the logic $\mathcal{ALC} + \mathbf{T}_{\mathbf{R}}$ one can consistently express exceptions and reason about defeasible inheritance as well. For instance, a knowledge base can consistently express that "typical students are young persons", whereas "normally, senior students are not young persons" by $\mathbf{T}(Student) \sqsubseteq Young$ and $\mathbf{T}(SeniorStudent) \sqsubseteq \neg Young$, given a knowledge base also containing the standard inclusion $SeniorStudent \sqsubseteq Student$, representing that all senior students are students. The semantics of the $\mathbf{T}$ operator is characterized by the properties of *rational logic* [7], recognized as the core properties of nonmonotonic reasoning. The Description Logic $\mathcal{ALC} + \mathbf{T}_{\mathbf{R}}$ is characterized by a minimal model semantics corresponding to an extension to DLs of a notion of *rational closure* as defined in [7] for propositional logic: the idea is to adopt a preference relation among $\mathcal{ALC} + \mathbf{T}_{\mathbf{R}}$ models, where intuitively a model is preferred to another one if it contains less exceptional elements, as well as a notion of *minimal entailment* restricted to models that are minimal with respect to such preference relation. As a consequence, the operator $\mathbf{T}$ inherits well-established properties like *specificity* and *irrelevance*; in the example, the Description Logic $\mathcal{ALC} + \mathbf{T}_{\mathbf{R}}$ allows one to infer that $\mathbf{T}(Student \sqcap Italian) \sqsubseteq Young$ (being Italian is irrelevant with respect to being young) and, if one knows that Rachel is a typical senior student, to infer that she is not young, giving preference to the most specific information.

A model $\mathcal{M}$ of $\mathbf{T}^{CL}$ extends standard $\mathcal{ALC}$ models by a preference relation among domain elements as in the logic of typicality [5]. In this respect, $x < y$ means that x is "more normal" than y, and that the typical members of a concept C are the minimal elements of C with respect to this relation. An element $x \in \Delta^{\mathcal{I}}$ is a *typical instance* of some concept C if $x \in C^{\mathcal{I}}$ and there is no C-element in $\Delta^{\mathcal{I}}$ *more normal* than x.

Definition 1 (Model of $\mathbf{T}^{CL}$). *A model $\mathcal{M}$ is any structure $\langle \Delta^{\mathcal{I}}, <, .^{\mathcal{I}} \rangle$ where: (i) $\Delta^{\mathcal{I}}$ is a non empty set of items called the domain; (ii) $<$ is an irreflexive, transitive, well-founded and modular (for all x, y, z in $\Delta^{\mathcal{I}}$, if $x < y$ then either $x < z$ or $z < y$) relation over $\Delta^{\mathcal{I}}$; (iii) $.^{\mathcal{I}}$ is the extension function that maps each atomic concept C to $C^{\mathcal{I}} \subseteq \Delta^{\mathcal{I}}$, and each role R to $R^{\mathcal{I}} \subseteq \Delta^{\mathcal{I}} \times \Delta^{\mathcal{I}}$, and is extended to complex concepts in the standard way for standard connectives, whereas for the typicality operator we have $(\mathbf{T}(C))^{\mathcal{I}} = Min_<(C^{\mathcal{I}})$, where $Min_<(C^{\mathcal{I}}) = \{x \in C^{\mathcal{I}} \mid \nexists y \in C^{\mathcal{I}} \text{ s.t. } y < x\}$.*

In order to perform useful nonmonotonic inferences, in [5] the above semantics is strengthened by restricting entailment to a class of minimal models. Intuitively, the idea is to restrict entailment to models that *minimize the atypical instances of a concept*. The resulting logic corresponds to a notion of *rational closure* on top of $\mathcal{ALC} + \mathbf{T_R}$. Such a notion is a natural extension of the rational closure construction provided in [7] for the propositional logic. This nonmonotonic semantics relies on minimal rational models that minimize the *rank of domain elements*. Informally, given two models of KB, one in which a given domain element x has rank 2 (because for instance $z < y < x$), and another in which it has rank 1 (because only $y < x$), we prefer the latter, as in this model the element x is assumed to be "more typical" than in the former. Query entailment is then restricted to minimal *canonical models*. The intuition is that a canonical model contains all the individuals that enjoy properties that are consistent with KB.

The Description Logic $\mathbf{T}^{CL}$ considers a distributed semantics similar to DISPONTE [21] for probabilistic DLs. This logic allows one to label inclusions $\mathbf{T}(C) \sqsubseteq D$ with a real number between 0.5 and 1, representing its degree of belief, assuming that each axiom is independent from each others. Degrees in typicality inclusions allow one to define a probability distribution over *scenarios*: intuitively, a scenario is obtained by choosing, for each typicality inclusion, whether it is considered as true or false. In an extension of the above example, we could have the following KB:

(1) $SeniorStudent \sqsubseteq Student$
(2) $0.70 :: \mathbf{T}(Student) \sqsubseteq Young$
(3) $0.95 :: \mathbf{T}(SeniorStudent) \sqsubseteq \neg Young$
(4) $0.85 :: \mathbf{T}(SeniorStudent) \sqsubseteq Married$

We consider eight different scenarios, representing all possible combinations of typicality inclusion, for instance $\{((2), 1), ((3), 1), ((4), 0)\}$ represents the scenario in which (2) and (3) hold, whereas (4) is not considered. The standard inclusion (1) holds in every scenario, representing a rigid property not admitting exceptions. We equip each scenario with a probability depending on those of the involved inclusions: the scenario of the example has probability $0.7 \times 0.95 \times (1 - 0.85)$, since 2 and 3 are involved, whereas 4 is not. Such probabilities are then taken into account in order to select the most adequate scenario describing the prototype of the combined concept.

Last, the logic $\mathbf{T}^{\mathsf{CL}}$ exploits a method inspired by cognitive semantics [6] for the identification of a dominance effect between the concepts to be combined: for every combination, we distinguish a HEAD, representing the stronger element of the combination, and a MODIFIER. The basic idea is: given a KB and two concepts C_H (HEAD) and C_M (MODIFIER) occurring in it, we consider only *some* scenarios in order to define a revised knowledge base, enriched by typical properties of the combined concept $C \sqsubseteq C_H \sqcap C_M$.

Given a KB $\mathcal{K} = \langle \mathcal{R}, \mathcal{T}, \mathcal{A} \rangle$ and given two concepts C_H and C_M occurring in $\mathcal{K}$, the logic $\mathbf{T}^{\mathsf{CL}}$ allows defining a prototype of the combined concept C as the combination of the HEAD C_H and the MODIFIER C_M, where the typical properties of the form $\mathbf{T}(C) \sqsubseteq D$ (or, equivalently, $\mathbf{T}(C_H \sqcap C_M) \sqsubseteq D$) to ascribe to the concept C are obtained by considering blocks of scenarios with the same probability, in decreasing order starting from the highest one. We first discard all the inconsistent scenarios, then: (1) we discard those scenarios considered as *trivial*, consistently inheriting all the properties from the HEAD from the starting concepts to be combined. This choice is motivated by the challenges provided by task of commonsense conceptual combination itself: in order to generate plausible and creative compounds it is necessary to maintain a level of surprise in the combination. Thus both scenarios inheriting all the properties of the two concepts and all the properties of the HEAD are discarded since they prevent this surprise; (2) among the remaining ones, we discard those inheriting properties from the MODIFIER in conflict with properties that could be consistently inherited from the HEAD; (3) if the set of scenarios of the current block is empty, i.e. all the scenarios have been discarded either because trivial or because preferring the MODIFIER, we repeat the procedure by considering the block of scenarios, having the immediately lower probability. Remaining scenarios are those selected by the logic $\mathbf{T}^{\mathsf{CL}}$.

The output of this mechanism is a knowledge base in the logic $\mathbf{T}^{\mathsf{CL}}$ whose set of typicality properties is enriched by those of the compound concept C. Given a scenario w satisfying the above properties, we define the properties of C as the set of inclusions $p :: \mathbf{T}(C) \sqsubseteq D$, for all $\mathbf{T}(C) \sqsubseteq D$ that are entailed from w in the logic $\mathbf{T}^{\mathsf{CL}}$. The probability p is such that: (i) if $\mathbf{T}(C_H) \sqsubseteq D$ is entailed from w, that is to say D is a property inherited either from the HEAD (or from both the HEAD and the MODIFIER), then p corresponds to the degree of belief of such inclusion of the HEAD in the initial knowledge base, i.e. $p : \mathbf{T}(C_H) \sqsubseteq D \in \mathcal{T}$; (ii) otherwise, i.e. $\mathbf{T}(C_M) \sqsubseteq D$ is entailed from w, then p corresponds to the degree of belief of such inclusion of a MODIFIER in the initial knowledge base, i.e. $p : \mathbf{T}(C_M) \sqsubseteq D \in \mathcal{T}$.

The knowledge base obtained as the result of combining concepts C_H and C_M into the compound concept C is called *C-revised* knowledge base, and it is defined as:

$$\mathcal{K}_C = \langle \mathcal{R}, \mathcal{T} \cup \{p : \mathbf{T}(C) \sqsubseteq D\}, \mathcal{A} \rangle,$$

for all D such that either $\mathbf{T}(C_H) \sqsubseteq D$ is entailed in w or $\mathbf{T}(C_M) \sqsubseteq D$ is entailed in w, and p is defined as above.

It turns out that reasoning in $\mathbf{T}^{\mathsf{CL}}$ is EXPTIME-complete, namely it remains in the same complexity class of standard Description Logic $\mathcal{ALC}$ [10].

3   The Tool NERVOUS: Automated Generation of Prototypical Descriptions of Musical Genres

The tool NERVOUS is implemented in Python, with a web interface in Flutter, and it makes use of the library `owlready2` (https://pythonhosted.org/Owlready2/) for relying on the services of efficient DL reasoners (like HermiT). NERVOUS first builds a prototypical description of basic musical genres available in AllMusic, like blues, classical, country, folk, jazz, rap, pop-rock. A screenshot of the platform AllMusic is reported in Fig. 1.

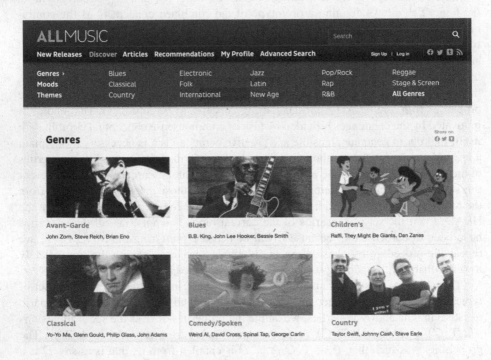

Fig. 1. A screenshot of the AllMusic platform.

To this aim, a web crawler extracts metadata from the information available on All-Music by means of the Python library BeautifulSoap 4. More in detail, for each basic genre, the crawler extracts metadata of the 50 songs belonging to the "highlight" section for that genre; for each song the crawler then extracts a list of properties, that AllMusic calls Styles, Moods, and Themes: these properties are those that will be used to describe the prototype of genres. More in detail, for each property the system counts the number of songs having that property, then the properties are considered in a descending order and equipped by a normalized probability. As an example, consider the genre Blues and the 50 songs belonging to such a genre: the property with the highest frequency is "Regional Blues", occurring in 40 songs over 50, followed by "Earthy" (35 over 50), "Gritty" (35 over 50), "Passionate" (29 over 50) and so on. These information are used in order to provide a description of each basic genre in terms of its typical properties in the logic $\mathbf{T}^{CL}$, where the frequency of a property for a genre is obtained from the number of occurrences of such property in descriptions of the songs belonging to that genre. The six properties with the highest frequency are included in the prototypical description of each basic genre, as well as the two properties with the lowest probabilities, that are added as negated properties. Formally, we have:

Definition 2. *Given a basic genre* Genre, *let* $\mathcal{MI}$ *be the set of songs classified in* Genre, *and let* S_{Genre} *be the set of the concepts occurring in the songs classified in that genre by AllMusic, i.e.* $S_{Genre} = \bigcup_{m \in \mathcal{MI}} S_m$, *where* S_m *is the set of properties extracted for* m *by the web crawler. Given a concept* Concept $\in S_{Genre}$, *let* $n_{Genre,Concept}$ *the number of songs in* $\mathcal{MI}$ *whose description contain* Concept, *we define the frequency of a concept* Concept *for a genre* Genre, *written* $f_{Genre,Concept}$, *as follows:*

$$f_{Genre,Concept} = \frac{n_{Genre,Concept}}{|\mathcal{MI}|}.$$

The prototypical description of a basic Genre in the logic $\mathbf{T}^{CL}$ is defined as the set of inclusions $p_1 :: \mathbf{T}(Genre) \sqsubseteq TypicalConcept_1$, $p_2 :: \mathbf{T}(Genre) \sqsubseteq TypicalConcept_2$, ..., $p_6 :: \mathbf{T}(Genre) \sqsubseteq TypicalConcept_6$, ..., where $TypicalConcept_1$, $TypicalConcept_2$, ..., $TypicalConcept_6$ are the six concepts in S_{Genre} with the highest frequencies; frequencies are then also normalized and used as degrees of belief of the respective inclusions. The two properties with the lowest frequencies are included as negated ones with a fixed probability of 0.9.

Definition 3. *Given a genre* Genre, *let the set of concepts* S_{Genre} *of Definition 2 in descending order by the frequencies* $f_{Genre,Concept}$ *of Definition 2:*

$$S_{Genre} = \langle C_1, C_2, \ldots, C_k \rangle$$

where $f_{Genre,C_1} \geq f_{Genre,C_2} \geq \cdots \geq f_{Genre,C_k}$. *The prototypical description of* Genre *in the logic* $\mathbf{T}^{CL}$ *is defined as the set of inclusions* $f_{Genre,C_1} :: \mathbf{T}(Genre) \sqsubseteq C_1$, $f_{Genre,C_2} :: \mathbf{T}(Genre) \sqsubseteq C_2$, ..., $f_{Genre,C_6} :: \mathbf{T}(Genre) \sqsubseteq C_6$, $0.9 :: \mathbf{T}(Genre) \sqsubseteq \neg C_{k-1}$, $0.9 :: \mathbf{T}(Genre) \sqsubseteq \neg C_k$.

Observed that the least frequent concepts in blues songs are "The Creative Side" and "Day Driving", the prototype of the genre Blues computed by the tool NERVOUS is therefore as follows:

$0.90 :: \mathbf{T}(Blues) \sqsubseteq RegionalBlues$
$0.86 :: \mathbf{T}(Blues) \sqsubseteq Earthy$
$0.86 :: \mathbf{T}(Blues) \sqsubseteq Gritty$
$0.82 :: \mathbf{T}(Blues) \sqsubseteq Passionate$
$0.82 :: \mathbf{T}(Blues) \sqsubseteq LateNight$
$0.76 :: \mathbf{T}(Blues) \sqsubseteq HangingOut$
$0.90 :: \mathbf{T}(Blues) \sqsubseteq \neg TheCreativeSide$
$0.90 :: \mathbf{T}(Blues) \sqsubseteq \neg DayDriving$

As mentioned, the logic $\mathbf{T}^{CL}$ allows one to also "manually" add rigid properties, for instance to express legal constraints, thus integrating the bottom-up, data-driven, process of prototype formation with top down expert knowledge. However, actually there is no convergence about the identification of rigid properties for describing a music genre, therefore we have chosen to avoid such properties and we have adopted typical properties only, but the reasoning mechanism provided by NERVOUS is already able to deal also with rigid properties.

4   The Tool NERVOUS: Generation of Novel Musical Genres

NERVOUS generates novel genres by combining existing ones by means of the reasoning mechanism provided by the logic $\mathbf{T}^{CL}$. Given the prototypical description of basic genres, the system NERVOUS combines two basic genres in order to build a prototype of the derived genre, by exploiting the logic $\mathbf{T}^{CL}$. To this aim, NERVOUS relies on a variant of CoCoS [14], a Python implementation of reasoning services for the logic $\mathbf{T}^{CL}$ in order to exploit efficient DLs reasoners for checking both the consistency of each generated scenario and the existence of conflicts among properties. More in detail, NERVOUS considers both the available choices for the HEAD and the MODIFIER, and it allows one to restrict its concern to a given and fixed number of inherited properties.

NERVOUS improves its ancestor, DENOTER [3], in several aspects:

- it implements a "smart" generation of scenarios, namely it beforehand discards scenarios that are inconsistent "at a glance", i.e. where P is a rigid property of the HEAD (resp. MODIFIER) and $\neg P$ is a rigid property of the MODIFIER (resp. HEAD). Moreover, similar potential conflicts among typical properties (e.g. P is a typical property of the MODIFIER whereas $\neg P$ is a typical property of the HEAD) are beforehand handled by means of suitable data structures;
- trivial scenarios are beforehand discarded;
- each scenario is equipped by a probability/score, computed by trying to assign a higher score to scenarios containing more properties, since they are considered more significant with statistic probability at hand;
- the user has the opportunity of choosing a scenario with a fixed number of properties for the combined genre rather than the one(s) with the higher probability/score.

As an example, consider the following prototype of genre Avant-garde:

$0.90 :: \mathbf{T}(AvantGarde) \sqsubseteq \neg Freedom$
$0.90 :: \mathbf{T}(AvantGarde) \sqsubseteq \neg Drammatic$
$0.90 :: \mathbf{T}(AvantGarde) \sqsubseteq TheCreativeSide$
$0.84 :: \mathbf{T}(AvantGarde) \sqsubseteq Cerebral$
$0.78 :: \mathbf{T}(AvantGarde) \sqsubseteq Uncompromising$
$0.78 :: \mathbf{T}(AvantGarde) \sqsubseteq Provocative$
$0.78 :: \mathbf{T}(AvantGarde) \sqsubseteq Revolutionary$
$0.78 :: \mathbf{T}(AvantGarde) \sqsubseteq ModernComposition$

The tool NERVOUS generates the prototype of the combined concept between Avant-garde (HEAD) and Blues (MODIFIER). The new, derived genre has the following $\mathbf{T}^{CL}$ description:

$$0.90 :: \mathbf{T}(AvantGarde \sqcap Blues) \sqsubseteq \neg DayDriving$$
$$0.90 :: \mathbf{T}(AvantGarde \sqcap Blues) \sqsubseteq RegionalBlues$$
$$0.86 :: \mathbf{T}(AvantGarde \sqcap Blues) \sqsubseteq Earthy$$
$$0.86 :: \mathbf{T}(AvantGarde \sqcap Blues) \sqsubseteq Gritty$$
$$0.82 :: \mathbf{T}(AvantGarde \sqcap Blues) \sqsubseteq Passionate$$
$$0.82 :: \mathbf{T}(AvantGarde \sqcap Blues) \sqsubseteq LateNight$$
$$0.76 :: \mathbf{T}(AvantGarde \sqcap Blues) \sqsubseteq HangingOut$$
$$0.90 :: \mathbf{T}(AvantGarde \sqcap Blues) \sqsubseteq \neg Freedom$$
$$0.90 :: \mathbf{T}(AvantGarde \sqcap Blues) \sqsubseteq \neg Dramatic$$

Rigid properties of basic concepts, if any, would be inherited by the derived concept too.

5   The Tool NERVOUS: Reclassifications and Recommendations

The tool NERVOUS is also able to reclassify songs of AllMusic within the novel derived genres. As mentioned, each song is equipped by some information available in AllMusic: NERVOUS extracts such information and then it computes a score, in order to compare them with the properties of a derived genre. Scores are provided by the portal users, who can mark each property of each song. All the metadata extracted by the crawler are stored in a JSON file.

Given a song m and a genre $Genre$, for each property C of m itself, the tool NERVOUS computes a score of compatibility of m with respect to $Genre$: intuitively, this is obtained as the combination of the frequencies of "compatible" concepts, i.e. concepts belonging to both the song and the prototypical description of the genre. More in detail, NERVOUS checks whether the property C is either a rigid or a typical property of the prototype of $Genre$: if this is the case, the score of the song is incremented by a positive number (1 in case of a rigid property, otherwise the product of the probability $f_{Genre,C}$ and the score of C in m). If $\neg C$ belongs to the typical properties of $Genre$, similarly the score is updated by a negative number. NERVOUS re-classifies the song m in the novel genre $Genre$ if the score so obtained is higher than 0, then it suggests the set of classified contents, in a descending order of compatibility.

Definition 4. *Given a song m, let $DerivedGenre$ be a derived genre as defined in Sect. 3 and let $\mathcal{S}_m$ be the set of properties occurring in the description of m and, given a concept $C \in \mathcal{S}_m$, let s_{m_C} be the score of C in the description of m. We define the score (rank) of compatibility as $r = \sum_{C \in \mathcal{S}_m} \theta_{C_{m,Genre}}$, where:*

- $\theta_{C_{m,Genre}} = p \times s_{m_C}$, *if* $p :: \mathbf{T}(Genre) \sqsubseteq C \in \mathcal{K}_C$
- $\theta_{C_{m,Genre}} = 1$, *if* $Genre \sqsubseteq C \in \mathcal{K}_C$
- $\theta_{C_{m,Genre}} = -p \times s_{m_C}$, *if* $p :: \mathbf{T}(Genre) \sqsubseteq \neg C \in \mathcal{K}_C$
- $\theta_{C_{m,Genre}} = -999$, *if* $Genre \sqsubseteq \neg C \in \mathcal{K}_C$

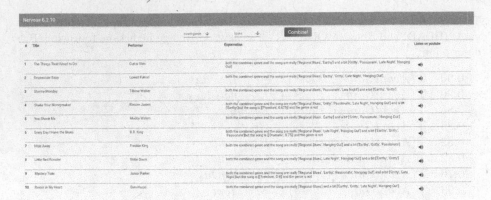

Fig. 2. A screenshot of the interface of NERVOUS.

As an example, consider the above derived genre *AvantGarde* ⊓ *Blues*, and the song "The Things That I Used to Do" by Guitar Slim. It is reclassified in the novel, generated genre *AvantGarde* ⊓ *Blues*, since its score is ... > 0. This song will be then recommended by NERVOUS, as it can be seen in Fig. 2, where a picture of NERVOUS's interface is shown. It is worth noticing that, in order to provide a "white-box" recommender system, each recommended song is equipped by an explanation, relying on the pipeline implemented by system of concept combination.

Let us conclude this section by observing that the fact that a recommended song belongs to both original, basic genres that have been combined is far from being obvious: indeed, the system NERVOUS suggests also the song "Moanin" by Art Blakey & the Jazz Messengers, which is classified by AllMusic as belonging to the genre Jazz. In our opinion, this is a further interesting mechanism providing the required component of surprise in the recommendation, justified by the fact that the description of the song matches the one of the novel genre, the last one only partially inheriting properties from the basic genres whose combination lead to such a new genre.

The tool NERVOUS is available at https://github.com/Mattia98779/Nervous. A preliminary version of a web interface is available at https://mattia98779.github.io/#/: by means of such a web interface, a user can select two basic genres and then obtain the list of suggested songs, together with an explanation.

6   Evaluation and Discussion

In this section we provide a preliminary evaluation of our tool NERVOUS. We have tested it in two different ways. The first evaluation is completely automatic and inheres the capability of the system of generating novel hybrid genres that are able to be populated by the original content of the AllMusic platform via a re-classification mechanism involving the 599 songs of the platform. In this case, the success criterion concerns the avoidance of the creation of empty boxes corresponding to the new generated combined genres. More in detail, at least 69 songs are re-classified by the tool NERVOUS for each derived music genre (the second genre containing "few" songs contains 138

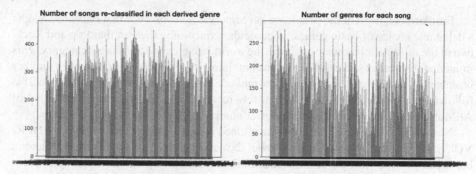

Fig. 3. Some statistics about the re-classification of NERVOUS.

items), with an average of 307 songs per derived genre. This is summarized in Fig. 3, picture in the left, whereas from the picture on the right we can observe that only 7 out of 599 songs on AllMusic (with very few attributes) are not re-classified in any genre by the system, whereas all the other ones (98.83%) are re-classified in at least one genre.

The second evaluation consisted in a user study involving 22 persons (11 females, 11 males, aged 14–72) that evaluated a total of 260 recommendations generated by the system. It is worth observing that this is one of the most commonly used methodology for the evaluation of recommender systems based on controlled small groups analysis [22]. The idea was to estimate the satisfaction of the potential users of the platform when exposed to the contents of the novel categories suggested by NERVOUS: all the participants were voluntary people using an availability sampling strategy. Participants were all naive to the experimental procedure and to the aims of the study. This evaluation was carried out as a classical *"one to one"* lab controlled experiment (i.e. one person at time with one expert interviewer) and we adopted a thinking aloud protocol, consisting in recording the verbal explanations provided by the people while executing a given laboratory task [16, 17]. In this setting, the users had to start the interview by indicating a couple of preferred genres among those available in AllMusic. This selection triggered both the activation of a novel hybrid prototypical genre by NERVOUS and the corresponding reclassification of the AllMusic songs based on such selection. The output of the system, pruned to show the top 10 best results, was then evaluated with a 1–10 voting scale expressing the satisfaction of the received recommendations.

The results we have obtained seem promising: the average score assigned by the users to the recommendations of the reclassified elements is 7.44 out of 10. This score was calculated by considering, for each new category, the score assigned to the top 10 reclassified songs, since they were provided, to the users, as recommendations for the novel genres.

It is worth observing that, in few cases, the creative classification performed by the tool NERVOUS has lead to counter-intuitive results. As an example, the song "I'm eighteen" by Alice Cooper, known as "The Godfather of Shock Rock", is classified as belonging to the derived genre result of the combination between Rap and Avant-garde. We strongly conjecture that these situations could be easily avoided by introducing constraints on some genres by means of rigid negated properties.

Furthermore, most of the people we have interviewed observed that AllMusic adopts a debatable choice of basic genres, in particular concerning the fact that Pop and Rock, two of the most popular music genres in the world, are grouped in a single category. This immediately implies some difficulties in combining its prototype with the one of another basic genre. Moreover, some of the (low ranked) items corresponded to old songs. This follows immediately from the fact that few recent songs belong to the highlights of AllMusic, since they have received a lower number of scores by the portal's users.

Notably the first two of the above mentioned issues are not directly related to NER-VOUS, since: i) the system can not know if the association description/item is coherent, but it just provides (for the recommended output) the correspondence already in place in AllMusic; ii) the recommendations of old editorial contents is based on the actual dataset of AllMusic (collecting about six hundred songs). This element can be overcome by simply adding an additional filter about the period preferences of the users.

7   Conclusions and Future Works

In this work we have presented NERVOUS, a knowledge-based system for the dynamic generation of novel contents about music, exploiting the reasoning mechanism of the logic $\mathbf{T}^{CL}$ in order to generate, reclassify and suggest novel content genres in the context of AllMusic, an online platform collecting in-depth information about music genres, albums, musicians and songs. The core component of the system NERVOUS relies on CoCoS, a tool for combining concepts in the logic $\mathbf{T}^{CL}$.

According to [23] recommender systems "try to identify the need and preferences of users, filter the huge collection of data accordingly and present the best suited option before the users by using some well-defined mechanism". The literature is rich of proposals, that we can partition in three main groups of recommender systems:

- collaborative filtering, which exploits similarities of usage patterns among mutually similar users;
- content-based filtering, which exploits content similarity;
- hybrid filtering, which combines the two approaches.

It is easy to observe that the tool NERVOUS could be considered an hybrid recommender system, since in its current form it makes use of content description as the input. However, it differs from the state of the art approaches since it exploits the reasoning power of a logic framework capable of representing new intuitive principles influencing user preferences and usage attitudes which cannot be derived from the pure analysis of content and/or the comparison of similar users.

The system NERVOUS has been tested in a twofold evaluation showing promising results for both the automatic evaluation and the user acceptability of the recommended items. With evaluation results at hand, we can observe that NERVOUS represents a good approach at addressing the very well known filter bubble effect [19], since it introduces mechanisms that add a sort of "plausible creativity" and a "reasonable serendipity" in content discovery by users.

In future research, we aim at extending our work in several directions. On the one hand, we aim at studying the application of optimization techniques in [1] in order to improve the efficiency of CoCoS and, as a consequence, of the proposed knowledge generation system. On the other hand, we aim at conducting a large scale experiment to further validate the effectiveness of the proposed approach, including people with sensory impairments, with the objective of promoting empathy, cohesion and inclusion across social groups, partially neglected by state-of-the-art recommender systems.

References

1. Alberti, M., Bellodi, E., Cota, G., Riguzzi, F., Zese, R.: cplint on SWISH: probabilistic logical inference with a web browser. Intelligenza Artificiale **11**(1), 47–64 (2017). https://doi.org/10.3233/IA-170106
2. Boden, M.A.: Creativity and artificial intelligence. Artif. Intell. **103**(1–2), 347–356 (1998)
3. Chiodino, E., Di Luccio, D., Lieto, A., Messina, A., Pozzato, G.L., Rubinetti, D.: A knowledge-based system for the dynamic generation and classification of novel contents in multimedia broadcasting. In: De Giacomo, G., et al., (eds.) ECAI 2020–24th European Conference on Artificial Intelligence, 29 August - 8 September 2020, Santiago de Compostela, Spain, 29 August - 8 September 2020. Frontiers in Artificial Intelligence and Applications, vol. 325, pp. 680–687. IOS Press (2020). https://doi.org/10.3233/FAIA200154
4. Frixione, M., Lieto, A.: Representing and reasoning on typicality in formal ontologies. In: Ghidini, C., Ngomo, A.N., Lindstaedt, S.N., Pellegrini, T. (eds.) Proceedings of the 7th International Conference on Semantic Systems, pp. 119–125. ACM International Conference Proceeding Series, ACM (2011). https://doi.org/10.1145/2063518.2063534
5. Giordano, L., Gliozzi, V., Olivetti, N., Pozzato, G.L.: Semantic characterization of rational closure: from propositional logic to description logics. Artif. Intell. **226**, 1–33 (2015). https://doi.org/10.1016/j.artint.2015.05.001
6. Hampton, J.A.: Inheritance of attributes in natural concept conjunctions. Memory Cognition **15**(1), 55–71 (1987)
7. Lehmann, D., Magidor, M.: What does a conditional knowledge base entail? Artif. Intell. **55**(1), 1–60 (1992). https://doi.org/10.1016/0004-3702(92)90041-U
8. Lieto, A., Perrone, F., Pozzato, G.L., Chiodino, E.: Beyond subgoaling: a dynamic knowledge generation framework for creative problem solving in cognitive architectures. Cogn. Syst. Res. **58**, 305–316 (2019). https://doi.org/10.1016/j.cogsys.2019.08.005
9. Lieto, A., Pozzato, G.L.: A description logic of typicality for conceptual combination. In: Ceci, M., Japkowicz, N., Liu, J., Papadopoulos, G.A., Raś, Z.W. (eds.) ISMIS 2018. LNCS (LNAI), vol. 11177, pp. 189–199. Springer, Cham (2018). https://doi.org/10.1007/978-3-030-01851-1_19
10. Lieto, A., Pozzato, G.L.: A description logic framework for commonsense conceptual combination integrating typicality, probabilities and cognitive heuristics. J. Exp. Theor. Artif. Intell. **32**(5), 769–804 (2020). https://doi.org/10.1080/0952813X.2019.1672799
11. Lieto, A., Pozzato, G.L., Perrone, F.: A dynamic knowledge generation system for cognitive agents. In: 31st IEEE International Conference on Tools with Artificial Intelligence, ICTAI 2019, Portland, OR, USA, 4–6 November 2019, pp. 676–681. IEEE (2019). https://doi.org/10.1109/ICTAI.2019.00099
12. Lieto, A., Pozzato, G.L., Perrone, F., Chiodino, E.: Knowledge capturing via conceptual reframing: a goal-oriented framework for knowledge invention. In: Proceedings of the 10th ACM Conference on Knowledge Capture, K-CAP 2019, Marina del Rey, pp. 109–114. ACM (2019)

13. Lieto, A., Pozzato, G.L., Striani, M., Zoia, S., Damiano, R.: Degari 2.0: a diversity-seeking, explainable, and affective art recommender for social inclusion. Cognitive Syst. Res. **77**, 1–17 (2023). https://doi.org/10.1016/j.cogsys.2022.10.001, https://www.sciencedirect.com/science/article/pii/S1389041722000456
14. Lieto, A., Pozzato, G.L., Valese, A.: COCOS: a typicality based concept combination system. In: Felli, P., Montali, M. (eds.) Proceedings of the 33rd Italian Conference on Computational Logic, Bolzano, Italy, 20–22 September 2018. CEUR Workshop Proceedings, vol. 2214, pp. 55–59. CEUR-WS.org (2018). https://ceur-ws.org/Vol-2214/paper6.pdf
15. Lieto, A., Pozzato, G.L., Zoia, S., Patti, V., Damiano, R.: A commonsense reasoning framework for explanatory emotion attribution, generation and re-classification. Knowl.-Based Syst. **227**, 107166 (2021)
16. Newell, A., Shaw, J.C., Simon, H.A.: Report on a general problem solving program. In: IFIP Congress, vol. 256, p. 64. Pittsburgh, PA (1959)
17. Newell, A., Simon, H.A.: Human Problem Solving, vol. 104, n. 9. Prentice-Hall, Englewood Cliffs (1972)
18. Osherson, D.N., Smith, E.E.: On the adequacy of prototype theory as a theory of concepts. Cognition **9**(1), 35–58 (1981)
19. Parisier, E.: The Filter Bubble: What the Internet Is Hiding from You (2012)
20. Riguzzi, F., Bellodi, E., Lamma, E., Zese, R.: Probabilistic description logics under the distribution semantics. Semant. Web **6**(5), 477–501 (2015). https://doi.org/10.3233/SW-140154
21. Riguzzi, F., Bellodi, E., Lamma, E., Zese, R.: Reasoning with probabilistic ontologies. In: Yang, Q., Wooldridge, M. (eds.) Proceedings of IJCAI 2015, pp. 4310–4316. AAAI Press (2015). https://ijcai.org/proceedings/2015
22. Shani, G., Gunawardana, A.: Evaluating recommendation systems. In: Ricci, F., Rokach, L., Shapira, B., Kantor, P.B. (eds.) Recommender Systems Handbook, pp. 257–297. Springer, Boston, MA (2011). https://doi.org/10.1007/978-0-387-85820-3_8
23. Sohail, S.S., Siddiqui, J., Ali, R.: Classifications of recommender systems: a review. Eng. Sci. Technol. Rev. **10**(4), 132–153 (2017)

Why Can Neural Networks Recognize Us by Our Finger Movements?

Elena Mariolina Galdi[1(✉)], Marco Alberti[2], Alessandro D'Ausilio[3], and Alice Tomassini[4]

[1] Dipartimento di Ingegneria, Universitá di Ferrara, Ferrara, Italy
elenamarioli.galdi@edu.unife.it
[2] Dipartimento di Matematica e Informatica, Universitá di Ferrara, Ferrara, Italy
marco.alberti@unife.it
[3] Dipartimento di Neuroscienze e Riabilitazione, Universitá di Ferrara, Ferrara, Italy
alessandro.dausilio@unife.it
[4] Istituto Italiano di Tecnologia, Ferrara, Italy
alice.tomassini@iit.it

Abstract. Neurobehavioral evidence suggests that human movement may be characterized by relatively stable individual differences (i.e. individual motor signatures or IMS). While most research has focused on the macroscopic level, all attempts to extract IMS have overlooked the fact that functionally relevant discontinuities are clearly visible when zooming into the microstructure of movements. These recurrent (2–3 Hz) speed breaks (sub-movements) reflect an intermittent motor control policy that might provide a far more robust way to identify IMSs.

In this study, we show that individuals can be recognized from motion capture data using a neural network. In particular, we trained a classifier (a convolutional neural network) on a data set composed of time series recording the positions of index finger movements of 60 individuals; in tests, the neural network achieves an accuracy of 80%.

We also investigated how different pre-processing techniques affect the accuracy in order to assess which motion features more strongly characterize each individual and, in particular, whether the presence of submovements in the data can improve the classifier's performance.

Keywords: Explainable AI · Convolutional neural networks · Motion capture · Movement analysis · Individual motor signature

1 Introduction

The possibility of recognizing an individual on the basis of his/her movements or gestures has been studied in depth in the past years due to its significant applications in the security and medical areas. Many researches focused on whole-body

This work was partly supported by the University of Ferrara FIRD 2022 project "Analisi di serie temporali da motion capture con tecniche di machine learning".

movements such as gait [22, 23] and most of these analyzed two dimensional input as images or videos. Gohar [14] proposed the use of Inertial Measurement Units or IMU to identify individuals based on gait. The reason for this different approach, namely, a one-dimensional time series instead of two-dimensional image analysis, lies in the fact that "image-based gait analysis often fails to extract quality measurements of an individual's motion patterns owing to problems related to variations in viewpoint, illumination (daylight), clothing, worn accessories, etc." [14]. The latter study showed that individuals could be identified based on an analysis of their gait with considerable accuracy (approximately 75%).

However, whole-body data may not be available for person identification in many applications. In addition, very little research has been devoted to investigating individual motor signatures during distal hand movement. The objective of our research is to investigate whether it is possible to identify a subject from the simplest possible movement (i.e., index finger extension and flexion) using a convolutional neural network (CNN). Although CNNs were initially proposed to classify images [17–19, 32], the choice of a CNN for multiclass classification, even with time series tasks, has been shown to be effective [8, 10, 34].

The data we used derive from a recent neuroscience project on interpersonal behavioral coordination across multiple temporal scales [30]. This study was aimed at investigating whether the recurrent discontinuities that characterize the microstructure of human movement composition (tiny recorrective speed-bumps in the range of 2–3 Hz which are often called sub-movements), are finely co-regulated when participants are required to synchronize at the macroscopic scale only. The experimental settings and their speed profile are shown in Fig. 1. The goal of the present work is very different and we thus adopt a radically different analytical approach. In fact, we here investigated whether these microscopic movement characteristics can be used for the identification of individual movement fingerprints.

In our research, we first wanted to determine whether finger movements contain sufficient information to allow the neural network to recognize the individual who generated the movements. In addition, we intend to carry out an in-depth post-hoc interpretation [24] of our results to understand the movement characteristics that are more relevant for identification. This latter goal is fully in line with the current interest in explainable artificial intelligence (XAI) [1, 26]. The reasons that led to the emergence of this research field have to be found in the necessity of providing an explanation before making any decision informed by an aseptic algorithm. In medical applications, a reasonable explanation is sometimes more important than a correct diagnosis [2, 11, 15]. The same applies to the security domain [9], and considering the implications of recognizing the identity of an individual from minimal bodily movements, it is self-evident how important explainability should be. The European GDPR makes this point very clear, considering that there are more than one article (13–15, 22) that focus on the importance of correctly motivating the decisions and forecasts made by any automated decision-making process [28]. XAI in machine learning is a well known problem [4, 5, 7, 13, 31], which has received significant attention also in the field of Deep Learning [3, 20, 24].

Samek [27] provided an extensive description of this field and the tools developed for it. Simic [29] reviewed XAI methods for neural time-series classification, highlighting the class activation maps method or CAM [35], which was also used by Goodfellow [15]. Nevertheless, we explored a simpler path that, based on neurophysiological knowledge of the multiscale nature of human movements [30], grants easier and more straightforward interpretability. To investigate which movement features (i.e. temporal scales) are more relevant for the neural network, we decided to decompose the time series on the basis of their spectral content and we evaluated their impact of this and other key preprocessing choices on recognition accuracy. To the best of our knowledge, there is no evidence in the literature on a similar analytic approach to solving an analogous problem (i.e., person identification from minimal kinematic data). Instead, time-series analysis in the frequency domain is standard in speech technologies [12]. In particular, we show which frequencies produce the largest impact on the ability of a CNN to recognize individuals from the movement of their finger.

The remainder of this paper is organized as follows. The experimental settings are described in Sect. 2. We show the most significant experimental results in Sect. 3. We conclude the paper (Sect. 4) with a discussion of the results and possible directions for future research.

2 Experimental Settings

In this section, after a brief introduction to the dataset we worked on (Sect. 2.1), we explain our application's architecture (Sect. 2.2). Then, we will deepen into two main parts: first, we list the preprocessing techniques we chose (Sect. 2.3) as series segmentation, series filtering, and series normalization; in the second part, the neural network model (Sect. 2.4) is described.

2.1 Dataset

The dataset we have been working on comes from previous research; all experimental instrumentation is described in depth in [30]. In total, 60 participants, forming 30 couples, performed a movement synchronization task. As shown in Fig. 1, participants were asked to keep their right index fingers pointing toward each other (without touching) and perform rhythmic flexion-extension movements around the metacarpophalangeal joint as synchronously as possible, either in-phase (toward the same direction) or anti-phase (toward opposite directions). Participants were instructed to maintain a slow movement pace (full movement cycle: single flexion/extension movements) by having them practice in a preliminary phase with a reference metronome set at 0.25 Hz. Each participant also performed the same finger movements alone (solo condition) with the only requirement of complying with the instructed pace (0.25 Hz). Finger movements were recorded using retroreflective markers tracked by a 3D real-time motion capture system (Vicon), providing continuous kinematic data sampled at 300

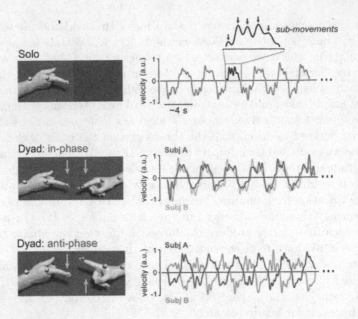

Fig. 1. On the left, the experimental setup for data collection. From top to bottom, there are three settings for the solo, in-phase, and anti-phase tasks. The right panel shows the speed profile for the three different cases. Figure granted by the research of Tomassini et al. [30]

Hz. Each trial had a duration of 2,5 min for a total of 45000 points for each time series. In addition, each of the three different experiments (solo, dyadic in-phase, dyadic antiphase) was repeated twice. This means that for each subject, we had six series, each made of 45000 points. As the first approximation, in this work, we considered that the finger movement was essentially only in one dimension along the x-axis.

To augment our dataset, we segmented each series. As we will describe later in Sect. 2.3, we decided to test two different types of cutting: cutting at the maximum of the position data in order to have a complete movement (index extension and flexion), and cutting sub-series with fixed length with a specified gap smaller than the subseries dimension. Considering natural movement variability, the first choice further requires a resizing of the subseries because the convolutional network needs all inputs with the same dimension. The second method was used by Yang [33] to segment the time-series signal into a collection of shorter pieces.

To investigate which movement features (i.e., temporal scales) are more relevant for the neural network, we decomposed the time series based on their spectral content. In particular, we applied different types of filters and studied their influence on the output accuracy of the CNN.

Two different type of filtering operations have been investigated: moving average window and band-pass frequency filter. The two techniques are described in Sect. 2.3.

Another important variable is related to the choice of applying or not a normalization to our signal, see Sect. 2.3.

Finally, we decided to investigate if differentiating the signal would provide different information. Thus, we investigated the accuracy of our neural networks with different types of inputs, namely, position, speed, and acceleration data.

2.2   Application Architecture

We decided to develop our AI program with Python. The software was essentially split in two main components: a first module assigned to the preprocessing, a second module for the neural network model.

The first module as described in Sect. 2.1, has a composite structure with different possible choices to preprocess the data and different parameters to set. As shown in Fig. 2, it is possible to independently choose the series type, filter method, type of segmentation, and whether the series must be normalized. Depending on the choice made, it is necessary to specify different input parameters. Table 1 lists the different parameters required for each pre-processing choice. Once the data preprocessing has been completed, the segmented series are sent

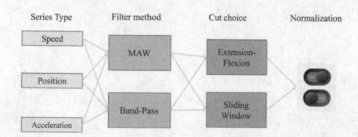

Fig. 2. Modular structure: *Series Type* = Speed, Position, Acceleration; *Filter Methods* = MAW (Moving Average Window), Band Pass Frequency Filter; *Cut Choice* = Complete movement (extension + flexion), Fixed Dimension Windows sliding with known gap

Table 1. Parameters needed in function of different choices

Choice	Parameter
MAW	Window dimension
Band pass	Low and high frequency cut
Extension-flexion	Resized subseries dimension
Sliding window	Subseries dimesion and gap

to the neural network. The TensorFlow Keras library was used to generate the neural network model. A Convolutional Neural Network (CNN) as been built for multiclass classification. It's known that CNN is the most suitable architecture for classifying data among more classes. Usually, it is applied to 2D input data (i.e., images) [16,17] but it also shows good results for 1D input (i.e., time-series data) [14].

2.3   Preprocessing Techniques

Series Cut. We considered two different methods to cut the series. As a first approach, we cut the time series corresponding to the maximum finger positions on the x-axis. In this way, each sub-series represents the complete movement, extension, and flexion of the index finger (see Fig. 3. This type of cutting is functionally defined, and each subseries contains information about the entire movement. However, this type of cut creates a subset of different lengths that cannot be directly used as an input to a CNN. This means that we had to resize the subseries using the TimeSeriesResampler component from the Python library tslearn.preprocessing. Figure 3 shows the result of resizing on different subseries.

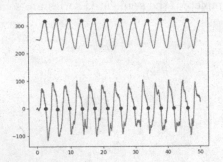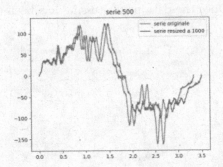

Fig. 3. On the left: the blue line represents the position in function of time while the orange line is the derived speed; with the red spot, we highlighted where the cut was operated, which corresponds to the maximum finger positions. **On the right:** the effect of resizing after cutting on functionally defined kinematic landmarks; the blue line is the original time-series and the orange one is the resized (Color figure online)

The second option to cut the time series is to decide a priori the dimension of the subseries we want to obtain and the gap between the following two subseries, as shown in Fig. 4. We applied this method to investigate whether there was any hidden information in the time series that was not locked to the entire movement cycle (extension-flexion). However, we have identified two main issues with this method. First, the dataset increases exponentially with a significant increase in program execution times. The second point was that, whereas in the previous case, we had the whole set of sub-series and we could randomly choose the data for training and testing, in this case, to avoid overlapping of the data, we had to cut the main series into two parts: the first 75% for the training set and the last 25% for testing. Consequently, we cannot exclude the possibility that the data organized in such a way is not biased in some ways.

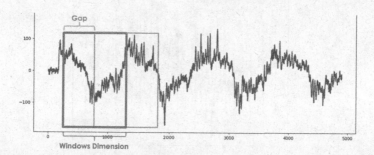

Fig. 4. Time series example with highlighted the sliding windows and gaps to shows how the second segmentation strategy was done.

Series Filtering. We also investigated the influence of the filtering time series. Therefore, we applied two different types of filters to our data.

Moving Average Window (MAW), is a very basic tool commonly used in time series to smooth signals. For each point of the set, a fixed number of subsequent points was averaged, and the result replaced the starting point. Obviously, we obtain different signals depending on the dimension of the window in which we calculate the average (see Fig. 5); the larger it is, the smoother the signal will be.

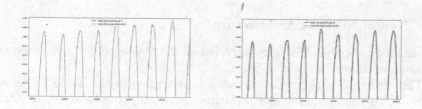

Fig. 5. Result of MAW with different windows dimension.

We also analyzed the effects of different **frequency filters** on the accuracy of the CNN. Essentially, we created a band-pass filter where we could set low and high frequencies. We created a Butterworth filter using the predefined function in Python's scipy. signal library, with the order set at 4. Thus, it is possible to set low and high frequencies. If the low-frequency cut was set to 0, it was applied as a low-pass filter (Fig. 6).

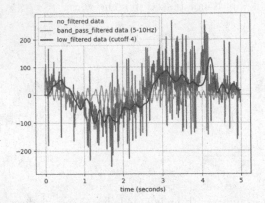

Fig. 6. Effect of different types of filters on the raw speed's time series.

Series Normalization. As a final step, we explored the effect of normalization on our dataset in terms of accuracy gains. In general, we know that when the data have a comparable scale, as in our case where the movement and its rhythm are predefined, the normalization does not improve the accuracy because it can destroy important information hidden in the dataset. Nevertheless, we performed experiments with and without normalization. To set the range of values within which we calculated the maximum and minimum of the normalization, we considered the entire series.

2.4   Neural Network Architecture

We decided to apply a CNN, as suggested in the literature, for multi-class classification of time series data [8,10,34].

The structure of the neural network is described in the Table 2. We used RMSprop as the optimizer and performed early stopping to avoid overfitting. We compared the results obtained with this neural network with a similar network made with a pytorch instead of tensorflow.keras. The results of these two networks are very similar.

Table 2. CDNN model.

1D convolution
Kernel: 3@64 ActFunct: ReLU
1D convolution
Kernel: 3@64 ActFunct: ReLU
1D max pooling
Pool size: 2
1D convolution
Kernel: 3@64 ActFunct: ReLU
1D convolution
Kernel: 3@64 ActFunct: ReLU
1D max Pooling
Pool size: 2
Dense
Dense
Softmax

3 Results

To evaluate the impact of different parameters on recognition performance, we examined the accuracy of our CNN. First, we show how accuracy is affected by the choice of the type of time series (see Table 3 below).

Table 3. The accuracy for the different series types was calculated using a low-pass filter set at 50 Hz and cut based on the maximum finger position.

Series's type	w Norm	w/o Norm
Position	2%	35%
Speed	69%	71%
Acceleration	2%	65%

It's evident the improvement of the accuracy for the acceleration and position once the normalization is applied. Nevertheless, the accuracy of the speed data was still the highest; therefore, it was used as a reference for the following experiments.

The experiment comparing the two types of series segmentation doesn't show significant differences in terms of accuracy, while the computational time was drastically longer when the data was cut with **sliding windows**. This convinced us to choose the **cut at the maximum finger position** as the standard segmentation method for our series.

MAW, as shown in Fig. 7, has a maximum performance at 0 or when no moving average has actually been applied. By increasing the dimension of its window, its accuracy decreased until it reached 30% with a 100 points window. Remember that when the MAW windows include 100 points, only the main shape of the movement is visible (see Fig. 5).

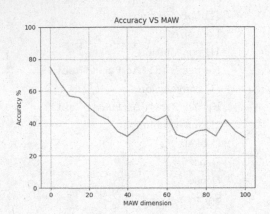

Fig. 7. The figure shows how the accuracy changed as a function of the number of points included in the moving average.

Figure 8 report how the accuracy changes with different **Frequency Filters**. As we can clearly see the fundamental frequency (i.e., 0.25 Hz or the instructed finger flexion-extension rhythm) is the most meaningful frequency and if we remove it from our signal no recognition can be done. The fact that each individual is characterized by their own preferred (self-paced) tapping tempo is well known in neurophysiology literature [25]. In addition, our experiments show that it is clear that this frequency alone is not sufficient, and the accuracy increases as we add more frequencies. Interestingly, in neurophysiology, it is well known [6] that in movement, albeit with the differences that may exist between moving a finger or leg, frequencies above 15 Hz begin to be attenuated. From to 20–30 onwards, there is no physiological relevance anymore. Instead, in our experiments, we still see further increases when adding frequencies above 30 Hz, which means that the network is still learning something. Future in-depth analysis will have to investigate what our neural network is learning in the range of 30 Hz to 70 Hz. More importantly, at 20 Hz, the accuracy is already 65%, which is a very good performance for classification among the 60 classes.

If look at Fig. 9 we can see the results obtained by applying a frequency domain filter and a simple MAW. We can see that we have similar results with a 1 Hz band low-pass filter and an MAW with a window of 100 points (approximately 30% accuracy). Instead, if we did not apply any MAW or filter, or we used a low-pass filter with a band higher than 60 Hz, we found a maximum accuracy of approximately 75%. Because one of our initial goals was to investigate the role of sub-movements in defining individual motor signatures, we focused our attention

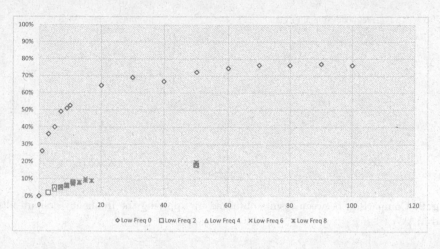

Fig. 8. In the figure, it is reported how the accuracy changes for different band pass filters: each curve corresponds to a filter with a specific low-frequency cut (0 Hz, 2 Hz, 4 Hz, 6 Hz, 8 Hz), while in the x-axis, the high-frequency cut is reported.

on the 2–4 Hz frequencies in Fig. 10. Although we did not notice any significant variation in the accuracy for the bandpass filter with a low cut at 2 Hz and a high cut at 4 Hz, we could clearly observe a significant slope increase for the low-pass filter around these frequencies. As explained earlier, the fundamental frequency (0.25 Hz) probably contained most of the information (less than 30% accuracy). However, the performance is far from its plateau; rather, the model largely improves by adding the sub-movement range. Future research should further investigate this aspect.

4 Discussion

The proposed work demonstrates that it is possible to recognize subjects by starting from their index finger movements. Interestingly, we achieved the same accuracy obtained by Gohar [14] even if he worked with human gait instead of finger movement.

In addition we found that the fundamental frequency is undoubtedly the pivotal aspect in the recognition of subjects, but not alone. Higher frequencies contribute significantly to an increase in accuracy, but only in the presence of fundamental frequency. For instance, we have not yet explained the gap we have from the 30% accuracy obtained with the fundamental frequency only, and 75% obtained with a low-pass filter with a bandwidth of 60–70 Hz (Fig. 11).

At this point of the research, it is not yet fully demonstrated whether sub-movements play a central role in the recognition process, but we have some clues. The slope of the accuracy curve may provide some hints for future investigations. It is possible to design more targeted experiments to investigate a range of frequencies with greater granularity. However, this work had to first

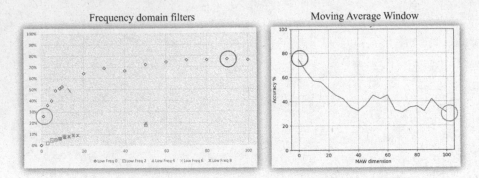

Fig. 9. Comparison between results obtained by applying the frequency-domain filter and MAW.

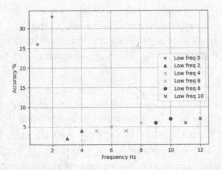

Fig. 10. The figure shows the accuracy of the band-pass filter with different low-frequency cut (0 Hz, 2 Hz, 4 Hz, 6 Hz, 8 Hz).

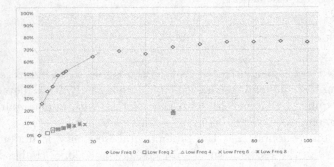

Fig. 11. The figure shows that the accuracy increases as the frequencies change. In particular, the slope in the accuracy from 0 to 4 Hz is shown in red, and that from 6 to 20 Hz is shown in blue. (Color figure online)

test several design choices, such as data type, segmentation, normalization, or filtering strategy, which, as we demonstrated here, have a dramatic impact on model performance. After all these tests, we can say that our approach, with few key design choices, has an interesting potential in recognizing individual motor signatures. In our future work, we will build from this work to better investigate the role of the different time scales of movement composition to differentiate and explore the interaction between macro- and microscopic movement features in defining individual movement fingerprints. Moreover, we do not exclude the possibility of answering this question by applying more structured tools such as class activation maps [35], or a clustering method based on PLif, as suggested by Li [21] in order to determine which other signal characteristics affect CNN classification the most.

References

1. Adadi, A., Berrada, M.: Peeking inside the black-box: a survey on explainable artificial intelligence (XAI). IEEE Access **6**, 52138–52160 (2018). https://doi.org/10.1109/ACCESS.2018.2870052
2. Ahmad, M.A., Eckert, C., Teredesai, A.: Interpretable machine learning in healthcare. In: Proceedings of the 2018 ACM International Conference on Bioinformatics, Computational Biology, and Health Informatics, BCB 2018, pp. 559–560. Association for Computing Machinery, New York (2018). https://doi.org/10.1145/3233547.3233667
3. Assaf, R., Schumann, A.: Explainable deep neural networks for multivariate time series predictions. In: Proceedings of the Twenty-Eighth International Joint Conference on Artificial Intelligence, pp. 6488–6490. International Joint Conferences on Artificial Intelligence Organization, Macao (2019). https://doi.org/10.24963/ijcai.2019/932
4. Baehrens, D., Schroeter, T., Harmeling, S., Kawanabe, M., Hansen, K.: How to explain individual classification decisions, p. 29 (2010)
5. Burkart, N., Huber, M.F.: A survey on the explainability of supervised machine learning. J. Artif. Intell. Res. **70**, 245–317 (2021). https://doi.org/10.1613/jair.1.12228
6. Burke, R.E.: Motor units: anatomy, physiology, and functional organization, pp. 345–422. Wiley (2011). https://doi.org/10.1002/cphy.cp010210, https://onlinelibrary.wiley.com/doi/abs/10.1002/cphy.cp010210
7. Burrell, J.: How the machine 'thinks': understanding opacity in machine learning algorithms. Big Data Soc. **3**(1), 205395171562251 (2016). https://doi.org/10.1177/2053951715622512
8. Cui, Z., Chen, W., Chen, Y.: Multi-scale convolutional neural networks for time series classification (2016)
9. Ernst, C.: Artificial intelligence and autonomy: self-determination in the age of automated systems. In: Wischmeyer, T., Rademacher, T. (eds.) Regulating Artificial Intelligence, pp. 53–73. Springer, Cham (2020). https://doi.org/10.1007/978-3-030-32361-5_3
10. Ismail Fawaz, H., Forestier, G., Weber, J., Idoumghar, L., Muller, P.-A.: Deep learning for time series classification: a review. Data Min. Knowl. Disc. **33**(4), 917–963 (2019). https://doi.org/10.1007/s10618-019-00619-1
11. Foster, K.R., Koprowski, R., Skufca, J.D.: Machine learning, medical diagnosis, and biomedical engineering research - commentary. Biomed. Eng. Online **13**(1), 94 (2014). https://doi.org/10.1186/1475-925X-13-94

12. Gee, A.H., Garcia-Olano, D., Ghosh, J., Paydarfar, D.: Explaining deep classification of time-series data with learned prototypes, p. 8 (2019)
13. Gilpin, L.H., Bau, D., Yuan, B.Z., Bajwa, A., Specter, M., Kagal, L.: Explaining explanations: an overview of interpretability of machine learning. In: 2018 IEEE 5th International Conference on Data Science and Advanced Analytics (DSAA), pp. 80–89 (2018). https://doi.org/10.1109/DSAA.2018.00018
14. Gohar, I., et al.: Person re-identification using deep modeling of temporally correlated inertial motion patterns. Sensors 20(3), 949 (2020). https://doi.org/10.3390/s20030949
15. Goodfellow, S.D., Goodwin, A., Greer, R., Laussen, P.C., Mazwi, M., Eytan, D.: Towards understanding ECG rhythm classification using convolutional neural networks and attention mappings, p. 18 (2018)
16. Heenaye-Mamode Khan, M., et al.: Multi- class classification of breast cancer abnormalities using deep convolutional neural network (CNN). PLOS One 16(8), 1–15 (2021). https://doi.org/10.1371/journal.pone.0256500
17. Hu, Y., Sokolova, M.: Convolutional neural networks in multi-class classification of medical data, p. 13 (2020)
18. Kim, Y.: Convolutional neural networks for sentence classification (2014)
19. LeCun, Y., et al.: Backpropagation applied to handwritten zip code recognition. Neural Comput. 1(4), 541–551 (1989). https://doi.org/10.1162/neco.1989.1.4.541
20. Leventi-Peetz, A.M., Östreich, T.: Deep learning reproducibility and explainable AI (XAI) (2022)
21. Li, L., Prakash, B.A., Faloutsos, C.: Parsimonious linear fingerprinting for time series. Proc. VLDB Endow. 3(1–2), 385–396 (2010). https://doi.org/10.14778/1920841.1920893
22. Little, J.J., Boyd, J.E.: Recognizing people by their gait: the shape of motion, p. 33 (1998)
23. Park, G., Lee, K.M., Koo, S.: Uniqueness of gait kinematics in a cohort study. Sci. Rep. 11(1), 15248 (2021). https://doi.org/10.1038/s41598-021-94815-z
24. Preece, A.: Asking 'Why' in AI: explainability of intelligent systems – perspectives and challenges. Intell. Syst. Account. Financ. Manage. 25(2), 63–72 (2018). https://doi.org/10.1002/isaf.1422
25. Repp, B.H., Su, Y.-H.: Sensorimotor synchronization: a review of recent research (2006–2012). Psychon. Bull. Rev. 20(3), 403–452 (2013). https://doi.org/10.3758/s13423-012-0371-2
26. Ribeiro, M.T., Singh, S., Guestrin, C.: "Why should i trust you?": explaining the predictions of any classifier (2016)
27. Samek, W., Montavon, G., Lapuschkin, S., Anders, C.J., Müller, K.R.: Explaining deep neural networks and beyond: a review of methods and applications. Proc. IEEE 109(3), 247–278 (2021). https://doi.org/10.1109/JPROC.2021.3060483
28. Selbst, A.D., Powles, J.: Meaningful information and the right to explanation. Int. Data Priv. Law 7(4), 233–242 (2017). https://doi.org/10.1093/idpl/ipx022
29. Šimić, I., Sabol, V., Veas, E.: XAI methods for neural time series classification: a brief review (2021)
30. Tomassini, A., et al.: Interpersonal synchronization of movement intermittency. iScience 25(4), 104096 (2022). https://doi.org/10.1016/j.isci.2022.104096
31. Vale, D., El-Sharif, A., Ali, M.: Explainable artificial intelligence (XAI) post-hoc explainability methods: risks and limitations in non-discrimination law. AI Ethics (2022). https://doi.org/10.1007/s43681-022-00142-y

32. Woan Ching, S.L., et al.: Multiclass convolution neural network for classification of COVID-19 CT images. Comput. Intell. Neurosci. **2022**, 1–15 (2022). https://doi.org/10.1155/2022/9167707

33. Yang, J.B., Nguyen, M.N., San, P.P., Li, X.L., Krishnaswamy, S.: Deep convolutional neural networks on multichannel time series for human activity recognition, p. 7 (2015)

34. Zheng, Y., Liu, Q., Chen, E., Ge, Y., Zhao, J.L.: Time series classification using multi-channels deep convolutional neural networks. In: Li, F., Li, G., Hwang, S., Yao, B., Zhang, Z. (eds.) WAIM 2014. LNCS, vol. 8485, pp. 298–310. Springer, Cham (2014). https://doi.org/10.1007/978-3-319-08010-9_33

35. Zhou, B., Khosla, A., Lapedriza, A., Oliva, A., Torralba, A.: Learning deep features for discriminative localization. In: 2016 IEEE Conference on Computer Vision and Pattern Recognition (CVPR), pp. 2921–2929 (2016). https://doi.org/10.1109/CVPR.2016.319

Miscellany

Labelled Sequent Calculi for Conditional Logics: Conditional Excluded Middle and Conditional Modus Ponens Finally Together

Nicola Olivetti[1], Nikola Panic[2], and Gian Luca Pozzato[2(✉)] ⓘ

[1] Aix Marseille Université, CNRS, ENSAM, Université de Toulon,
LSIS UMR 7296, Marseille, France
nicola.olivetti@univ-amu.fr
[2] Dipartimento di Informatica, Università di Torino, Turin, Italy
nikola.panic@edu.unito.it, gianluca.pozzato@unito.it

Abstract. We introduce labelled sequent calculi for Conditional Logics with a selection function semantics. Conditional Logics are a sort of generalization of multimodal logics where modalities are labelled by formulas of the same language. Recently, they received a renewed attention and have found several applications in knowledge representation and artificial intelligence. In a previous work, we have considered the basic system CK and extensions with well known conditions ID, MP, CS and CEM, with the exception of those admitting both conditions CEM and MP, obtaining labelled sequent calculi called SeqS. Here we provide calculi for the whole cube of the extensions of CK generated by the above axioms, including also those with both CEM and MP: the basic idea is that of replacing the rule dealing with CEM in SeqS, which performs a label substitutions in both its premises, by a new one that avoids such a substitution and adopts a conditional formula on the right-hand side of a sequent as its principal formula. We have also implemented the proposed calculi in Prolog following the "lean" methodology, then we have tested the performances of the new prover, called CondLean2022, and compared them with those of CondLean, an implementation of SeqS, on the common systems. The performances of CondLean2022 are promising and seem to be better than those of CondLean, witnessing that the proposed calculi also provide a more efficient theorem prover for Conditional Logics.

1 Introduction

Conditional Logics have a long history, starting with the seminal works by [5,17,18,24], and [4] in the seventies. Recently, Conditional Logics have found a renewed interest in several fields of artificial intelligence and knowledge representation, from hypothetical reasoning to belief revision, from diagnosis to nonmonotonic reasoning and planning [6,8–16,23].

Conditional Logics are extensions of classical logic by a binary operator $\Rightarrow$, called *conditional operator*, used in order to express conditional formulas of the form $A \Rightarrow B$. Similarly to modal logics, the semantics of Conditional Logics can be defined in terms of possible world structures. In this respect, Conditional Logics can be seen as a generalization of modal logics (or a type of multi-modal logic) where the conditional operator is a sort of modality indexed by a formula of the same language. However,

© The Author(s), under exclusive license to Springer Nature Switzerland AG 2023
A. Dovier et al. (Eds.): AIxIA 2022, LNAI 13796, pp. 345–357, 2023.
https://doi.org/10.1007/978-3-031-27181-6_24

as a difference with modal logics, the lack of a universally accepted semantics led to a partial underdevelopment of proof methods and theorem provers for these logics.

An effort in the direction of filling this gap is provided in [19]. The semantics considered in this work is the *selection function semantics* introduced by Nute in [18], where truth values are assigned to formulas depending on a world. Intuitively, the selection function f selects, for a world w and a formula A, the set of worlds $f(w, A)$ which are "most-similar to w" given the information A. In *normal* conditional logics, f depends on the set of worlds satisfying A rather than on A itself, so that $f(w, A) = f(w, A')$ whenever A and A' are true in the same worlds. A conditional formula $A \Rightarrow B$ is true in w whenever B is true in every world selected by f for A and w.

With the selection function semantics at hand, CK is the fundamental system and it has the same role as the system K in modal logic. Formulas valid in CK are exactly those ones that are valid in every selection function model. Extensions are then obtained by imposing restrictions on the selection function. In [19], a labelled sequent calculus for CK and some standard extensions with conditions ID (conditional identity), MP (conditional modus ponens), CEM (conditional third excluded middle), and CS (conditional strong centering) are considered, as well as most of the combinations of them. The proposed calculi, called SeqS, are modular and, in some cases, optimal. The authors also introduce CondLean, a theorem prover implementing the calculi SeqS in Prolog.

In [19], however, all the systems including both the axioms CEM and MP are neglected: the reason is that the proof of cut elimination, needed in order to prove the completeness of the calculi, does not work when such axioms are considered together. In this paper we provide labelled sequent calculi, that we call SeqS22, for the whole cube of the extensions of CK generated by the above mentioned axioms, including those with both CEM and MP, filling the existing gap. The basic idea is that of replacing the rule dealing with CEM in SeqS, which performs a label substitution in both its premises, by a new one that avoids such a substitution and adopts a conditional formula on the right-hand side of a sequent as its principal formula.

We show that one can derive a decision procedure from the cut-free calculi, providing a constructive proof of decidability of the logics considered. By estimating the size of the finite derivations of a given sequent, we also obtain a polynomial space complexity bound for these logics. Furthermore, we sketch an implementation of the proposed calculi SeqS22: the program, called CondLean2022, is implemented in Prolog and it is inspired by the "lean" methodology, whose aim is to write short programs and exploit the power of Prolog's engine as much as possible: in this respect, every clause of a single predicate, called `prove`, implement an axiom or rule of the calculi and the proof search is provided for free by the mere depth-first search mechanism of Prolog, without any additional ad hoc mechanism. We have tested the performances of CondLean2022 and compared them with those of CondLean, obtaining encouraging results that allow us to conclude that the new rule for CEM, on the one hand, makes it possibile to conclude the proof of cut elimination also in systems with MP, on the other hand, avoiding label substitution leads to a significant improvement of the performance of the prover.

2   Conditional Logics with Selection Function Semantics

In this section we briefly recall propositional Conditional Logics. A propositional conditional language $\mathcal{L}$ contains: (i) a set of propositional variables ATM; (ii) the constants

$\perp$ and $\top$; (iii) a set of connectives $\neg$ (unary), $\wedge$, $\vee$, $\rightarrow$, $\Rightarrow$ (binary). Formulas of $\mathcal{L}$ include formulas of classical logic $\neg A, A \wedge B, A \vee B, A \rightarrow B$, to which we add conditional formulas of the form $A \Rightarrow B$.

We define the *selection function semantics* as follows: given a non-empty set of possible worlds $\mathcal{W}$, the selection function f selects, for a world w and a formula A, the set of worlds of $\mathcal{W}$ which are *closer* to w given the information A. A conditional formula $A \Rightarrow B$ holds in a world w if the formula B holds in *all the worlds selected by f for w and A*.

Definition 1 (Selection function semantics). *A model is a triple* $\mathcal{M} = \langle \mathcal{W}, f, [\ ] \rangle$ *where: i)* $\mathcal{W}$ *is a non-empty set of* worlds; *ii)* f *is the* selection function $f : \mathcal{W} \times 2^{\mathcal{W}} \longrightarrow 2^{\mathcal{W}}$ *iii)* $[\ ]$ *is the* evaluation function, *which assigns to an atom* $P \in ATM$ *the set of worlds where* P *is true, and is extended to the other formulas in the usual way for classical connectives, whereas for conditional formulas we have* $[A \Rightarrow B] = \{w \in \mathcal{W} \mid f(w, [A]) \subseteq [B]\}$.

It is worth noticing that we have defined f taking $[A]$ rather than A (i.e. $f(w, [A])$ rather than $f(w, A)$) as an argument; this is equivalent to define f on formulas, i.e. $f(w, A)$ but imposing that if $[A] = [A']$ in the model, then $f(w, A) = f(w, A')$. This condition is called *normality*.

The semantics above characterizes the basic conditional logic CK. An axiomatization of this system is given by:

- any axiomatization of classical propositional calculus;
- (Modus Ponens) $\dfrac{A \quad A \rightarrow B}{B}$
- (RCEA) $\dfrac{A \leftrightarrow B}{(A \Rightarrow C) \leftrightarrow (B \Rightarrow C)}$
- (RCK) $\dfrac{(A_1 \wedge \cdots \wedge A_n) \rightarrow B}{(C \Rightarrow A_1 \wedge \cdots \wedge C \Rightarrow A_n) \rightarrow (C \Rightarrow B)}$

As for modal logics, we can consider extensions of CK by assuming further properties on the selection function. We consider the following ones:

Logic	Axiom	Model condition
ID	$A \Rightarrow A$	$f(w, [A]) \subseteq [A]$
CS	$(A \wedge B) \rightarrow (A \Rightarrow B)$	$w \in [A] \rightarrow f(w, [A]) \subseteq \{w\}$
CEM	$(A \Rightarrow B) \vee (A \Rightarrow \neg B)$	$\mid f(w, [A]) \mid \leq 1$
MP	$(A \Rightarrow B) \rightarrow (A \rightarrow B)$	$w \in [A] \rightarrow w \in f(w, [A])$

The above axiomatizations are complete with respect to the respective semantics [18].

It is worth noticing that:

Proposition 1. *In systems with both axioms (CEM) and (MP), axiom (CS) is derivable.*

Proof. For (CEM) we have that $\mid f(w, [A]) \mid \leq 1$. For (MP), we have that, if $w \in [A]$, then $w \in f(w, [A])$. Therefore, it follows that if $w \in [A]$, then $f(w, [A]) = \{w\}$, satisfying the (CS) condition. $\square$

3   SeqS22: A Sequent Calculus for Conditional Logics

In this section we introduce SeqS22, a family of labelled sequent calculi for the conditional systems under consideration. The calculi are modular and they are able to deal with the basic system CK as well as with the whole cube of extensions with axioms ID, CS, CEM and MP. Given Proposition 1, it is worth noticing that, concerning systems admitting the axiom (CS), the calculi SeqS22 offer two alternative calculi: on the one hand, the calculus obtained by adding the suitable rule (CS), as in SeqS [19], on the other hand, the calculus obtained by including the rules for (MP) and (CEM) and omitting the rule for (CS), thus avoiding the mechanism of label substitution required by such a rule.

The calculi make use of labels to represent possible worlds. We consider a language $\mathcal{L}$ and a denumerable alphabet of labels $\mathcal{A}$, whose elements are denoted by $x, y, z, ...$. There are two kinds of labelled formulas:

- *world formulas*, denoted by x: A, where $x \in \mathcal{A}$ and $A \in \mathcal{L}$, used to represent that A holds in a world x;
- *transition formulas*, denoted by $x \xrightarrow{A} y$, where $x, y \in \mathcal{A}$ and $A \in \mathcal{L}$. A transition formula $x \xrightarrow{A} y$ represents that $y \in f(x, [A])$.

A *sequent* is a pair $\langle \Gamma, \Delta \rangle$, usually denoted with $\Gamma \vdash \Delta$, where Γ and Δ are multisets of labelled formulas. The intuitive meaning of $\Gamma \vdash \Delta$ is: every model that satisfies all labelled formulas of Γ in the respective worlds (specified by the labels) satisfies at least one of the labelled formulas of Δ (in those worlds). Formally, given a model $\mathcal{M} = \langle \mathcal{W}, f, [\,] \rangle$ for $\mathcal{L}$, and a label alphabet $\mathcal{A}$, we consider any *mapping* $I : \mathcal{A} \to \mathcal{W}$. Let F be a labelled formula, we define $\mathcal{M} \models_I F$ as follows:

- $\mathcal{M} \models_I x$: A if and only if $I(x) \in [A]$
- $\mathcal{M} \models_I x \xrightarrow{A} y$ if and only if $I(y) \in f(I(x), [A])$

We say that $\Gamma \vdash \Delta$ is *valid* in $\mathcal{M}$ if for every mapping $I : \mathcal{A} \to \mathcal{W}$, if $\mathcal{M} \models_I F$ for every $F \in \Gamma$, then $\mathcal{M} \models_I G$ for some $G \in \Delta$. We say that $\Gamma \vdash \Delta$ is valid in a system (CK or any extension of it) if it is valid in every $\mathcal{M}$ satisfying the specific conditions for that system.

We say that a sequent $\Gamma \vdash \Delta$ is *derivable* if it admits a derivation in SeqS22, i.e. a proof tree, obtained by applying backwards the rules of the calculi, having $\Gamma \vdash \Delta$ as a root and whose leaves are all instances of (AX). As usual, the idea is as follows: in order to prove that a formula F is valid in a conditional logic, then one has to check whether the sequent $\vdash x : F$ is derivable in SeqS22, i.e. if we can obtain a proof tree by applying backwards the rules, starting from the root $\vdash x : F$.

As a difference with the sequent calculi SeqS introduced in [19], the calculi SeqS22 follows the basic idea of the calculus introduced in [22], which in this paper is extended in order to deal also with MP. Such an idea is that of dealing with the CEM condition by means of a second rule having a conditional $A \Rightarrow B$ on the right-hand side of a sequent as a principal formula, rather than the one in SeqS, where the condition on the cardinality (at most 1) of the set of worlds selected by the selection function is captured by means of a label substitution mechanism: roughly speaking, given $x \xrightarrow{A} y$, in order to prove $x \xrightarrow{A} z$, we replace both y and z with a new label u, following the observation that they represent the same world. The "old" rule in SeqS is as follows:

$$\frac{\Gamma, x \xrightarrow{A} y \vdash \Delta, x \xrightarrow{A} z \quad (\Gamma, x \xrightarrow{A} y \vdash \Delta)[y/u, z/u]}{\Gamma, x \xrightarrow{A} y \vdash \Delta} (CEM)$$

where $\Sigma[x/u]$ is used to denote the multiset obtained from Σ by replacing, as mentioned here above, the label x by u wherever it occurs, and where it holds that $y \neq z$ and $u \notin \Gamma, \Delta$.

The novel rule introduced in SeqS22 is as follows:

$$\frac{\Gamma \vdash \Delta, x : A \Rightarrow B, x \xrightarrow{A} y \quad \Gamma \vdash \Delta, x : A \Rightarrow B, y : B}{\Gamma \vdash \Delta, x : A \Rightarrow B} (\textbf{CEM})$$

Intuitively, given a conditional formula $x : A \Rightarrow B$ on the right-hand side of a sequent, the calculi apply the rule ($\Rightarrow \textbf{R}$) only one time, introducing a new label y representing the single world selected by the selection function, then the new rule ($\textbf{CEM}$) makes use of such a label y for all other conditional formulas of the form $x : A' \Rightarrow B'$. As an example, Fig. 2 shows a derivation of an instance of the characterizing axiom (CEM).

The calculi SeqS22 are shown in Fig. 1. They satisfy basic structural properties, namely height-preserving admissibility of weakening, height-preserving invertibility of the rules (with the exception of ($\textbf{EQ}$)), height-preserving admissibility of contraction. These are needed in order to show that the following *cut* rule is admissible:

Theorem 1. *The* cut *rule:*

$$\frac{\Gamma \vdash \Delta, F \quad F, \Gamma \vdash \Delta}{\Gamma \vdash \Delta} (cut)$$

where F is any labelled formula, is admissible in SeqS22, i.e. if $\Gamma \vdash \Delta, F$ and $F, \Gamma \vdash \Delta$ are derivable, so is $\Gamma \vdash \Delta$.

Proof. As usual, the proof proceeds by a double induction over the complexity of the cut formula and the sum of the heights of the derivations of the two premises of cut, in the sense that we replace one cut by one or several cuts on formulas of smaller complexity, or on sequents derived by shorter derivations. We show two of the most interesting cases involving the novel rule ($\textbf{CEM}$).

Let us first consider the case involving the rules ($\textbf{CEM}$) and ($\textbf{MP}$), those rules that caused the failure of the proof of admissibility of cut in [19]. We consider the case in which the cut formula is principal in the application of the ($\textbf{MP}$) rule only, as follows:

$$\frac{\dfrac{\Gamma \vdash \Delta, x : A \Rightarrow B, x \xrightarrow{A} x, x : A}{(3)\ \Gamma \vdash \Delta, x : A \Rightarrow B, x \xrightarrow{A} x} (\textbf{MP}) \quad \dfrac{\begin{array}{l}(1)\ x \xrightarrow{A} x, \Gamma \vdash \Delta, x : A \Rightarrow B, x \xrightarrow{A} y \\ (2)\ x \xrightarrow{A} x, \Gamma \vdash \Delta, x : A \Rightarrow B, y : B\end{array}}{x \xrightarrow{A} x, \Gamma \vdash \Delta, x : A \Rightarrow B} (\textbf{CEM})}{(4)\ \Gamma \vdash \Delta, x : A \Rightarrow B} (cut)$$

SeqS22

CK

(AX) $\Gamma, x : P \vdash \Delta, x : P$ $(P \in ATM)$ (AX) $\Gamma, x : \bot \vdash \Delta$ (AX) $\Gamma \vdash \Delta, x : \top$

$(\neg L) \dfrac{\Gamma \vdash \Delta, x : A}{\Gamma, x : \neg A \vdash \Delta}$ $(\neg R) \dfrac{\Gamma, x : A \vdash \Delta}{\Gamma \vdash \Delta, x : \neg A}$ $(\vee L) \dfrac{\Gamma, x : A \vdash \Delta \qquad \Gamma, x : B \vdash \Delta}{\Gamma, x : A \vee B \vdash \Delta}$

$(\vee R) \dfrac{\Gamma \vdash \Delta, x : A, x : B}{\Gamma \vdash \Delta, x : A \vee B}$ $(\wedge L) \dfrac{\Gamma, x : A, x : B \vdash \Delta}{\Gamma, x : A \wedge B \vdash \Delta}$ $(\wedge R) \dfrac{\Gamma \vdash \Delta, x : A \qquad \Gamma \vdash \Delta, x : B}{\Gamma \vdash \Delta, x : A \wedge B}$

$(\to L) \dfrac{\Gamma \vdash \Delta, x : A \qquad \Gamma, x : B \vdash \Delta}{\Gamma, x : A \to B \vdash \Delta}$ $(\to R) \dfrac{\Gamma, x : A \vdash \Delta, x : B}{\Gamma \vdash \Delta, x : A \to B}$

$(EQ) \dfrac{u : A \vdash u : B \qquad u : B \vdash u : A}{\Gamma, x \xrightarrow{A} y \vdash \Delta, x \xrightarrow{B} y}$ $(\Rightarrow R) \dfrac{\Gamma, x \xrightarrow{A} y \vdash \Delta, x : A \Rightarrow B, y : B}{\Gamma \vdash \Delta, x : A \Rightarrow B}$ $(y \notin \Gamma, \Delta)$

$(\Rightarrow L) \dfrac{\Gamma, x : A \Rightarrow B \vdash \Delta, x \xrightarrow{A} y \qquad \Gamma, x : A \Rightarrow B, y : B \vdash \Delta}{\Gamma, x : A \Rightarrow B \vdash \Delta}$

extensions

$(CS) \dfrac{\Gamma, x \xrightarrow{A} y \vdash \Delta, x : A \qquad \Gamma[x/u, y/u], u \xrightarrow{A} u \vdash \Delta[x/u, y/u]}{\Gamma, x \xrightarrow{A} y \vdash \Delta}$ $(x \neq y, u \notin \Gamma, \Delta)$ $(ID) \dfrac{\Gamma, x \xrightarrow{A} y, y : A \vdash \Delta}{\Gamma, x \xrightarrow{A} y \vdash \Delta}$

$(CEM) \dfrac{\Gamma \vdash \Delta, x : A \Rightarrow B, x \xrightarrow{A} y \qquad \Gamma \vdash \Delta, x : A \Rightarrow B, y : B}{\Gamma \vdash \Delta, x : A \Rightarrow B}$ $(MP) \dfrac{\Gamma \vdash \Delta, x \xrightarrow{A} x, x : A}{\Gamma \vdash \Delta, x \xrightarrow{A} x}$

Fig. 1. Rules of sequent calculi SeqS22

$$\dfrac{\dfrac{}{u : A \vdash u : A} (AX)}{\dfrac{}{x \xrightarrow{A} y \vdash x : A \Rightarrow B, x : A \Rightarrow \neg B, y : B, x \xrightarrow{A} y}} (EQ) \qquad \dfrac{\dfrac{}{u : A \vdash u : A} (AX) \qquad \dfrac{}{x \xrightarrow{A} y, y : B \vdash x : A \Rightarrow B, x : A \Rightarrow \neg B, y : B} (AX)}{\dfrac{x \xrightarrow{A} y \vdash x : A \Rightarrow B, x : A \Rightarrow \neg B, y : B, y : \neg B} (\neg R)}$$

$$\dfrac{x \xrightarrow{A} y \vdash x : A \Rightarrow B, x : A \Rightarrow \neg B, y : B}{\dfrac{\vdash x : A \Rightarrow B, x : A \Rightarrow \neg B}{\vdash x : (A \Rightarrow B) \vee (A \Rightarrow \neg B)} (\vee R)} (\Rightarrow R)$$

Fig. 2. A derivation of CEM in SeqS22.

Since weakening is height-preserving admissible, since (3) is derivable, so are (3') $\Gamma \vdash \Delta, x : A \Rightarrow B, x \xrightarrow{A} x, x \xrightarrow{A} y$ and (3'') $\Gamma \vdash \Delta, x : A \Rightarrow B, x \xrightarrow{A} x, y : B$ with derivations of no greater heights. We can then apply the inductive hypothesis on the height of the derivations to (3') and (1), obtaining a derivation of (5) $\Gamma \vdash \Delta, x : A \Rightarrow B, x \xrightarrow{A} y$, as well as to (3'') and (2), obtaining a derivation of (6) $\Gamma \vdash \Delta, x : A \Rightarrow B, y : B$. We conclude that (4) can be derived by an application of **(CEM)** to (5) and (6).

Let us now take into account the case in which the cut formula is the principal formulas in both the premises of (cut), and the rules applied to it are $(\mathbf{CEM})$ and $(\Rightarrow \mathbf{L})$. The situation is as follows:

$$
\frac{
\begin{array}{c}
(7)\ \Gamma \vdash \Delta, x : A \Rightarrow B, x \xrightarrow{A} y \\
(8)\ \Gamma \vdash \Delta, x : A \Rightarrow B, y : B
\end{array}
}{(11)\ \Gamma \vdash \Delta, x : A \Rightarrow B} \ (\mathbf{CEM})
\qquad
\frac{
\begin{array}{c}
(9)\ \Gamma, x : A \Rightarrow B \vdash \Delta, x \xrightarrow{A} y \\
(10)\ \Gamma, x : A \Rightarrow B, y : B \vdash \Delta
\end{array}
}{(12)\ \Gamma, x : A \Rightarrow B \vdash \Delta} \ (\Rightarrow \mathbf{L})
$$

$$
\frac{\qquad\qquad\qquad\qquad\qquad\qquad\qquad\qquad\qquad\qquad\qquad\qquad}{\Gamma \vdash \Delta} \ (cut)
$$

Since weakening is height-preserving admissible, we can obtain a proof (with a derivation of at most the same height of (11)) for $(11')\ \Gamma \vdash \Delta, x : A \Rightarrow B, y : B$. By inductive hypothesis on the height of the derivations, we can cut (10) and $(11')$, obtaining a derivation of $(13)\ \Gamma, y : B \vdash \Delta$. Since weakening is height-preserving admissible, we can obtain a proof (with a derivation of at most the same height of (12)) for $(12')\ \Gamma, x : A \Rightarrow B \vdash \Delta, y : B$. By inductive hypothesis on the height of the derivations, we can cut (8) and $(12')$, obtaining a derivation of $(14)\ \Gamma \vdash \Delta, y : B$. We can then apply the inductive hypothesis on the complexity of the cut formula to cut (13) and (14), and we are done with a derivation of $\Gamma \vdash \Delta$. Due to space limitations, the other cases are omitted and left to the reader. $\qquad\qquad\qquad\qquad\qquad\qquad\quad\square$

Theorem 2 (Soundness and completeness). *Given a conditional formula F, it is valid in a conditional logic if and only if it is derivable in the corresponding calculus of SeqS22, that is to say $\models F$ if and only if $\vdash x : F$ is derivable in SeqS22.*

Proof. (Soundness) We have to prove that, if a sequent $\Gamma \vdash \Delta$ is derivable, then the sequent is valid. This can be done by induction on the height of the derivation of $\Gamma \vdash \Delta$. The basic cases are those corresponding to derivations of height 0, that is to say instances of (AX). It is easy to see that, in all these cases, $\Gamma \vdash \Delta$ is a valid sequent. As an example, consider $\Gamma, x : P \vdash \Delta, x : P$: consider every model $\mathcal{M}$ and every mapping I satisfying all formulas in the left-hand side of the sequent, then also $x : P$. This means that $I(x) \in [P]$, but then we have that $\mathcal{M}$ satisfies via I at least a formula in the right-hand side of the sequent, the same $x : P$. For the inductive step, we proceed by considering each rule of the calculi SeqS22 in order to check that, if the premise(s) is (are) valid sequent(s), to which we can apply the inductive hypothesis, so is the conclusion. To save space, we only present the cases of $(\mathbf{MP})$ and of the new rule $(\mathbf{CEM})$, the other ones are left to the reader. Let us start with $(\mathbf{MP})$ and a derivation ended as follows:

$$
\frac{(1)\ \Gamma \vdash \Delta, x \xrightarrow{A} x, x : A}{(2)\ \Gamma \vdash \Delta, x \xrightarrow{A} x} \ (\mathbf{MP})
$$

By inductive hypothesis, the sequent (1) is valid. By absurd, suppose that (2) is not: this means that there exists a model $\mathcal{M}$ and a mapping I satisfying all formulas in Γ but falsifying all formulas in the right-hand side of the sequent, namely all formulas in Δ and $x \xrightarrow{A} x$. Since (1) is valid, every model with any mapping satisfying all formulas in Γ satisfies also at least a formula in the right-hand side of the sequent: since $\mathcal{M}$ falsifies all formulas in Δ and $(*)\ x \xrightarrow{A} x$ via I, it must be that $\mathcal{M} \models_I x : A$, that is to say the world w represented by $I(x)$ is an A-world, i.e. $w \in [A]$. By the condition (MP), this implies that also $w \in f(w, [A])$, however this would mean that $I(x) \in f(I(x), [A])$, i.e. $\mathcal{M} \models_I x \xrightarrow{A} x$, against $(*)$.

Let us now consider the rule (**CEM**) and a proof ended as:

$$\frac{(3)\ \Gamma \vdash \Delta, x : A \Rightarrow B, x \xrightarrow{A} y \qquad (4)\ \Gamma \vdash \Delta, x : A \Rightarrow B, y : B}{(5)\ \Gamma \vdash \Delta, x : A \Rightarrow B} \text{(\textbf{CEM})}$$

By inductive hypothesis, both (3) and (4) are valid. Again by absurd, suppose (5) is not, that is to say there exists a model $\mathcal{M}'$ and a mapping I' satisfying all formulas in Γ but falsifying all formulas in Δ as well as $x : A \Rightarrow B$. Since (3) is valid, since $\mathcal{M}'$ and I' falsify all formulas in Δ and $x : A \Rightarrow B$, necessarily we have that $\mathcal{M}' \models_{I'} x \xrightarrow{A} y$, that is to say $I'(y) \in f'(I'(x), [A])$. By the (CEM) semantic condition, it follows that $(**)\ f'(I'(x), [A]) = \{I(y)\}$. Analogously, by the validity of (4) we have that $\mathcal{M}' \models_{I'} y : B$. If $\mathcal{M}' \not\models_{I'} x : A \Rightarrow B$ in (5), there exists a world w such that $w \in f'(I'(x), [A])$ and $w \notin [B]$, however, since $(**)$, we have that $I'(y) = w$, against the validity of (4), and we are done.

(Completeness) The completeness is an easy consequence of the admissibility of the *cut* rule (Theorem 1). We show that if a formula F is valid in a conditional logic, then $\vdash x : F$ is derivable in SeqS22. We proceed by induction on the complexity of the formulas, therefore we show that the axioms are derivable and that the set of derivable formulas is closed under (Modus Ponens), (RCEA), and (RCK). A derivation of axioms (**ID**), (**CS**) and (**MP**) can be obtained as in SeqS [19]. A derivation of (CEM) is provided in Fig. 2. For (Modus Ponens), suppose that $\vdash x : A \rightarrow B$ and $\vdash x : A$ are derivable. We easily have that $x : A \rightarrow B, x : A \vdash x : B$ is derivable too by applying $(\rightarrow \text{L})$. Since cut is admissible by Theorem 1, by two cuts we obtain $\vdash x : B$ (weakenings are omitted to increase readability):

$$\frac{\dfrac{x : A \rightarrow B, x : A \vdash x : B \quad \vdash x : A \rightarrow B}{x : A \vdash x : B} \text{(cut)} \qquad \vdash x : A}{\vdash x : B} \text{(cut)}$$

For (RCEA), we have to show that if $A \leftrightarrow B$ is derivable, then also $(A \Rightarrow C) \leftrightarrow (B \Rightarrow C)$ is so. The formula $A \leftrightarrow B$ is an abbreviation for $(A \rightarrow B) \wedge (B \rightarrow A)$. Suppose that $\vdash x : (A \rightarrow B) \wedge (B \rightarrow A)$ is derivable, then also $x : A \vdash x : B$ and $x : B \vdash x : A$ are derivable since rules are height-preserving invertible. We can derive $x : A \Rightarrow C \vdash x : B \Rightarrow C$ as follows:

$$\frac{\dfrac{x : A \vdash x : B \qquad x : B \vdash x : A}{x \xrightarrow{B} y, x : A \Rightarrow C \vdash x : B \Rightarrow C, y : C, x \xrightarrow{A} y \quad y : C, x \xrightarrow{B} y, x : A \Rightarrow C \vdash x : B \Rightarrow C, y : C} \text{(EQ)}}{\dfrac{x \xrightarrow{B} y, x : A \Rightarrow C \vdash x : B \Rightarrow C, y : C}{x : A \Rightarrow C \vdash x : B \Rightarrow C} (\Rightarrow \text{R})} (\Rightarrow \text{L})$$

The other half is symmetric. For (RCK), suppose that $\vdash x : B_1 \wedge B_2 \cdots \wedge B_n \rightarrow C$ is derivable, by the height-preserving invertibility of the rules also $y : B_1, \ldots, y : B_n \vdash$

$y : C$ is derivable, then so is $(*)$ $x : A \Rightarrow B_1, x : A \Rightarrow B_2, \ldots, x : A \Rightarrow B_n, y : B_1, \ldots, y : B_n \vdash x : A \Rightarrow C, y : C$ by admissibility of weakening. We have:

$$
\cfrac{x \xrightarrow{A} y \vdash x \xrightarrow{A} y \quad (*)\, x : A \Rightarrow B_1, \ldots, y : B_1, \ldots, y : B_n \vdash x : A \Rightarrow C, y : C}{x \xrightarrow{A} y, x : A \Rightarrow B_1, \ldots, x : A \Rightarrow B_n, y : B_1, \ldots, y : B_{n-1} \vdash x : A \Rightarrow C, y : C} \ (\Rightarrow \mathbf{L})
$$

$$
\vdots
$$

$$
\cfrac{\cfrac{x \xrightarrow{A} y \vdash x \xrightarrow{A} y \qquad x \xrightarrow{A} y, x : A \Rightarrow B_1, \ldots, x : A \Rightarrow B_n, y : B_1 \vdash x : A \Rightarrow C, y : C}{\cfrac{x \xrightarrow{A} y, x : A \Rightarrow B_1, \ldots, x : A \Rightarrow B_n \vdash x : A \Rightarrow C, y : C}{x : A \Rightarrow B_1, \ldots, x : A \Rightarrow B_n \vdash x : A \Rightarrow C} \ (\Rightarrow \mathbf{R})} \ (\Rightarrow \mathbf{L})}
$$

$\square$

The presence of labels and of the rules $(\Rightarrow \mathbf{L})$, $(\Rightarrow \mathbf{R})$, $(\mathbf{ID})$, $(\mathbf{MP})$, $(\mathbf{CEM})$, and $(\mathbf{CS})$, which increase the complexity of the sequent in a backward proof search, is a potential cause of a non-terminating proof search. However, with a similar argument to the one proposed in [19], we can define a procedure that can apply such rules in a controlled way and introducing a finite number of labels, ensuring termination. Intuitively, it can be shown that it is useless to apply $(\Rightarrow \mathbf{L})$ and $(\Rightarrow \mathbf{R})$ on $x : A \Rightarrow B$ by introducing (looking backward) the same transition formula $x \xrightarrow{A} y$ more than once in each branch of a proof tree. Similarly, it is useless to apply $(\mathbf{ID})$, $(\mathbf{MP})$, $(\mathbf{CEM})$, and $(\mathbf{CS})$ on the same transition formula more than once in a backward proof search in each branch of a derivation. This leads to the decidability of the given logics:

Theorem 3 (Decidability). *Conditional Logics CK and all its extensions with axioms ID, MP, CS, CEM and all their combinations are decidable.*

It can be shown that provability in all the Conditional Logics considered is decidable in $O(n^2 \log n)$ space, we omit the proof which is essentially the same as in [19].

4   A Theorem Prover for Conditional Logics with CEM

In this section we briefly present CondLean22 (https://gitlab2.educ.di.unito.it/pozzato/condlean4), a Prolog implementation of the calculi SeqS22 introduced in the previous section. The prover is in the line of the existing provers for that logics [20,21] and it follows the "lean" methodology, introduced by Beckert and Posegga in the middle of the 90s [2,3,7]: they have proposed a very elegant and extremely efficient first-order theorem prover, called leanT^AP, consisting of only five Prolog clauses. The basic idea of the "lean" methodology is "to achieve maximal efficiency from minimal means" [2] by writing short programs and exploiting the power of Prolog's engine as much as possible. Moreover, it is straightforward to prove soundness and completeness of the theorem prover by exploiting the one to one correspondence between axioms/rules of SeqS22 and clauses of CondLean2022.

We implement each component of a sequent by a list of formulas, partitioned into three sub-lists: atomic formulas, transitions and complex formulas. Atomic and complex formulas are implemented by a Prolog list of the form [x, a], where x is a Prolog constant and a is a formula. A transition formula $x \xrightarrow{A} y$ is implemented by a Prolog list of the form [x,a,y]. Labels are implemented by Prolog constants. The sequent calculi are implemented by the predicate

prove(Gamma, Delta, Labels, Rcond, LCond, Tree)

which succeeds if and only if $\Gamma \vdash \Delta$ is derivable in SeqS, where Gamma and Delta are the lists implementing the multisets Γ and Δ, respectively and Labels is the list of labels introduced in that branch. As we will describe later on, arguments RCond and LCond are used in order to ensure the termination of the proof search by restricting the application of some crucial rules. Tree is an output term: if the proof search succeeds, it matches a Prolog representation of the derivation found by the theorem prover.

Each clause of the prove predicate implements one axiom or rule of SeqS22. The theorem prover proceeds as follows. First of all, if $\Gamma \vdash \Delta$ is an axiom, then the goal will succeed immediately by using the clauses for the axioms. If it is not, then the first applicable rule is chosen. The ordering of the clauses is such that the application of the branching rules is postponed as much as possible. Concerning the rules for $\Rightarrow$ on the right-hand side of a sequent, the rule $(\Rightarrow R)$, which introduces a new label in a backward proof search, is first applied to a sequent of the form $\Gamma \vdash \Delta, x : A \Rightarrow B$. If this does not lead to a derivation, the new rule for CEM is then applied. As mentioned here above, arguments RCond and LCond are used in order to ensure the termination of the proof search by controlling the application of the rules $(\Rightarrow \mathbf{L})$ and $(\Rightarrow \mathbf{R})$: indeed, these rules copy the conditional formula $x : A \Rightarrow B$ to which they are applied in their premises, therefore we need to avoid redundant applications that, otherwise, would lead to expand an infinite branch. For instance, RCond is a Prolog list containing all the formulas $x : A \Rightarrow B$ to which the rule $(\Rightarrow \mathbf{R})$ has been already applied in the current branch: such a rule will be then applied to $x : A \Rightarrow B$ only if it does not belong to the list RCond. A similar mechanism is implemented for extensions of CK, namely further suitable arguments are added to the predicate prove to keep track of the information needed to avoid useless and uncontrolled applications of the rules $(\mathbf{MP})$, $(\mathbf{ID})$, $(\mathbf{CEM})$, and $(\mathbf{CS})$, which copy their principal formulas in their premise(s). As an example, in systems with condition (CEM), a further argument is a Prolog list, called CEM, whose elements are pairs $(y, x : A \Rightarrow B)$ representing that the rule $(\mathbf{CEM})$ has been already applied (in a backward proof search) to a conditional formula $x : A \Rightarrow B$ by using the label y in the premises, i.e. by introducing $x \xrightarrow{A} y$ and $y : B$ in the two premises of the rule. In order to apply the rule $(\mathbf{CEM})$ to a formula $x : A \Rightarrow B$, the clause implementing it will choose a label y in the list Labels such that the pair $(y, x : A \Rightarrow B)$ does not belong to the list CEM.

Let us now present some clauses of CondLean2022. As a first example, the clause for the axiom checking whether the same atomic formula occurs in both the left and the right hand side of a sequent is implemented as follows:

```
prove([LitGamma,_,_],[LitDelta,_,_],_,_,_,tree(ax)):-
    member(F,LitGamma),member(F,LitDelta),!.
```

It is easy to observe that the rule succeeds when the same labelled formula F belongs to both the right and the left hand side of the sequent under investigation, completing the proof search: indeed, no recursive call to the predicate `prove` is performed, and the output term `Tree` matches a representation of a leaf in the derivation (`tree(ax)`).

As another example, we show the code of the novel rule (**CEM**):

```
prove([LitGamma,TransGamma,ComplexGamma],[LitDelta,TransDelta,ComplexDelta],
        Labels, RCond, LCond, CEM, tree(cem,SubTree1,SubTree2)):-
    member([X,A => B],ComplexDelta),
    member([Y,Labels),
    \+member([Y,[X,A => B]],CEM), !,                                    (*)
    put([Y,B],LitDelta,ComplexDelta,NewLitDelta,NewComplexDelta),
    prove([LitGamma,TransGamma,ComplexGamma],
        [LitDelta,[[X,A,Y] | TransDelta],ComplexDelta],
        Labels, RCond, LCond, [ [Y,[X,A => B]] | CEM], SubTree1),
    prove([LitGamma,TransGamma,ComplexGamma],
        [NewLitDelta,TransDelta,NewComplexDelta],
        Labels, RCond, LCond, [ [Y,[X,A => B]] | CEM], SubTree2).
```

The predicate `put` is used to put `[Y,B]` in the proper sub-list of the antecedent. The recursive calls to `prove` implement the proof search on the two premises. As mentioned, in order to ensure termination, in line $(*)$ the theorem prover checks whether (**CEM**) has been already applied in the current branch by using the same label y to the conditional formula $x : A \Rightarrow B$: to this aim, CondLean2022 looks for the pair `[Y,[X,A => B]]` in the list `CEM` and, if needed, it avoids a further, useless application.

In order to search a derivation of a sequent $\Gamma \vdash \Delta$, the theorem prover proceeds as follows. First, if $\Gamma \vdash \Delta$ is an axiom, the goal will succeed immediately by using the clauses for the axioms. If it is not, then the first applicable rule is chosen, e.g. if `ComplexDelta` contains a formula `[X,A -> B]`, then the clause for $(\rightarrow R)$ rule is used, invoking `prove` on the unique premise of $(\rightarrow R)$. The prover proceeds in a similar way for the other rules. The ordering of the clauses is such that the application of the branching rules is postponed as much as possible.

In order to check whether a formula is valid in one of the considered system, one has just to invoke the following auxiliary predicate:

pr(Formula)

which wraps the `prove` predicate by a suitable initialization of its arguments.

In order to provide a first evaluation of the performance of the theorem prover, we have tested both CondLean and CondLean2022 over (i) a set of formulas holding only in systems with CEM, as well as over (ii) a set of randomly generated formulas, either valid or not. We have observed that, over a set of valid formulas, the performances of CondLean2022 are improved of $20, 57\%$ with respect to CondLean. As an example, running both the provers over the formula

$$(A \Rightarrow (B_1 \vee \ldots B_5)) \Rightarrow ((A \Rightarrow B_1) \vee \ldots \vee (A \Rightarrow B_5))$$

CondLean2022 is able to build a derivation in 94 ms, against the 266 ms needed by CondLean. Over randomly generated formulas, the statistics are even better: CondLean2022 provides an improvement of the performances of $48,27\%$ with respect to CondLean.

The performance of CondLean2022 are promising, especially concerning all cases in which it has to answer *no* for a not valid formula: this is justified by the fact that CondLean has to make a great effort in order to explore the whole space of alternative choices in label substitution, needed in order to conclude the proof. The current version of the theorem prover CondLean2022 is available for free download at https://gitlab2.educ.di.unito.it/pozzato/condlean4, where one can also find an updated version of CondLean in order to compare the two provers on common systems.

5   Conclusions and Future Works

In this work we have introduced labelled sequent calculi for Conditional Logics with the selection function semantics, including the basic system CK as well as extensions with well established axioms ID, MP, CEM, and CS and all their combinations. As a difference with the seminal work in [19], we are also able to deal with systems combining the condition of the conditional third excluded middle (CEM) and conditional modus ponens (MP), where the conditional strong centering (CS) is a derived condition. The same extensions, with condition (CSO) in place of (CS), are considered in [1].

We have provided alternative calculi, where the original rule for CEM, based on an expensive mechanism of label substitution, has been replaced by a "standard" rule, called $(\mathbf{CEM})$ inspired to the one introduced in [22] and specifically tailored for handling conditional formulas $A \Rightarrow B$ in these systems. We have also implemented the proposed calculi and compared the obtained theorem prover, called CondLean2022, with its ancestor CondLean. The promising performance we obtained provide an empirical proof that the proposed system not only fills a gap in terms of considered Conditional Logics, but is also a concrete step in the direction of efficient theorem proving for them.

We plan to extend our work in several directions. First, we aim at extending the calculi and the implementation to stronger Conditional Logics. Moreover, we aim at extending the theorem prover CondLean2022 towards a "concrete" theorem prover: in particular, we aim at implementing state of the art heuristics, data structures and suitable refinements, as well as a graphical web interface for it. Last, we aim at extending the set of formulas adopted in the performance evaluation.

Acknowledgement. This work has been partially supported by the INdAM - GNCS Project cod. CUP_E55F22000270001 "LESLIE: LogichE non-claSsiche per tooL Intelligenti ed Explainable".

References

1. Alenda, R., Olivetti, N., Pozzato, G.L.: Nested sequent calculi for normal conditional logics. J. Log. Comput. **26**(1), 7–50 (2016). https://doi.org/10.1093/logcom/ext034
2. Beckert, B., Posegga, J.: leanTAP: lean tableau-based deduction. J. Autom. Reason. **15**(3), 339–358 (1995)
3. Beckert, B., Posegga, J.: Logic programming as a basis for lean automated deduction. J. Log. Program. **28**(3), 231–236 (1996)
4. Burgess, J.P.: Quick completeness proofs for some logics of conditionals. Notre Dame J. Formal Log. **22**, 76–84 (1981)
5. Chellas, B.F.: Basic conditional logics. J. Philos. Log. **4**, 133–153 (1975)
6. Delgrande, J.P.: A first-order conditional logic for prototypical properties. Artif. Intell. **33**(1), 105–130 (1987)
7. Fitting, M.: leanTAP revisited. J. Log. Comput. **8**(1), 33–47 (1998)
8. Friedman, N., Halpern, J.Y.: Plausibility measures and default reasoning. J. ACM **48**(4), 648–685 (2001)
9. Gabbay, D.M., Giordano, L., Martelli, A., Olivetti, N., Sapino, M.L.: Conditional reasoning in logic programming. J. Log. Program. **44**(1–3), 37–74 (2000)
10. Genovese, V., Giordano, L., Gliozzi, V., Pozzato, G.L.: Logics in access control: a conditional approach. J. Log. Comput. **24**(4), 705–762 (2014)
11. Giordano, L., Gliozzi, V., Olivetti, N.: Iterated belief revision and conditional logic. Stud. Log. **70**(1), 23–47 (2002)
12. Giordano, L., Gliozzi, V., Olivetti, N.: Weak AGM postulates and strong Ramsey test: a logical formalization. Artif. Intell. **168**(1–2), 1–37 (2005)
13. Giordano, L., Schwind, C.: Conditional logic of actions and causation. Artif. Intell. **157**(1–2), 239–279 (2004)
14. Giordano, L., Gliozzi, V., Olivetti, N., Pozzato, G.L.: Analytic tableaux for KLM preferential and cumulative logics. In: Sutcliffe, G., Voronkov, A. (eds.) LPAR 2005. LNCS (LNAI), vol. 3835, pp. 666–681. Springer, Heidelberg (2005). https://doi.org/10.1007/11591191_46
15. Grahne, G.: Updates and counterfactuals. J. Log. Comput. **8**(1), 87–117 (1998)
16. Kraus, S., Lehmann, D., Magidor, M.: Nonmonotonic reasoning, preferential models and cumulative logics. Artif. Intell. **44**(1–2), 167–207 (1990)
17. Lewis, D.: Counterfactuals. Basil Blackwell Ltd. (1973)
18. Nute, D.: Topics in Conditional Logic. Reidel, Dordrecht (1980)
19. Olivetti, N., Pozzato, G.L., Schwind, C.B.: A sequent calculus and a theorem prover for standard conditional logics. ACM Trans. Comput. Log. (ToCL) **8**(4), 22-es (2007)
20. Olivetti, N., Pozzato, G.L.: CondLean: a theorem prover for conditional logics. In: Cialdea Mayer, M., Pirri, F. (eds.) TABLEAUX 2003. LNCS (LNAI), vol. 2796, pp. 264–270. Springer, Heidelberg (2003). https://doi.org/10.1007/978-3-540-45206-5_23
21. Olivetti, N., Pozzato, G.L.: CondLean 3.0: improving CondLean for stronger conditional logics. In: Beckert, B. (ed.) TABLEAUX 2005. LNCS (LNAI), vol. 3702, pp. 328–332. Springer, Heidelberg (2005). https://doi.org/10.1007/11554554_27
22. Panic, N., Pozzato, G.L.: Efficient theorem proving for conditional logics with conditional excluded middle. In: Calegari, R., Ciatto, G., Omicini, A. (eds.) Proceedings of the 37th Italian Conference on Computational Logic, Bologna, Italy, 29 June–1 July 2022. CEUR Workshop Proceedings, vol. 3204, pp. 217–231. CEUR-WS.org (2022). https://ceur-ws.org/Vol-3204/paper_22.pdf
23. Schwind, C.B.: Causality in action theories. Electron. Trans. Artif. Intell. (ETAI) **3**(A), 27–50 (1999)
24. Stalnaker, R.: A theory of conditionals. In: Rescher, N. (ed.) Studies in Logical Theory, pp. 98–112. Blackwell (1968)

Deep Learning for ECoG Brain-Computer Interface: End-to-End vs. Hand-Crafted Features

Maciej Śliwowski[1,2]([✉])(iD), Matthieu Martin[1](iD), Antoine Souloumiac[2], Pierre Blanchart[2], and Tetiana Aksenova[1](iD)

[1] Univ. Grenoble Alpes, CEA, LETI, Clinatec, 38000 Grenoble, France
macieksliwowski@gmail.com, tetiana.aksenova@cea.fr
[2] Université Paris-Saclay, CEA, List, 91120 Palaiseau, France

Abstract. In brain signal processing, deep learning (DL) models have become commonly used. However, the performance gain from using end-to-end DL models compared to conventional ML approaches is usually significant but moderate, typically at the cost of increased computational load and deteriorated explainability. The core idea behind deep learning approaches is scaling the performance with bigger datasets. However, brain signals are temporal data with a low signal-to-noise ratio, uncertain labels, and nonstationary data in time. Those factors may influence the training process and slow down the models' performance improvement. These factors' influence may differ for end-to-end DL model and one using hand-crafted features.

As not studied before, this paper compares the performance of models that use raw ECoG signals with time-frequency features-based decoders for BCI motor imagery decoding. We investigate whether the current dataset size is a stronger limitation for any models. Finally, obtained filters were compared to identify differences between hand-crafted features and optimized with backpropagation. To compare the effectiveness of both strategies, we used a multilayer perceptron and a mix of convolutional and LSTM layers that were already proved effective in this task. The analysis was performed on the long-term clinical trial database (almost 600 min of recordings over 200 days) of a tetraplegic patient executing motor imagery tasks for 3D hand translation.

For a given dataset, the results showed that end-to-end training might not be significantly better than the hand-crafted features-based model. The performance gap is reduced with bigger datasets, but considering the increased computational load, end-to-end training may not be profitable for this application.

Keywords: Deep learning · ECoG · Brain-computer interfaces · Dataset size · Motor imagery · End-to-end

1 Introduction

In the last decade, deep learning (DL) models achieved extraordinary performance in a variety of complex real-life tasks, e.g., computer vision [4], natural

A. Dovier et al. (Eds.): AIxIA 2022, LNAI 13796, pp. 358–373, 2023.
https://doi.org/10.1007/978-3-031-27181-6_25

language processing [2], compared to previously developed models. This was possible mainly thanks to the improvements of data processing units and, most importantly, increased dataset sizes [4]. Generally, in brain-computer interfaces (BCI) research, access to large databases of brain signals is limited due to the experimental and medical constraints as well as the immensity of paradigms/hardware combinations. Given limited datasets, can we still train end-to-end (E2E) DL models for the medical BCI application as effectively as in computer vision?

In 2019, Roy et al. [12] reported that the number of studies classifying EEG signals with deep learning using hand-crafted features (mainly frequency domain) and raw EEG signals (end-to-end) was similar. This indicates that decoding raw EEG signals, without feature extraction, is indeed possible. However, in many articles, researchers decided to use harder to design hand-crafted features. While end-to-end models dominated computer vision, in brain signals processing, it is still common to use features extracted as an input to the DL models. It is unclear whether specific signal characteristics cause this, e.g., nonstationarity in time making the creation of a homogeneous dataset impractical, low signal-to-noise ratio complicating the optimization process and favoring overfitting, labels uncertainty originating from human-in-the-loop experimental setup, or researchers' bias toward solutions better understood and more explainable.

Most studies do not directly compare DL using end-to-end and hand-crafted features approaches. Usually, DL architectures are compared with each other and with an additional 'traditional' ML pipeline, e.g., filter-bank common spatial pattern (FBCSP) in [15], xDAWN and FBCSP in [5], SVM and FBCSP in [17]. In Fig. 1, we aggregated studies analyzed[1] by Roy et al. [12] to present the accuracy improvement of the best proposed DL model in every article compared to the 'traditional' baseline depending on the recording time and the number of examples in the dataset. The gap between performance improvement of DL compared to the 'traditional' baseline increases with the dataset size (except for the last points on the plot, which contain significantly fewer studies). In the right plot, the difference between models using raw EEG and frequency domain features increases which may exhibit a boost of end-to-end models with access to bigger datasets compared to hand-crafted features. As the proposed DL models are usually compared to the baseline, the boost of end-to-end models cannot be clearly stated because the accuracy difference depends strongly on the 'traditional' baseline model performance and the particular task tackled in the study.

While EEG and ECoG signals share many characteristics—both are multi-channel temporal signals with information encoded in frequency and space, with low signal-to-noise ratio and noisy labels—there are also differences, e.g., a higher spatial resolution of ECoG, higher signal-to-noise ratio and higher contribution of informative high gamma band ($>70\,Hz$). In motor imagery ECoG decoding, end-to-end DL is not commonly used. Instead, 'traditional' ML classifiers are

---

[1] limited to the articles that contained all the required information, code adapted from [12].

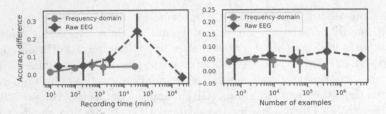

Fig. 1. Binned average accuracy difference between best proposed DL model and 'traditional' baseline on EEG datasets. Error bars denote one standard deviation of the values in the bin. Bins are equal in size on a logarithmic scale. Points x-axis position denotes the average dataset size in a bin.

usually preceded by a feature extraction step creating brain signals representation, typically in the form of time-frequency features, containing information about power time course in several frequency bands [8,14] or focused only on low-frequency component (LFC)/Local Motor Potential (LMP) [14] (detailed analysis can be found in [19]).

However, a successful application of an end-to-end DL model to motor imagery decoding of finger movements trajectory from ECoG was performed with convolutional layers filtering the raw signal both in temporal and spatial domains followed by LSTM layers [20]. Nevertheless, an average improvement from training the weights compared to fixed hand-crafted features can be estimated as 0.022 ± 0.0393 of Pearson r correlation coefficient, which is relatively small, with 66% of cases noticeable improvement from end-to-end training. As this was not studied before, we investigated the differences in data requirements between an end-to-end model and one using hand-crafted features on a long-term clinical trial BCI dataset of 3D target reach task. Unique long-term recordings (several months of experiments, more than 600 min duration in total, compared to few minutes of ECoG recording available in previous studies, e.g., [20]) allowed us to explore the relationship between dataset size and the type of feature used for ECoG signal decoding. In this study, we used architectures previously applied to the ECoG dataset for decoding motor imagery signals with hand-crafted time-frequency features as input [16]. In addition, we optimized the temporal filtering layer with backpropagation seeking a more efficient set of filters that were initialized to reproduce continuous wavelet transform. We also investigated whether both approaches react differently to training dataset perturbations which may be the case due to distinct model properties and may influence the choice of optimal data processing pipeline for ECoG BCI.

2   Methods

2.1   Dataset

The dataset used in this study was collected as a part of the clinical trial 'BCI and Tetraplegia' (ClinicalTrials.gov identifier: NCT02550522, details in [1]) approved by the ethical Committee for the Protection of Individuals (Comité de Protection des Personnes-CPP) with the registration number: 15-CHUG-19 and the Agency for the Safety of Medicines and Health Products (Agence nationale de sécurité du médicament et des produits de santé—ANSM) with the registration number: 2015-A00650-49 and the ethical Committee for the Protection of Individuals (Comité de Protection des Personnes—CPP) with the registration number: 15-CHUG-19.

In the experiment, a 28-years-old tetraplegic patient after spinal cord injury was asked to move the hands of a virtual avatar displayed on a screen (see Fig. 2) using motor imagery patterns—by repeatedly imaging/attempting hand/fingers/arm movements (without actual movements) that influence brain activity in the motor cortex. These changes were then recorded with two WIMAGINE [10] implants placed over the primary motor and sensory cortex bilaterally. Each implant consisted of 8×8 grid of electrodes with recording performed using 32 electrodes selected in a chessboard-

Fig. 2. Screenshot from the virtual environment. The patient is asked to reach the yellow square (target) with the left hand (effector) using motor imagery. (Color figure online)

like manner due to limited data transfer with a sampling frequency equal to 586 Hz. Signals from implants were transferred to the decoding system that performed online predictions. First, one out of 5 possible states (idle, left and right hand translation, left and right wrist rotation) was selected with a state decoder. Then, for every state (except idle), a multilinear REW-NPLS model [3] updated online was used to predict 3D movements or 1D wrist rotation. The dataset consisted of 44 experimental sessions recorded over more than 200 days. It constitutes 300 and 284 min for left and right hand translation, respectively.

2.2   Data Representation and Problem

From the recorded signals, we extracted two datasets for left and right hand translation. The raw signal representation was created from 1-second long windows of ECoG signal with 90% overlap. Every observation $\mathbf{X}_i \in \mathbb{R}^{64 \times 590}$ contained 590 samples[2] for each of the 64 channels corresponding to the number of electrodes recording the signal.

Every signal window $\mathbf{X}_i$ was paired with the corresponding desired trajectory $\mathbf{y}_i \in \mathbb{R}^3$ that the patient was asked to follow, i.e., the straight line connecting the tip of the hand to the target. The trajectories were computed in the 3D virtual avatar coordinate system mounted in the pelvis of the effector.

Before feeding the data to the models, datasets were cleaned from data loss artifacts that were not caught during the online recordings. Additionally, observations for which the predicted and desired state did not match due to state

---

[2] instead of 586 samples due to 100 ms buffer during recording.

decoder errors were also removed to reduce the number of mislabelled observations (e.g., when the patient was asked to control left hand translation but instead left wrist was rotating).

Then, all the models were trained to find the mapping between $\mathbf{X}_i$ ECoG signal and $\mathbf{y}_i$ desired trajectories that the hand should follow in the case of optimal prediction. As a performance metric we used cosine similarity (Eq. 1) measuring cosine of the angle α_i between prediction $\hat{\mathbf{y}}_i$ and the desired trajectory $\mathbf{y}_i$.

$$\mathrm{CS}(\mathbf{y}_i, \hat{\mathbf{y}}_i) = \frac{\mathbf{y}_i \cdot \hat{\mathbf{y}}_i}{\|\mathbf{y}_i\| \cdot \|\hat{\mathbf{y}}_i\|} = \cos\alpha_i \qquad (1)$$

Cosine loss defined as $\mathrm{CL}(\mathbf{y}_i, \hat{\mathbf{y}}_i) = 1 - \mathrm{CS}(\mathbf{y}_i, \hat{\mathbf{y}}_i)$ was used as optimization objective.

2.3 Hand-Crafted Features Extraction and DL Optimization

'Traditional' hand-crafted features were extracted using complex continuous wavelet transform (CWT). CWT was performed with Morlet wavelets with central frequencies ranging from 10 to 150 Hz (broad band as ECoG contains higher frequencies than EEG) with a step of 10 Hz. Each wavelet support consisted of 118 samples (0.2 s) centered on its maximum value. Features were obtained by applying CWT on one-second-long signals, computing the module of the complex signals, and performing an average pooling of 0.1 s. The resulting feature tensor was of shape $64 \times 15 \times 10$, with dimensions corresponding to channels, frequency bands, and time steps.

CWT can be represented as a convolution between a set of filters and a signal in the temporal domain. In the standard case, the filters are fixed and constitute a basis for feature extraction where every filter detects brain activity in a different frequency band. As every spatial channel is convolved separately in time, we obtained a time-frequency-space representation of the ECoG signal (see Table 1 for feature extractor architecture specification).

Here, we propose to adjust the filters during backpropagation together with all other parameters of the models. In the first scenario, the filters were initialized to Morlet wavelets with 15 central frequencies, resulting in 30 kernels (real and imaginary parts). Note that at the beginning of training, the first layer reproduces 'traditional' hand-crafted feature extraction. The filters were fixed for 5 epochs of so-called pre-training, then they were unfreezed and optimized freely (without any additional constraints imposing specific filter shape) for the following 50 epochs. The pre-training was used to not distort the wavelets drastically in the first epochs when parameters of the rest of the network are randomly initialized. We also evaluated random weights initialization from uniform distribution as a solution that does not incorporate prior knowledge about the system.

In the second scenario, an alternative approach was used to maintain the wavelet structure by optimizing only the parameters used to generate the wavelets instead of modifying all filters' parameters. In our case, the function generating the wavelets was defined as:

$$\Psi(t, f) = \frac{1}{\sqrt{\pi}} \frac{1}{\sqrt{\frac{f_s}{f}}} e^{-(tf)^2} e^{2i\pi tf} \tag{2}$$

where central frequency parameter f defines the center of the frequency band analyzed by the wavelet and f_s is the signal sampling frequency. In the central frequency optimization (CFO) scenario, we optimized only the central frequency f parameters (one per wavelet), so the filters after training are still from the Morlet wavelets family.

Table 1. The architecture used to reproduce hand-crafted feature extraction with CWT. Only one convolutional layer (conv time) was used in computations according to the performed experiment E2E/E2E CFO.

Layer	Kernel shape	Output shape	Param #	Mult-adds
Input	–	[200, 1, 590, 8, 8]	–	–
Conv time	[1, 30, 118, 1, 1]	[200, 30, 590, 8, 8]	3,570	27,006,336,000
Conv time CFO	[1, 30, 118, 1, 1]	[200, 30, 590, 8, 8]	15	27,006,336,000
Square	–	[200, 30, 590, 8, 8]	–	–
Sum real and imaginary	–	[200, 15, 590, 8, 8]	–	–
Square root	–	[200, 15, 590, 8, 8]	–	–
Dropout	–	[200, 15, 590, 8, 8]	–	–
AvgPool	–	[200, 15, 10, 8, 8]	–	–
BatchNorm	[15]	[200, 15, 10, 8, 8]	30	6,000

2.4 DL Architectures

In this study, we used two architectures proposed in [16], i.e., CNN+LSMT+MT, which showed the best performance, and MLP, which was the simplest approach. In the baseline approach, the hand-crafted feature extraction was followed with fully connected or convolutional layers. When optimizing the first convolutional layer, we kept the rest of the network the same to isolate the influence of the training feature extraction step. Details of the tested DL architectures are described below and in [16]. Additionally, we used ShallowFBCSPNet and Deep4Net [15] as end-to-end DL baseline.

MLP. The most basic DL architecture evaluated in the study was multilayer perceptron (MLP), consisting of two fully connected layers. Dropout and batch normalization layers were placed between fully connected layers for stronger regularization (see Table 2).

Table 2. MLP architecture from [16].

Layer	Kernel shape	Output shape	Param #	Mult-adds
Flatten	–	[200, 9600]	–	–
Fully connected	[9600, 50]	[200, 50]	480,050	96,010,000
BatchNorm	[50]	[200, 50]	100	20,000
ReLU	–	[200, 50]	–	–
Dropout	–	[200, 50]	–	–
Fully connected	[50, 50]	[200, 50]	2,550	510,000
ReLU	–	[200, 50]	–	–
Dropout	–	[200, 50]	–	–
Fully connected	[50, 3]	[200, 3]	153	30,600

CNN+LSTM+MT. In the CNN+LSTM+MT architecture, CWT features were further analyzed with 3×3 convolutional layers in space (electrodes organized on an array 4×8 reflecting positions of electrodes on implants). After two convolutional layers, two LSTM layers were applied to analyze temporal information from 10 timesteps. Finally, every output of the last LSTM layer was used for training to compute loss based on all predicted and ground truth trajectories corresponding to 1 s (10 timesteps) of signal analyzed (see Table 3).

Table 3. CNN+LSTM+MT architecture from [16].

Layer	Kernel shape	Output shape	Param #	Mult-adds
Input		[200, 15, 8, 8, 10]	–	
Input per implant		[200, 15, 8, 4, 10]	–	
Conv space	[15, 32, 3, 3, 1]	[200, 32, 6, 4, 10]	4,352	208,896,000
ReLU	–	[200, 32, 6, 4, 10]	–	–
BatchNorm	[32]	[200, 32, 6, 4, 10]	64	12,800
Dropout	–	[200, 32, 6, 4, 10]	–	–
Conv space	[32, 64, 3, 3, 1]	[200, 64, 4, 2, 10]	18,496	295,936,000
ReLU	–	[200, 64, 4, 2, 10]	–	–
Dropout	–	[200, 64, 4, 2, 10]	–	–
LSTM	–	[200, 10, 50]	215,200	430,400,000
LSTM	–	[200, 10, 3]	660	

Models Training and Hyperparameters. For every model evaluation, we used 90% and 10% of the training dataset for training and validation, respectively. The validation dataset was used for early stopping after 20 epochs without improvement. All the models used a fixed set of hyperparameters, i.e., learning rate of 0.001, weight decay of 0.01, batch size of 200, and ADAM optimizer [9]. To train DL models we used PyTorch [11], skorch [18], and braindecode [15].

2.5   Offline Experiments

First, we computed results in a classical evaluation scenario, i.e., train/valid/test split. We used the calibration dataset (first six sessions, approximately 10% of the dataset) as the training dataset. The rest of the data (online evaluation dataset) was used as the test set.

Additionally, we gradually increased the training dataset size from one session up to 22 with a step of 2. As different models may have different dataset requirements, we wanted to verify whether collecting more data can be more profitable for one of the evaluated optimization/architecture combinations.

To investigate the possible influence of end-to-end learning on models' robustness against data mislabelling, we perturbed the dataset to make training more challenging. In the BCI, part of observations is often mistakenly labeled due to lack of subject attention, tiredness, experimental setup, etc. Therefore, we randomly selected a fraction of observations in which targets were shuffled between samples so they no longer have a meaningful connection with the ECoG signal while preserving the same distribution. At the same time, we kept the test set unchanged.

3   Results

Table 4. Test cosine similarity computed in the train-valid-test split scenario. Values are sorted by average performance and represent the mean and standard deviation of 5 runs.

	Left hand	Right hand
E2E CNN+LSTM+MT CFO	**0.304 ± 0.005**	0.266 ± 0.020
CNN+LSTM+MT	0.297 ± 0.008	0.270 ± 0.011
E2E CNN+LSTM+MT	0.289 ± 0.007	**0.273 ± 0.015**
E2E MLP CFO	0.254 ± 0.012	0.230 ± 0.013
MLP	0.247 ± 0.023	0.232 ± 0.005
E2E MLP	0.243 ± 0.014	0.234 ± 0.020
ShallowFBCSPNet [15]	0.235 ± 0.010	0.236 ± 0.011
E2E CNN+LSTM+MT random init	0.216 ± 0.008	0.230 ± 0.020
E2E MLP random init	0.181 ± 0.029	0.223 ± 0.008
Deep4Net [15]	0.111 ± 0.021	0.259 ± 0.013

We started the analysis by comparing different model training scenarios when trained on the first six sessions (online calibration dataset). The results for the train/test split can be found in Table 4. Differences between scenarios are rather small, with only small performance improvement coming from full end-to-end optimization. The best performance was achieved by models using CFO. However, the gap between the hand-crafted features approach and CFO is relatively small, considering standard deviations of the computed values. The worst performance was achieved for Deep4Net (especially low performance for the left hand dataset) and both MLP and CNN+LSTM+MT models with random weights initialization, suggesting the high importance of the prior signal processing knowledge used to define the wavelet shape of the filters at the beginning of the training.

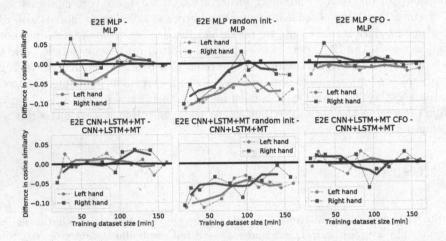

Fig. 3. Difference between cosine similarity of end-to-end model and its counterpart using hand-crafted features. The bold line denotes the moving average with a window of size 3.

We did not notice significant improvements coming from end-to-end optimization, so we wanted to verify the hypothesis of different dataset size requirements for different optimization methods. Therefore, the differences between end-to-end models and their hand-crafted features counterparts for several training dataset sizes are presented in Fig. 3. In some cases, end-to-end models increase the cosine similarity faster than the models using fixed features, so the gap between models can be reduced for approaches using random weights initialization. However, only for models initialized to wavelets and optimized directly, an improvement over hand-crafted features can be observed for some points (up to 0.05 of cosine similarity for the right hand dataset).

When comparing CFO and standard E2E optimization in Fig. 4, higher effectiveness of CFO for small training datasets can be observed. CFO may limit overfitting as the functions represented by the convolutional filters are constrained to the wavelet family. It may be interpreted as an additional optimization constraint imposed on model parameters. Note that diminished gap between CFO and standard end-to-end in Fig. 4 show only relative decrease of CFO performance.

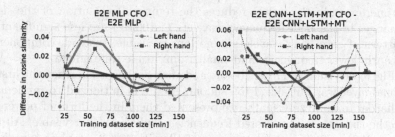

Fig. 4. Difference between cosine similarity of the CFO model and its counterpart using constraint-free end-to-end optimization. The bold line denotes the moving average with a window of size 3.

3.1 Filters Visualization

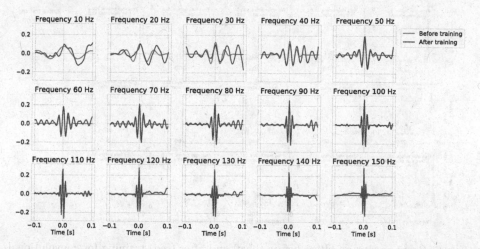

Fig. 5. Visualized filters before (blue) and after (red) training for the models with parameters optimized freely. Note that only real part of the wavelet was visualized for clarity. Plot titles denote central wavelet frequency at initialization. (Color figure online)

We visualized the filters before and after training to analyze the characteristics of learned feature extraction. In Fig. 5, we presented the filters modified without additional constraints. The biggest change can be observed in the central frequencies between 30 Hz and 80 Hz. In most cases, the initial central frequency was maintained, while the wavelets got extended with a signal similar to the sine wave in the central wavelet frequency. This could indicate the importance of information about frequencies from which the signal is composed. At the same time, extending wavelets reduces the temporal resolution of the signals. The changes in the high-frequency wavelets (>100 Hz) are less significant, and the pattern of extending wavelets is no longer visible. Instead, components of significantly lower frequencies and smaller amplitude were added.

In Fig. 6, we visualized filters before and after optimization when the first convolutional layer was initialized to random. As filters initialized to random were much harder to analyze visually, we presented them in the form of power spectra, so the changes in the filtered frequencies could be better visible. All filters have a maximum power peak lower than 65 Hz with 40% of maxima contained in the frequency range 25–30 Hz. Compared to hand-crafted features, end-to-end filters initialized to random covered only approximately half of the frequency band analyzed by the fixed hand-crafted feature extraction pipeline. However, in the higher frequencies, there are smaller peaks which can also contribute to the extracted representation and may cover the missing frequency band.

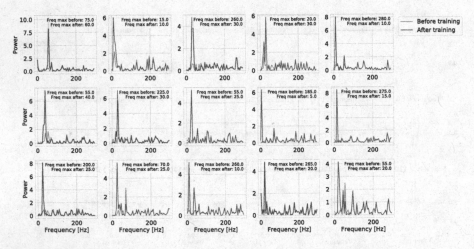

Fig. 6. Power spectra of filters before (blue) and after (red) training for convolutional layer initialized to random. The plots denoted frequencies for which maximum power spectra were observed before and after training. (Color figure online)

In Fig. 7a, we presented the difference between initialized central wavelet frequency and the one obtained after the training. We observed a decrease in almost all frequencies when training the models. The decrease was higher for higher frequencies. This may suggest that more information can be extracted from lower frequencies. However, in our preliminary results, we noticed that adapting the learning rate for the convolutional layer may significantly change the frequency behavior (see Fig. 7b), which should be taken into account when analyzing the results. This may lead to different changes in the central frequencies than in the base model. The gradient was increased 150 times by squeezing central frequencies from 10–150 Hz to 0–1. In the case of initialization to wavelet, a network may start the training near a local minimum found by the manual design of feature extraction that can be hard to move out. Setting a higher learning rate may enable reaching different regions on the loss function surface. The performance achieved with a higher learning rate was similar to the standard CFO results with a cosine similarity of 0.283 ± 0.014 (left hand) and 0.270 ± 0.011 (right hand) for CNN+LSTM+MT and 0.262 ± 0.01 (left hand) and 0.227 ± 0.007 (right hand) for MLP.

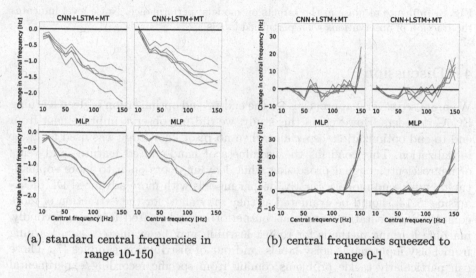

(a) standard central frequencies in range 10-150

(b) central frequencies squeezed to range 0-1

Fig. 7. Difference between central wavelet frequencies before and after CFO. Models for left hand translation are presented in the left column, for the right hand in the right column. Note that the scale is different for (a) and (b).

3.2   Target Perturbation

In the case of perturbed ground-truth (Fig. 8), CNN+LSTM+MT models were more robust to noise in the targets with increased stability (especially for the left hand) of hand-crafted features and CFO models compared to models optimized freely. On the other hand, in the case of MLP models, almost no differences between different optimization methods in the influence of noise on the performance were noticed.

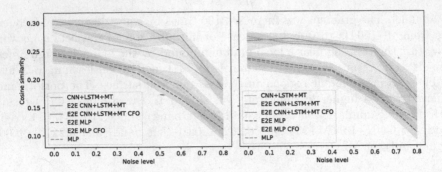

Fig. 8. Influence of noise in the targets on models' performance. Noise level indicates the fraction of observations with perturbed labels.

4 Discussion

We proposed several approaches for the end-to-end optimization of deep learning ECoG decoders. However, in this study, we did not observe improvement from end-to-end optimization, especially when no prior knowledge was used for filter initialization. This confirms the usefulness of hand-crafted features and years of neuroscientific signal processing while leaving doors open to more sophisticated end-to-end models. Firstly, deeper models with more advanced DL mechanisms [6,13] should be evaluated as they may allow for the extraction of more complex representations and thus outperform hand-crafted features. Secondly, machine learning methods for robust learning may be evaluated, e.g., learning from noisy input data, noisy labels, and out-of-distribution samples [7]. Those can particularly tackle problems coming from specific recording/experimental circumstances.

The reasoning behind our study is focused on the specificity of ECoG brain signals and the adequacy of selected DL methods to the problem. The specificity originates from experimental constraints caused by the presence of a human in the loop but also signals characteristics, hardware capabilities, etc. It results in a distorted dataset with a low signal-to-noise ratio, short signal stationarity interval, and uncertain labels. This is quite different from computer vision problems, usually with well-defined labels and images understandable with a naked eye. Improving information extraction from noisy data may be especially important in the light of increased robustness to noise in targets shown by the CNN+LSTM+MT model compared to MLP. Using all 10 targets recorded during a 1-s window decreases the influence of single perturbed points on the performance because the information can be efficiently extracted even for 40% or 60% of perturbed targets. In this case, the CNN+LSTM+MT model using hand-crafted features maintains high performance for a higher noise level than the end-to-end model. However, an important point in the discussion is that our dataset, even after data cleaning, still contains a significant, unknown amount of observations with incorrect labels. Thus, in Fig. 8, a noise level equal to zero corresponds to an unknown noise level in labels originating from the experimental setup. Thus, generative models should be used to create datasets with a known level of noise and analyze the influence of perturbations on the performance in the case of less distorted datasets.

All the results were computed offline on datasets recorded with only one patient. These kinds of datasets are hardly accessible due to experimental and legal constraints. It makes the generalization of the results to other patients and datasets hard to estimate. Thus, more simulations should be performed to confirm our conclusions, ideally with more patients and tasks. This should also include hyperparameters search, like learning rate, batch size, weight decay, as those could vary between different approaches. However, performing hundreds of evaluations is time-consuming, and the problem is magnified in the case of end-to-end models due to increased computational load. Our study focused on feature extraction based on wavelet transform, which was previously used in this problem. As we optimized the parameters of the wavelet transform without changing other parts of the model, we isolated the influence of end-to-end optimization on models' performance. While this simplified the problem, our study did not evaluate other feature extraction pipelines that could behave differently. Thus, an extended analysis of several feature extraction pipelines compared to their end-to-end counterparts would allow for broader generalization and therefore is of great interest.

While this article and [20] analyzed ECoG signals, targets used for training models in [20] were actual fingers trajectories recorded while subjects performed real movements. In our case, targets are much noisier due to the lack of labeling based on the hand movements of a tetraplegic patient. This may favor hand-crafted features, as could be seen for CNN+LSTM+MT in Fig. 8. Finally, our conclusions are in line with [20] who observed relatively small improvement from optimizing hand-crafted features and worse performance/longer training time when initializing the model to random. In our case, end-to-end models achieved the same performance as models using CWT features only with smart weights initialization, which emphasizes the importance of prior signal processing knowledge in designing DL for ECoG analysis.

Acknowledgement. Clinatec is a Laboratory of CEA-Leti at Grenoble and has statutory links with the University Hospital of Grenoble (CHUGA) and University Grenoble Alpes (UGA). This study was funded by CEA (recurrent funding) and the French Ministry of Health (Grant PHRC-15-15-0124), Institut Carnot, Fonds de Dotation Clinatec. Matthieu Martin was supported by the cross-disciplinary program on Numerical Simulation of CEA. Maciej Śliwowski was supported by the CEA NUMERICS program, which has received funding from European Union's Horizon 2020 research and innovation program under the Marie Sklodowska-Curie grant agreement No 800945—NUMERICS—H2020-MSCA-COFUND-2017.

References

1. Benabid, A.L., et al.: An exoskeleton controlled by an epidural wireless brain-machine interface in a tetraplegic patient: a proof-of-concept demonstration. Lancet Neurol. **18**(12), 1112–1122 (2019). https://doi.org/10.1016/S1474-4422(19)30321-7

2. Devlin, J., Chang, M., Lee, K., Toutanova, K.: BERT: pre-training of deep bidirectional transformers for language understanding. In: Burstein, J., Doran, C., Solorio, T. (eds.) Proceedings of the 2019 Conference of the North American Chapter of the Association for Computational Linguistics: Human Language Technologies, NAACL-HLT 2019, Minneapolis, MN, USA, 2–7 June 2019, Volume 1 (Long and Short Papers), pp. 4171–4186. Association for Computational Linguistics (2019). https://doi.org/10.18653/v1/n19-1423

3. Eliseyev, A., et al.: Recursive exponentially weighted N-way partial least squares regression with recursive-validation of hyper-parameters in brain-computer interface applications. Sci. Rep. **7**(1), 16281 (2017). https://doi.org/10.1038/s41598-017-16579-9

4. Krizhevsky, A., Sutskever, I., Hinton, G.E.: ImageNet classification with deep convolutional neural networks. In: Pereira, F., Burges, C., Bottou, L., Weinberger, K. (eds.) Advances in Neural Information Processing Systems, vol. 25. Curran Associates, Inc. (2012). http://proceedings.neurips.cc/paper/2012/file/c399862d3b9d6b76c8436e924a68c45b-Paper.pdf

5. Lawhern, V.J., Solon, A.J., Waytowich, N.R., Gordon, S.M., Hung, C.P., Lance, B.J.: EEGNet: a compact convolutional neural network for EEG-based brain-computer interfaces. J. Neural Eng. **15**(5), 056013 (2018). https://doi.org/10.1088/1741-2552/aace8c

6. Lee, Y.E., Lee, S.H.: EEG-transformer: self-attention from transformer architecture for decoding EEG of imagined speech (2021). https://doi.org/10.48550/ARXIV.2112.09239

7. Li, J., Xiong, C., Hoi, S.C.: Learning from noisy data with robust representation learning. In: 2021 IEEE/CVF International Conference on Computer Vision (ICCV), pp. 9465–9474 (2021). https://doi.org/10.1109/ICCV48922.2021.00935

8. Liang, N., Bougrain, L.: Decoding finger flexion from band-specific ECoG signals in humans. Front. Neurosci. **6**, 91 (2012). https://doi.org/10.3389/fnins.2012.00091

9. Loshchilov, I., Hutter, F.: Decoupled weight decay regularization. In: International Conference on Learning Representations (2019). http://openreview.net/forum?id=Bkg6RiCqY7

10. Mestais, C.S., Charvet, G., Sauter-Starace, F., Foerster, M., Ratel, D., Benabid, A.L.: WIMAGINE: wireless 64-channel ECoG recording implant for long term clinical applications. IEEE Trans. Neural Syst. Rehabil. Eng. **23**(1), 10–21 (2015). https://doi.org/10.1109/TNSRE.2014.2333541

11. Paszke, A., et al.: PyTorch: an imperative style, high-performance deep learning library. In: Advances in Neural Information Processing Systems, vol. 32, pp. 8024–8035. Curran Associates, Inc. (2019). https://papers.neurips.cc/paper/9015-pytorch-an-imperative-style-high-performance-deep-learning-library.pdf

12. Roy, Y., Banville, H., Albuquerque, I., Gramfort, A., Falk, T.H., Faubert, J.: Deep learning-based electroencephalography analysis: a systematic review. J. Neural Eng. **16**(5), 051001 (2019). https://doi.org/10.1088/1741-2552/ab260c

13. Santamaría-Vázquez, E., Martínez-Cagigal, V., Vaquerizo-Villar, F., Hornero, R.: EEG-inception: a novel deep convolutional neural network for assistive ERP-based brain-computer interfaces. IEEE Trans. Neural Syst. Rehabil. Eng. **28**(12), 2773–2782 (2020). https://doi.org/10.1109/TNSRE.2020.3048106
14. Schalk, G., et al.: Decoding two-dimensional movement trajectories using electrocorticographic signals in humans. J. Neural Eng. **4**(3), 264–275 (2007). https://doi.org/10.1088/1741-2560/4/3/012
15. Schirrmeister, R.T., et al.: Deep learning with convolutional neural networks for EEG decoding and visualization. Hum. Brain Mapp. **38**(11), 5391–5420 (2017). https://doi.org/10.1002/hbm.23730
16. Śliwowski, M., Martin, M., Souloumiac, A., Blanchart, P., Aksenova, T.: Decoding ECoG signal into 3D hand translation using deep learning. J. Neural Eng. **19**(2), 026023 (2022). https://doi.org/10.1088/1741-2552/ac5d69
17. Tabar, Y.R., Halici, U.: A novel deep learning approach for classification of EEG motor imagery signals. J. Neural Eng. **14**(1), 016003 (2016). https://doi.org/10.1088/1741-2560/14/1/016003
18. Tietz, M., Fan, T.J., Nouri, D., Bossan, B., skorch Developers: SKORCH: a scikit-learn compatible neural network library that wraps PyTorch (2017). http://skorch.readthedocs.io/en/stable/
19. Volkova, K., Lebedev, M.A., Kaplan, A., Ossadtchi, A.: Decoding movement from electrocorticographic activity: a review. Front. Neuroinform. **13**, 74 (2019). https://doi.org/10.3389/fninf.2019.00074
20. Xie, Z., Schwartz, O., Prasad, A.: Decoding of finger trajectory from ECoG using deep learning. J. Neural Eng. **15**(3), 036009 (2018). https://doi.org/10.1088/1741-2552/aa9dbe

Quantum Circuit Compilation for the Graph Coloring Problem

Angelo Oddi[1](✉)(iD), Riccardo Rasconi[1](iD), Marco Baioletti[2](✉)(iD),
Vieri Giuliano Santucci[1](iD), and Hamish Beck[3]

[1] Institute of Cognitive Sciences and Technologies (ISTC-CNR), Rome, Italy
{angelo.oddi,riccardo.rasconi,vieri.santucci}@istc.cnr.it
[2] University of Perugia, Perugia, Italy
marco.baioletti@unipg.it
[3] Advanced Concepts Team, ESA European Space Research and Technology Centre,
Noordwijk, The Netherlands

Abstract. In this work we investigate the performance of greedy randomised search (GRS) techniques to the problem of compiling quantum circuits that solve instances of the Graph Coloring problem. Quantum computing uses *quantum gates* that manipulate multi-valued bits (*qubits*). A quantum circuit is composed of a number of qubits and a series of quantum gates that operate on those qubits, and whose execution realises a specific quantum algorithm.

Current quantum computing technologies limit the qubit interaction distance allowing the execution of gates between adjacent qubits only. This has opened the way to the exploration of possible techniques aimed at guaranteeing nearest-neighbor (NN) compliance in any quantum circuit through the addition of a number of so-called *swap* gates between adjacent qubits. In addition, technological limitations (*decoherence* effect) impose that the overall duration (i.e., *depth*) of the quantum circuit realization be minimized.

One core contribution of the paper is the application of an upgraded version of the greedy randomized search (GRS) technique originally introduced in the literature that synthesises NN-compliant quantum circuits realizations, starting from a set of benchmark instances of different size belonging to the *Quantum Approximate Optimization Algorithm* (QAOA) class tailored for the Graph Coloring problem. We propose a comparison between the presented method and the SABRE compiler, one of the best-performing compilation procedures present in Qiskit, an open-source SDK for quantum development, both from the CPU efficiency and from the solution quality standpoint.

Keywords: Randomized search · Quantum circuit compilation · Planning · Scheduling · Optimization

© The Author(s), under exclusive license to Springer Nature Switzerland AG 2023
A. Dovier et al. (Eds.): AIxIA 2022, LNAI 13796, pp. 374–386, 2023.
https://doi.org/10.1007/978-3-031-27181-6_26

1   Introduction

Quantum algorithms process information represented as qubits, the basic unit of quantum information, and quantum operations (called gates) are the building blocks of quantum algorithms. In order to be run on real quantum computing hardware, quantum algorithms must be compiled into a set of elementary machine instructions (or *gates*). Since currently available quantum devices suffer a number of technological problems such as noise and *decoherence*, it is important that the process that carries out the quantum computation be somehow adapted to the physical limitations of the quantum hardware of interest, by means of a proper compilation.

For practical applications, it is essential to make quantum computation able to tackle problem instances of more and more realistic size. To this aim, the ability to produce compiled quantum circuits of good quality is of paramount importance. In this paper, we focus our efforts on the so-called Quantum Alternate Operator Ansatz (QAOA) algorithms [9] applied on the gate-model noisy intermediate-scale quantum (NISQ) processor units [18]. Our approach intends to improve over the compilation algorithms employed in the Qiskit quantum computing software development kit [1], and devise solutions that are easily adaptable to different classes of problems. In the NISQ era, the leading quantum processors are characterized by about 50 to a few hundred qubits but are not advanced enough to reach fault tolerance, nor large or sophisticated enough to continuously implement quantum error correction. The term "noisy" refers to the fact that quantum processors are very sensitive to the environment and may lose their quantum state due to quantum decoherence. The term "intermediate-scale" refers to the relatively small number of qubits and moderate gate fidelity. The term *NISQ algorithms* refers to algorithms designed for NISQ quantum processors. For example, the Variational Quantum Eigensolver (VQE) or the Quantum Alternate Operator Ansatz (QAOA) (and its sub-class, the Quantum Approximate Optimization Algorithm [6,8]) are *hybrid* algorithms that use NISQ devices but reduce the calculation load by implementing some parts of the algorithm in usual classical processors.

Usually, NISQ algorithms require error mitigation techniques to recover useful data, which however make use of precious qubits to be implemented. Thus, the creation of a computer with tens of thousands of qubits and sufficient error correction capabilities would eventually end the NISQ era. These "beyond-NISQ" devices would be able, for example, to implement Shor's algorithm, for very large numbers, and break RSA encryption. Until that point however, the need to produce circuits runnable in the current (or near-future) quantum architectures in a reasonably reliable manner (i.e., counting on noise minimization techniques rather than on error-correcting techniques) will stand. Hence, the need to provide quantum circuit compilation procedures that minimize the effects of decoherence by minimizing the circuit's depth.

In this work, we investigate the performance of an upgraded version of the greedy randomized search (GRS) technique [10,16,19] originally introduced in [17] applied to the problem of compiling quantum circuits to emerging quantum hardware. In particular, we experiment on a set of benchmark instances belonging to the Quantum Alternate Operator Ansatz (QAOA) class tailored for the Graph Coloring problem, and devised to be executed on top of a hardware architecture inspired by Rigetti Computing Inc. [20]. We compare our algorithm's performance against the SABRE compiler [13], one of the best compilers present in the Qiskit framework, and demonstrate the superiority of our approach.

The paper is organized as follows. Section 2 provides some background information. Section 3 formally describes the problem, whereas Sect. 4 describes the proposed heuristic solving algorithms and the Greedy Randomised Search approach. Finally, an empirical comparison with the results obtained from the SABRE compiler [1] and some conclusions close the paper.

2   Background

Quantum computing is based on the manipulation of qubits rather than conventional bits; a quantum computation is performed by executing a set of quantum gates on the qubits. A gate whose execution involves k qubits is called k-qubit quantum gate. Current NISQ devices only allow the direct execution of 1-qubit and 2-qubit quantum gates. In order to be executed, a quantum circuit must be mapped on a quantum chip which determines the circuit's hardware architecture specification [14]. The chip can be seen as an undirected multigraph whose nodes represent the qubits (quantum physical memory locations) and whose edges represent the types of gates that can be physically implemented between adjacent qubits of the physical hardware (see Fig. 1 as an example of three chip topologies of increasing size). Since a 2-qubit gate requiring two specific qstates can only be executed on a pair of adjacent (NN) qubits, the required qstates must be made nearest-neighbors prior to gate execution. NN-compliance can be obtained by adding a number of *swap* gates so that every pair of qstates involved in the quantum gates can be eventually made adjacent, allowing all gates to be correctly executed.

Figure 2 shows an example of quantum circuit that only uses the first three qubits of the chip ($N = 8$) of Fig. 1, which assumes that qstates q_1, q_2 and q_3 are initially allocated to qubits n_1, n_2 and n_3. The circuit is composed of four generic 2-qubit gates (i.e., CNOT gates) and one generic 1-qubit gate (i.e., the Hadamard gate). Note that the circuit is not NN-compliant as the last gate involves two qstates resting on to two non-adjacent qbits (n_1 and n_3). The right side of Fig. 2 shows the same circuit made NN-compliant through the insertion of a swap gate.

In this work, we tackle the compilation problem of quantum circuit following a scheduling-oriented formulation, as described in the next sections. In particular, our approach is related to a body of heuristic efforts available in the current literature, see [11,12] for two relatively recent representative works. Even though these papers pursue the same objective, i.e., optimizing the realization of *nearest-neighbor* compliant quantum circuits, they focus on quantum circuits characterized by pre-ordered non-commutative gates. On the contrary, our approach

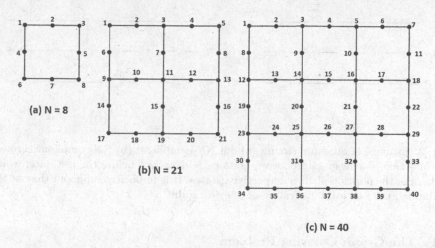

Fig. 1. Three quantum chip designs characterized by an increasing number of qubits ($N = 8, 21, 40$) inspired by Rigetti Computing Inc. Every qubit is located at a different location (node), and the integers at each node represent the qubit's identifier.

leverages the parallel nature of the considered planning/scheduling problem, and proposes a greedy randomized algorithm that exploits gate commutativity through a heuristic ranking function for quantum gate selection.

3   The QCC Problem

The problem tackled in this work consists in compiling a given quantum circuit on a specific quantum hardware architecture. To this aim, we focus on the Quantum Alternating Operator Ansatz (QAOA) framework [9] a generalization of the *Quantum Approximate Optimization Algorithm* (QAOA) circuits [6,8], a class of hybrid quantum algorithms used in the literature to solve problems like the Max-Cut, while the Graph Coloring problem has received much less attention. The quantum hardware architecture we consider is inspired by the one proposed by Rigetti Computing Inc. [20]. The quantum circuits that solve the benchmark problems considered in this work are characterized by a high number of commuting quantum gates (i.e., gates among which no particular order is superimposed) that allow for great flexibility and parallelism in the solution, which makes the corresponding optimization problem very interesting and allows for an a significant depth minimization potential to limit circuit's decoherence [21].

The rest of this section is devoted to: (i) describing the Graph Coloring problem and (ii) providing a formulation of the Quantum Circuit Compilation Problem (QCCP).

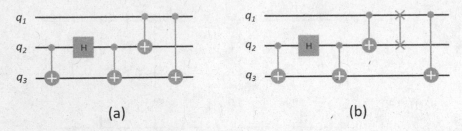

Fig. 2. Example of quantum circuit: (a) not NN-compliant; (b) NN-compliant through the insertion of a swap gate between qbits n_1 and n_2 just before the last gate, which exchanges the position of their respective qstates. It is implicitly supposed that at the beginning, the i-th qstate is resting on the i-th qubit.

3.1   The Graph Coloring Problem

Given a graph $G(V, E)$ with $n = |V|$ nodes and $m = |E|$ edges, the objective is to maximize the number of edges in E that have end points with different colours, using for each node one among k available colours ($k > 2$), see Fig. 3a. Similarly to the MaxCut problem case, the quantum state preparation circuit within the QAOA solving framework relative to the Graph Coloring problem is divided in the following ordered phases: (i) *initial state preparation* (INIT block), (ii) *phase-shift* (P-S block), and (iii) *mixing* (MIX block) (see Fig. 3b).

Specifically, the initial state preparation phase serves the purpose of initializing the quantum states to represent a *feasible* initial assignment, and its objective is to create a superposition with equal coefficients of all the k^n possible colorings (W_N state [4]), following the *one-hot encoding* [7]. According to the one-hot encoding, k qubits are required to represent the color of each vertex, where all but the i-th qubit ($1 \leq i \leq k$) are assigned the $|0\rangle$ value and the i-th qubit, which is assigned the $|1\rangle$ value, indicates whether that node is coloured with the colour i. As a consequence, in order to solve a Graph Coloring instance characterized by n nodes and k colors following the one-hot encoding, it is necessary to use quantum machines with at least nk qubits. More concretely, the feasible initial state assignment is obtained through the utilization of a series of *controlled-$G(p)$* rotations followed by an inverted CNOT (W_N gates, see Fig. 3c). The analysis of the specific circuitry necessary to develop the W_N quantum state is beyond the scope of this paper; the interested reader may refer to [4].

The P-S-phase is composed of a series of phase-shift (R_{ZZ}) gates whose task is counting the edges colored with different colors. For this purpose, an R_{ZZ} gate (see Fig. 3c) is applied to all the $(k^2 - k)/2$ combinations of different colors associated to the end-points of any edge of the graph to be colored. All the phase-shift gates are commutative, so the compilation process does not need to worry about their order in the final circuit.

Finally, the MIX phase serves the purpose of implementing the rotation of all the k colors on every node on the graph, thus potentially allowing any possible color assignment. The basic component of the MIX phase is the $R_{XX}R_{YY}$ (or MIX_{XY}) gate (see Fig. 3c), applied to each vertex of the graph to be colored, and for each pair of adjacent colors in the graph that represents the color rotation on each vertex. The placement of the MIX_{XY} gates in the compiled circuit requires some attention, as these gates are only partially commutative (see the next section).

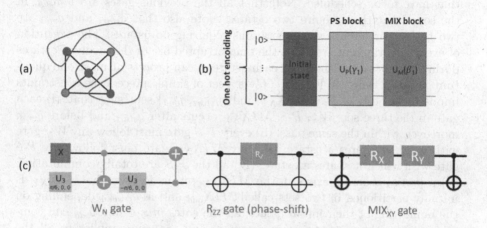

Fig. 3. (a) An example of Graph Coloring instance with $k = 3$ colors. (b) Schema of the quantum state preparation circuit within the QAOA framework, composed of the initialization block, P-S- (phase-shift) block and MIX block. (c) Decomposition in terms of unary and binary basic gates of the quantum gates that respectively compose the three previous blocks.

Figure 3a shows an example of the graph G that represents a Graph Coloring problem instance composed of 5 vertices, 8 edges and $k = 3$ colors. Figure 3b, presents the quantum state preparation schema of the QAOA framework, typically composed of the initial qubit allocation block (state initialization), the P-S (phase-shift) block and the MIX block. In the Graph Coloring problem case, each of the previous three blocks are composed of particular quantum gate aggregations, the W_N, the R_{ZZ} (phase-shift), and the MIX_{XY} gates respectively, shown in Fig. 3c. Generally, the P-S and the MIX blocks within the QAOA framework can be executed along multiple passes (p) in order to obtain more accurate results; in the context of this work, we consider quantum circuits composed of two passes $(p = 2)$.

3.2 Quantum Gate Compilation Problem

Formally, the Quantum Circuit Compilation Problem (QCCP) is a tuple $P = \langle C_0, L_0, QM \rangle$, where C_0 is the input quantum circuit, representing the execution of the Graph Coloring algorithm, L_0 is the initial assignment of the i-th *qstate* q_i to the i-th qubit n_i, and QM is a representation of the quantum hardware as a multigraph.

- The input quantum circuit is a tuple $C_0 = \langle Q, V_{C_0}, TC_0 \rangle$, where: (1) $Q = \{q_1, q_2, \ldots, q_N\}$ is the set of qstates which, from a planning & scheduling perspective, represent the *resources* necessary for each gate's execution (see for example [15], Chap. 15); (2) $V_{C_0} = W_N \cup P\text{-}S \cup MIX_{XY} \cup \{g_{start}, g_{end}\}$ represents the set of *state initialization*, *phase-shift* and *mix* gate *operations* that have to be scheduled. Note that all the previous gates are *binary*, in the sense that they require two qstates. Note also that g_{start} and g_{end} are two fictitious reference gate operations requiring no qstates. The execution of every quantum gate requires the uninterrupted use of the involved qstates during its processing time, and each qstate q_i can process at most one quantum gate at a time. (3) Finally, TC_0 is a set of simple precedence constraints imposed on the W_N, $P\text{-}S$, MIX_{XY} and $\{g_{start}, g_{end}\}$ sets, such that: (i) each gate in the three sets W_N, $P\text{-}S$, MIX_{XY} occurs after g_{start} and before g_{end}; moreover, within the same pass: (ii) every $P\text{-}S$ gate must follow any W_N gate with which it shares a qstate; (iii) any MIX_{XY} gate must follow any $P\text{-}S$ gate with which it shares a qstate; (iv) all the $P\text{-}S$ are totally commutative; (v) a partial ordering exists in the MIX_{XY} set, as follows: the MIX_{XY} is initially partitioned in two sets called MIX_{odd} and MIX_{even} depending on the numbering of their initial qstate; all the gates $mix \in MIX_{odd}$ can commute as they have no qstate in common, and the same applies to all the gates $mix \in MIX_{even}$, while there exists a precedence imposed between a $mix \in MIX_{odd}$ and a $mix \in MIX_{even}$ if and only if they share at least one qstate.
  Between two consecutive passes, no $P\text{-}S$ gate that belongs to the $i+1$-th pass can be executed before any MIX_{XY} gate that belongs to the i-th pass if they share at least one qstate.
- L_0 is the initial assignment at the time origin $t = 0$ of qstates q_i to qubits n_i.
- QM is a representation of the quantum hardware as an undirected multigraph $QM = \langle V_N, E_{W_N}, E_{p\text{-}s}, E_{swap} \rangle$, where $V_N = \{n_1, n_2, \ldots, n_N\}$ is the set of qubits (nodes), $E_{p\text{-}s}$, E_{swap} or E_{W_N} is a set of undirected edges (n_i, n_j) representing the set of *adjacent* locations the qstates q_i and q_j of the gates $p\text{-}s(q_i, q_j)$, $swap(q_i, q_j)$ or $W_N(q_i, q_j)$ can potentially be allocated to. Figure 1 shows an example of quantum hardware.

A feasible solution is a tuple $S = \langle SWAP, TC \rangle$, which extends the initial circuit C_0 to a circuit $C_S = \langle Q, V_{C_S}, TC_S \rangle$, such that $V_{C_S} = SWAP \cup W_N \cup P\text{-}S \cup MIX \cup \{g_{start}, g_{end}\}$ and $TC_S = TC_0 \cup TC$ where: (i) $SWAP$ is a set of additional $swap(q_i, q_j)$ gates added to guarantee the adjacency constraints for the set of W_N, $P\text{-}S$ and MIX_{XY} gates, and (ii) TC is a set of additional simple precedence constraints such that:

- for each qstate q_i, a total order $\preceq_i$ is imposed among the set Q_i of operations requiring q_i, with $Q_i = \{op \in W_N \cup P\text{-}S \cup MIX_{XY} \cup SWAP : op \; requires \; q_i\}$;

Algorithm 1. Greedy Randomized Search

Require: An problem P, stop criterion
   $S_{best} \leftarrow$ COMPILECIRCUIT(P)
  while (stopping criterion not satisfied) **do**
     $S \leftarrow$ COMPILECIRCUIT(P)
     if (depth(S) $<$ depth(S_{best})) **then**
       $S_{best} \leftarrow S$
     end if
  end while
  return (S_{best})

- all the $w_N(q_i, q_j)$, $p\text{-}s(q_i, q_j)$, $mix_{XY}(q_i, q_j)$ and $swap(q_i, q_j)$ gate operations are allocated on adjacent qubits in QM;
- the graph $\langle V_{C_S}, TC_S \rangle$ does not contain cycles.

Given a solution S, a path between the two fictitious gates g_{start} and g_{end} is a sequence of gates $g_{start}, op_1, op_2, \ldots, op_k, g_{end}$, with $op_j \in W_N \cup P\text{-}S \cup MIX_{XY} \cup SWAP$, such that $g_{start} \preceq op_1, op_1 \preceq op_2, \ldots, op_k \preceq g_{end} \in TC_0 \cup TC_S$. The length of the path is the number of all the path's gates and $depth(S)$ is the length of the longest path from g_{start} to g_{end}. An optimal solution S is a feasible solution characterized by the minimum depth.

4   A Greedy Randomized Search Algorithm

In this section we provide a detailed description of the *Greedy Randomized Search (GRS)* procedure used to compile the circuit introduced in previous Sect. 3. *GRS* has traditionally proved to be a very effective method for the resolution of complex optimization problems (such as the *QCCP*), as it realizes a simple optimization process that quickly guides the search towards good solutions [10,16,19]). The *GRS* is particularly useful in cases where a high-quality solution is needed in a relatively short time. Among other applications, it is particularly suitable for constraint-based scheduling problems; since the *QCCP* can be reduced to a Planning and Scheduling (P&S) problem [17,21].

Algorithm 1 depicts the complete randomized search algorithm for generating a near-optimal solutions, which is designed to invoke the COMPILECIRCUIT() procedure until a stop criterion is satisfied. It essentially realizes an optimization cycle in which a new solution S is computed at each iteration through the COMPILE-CIRCUIT() algorithm, and its depth $(depth(S))$ is compared with the best depth found so far $(depth(S_{best}))$ in the iterative process. In case $depth(S)$ is smaller than $depth(S_{best})$, then the current solution S becomes the new best solution S_{best}. The optimization process continues until a stopping condition (generally a max time limit) is met, where the *GRS* procedure returns the best solution found. As can be readily observed, the efficacy of the *GRS* mainly depends on the efficacy of the

---

Algorithm 2. Compile Circuit

Require: A problem $P = \langle C_0, L_0, QM \rangle$
  $S \leftarrow$ INITSOLUTION(P);
  $t \leftarrow 0$
  while not all the P-S and MIX operations are inserted in S **do**
    $op \leftarrow$ SELECTEXECUTABLEGATE(P, S, t)
    if $op \neq nil$ **then**
      $S \leftarrow$ INSERTGATE(op, S, t)
    else
      $t \leftarrow t + 1$
    end if
  end while
  return S

COMPILECIRCUIT() procedure (described in the following section), which has the task of synthesizing increasingly better solutions.

4.1 Compile Circuit Algorithm

Algorithm 2 is a randomized algorithm, it operates on *macro-gates* containing primitive gates that use two qstates at most. Indeed, Algorithm 2 is in itself a heuristically-based iterative algorithm that implements a constructive methodology where a solution is built from scratch using a randomized ranking heuristic. This heuristic returns a ranking among the gates that takes into account the "neighbouring cost" of all the gates that have yet to be inserted in the solution. At each iteration, a subset of gates that guarantee the fastest realization of the neighbouring conditions of all the remaining gates is generated and one gate is selected at random from this subset, for insertion in the current partial solution.

Algorithm 2 takes as input a $QCCP$ problem $P = \langle C_0, L_0, QM \rangle$, and proceeds by *chronologically* inserting in the *partial solution* S one gate operation at a time until all the gates in the set $W_N \cup P\text{-}S \cup MIX_{XY}$ are in S. Let $op \in Q_i$ be a general gate operation that involves qstate q_i, we define a *chain* $ch_i = \{op \in Q_i : op \in S\}$ as the set of gates involving q_i and currently present in the partial solution S, among which a total order is imposed. Let us also define $last(ch_i)$ as the last gate in the chain ch_i according to the imposed total order and $nlast(ch_i)$ as the QM node at which the last operation in the chain ch_i terminates its execution. Finally, we define the state of a partial solution as follows. Given a partial solution S, the *state* L_S is the tuple $L_S = \langle nlast(ch_1), nlast(ch_2), \ldots, nlast(ch_N) \rangle$ of QM locations (nodes) where each last chain operation $last(ch_i)$ terminates its execution. The first step of Algorithm 2 is the initialisation of the partial solution S; in particular, it sets the current state L_S to the init value L_0 by initialising the locations of every qstate q_i (i.e., for every chain ch_i) at the time origin[1] $t = 0$.

---

[1] It is implicitly supposed that at the beginning, the i-th qstate is initialized at the i-th location.

The core of the algorithm is the function SELECTEXECUTABLEGATE(), which returns at each iteration either one of the gates in the set $W_N \cup P\text{-}S \cup MIX_{XY}$ or a $swap(q_i, q_j)$ gate in the $SWAP$ set necessary to guarantee NN-compliance as described in the previous Sect. 3.

Indeed, it is a random algorithm targeted to minimize the solution depth, in particular its implementation is inspired to [3], such that the selection of a gate is based on two criteria: (i) the earliest start time gate selection (a value correlated to depth minimization); (ii) a metric to minimize the number of swaps. At each iteration, SELECTEXECUTABLEGATE(P, S, t) selects the next gate to be inserted in the solution by means of the INSERTGATE(op, S, t) method. In all time instants t where no quantum gate can be selected for insertion, the current time t is increased ($t = t+1$). In particular, SELECTEXECUTABLEGATE() resembles Algorithm 3 (see [2], page 8) with the following important difference: while the cited Algorithm 3 generates a set of *eligible gates* Ω and then selects a gate at random on the basis the proposed *pheromone model* (see [2]), the SELECTEXECUTABLEGATE() procedure chooses one gate at random following the same strategy proposed in [17], so that a set of equivalent gates Ω^*, is extracted from Ω by identifying one gate op^* associated with the minimal lexicographic heuristic value $\Delta_{sum}(op^*)$ (see [17] for further details on its definition) and by considering equivalent to op^* all the gates op such that $\Delta_{sum}(op) = \Delta_{sum}(op^*)$, $\Omega^* = \{op : op \in \Omega, \Delta_{sum}(op) = \Delta_{sum}(op^*)\}$. A full description of the procedure SELECTEXECUTABLEGATE() is given in [2]. The randomly selected gate $op \in \Omega^*$ is inserted in the partial solution S *at the earliest feasible time* as the last operation of the chains relative to the qstates involved in op: $last(ch_i) \leftarrow op$; subsequently, the state L_S of the partial solution is updated accordingly. Algorithm 2 proceeds until a complete solution is built.

5 Experimental Evaluation

We have implemented and tested the proposed ideas leveraging the Qiskit open-source quantum-related framework [1]. Qiskit is a known open-source Software Development Kit for working with quantum computers at the level of pulses, circuits and application modules. It allows for the creation, modification, simulation, and optimization of quantum circuits on a set of both simulated and real quantum architectures, as well as allowing the possibility to test mapping algorithms on arbitrary quantum hardware topologies.

Our contribution for this study focuses on the process of quantum circuit compilation with reference to a given hardware topology with the aim of minimizing the circuit's depth. The proposed procedure was implemented in Python in order to allow its integration within Qiskit. The performance of the algorithm was tested on a benchmark set specifically created to represent the application of quantum computing to the Graph Coloring problem.

5.1 Setup

The benchmark set for the graph colouring circuits is obtained as an extension of part of the $N8$ benchmark set for the Max-Cut problem [21]. Following the

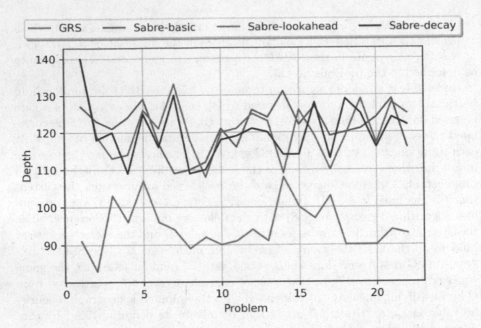

Fig. 4. Comparison between GRS and SABRE

approach in [21], the graph G for which the optimal coloring assignment needs to be found are randomly generated as Erdös-Rényi graphs [5]. In particular, 100 graphs are generated for the $N = 8$ qubit case. Half (50 problems) are generated by choosing N of $N(N-1)/2$ edges over 7 qstates randomly located on the circuit of size 8 qubits (referred as 'Utilization' $u = 90\%$). The other 50 problems are generated by choosing N edges over 8 qstates - referred as utilization $u = 100\%$. For the graph colouring benchmark, we only consider the $N8$ problems with utilization $u = 100\%$, and such that the connected graph contains exactly 7 nodes, assigning three colours ($k = 3$) to each node of the graph, for a total of 22 graph instance problems. Hence, quantum processors with at least 21 qubits (7 nodes times 3 colours) are necessary for the execution of such instances (see Sect. 3.1). More specifically, we consider a Rigetti-inspired 21 qubit processor and set $p = 2$ (two PS-mixing passes).

5.2   Results

The Python version of the proposed greedy randomized search (GRS) algorithm compiles a $QAOA$ circuit with the following choices: (i) a *one-hot* encoding to represent the graph-coloring problems [7], and (ii) a decomposition procedure for the $QAOA$ blocks based on the identification of odd and even MIX_{XY} gates [9,22], as explained in Sect. 3.2.

Figure 4 compares the proposed GRS algorithm with the SABRE compiler available in Qiskit (*SabreSwap*), launched according to its three different heuristics (*basic*, *lookahead*, and *decay*). The algorithms are compared with respect to the depth of the compiled circuits (the circuit's depth represents the longest path in the compiled circuit graph). For each algorithm, a CPU time limit of 10 seconds is imposed on each run.

From the results in Fig. 4 it is clear that GRS outperforms SABRE in all the latter's execution modes. One possible explanation for the superiority of GRS is its capability to better exploit the commutativity rules of the gates in the QAOA-based Graph Coloring quantum circuit instances. Indeed, our algorithm imposes no particular order in the selection of the W_N, $P\text{-}S$, and MIX_{XY} macro-gates as the solution is built, beyond the precedence constraints originally present in the input quantum circuit, contained in the TC_0 set described in Sect. 3.2. As opposed to GRS, SABRE performs the SWAP addition process reasoning directly on the circuit expressed in terms of basic gates, and it is not capable of changing the order of such gates after the circuit is loaded.

6   Conclusions

This study focused on quantum computing as an accelerator for optimization problem resolution. We have considered the compilation techniques for Noisy Intermediate-Scale Quantum (NISQ) devices [18]. In particular, we have explored the Quantum Alternating Operator Ansatz (QAOA) framework [9] for solving optimization problems and studied the quantum circuits for the Graph Coloring reference problem. We have proposed a greedy randomized search (GRS) algorithm targeted at optimizing the compilation of quantum circuits and defined an original benchmark set for testing compilation algorithms. On the basis of our empirical validation the proposed GRS algorithm outperforms other compilation algorithms available in the Qiskit framework.

Acknowledgement. This work is the result of an Ariadna study, a joint collaborative research project with the Advanced Concepts Team (ACT) of the European Space Agency (ESA): Meta-Heuristic Algorithms for the Quantum Circuit Compilation Problem, ESA Contract No. 4000134995/21/NL/GLC/my.

References

1. Qiskit: an open-source framework for quantum computing (2021). https://doi.org/10.5281/zenodo.2573505
2. Baioletti, M., Rasconi, R., Oddi, A.: A novel ant colony optimization strategy for the quantum circuit compilation problem. In: Zarges, C., Verel, S. (eds.) EvoCOP 2021. LNCS, vol. 12692, pp. 1–16. Springer, Cham (2021). https://doi.org/10.1007/978-3-030-72904-2_1
3. Chand, S., Singh, H.K., Ray, T., Ryan, M.: Rollout based heuristics for the quantum circuit compilation problem. In: 2019 IEEE Congress on Evolutionary Computation (CEC), pp. 974–981 (2019)
4. Cruz, D., et al.: Efficient quantum algorithms for GHZ and w states, and implementation on the IBM quantum computer. Adv. Quant. Technol. **2**(5–6), 1900015 (2019)

5. Erdos, P., Renyi, A.: On the evolution of random graphs. Publ. Math. Inst. Hungary. Acad. Sci. **5**, 17–61 (1960)
6. Farhi, E., Goldstone, J., Gutmann, S.: A quantum approximate optimization algorithm. arXiv preprint arXiv:1411.4028 (2014)
7. Fuchs, F.G., Kolden, H.Ø., Aase, N.H., Sartor, G.: Efficient encoding of the weighted max k-cut on a quantum computer using QAOA. SN Comput. Sci. **2**(2), 89 (2021). https://doi.org/10.1007/s42979-020-00437-z
8. Guerreschi, G.G., Park, J.: Gate scheduling for quantum algorithms. arXiv preprint arXiv:1708.00023 (2017)
9. Hadfield, S., Wang, Z., O'Gorman, B., Rieffel, E., Venturelli, D., Biswas, R.: From the quantum approximate optimization algorithm to a quantum alternating operator ansatz. Algorithms **12**(2), 34 (2019)
10. Hart, J., Shogan, A.: Semi-greedy heuristics: an empirical study. Oper. Res. Lett. **6**, 107–114 (1987)
11. Kole, A., Datta, K., Sengupta, I.: A heuristic for linear nearest neighbor realization of quantum circuits by swap gate insertion using n-gate lookahead. IEEE J. Emerg. Sel. Topics Circuits Syst. **6**(1), 62–72 (2016). https://doi.org/10.1109/JETCAS.2016.2528720
12. Kole, A., Datta, K., Sengupta, I.: A new heuristic for n-dimensional nearest neighbor realization of a quantum circuit. IEEE Trans. Comput. Aided Des. Integr. Circuits Syst. **37**(1), 182–192 (2018). https://doi.org/10.1109/TCAD.2017.2693284
13. Li, G., Ding, Y., Xie, Y.: Tackling the qubit mapping problem for NISQ-era quantum devices. CoRR abs/1809.02573 (2018). https://arxiv.org/1809.02573 arxiv.org/abs/1809.02573
14. Maslov, D., Falconer, S.M., Mosca, M.: Quantum circuit placement: optimizing qubit-to-qubit interactions through mapping quantum circuits into a physical experiment. In: Proceedings of the 44th Annual Design Automation Conference, DAC'07, pp. 962–965. ACM, New York, NY, USA (2007). https://doi.org/10.1145/1278480.1278717
15. Nau, D., Ghallab, M., Traverso, P.: Automated Planning: Theory & Practice. Morgan Kaufmann Publishers Inc., San Francisco (2004)
16. Oddi, A., Smith, S.: Stochastic procedures for generating feasible schedules. In: Proceedings 14th National Conference on AI (AAAI-97), pp. 308–314 (1997)
17. Oddi, A., Rasconi, R.: Greedy randomized search for scalable compilation of quantum circuits. In: van Hoeve, W.J. (ed.) Integration of Constraint Programming, Artificial Intelligence, and Operations Research, pp. 446–461. Springer International Publishing, Cham (2018). https://doi.org/10.1007/978-3-319-93031-2_32
18. Preskill, J.: Quantum computing in the NISQ era and beyond. Quantum **2**, 79 (2018). https://doi.org/10.22331/q-2018-08-06-79
19. Resende, M.G., Werneck, R.F.: A hybrid heuristic for the p-median problem. J. Heuristics **10**(1), 59–88 (2004)
20. Sete, E.A., Zeng, W.J., Rigetti, C.T.: A functional architecture for scalable quantum computing. In: 2016 IEEE International Conference on Rebooting Computing (ICRC), pp. 1–6 (2016).https://doi.org/10.1109/ICRC.2016.7738703
21. Venturelli, D., Do, M., Rieffel, E., Frank, J.: Temporal planning for compilation of quantum approximate optimization circuits. In: Proceedings of the 26th International Joint Conference on Artificial Intelligence, IJCAI-17, pp. 4440–4446 (2017). https://doi.org/10.24963/ijcai.2017/620
22. Wang, Z., Rubin, N.C., Dominy, J.M., Rieffel, E.G.: xy mixers: analytical and numerical results for the quantum alternating operator ansatz. Phys. Rev. A **101**, 012320 (2020)

Toward a Heterogeneous Multi-robot Framework for Priority-Based Sanitization of Railway Stations

Riccardo Caccavale[1], Mirko Ermini[2], Eugenio Fedeli[2], Alberto Finzi[1], Vincenzo Lippiello[1], and Fabrizio Tavano[1,2]

[1] Università degli studi di Napoli "Federico II", via Claudio 21, 80125 Naples, Italy
{riccardo.caccavale,alberto.finzi,vincenzo.lippiello}@unina.it
[2] Rete Ferroviaria Italiana, Piazza della Croce Rossa 1, 00161 Rome, Italy
{mi.ermini,e.fedeli}@rfi.it, fabrizio.tavano@unina.it

Abstract. We present a new framework for the prioritized multi-robot sanitization of railway stations based on Deep Reinforcement Learning. The proposed framework allows us to define teams of robots having different sanitizing strategies/capabilities, e.g., faster robots rapidly sanitizing small areas in cooperation with slower but long-range ones. Here, robot-specific policies are defined in order to accommodate the different capabilities of the single agents, while two global metrics are defined to assess the performance of the overall team. This capability of managing heterogeneous teams is an important requirement for the infrastructure manager Rete Ferroviaria Italiana S.p.A., which plans to verify to what extent different technologies or different strategies can be combined to reduce costs or increase cleaning efficiency. We tested our framework considering real data collected by the WiFi network of the main Italian railway station, Roma Termini, comparing its results with a similar Deep Reinforcement Learning system where homogeneous robots are employed.

Keywords: Heterogeneous multi-robot system · Deep reinforcement learning · Priority-based sanitization

1 Introduction

The work illustrated in this paper is motivated by a request from the Italian railway infrastructure manager Rete Ferroviaria Italiana concerned about the spread of Covid-19 disease in the common areas of railway stations. A recent [15] study shows that in train stations there is a high probability of being infected during the pandemic: passengers gathered in the corridors and platforms of stations, eating at restaurants, getting on trains, facilitates the transmission of diseases. The pandemic caused by the SARS-CoV-2 has spawned a crisis that has affected the railway sector in a significant way [31], for example, by inducing people to prefer

A. Dovier et al. (Eds.): AIxIA 2022, LNAI 13796, pp. 387–401, 2023.
https://doi.org/10.1007/978-3-031-27181-6_27

cars instead of trains [4]. It is then strategic for the infrastructure managers (such as the Italian Rete Ferroviaria Italiana) to deploy adequate and modern tools to prevent future contagion inside railway stations [26]. In the last two decades, we have seen the spreading in the world of diseases such as SARS-CoV, MERS-CoV, or COVID-19 with different waves [9,33]. In this regard, disinfectant robot technologies are proven very useful in fighting global pandemics [32] by reducing the number of people involved in the cleaning process and by optimizing sterilization. In this work, we propose a multi-robot sanitizing framework specific for teams of robots capable of cleaning human-populated environments [20] as railway stations. Our main goal is to provide a strategy in which a team of autonomous and heterogeneous indoor cleaning robots executes the sanitizing activities by exploiting both the specific capabilities offered by the different robots and the information about human presence. The latter knowledge is stored in a shared heatmap representing the most populated areas retrieved from the station' WIFI infrastructure. The proposed work is an extended version of our previous multi-robot sanitizing framework [3] where heterogeneous agents are considered. Specifically, we extended the framework by allowing different robots with different features - such as cleaning range, the shape of the cleaning area, or speed - to cooperate during the execution of the shared cleaning task. Analogously to [3], we propose a framework based on a decentralized deep reinforcement learning, where each robot of the team performs its own learning process. Our claim is that the robot-specific policies produced by this approach permits cooperation between the heterogeneous robots without performance degradation of the overall team. The need to consider heterogeneous robots is relevant for the infrastructure manager. Different typologies of robots with different cleaning strategies can be deployed, for instance, by integrating several small (low-cost) robots, having limited sanitizing capabilities, in alternative to bigger but more performing ones. The possibility to increase the number of robots in a team with different or less expensive models without reducing the cleaning performance of the overall system may be convenient in terms of costs but also in terms of hardware and software maintenance [10], especially over prolonged usage periods [24]. In the literature, frameworks that simulate heterogeneous teams of robots are often considered and deployed in several different contexts [28]. For instance, in the pursuit-evasion class of games, robots with different capabilities cooperate to catch moving targets in a shared environment and their pursuit strategies must be adapted with respect to the behavior of the opponent [30,34]. This case is similar to our domain, where clusters of people appear/disappear/move around the station and the robots' cleaning strategy should be adapted accordingly. The benefit of the coordinated heterogeneous robots is also emphasized in [35] where different robots (aerial and ground vehicles) are deployed. In the cleaning context, several multi-robot frameworks have been proposed based on Coverage Path Planning (CPP) [11–14,17,21–23]. In these works, each robot is assigned to a specific area of the environment executing fixed shaped paths (spirals, rectangles, etc.) to cover them. These methods are effective in providing a continuous cleaning service which maximizes the coverage and minimizes the idleness of the agents, but priority-based cleaning is hardly considered. Priority issues are instead considered in Persistent CPP [16,19,25,29], where robots' paths have to be adjusted in order to ensure that static prioritized locations are visited within the pre-specified time period. These approaches often consider static priorities and a graph-based representation of the environments with only a limited number of nodes. Deep Q-Learning (DQN) methods for sanitization are considered in [11,22], but in a single robot framework. In contrast, our approach is to dynamically update the behavior of a team of heterogeneous robots by considering the continuous evolution about the positions of the people and the diffusion of the contaminants in the map. Moreover, we are interested in finding a multi-robot sanitization strategy considering heterogeneous teams and high resolution priorities in very large railway stations. For this reason, we proposed a solution based on Multi-Agent Reinforcement Learning [3] capable of adapting the cleaning strategy to the continuous changes in a very large dynamic environment. In this work, our main contribution is the design of a heterogeneous framework where multiple mobile robots of different characteristics and typologies learn to cooperate during the execution of cleaning tasks. To evaluate the approach, we consider a very large crowded environment from a real railway station, exploiting WiFi information about the distribution of people in order to assess the performance of different heterogeneous teams of robots. We also propose an assessment of a heterogeneous robotic team in a real case study, using a one-day data recording of the people's movements inside the Roma Termini station, retrieved from the Meraki Cisco System WiFi Network. In this context, the empirical results collected show that the performance of the heterogeneous team is comparable to that of the homogeneous team working under the same conditions. The rest of the paper is structured as follows. In Sect. 2, we describe the architecture of the proposed framework along with the main components and the overall learning process. In Sect. 3, we focus on the experiments about the convergence and performance of the proposed heterogeneous team in comparison with the homogeneous one. Finally, Sect. 4 concludes the paper and discusses future works.

2   The Architecture

The multi-robot DQN approach proposed in this work is an evolution of the decentralized client-server architecture presented in [3], where it is now possible to specify different characteristics of each single robot. In particular, the team is composed of k robots with different capabilities, each endowed with a robot-specific policy. The robots interact with a central system (server) that maintains/updates a shared representation of the station in the form of a heatmap whose hot spots are areas to be sanitized. Specifically, we represent the environment as a 2-dimensional gridmap whose grids outline 1 m^2 areas of the station. Grids are then associated with a priority level (the heatmap), which depends on the distribution of people in the station and indicates how risky the area is and how urgently the robots should sterilize it. The goal of the agents is to

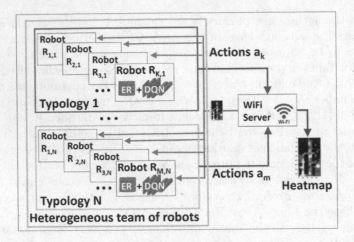

Fig. 1. Graphical representation of the framework including multiple agents (left), each endowed with agent-specific experience replay buffers and networks, along with a single server (right) that exploits WiFi statistics to provide a heatmap of priorities (red to yellow spots) for the agents. (Color figure online)

suitably navigate the gridmap cleaning the traversed grids in the process, in so minimizing the risky areas and reducing the level of priority on the overall map. We formalize our domain as a distributed multi-robot Deep Q-Learning problem [1] where a set of agent-specific policies $(\pi_1, \ldots, \pi_k)$ should be found for the k robots in order to guide each agent toward the cleaning targets. More formally, we define M as the gridmap of the station, X as the set of all free-obstacle grids in the map, S as the set of possible heatmaps (i.e., priority distributions) on the map M and A as the set of actions available for a single agent, where $a_i \in A$ drives the agent i from the current grid to an adjacent one. The aim is to find, for each robot i, a suitable policy $\pi_i : S \times X \to A$ associating the agent positions $x_i \in X$ and the distributions of priority in the map $s \in S$ to robot-specific actions $a_i \in A$, driving the agent from the current grid to the next grid to be sanitized. A representation of the overall architecture is depicted in Fig. 1. The framework includes a team of different typologies of mobile cleaning robots. Every typology is characterized by a different dimension of the area that agents sanitize during their movements in the environment. Each robot communicates with a single shared WiFi server that is responsible for building a heatmap of the Roma Termini railway station. The server updates the heatmap considering the information about the agents' cleaning activities and the (anonymized) data on the location of people, which are used to define the risky areas to be sterilized. The role of each agent is to elaborate the heatmap by means of an agent-specific DQN and to update the local strategy π_i considering their specific capabilities, the environmental settings and the priorities in the map.

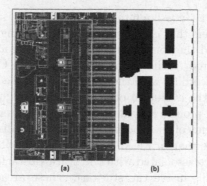

Fig. 2. Planimetry of the Roma Termini shared by Rete Ferroviaria Italiana (a) and the selected occupancy gridmap (b). (Color figure online)

2.1   Heatmap Definition and Update

The gridmap representing the environment is built from the real planimetry of the Roma Termini railway station, which has been provided to us by Italian Infrastructure Manager Rete Ferroviaria Italiana. The area of the station selected for our experiments is depicted in Fig. 2 (yellow box). We defined this area because, on the one hand, it represents the indoor part of the station, where open air and wind cannot attenuate contamination and, on the other hand, it includes the areas of the station where it is more likely to have crowed areas. Selected sectors include: access gates for the railway lines, commercial activities like shops, restaurants, ticket offices, waiting rooms, and luggage storage. Starting from this gridmap, we design a heatmap where populated areas are associated with colored spots (from red to yellow) representing the cleaning priority that the heterogeneous team should take into account during the sanitizing process. More specifically, the resulting heatmap has a dimension of 100×172 pixels and a resolution of $1 \ m^2$ per pixel. During every step of the execution, each robot of the team decides the new position to reach in order to start the cleaning action depending on its own specific capability. After a movement, each robot cleans at a fixed cleaning rate (i.e., 4 pixels per step) a cleaning area of fixed dimensions and shape. Each robot in the team has its assigned dimension and shape of the cleaning area. This area-cleaning process is simulated by holding the robot in the current pose for a certain number of steps which depends by its cleaning rate. In our framework, the WiFi Server constantly communicates with all the members of the team to update of the shared heatmap. Specifically, the server updates the heatmap by removing the cleaning priorities of areas sanitized by the robots, while new priorities are also added as colored spots at the positions of newly detected people. Furthermore, at every step of the execution, the server updates the priorities on the heatmap by simulating the natural spreading and the attenuation of contamination over time. This effect is computed from the position of people (clusters) by modeling the possible spreading of viruses or bacteria using a Gaussian model of dispersion [7]. Specifically, we exploit the periodic convolution of a Gaussian filter $\mathcal{N}(\mu, \sigma^2)$ every ψ steps, where μ, σ^2 and ψ are suitable parameters that can be regulated depending on the meters/pixels ratio, the timestep, and the considered typology of spreading (in this work we assume a setting inspired to the aerial diffusion of the Covid-19 [27]). In our case, we set μ and σ according with the spreading parameters proposed in [2,8]. An exemplification of the evolution of a heatmap configuration is provided in Fig. 3. The convolution process acts at every step by incrementally reducing the magnitude of the elements of the heatmap matrix, while distributing the priority on a wider area. Notice that in Fig. 3 there are several black areas (0 priority) that are regions of space associated with the static obstacles of the environment (shops, rooms and walls inside the station). These areas are assumed to be always clean, hence unattractive for the robots. When an agent moves with an action $a_i \in A$, it sends the new position to the WiFi Server. The region of the heatmap in the neighborhood of the newly reached position, with the cleaning area assigned to the agent, is cleaned by the server, which then sets to 0 the associated priority level when updating the heatmap.

2.2   Multi-agent Experience Replay and the Learning Process

In our framework, we propose a multi-agent variation of the experience replay method proposed in [1,3,18]. In particular, our training scheme exploits a Distributed Training Decentralized Execution (DTDE) approach [6], where each robot is independent during both the execution phase and the training phase, while its own individual policy is updated by considering only its own experience, without explicit information exchange between robots. In this framework, our idea is to exploit this DTDE approach to allow robots of different types to cooperate in a heterogeneous team. Robot-specific capabilities are: the travelling speed of the robot in the map (denoted by the movement length in Table 1), the shape and the dimensions of the areas that the robots are able to clean after each movement, and the time that the robot takes to clean the reached area (denoted by the cleaning speed in Table 1). In order to ensure that every robot learns by its own experience, each of the k agents is endowed with a specific replay buffer, along with specific *target* and *main* DQNs, which are synchronously updated with respect to the position of the agent and to the shared environment provided by the server (see Fig. 1). The target and the main networks are two identical convolutional neural-network composed of the following layers: the first layer is a 2D convolutional layer with 32 filters 8×8, strides $(4, 4)$ and ReLU activation; the second is a 2D convolutional layer with 64 filters 4×4, strides $(2, 2)$ and ReLU activation; the third is a 2D convolutional layer with 64 filters 3×3, strides $(1, 1)$ and ReLU activation; the fourth is a flatten layer; the fifth layer is a dense layer of 512 neurons still with ReLU activation; finally, the output layer is a dense layer composed of 8 neurons with linear activation. The input of the neural network is an image with 2 channels of dimensions 100×172 pixels. In the first channel there is the heatmap, represented as matrix where each element is a real number in the interval $[0, 1]$ where 1 is the maximum priority and 0 means that no cleaning is needed. This matrix can be displayed as a color-coded

Table 1. Parameters of the framework

Actor	Parameter	Value
Exp. replay	Discount factor γ	0.99
	Maximum ϵ	1.0
	Minimum ϵ	0.1
	Decay ϵ	$9 \cdot 10^{-7}$
	Replay buffer size	10^4
	Target network update	10^4 steps
	Main network update	4 steps
	Batch size	32
WiFi server	Refresh period	60 steps
Cluster of people	Diameter	1 px
Long-range robot	Cleaning area	25 px
	Cleaning speed	4 px/step
	Movement length	2 px
	Cleaning shape	Square
Mid-range robot	Cleaning area	17 px
	Cleaning speed	4 px/step
	Movement length	2 px
	Cleaning shape	Hexagon
Short-range robot	Cleaning area	9 px
	Cleaning speed	4 px/step
	Movement length	1 px
	Cleaning shape	Square
Spreading	Diameter	5 px
	μ	0
	σ	0.9
Environment	Dimensions	100×172 px

image (see map in Fig. 3), where black pixels are associated with 0 priority areas, while colors from red to yellow are for increasingly higher priorities. The second channel x is a binary $m \times n$ matrix (100×172 pixels in our case) representing the position and size of the cleaning area of the robot in the heatmap, which is 1 for the portions of the environment that are currently in the range of the robot cleaning effect, and 0 otherwise. In order to update the networks, we apply the Adam optimizer with learning rate $\alpha = 0.00025$. A local reward function r_i is defined, to permit each agent to evaluate its performance during the cleaning activity in the training process. The local *reward* function r_i is designed to give a benefit to the agents that reach prioritized areas of the environment (hot points), while there is a penalty if a robot meets a fixed obstacle or an already

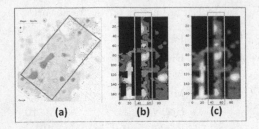

Fig. 3. Generation of the heatmap from Meraki data. From left to right, the starting georeferenced Meraki data (a) are converted into a robot-frame heatmap (b), which is then updated by the server through Gaussian convolution after 100 timesteps(c).

visited area (cold point) in the heatmap. In this direction, we firstly introduce a cumulative priority function cp_i that summarizes the importance of a cleaned area,

$$cp_i = \sum_{(j,l)} s_i(j,l)x_i(j,l) \tag{1}$$

represented in Eq. 1 as the sum of the element-wise priorities from matrix s_i in the area sterilized by the agent i (where $x_i(j,l) = 1$). Such value is then exploited to define the reward r_i for the agent i as follows:

$$r_i = \begin{cases} cp_i & \text{if } cp_i > 0; \\ penalty & \text{otherwise.} \end{cases} \tag{2}$$

Specifically, when an agent i sanitizes a priority area, the reward is equal to the cumulative value cp_i; otherwise, if no priority is associated with the cleaned area (i.e., $cp_i = 0$) a negative reward $penalty < 0$ is earned [5] (we empirically set $penalty = -2$ for our case studies). This way, agents receive a reward that is proportional to the importance of the sanitized area, while routes toward zero-priority areas, such as obstacles or clean regions, are discouraged. Notice that in this framework, when the action of an agent leads to an obstacle (collision), no motion is performed. This behavior penalizes the agent (no further cleaning is performed), thus producing an indirect drive toward collision-free paths. We define also an *overall reward* function $r = \sum_i^k r_i$ to summarize and evaluate the team performance as illustrated in Fig. 4.

3   Experiments

In this section, we show how the proposed heterogeneous multi-robot framework can be deployed in a realistic environment. As illustrated in the previous sections, we consider Roma Termini station (the largest and most populated Italian railway station) as the environment for our experiments. The station is endowed with several access points managed through a Meraki platform of Cisco System WiFi Network that allows remote operators to monitor the information about the presence and the positions of mobile devices (smartphones) all over the station. This information is exploited by the system (WiFi Server) to estimate the distribution of people and then to update the heatmap shared by the heterogeneous team. An example of the distribution of people retrieved from the Meraki system can be found in Fig. 3(a). We consider the WiFi Server to receive an updated distribution of people every 1 h. The information from the Meraki is then converted into a heatmap for the robots by associating each location with a priority value proportional to the density of people. Since the information from the Meraki are georeferenced, the retrieved value are finally rotated, translated and scaled in order to match the reference frame of the robots (see Fig. 3(b)). Thanks to the collaboration with Rete Ferroviaria Italiana, we obtained an entire day of recording of the Meraki system (2 September 2021) to be exploited for our experiments. In order to assess the performance of the proposed heterogeneous framework, we compare its performance with respect to a similar framework in which a homogeneous team is deployed. Specifically, we assume two teams, both composed of 4 robots: the first team (homogeneous) is composed of 4 mid-range sanitizing robots, while the second team (heterogeneous) is composed of 2 types of agents, namely, 2 short-range robots and 2 long-range ones. The parameters (ranges and velocities) for these 3 categories are shown in Table 1. In our tests, we consider for each robot the same cleaning speed. The two teams are associated with equal values of the total sum of the cleaning areas. The movement length of each robot, after the conclusion of the sanitization of its cleaning area, is equal to the ray of its own cleaning area. In the first case study we have compare the convergence of the two teams during the training phase by randomly generating heatmaps to be sanitized by the robots. In the second case, we exploit the one-day recorded data from the Meraki system to test and compare the cleaning performance of the 2 teams in a realistic scenario.

3.1 Case 1: The Training Process

In this case study, we compare the convergence of the two teams (heterogeneous and homogeneous) during the training phase. At every training episode we randomly generate priority distributions over the station. The resulting heatmap is left evolving by Gaussian convolution at every timestep, in order to emulate the spreading of the contaminants over time (see Fig. 3(c)). The task of the two teams is then to clean the whole map (maximize reward) by avoiding robots overlapping or transitions on clean areas (minimize penality). More specifically, at the beginning of every episode, the framework generates a new configuration of the map by uniformly distributing clusters of people inside the heatmap. Each location of the map has a 0.02 probability to generate a new cluster. The positions of the clusters, which represents the priority that the robots must sanitize, do not change position for the whole duration of the episode. Notice that in a real case, people are not equally distributed in a station. The training process is designed to generate a challenging context for the teams, while supporting the robots to build a generic policy, which is able to cope with a wider range of possible distributions. In every step of the episode, the WiFi server is responsible

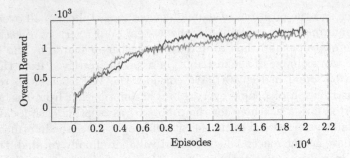

Fig. 4. Comparison of the convergence between the heterogeneous team (green) and the homogeneous team (blue). (Color figure online)

for the update of the heatmap: the server firstly deletes the priorities of the areas corresponding to spots cleaned by the robots, secondly it applies the Gaussian convolution to simulate the evolution of the contaminants in the indoor environment. The updated heatmap is exploited by the robots to decide in which direction the next cleaning should be performed. The action of moving toward a location and cleaning the related area is performed according to the specific robot type (Table 1). For instance, a mid-range robot (such as the ones of the homogeneous team) is able to cover a distance of 2 px and to clean an hexagonal area of 17 px in 4 steps (around 5 m^2 in 4 min). The episode ends when agents successfully clean up to the 98% of the map or when a suitable timeout is reached (400 steps in this setting). During the training process we monitor as quantitative performance measures the overall reward, i.e., the sum of the reward earned by every agent during one episode, and the number of steps needed to accomplish the task. The convergence of the training process for the two teams is depicted in Fig. 4. We can observe that the two teams are able to converge to a total reward of about 1200 in 20000 episodes. Despite the overall performance seems quite comparable, the homogeneous team converges slightly faster than the heterogeneous one. This was expected given the additional complexity associated with the heterogeneous case, in which the robots are to learn how to suitably combine their different capabilities in order to effectively accomplish the shared task.

3.2   Case 2: Testing with Real Data

In a second case study, we considered a more realistic scenario in which the real data from the Meraki system are used to continuously update the heatmap (once every 60 min). In order to assess the performance of the teams, we introduce two simple metrics to evaluate the efficiency of the cleaning actions of the two teams. Specifically, given the heatmap, we measure how clean it is (in percentage) with the c_perc value defined as follows:

$$c\_perc = ((x_{tot} - s_{curr})/x_{tot}) \cdot 100, \tag{3}$$

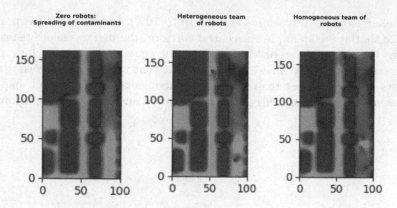

Fig. 5. Snapshots of the 3 settings at work: no-robot baseline, heterogeneous and homogeneous teams (from left to right).

where $x_{tot} = |X|$ is the number of free-obstacles cells of the map, while $s_{curr} = \sum_{(i,j)} s(i,j)$ is the sum of the current priorities for each cell of the heatmap. Notice that the c_perc is 100% if the map is totally clean (i.e., each cell has 0 priority) and 0% if every cell of the map has maximum priority. We also in introduce the value n_perc representing the percentage of safe spots in the map, i.e., the percentage of number of cells whose priority/risk level is less than a given threshold:

$$n\_perc = (x_{le}/x_{tot}) \cdot 100, \tag{4}$$

in this case x_{le} represents the number of cells with low priority. For this experiment, we empirically set the safety-threshold to 0.2. In this way we can measure the percentage of the cleaned surface, given the resolution 1 m^2 for pixel of the heatmap. The above metrics are used to assess the performance of the teams over the whole map. On the other hand, since the distribution of people in the station is not uniform, there are some areas of the station that are generally more populated. This is the case, for example, of the central corridor of the state (green rectangles in Fig. 3), which is close to the access gates, where people usually crowd. To provide an additional assessment of the performance of the teams, we also measure the c_perc_z and n_perc_z values of the central corridor. In Fig. 5, we show some snapshots of the system at work. The results of the cleaning process over 13 h of execution (from 6:00 a.m. to 7:00 p.m, i.e., the busiest time of the day) are illustrated in Fig. 6. In the latter charts, we compare the performance of the heterogeneous team (green) with respect to the homogeneous one (blue) and a no-robot baseline (grey), where the contamination evolves naturally. From the charts we can notice that both teams obtain similar results. Considering the overall c_perc values (upper charts), the homogeneous team performs slightly better than the heterogeneous one, with an average difference of about 2%. For both teams the improvement with respect to the baseline becomes more evident (over 5%) when the station becomes more crowded (after 2:00 p.m.). As for the c_perc_z measurement, for both teams the improved performance with respect to the baseline looks slightly more evident (up to 10%). In this case, it is possible to notice that at 9:00 a.m., in the central corridor, the heterogeneous team outperforms the homogeneous one by a mean value equal to 4% and 7% for c_perc_z and n_perc_z respectively. These results suggest that while a homogeneous team of robots performs better than the heterogeneous one on the overall map, the latter seems to work more effectively on restricted and highly populated areas.

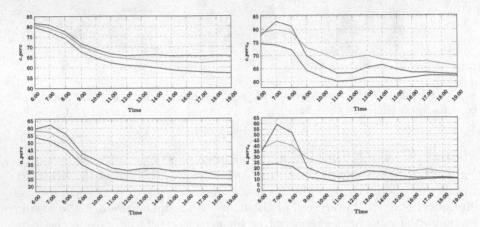

Fig. 6. Plots of the values c_perc, c_perc_z, n_perc and n_perc_z for the heterogeneous team (green), the homogeneous team (blue) and the baseline with zero robots (grey). (Color figure online)

4   Conclusions and Future Works

In this work, we proposed a DQN framework for multi-robot sanitization of large indoor environments. Specifically, we deployed a DTDE approach to train a cooperative team of heterogeneous robots for the execution of a shared sanitization task. To evaluate the framework we proposed a comparison between heterogeneous and homogeneous teams of robots in a realistic domain obtained from a dataset that collects 1 day of data recording of the WiFi network of the Roma Termini railway station. The empirical results show that, despite the additional complexity given by heterogeneity, the heterogeneous system behaves similarly to the homogeneous version of the approach in terms of training convergence. On the other hand, the heterogeneous system works better than the homogeneous one in restricted and populated environments, while the cleaning performance on the overall map is slightly reduced when compared to the homogeneous case. As a future work, we plan to investigate larger robot teams equipped with more complex high-level heuristics suitable for increasingly larger real-world environments.

References

1. Bae, H., Kim, G., Kim, J., Qian, D., Lee, S.: Multi-robot path planning method using reinforcement learning. Appl. Sci. **9**(15) (2019). https://doi.org/10.3390/app9153057, https://www.mdpi.com/2076-3417/9/15/3057
2. Buonanno, G., Morawska, L., Stabile, L.: Quantitative assessment of the risk of airborne transmission of SARS-CoV-2 infection: prospective and retrospective applications. Environ. Int. **145**, 106112 (2020). https://doi.org/10.1016/j.envint.2020.106112, https://www.sciencedirect.com/science/article/pii/S0160412020320675
3. Caccavale, R., Calà, V., Ermini, M., Finzi, A., Lippiello, V., Tavano, F.: Multi-robot sanitization of railway stations based on deep Q-learning. In: AIRO 2021: 8th Italian Workshop on Artificial Intelligence and Robotics of the 20th International Conference of the Italian Association for Artificial Intelligence (AI*IA 2021) (2021)
4. Ciuffini, F., Tengattini, S., Bigazzi, A.Y.: Mitigating increased driving after the COVID-19 pandemic: an analysis on mode share, travel demand, and public transport capacity. Transp. Res. Rec. 03611981211037884 (2021). https://doi.org/10.1177/03611981211037884
5. Duan, J., et al.: Deep-reinforcement-learning-based autonomous voltage control for power grid operations. IEEE Trans. Power Syst. **35**(1), 814–817 (2020). https://doi.org/10.1109/TPWRS.2019.2941134
6. Gronauer, S., Diepold, K.: Multi-agent deep reinforcement learning: a survey. Artif. Intell. Rev. 1–49 (2021)
7. Hanna, S.: Transport and dispersion of tracers simulating COVID-19 aerosols in passenger aircraft. Indoor Air **32**(1), e12974 (2022). https://doi.org/10.1111/ina.12974, https://onlinelibrary.wiley.com/doi/abs/10.1111/ina.12974
8. Harmon, M., Lau, J.: The facility infection risk estimator^{TM}: a web application tool for comparing indoor risk mitigation strategies by estimating airborne transmission risk. Indoor Built Environ. 1420326X211039544 (2022). https://doi.org/10.1177/1420326X211039544
9. Hossam, M., et al.: Effect of mutation and vaccination on spread, severity, and mortality of COVID-19 disease. J. Med. Virol. **94**(1), 197–204 (2022)
10. Howard, A., Parker, L.E., Sukhatme, G.S.: Experiments with a large heterogeneous mobile robot team: exploration, mapping, deployment and detection. Int. J. Robot. Res. **25**(5–6), 431–447 (2006). https://doi.org/10.1177/0278364906065378
11. Lakshmanan, A.K., et al.: Complete coverage path planning using reinforcement learning for tetromino based cleaning and maintenance robot. Autom. Constr. **112**, 103078 (2020)
12. Lee, T.K., Baek, S.H., Choi, Y.H., Oh, S.Y.: Smooth coverage path planning and control of mobile robots based on high-resolution grid map representation. Robot. Auton. Syst. **59**(10), 801–812 (2011). https://doi.org/10.1016/j.robot.2011.06.002, https://www.sciencedirect.com/science/article/pii/S0921889011000996
13. Lee, T.K., Baek, S.H., Oh, S.Y., Choi, Y.H.: Complete coverage algorithm based on linked smooth spiral paths for mobile robots. In: 2010 11th International Conference on Control Automation Robotics Vision, pp. 609–614 (2010). https://doi.org/10.1109/ICARCV.2010.5707264
14. Lee, T.K., Baek, S., Oh, S.Y.: Sector-based maximal online coverage of unknown environments for cleaning robots with limited sensing. Robot. Auton. Syst. **59**(10), 698–710 (2011). https://doi.org/10.1016/j.robot.2011.05.005, https://www.sciencedirect.com/science/article/pii/S0921889011000893

15. Li, D., Yin, Y., Zhang, S., Wu, L.: How does railway respond to COVID-19 spreading. Countermeasure Analysis and Evaluation around the World (2020)
16. Mallya, D., Kandala, S., Vachhani, L., Sinha, A.: Priority patrolling using multiple agents. In: 2021 IEEE International Conference on Robotics and Automation (ICRA), pp. 8692–8698 (2021). https://doi.org/10.1109/ICRA48506.2021.9561785
17. Miao, X., Lee, J., Kang, B.Y.: Scalable coverage path planning for cleaning robots using rectangular map decomposition on large environments. IEEE Access **6**, 38200–38215 (2018). https://doi.org/10.1109/ACCESS.2018.2853146
18. Mnih, V., et al.: Human-level control through deep reinforcement learning (2015). https://www.nature.com/articles/nature14236#article-info
19. Murtaza, G., Kanhere, S., Jha, S.: Priority-based coverage path planning for aerial wireless sensor networks. In: 2013 IEEE Eighth International Conference on Intelligent Sensors, Sensor Networks and Information Processing, pp. 219–224 (2013). https://doi.org/10.1109/ISSNIP.2013.6529792
20. Narang, M., et al.: Fighting COVID: an autonomous indoor cleaning robot (AICR) supported by artificial intelligence and vision for dynamic air disinfection. In: 2021 14th IEEE International Conference on Industry Applications (INDUSCON), pp. 1146–1153 (2021). https://doi.org/10.1109/INDUSCON51756.2021.9529813
21. Nasirian, B., Mehrandezh, M., Janabi-Sharifi, F.: Efficient coverage path planning for mobile disinfecting robots using graph-based representation of environment. Front. Robot. AI **8** (2021). https://doi.org/10.3389/frobt.2021.624333, https://www.frontiersin.org/article/10.3389/frobt.2021.624333
22. Nasirian, B., Mehrandezh, M., Janabi-Sharifi, F.: Efficient coverage path planning for mobile disinfecting robots using graph-based representation of environment. Front. Robot. AI **8**, 4 (2021)
23. Oh, J.S., Choi, Y.H., Park, J.B., Zheng, Y.: Complete coverage navigation of cleaning robots using triangular-cell-based map. IEEE Trans. Industr. Electron. **51**(3), 718–726 (2004). https://doi.org/10.1109/TIE.2004.825197
24. Parker, L.E.: Lifelong adaptation in heterogeneous multi-robot teams: response to continual variation in individual robot performance (2000)
25. Pasqualetti, F., Durham, J.W., Bullo, F.: Cooperative patrolling via weighted tours: performance analysis and distributed algorithms. IEEE Trans. Rob. **28**(5), 1181–1188 (2012). https://doi.org/10.1109/TRO.2012.2201293
26. Poliński, J., Ochociński, K.: Impact of COVID-19 on the functioning of passenger rail transport. Probl. Kolejnictwa **Z. 190**, 103–124 (2021)
27. Setti, L., et al.: Airborne transmission route of COVID-19: why 2 meters/6 feet of inter-personal distance could not be enough (2020). https://www.ncbi.nlm.nih.gov/pmc/articles/PMC7215485/
28. Stegagno, P., Cognetti, M., Rosa, L., Peliti, P., Oriolo, G.: Relative localization and identification in a heterogeneous multi-robot system. In: 2013 IEEE International Conference on Robotics and Automation, pp. 1857–1864 (2013). https://doi.org/10.1109/ICRA.2013.6630822
29. Stump, E., Michael, N.: Multi-robot persistent surveillance planning as a vehicle routing problem. In: 2011 IEEE International Conference on Automation Science and Engineering, pp. 569–575 (2011). https://doi.org/10.1109/CASE.2011.6042503
30. Tanner, H.G.: Switched UAV-UGV cooperation scheme for target detection. In: Proceedings 2007 IEEE International Conference on Robotics and Automation, pp. 3457–3462 (2007). https://doi.org/10.1109/ROBOT.2007.364007
31. Tardivo, A., Zanuy, A.C., Martín, C.S.: COVID-19 impact on transport: a paper from the railways' systems research perspective. Transp. Res. Rec. **2675**(5), 367–378 (2021). https://doi.org/10.1177/0361198121990674

32. Tavakoli, M., Carriere, J., Torabi, A.: Robotics, smart wearable technologies, and autonomous intelligent systems for healthcare during the COVID-19 pandemic: an analysis of the state of the art and future vision. Adv. Intell. Syst. **2**(7), 2000071 (2020). https://doi.org/10.1002/aisy.202000071, https://onlinelibrary.wiley.com/doi/abs/10.1002/aisy.202000071

33. To, K.K., Hung, I.F., Chan, J.F., Yuen, K.Y.: From SARS coronavirus to novel animal and human coronaviruses. J. Thorac. Dis. **5**(Suppl 2), S103 (2013)

34. Vidal, R., Shakernia, O., Kim, H., Shim, D., Sastry, S.: Probabilistic pursuit-evasion games: theory, implementation, and experimental evaluation. IEEE Trans. Robot. Autom. **18**(5), 662–669 (2002). https://doi.org/10.1109/TRA.2002.804040

35. Waslander, S.L.: Unmanned aerial and ground vehicle teams: recent work and open problems. In: Nonami, K., Kartidjo, M., Yoon, K.J., Budiyono, A. (eds.) Autonomous Control Systems and Vehicles. Intelligent Systems, Control and Automation: Science and Engineering, vol. 65, pp. 21–36. Springer, Tokyo (2013). https://doi.org/10.1007/978-4-431-54276-6_2

Simulated Annealing for the Home Healthcare Routing and Scheduling Problem

Sara Ceschia[ID], Luca Di Gaspero[ID], and Andrea Schaerf[(✉)][ID]

DPIA, Università degli Studi di Udine, via delle Scienze 206, 33100 Udine, Italy
{sara.ceschia,luca.digaspero,andrea.schaerf}@uniud.it

Abstract. Home healthcare services are carried out by trained caregivers who visit the patient's home, perform their service operations that depend on the patient's need (e.g., medical care or just instrumental activities of daily living), and then move to the next patient.

We consider the home healthcare scheduling and routing problem, in the formulation proposed by Mankowska et al. (2014), which includes synchronization among services and time windows for patients. For this problem, we propose a local search approach based on a novel neighborhood operator and guided by the Simulated Annealing metaheuristic.

We show that our approach, properly tuned in a statistically-principled way, is able to outperform state-of-the-art methods on most of the original instances made available by Mankowska et al.

Keywords: Simulated annealing · Healthcare · Scheduling · Routing

1 Introduction

In the last twenty years we assisted to the relocation of supportive and geriatric care from institutional places, usually rest or nursing homes, to the patients' domicile. The reasons of this shift is twofold: on the one hand, the possibility to stay in a habitual environment increases the quality of life of the patient, on the other hand, this situation has a significant positive impact on decreasing the healthcare costs [13].

Home Healthcare services are carried out by trained caregivers who visit the patient's home within a predefined time window, perform their service operations that depend on the patient's need (e.g., medical care or just instrumental activities of daily living), and then move to the next patient. This specific feature makes the problem peculiar. Indeed, the decisions required in the classical activity scheduling problems in hospitals or other healthcare institutions involve only the temporal aspects, whereas in Home Healthcare also a spatial dimension and the related traveling times have to be considered.

One of the most peculiar type of constraints for this problem are the synchronization ones that induce temporal dependencies among the activities.

© The Author(s), under exclusive license to Springer Nature Switzerland AG 2023
A. Dovier et al. (Eds.): AIxIA 2022, LNAI 13796, pp. 402–412, 2023.
https://doi.org/10.1007/978-3-031-27181-6_28

For example, some medical care activities (e.g., physiotherapy) requires the simultaneous presence of more than a single caregiver (e.g., for raising the patient from his/her bed); other activities (e.g., medicine administration/lunch preparation) might require that subsequent activities should take place after a given time interval (e.g., one administration in the morning, the other in the evening/dishes cleaning). Since the caregiver transit from one patient to the next requires a non negligible traveling time, these constraints make the routing component of the problem pretty hard with respect to the standard vehicle routing problems.

In this work we propose a metaheuristic approach for solving a standardized formulation of the problem introduced by Mankowska et al. [21]. The solution method is based on local search and makes use of an original neighborhood operator. In particular, the solution process is driven by a Simulated Annealing (SA) procedure [16]. The approach outperforms alternative methods that appeared in the literature [18–21] and is able to improve the current state-of-the-art results on the set of benchmark instances.

The rest of the work is organized as follows: Sect. 2 briefly surveys related work about Home Healthcare services whereas Sect. 3 presents an informal description of the specific problem statement. The metaheuristic solution method is reported in Sect. 4 that illustrates the modeling of the problem into the local search framework (Sect. 4.1), and a detailed description of the novel neighborhood operator (Sect. 4.2). Moreover, Sect. 4.3 outlines the Simulated Annealing procedure that drives the search process. An experimental analysis of the proposed solution method, including the details of the tuning process, is reported in Sect. 5, where the proposed method is compared with the alternative approaches. Finally, Sect. 6 contains some conclusions.

2   Related Work

The problem of scheduling Home Healthcare services has been studied since the late 1990s, in particular Begur et al. [1] first take into consideration the problem and employ a simple scheduling heuristic to solve it, whereas Cheng and Rich [7] were the first to formulate a mixed integer linear programming model.

Following solution attempts look at the problem from a *set covering* perspective. Specifically, Eveborn et al. [10] proposed a working system for healthcare planning, while Rasmussen et al. [22] were the first to consider also temporal dependencies among the activities. Bredström and Rönnqvist [5] also worked on a similar synchronization problem although from a vehicle routing perspective and without an explicit consideration of the healthcare nature of the provided services.

The provision of services in a metropolitan area, where the transit from one patient to the next could take place using a public transportation network instead of a dedicated car, has been considered by Bertels and Fahle [3] and Rendl et al. [23]. The latter work also take into account the possibility of changing the transportation mean during the transit, leading to multi-modal trips.

Di Gaspero and Urli [9] worked on a similar problem, although with a different perspective. In particular, the considered temporal horizon spans on multiple days and a balancing of the caregivers workload, including minimizing overtime work, is also taken into account. Moreover, in that work there is the possibility to leave some patient's activity unscheduled so as to deal with overconstrained problems (and possibly hire further occasional caregivers). The problem is modeled in the Constraint Programming framework and solved with special-purpose branching heuristics and a Large Neighborhood Search approach.

A somehow standardized formulation of the problem along with a number of benchmark instances has been provided by Mankowska et al. [21]. The problem formulation (refer to Sect. 3 for an informal presentation) considers synchronization constraints at patients' homes between at most two activities and the solution quality is basically measured in terms of traveling times and tardiness of the service activities with respect to the patients' time windows. For this problem, Mankowska et al. developed an Adaptive Variable Neighborhood Search method implementing eight different neighborhood operators.

In 2017, Fikar and Hirsch [11] provided a survey on the topic. Later developments include the work of Lasfargeas et al. [20], who proposed a local search based method equipped in a Variable Neighborhood Search solution procedure and tested it on Mankowska et al. benchmarks. Population based approaches were tried by a number of authors, in different problem settings. Specifically, Decerle et al. [8], Grenouilleau et al. [14] devise memetic algorithms (i.e., genetic algorithms followed by a local search) for the problem. Similarly to Di Gaspero and Urli [9], also Grenouilleau et al. [14] considered a multi-day horizon and the balancing of overtime work among caregivers but their underlying routing problem is more sophisticated as it takes also hourly dependent traveling times due to traffic. Xiang et al. [25] considered the problem from a multi-objective perspective trying to balance the total operating cost with caregivers/patients satisfaction and solved the problem through a NSGA-II genetic algorithm.

The formulation of Mankowska et al. [21] has attracted the attention of Kummer et al. [17–19] who devise and employ Biased Random Key Genetic Algorithms for solving the problem. Their results are currently the state-of-the-art with respect of these benchmarks.

3   Problem Statement

The Home Health Care Routing and Scheduling Problem (HHCRSP) has been formally defined by Mankowska et al. [21, Section 3] using a mathematical model. In order to make the paper self-contained, we briefly recall its definition here.

The main entities involved in the problem are the following ones:

Times and Horizon: The problem regards one single day of planning. The times are expressed in minutes, starting from 0 which represents the beginning of the activities for the day (e.g., 6:00AM). There is no explicit horizon and the activities are constrained by the time windows of the patients. Distances between patients themselves and with the depot are given directly in minutes necessary to cover them.

Patients: Patients are divided into two classes: *single-service* patients and *double-service* ones, which need to be served within their time window by one or two caregivers, respectively. In the case of double-service patients, the minimum and maximum time distance between the two services are specified. When simultaneous services are needed both distances are set to 0.

Caregivers: Each caregiver has a given set of services that she/he can provide (abilities) and performs a single specific service to the patient. All caregivers start their daily activity from the depot and return to it at the end of the working day.

The service time, in principle, can vary depending on the service, the patient, and the caregiver, but in the available instances is actually assumed identical. The possibility that a single caregiver provides both services for the same patient is forbidden, even in the case of non-simultaneous services.

The fact that the caregiver performing a service must have the corresponding ability (qualification) is a hard constraint. Similarly, the service cannot start before the beginning of the time window of the patient. In case of early arrival it is allowed that the caregiver waits until the time window of the patient starts. Conversely, the possibility that a patient is served late is acceptable, and the tardiness contributes to the objective function.

The objective function has three components: the total travel time, the total tardiness (for all services), and the largest tardiness. The latter objective is used to ensure some fairness among patients, such that the best solution cannot be obtained at the expense of one single patient. For double service patients, each service contributes to total tardiness independently.

Notice that it is possible that some caregivers are not assigned to any patient, thus they have an empty route.

4 Solution Technique

We propose a search method based on local search. In the following sections, we describe in turn the key features of the local search approach, namely the search space and the initial solution strategy, the neighborhood relation, and the metaheuristic that guides the search.

4.1 Search Space and Initial Solution

Following Mankowska et al. [21], the search space is represented by a vector Π of size P (total number of patients) containing a permutation of the values $0, \ldots, P - 1$, which represents a global ordering of the patients. This vector is completed by a vector Θ of size P of pairs $\langle c_1, c_2 \rangle$ that stores for each patient p the caregivers that serve her/him. In case of single-service patients, the second element of the pair c_2 is marked as unused.

The routes of the caregivers and the corresponding times are deterministically constructed starting from Π and Θ. The procedure starts with all routes empty, and processes one patient p at the time according to the Π ordering. The patient p is inserted as the last element in the route(s) obtained according to the values $\langle c_1, c_2 \rangle$ stored in Θ.

The service start times are computed *at the earliest* taking into account the time window of p. That is, the service start time of c_1 to p is the maximum between the beginning of the time window of p and the earliest time in which c_1 can reach p (according to previous duties and travel time). For the second service (if it exists) the service start time of c_2 to p is the maximum between the minimum separation between the two services for p and the earliest time in which c_2 can reach the patient.

In the case in which c_2 reaches the patient later than the maximum separation of the two services, the service of c_1 is postponed as much as necessary. With this construction, earliness and missing separations can never happen, whereas tardiness is possible. Given that tardiness is considered a soft constraint in this formulation, the feasibility of the solution is guaranteed.

The Π and Θ vectors are sufficient to represent and build the full solution. Nonetheless, they are complemented by various redundant data structures, used to speed-up the computation of moves and costs.

The initial solution is built at random. First, a random permutation is selected for the Π vector, then one or two (distinct) caregivers are randomly drawn for each patient. The caregivers are selected among those that have the necessary ability to fulfill the service.

4.2   Neighborhood Operator

Regarding the neighborhood operator, Mankowska et al. [21] consider the possibility of repositioning a patient in the global order, changing the caregiver(s), or swapping either the position or the caregiver(s). We consider, instead, a larger neighborhood which consists in repositioning one patient in the global ordering *and* assigning new caregiver(s) to her/him, in one single move. More formally, we define the following neighborhood:

– MovePatient(MP): the move $\mathrm{MP}\langle p, i, c_1, c_2 \rangle$ inserts patient p in the position i in the global order Π, with caregivers c_1 and (if requested) c_2.

The position i can also be the current one of p, so that the move results in a change of caregiver(s) only. Similarly, one or both caregivers can remain unchanged, so that the move can represent only a change in the order in the routes. Consequently, all quadruples $\langle p, i, c_1, c_2 \rangle$ (or triples $\langle p, i, c_1 \rangle$, for single service patients) are legal moves, except for the following cases:

1. **null move:** all three elements $\langle i, c_1, c_2 \rangle$ (resp. two elements $\langle i, c_1 \rangle$) are equal to the current ones of p;
2. **same caregiver:** c_1 is equal to c_2;
3. **missing ability:** c_1 or c_2 do not have the ability for the corresponding service.

4.3   Simulated Annealing

We use Simulated Annealing [16] to guide the local search. For a review of the different variants of SA, we refer the interested reader to the work by Franzin and Stützle [12].

The SA procedure starts from the initial solution built as described in Sect. 4.1 and then, at each iteration, uniformly selects a legal move in the neighborhood.

The move is always accepted if the difference of cost Δ is null or negative (i.e., the value of the objective function improves o remains equal), whereas if $\Delta > 0$ it is accepted with probability $\exp^{-\Delta/T}$, where T is a control parameter called *temperature*. Indeed, SA starts with an initial temperature T_0, which is decreased according to the classical geometric cooling scheme ($T_i = c \cdot T_{i-1}$) after a fixed number of samples n_s. To the basic SA procedure, we add the *cut-off* mechanism such that the temperature decreases also if a maximum number of moves has been accepted. This is expressed as a fraction ρ of the number of iterations n_s (with $0 \leq \rho \leq 1$). In order to guarantee the same running time to all configurations of SA, we use the total number of iterations $\mathcal{I}$ as stop criterion. To keep $\mathcal{I}$ fixed, we recompute n_s from $n_s = \mathcal{I} \Big/ \left(\frac{\log(T_f/T_0)}{\log c} \right)$, where T_f is the final temperature.

5   Experimental Results

The SA method has been implemented in C++. The experiments have been run on an Ubuntu Linux 20.4 machine with 4 cores Intel® i7-7700 (3.60 GHz), with a single core dedicated to each experiment.

5.1   Instances

The original dataset of Mankowska et al. [21] comprises 7 groups of 10 instances each, with 10, 25, 50, 75, 100, 200, 300 patients, respectively. The groups are labeled with the letters from A to G, so that instance names are $A_1, A_2, \ldots, G_{10}$. We excluded from our analysis the group A as all 10 instances are always consistently solved to optimality, so that they are not sufficiently challenging.

Table 1 presents the main features of the dataset in terms of number of patients, services, caregivers, percentage of double service (DS) patients, length of the time windows, compatibility between patients and caregivers (per service), average (Euclidean) distance in minutes between patients and with depot. Notice that instances of different groups are quite homogeneous; this is probably due to the fact that they were created by the same generator.

5.2   Parameter Tuning

The tuning procedure of the SA parameters was performed using the tool JSON2RUN [24], which samples the configurations using the *Hammersley point set* [15], and implements the F-Race procedure [4] to compare them.

Table 1. Summary of features of the different instance groups.

Group	A	B	C	D	E	F	G
# Patients	10	25	50	75	100	200	300
# Services	6	6	6	6	6	6	6
# Caregivers	3	5	10	15	20	30	40
% DS patients	30%	32%	30%	31%	30%	30%	33%
Time window size	120	120	120	120	120	120	120
Compatibility	0.33–0.56	0.35–0.52	0.34–0.49	0.33–0.46	0.37–0.43	0.38–0.46	0.37–0.42
Average travel time	39.6–50.1	38.4–45.9	39.5–45.0	39.3–44.7	39.4–44.7	38.9–42.0	39.2–42.1

Table 2. Parameter settings.

Name	Description	Value	Range
T_0	Initial temperature	7.86	3–10
T_f	Final temperature	0.28	0.1–0.3
c	Cooling rate	0.992	0.985–0.995
ρ	Accepted moves ratio	0.15	0.05–0.20

We tested 30 Hammersley points, and the resulting best one is shown in Table 2, which reports also the initial range, that have been selected based on preliminary experiments. For the tuning phase, the maximum number of iterations $\mathcal{I}$ was fixed to $5 \cdot 10^7$, resulting in an average running time of about 88 s on our machine.

5.3   Comparative Results

We compared our results with the best ones in the literature, obtained by Mankowska et al. [21] and Lasfargeas et al. [20] using Variable Neighborhood Search and by Kummer et al. [18,19] using Biased Random-Key Genetic Algorithms.

We run ten replicates of our solver for each instance, fixing the number of iterations $\mathcal{I} = 10^8$, which corresponds to about 6 min for the larger instances (group G). This is less than the time granted by the others for the same instances, but resulted in much longer times (up to 2 orders of magnitude) for us for the smaller instances, as our solver scales more linearly then the competitors.

The results are reported in Tables 3 and 4, in which average best results are in boldface, and the best known ones are in italics. Table 4 has one less entry as Lasfargeas et al. [20] did not consider groups E, F, and G. In the tables, we report also the lower bounds obtained by Kummer et al. [18] starting from the MIP (mixed integer programming) model by Mankowska et al. [21].[1]

---

[1] All our results have been validated using the MIP model by Mankowska et al. [21], implemented and kindly supplied to us by Alberto Kummer.

Table 3. Comparative results on instances of groups $B - D$.

Inst.	[18]	[21]		[20]			[19]			[18]			SA		
	LB	cost	t[s]	best	avg	t[s]	best	avg	t[s]	best	avg	t[s]	best	avg	t[s]
B_1	428.10	458.9	<1	434.1	552.8	53.1	*428.10*	428.26	8.6	*428.10*	428.53	0.8	*428.10*	**428.10**	70.2
B_2	476.05	476.2	36000	*476.0*	561.3	27.7	483.63	485.66	8.4	*476.05*	476.92	0.9	*476.05*	**476.05**	68.9
B_3	399.09	399.2	36000	*399.1*	527.6	63.5	402.80	402.80	9.0	402.80	409.29	1.0	*399.09*	**399.09**	70.7
B_4	411.30	576.0	36000	414.0	509.7	66.8	420.29	431.87	8.2	422.06	430.46	1.1	*411.30*	**411.30**	68.7
B_5	366.34	391.1	<1	385.6	496.9	13.7	372.16	374.24	8.2	369.44	375.15	1.0	*366.34*	**366.34**	68.8
B_6	405.58	534.7	<1	*447.8*	611.8	443.7	471.00	471.87	8.9	470.59	470.70	1.2	*464.62*	**464.62**	70.1
B_7	328.67	355.5	<1	*328.7*	398.8	61.5	328.67	328.67	9.5	*328.67*	328.67	0.9	*328.67*	**328.67**	68.6
B_8	357.68	357.8	36000	359.7	488.7	79.3	359.70	359.70	9.2	*357.68*	359.40	0.7	*357.68*	**357.68**	70.6
B_9	330.30	403.8	36000	404.1	483.4	62.1	*402.67*	404.27	10.0	404.11	404.29	0.9	*402.67*	**402.67**	71.9
B_{10}	420.99	500.4	<1	*462.7*	616.8	8.7	469.58	469.58	9.2	469.58	469.58	0.9	462.75	**462.75**	69.8
Avg		445.4		411.2	524.8	88.0	413.86	415.69	8.9	412.91	415.30	0.9	409.73	409.73	69.8
C_1	459.25	1123.6	<1	974.2	1350.4	96.2	965.15	975.59	36.9	969.11	973.87	3.1	*943.73*	**946.34**	96.0
C_2	373.94	673.8	<1	605.1	685.5	106.4	583.39	590.48	39.0	584.18	587.00	2.9	*569.12*	**572.45**	93.9
C_3	390.48	642.4	<1	562.9	698.2	109.8	548.79	559.05	37.4	549.63	**552.52**	2.9	*537.79*	554.68	94.7
C_4	371.99	580.4	<1	521.9	630.4	112.4	519.91	530.59	36.2	520.13	524.15	3.0	*495.17*	**497.75**	94.0
C_5	464.97	754.6	<1	683.1	822.6	114.9	678.61	702.92	31.4	668.65	685.92	3.4	*655.72*	**661.02**	93.2
C_6	360.73	951.6	<1	854.6	1010.6	115.9	840.69	845.49	37.2	841.48	846.83	2.9	*815.19*	**828.79**	96.0
C_7	354.15	577.4	<1	529.2	572.5	109.4	534.85	540.39	42.2	533.92	541.88	3.4	*514.06*	**515.53**	92.8
C_8	375.52	540.6	<1	471.0	522.8	110.8	474.55	480.06	36.5	475.96	478.39	3.5	*469.48*	**470.14**	93.7
C_9	355.29	608.7	<1	551.1	642.7	115.4	534.30	551.14	42.8	545.18	558.54	3.4	*533.05*	**535.73**	94.5
C_{10}	431.18	679.3	<1	608.9	653.0	99.0	611.25	618.27	35.3	611.03	614.59	2.7	*590.26*	**590.26**	93.5
Avg		713.2		636.2	758.9	109.0	629.15	639.40	37.5	629.93	636.37	3.1	612.36	617.27	94.2
D_1	492.09	1321.8	5	1278.2	1498.8	143.0	1186.20	1209.62	93.7	1193.21	1215.79	8.0	*1122.81*	1174.49	120.6
D_2	384.68	892.7	4	746.9	914.3	168.7	693.28	718.03	82.9	679.58	695.99	7.2	*649.13*	**660.54**	119.0
D_3	380.05	819.4	4	678.6	817.8	155.4	635.67	651.35	102.2	644.16	650.22	8.5	*616.44*	**629.97**	118.8
D_4	418.94	877.4	4	809.7	1073.1	148.5	814.35	841.64	82.3	795.15	827.28	7.2	*776.60*	**779.76**	119.5
D_5	415.81	872.1	5	777.0	924.9	150.3	691.50	703.12	92.4	693.83	702.68	7.7	*656.90*	**657.73**	120.2
D_6	392.08	835.2	5	768.6	886.6	154.6	733.67	744.70	105.8	731.71	743.64	7.9	*688.63*	**696.72**	119.3
D_7	372.49	706.3	6	600.1	680.4	168.1	590.64	604.75	112.8	586.10	597.25	7.8	*566.18*	**569.28**	118.7
D_8	409.35	811.4	4	715.5	775.8	149.8	661.78	680.31	102.7	658.49	669.83	8.1	*650.01*	**659.93**	117.4
D_9	385.89	842.7	6	741.0	818.2	156.0	706.08	723.45	92.6	689.83	710.32	9.2	*651.39*	**660.49**	119.2
D_{10}	485.63	1306.6	3	1424.6	1867.7	173.1	1208.71	1290.56	77.7	1189.32	1280.92	6.9	*1157.58*	**1165.72**	120.4
Avg		928.6	4.6	854.0	1025.8	156.8	792.19	816.75	94.5	786.14	809.39	7.9	753.57	765.46	119.3

Even though a totally fair comparison is not possible due to different running time and different processors, we can see that our best and average results are consistently better that the others. This is confirmed by the results averaged on each group reported in the Avg rows in the tables. We also noticed that we found the optimal solutions for seven out of ten instances of group B.

Table 4. Comparative results on instances of groups $E - G$.

Inst.	[18]	[21]		[19]			·[18]			SA		
	LB	cost	t[s]	best	avg	t[s]	best	avg	t[s]	best	avg	t[s]
E_1	430.36	1604.9	17	1331.49	1352.32	193.6	1327.72	1340.36	17.2	1260.61	**1282.34**	142.7
E_2	444.88	1101.9	10	848.08	871.25	192.0	829.79	865.05	17.1	782.08	**789.96**	139.6
E_3	454.27	986.4	14	788.03	814.23	182.9	789.56	806.53	16.7	763.35	**774.57**	142.2
E_4	412.08	871.0	19	711.19	729.93	196.5	723.87	728.96	14.8	691.18	**697.45**	142.2
E_5	416.62	1018.0	19	781.50	803.86	182.3	780.04	817.13	17.0	713.78	**734.20**	142.1
E_6	416.60	1003.0	19	790.47	804.16	177.6	779.82	793.68	18.3	753.56	**762.38**	143.3
E_7	389.57	921.1	20	711.11	733.91	191.8	705.79	715.46	18.0	682.66	**693.81**	141.6
E_8	433.89	884.6	19	752.35	761.97	168.8	733.90	750.59	17.2	710.46	**717.42**	143.5
E_9	446.49	1131.7	18	921.78	951.91	163.1	893.35	916.56	16.4	859.18	**872.41**	141.3
E_{10}	455.07	1053.6	11	825.24	845.10	174.5	822.85	841.57	16.0	788.71	**799.98**	140.7
Avg		1057.6	16.6	846.12	866.86	182.3	838.67	857.59	16.9	800.56	812.45	141.9
F_1	548.88	1721.4	889	1401.96	1425.97	745.5	1311.10	1351.20	124.4	1246.11	**1274.45**	248.2
F_2	543.32	1763.8	909	1336.33	1383.58	812.1	1298.31	1337.41	121.7	1226.08	**1246.20**	246.1
F_3	547.64	1549.6	868	1263.39	1285.81	780.3	1215.96	1272.23	116.5	1161.88	**1172.23**	245.6
F_4	531.84	1420.4	1321	1124.24	1146.22	901.9	1100.66	1134.66	136.0	1055.16	**1072.77**	246.9
F_5	538.14	1701.9	1145	1329.29	1365.17	826.1	1298.55	1331.09	119.8	1231.57	**1251.21**	246.1
F_6	518.47	1639.7	836	1332.14	1373.32	649.8	1292.52	1368.41	109.6	1237.13	**1270.02**	247.9
F_7	512.98	1384.3	1294	1131.27	1157.35	817.0	1084.57	1125.37	120.5	1073.17	**1095.17**	245.5
F_8	536.15	1544.6	924	1132.77	1165.15	716.4	1123.22	1140.42	107.7	1089.42	**1111.02**	246.4
F_9	543.16	1572.9	1642	1311.43	1345.01	770.4	1263.19	1344.62	125.4	1204.15	**1233.04**	246.8
F_{10}	546.84	1581.0	1326	1418.53	1446.35	740.3	1383.08	1419.76	119.6	1270.52	**1310.33**	248.6
Avg		1588.0	1115.4	1278.14	1309.39	776.0	1237.12	1282.52	120.1	1179.52	1203.64	246.8
G_1	612.37	2248.0	7200	1778.54	1855.17	1949.8	1744.14	1824.34	439.4	1681.09	**1715.06**	367.7
G_2	605.84	2316.1	7200	1824.74	1897.99	2115.1	1709.70	1799.78	519.5	1652.69	**1677.10**	362.0
G_3	614.20	1885.3	7147	1514.23	1546.53	1935.1	1464.69	1511.86	461.6	1432.36	**1454.04**	367.4
G_4	604.30	2023.2	7200	1564.42	1599.39	2137.6	1508.94	1569.01	529.0	1458.50	**1488.28**	373.6
G_5	633.66	2247.6	7200	1698.28	1749.10	1840.9	1652.88	1681.00	466.6	1550.76	**1585.98**	371.3
G_6	621.46	2144.4	7200	1714.38	1777.39	2014.4	1681.64	1719.18	570.5	1654.66	**1684.79**	371.5
G_7	602.42	1971.5	6934	1640.07	1677.92	1844.3	1536.00	1604.96	522.4	1493.87	**1544.63**	365.1
G_8	618.74	1987.4	7200	1547.63	1583.86	1799.1	1498.38	1535.90	531.7	1456.98	**1483.25**	367.3
G_9	662.70	2415.5	7023	1942.21	1972.48	1810.7	1850.07	1976.27	446.6	1768.87	**1814.84**	371.3
G_{10}	633.76	2373.4	7003	1872.08	1932.27	1649.6	1785.37	1868.56	482.8	1690.62	**1723.49**	372.4
Avg		2161.2	7130.7	1709.66	1759.21	1909.7	1643.18	1709.09	497.0	1584.04	1617.15	369.0

6   Conclusions

In this work, we propose a local search based approach using a neighborhood larger than the previous ones proposed in the literature. The use of this large neighborhood does not compromise the efficiency of the method thanks to the fact that it is not explored exhaustively, due to the random selection criterion typical of SA. The SA approach has been able to compare favorably with respect to all state-of-the-art methods in the literature, obtaining the best known results for most of the instances, although with larger (but still acceptable) running time on small instances.

For the future work, we plan to improve the solution method by implementing different neighborhoods, in particular those based on the swap of caregivers, and using them in a multi-neighborhood approach [2,6].

As a longer term project, we plan to extend the problem formulation by including other real-world features such as multi-day horizon, synchronization based on mobile equipment, and multiple depots. For this general problem, we aim at designing a more flexible and robust file format for the input and output data, and to translate other datasets such as the ones by Bredström and Rönnqvist [5], Grenouilleau et al. [14], and Di Gaspero and Urli [9] in this new format.

Acknowledgements. We wish to thank Alberto Kummer for answering our questions about the work of his research group and for providing us the CPLEX source code of the MIP model.

This research is part of the project "Models and algorithms for the optimization of integrated healthcare management" (no. 2020LNEZYC) supported by the Italian Ministry of University and Research (MUR) under the PRIN-2020 program.

References

1. Begur, S.V., Miller, D.M., Weaver, J.R.: An integrated spatial DSS for scheduling and routing home-health-care nurses. Interfaces **27** (1997)
2. Bellio, R., Ceschia, S., Di Gaspero, L., Schaerf, A.: Two-stage multi-neighborhood simulated annealing for uncapacitated examination timetabling. Comput. Oper. Res. **132**, 105300 (2021)
3. Bertels, S., Fahle, T.: A hybrid setup for a hybrid scenario: combining heuristics for the home health care problem. Comput. Oper. Res. **33** (2006)
4. Birattari, M., Yuan, Z., Balaprakash, P., Stützle, T.: F-Race and iterated F-Race: an overview. In: Bartz-Beielstein, T., Chiarandini, M., Paquete, L., Preuss, M. (eds.) Experimental Methods for the Analysis of Optimization Algorithms, pp. 311–336. Springer, Heidelberg (2010). https://doi.org/10.1007/978-3-642-02538-9_13
5. Bredström, D., Rönnqvist, M.: Combined vehicle routing and scheduling with temporal precedence and synchronization constraints. Eur. J. Oper. Res. **191**(1), 19–31 (2008)
6. Ceschia, S., Di Gaspero, L., Rosati, R.M., Schaerf, A.: Multi-neighborhood simulated annealing for the minimum interference frequency assignment problem. EURO J. Comput. Optim. 1–32 (2021)
7. Cheng, E., Rich, J.: A home health care routing and scheduling problem. Technical report. CAAM TR98-04, Rice University (1998)
8. Decerle, J., Grunder, O., El Hassani, A.H., Barakat, O.: A memetic algorithm for a home health care routing and scheduling problem. Oper. Res. Health Care **16**, 59–71 (2018)
9. Di Gaspero, L., Urli, T.: A CP/LNS approach for multi-day homecare scheduling problems. In: Blesa, M.J., Blum, C., Voß, S. (eds.) HM 2014. LNCS, vol. 8457, pp. 1–15. Springer, Cham (2014). https://doi.org/10.1007/978-3-319-07644-7_1
10. Eveborn, P., Flisberg, P., Rönnqvist, M.: Laps care–an operational system for staff planning of home care. Eur. J. Oper. Res. **171** (2006)
11. Fikar, C., Hirsch, P.: Home health care routing and scheduling: a review. Comput. Oper. Res. **77**, 86–95 (2017)
12. Franzin, A., Stützle, T.: Revisiting simulated annealing: a component-based analysis. Comput. Oper. Res. **104**, 191–206 (2019)

13. Genet, N., Boerma, W., Kroneman, M., Hutchinson, A., Saltman, R.B. (eds.): Homecare Across Europe. World Health Organization. European Observatory on Health Systems and Policies (2012)
14. Grenouilleau, F., Legrain, A., Lahrichi, N., Rousseau, L.M.: A set partitioning heuristic for the home health care routing and scheduling problem. Eur. J. Oper. Res. **275**(1), 295–303 (2019)
15. Hammersley, J.M., Handscomb, D.C.: Monte Carlo Methods. Chapman and Hall, London (1964)
16. Kirkpatrick, S., Gelatt, D., Vecchi, M.: Optimization by simulated annealing. Science **220**, 671–680 (1983)
17. Kummer, A.F.: A study on the home care routing and scheduling problem. Ph.D. thesis, Universidade Federal do Rio Grande do Sul (2021)
18. Kummer, A.F., de Araújo, O.C.B., Buriol, L.S., Resende, M.G.C.: A biased random-key genetic algorithm for the home health care problem (2022). arXiv preprint arXiv:2206.14347
19. Kummer, A.F., Buriol, L.S., de Araújo, O.C.: A biased random key genetic algorithm applied to the VRPTW with skill requirements and synchronization constraints. In: Proceedings of the 2020 Genetic and Evolutionary Computation Conference, pp. 717–724 (2020)
20. Lasfargeas, S., Gagné, C., Sioud, Á.: Solving the home health care problem with temporal precedence and synchronization. In: Talbi, E.-G., Nakib, A. (eds.) Bioinspired Heuristics for Optimization. SCI, vol. 774, pp. 251–267. Springer, Cham (2019). https://doi.org/10.1007/978-3-319-95104-1_16
21. Mankowska, D.S., Meisel, F., Bierwirth, C.: The home health care routing and scheduling problem with interdependent services. Health Care Manag. Sci. **17**(1), 15–30 (2014)
22. Rasmussen, M.S., Justesen, T., Dohn, A., Larsen, J.: The home care crew scheduling problem: preference-based visit clustering and temporal dependencies. Eur. J. Oper. Res. **219** (2012)
23. Rendl, A., Prandtstetter, M., Hiermann, G., Puchinger, J., Raidl, G.: Hybrid heuristics for multimodal homecare scheduling. In: Beldiceanu, N., Jussien, N., Pinson, É. (eds.) CPAIOR 2012. LNCS, vol. 7298, pp. 339–355. Springer, Heidelberg (2012). https://doi.org/10.1007/978-3-642-29828-8_22
24. Urli, T.: json2run: a tool for experiment design & analysis. CoRR abs/1305.1112 (2013)
25. Xiang, T., Li, Y., Szeto, W.Y.: The daily routing and scheduling problem of home health care: based on costs and participants' preference satisfaction. Int. Trans. Oper. Res. **30**, 39–69 (2021)

MAP Inference in Probabilistic Answer Set Programs

Damiano Azzolini[1]([✉]) [ID], Elena Bellodi[2] [ID], and Fabrizio Riguzzi[3] [ID]

[1] Dipartimento di Scienze dell'Ambiente e della Prevenzione,
Università di Ferrara, Ferrara, Italy
damiano.azzolini@unife.it
[2] Dipartimento di Ingegneria, Università di Ferrara, Ferrara, Italy
elena.bellodi@unife.it
[3] Dipartimento di Matematica e Informatica, Università di Ferrara, Ferrara, Italy
fabrizio.riguzzi@unife.it

Abstract. Reasoning with uncertain data is a central task in artificial intelligence. In some cases, the goal is to find the most likely assignment to a subset of random variables, named query variables, while some other variables are observed. This task is called Maximum a Posteriori (MAP). When the set of query variables is the complement of the observed variables, the task goes under the name of Most Probable Explanation (MPE). In this paper, we introduce the definitions of cautious and brave MAP and MPE tasks in the context of Probabilistic Answer Set Programming under the credal semantics and provide an algorithm to solve them. Empirical results show that the brave version of both tasks is usually faster to compute. On the brave MPE task, the adoption of a state-of-the-art ASP solver makes the computation much faster than a naive approach based on the enumeration of all the worlds.

Keywords: Probabilistic answer set programming · MAP inference · Statistical relational artificial intelligence

1 Introduction

The research field of Probabilistic Logic Programming (PLP) [20] aims to reason with logic programs where some of the facts, called *probabilistic facts*, are considered uncertain [11]. One of the most adopted semantics for these programs, the Distribution Semantics (DS) [21], assigns a meaning to probabilistic logic programs where every *world*, i.e., a logic program identified by the truth values of probabilistic facts, is required to have a total well-founded model [25].

Probabilistic Answer Set Programming (PASP) [10,19] extends the capabilities of Answer Set Programming (ASP) [9] and allows, as PLP, the definition of probabilistic facts. With PASP, however, every world is an answer set program and thus may have multiple answer sets. In this case, a semantics that can be adopted is the *credal semantics*, which assigns a probability range rather than

© The Author(s) 2023
A. Dovier et al. (Eds.): AIxIA 2022, LNAI 13796, pp. 413–426, 2023.
https://doi.org/10.1007/978-3-031-27181-6_29

a sharp probability value, as happens with the DS, to a query. This range is defined by a lower and an upper probability.

Maximum-a-Posteriori (MAP) inference is a central topic in machine learning, where the goal is to find, given a set of evidence variables, the most probable value to a subset of the random variables (called query variables). If the set of query variables is the complement of the set of evidence variables, the problem is called Most Probable Explanation (MPE).

In this paper, we propose an algorithm to perform both *cautious* MAP/MPE and *brave* MAP/MPE inference in probabilistic answer set programs, where we consider respectively the lower and the upper probability bound induced by the query variables. We test this algorithm on two datasets with different configurations. Moreover, we also compare our algorithm with the clingo's [13] `#maximize` statement for the brave MPE task.

The paper is structured as follows: in Sect. 2, we discuss some related works. Section 3 introduces the main concepts of PLP and PASP. Section 4 describes our algorithm to perform brave and cautious MAP/MPE inference in PASP and in Sect. 5 we discuss some experiments to test its performance. Section 6 concludes the paper with some final remarks and possible future works.

2   Related Work

The MAP/MPE task has received relatively small attention in PLP: in [22], the authors introduced an algorithm to compute the MAP/MPE for a given LPAD [26]. The program is converted into a compact form and then the result is computed by analysing it. Similar work can be found in [8]. However, both consider programs where every world has a unique model, so they cannot deal with probabilistic ASP programs, where every world may have multiple models.

The authors of [16] propose a tool to perform inference in ASP programs following the LP^{MLN} [17] semantics. Differently from them, we adopt a different semantics, the credal semantics [10], that we believe being more general and intuitive for PASP. Moreover, we consider the MAP/MPE task, not discussed in their work.

Inference in PASP has been considered in [24], where the authors introduced the PASOCS solver, but they do not explore the MAP/MPE task. Similar considerations can be applied to [23], where the authors discussed how to perform inference in ProbLog [11] programs under the stable model semantics, but still ignoring MAP/MPE.

3   Background

We assume that the reader is familiar with the basic concepts of Logic Programming [18]. Here we consider the Answer Set Programming (ASP) syntax [9] enriched with *aggregate atoms* [3]. An aggregate atom is composed by two *guards* that can be either constants or variables, denoted with g_0 and g_1, two comparison arithmetic operators, δ_0 and δ_1, an aggregate function symbol φ, and a set of expressions $\epsilon_0, \ldots, \epsilon_n$ where each ϵ_i has the form $t_1, \ldots, t_n : F$ and each t_i is a term whose variables appear in the conjunction of literals F. Given the previous elements, the syntax of an aggregate atom is $g_0 \delta_0 \, \#\varphi\{\epsilon_0; \ldots; \epsilon_n : F\} \, \delta_1 g_1$. An example of aggregate atom is `0 <= #sum{A : p(A)} <= 2`.

We denote a *disjunctive rule* (or simply *rule*) with the syntax

```
h1 ; ... ; hm :- b1, ..., bm.
```

where each `hi` is an atom and each `bi` is a literal. The disjunction of atoms at the left of the neck operator (`:-`) is called *head* while the conjunction of literals at its right is called *body*. If the head is empty and the body is not, the rule is called a *constraint* and if the body is empty and the head is not, the rule is a *fact*. We restrict ourselves to *safe rules*, i.e., rules where every variable in the head also appears in a positive literal in the body. Finally, if a rule does not contain variables it is called *ground*. A program is a finite set of rules.

To provide the definition of answer set, we need to introduce some more concepts. If we consider an answer set program $\mathcal{P}$, with $B_{\mathcal{P}}$ we denote the set of ground atoms that can be constructed with the symbols in $\mathcal{P}$. $B_{\mathcal{P}}$ is also called Herbrand base. An interpretation I of $\mathcal{P}$ is such that $I \subset B_{\mathcal{P}}$. I satisfies a ground rule if at least one head atom is true in it when all the literals in the body are true in it, and it is called a *model* if it satisfies all the groundings of the rules of $\mathcal{P}$. The *reduct* [12] of a ground program $\mathcal{P}_g$ w.r.t. an interpretation I is obtained by removing from $\mathcal{P}_g$ the rules where at least one literal in the body is false in I. Finally, an *answer set* (or stable model) for a program $\mathcal{P}$ is defined as an interpretation that is a minimal (under set inclusion) model of $\mathcal{P}_g$. We indicate with $AS(\mathcal{P})$ the set of all the answer sets of a program $\mathcal{P}$. Finally, the *projective solutions* [14] onto a set of ground atoms B are given by the set $AS_B(\mathcal{P}) = \{A \cap B \mid A \in AS(\mathcal{P})\}$.

Probabilistic Logic Programming [20] allows the definition of uncertain data in logic programs. For example, ProbLog [11] allows *probabilistic facts*. Each probabilistic fact has the form $\Pi :: f$ where $\Pi \in \,]0, 1]$ and f is an atom. According to the Distribution Semantics [21], an assignment of truth value, true ($\top$) or false ($\bot$), for every probabilistic fact f_i in the program identifies a *world* w whose probability $P(w)$ can be computed as

$$P(w) = \prod_{i|f_i=\top} \Pi_i \cdot \prod_{i|f_i=\bot} (1 - \Pi_i) \tag{1}$$

If we are given a query q, i.e., a conjunction of ground literals, its probability is the sum of the probability of the worlds where the query is true:

$$P(q) = \sum_{w \models q} P(w) \tag{2}$$

The Distribution Semantics assumes that all the probabilistic facts are independent and that every world is a logic program with a two-valued well-founded model [25]. However, when we consider Probabilistic Answer Set Programming, the latter condition usually does not hold. For PASP, we consider here the credal semantics (CS) [10,19]. Under the CS, every query q is associated with a probability interval defined by a lower bound $\underline{P}(q)$ and an upper bound $\overline{P}(q)$. A world contributes to the upper probability if the query is present in *at least one* of its answer sets and contributes to the lower probability if the query is present in *all* its answer sets. In formulas,

$$\overline{P}(q) = \sum_{w_i | \exists m \in AS(w_i),\ m \models q} P(w_i)$$

$$\underline{P}(q) = \sum_{w_i | |AS(w_i)| > 0\ \wedge\ m \in AS(w_i),\ m \models q} P(w_i)$$

These formulas are valid only if every world has at least one answer set, so in this paper we consider only programs that satisfy this requirement. If every world has exactly one answer set, the CS coincides with the DS and the query has a sharp probability value. Consider the following program.

Example 1. Gold example

```
1  0.2::gold(1).
2  0.3::gold(2).
3  0.7::gold(3).
4  valuable(X) ; not_valuable(X):- gold(X).
5  :- #count{X:valuable(X), gold(X)} = VG,
6     #count{X:gold(X)} = G, 10*VG < 6*G.
```

The first three lines introduce three probabilistic facts `gold/1` indicating that the objects identified with 1, 2, and 3 could be made of gold with different probabilities. Line 4 states that an object made of gold may be valuable or not. Line 5 represents a constraint saying that 60% of the objects made of gold are valuable. This program has $2^3 = 8$ worlds listed in Table 1. If we consider the query q `valuable(1)`, $\underline{P}(q) = 0.158$ (corresponding to $P(w_4) + P(w_5) + P(w_6)$) and $\overline{P}(q) = 0.2$ (corresponding to $P(w_4) + P(w_5) + P(w_6) + P(w_7)$).

Table 1. Worlds for Example 1. Predicate 'g' stands for **gold**. Column 'mq' indicates whether there is at least one model of the world where the query **valuable(1)** is true and column 'mnq' indicates whether there is at least one model of the world where the query is false.

world	g(1)	g(2)	g(3)	P(w)	mq	mnq
0	0	0	0	0.168	F	T
1	0	0	1	0.392	F	T
2	0	1	0	0.392	F	T
3	0	1	1	0.168	F	T
4	1	0	0	0.042	T	F
5	1	0	1	0.098	T	F
6	1	1	0	0.018	T	F
7	1	1	1	0.042	T	T

4 MAP Inference in Probabilistic Answer Set Programming

In PLP, the MAP task [8,22] consists in finding a possible truth value assignment to a subset of probabilistic facts such that a given evidence is satisfied and the sum of the probabilities of the possible worlds identified by the truth values' choices is maximized. More formally, given a probabilistic logic program, a set of ground atoms e, and a set of query random variables (also called query variables) Q, the goal is to solve

$$\arg\max_q P(Q = q \mid e)$$

If all the program variables are query variables, the task is called MPE.

If we consider PASP, every world may have multiple models so the previous definition must be extended. We now introduce the *cautious* MAP and *brave* MAP tasks:

Definition 1. *Cautious and brave MAP/MPE. Given a PASP program $\mathcal{P}$, a set of ground atoms e (call it evidence), and a set of query probabilistic facts Q:*

– *the cautious MAP problem consists in finding a truth assignment q to query facts Q such that $\underline{P}(q \mid e)$ is maximized, i.e., in solving:*

$$\underline{\mathrm{MAP}}(e) = \arg\max_q \underline{P}(Q = q \mid e) = \arg\max_q \sum_{w_i \mid \forall m \in AS(w_i),\, m \models q \wedge m \models e} P(w_i)$$

– *the brave MAP problem consists in finding a truth assignment q to query facts Q such that $\overline{P}(q \mid e)$ is maximized, i.e., in solving:*

$$\overline{\mathrm{MAP}}(e) = \arg\max_q \overline{P}(Q = q \mid e) = \arg\max_q \sum_{w_i \mid \exists m \in AS(w_i),\, m \models q \wedge m \models e} P(w_i)$$

The definition of cautious and brave MPE inference for a query e, denoted with $\underline{\mathrm{MPE}}(e)$ and $\overline{\mathrm{MPE}}(e)$ respectively, is similar.

Note that this task is different from computing the conditional probability of a query given evidence. Given the previous definitions, for a query e we have that $P(\underline{\mathrm{MAP}}(e)) \leq P(\overline{\mathrm{MAP}}(e))$ and $P(\underline{\mathrm{MPE}}(e)) \leq P(\overline{\mathrm{MPE}}(e))$.

If we consider all the three probabilistic facts gold/1 of Example 1 as query variables (denoted by prepending the functor map), the cautious MPE state (all the probabilistic facts are query variables) for the query valuable(1) is given by {gold(1), not gold(2), gold(3)} with an associated probability of 0.098 (world 5 of Table 1). With not gold(2) we indicate that the probabilistic fact gold(2) should be false. The same state is also the brave MPE state. The cautious MAP/MPE and the brave MAP/MPE state do not necessarily coincide. For example, if we consider gold(1) and gold(3) as query variables, the cautious MAP state for the evidence valuable(1) is {gold(1), not gold(3)} with a probability of 0.06 (sum of the probabilities of the worlds 4 and 6 of Table 1) while the brave MAP state is {gold(1), gold(3)} with a probability of 0.14 (sum of the probabilities of the worlds 5 and 7 of Table 1). Finally, there can be multiple cautious/brave MAP/MPE states. If we consider again Example 1 but with all the probabilities set to 0.5 and all the three probabilistic facts as query variables, there are 3 cautious MPE states for the query `valuable(1)`, all with an associated probability of 0.125: {`gold(1)`, `gold(2)`, `not gold(3)`}, {`gold(1)`, `not gold(2)`, `gold(3)`}, and {`gold(1)`, `not gold(2)`, `not gold(3)`}.

4.1 Algorithm

To solve the cautious/brave MAP/MPE task[1], we developed an algorithm that works in two steps: first, it translates the PASP program into an ASP program by rewriting probabilistic facts and query variables into ASP choice rules. It is shown in Algorithm 1 and it proceeds as follows: first, the function CON-VERTVARIABLES converts probabilistic facts and query variables into an ASP representation. Every probabilistic fact `p::f` and every query variable `map p::f` (note that `f` may also have arguments) is transformed into `0{f}1`. Moreover, we add the rule `not_f:- not f`. Function COMPUTEMINIMALSET [5] extracts the minimal set of probabilistic facts by computing the cautious consequences (intersection of all models). The facts in this set must always be true, so we can remove the choices for them and fix their value. For every element in this set, we add a constraint imposing that it must be true (line 5). This is possible since every world is required to have at least one answer set. Now, if we want to perform brave MAP (i.e., considering the upper probability) given an evidence e, we insert the rule `:- not e` (a constraint imposing that the evidence must always be true) to the program and project the solutions on the probabilistic facts (line 9). Otherwise, if we consider cautious MAP (lower probability), we add the rules `q:- e` and `nq:- not e` and still project the solutions on the atoms `q/0` and `nq/0` (line 12). Finally, we extract every world and its contribution to the probability with the function COMPUTECONTRIBUTION and identify the MAP state (function COMPUTEMAPSTATE).

To better understand how the algorithm works, consider the program shown in Example 1 with `gold(1)` and `gold(3)` as query variables and `valuable(1)` as evidence. After the execution of function CONVERTVARIABLES, the probabilistic fact and the two query variables become `0{gold(2)}1`, `0{gold(1)}1`, and `0{gold(3)}1`. The minimal set of atoms, obtained by computing the cautious consequences on the converted program with an additional rule `:- not valuable(1)`, contains `gold(1)`, so we add the constraint `:- not gold(1)` to the program. If we consider *brave* MAP, by adding again `:- not valuable(1)` to the program and projecting the solutions on the probabilistic facts (function PROJECTSOLUTIONS, line 9), we get 4 answer sets:

`AS1 = {gold(1) not_gold(2) not_gold(3)}`,
`AS2 = {gold(1) not_gold(2) gold(3)}`,

---

[1] We will usually only write MAP to simplify the notation, since MPE is a special case of MAP.

    AS3 = {gold(1) gold(2) not_gold(3)}, and
    AS4 = {gold(1) gold(2) gold(3)},

where with not_gold(i) we indicate that the probabilistic fact or query variable is not selected. These four answer sets (worlds) have respectively probability $0.2 \cdot (1-0.3) \cdot (1-0.7) = 0.042$, $0.2 \cdot (1-0.3) \cdot 0.7 = 0.098$, $0.2 \cdot 0.3 \cdot (1-0.7) = 0.018$, and $0.2 \cdot 0.3 \cdot 0.7 = 0.042$, that are computed with the function COMPUTECONTRIBUTION. Finally, if we group these answer sets by query variables (function COMPUTEMAPSTATE), we get two sets representing two different MAP states: MAP1 = {AS1, AS3} (gold(1) and not_gold(3)) and MAP2 = {AS2, AS4} (gold(1) and gold(3)). MAP1 has probability $0.042 + 0.018 = 0.06$ while MAP2 has probability $0.098 + 0.042 = 0.14$ so MAP2 is selected as MAP state since it gives the highest upper probability for the evidence valuable(1).

    If we consider instead *cautious* MAP, the process in analogous, but we cannot add the constraint :- not valuable(1) since we need to consider the lower probability: in this case, a world contributes to the lower probability if the evidence is true in every answer set. If we add the constraint imposing that the evidence must be true in every answer set, we cannot identify the worlds that have at least one answer set where the evidence is false (and thus do not contribute to the lower probability). We now get 5 answer sets:

    {gold(1) gold(2) gold(3) nq},
    {gold(1) gold(2) gold(3) q},
    {gold(1) gold(2) not_gold(3) q},
    {gold(1) not_gold(2) gold(3) q}, and
    {gold(1) not_gold(2) not_gold(3) q}.

The world identified by the first two answer sets is the same (all the three variables true) but in the first there is nq and in the second q. Thus, the first answer set indicates that there is at least one answer set of this world where the query is false, so it does not contribute to the lower probability (and can be discarded). For the remaining three worlds there is only one answer set each and it has q inside, so they contribute to both the lower and the upper probability. By applying, as before, functions COMPUTECONTRIBUTION and then COMPUTEMAPSTATE, we get {gold(1), not gold(3)} as MAP state (third and fifth answer set) with an associated probability of $0.2 \cdot 0.3 \cdot (1 - 0.7) + 0.2 \cdot (1 - 0.3) \cdot (1 - 0.7) = 0.06$.

    For both brave and cautious MAP tasks we need to generate at worst 2^n answer sets, where n is the number of probabilistic facts, thus the algorithm is exponential in n. The reason is that we need to know if there is at least one answer set for every world where the query is true for the brave MAP and if in all the models for every world the query is true for cautious MAP. However, the number of generated models for brave MAP is usually smaller than the number of generated models for cautious MAP, due to the additional constraint removing the models where the query is false. However, this additional constraint plus possibly the constraints given by the elements in the minimal set of atoms does not reduce the complexity of the task.

Algorithm 1. Function COMPUTEMAPSTATE: computation of the MAP/MPE state given a query e in a PASP program $\mathcal{P}$.

```
 1: function COMPUTEMAPSTATE(e, P, mode)
 2:     PASP_p, mapVariables ← CONVERTVARIABLES(P)
 3:     minSet ← COMPUTEMINIMALSET(PASP_p ∪ {: − not e.})
 4:     for all a ∈ minSet do                              ▷ a represents a probabilistic fact
 5:         PASP_p ← PASP_p ∪ {: − not a.}
 6:     end for
 7:     if mode is brave then                              ▷ Brave MAP
 8:         PASP_p ← PASP_p ∪ {: − not e.}
 9:         AS ← PROJECTSOLUTIONS(PASP_p, probFacts)
10:     else                                               ▷ Cautious MAP
11:         PASP_p ← PASP_p ∪ {q : − e., nq : − not e.}
12:         AS ← PROJECTSOLUTIONS(PASP_p, probFacts, q ∪ nq)
13:     end if
14:     worldsList ← COMPUTECONTRIBUTION(AS)
15:     return COMPUTEMAPSTATE(worldsList, mapVariables)
16: end function
```

We propose another possible encoding for the brave MPE task. For each query variable `map p::f`, we add: a rule `0{f}1`, a rule `f(lp):- f` and a rule `not_f(nlp):- not f`. `lp` is given by $10^n \cdot log(p)$ and `nlp` is given by $10^n \cdot log(1-p)$, where n is an integer that denotes its scale. The multiplications by 10^n are needed since ASP does not handle floating points. For example, if we set n to 3, the fact `0.2::gold(1)` of Example 1 is expanded in: `0{gold(1)}1`, `gold(1,-1609):- gold(1)`, and `not_gold(1,-223):- not gold(1)`, where $10^3 \cdot log(0.2) = -1609$ and $10^3 \cdot log(0.8) = -223$. With this log-encoding, we can leverage the property $log(a \cdot b) = log(a) + log(b)$ and thus use the `#sum` aggregate. By multiplying by 10^n, it is not straightforward to obtain the original probabilities once we have the brave MPE state. However, once we get the combination of variables in this state, we can simply look up the initial probabilities in the program. Finally, since we have the (converted) probability as argument of the atoms, we can use the clingo [13] `#maximize` to find the combination of query variables resulting in the brave MPE state. If we consider again Example 1, with all the probabilistic facts converted as previously described, we can compute the brave MPE state with `#maximize{ P : wp(P) }` where `wp/1` is defined as

```
1   wp(P):-
2       PS = #sum{X,Y : gold(Y,X)},
3       PNS = #sum{X,Y : not_gold(Y,X)},
4       P = PS + PNS.
```

This is a naive encoding that requires the enumeration of all the answer sets. An alternative ASP encoding, we call it *improved*, for the solution of the brave MPE task for the same example, that does not require the enumeration of all the answer sets, is `#maximize{X,Y:gold(Y,X); X,Y:not_gold(Y,X)}`. In the next section, we test our algorithm for cautious and brave MAP and MPE and compare the execution time between our brave MPE proposal and the clingo `#maximize` statement.

5   Experiments

We implemented the algorithm in Python and we used the clingo APIs [13] to compute the answer sets[2]. To test the performance, we ran some experiments on a computer with Intel® Xeon® E5-2630v3 running at 2.40 GHz with 8 Gb of RAM and a time limit of 8 h. Execution times are computed with the bash command `time`. The reported values are from the `real` field.

The first dataset, `gold`, contains a set of programs with the structure of Example 1. The size of a program is given by the number of probabilistic facts `gold/1`. Example 1 has size 3. For the MAP task, 50% of the `gold/1` facts are considered query variables. We randomly set the probability of probabilistic facts. The query is `valuable(1)`. Results are shown in Fig. 1a. We removed the results for size less than 19 since their execution times were negligible. The computation of the brave MAP state seems the fastest one, followed by the brave MPE state. This is due to the additional constraint inserted into the program, which removes some of the possible answer sets. Cautious MAP and cautious MPE have comparable execution times. In all the cases, for size greater than 25 we get a memory error.

The second dataset, `smoke`, describes a network of friends where some of them smoke. An example of program of size (number of people) 4 is:

```
1  0.73::e(0,1). 0.59::e(0,2).
2  0.08::e(0,3). 0.19::e(2,3).
3
4  smokes(0). smokes(2).
5  friend(X,Y):- e(X,Y). friend(X,Y):- e(Y,X).
6  smokes(X); no_smokes(X):- friend(X,Y),smokes(Y).
7
8  :- #count{X:no_smokes(X)} = N,
9     #count{X:smokes(X)} = S, 10*S < 8*(N+S).
```

A person X smokes if she has at least one friend Y that smokes. The constraint imposes that at least 80% of the people smoke. The goal is to compute the MAP/MPE state for the query `smokes(n)` where `n` is the number of people involved (here 4). Half of the people of the network certainly smoke. If the number of people is odd, we round the result to the next integer. As before, for the MAP experiments, 50% of `e/2` facts are query The number of probabilistic facts follows a Barabási-Albert preferential attachment model generated with the `networkx` [15] Python package. We set as initial number of nodes of the graph (n) the size of the instance and as the number of edges that connect a new node to an existing one (m) 2. Results are shown in Fig. 1b. As for the `gold` dataset, also here brave MAP and brave MPE seem the fastest, and their execution times are similar (the red and black curves in the plot overlap). In all cases, for size greater than 14 we get a memory error.

In a second set of experiments we verified whether and how the execution time of the algorithm varies when there is an increasing number of MAP/MPE states.

---

[2] Source code and datasets available at https://github.com/damianoazzolini/pasta.

To do this, we generated two versions of the gold dataset, one with random probabilities and one with all the probabilities set to 0.5. The remaining parts of the programs are equal to Example 1. Figure 2a shows the execution times of the cautious and brave MAP and MPE task on the dataset with all the probabilities set to 0.5. As before, brave MAP/MPE are the fastest. Also here, datasets with size larger than 25 cause a memory error, except for brave MPE that stops at size 23. Execution times for cautious MPE/MAP are almost identical. In Fig. 2b we compare the two versions of the datasets on the brave MPE task. Brave MAP with all probabilities set to 0.5 and brave MPE with random probabilities seem to take the same time to complete. Execution times for random probabilities are slightly smaller since there is usually only one MAP/MPE state in this case. Moreover, the MAP/MPE task where all the probabilities are equal gives a memory error starting from size 24, while, when the probabilities are all different, we get a memory error starting from size 26. A similar trend (exponential) was observed in the case of cautious MAP/MPE, but with the same differences found in Fig. 2a.

Lastly, we compared our algorithm with the #maximize statement of clingo on the brave MPE task for the gold dataset. As before, we generate a set of programs with random probabilities and a set of programs with all the probabilities set to 0.5. For a fair comparison, we set all the elements of the minimal set of atoms to be true in the program that will use the clingo statement and we add the constraint imposing that the query must be true. We ran two tests: one that outputs only one brave MPE state (even if there may be more) and one that outputs all the states, by using the flag --opt-mode=optN. We only considered the naive encoding, since the improved one is order of magnitude faster than the other and than our tool. For example, with 30 probabilistic facts and the improved encoding, the result is computed in a fraction of a second. Results in Fig. 3a show that the execution time for the computation of the brave MPE state oscillates when we want only one solution when probabilities are all equals. The computation of all the solutions when the probabilities are all set to 0.5 is the fastest one. For random probabilities, in both cases (the two curves overlap) the programs of size larger than 12 give a memory error. Figure 3b shows that clingo's #maximize statement is slower than our algorithm but it can handle larger instances when we want to compute all the solutions of the brave MPE task when all the probabilities of the states are equal (red and yellow curves). This may be due to a better memory management of the program and a possibly better search strategy. Moreover, the computation of 1 MPE state in clingo (blue curve) stops for the time limit, rather than the memory limit as the others.

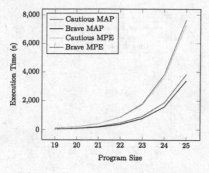

(a) Results for the **gold** dataset.

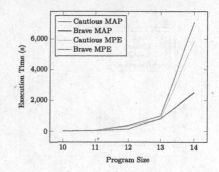

(b) Results for the **smoke** dataset.

Fig. 1. Results for cautious and brave MAP and MPE tasks for the **gold** and **smoke** datasets in terms of inference time as the program size (number of probabilistic facts) increases.

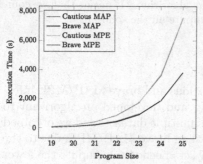
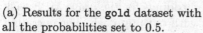

(a) Results for the **gold** dataset with all the probabilities set to 0.5.

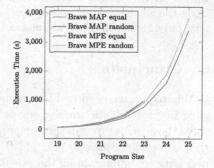

(b) Comparison between random and equal probabilities for the brave MAP/MPE task for the **gold** dataset.

Fig. 2. Comparisons between the two **gold** dataset versions.

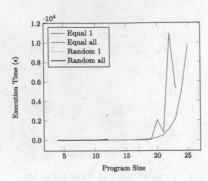

(a) Results obtained using the #maximize aggregate in clingo on the gold dataset.

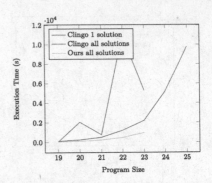

(b) Comparison between clingo #maximize statement and our algorithm on the gold dataset with probabilities set to 0.5.

Fig. 3. Results for the brave MPE task computed with clingo's #maximize statement using the naive encoding and comparison with our algorithm. '1' means that we compute only 1 solution while 'all' means that we compute all the solutions.

6   Conclusions

In this paper, we proposed the concepts of cautious and brave MAP/MPE inference in probabilistic answer set programming and developed an algorithm to solve these tasks. We ran some experiments on multiple datasets and we obtained that, generally, cautious MAP/MPE is slower than brave MAP/MPE, due to the necessity to enumerate all the possible answer sets needed to compute the lower probability. We also proposed two alternative encodings for the brave MPE task and compare the clingo #maximize statement with our approach. The encoding that does not require the enumeration of all the answer sets is order of magnitude faster than the other and than our tool. However, if we consider the naive encoding, when all the probabilities are set to 0.5, clingo is slower than our algorithm but it seems to be able to solve larger instances with less memory requirements. In the future, we plan to test other ASP solvers such as WASP [1,2], adopt approximate algorithms based on sampling [6,7], and consider the concept of abduction [4] in PASP.

Acknowledgements. This research was partly supported by TAILOR, a project funded by EU Horizon 2020 research and innovation programme under GA No. 952215. Damiano Azzolini was supported by IndAM - GNCS Project with code CUP_E55F22000270001.

References

1. Alviano, M., Dodaro, C., Leone, N., Ricca, F.: Advances in WASP. In: Calimeri, F., Ianni, G., Truszczynski, M. (eds.) LPNMR 2015. LNCS (LNAI), vol. 9345, pp. 40–54. Springer, Cham (2015). https://doi.org/10.1007/978-3-319-23264-5_5

2. Alviano, M., Dodaro, C., Marques-Silva, J., Ricca, F.: Optimum stable model search: algorithms and implementation. J. Log. Comput. **30**(1), 863–897 (2020). https://doi.org/10.1093/logcom/exv061

3. Alviano, M., Faber, W.: Aggregates in answer set programming. KI-Künstliche Intelligenz **32**(2), 119–124 (2018). https://doi.org/10.1007/s13218-018-0545-9

4. Azzolini, D., Bellodi, E., Ferilli, S., Riguzzi, F., Zese, R.: Abduction with probabilistic logic programming under the distribution semantics. Int. J. Approx. Reason. **142**, 41–63 (2022). https://doi.org/10.1016/j.ijar.2021.11.003

5. Azzolini, D., Bellodi, E., Riguzzi, F.: Statistical statements in probabilistic logic programming. In: Gottlob, G., Inclezan, D., Maratea, M. (eds.) Logic Programming and Nonmonotonic Reasoning, pp. 43–55. Springer International Publishing, Cham (2022). https://doi.org/10.1007/978-3-031-15707-3_4

6. Azzolini, D., Riguzzi, F., Lamma, E.: An analysis of Gibbs sampling for probabilistic logic programs. In: Dodaro, C., et al. (eds.) Workshop on Probabilistic Logic Programming (PLP 2020). CEUR-WS, vol. 2678, pp. 1–13. Sun SITE Central Europe, Aachen, Germany (2020)

7. Azzolini, D., Riguzzi, F., Masotti, F., Lamma, E.: A comparison of MCMC sampling for probabilistic logic programming. In: Alviano, M., Greco, G., Scarcello, F. (eds.) AI*IA 2019. LNCS (LNAI), vol. 11946, pp. 18–29. Springer, Cham (2019). https://doi.org/10.1007/978-3-030-35166-3_2

8. Bellodi, E., Alberti, M., Riguzzi, F., Zese, R.: MAP inference for probabilistic logic programming. Theor. Pract. Log. Prog. **20**(5), 641–655 (2020). https://doi.org/10.1017/S1471068420000174

9. Brewka, G., Eiter, T., Truszczyński, M.: Answer set programming at a glance. Commun. ACM **54**(12), 92–103 (2011). https://doi.org/10.1145/2043174.2043195

10. Cozman, F.G., Mauá, D.D.: The joy of probabilistic answer set programming: semantics, complexity, expressivity, inference. Int. J. Approx. Reason. **125**, 218–239 (2020). https://doi.org/10.1016/j.ijar.2020.07.004

11. De Raedt, L., Kimmig, A., Toivonen, H.: ProbLog: a probabilistic Prolog and its application in link discovery. In: Veloso, M.M. (ed.) IJCAI 2007. vol. 7, pp. 2462–2467. AAAI Press/IJCAI, California (2007)

12. Faber, W., Leone, N., Pfeifer, G.: Recursive aggregates in disjunctive logic programs: semantics and complexity. In: Alferes, J.J., Leite, J. (eds.) JELIA 2004. LNCS (LNAI), vol. 3229, pp. 200–212. Springer, Heidelberg (2004). https://doi.org/10.1007/978-3-540-30227-8_19

13. Gebser, M., Kaminski, R., Kaufmann, B., Schaub, T.: Multi-shot asp solving with clingo. Theory Pract. Logic Program. **19**(1), 27–82 (2019). https://doi.org/10.1017/S1471068418000054

14. Gebser, M., Kaufmann, B., Schaub, T.: Solution enumeration for projected Boolean search problems. In: van Hoeve, W.-J., Hooker, J.N. (eds.) CPAIOR 2009. LNCS, vol. 5547, pp. 71–86. Springer, Heidelberg (2009). https://doi.org/10.1007/978-3-642-01929-6_7

15. Hagberg, A.A., Schult, D.A., Swart, P.J.: Exploring network structure, dynamics, and function using networkx. In: Varoquaux, G., Vaught, T., Millman, J. (eds.) Proceedings of the 7th Python in Science Conference, pp. 11–15. Pasadena, CA USA (2008)

16. Hahn, S., Janhunen, T., Kaminski, R., Romero, J., Rühling, N., Schaub, T.: Plingo: a system for probabilistic reasoning in clingo based on LPMLN (2022). https://doi.org/10.48550/ARXIV.2206.11515

17. Lee, J., Wang, Y.: Weighted rules under the stable model semantics. In: Baral, C., Delgrande, J.P., Wolter, F. (eds.) Principles of Knowledge Representation and Reasoning: Proceedings of the Fifteenth International Conference, KR 2016, Cape Town, South Africa, 25–29 April 2016. pp. 145–154. AAAI Press (2016)
18. Lloyd, J.W.: Foundations of Logic Programming, 2nd edn. Springer, Heidelberg (1987). https://doi.org/10.1007/978-3-642-83189-8
19. Mauá, D.D., Cozman, F.G.: Complexity results for probabilistic answer set programming. Int. J. Approx. Reason. **118**, 133–154 (2020). https://doi.org/10.1016/j.ijar.2019.12.003
20. Riguzzi, F.: Foundations of Probabilistic Logic Programming: Languages, Semantics, Inference and Learning. River Publishers, Gistrup (2018)
21. Sato, T.: A statistical learning method for logic programs with distribution semantics. In: Sterling, L. (ed.) ICLP 1995, pp. 715–729. MIT Press (1995). https://doi.org/10.7551/mitpress/4298.003.0069
22. Shterionov, D., Renkens, J., Vlasselaer, J., Kimmig, A., Meert, W., Janssens, G.: The most probable explanation for probabilistic logic programs with annotated disjunctions. In: Davis, J., Ramon, J. (eds.) ILP 2014. LNCS (LNAI), vol. 9046, pp. 139–153. Springer, Cham (2015). https://doi.org/10.1007/978-3-319-23708-4_10
23. Totis, P., Kimmig, A., Raedt, L.D.: Smproblog: stable model semantics in problog and its applications in argumentation. arXiv abs/2110.01990 (2021). https://doi.org/10.48550/ARXIV.2110.01990
24. Tuckey, D., Russo, A., Broda, K.: PASOCS: a parallel approximate solver for probabilistic logic programs under the credal semantics. arXiv abs/2105.10908 (2021). https://doi.org/10.48550/ARXIV.2105.10908
25. Van Gelder, A., Ross, K.A., Schlipf, J.S.: The well-founded semantics for general logic programs. J. ACM **38**(3), 620–650 (1991)
26. Vennekens, J., Verbaeten, S., Bruynooghe, M.: Logic programs with annotated disjunctions. In: Demoen, B., Lifschitz, V. (eds.) ICLP 2004. LNCS, vol. 3132, pp. 431–445. Springer, Heidelberg (2004). https://doi.org/10.1007/978-3-540-27775-0_30

Verifying a Stochastic Model for the Spread of a SARS-CoV-2-Like Infection: Opportunities and Limitations

Marco Roveri[✉][iD], Franc Ivankovic, Luigi Palopoli[iD], and Daniele Fontanelli[iD]

Department of Information Engineering and Computer Science, University of Trento,
Via Sommarive 9, 38123 Povo, Trento, Italy
{marco.roveri,franc.ivankovic,luigi.palopoli,
daniele.fontanelli}@unitn.it

Abstract. There is a growing interest in modeling and analyzing the spread of diseases like the SARS-CoV-2 infection using stochastic models. These models are typically analyzed quantitatively and are not often subject to validation using formal verification approaches, nor leverage policy syntheses and analysis techniques developed in formal verification.

In this paper, we take a Markovian stochastic model for the spread of a SARS-CoV-2-like infection. A state of this model represents the number of subjects in different health conditions. The considered model considers the different parameters that may have an impact on the spread of the disease and exposes the various decision variables that can be used to control it. We show that the modeling of the problem within state-of-the-art model checkers is feasible and it opens several opportunities. However, there are severe limitations due to i) the espressivity of the existing stochastic model checkers on one side, and ii) the size of the resulting Markovian model even for small population sizes.

1 Introduction

The recent COVID-19 pandemic highlighted the importance to develop reliable models to study, predict and control the evolution and spread of diseases. Several analytical models have been proposed in the literature [1,3–5,10,11,15,16,25]. All these models are deterministic and aims at capturing the disease dynamics. These studies have been complemented with studies proposing stochastic models, that differently from deterministic ones, allows to derive richer set of informations like e.g. show converge to a disease-free state even if the corresponding deterministic models converge to an endemic equilibrium [2]; computing the probability of an outbreak, the distribution of the final size of a population or the expected duration of an epidemic [5,23]; computing the probability of transition between different state of COVID-19-affected patients based on the age class [26]; or evaluating the effects of lock-down policies [21]. Recently, the evolution of diseases has also been modeled with stochastic models in form of Markov Processes [1,6,19]. The use of stochastic models opens for the

---

This work is partially funded by the grant MOSES, Bando interno 2020 Università di Trento "Covid 19".

A. Dovier et al. (Eds.): AIxIA 2022, LNAI 13796, pp. 427–440, 2023.
https://doi.org/10.1007/978-3-031-27181-6_30

possibility to use Stochastic Model Checking techniques to i) validate the model using probabilistic temporal properties of the model as well as compute quantitative measures of the degree of satisfaction of a given temporal property [20]; ii) evaluate the effects of a strategy on a population during the evolution of a disease [7,8]. The work in [19] describes a stochastic compartmental model (the population has been broken down into several compartments) for the spread of COVID-19like diseases, with some preliminary results on the use of stochastic model checking techniques to analyze a simplified version of the epidemic model.

In this paper we make the following contributions. First, we consider the epidemic model presented in [19] and we show how to encode it into languages suitable for being analyzed with state-of-the-art stochastic model checkers. To this extent, we developed a C++ open source tool that given the parameters of the epidemic model is able to generate models in the PRISM formalism [17] to be then analyzed by tools supporting that formalism (e.g. the PRISM [17] and the STORM [14] model checkers). Second, we show that the encoding of the considered model in the language accepted by model checkers is out of the espressivity capabilities of the input languages, and even for small population sizes it results in very large files that easily reach unacceptable timings for the storage and parsing of such models, thus preventing any further analysis. To this extent, we modified the developed tool to link with the STORM model checker to pass the model directly in memory without the use of intermediate files. Third, we used the developed tool to study the model with increasing population sizes, analyzing the models against given temporal properties, and evaluating the effects of different control policies. These results show that the approach is feasible, but they confirm the scalability issues first noticed in [12,18], and pose challenges to the community to address large population sizes on one hand, and espressivity requirements on the input languages, on the other hand, to facilitate the specification of such complex mathematical models.

This paper is organized as follows. In Sect. 2 we briefly summarize the basic concepts. In Sect. 3 we discuss the model presented in [19] and we show how to compute the probabilistic transition function. In Sect. 4 we describe the tools and the experiments carried out. In Sect. 5 we discuss the related works, an finally in Sect. 6 we draw conclusions and discuss possible future works.

2   Background

A Markov Decision Process (MDP) is a tuple $\langle S, S_I, A, T, R \rangle$ where S is a finite set of states, $S_I \subseteq S$ is the set of initial states, A is a finite set of actions (i.e. control variables), $T : S \rightarrow 2^{A \times S \times \mathbb{R}}$ is the transition probability function that associates to a state $s \in S$ and an action $a \in A$, the probability p to end up in state s', $R : S \times A \rightarrow \mathbb{R}$ is the reward function, giving the expected immediate reward r gained for taking action $a \in A$ in state $s \in S$ (we remark that, in many cases there is no reward function). A Discrete Time Markov Chain (DTMC) is an MDP such that in each state $s \in S$ there is only one action to be considered with an associated probability to end-up in a state $s' \in S$ (i.e. there is a single probability distribution over successor states). Partially Observable MDPs, extend MDPs by a set of observations and label every state with one of these observations. Thus, the states labeled by the same observation must be considered undistinguishable.

Several formalisms have been proposed to specify (PO)MDPs and DTMCs. We refer to [14] for a thorough overview. In the following we briefly describe the PRISM language [17] supported by the PRISM and STORM stochastic model checkers. The PRISM language is a simple state-based language such that i) the user specifies variables with a finite domain (a complete assignment of a value to these variables at any given time constitutes a possible state of the system); ii) the behavior is specified through commands of the form [action] guard -> prob_1 : update_1 + ... + prob_n : update_n where: guard is a predicate over all the variables in the model, each update_i describes a transition which the model can make if the guard is true (a transition specifies the new values of the variables, and is associated to the probability/rate prob_i to take that update), and to an optional annotation action (modeling a control variable). On a (PO)MDP/DTMC model one can check several kind of properties, like e.g., temporal logic formulas based on PCTL [13] (e.g., property $\mathbf{P}_{<0.25}[\mathbf{F}\,O_k = C]$ means the probability of reaching a state where the variable O_k is equal to C is less than 0.25), or compute the probability with which a system reaches a certain state (e.g., $\mathbf{P}_{=?}[\mathbf{F}\,O_k = C]$ to compute the probability to reach a state where O_k is equal to C), or perform conditional probability and cost queries, or compute long-run average values (also known as steady-state or mean payoff values), or synthesize a policy to satisfy a certain PCTL property. We refer the reader to [13, 14, 17] for a thorough discussion of possible queries.

In the following, we denote with $n! = n \cdot (n-1) \cdot \ldots \cdot 1$ the factorial (i.e. the permutations of n elements), with $\binom{n}{k} = \frac{n!}{k! \cdot (n-k)!}$ the binomial coefficient, with $\mathbb{M}_{n,n_1,n_2,\ldots,n_{k-1}} = \binom{n}{n_1,n_2,\ldots,n_k} = \frac{n!}{\prod_{i=1}^{k} n_i!}$ the multinomial coefficient (i.e. the permutations with repetitions obtained computing all the permutations of n elements taken from k sets with $n_1, n_2, \ldots, n_k$ elements such that $n_k = n - \sum_{i=1}^{k-1} n_i$), and with $\mathcal{B}(N, p)_X = \binom{N}{X} p^X (1-p)^{N-X}$ the binomial probability distribution function where X is the total number of successes, p is the probability of success on an individual trial, and N is the number of trials.

3   A Stochastic Model for SARS-CoV-2-Like Infection's Spread

We model a subject of the population as a stochastic discrete–time system with 8 states, as illustrated in Fig. 1, each representing a possible state of the subject: the susceptible S, infected I, recovered R, asymptomatic A (i.e., a group of infected people that do not exhibit symptoms but are infective), hospitalised O, dead D, recovered Ra from an asymptomatic state, and the case of swab-tested people that are quarantined (denoted with Q) if they result positive. The evolution is observed at discrete time k and each subject can belong to one of eight possible states. The subjects who are in a state at step k will be denoted by a calligraphic letter (e.g., $\mathcal{S}_k$ is the set of susceptible subjects). Figure 2 reports the symbols used to denote the different sets, their cardinality (e.g., S_k is the cardinality of $\mathcal{S}_k$) and the different probabilities governing the transition of a subject between the different sets. The states of the discrete–time Markov chain can be characterized by a vector $\vec{V}_k = [S_k, A_k, I_k, R_k, O_k, D_k, Q_k, Ra_k]$ such that the values of all the different quantities are non-negative integers representing the cardinality of their respective sets.

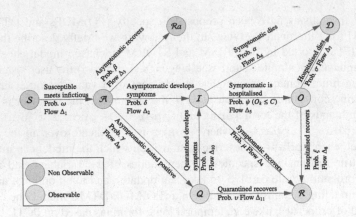

Fig. 1. Transitions between the different states of a single subject of the entire population.

Sets			
$S_k = |\mathcal{S}_k|$	N. of susceptible sub. $\mathcal{S}_k$ at step k,	$A_k = |\mathcal{A}_k|$	N. of asymptomatic sub. $\mathcal{A}_k$ at step k,
$I_k = |\mathcal{I}_k|$	N. of symptomatic sub. $\mathcal{I}_k$ at step k,	$R_k = |\mathcal{R}_k|$	N. of recovered sub. $\mathcal{R}_k$ at step k,
$Ra_k = |\mathcal{R}a_k|$	N. of asympt. recovered sub. $\mathcal{R}a_k$ at step k,	$O_k = |\mathcal{O}_k|$	N. of hospitalised sub. $\mathcal{O}_k$ at step k,
$D_k = |\mathcal{D}_k|$	N. of deceased sub. $\mathcal{D}_k$ at step k,	$Q_k = |\mathcal{Q}_k|$	N. of quarantined sub. $\mathcal{Q}_k$ at step k,
$Q_k^{(R)} = |\mathcal{Q}_k^{(R)}|$	N. of quarantined sub. recovered $\mathcal{Q}_k^{(R)}$ at step k.		

Deterministic Parameters			
N	Total number of subjects,	C	Available beds in hospital facilities.

Probabilistic Parameters			
ω	Prob. to contract the infection in one meeting,	β	Prob. for an infectious asympt. sub. to recover,
δ	Prob. for an asympt. sub. to devel symptoms,	μ	Prob. for a symptomatic sub. to recover,
α	Prob. for a symptomatic sub. to die,	σ	Prob. for an hospitalised sub. to die,
ξ	Prob. for an hospitalised sub. to recover,	γ	Prob. for a tested infectious sub. to be positive,
ψ	Prob. for a symptomatic sub. to be hospitalised,	ι	Prob. that a quarantined sub. devel symptoms,
υ	Prob. that a quarantined sub. recovers.		

Command Variables			
M_k	Num. of people met by any subject,	t_k	Num. of people tested.

Fig. 2. Summary of symbols.

This model is based on the following assumptions: i) the presence of a virus can be detected either if the subject starts to develop symptoms of the disease or when the subject is tested positive; ii) if a subject is tested positive (i.e. infectious) she/he becomes quarantiened until recovery; iii) a quarantined subject either recovers or develops the symptoms and becomes infectious; iv) a recovered subject cannot be re-infected; v) since it is not possible to distinguish a subject who is susceptible, asymptomatic or recovered without having developed symptoms, the states $\mathcal{S}$, $\mathcal{A}$, $\mathcal{R}a$ are not observable, while all the other states $\mathcal{Q}$, $\mathcal{I}$, $\mathcal{O}$, $\mathcal{D}$, $\mathcal{R}$ are observable; vi) the hospitals have a maximum capacity of $C \leq N$.

The elements of the vector $\vec{V}_k = [S_k, A_k, I_k, R_k, O_k, D_k, Q_k, Ra_k]$ are subject to the following constraints: $S_k + A_k + I_k + R_k + Ra_k + Q_k + O_k + D_k = N$, $O_k \leq C$. We denote with $\vec{\Delta v} = V_{k+1} - V_k = [\Delta_S, \Delta_A, \Delta_I, \Delta_R, \Delta_O, \Delta_D, \Delta_Q, \Delta_{Ra}]^T$ the change of the state vector from $\vec{V}_k$ to V_{k+1}, such that the input/output flow from each state of Fig. 1 is respected (i.e. $\Delta_S = -\Delta_1$, $\Delta_A = \Delta_1 - \Delta_2 - \Delta_3 - \Delta_9$, $\Delta_I = \Delta_{10} + \Delta_2 - \Delta_4 - \Delta_5 - \Delta_6$, $\Delta_R = \Delta_4 + \Delta_8 + \Delta_{11}$, $\Delta_O = \Delta_5 - \Delta_7 - \Delta_8$, $\Delta_D = \Delta_6 + \Delta_7$, $\Delta_Q = \Delta_9 - \Delta_{10} - \Delta_{11}$, $\Delta_{Ra} = \Delta_3$). Hereafter, we will refer to these equations with name *balance equations*. To ensure that different subjects in the different states of this model are non-negative we also enforce the following constraints: $\Delta_1 \leq S_k$, $\Delta_2 + \Delta_3 + \Delta_9 \leq A_k$, $\Delta_{10} + \Delta_{11} \leq Q_k$, $\Delta_4 + \Delta_5 + \Delta_6 \leq I_k$, and $\Delta_7 + \Delta_8 \leq O_k$.

We denote by $l(\cdot)$ an assignment of variables: $\Delta_i = \delta_i$, for $i = 1, \ldots, 11$. For an assignment of variable $l(\cdot)$ we use $l(\cdot) \models \varphi$ to mean that the assignment $l(\cdot)$ satisfies formula φ. For instance, $l\,(\Delta_4 = \delta_4,\ \Delta_8 = \delta_8,\ \Delta_{11} = \delta_{11}) \models \Delta_R = \Delta_4 + \Delta_8 + \Delta_{11}$ means that the assignment $\delta_4, \delta_8, \delta_{11}$ to the variables Δ_4, Δ_8 and Δ_{11} satisfies balance equation $\Delta_R = \Delta_4 + \Delta_8 + \Delta_{11}$. We also introduce the following notations:

- l_1 is an assignment linking the variable Δ_1 defined via B_1 as: $l_1 : (\delta_1 = -\Delta_S)$;
- l_2 is a function linking the variables Δ_2, Δ_3 and Δ_9 (with the variable Δ_9 obtained via equation B_2, and the variable Δ_3 obtained via equation B_8), defined as: $l_2 :$ $(\Delta_2 = \delta_2, \Delta_3 = \Delta_{R_a},\ \Delta_9 = -\Delta_S - \Delta_A - \Delta_{R_a} - \delta_2)$;
- l_3 is a function linking Δ_4, Δ_5, Δ_6 and given by: $l_3 : (\Delta_4 = \delta_4, \Delta_5 = \delta_5, \Delta_6 = \delta_6)$;
- l_4 is an assignment linking the remaining variables defined as: $l_4 : (\Delta_7 = \Delta_D - \delta_6,\ \Delta_8 = \delta_5 + \delta_6 - \Delta_D - \Delta_O,\ \Delta_{10} = \Delta_I - \delta_2 + \delta_4 + \delta_5 + \delta_6, \Delta_{11} = \Delta_R + \Delta_D + \Delta_O - \delta_4 - \delta_5 - \delta_6)$;
- l_5, finally, assigns $(\Delta_2 = \delta_2, \Delta_3 = \delta_3, \Delta_9 = \delta_9)$.

Finally, we also consider the following terms: $C_{\beta,\delta} = (1 - \beta - \delta) \geq 0$, $C_{\mu,\psi,\alpha} = (1 - \mu - \psi - \alpha) \geq 0$, $C_{\sigma,\xi} = (1 - \sigma - \xi) \geq 0$, $C_{\iota,\upsilon} = (1 - \iota - \upsilon) \geq 0$.

The probability associated with a transition from state vector $\vec{V}_k$ to state vector $\vec{V}_{k+1}$, such that exactly M_k encounters between susceptible subjects can happen and exactly t_k tests are performed, denoted with $\Pr\{\vec{V}_{k+1} | \vec{V}_k\}$ can be computed as follows:

$$\Pr\{\vec{V}_{k+1} | \vec{V}_k\} = \Pr\{l_1 | \vec{V}_k\} \cdot \sum_{\delta_2=0}^{-\Delta_S - \Delta_A - \Delta_{R_a}} \Pr\{l_2 | \vec{V}_k \wedge l_1\}$$

$$\cdot \sum_{\delta_4=0}^{\delta_2 - \Delta_I} \sum_{\delta_5=0}^{\delta_2 - \Delta_I - \delta_4} \sum_{\delta_6=0}^{\delta_2 - \Delta_I - \delta_4 - \delta_5} \Pr\{l_3 | \vec{V}_k \wedge l_1 \wedge l_2\} \qquad (1)$$

$$\cdot \Pr\{l_4 | \vec{V}_k \wedge l_1 \wedge l_2 \wedge l_3\}$$

where:

- $\Pr\{l_1 | \vec{V}_k\}$ is the probability that exactly δ_1 susceptible become asymptomatic, and is computed as $\Pr\{l_1 | \vec{V}_k\} = \mathcal{B}(S_k, \Pr\{g_k | \vec{V}_k\}_{M_k})_{-\Delta_S}$ where, and $\Pr\{g_k | \vec{V}_k\}_{M_k} = 1 - \left(1 - \frac{\omega A_k}{N - D_k - I_k - O_k - Q_k}\right)^{M_k}$.
- $\Pr\{l_2 | \vec{V}_k \wedge l_1\}$ is defined as $\sum_{H=\delta_9}^{t_k} \Pr\{s_H\} \sum_{F=0}^{\delta_9} \rho(\delta_2, \delta_3 + F, \vec{V}_k) \binom{A_k}{H}^{-1} K$

where t_k are the tests performed in the transition from $\vec{V}_k$ to $\vec{V}_{k+1}$, $K = \binom{\delta_3 + F}{F} \binom{A_k - (\delta_2 + \delta_3 + F)}{\delta_9 - F} \binom{\delta_2}{H - \delta_0}$, $\rho(\delta_2, \delta_3, \vec{V}_k) = \frac{A_k! \, \beta^{\delta_3} \, \delta^{\delta_2} \, C_{\beta,\delta}^{A_k - \delta_2 - \delta_3}}{\delta_2! \delta_3! (A_k - \delta_2 - \delta_3)!}$, and $\Pr\{s_H\} = \binom{N_k}{t_k}^{-1} \sum_{p=0}^{t_k} \binom{S_k + R_{a_k}}{t_k - p} \binom{A_k}{p} \mathcal{B}(p, \gamma)_H$.

– $\Pr\{l_3 \,|\, \vec{V}_k \wedge l_1 \wedge l_2\}$ is defined as

$$
\Pr\{l_3 \,|\, \vec{V}_k \wedge l_1 \wedge l_2\} = \begin{cases} 0 & \text{if } \delta_4 + \delta_5 + \delta_6 > I_k \vee \delta_5 > C - O_k \\ M(\delta_4, \delta_5, \delta_6) & \text{if } \delta_5 < C - O_k \wedge \delta_4 + \delta_5 + \delta_6 \leq I_k \\ M'(\delta_4, \delta_6) & \text{if } \delta_5 = C - O_k \wedge \delta_4 + \delta_5 + \delta_6 \leq I_k \end{cases}
$$

where $M(\delta_4, \delta_5, \delta_6) = \mathbb{M}_{I_k, \delta_4, \delta_5, \delta_6} \mu^{\delta_4} \psi^{\delta_5} \alpha^{\delta_6} C_{\mu, \psi, \alpha}^{I_k - \delta_4 - \delta_5 - \delta_6}$ and $M'(\delta_4, \delta_6) = \sum_{h=0}^{I_k - \delta_4 - \delta_6 - (C - O_k)} M(\delta_4, (C - O_k) + h, \delta_6)$;

– $\Pr\{l_4 \,|\, \vec{V}_k \wedge l_1 \wedge l_2 \wedge l_3\}$ is defined as $\zeta(\Delta_D - \delta_6, \delta_5 + \delta_6 - \Delta_D - \Delta_O, \vec{V}_k) \cdot \chi(\Delta_I - \delta_2 + \delta_4 + \delta_5 + \delta_6, \Delta_R + \Delta_D + \Delta_O - \delta_4 - \delta_5 - \delta_6, \vec{V}_k)$ where $\zeta(\delta_7, \delta_8, \vec{V}_k) = \mathbb{M}_{O_k, \delta_7, \delta_8} \sigma^{\delta_7} \xi^{\delta_8} C_{\sigma, \xi}$, and $\chi(\delta_{10}, \delta_{11}, \vec{V}_k) = \mathbb{M}_{Q_k, \delta_{10}, \delta_{11}} \iota^{\delta_{10}} \upsilon^{\delta_{11}} C_{\iota, \upsilon}^{Q_k - \delta_{10} - \delta_{11}}$.

All the mathematical details and proofs to show the correctness of the above formulation for computing the probability of a transition from $\vec{V}_k$ to $\vec{V}_{k+1}$ subject to having exactly M_k meetings and performing exactly t_k tests for the model depicted in Fig. 1 are out of the scope of this paper and can be found in [19].

Given the above definitions, we can compute the transitions and the associated probabilities from a state vector $\vec{V}_k$ given exactly M_k encounters, and exactly t_k tests by enumerating all possible configurations V_{k+1} that are compatible with the *balance equations* at page 4. Algorithm 1 in [22] shows how to perform this enumeration.

The transitions from a state vector $\vec{V}_k$ subjected to encounters from a set of minimum encounters M_{min} to a maximum of M_{max} encounters, and tests from a minimum of T_{min} to a maximum of T_{max} can be computed by enumerating all possible (m, t) such that $m \in [M_{min}, M_{max}]$ and $t \in [T_{min}, T_{max}]$ using previous algorithm (see Algorithm 2 in [22] for details). These algorithms are the building blocks for computing the MDP for the full stochastic model for the spread of a SARS-CoV-2-like infection for a population of size N such that each subject evolves as illustrated in Fig. 1. The set of states of the MDP are all those vector states $\vec{V}_k = [S_k, A_k, I_k, R_k, O_k, D_k, Q_k, Ra_k]$ such that they satisfy the constraint $S_k + A_k + I_k + R_k + O_k + D_k + Q_k + Ra_k = N$ for a population of N subjects[1]. The set of actions can be computed as $A = \{\langle M_k, t_k \rangle \,|\, M_k \in [M_{min}, M_{max}], t_k \in [t_{min}, t_{max}]\}$, for the possibility to meet subjects from M_{min} to M_{max}, and to perform tests from t_{min} to t_{max}. The transition probability function $T = \{\langle \vec{V}_k, \langle M_k, t_k \rangle, \vec{V}_{k+1}, \Pr\{\vec{V}_{k+1} \,|\, \vec{V}_k\}\rangle \,|\, \langle M_k, t_k \rangle \in A, \vec{V}_k \in S, \langle \vec{V}_k, \langle M_k, t_k \rangle, \vec{V}_{k+1}, \Pr\{\vec{V}_{k+1} \,|\, \vec{V}_k\}\rangle \in \textsc{Transitions}(\vec{V}_k, M_k, t_k)\}$. Finally, $S_I \subseteq S$ is the set of initial states. In this model, we do not consider any reward function.

This framework allows for the application of several policies to control the (PO)MDP. To this extent, we see a policy as a function $\mathcal{P}(\vec{V}_k) \to 2^A$ that associates with a state $\vec{V}_k$ a pair $\langle M_k, t_k \rangle$ such that $M_k \in [M_{min}, M_{max}]$ and $t_k \in [t_{min}, t_{max}]$. This can be achieved by restricting the transition probability function to follow policy $\mathcal{P}$ as follows: $T = \{\langle \vec{V}_k, \langle M_k, t_k \rangle, \vec{V}_{k+1}, \Pr\{\vec{V}_{k+1} \,|\, \vec{V}_k\}\rangle \,|\, \langle M_k, t_k \rangle \in \mathcal{P}(\vec{V}_k) \subseteq A, \vec{V}_k \in S, \langle \vec{V}_k, \langle M_k, t_k \rangle, \vec{V}_{k+1}, \Pr\{\vec{V}_{k+1} \,|\, \vec{V}_k\}\rangle \in \textsc{Transitions}(\vec{V}_k, M_k, t_k)\}$. Algorithms 1

---

[1] As shown in [19], this model is such that, for a population of N subjects, assuming there are n possible configurations (in our case $n = 8$), the maximum number of possible states that can be generated is $\binom{N+n-1}{N}$ that corresponds to the Bose-Einstein statistics.

and 2 in [22] can be easily adapted to restrict the actions to obey a given policy $\mathcal{P}(\vec{V}_k)$. In particulara, it is sufficient in Algorithm 2 to replace the two nested for loops with a single loop over elements of a set of pairs $\langle m, t \rangle \in \mathcal{P}(\vec{V}_k)$.

4   Experimenting with State-of-the-art Stochastic Model Checkers

Once the (PO)MDP model has been built, one can convert it into the input format of a stochastic model checker like e.g. PRISM [17] or STORM [14], and use this model to verify PCTL [13] properties, for synthesizing policies satisfying a given PCTL property, to evaluate formally the effects of a policy, and to compute steady state probabilities.

To this extent, we have developed a C++ proof of concept open-source tool, named covid_tool[2]. As an input, this tool receives (encoded in a json file) the population size N, all the probability parameters described in Fig. 2, the $M_{min}, M_{max}, t_{min}, t_{max}$ and the hospital capacity C. The tool also accepts in input a set of possible initial states where each initial state is fully specified by the respective $\vec{V}$. Moreover, to evaluate the possible effects of manually specified control policies, we integrated in the tools four policies $\mathcal{P}_{-1}, \mathcal{P}_0, \mathcal{P}_1$, and $\mathcal{P}_2$. $\mathcal{P}_{-1}$ corresponds to not applying any policy, and this results in generating all possible pairs in A (see e.g., Algorithm 2 from [22]). $\mathcal{P}_0$ is a constant policy that regardless of the state $\vec{V}_k$ returns a singleton element $\langle M, t \rangle$ (i.e., $\forall \vec{V}_k \in S. \mathcal{P}_0(\vec{V}_k) = \{\langle M, t \rangle\}$). Policies $\mathcal{P}_1$ and $\mathcal{P}_2$ have the following form $\mathcal{P}(\vec{V}_k) = \{\langle M_k, t \rangle | M_k = \mathcal{F}(\vec{V}_k), t \in [t_{min}, t_{max}]\}$ where

$$\mathcal{F}(\vec{V}_k) = \begin{cases} M_{max} & \text{if } f(\vec{V}_k) \leq T_\downarrow \\ M_{min} & \text{if } f(\vec{V}_k) \geq T_\uparrow \\ M_{max} + (M_{min} - M_{max}) \frac{f(\vec{V}_k) - T_\downarrow}{T_\uparrow - T_\downarrow} & \text{otherwise.} \end{cases} \quad (2)$$

$\mathcal{P}_1$ uses $f(\vec{V}_k) = I_k + O_k/(N - D_k)$ while $\mathcal{P}_2$ uses $f(\vec{V}_k) = A_k/(N - D_k)$. In $\mathcal{P}_1$ when the percentage of the number of symptomatic and hospitalized patients over the living population is below the threshold $T_\downarrow$, we impose no restrictions for social life. If this number is above a threshold $T_\uparrow$, we adopt the maximum restriction (the minimum value M_{min} for M). Otherwise we adopt a linear interpolation between the minimum and the maximum values of M. $\mathcal{P}_2$ is similar to $\mathcal{P}_1$, but here we consider the ratio between asymptomatic infected subjects and the living population. The tool and all the material to reproduce the experiments reported hereafter are available at https://bitbucket.org/luigipalopoli/covd_tool.

This tool uses Algorithms 1 and 2 from [22] to build the MDP for the model of Fig. 1, and the respective adaptation of such algorithms to generate the DTMCs resulting from the application of a given pre-defined policy $\mathcal{P}$. Among the different possibilities this tool provides, we highlight here the ability to generate a (PO)MDP symbolic model as accepted by PRISM and STORM. The symbolic model encodes the state vector $\vec{V}$ with 8 integer variables (S, A, I, R, O, D, Q, Ra) with values ranging from 0 to N. We encode actions with a label action_m_t for meeting exactly m subjects and performing exactly t tests. Then using Algorithm 1 from [22] to compute the possible

---

[2] https://bitbucket.org/luigipalopoli/covd_tool.

```
mdp // The kind of model
module covid_mdp // The main module
  // The variables
  nS : [0..10]; nA : [0..10]; nI : [0..10]; nR : [0..10]; nO : [0..10]; nD : [0..10];
  ... // omitted for lack of space
  [act_M_is_5]  ((nS = 0) & (nA = 0) & (nI = 0) & (nR = 0) & (nO = 1) & (nD = 9)) ->
           0.5 : (nS' = 0) & (nA' = 0) & (nI' = 0) & (nR' = 1) & (nO' = 0) & (nD' = 9)
         + 0.2 : (nS' = 0) & (nA' = 0) & (nI' = 0) & (nR' = 0) & (nO' = 1) & (nD' = 9)
         + 0.3 : (nS' = 0) & (nA' = 0) & (nI' = 0) & (nR' = 0) & (nO' = 0) & (nD' = 10);
  ... // omitted for lack of space
endmodule
init // The set of initial states
   (  (nS = 7) & (nA = 3) & (nI = 0) & (nR = 0) & (nO = 0) & (nD = 0)
    | (nS = 9) & (nA = 1) & (nI = 0) & (nR = 0) & (nO = 0) & (nD = 0) )
endinit
```

Listing 1.1. Excerpt of a PRISM file generated for a SAIROD model with a population of 10 individuals. The entire file is about 103Mb on disk.

next states and respective probabilities. The tool is also able to generate a symbolic Partially Observable Markov Decision Problems in PRISM format by specifying that the S, A, Ra are not observable. Moreover, the tool can handle two cases, the full model with all the eight states as per Fig. 1, and a simplified model that does not considers quarantined and the possibility to recover from asymptomatic state (that corresponds to a SAIROD model). We introduced this possibility for two main reasons. First, the SAIROD model has been already studied, and it is easier to retrieve the parameters governing the behavior [11]. Second, as we will see later on, the full model is subject to scalability issues much quickly than the simple SAIROD one. Listing 1.1 is an excerpt of a simple PRISM model corresponding to a population composed of 10 subjects.

The generation of models in PRISM language is subject to severe efficiency and espressivity problems. First, the PRISM language can represent symbolically the transitions once the $\Pr\{\vec{V}_{k+1}|\vec{V}_k\}$ are pre-computed for each transition, but there is no efficient way to encode $\Pr\{\vec{V}_{k+1}|\vec{V}_k\}$ in the language due to the limited espressivity of the PRISM language (the involved math is not supported by the language). A possibility that we considered was to build a defined symbols to represent the $\Pr\{\vec{V}_{k+1}|\vec{V}_k\}$ for all possible values of the $\vec{V}_k$, M_k, and t_k, however the resulting file will be huge (larger than a gigabyte) even for a very small population (<10 subjects). Thus, we ended up pre-computing such probabilities, and associating the resulting value with each transition. The size of the file is problematic for two reasons: i) a storage problem; ii) assuming

Table 1. Experiments using the extended model, no policy ($\mathcal{P}_{-1}$).

N	C	P_{min}	P_{max}	Creation of T (s)	STORM model creation (s)	STORM model checking (s)
5	1	0.250	0.312	0.088	0.297	0.005
10	1	0.260	0.346	25.161	58.705	56.955
15	1	0.264	0.382	1118.465	3205.290	33.257
20	1		Memout			
10	2	0.005	0.019	36.080	103.292	2.191
15	3			Memout		

the huge file has been generated successfully, the PRISM and STORM model checkers require a large amount of memory and huge timing (days) to parse the file before even starting verification on modern high-performance computers equipped with large memory (Terabytes). Here we remark that STORM is slightly more efficient than PRISM in handling large input files. This might be due to a number of reasons, notably the fact that STORM uses an efficient C++ parser, while PRISM uses Java. To overcome these limitations, we considered two directions: i) the possibility to generate the explicit transition matrix files in the different formats accepted by the STORM and PRISM model checkers (the generated files with this flow are smaller than the symbolic approach, but still large and requiring large computation and memory to handle them); ii) the possibility to have a more strict integration with the model checker by linking the model checker in memory (thus avoiding intermediate file generation). In particular, we did a tight integration with the STORM model checker by directly building in memory the data structures to enable model checking. We have chosen STORM since it is written in C++ while PRISM is written in Java. Moreover, STORM provides a clear C/C++ API to facilitate the integration in other tools. Currently, we are only building the sparse matrix representation [14], and thus we are limited to the verification capabilities by STORM with this model representation. (See https://www.stormchecker.org/ for further details.)

All the experiments have been executed on a cluster equipped with 112 Intel(R) Xeon(R) CPU cores 2.20GHz and 256Gb of RAM. We considered a memory limit of 256GB and a CPU time limit of 5400 s seconds.

We conducted experiments with varying population sizes N, hospital capacities C and policies used. The values of M_{min} and M_{max} used were 1 and 5, respectively. The values of t_{min} and t_{max} used were 1 and 3, respectively. These values are reasonable for the population sizes we managed to consider (see the results later in this section). All the values of the parameters (e.g., transition probabilities) were based on discussions with experts. The precise values used in all these experiments can be found in the aforementioned bitbucket Git repository of the tool. We performed the experiments on two versions of the model: i) the "*full*" model described in previous section (the results are reported in Tables 4 and 5 in [22]), and ii) the "*reduced*" model, which does not consider the possibility of entering in quarantine ($\mathcal{Q}$) and the possibility for an asymptomatic to recover ($\mathcal{R}a$) (the results are reported in Tables 4 and 5 in [22]). Moreover, we also considered the effects of the different considered policies. Tables 1 and 4 report the results for $\mathcal{P}_{-1}$, while Tables 2 and 5 show cases for policies $\mathcal{P}_0$, $\mathcal{P}_1$ and $\mathcal{P}_2$. In the experiments with policies $\mathcal{P}_0$, $\mathcal{P}_1$, $\mathcal{P}_2$ we considered the verification of the PCTL formula $\mathbf{P}_{=?}[\mathbf{F} O = C]$ (i.e. the probability of eventually reaching a state in which the hospital is saturated), while in the experiments with $\mathcal{P}_0$, we find minimum and maximum probabilities ($\mathbf{P}_{min=?}[\mathbf{F} O = C]$ and $\mathbf{P}_{max=?}[\mathbf{F} O = C]$, respectively). These properties were chosen given the interest of experts and decision makers of knowing the probabilities to saturate hospitals in different conditions. Constant policies ConstHigh and ConstLow use the M values of 1 and 5, respectively. With Adapt1 we denote the adaptive policy with $T_{\downarrow} = 0.1$ and $T_{\uparrow} = 0.5$. Adapt2 denotes the adaptive policy with $T_{\downarrow} = 0.05$ and $T_{\uparrow} = 0.15$.

For each experiment we report: i) the time in seconds required to build the complete transition matrix with the approach described in the previous section; ii) the time in seconds to fill and build the model in memory within the STORM model checker;

iii) the time in seconds required by STORM to model check the given property on the previously built model; iv) the computed probabilities for the considered properties.

The results in the tables clearly show that the time is mostly divided between computing the transition probability matrix and creating the STORM model (with checking the property taking relatively little time). This is due to the large number of states and

Table 2. Experiments using the extended model, policies $\mathcal{P}_0$, $\mathcal{P}_1$ and $\mathcal{P}_2$.

	Policy	N	C	P	Creation of T (s)	STORM model creation (s)	STORM model checking (s)
ConstLow	$\mathcal{P}_0$	5	1	0.280	0.088	0.178	0.001
	$\mathcal{P}_0$	10	1	0.300	25.111	33.044	0.170
	$\mathcal{P}_0$	15	1	0.308	1131.249	988.710	5.031
	$\mathcal{P}_0$	10	2	0.011	36.010	49.453	0.301
	$\mathcal{P}_0$	15	3	0.0006	2371.702	2179.716	16.505
	$\mathcal{P}_0$	20	4		Memout		
ConstHigh	$\mathcal{P}_0$	5	1	0.280	0.088	0.175	0.001
	$\mathcal{P}_0$	10	1	0.300	25.032	33.642	0.182
	$\mathcal{P}_0$	15	1,	0.308	1130.826	956.313	5.050
	$\mathcal{P}_0$	20	1		Timeout		
	$\mathcal{P}_0$	10	2	0.011	35.977	48.314	0.304
	$\mathcal{P}_0$	15	3	0.308	1130.826	956.313	5.051
	$\mathcal{P}_0$	20	4		Timeout		
Adapt1	$\mathcal{P}_1$	5	1	0.280	0.088	0.179	0.001
	$\mathcal{P}_1$	10	1	0.300	25.279	34.985	0.181
	$\mathcal{P}_1$	15	1	0.308	1132.725	957.143	5.005
	$\mathcal{P}_1$	20	1		Memout		
	$\mathcal{P}_1$	10	2	0.011	35.885	49.046	0.301
	$\mathcal{P}_1$	15	3		Timeout		
Adapt1	$\mathcal{P}_2$	5	1	0.280	0.088	0.187	0.001
	$\mathcal{P}_2$	10	1	0.300	25.062	32.684	0.184
	$\mathcal{P}_2$	15	1	0.308	1124.658	968.644	5.735
	$\mathcal{P}_2$	20	1		Memout		
	$\mathcal{P}_2$	10	2	0.011	35.931	48.781	0.306
	$\mathcal{P}_2$	15	3	0.0006	2528.367	2473.946	15.958
	$\mathcal{P}_2$	20	4		Timeout		
Adapt2	$\mathcal{P}_1$	5	1	0.280	0.087	0.179	0.001
	$\mathcal{P}_1$	10	1	0.300	25.048	32.583	0.169
	$\mathcal{P}_1$	15	1	0.308	1134.407	974.875	5.013
	$\mathcal{P}_1$	20	1		Memout		
	$\mathcal{P}_1$	10	2	0.011	35.885	48.797	0.316
	$\mathcal{P}_1$	15	3		Timeout		
Adapt2	$\mathcal{P}_2$	5	1	0.280	0.088	0.183	0.001
	$\mathcal{P}_2$	10	1	0.300	25.080	32.528	0.181
	$\mathcal{P}_2$	15	1	0.308	1124.280	949.528	5.051
	$\mathcal{P}_2$	20	1		Memout		
	$\mathcal{P}_2$	10	2	0.280	0.088	0.347	0.001
	$\mathcal{P}_2$	15	3		Timeout		

transitions even for the small population sizes considered. With the hardware at our disposal, we mostly manage to deal with population sizes up to 25. All the experiments ran out of memory with larger values of N while computing the transition probability matrix. We spent a significant engineering effort to limit this explosion trying to find efficient methods to represent states and transitions, as well as memorizing the result of the computation of the transition probabilities. However, despite this engineering effort, the large state space required reached easily the limits of the hardware at our disposal. We remark that, it is in principle possible to address scalability to large population size by considering a unit of population in the model as the representative of a (larger) number of people with a numerically quantifiable error (a similar approach has been discussed in [18], and is left as future work). The results also show that, as expected, the probability of hospitals being saturated increases with increasing population sizes and decreases with greater hospital capacities.

We remark that, despite the limited scalability issues we encountered, this work constitutes a basis to challenge stochastic model checkers along different directions (e.g., expressivity to allow for a concise representation of cases like this one, and efficiency to allow handle more realistic size scenarios). Moreover, it opens the possibility to leverage the feature provided by stochastic model checkers to compute policies to achieve given properties of interest for a decision maker (although we have not yet experimented with this feature, and we will leave as future work).

5 Related Works

There have been several works that addressed the problem of mathematically modeling the spread of diseases [1,3–5,10,11,15,16,25][3]. These works consider models where the population has been break down into several compartments like e.g. the Susceptible-Infected-Recovered (SIR) model which is a simplified version w.r.t. the one adopted in this paper. Some of the recent works (like e.g. [1,5]) focused on analyzing strategies to keep in check the evolution of the epidemic leveraging the control variables with the goal to construct interesting control theoretical results. For instance, in [11] has been presented a model with many compartments. In [16] has been analyzed the problem of stability, while policies for COVID-19 based on Optimal Control are discussed in [25]. All of these models are deterministic and aim at capturing the disease dynamics. Stochastic models, differently from deterministic ones, allows to derive richer set of informations. For instance, stochastic models i) may converge to a disease-free state even if the corresponding deterministic models converge to an endemic equilibrium [2]; ii) may allow for computing the probability of an outbreak, the distribution of the final size of a population or the expected duration of an epidemic (see e.g. [5,23]); iii) may allow to quantify the probability of transition between different state of COVID-19-affected patients based on the age class (see e.g. [26]); iv) allow to evaluate the effects of lock-down policies (see e.g. [21]). An important class of models amenable to analytical analysis are Markov Processes [1,6]. When we observe the system in discrete–time,

---

[3] We refer the reader to [19] for a more detailed discussion of the literature on modeling and analyzing the spread of diseases with analytical models.

Markov Models are called discrete-time Markov chains (DTMC). When command variables become part of the model, Markov Models are called Markov Decision Processes (MDP), and where not all states are directly observable (e.g., asymptomatic persons), we have a Partially Observable MDPs (POMDP). These models, contrary to other stochastic models such as Stochastic Differential Equations (SDE), adopt a numerable state space composed of discrete variables.

In the literature two paradigms have been adopted to model a disease spread as a DTMC, namely the Reed-Frost model and the Greenwood model [9,24]. In all these models the transition probabilities are governed by binomial random variables. Extensions of this model were presented by. The use of stochastic models opens for the possibility to use Stochastic Model Checking in order to study probabilistic temporal properties to evaluate the effects of a strategy on a population during the evolution of a disease [7,8,20]. An adapted version of the Susceptible-Exposed-Infectious-Recovered-Delayed-Quarantined (Susceptible/Recovered) continuous time Markov chain model has been used in [20] to analyze the spread of internet worms using the PRISM model checker [17]. A stochastic model to compute with the PRISM model checker the minimum number of influenza hemagglutinin trimmers required for fusion to be between one and eight has been proposed in [8]. The use of stochastic simulations to compute timing parameters for a timed automaton has been studied in [7]. All these stochastic models are rather simplified and abstract models of the disease spread, and the main reason for such is tractability. Indeed, considering large models with complex dynamics (as shown in this paper) reach quickly to computation limits even on recent computation infrastructures. Moreover, all these models, to make the model tractable by model checkers, enforce that only one subject can change her/his state across one transition or do not consider command variables. In this work, leveraging on the stochastic model defined in [19] we allow for multiple subjects to change state simultaneously across one transition, and we allow for command variables. In this work we show the limits of this more realistic model and show challenges for making next generation stochastic model checkers suitable for analyzing complex disease stochastic models.

The problem of scalability of epidemic models has been discussed in [12,18]. The work in [18] addressed the scalability to large population size by considering a unit of population in the model as the representative of a number of people. [12] addresses the problem by considering a graph of MDPs, each governed by the same update rules, that interact with their neighbors following the given graph topology. It would be interesting to see how verification techniques could leverage these abstractions to address the scalability issues. However, this is left to future work.

6   Conclusions and Future Works

In this paper we considered the study of an epidemic model for the evolution of diseases modeled with stochastic models in form of Markov Processes, and we showed how to encode such complex model into formalisms suitable for being analyzed with state-of-the-art stochastic model checkers. We developed an open source tool that given the parameters of the epidemic model is able to generate models in the PRISM formalism (a widely used formalism); as well as to build directly in memory the STORM sparse model by linking our tool with the STORM model checker. We used the developed tool to study the model with increasing population sizes, analyzing the models against given temporal properties, and evaluating the effects of different control policies w.r.t. some interesting temporal properties. The results showed that the approach is feasible, but it is subject to scalability issues even with small population sizes. Moreover, this work highlighted several challenges for the community to address large population sizes on one hand, and espressivity requirements on the input languages on the other hand to simplify the specification of such complex mathematical models.

As future work, we want to investigate the use of abstraction techniques to improve the performance and to handle large population sizes. Moreover, we aim also to leverage the framework to synthesize policies with a clear guarantee on the respective effects. In terms of modeling, the model could be further extended to consider the vaccinated population as well as vaccinations.

References

1. Allen, L., et al.: Mathematical Epidemiology. Lecture Notes in Mathematics, Springer, Berlin (2008)
2. Anderson, R., May, R.: Infectious Diseases of Humans: Dynamics and Control. OUP, Oxford (1992)
3. Bernoulli, D.: Essai d'une nouvelle analyse de la mortalite causee par la petite verole, et des avantage de l'inoculation pour la prevenir. Mem. phys. Acade. Roy. Sci. 1(6), 1-45 (1760)
4. Blanchini, F., Franco, E., Giordano, G., Mardanlou, V., Montessoro, P.L.: Compartmental flow control: decentralization, robustness and optimality. Automatica 64, 18–28 (2016)
5. Brauer, F., Castillo-Chavez, C., Feng, Z.: Mathematical Models in Epidemiology. Texts in Applied Mathematics, Springer, New York (2019)
6. Cassandras, C.G., Lafortune, S.: Introduction to Discrete Event Systems. Springer Science & Business Media, Berlin (2009)
7. Chauhan, K.: Epidemic analysis using traditional model checking and stochastic simulation. Master's thesis, Indian Institute of Technology Hyderabad (2015)
8. Dobay, M.P., Dobay, A., Bantang, J., Mendoza, E.: How many trimers? modeling influenza virus fusion yields a minimum aggregate size of six trimers, three of which are fusogenic. Mol. BioSyst. 7, 2741–2749 (2011)
9. Gani, J., Jerwood, D.: Markov chain methods in chain binomial epidemic models. Biometrics 27, 591–603 (1971)
10. Ghezzi, L.L., Piccardi, C.: PID control of a chaotic system: an application to an epidemiological model. Automatica 33(2), 181–191 (1997)
11. Giordano, G., et al.: Modelling the COVID-19 epidemic and implementation of population-wide interventions in Italy. Nature Med. 26(6), 1–6 (2020)
12. Haksar, R.N., Schwager, M.: Controlling large, graph-based MDPS with global control capacity constraints: an approximate LP solution. In: 2018 IEEE Conference on Decision and Control (CDC), pp. 35–42 (2018). https://doi.org/10.1109/CDC.2018.8618745
13. Hansson, H., Jonsson, B.: A logic for reasoning about time and reliability. Formal Aspects Comput. 6(5), 512–535 (1994)
14. Hensel, C., Junges, S., Katoen, J.-P., Quatmann, T., Volk, M.: The probabilistic model checker STORM. Int. J. Softw. Tools Technol. Trans. 24, 1–22 (2021). https://doi.org/10.1007/s10009-021-00633-z

15. Kermack, W.O., McKendrick, A.G., Walker, G.T.: A contribution to the mathematical theory of epidemics. In: Proceedings of the Royal Society of London. Series A, Containing Papers of a Mathematical and Physical Character, vol. 115, no. 772, pp. 700–721 (1927)

16. Khanafer, A., Başar, T., Gharesifard, B.: Stability of epidemic models over directed graphs: a positive systems approach. Automatica **74**, 126–134 (2016)

17. Kwiatkowska, M., Norman, G., Parker, D.: PRISM 4.0: verification of probabilistic real-time systems. In: Gopalakrishnan, G., Qadeer, S. (eds.) CAV 2011. LNCS, vol. 6806, pp. 585–591. Springer, Heidelberg (2011). https://doi.org/10.1007/978-3-642-22110-1_47

18. Nasir, A., Baig, H.R., Rafiq, M.: Epidemics control model with consideration of seven-segment population model. SN Appl. Sci. **2**(10), 1–9 (2020). https://doi.org/10.1007/s42452-020-03499-z

19. Palopoli, L., Fontanelli, D., Frego, M., Roveri, M.: A Markovian model for the spread of the SARS-CoV-2 virus. CoRR abs/2204.11317 (2022)

20. Razzaq, M., Ahmad, J.: Petri net and probabilistic model checking based approach for the modelling, simulation and verification of internet worm propagation. PLOS ONE **10**(12), 1–22 (2016)

21. Riccardo, F., Ajelli, M., Andrianou, X.D., et al.: Epidemiological characteristics of COVID-19 cases and estimates of the reproductive numbers 1 month into the epidemic, Italy, 28 January to 31 March 2020. Eurosurveillance **25**(49) (2020)

22. Roveri, M., Ivankovic, F., Palopoli, L., Fontanelli, D.: Verifying a stochastic model for the spread of a sars-cov-2-like infection: opportunities and limitations (2022). https://doi.org/10.48550/ARXIV.2211.00605, https://arxiv.org/abs/2211.00605

23. Sattenspiel, L.: Modeling the spread of infectious disease in human populations. Am. J. Phys. Anthropol. **33**(S11), 245–276 (1990)

24. Tuckwell, H.C., Williams, R.J.: Some properties of a simple stochastic epidemic model of sir type. Math. Biosci. **208**(1), 76–97 (2007)

25. Yousefpour, A., Jahanshahi, H., Bekiros, S.: Optimal policies for control of the novel coronavirus disease (COVID-19) outbreak. Chaos Solitons Fractals **136**, 109883 (2020)

26. Zardini, A., et al.: A quantitative assessment of epidemiological parameters required to investigate COVID-19 burden. Epidemics **37**, 100530 (2021)

Natural Language Processing

DelBERTo: A Deep Lightweight Transformer for Sentiment Analysis

Luca Molinaro[1]([✉]) [iD], Rosalia Tatano[1] [iD], Enrico Busto[1], Attilio Fiandrotti[2] [iD], Valerio Basile[2] [iD], and Viviana Patti[2] [iD]

[1] Addfor Industriale S.r.l., Turin, Italy
{l.molinaro,r.tatano,e.busto}@vargroup.it
[2] University of Turin, Turin, Italy
{attilio.fiandrotti,valerio.basile,viviana.patti}@unito.it

Abstract. This article introduces DelBERTo, a resource-efficient Transformer architecture for Natural Language Processing (NLP). Transformers replace convolutions and recurrence with the self-attention mechanism and represent the state-of-the-art in NLP. However, self-attention's complexity grows quadratically with the size of the input, which limits their applications. DelBERTo relies on adaptive input and on a deep yet lightweight Transformer architecture to reduce the number of learnable parameters, and relies on adaptive softmax to improve pre-training speed and memory footprint. We evaluate the proposed architecture in a sentiment analysis task and compare it against AlBERTo, a BERT model representing the state-of-the-art in sentiment analysis over Italian tweets. DelBERTo has only one-seventh of AlBERTo's learnable parameters, is faster, and requires less memory. Despite this, our experiments show that DelBERTo is competitive with AlBERTo over the three SENTIPOLC sub-tasks proposed at EVALITA 2016: subjectivity classification, polarity classification, and irony detection.

Keywords: Efficient transformer · Sustainable NLP · Sentiment analysis

1 Introduction

Natural Language Processing refers to the automated analysis of written text towards tasks such as machine translation, question answering, and sentiment analysis. In particular, sentiment analysis is the task of identifying the sentiment associated with a sentence [18]. As an example, this task is crucial to determining if reviews of a service express a positive or negative sentiment (polarity classification) or if messages on social media contain subjective or objective information (subjectivity classification). This task is especially challenging because it can be ambiguous due to the presence of irony and idioms.

This work was supported by Addfor Industriale S.r.l., (https://www.addforindustriale.com).

Techniques based on deep learning [13] represent the state-of-the-art in many NLP tasks. Among these, Recurrent Neural Networks (RNNs) [20] enjoyed widespread popularity due to their ability to process sequences of variable length via the recurrence mechanism. RNNs' main downside is that they suffer from the vanishing gradient problem, and they are not suitable to model long-term dependencies. Newer RNN architectures, such as Long Short Term Memory (LSTM) [10], overcome these limitations, but they still have one major downside: they are not able to take advantage of the parallelism of the hardware since they are sequential in nature. Other architectures, such as CNNs [24], are more parallelizable but cannot model long-term dependencies like LSTMs do.

Transformers [22] were introduced for machine translation tasks, and they simultaneously solve all of the previously mentioned problems. Transformers are based on the self-attention mechanism, which allows discovering relationships between different parts of a sentence. Based on such relationships, the network then assigns higher importance to some parts of the input and lower importance to other parts. The complexity of the self-attention mechanism, which grows quadratically with the size of the input, represents the main limiting factor in their practical adoption. In recent years, efforts have been made to improve the efficiency of the Transformer architecture [21]. Some of these efficiency-improving techniques directly target the computational complexity of the self-attention mechanism [5], while other ones target the model as a whole by making architectural changes aimed at reducing memory requirements and improving speed [6]. Despite efforts, this complexity problem is still not completely solved.

This paper presents DelBERTo, a transformer-based lightweight architecture for NLP. DelBERTo builds upon the *Deep and Light-weight Transformer* (DeLighT) [15], which reduces the parameters and redistributes them among the different parts of the network. In this work, we leverage *adaptive input* [1] and *adaptive softmax* [8] to further slash the complexity to a point where it becomes affordable for practical applications. We also modified the DeLighT architecture to be encoder-only, which is more suitable for classification and sequence labeling tasks. We evaluate DelBERTo over the SENTIPOLC 2016 challenge [2], which contains 7410 annotated tweets in Italian over the tasks of subjectivity classification, polarity classification, and irony detection. AlBERTo [19], a BERT [7] model for the Italian language, represents the best performer in this challenge. Our experiments show that DelBERTo achieves an F-score of 73% in subjectivity classification (AlBERTo 79%), 69% in polarity classification (AlBERTo 72%), and 62% in irony detection (AlBERTo 61%), despite having only one-seventh of AlBERTo's learnable parameters, being faster, and requiring much less memory.

2   Background and Related Work

The Transformer was originally proposed as an encoder-decoder architecture for NLP tasks. The key characteristic of the Transformer is the attention mechanism, which aims at uncovering the relationship between words in two input sentences. Input sentences are first preprocessed and then passed to an embedding layer.

Namely, a tokenizer breaks each sentence into tokens, which then are replaced with integer identifiers, from 0 to a given vocabulary size. Padding or truncation may be applied to reach a fixed sequence length. The embedding layer then maps every token ID to a continuous representation $x \in \mathbb{R}^{d_e}$, where d_e is the size of the embedding vectors. Finally, to encode the information about the position of the words in the sentence, a *positional encoding* is used. Positional encodings are stored in a matrix that is summed to the output of the embedding layer and can be fixed or learned during training.

The attention layer calculates the scaled dot product attention between input sentences. The inputs to this layer are three matrices: query $\mathbf{Q}$, key $\mathbf{K}$, and value $\mathbf{V}$. The attention mechanism gives the values weighted by the softmax of the dot-product of all the queries and all the keys. If the three input matrices are the same, it is called a *self-attention mechanism*; otherwise, we talk about *cross-attention*. To improve the model performance, the Transformer architecture runs different attention layers in parallel, a mechanism called *multi-head attention*.

After the introduction of the Transformer, several new variants were proposed. One of the most famous is BERT, the current state-of-the-art language understanding model. It is an encoder-only architecture that can be used in more than one NLP task by fine-tuning it to obtain a decoding layer with weights optimized for the specific task. During the learning phase in BERT, the text is scanned in both directions (left to right and right to left). In addition, BERT uses a *Masked Language Model* (MLM): during the training, random terms are masked in order to be predicted by the network. Finally, BERT employs a weight sharing technique to improve the efficiency of the Transformer, in particular, by reusing the embedding matrix in the output layer.

AlBERTo represents the first BERT model trained on tweets in Italian. In particular, it was pre-trained on TWITA [3], a dataset containing tweets in Italian that is constantly updated. The particular version used contains about 200 million tweets without annotations, which makes it ideal for pre-training models in a self-supervised way by using the MLM technique. AlBERTo was fine-tuned on the 3 tasks of SENTIPOLC 2016, reaching state-of-the-art results on this challenge. In Sect. 4.3, we compare our results to those of AlBERTo.

Even though transformers like BERT score top-notch performance in several NLP tasks, the computational complexity of the attention layer is a major drawback to their practical adoption. In fact, attention's complexity grows quadratically in the length of the input sequence. This makes it expensive to process long sequences.

In the last few years, new transformer architectures have been proposed to improve the efficiency of the attention mechanism. Some architectures, like Big-Bird [23], propose a sparsification of the attention matrix by means of a mask with a fixed pattern with the aim of effectively limiting the field of view of the attention. Other architectures use sparsification by means of patterns that are not predetermined but learned in a data-driven way, as in the case of the Reformer [11]. Efficiency is also achieved by rewriting the attention formula using kernels that avoid the explicit computation of the attention matrix, as done in

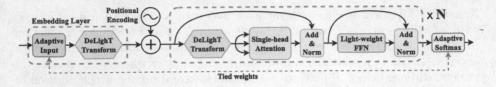

Fig. 1. Architecture of DelBERTo

the case of the Performer [5]. Finally, other techniques to improve efficiency do not modify the self-attention mechanism directly but act on the architecture itself, employing weight sharing, pruning, or pooling.

3   Proposed Method

This section introduces our transformer-based architecture for NLP, named Del-BERTo, short for *Deep and Light-weight Bidirectional Encoder Representations from Transformers*. First, the architecture is described in detail. Then, the relative data preparation procedure and the training process are discussed.

The architecture of DelBERTo is inspired by the DeLighT architecture, and it was designed by us to be encoder-only. Figure 1 depicts the architecture of DelBERTo. As shown, the embedding layer is composed of adaptive input followed by a DeLighT transformation (both explained later in this section). After the embedding layer, positional encodings are added, followed by a series of N DeLighT encoder blocks. These blocks are similar to the original Transformer's encoder blocks. The main differences are the fact that they start with a DeLighT transformation, the use of a single-head attention, and lastly, the fact that the fully connected network (FFN) first reduces the dimension of the hidden vectors and then expands it, thus saving parameters compared to doing the opposite. After the last encoder block, an adaptive softmax layer is employed. The weights of adaptive input and adaptive softmax are shared.

Adaptive Input and Adaptive Softmax. Transformer architectures that use large vocabularies have embedding layers characterized by a very large weight matrix. This is especially true for encoder-only transformer-based architectures like BERT. The output layer multiplies this weight matrix with the output of the previous layer during pre-training with MLM. This matrix multiplication is slow and problematic due to the large amount of GPU memory required for its calculation. In addition, having a big embedding matrix implies that the model has many parameters and will require gigabytes of available space on disk to be saved. These problems can be mitigated by substituting the embedding layer with an adaptive input layer and by using an adaptive softmax layer instead of the last matrix multiplication followed by the softmax function.

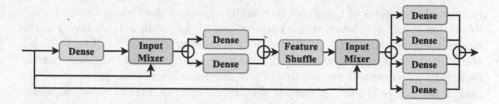

Fig. 2. Example of a DeLighT transformation during the expansion phase

Adaptive input is a drop-in replacement for the embedding layer, i.e., it does not require any modifications to the rest of the model's computational graph. To reduce the number of parameters, each token is assigned to one of n different clusters based on the token's frequency and has an embedding vector whose size depends on the cluster: the most frequent tokens are assigned to the first cluster and have embedding vectors of size d_e, while the others with lower frequency are assigned to subsequent clusters and have progressively smaller embedding vectors (of size d_e/k^{i-1}, where i is the index of the cluster, $1 \leq i \leq n$ and k represents the projection factor). The reduction of the embedding vector sizes produces, as an effect, a reduction in the number of parameters needed in the embedding layer.

In models that use the decoder-only or encoder-decoder architectures, the output of the network is the probability distribution for the next token, calculated using the softmax activation function. Adaptive softmax is a speedup technique used to replace the last dense layer with the softmax activation function in a neural network used for language modeling. Similarly to adaptive input, adaptive softmax performs a partition of the vocabulary into clusters. The first cluster contains the words occurring with the highest frequency, and it represents the distribution's head, while the other clusters contain words occurring with lower frequency and represent the tail of the distribution. Adaptive softmax takes inspiration from the class-based hierarchical softmax. The head cluster contains a special token for each tail cluster, which is used to model the probability that an output token belongs to the considered tail cluster. Then, since in the MLM task the labels are one-hot vectors indicating which token is the right one, the softmax output in the loss function is not explicitly calculated for all clusters, but only for the head cluster (containing the most frequent tokens) and for the cluster containing the token indicated by the one-hot vector (which might likely coincide with the head cluster). This optimized loss function makes it possible to save GPU memory and speed up the computation.

Finally, further parameter reduction can be achieved by sharing the embedding matrices of the clusters in adaptive input with the ones in adaptive softmax, as done in DelBERTo.

The DeLighT Transformation. Let us now describe what the DeLighT transformation actually is. As shown in Fig. 2, the DeLighT transformation is composed of a series of three different kinds of layers: the Group Linear Transformation (GLT) [16] layer, which corresponds to the parallel dense layers in the figure; the *input mixer* [17] layer; and the *feature shuffle* layer [25]. The DeLighT transformation is composed of two distinct phases: the expansion phase, characterized by an increase in the number of parallel dense layers (groups) in the GLTs and in the size of the GLTs' output vectors; and the reduction phase, in which the opposite situation occurs. In particular, during expansion (first $\lceil \frac{N_l}{2} \rceil$ layers, if N_l is the number of GLT layers), the vectors increase in size linearly until they reach a maximum size $d_{max} = w_m d_{in}$, where w_m is a configuration parameter called width multiplier, while during reduction (next $N_l - \lceil \frac{N_l}{2} \rceil$ layers), the vectors decrease in size linearly until they reach the desired size d_{out}.

Let us now describe the three layers of the DeLighT transformation. The GLT layer splits an input vector of size d_i into g vectors of size $\frac{d_i}{g}$. Each of these vectors is then passed as input to a different dense layer, which produces vectors of size $\frac{d_o}{g}$. Finally, the output vectors are concatenated into a single vector of size d_o. The splitting and concatenation operations are shown in Fig. 2 as circles. The maximum number of groups in a GLT layer is controlled by g_{max}. The feature shuffle layer performs a reshaping of the input vector $x \in \mathbb{R}^d$ into a matrix of size $g \times \frac{d}{g}$, then transposes this matrix and reshapes it back into a vector.

The input mixer layer takes two vectors $x \in \mathbb{R}^{d_x}$ and $y \in \mathbb{R}^{d_y}$ as input. It then splits each input vector into g vectors such that $x = \text{Concat}(x_1, \cdots, x_g)$, $y = \text{Concat}(y_1, \cdots, y_g)$ and produces an output vector $z = \text{Concat}(x_1, y_1, \cdots, x_g, y_g)$. This layer acts as a replacement for residual connections since they cannot be used in the DeLighT transformation because they require vectors of the same size. The input mixer's g hyperparameter is set to be equal to the g hyperparameter of the GLT that comes right after the input mixer. Each encoder layer has a different number of GLTs, which varies between N_{min} and N_{max}. The encoder layers in DelBERTo gradually become deeper and wider when moving from the first one to the last one.

Configuration. To instantiate DelBERTo, the vocabulary size V, the size of the embedding vectors d_e, and the maximum length of the input sequence take values of 128k, 768, and 128 respectively, as in AlBERTo. In adaptive input and adaptive softmax, the projection factor k is equal to 4 and the number n of clusters is 3. The first, second, and third clusters have 1960, 23708, and 102332 tokens, respectively. The size of the clusters was calculated with a script used to find the optimal size for a given vocabulary. The DelBERTo specific configuration hyperparameters have been set as described in Table 1. In the implementation of GLTs, it is possible to optionally use biases and to apply an activation function to the concatenated output of the GLTs. In particular, DelBERTo uses GELU [9] as an activation function for the GLTs and also uses biases.

3.1   Text Preprocessing

The text of each tweet is preprocessed as in [19]. First, tweets are converted to lowercase. Afterwards, URLs, emails, usernames, percents, money amounts,

Table 1. The top half of the table shows the hyperparameters of DelBERTo and their assigned values, while the bottom half shows the hyperparameters used to instantiate the DeLighT transformation in the embedding layer.

Hyperparam	Value	Description
d_{in}	768	DeLighT transformation's input vectors size (equal to d_e)
d_{out}	256	DeLighT transformation's output vectors size
g_{max}	16	Maximum number of groups in the GLTs
w_m	3	Base width multiplier for the GLTs
N	6	Number of DeLighT blocks
N_{min}	3	Minimum number of GLT layers in a DeLighT transformation
N_{max}	9	Maximum number of GLT layers in a DeLighT transformation
d_{in}	768	DeLighT transformation's input vectors size (equal to d_e)
d_{out}	768	DeLighT transformation's output vectors size (equal to d_e)
g_{max}	16	Maximum number of groups in the GLTs
w_m	3	Width multiplier for the GLTs
N_l	3	Number of GLT layers

phone numbers, dates, times, and numbers are normalized [4]. In particular, the normalization step consists in replacing those terms with an <[entity type]> token, where [entity type] can be, for example, url, if the term that was replaced was a URL. Next, hashtags are tagged and unpacked. The tagging operation consists in enclosing each hashtag with two tags, <hashtag> and </hashtag>, while the unpacking operation consists in segmenting the hashtag into known words. The next step is to delete every special character that is not an emoji, an accented letter, a question mark, or an exclamation mark. As an example, the tweet "#sport #news Liga, risultati e classifica della 19esima giornata http://t.co/OG8Recep" becomes "<hashtag> sport </hashtag> <hashtag> news </hashtag> liga risultati e classifica della esima giornata <url>".

Second, the tweets are tokenized. The SentencePiece library [12] was used since it is able to generate a vocabulary composed of the most common words and sub-words. By splitting words into sub-words, rare and misspelled words can be tokenized instead of simply using an unknown token for words not in the vocabulary. Once the vocabulary is created, every tweet in the dataset is tokenized. The tokenizer output is a vector that contains token IDs, which are integers. The last step consists in padding or truncating this vector to a specified length, which is equal to 128 tokens for DelBERTo and AlBERTo.

3.2 Training Procedure

The training procedure consists in a preliminary self-supervised pre-training stage over a larger dataset, followed by a supervised fine-tuning stage over a smaller dataset. Following AlBERTo's training procedure, the network is first trained on the TWITA dataset over the MLM task. In this task, a single sentence is used as input, and 15% of its tokens are randomly selected to be either masked, replaced with a random token, or left unchanged. For each selected token, one of these 3 transformations is chosen randomly. In particular, masking is chosen 80% of the time, while the other two transformations are chosen 10% of the time each. The network is then trained to predict the selected tokens, therefore learning a language model. As for AlBERTo, we did not use the Next Sentence Prediction task since the dataset is not structured in a suitable way.

Next, the fine-tuning stage consists in training DelBERTo on all the three tasks of the dataset provided for the SENTIPOLC 2016 challenge described in Sect. 4.1. In particular, we trained a DelBERTo binary classifier for each of the four labels in the dataset, as was done for AlBERTo. More details about how the training was performed in the different experiments can be found in Sect. 4.2.

4 Experiments

To evaluate the proposed architecture, we tested DelBERTo on the *SENTIment POLarity Classification Task 2016* (SENTIPOLC 2016). In this section, we first describe the SENTIPOLC 2016 dataset, and then we report the results of our experiments on this challenge, comparing them against the state-of-the-art.

4.1 Datasets

The SENTIPOLC 2016 challenge proposes three tasks on sentiment classification at the message level for Italian tweets: subjectivity classification, polarity classification, and irony detection. The training set of SENTIPOLC 2016 contains 7410 tweets in Italian. Each of them is annotated with six labels, of which four are used in the challenge. There is a binary label for irony (0 = non-ironic, 1 = ironic), a binary label for subjectivity (0 = objective, 1 = subjective), and two binary labels for polarity. The combination of these two labels can express positive, negative, neutral or mixed sentiment. There are also two more labels that represent literal polarity (they do not take into account irony), but, as explained before, these labels are not used.

4.2 Setup

All experiments except one were performed by using two Nvidia GTX 1080 Ti GPUs with 10 GB of memory each, for a total of about 20 GB of memory. Ideally, we wished to use the same training hyperparameters as AlBERTo to guarantee comparable results. However, the amount of GPU memory available forced us to adapt the hyperparameters to match the hardware constraints.

Pre-training. Like AlBERTo, we did use a sequence length of 128 tokens, and we also defined one epoch as equal to 2500 training steps. For the initial pre-training of DelBERTo, we did use the same batch size as AlBERTo (128) since the GPU memory was enough. We also used the same number of epochs, that is, 400 epochs. The number of examples used is $2500 * 400 * 128 = 128$ million, the same used by AlBERTo. The pre-training took about 9 days.

Fine-Tuning. We experimented with two different fine-tuning strategies, starting from the best checkpoint produced during pre-training. During fine-tuning, about 5% of the train set was left out for validation purposes, and the epoch was defined as one iteration of the dataset. In the following, the first fine-tuning strategy is referred to as *DelBERTo-1S*. In this case, we simply fine-tuned the entire network for 219 epochs with a learning rate (LR) of 2e−5, as for AlBERTo. Yet, due to GPU memory limitations, we could not afford AlBERTo's batches of 512 and had to use smaller batches of 128. The second fine-tuning strategy, *DelBERTo-2S*, relies on a more sophisticated two-stage approach. During the first stage, we froze the weights of all layers except the output layer and trained the network for 50 epochs with a LR of 1e−4. By training the output layer only, we could afford a larger batch size of 512 in this first stage. Furthermore, this prevents very large gradient updates, which would degrade the pre-trained weights since we are mixing pre-trained layers with a new, randomly initialized, output layer. Once convergence is reached, it is safe to proceed with the second stage, in which we trained all the layers with a lower LR of 1e−6 for 169 epochs. Due to the complexity of training all the layers, and to the fact that one GPU was not available to us for this fine-tuning, a smaller batch size of 64 was used.

Ablation Study. Finally, for the purpose of evaluating the impact of adaptive input and adaptive softmax in isolation, we consider another model that we call *AdalBERTo*. This model is based on BERT. The only difference is that AdalBERTo uses adaptive input and adaptive softmax instead of BERT's embedding layer and output layer. AdalBERTo was pre-trained and fine-tuned almost exactly like *DelBERTo-1S*. The only difference is that during pre-training and fine-tuning we had to use a batch size of 64 because of hardware limitations. Nonetheless, we compensate for the smaller batch size by using 800 epochs during pre-training and by doubling the number of train steps per epoch during fine-tuning. The pre-training took about 17 days, nearly twice as much as DelBERTo. All the models were fine-tuned once for each label, creating 4 binary classifiers like it was done for AlBERTo.

4.3 Results

Table 2 summarizes the results of our experiments. The top half contains the results of AlBERTo and other references from [19]. The bottom part contains the results for DelBERTo and AdalBERTo produced by our experiments. F1 Scores have been calculated by running the official evaluation script and using the official SENTIPOLC 2016 test set, which contains 2000 examples. For each of the three tasks, three columns are presented. The first two columns show the F1 Score of each class, while the F column represents the mean of the two columns. For the polarity task, since the number of classes is 4, the Pos column shows the mean of the F1 Scores for the positive class and the non-positive class, and the Neg column shows the mean of the F1 Scores for the negative class and the non-negative class. As shown in Table 2, *DelBERTo-2S* achieves results close to AlBERTo's at

Table 2. Results over the three SENTIPOLC 2016 classification tasks

	Subjectivity			Polarity			Irony			Params
	Obj	Subj	F	Pos	Neg	F	Non-I	Iro	F	[M]
AlBERTo	**73.98**	**84.15**	**79.06**	71.55	**72.91**	**72.23**	**94.08**	27.72	60.90	184
Unitor.1.u	67.84	81.05	74.44	63.54	68.85	66.20	n/a	n/a	n/a	n/a
UniPI.2.c	n/a	n/a	n/a	68.50	64.26	66.38	n/a	n/a	n/a	n/a
tweet2check16.c	n/a	n/a	n/a	n/a	n/a	n/a	91.15	17.10	54.12	n/a
AdalBERTo	71.74	78.38	75.06	**73.84**	64.76	69.30	93.79	17.20	55.50	97
DelBERTo-2S	68.11	78.34	73.22	70.43	68.93	69.68	93.00	**31.35**	**62.18**	24
DelBERTo-1S	68.29	76.03	72.16	59.30	63.31	61.31	93.05	26.59	59.82	

a fraction of the parameters. At the irony detection task, *DelBERTo-2S* gets better results than AlBERTo, whereas *DelBERTo-1S* is close but does not surpass it. The reason why *DelBERTo-2S* is better than *DelBERTo-1S* is the fact that it uses the two-stage fine-tuning process, which, as previously described, prevents the degradation of the pre-trained weights.

Complexity. For the purpose of comparing the computational complexity of DelBERTo with AlBERTo, we implemented the same BERT architecture used by AlBERTo. AdalBERTo uses the same code but with the modifications previously described, so as to minimize the differences in the implementation. For these benchmarks, we were given temporary access to one Nvidia A40 GPU with 48 GB of memory. In particular, we measured the computational performance differences in terms of the peak GPU memory consumption and the number of examples per second that the models were able to process. We measured these two metrics during pre-training, fine-tuning, and inference with different batch sizes (all the powers of two between 1 and 64 inclusive).

Figure 3 shows the results of the benchmarks. The first row is relative to pre-training, the second to fine-tuning, and the third to inference. The first column shows the speed of the models in steps per second, and the second column shows the peak GPU memory footprint. AlBERTo required more than the available memory for batch size 64 during pre-training, so the related plot point is missing.

Table 3 details the results of the three architectures and the gains relative to AlBERTo for a batch size of 32 examples. The first result to notice is the vast difference in speed and memory footprint between DelBERTo and the references during pre-training, which constitutes the bulk of the training time. Due to the lightweight DeLighT architecture and the adaptive input and adaptive softmax layers, DelBERTo is 4.03 times faster than AlBERTo for a batch size of 32. AdalBERTo shares the same BERT architecture as AlBERTo, yet it is still 2.57 times faster than AlBERTo thanks to adaptive input and adaptive softmax. So, we conclude that the DeLighT architecture, adaptive input, and adaptive softmax are about equally responsible for the faster training of DelBERTo. Regarding the memory footprint, DelBERTo and AdalBERTo use only 16.8% and 29.4% of the memory used by AlBERTo, respectively, with adaptive softmax representing the

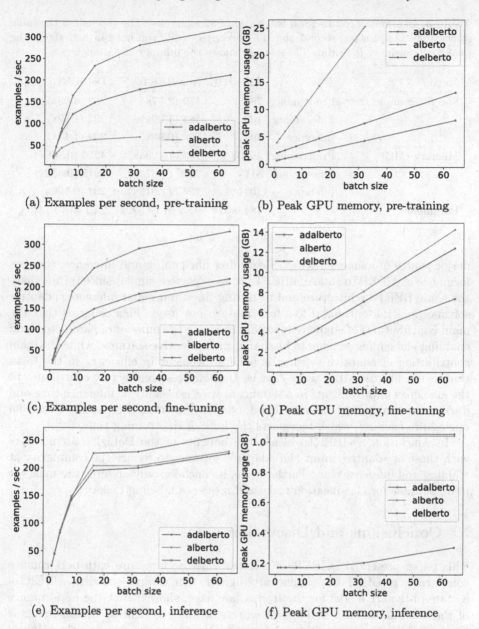

Fig. 3. Results of the benchmarks. The first column of figures shows the number of examples per second that the models are able to achieve, while the second column shows the peak GPU memory footprint. Each row corresponds to a different task, namely from top to bottom, pre-training, fine-tuning, and inference.

Table 3. Benchmark results for a batch size of 32 examples. The top half of the table shows the examples per second and the speedups, while the bottom half shows the peak GPU memory footprint. The last row shows the number of parameters.

Metric	Task	AlBERTo	AdalBERTo	DelBERTo
Speed (examples/sec)	Pre-training	70	179 (2.57x)	282 (4.03x)
	Fine-tuning	169	185 (1.09x)	291 (1.72x)
	Inference	204	200 (0.98x)	229 (1.12x)
Memory (MB)	Pre-training	25308	7435 (0.294x)	4250 (0.168x)
	Fine-tuning	8115	7090 (0.874x)	3915 (0.482x)
	Inference	1041	1043 (1.012x)	204 (0.196x)
Parameters		184.0 M	97.5 M (0.529x)	24.1 M (0.131x)

major source of memory savings. Regarding fine-tuning and inference, the performance of AlBERTo and AdalBERTo is, as expected, similar since i) they share the same BERT architecture and ii) during fine-tuning and inference, adaptive softmax and the optimized loss function are not used. This confirms that the main contributions of adaptive input are reducing the number of parameters and enabling embedding weights to be shared with adaptive softmax, while the main contribution of adaptive softmax is an improvement in efficiency in the tasks that use it, like the MLM task. That is, DelBERTo's architecture contributes to the efficiency improvements in a significant way, especially at inference time and during fine-tuning. On the other hand, adaptive softmax is especially beneficial during pre-training, which represents the bulk of the training time.

In conclusion, DelBERTo blends the benefits of the DeLighT architecture with those of adaptive input and adaptive softmax to reduce the complexity at training and inference time. Furthermore, its encoder-only architecture makes it more suitable for classification tasks and sequence labeling tasks.

5   Conclusions and Discussion

This paper presented DelBERTo, a transformer architecture with performance comparable to BERT but significantly lighter. Our comparison with AlBERTo, a state-of-the-art model for the Italian language, showed that the performance of the two models on a well-known sentiment analysis task on Italian tweets is similar, while the training time and memory footprint are significantly reduced.

While the results are promising, we consider these experiments preliminary. In particular, the hardware resources available at the time constrained our hyper-parameter choices; we expect that removing such constraints will boost performance. Finally, while the present work focused on the Italian language, DelBERTo is language-agnostic and can be deployed for tasks other than sentiment analysis. In the near future, we plan to further refine the model and evaluate it on the English IMDb Movie Reviews dataset [14].

References

1. Baevski, A., Auli, M.: Adaptive input representations for neural language modeling. In: International Conference on Learning Representations (2019). https://openreview.net/forum?id=ByxZX20qFQ

2. Barbieri, F., Basile, V., Croce, D., Nissim, M., Novielli, N., Patti, V.: Overview of the evalita 2016 sentiment polarity classification task. In: Proceedings of CLiC-it 2016 and EVALITA 2016, Napoli, Italy, 5-7 December 2016 (2016). http://ceur-ws.org/Vol-1749/paper_026.pdf

3. Basile, V., Lai, M., Sanguinetti, M.: Long-term social media data collection at the university of turin. In: Proceedings of the 5th Italian Conference on Computational Linguistics (CLiC-it 2018), Torino, Italy, 10-12 December 2018. (2018). http://ceur-ws.org/Vol-2253/paper48.pdf

4. Baziotis, C., Pelekis, N., Doulkeridis, C.: Datastories at semeval-2017 task 4: Deep LSTM with attention for message-level and topic-based sentiment analysis. In: Proceedings of the 11th International Workshop on Semantic Evaluation (SemEval-2017), pp. 747–754. Association for Computational Linguistics, Vancouver, Canada (2017)

5. Choromanski, K.M., et al.: Rethinking attention with performers. In: International Conference on Learning Representations (2021). https://openreview.net/forum?id=Ua6zuk0WRH

6. Dai, Z., Lai, G., Yang, Y., Le, Q.V.: Funnel-transformer: filtering out sequential redundancy for efficient language processing. In: Proceedings of the 34th International Conference on Neural Information Processing Systems, NIPS'20, Curran Associates Inc., Red Hook, NY, USA (2020)

7. Devlin, J., Chang, M.W., Lee, K., Toutanova, K.: BERT: pre-training of deep bidirectional transformers for language understanding. In: Proceedings of the 2019 Conference of the North American Chapter of the Association for Computational Linguistics: Human Language Technologies, vol. 1 (Long and Short Papers), pp. 4171–4186. Association for Computational Linguistics, Minneapolis, Minnesota (2019). https://doi.org/10.18653/v1/N19-1423, https://aclanthology.org/N19-1423

8. Grave, É., Joulin, A., Cissé, M., Grangier, D., Jégou, H.: Efficient softmax approximation for GPUs. In: Precup, D., Teh, Y.W. (eds.) Proceedings of the 34th International Conference on Machine Learning. Proceedings of Machine Learning Research, vol. 70, pp. 1302–1310. PMLR (2017). https://proceedings.mlr.press/v70/grave17a.html

9. Hendrycks, D., Gimpel, K.: Gaussian error linear units (gelus) (2020)

10. Hochreiter, S., Schmidhuber, J.: Long short-term memory. Neural Comput. **9**, 1735–80 (1997). https://doi.org/10.1162/neco.1997.9.8.1735

11. Kitaev, N., Kaiser, L., Levskaya, A.: Reformer: the efficient transformer. In: International Conference on Learning Representations (2020). https://openreview.net/forum?id=rkgNKkHtvB

12. Kudo, T., Richardson, J.: SentencePiece: a simple and language independent subword tokenizer and detokenizer for neural text processing. In: Proceedings of the 2018 Conference on Empirical Methods in Natural Language Processing: System Demonstrations, pp. 66–71. Association for Computational Linguistics, Brussels, Belgium (2018). https://doi.org/10.18653/v1/D18-2012, https://aclanthology.org/D18-2012

13. LeCun, Y., Bengio, Y., Hinton, G.: Deep learning. Nature **521**(7553), 436–444 (2015). https://doi.org/10.1038/nature14539

14. Maas, A.L., Daly, R.E., Pham, P.T., Huang, D., Ng, A.Y., Potts, C.: Learning word vectors for sentiment analysis. In: Proceedings of the 49th Annual Meeting of the Association for Computational Linguistics: Human Language Technologies, pp. 142–150. Association for Computational Linguistics, Portland, Oregon, USA (2011). http://www.aclweb.org/anthology/P11-1015

15. Mehta, S., Ghazvininejad, M., Iyer, S., Zettlemoyer, L., Hajishirzi, H.: Delight: deep and light-weight transformer. arXiv preprint arXiv:2008.00623 (2020)

16. Mehta, S., Koncel-Kedziorski, R., Rastegari, M., Hajishirzi, H.: Pyramidal recurrent unit for language modeling. In: Proceedings of the 2018 Conference on Empirical Methods in Natural Language Processing, pp. 4620–4630. Association for Computational Linguistics, Brussels, Belgium (Oct 2018). https://doi.org/10.18653/v1/D18-1491, https://aclanthology.org/D18-1491

17. Mehta, S., Koncel-Kedziorski, R., Rastegari, M., Hajishirzi, H.: Define: deep factorized input token embeddings for neural sequence modeling. In: 8th International Conference on Learning Representations, ICLR 2020, Addis Ababa, Ethiopia, 26-30 April 2020. OpenReview.net (2020), https://openreview.net/forum?id=rJeXS04FPH

18. Pang, B., Lee, L.: Opinion mining and sentiment analysis. Found. Trends Inf. Retr. **2**(1–2), 1–135 (2008). https://doi.org/10.1561/1500000011

19. Polignano, M., Basile, P., Degemmis, M., Semeraro, G., Basile, V.: Alberto: Italian Bert language understanding model for NLP challenging tasks based on tweets. In: CLiC-it (2019)

20. Rumelhart, D.E., Hinton, G.E., Williams, R.J.: Learning Internal Representations by Error Propagation, pp. 318–362. MIT Press, Cambridge (1986)

21. Tay, Y., Dehghani, M., Bahri, D., Metzler, D.: Efficient transformers: a survey. ACM Comput. Surv. (2022). https://doi.org/10.1145/3530811

22. Vaswani, A., et al.: Attention is all you need. In: Guyon, I., Luxburg, U.V., Bengio, S., Wallach, H., Fergus, R., Vishwanathan, S., Garnett, R. (eds.) Advances in Neural Information Processing Systems, vol. 30. Curran Associates, Inc. (2017). https://proceedings.neurips.cc/paper/2017/file/3f5ee243547dee91fbd053c1c4a845aa-Paper.pdf

23. Zaheer, M., et al.: Big bird: transformers for longer sequences. In: Larochelle, H., Ranzato, M., Hadsell, R., Balcan, M.F., Lin, H. (eds.) Advances in Neural Information Processing Systems, vol. 33, pp. 17283–17297. Curran Associates, Inc. (2020), https://proceedings.neurips.cc/paper/2020/file/c8512d142a2d849725f31a9a7a361ab9-Paper.pdf

24. Zhang, X., Zhao, J., LeCun, Y.: Character-level convolutional networks for text classification. In: Cortes, C., Lawrence, N., Lee, D., Sugiyama, M., Garnett, R. (eds.) Advances in Neural Information Processing Systems, vol. 28. Curran Associates, Inc. (2015). https://proceedings.neurips.cc/paper/2015/file/250cf8b51c773f3f8dc8b4be867a9a02-Paper.pdf

25. Zhang, X., Zhou, X., Lin, M., Sun, J.: Shufflenet: an extremely efficient convolutional neural network for mobile devices. In: 2018 IEEE/CVF Conference on Computer Vision and Pattern Recognition, pp. 6848–6856 (2018). https://doi.org/10.1109/CVPR.2018.00716

A BERT-Based Scoring System
for Workplace Safety Courses in Italian

Nicola Arici[1]([✉]), Alfonso E. Gerevini[1], Luca Putelli[1], Ivan Serina[1],
and Luca Sigalini[2]

[1] Università degli Studi di Brescia, Via Branze 38, Brescia, Italy
{nicola.arici,alfonso.gerevini,luca.putelli1,ivan.serina}@unibs.it
[2] Mega Italia Media, Via Roncadelle 70A, Castel Mella, Italy
luca.sigalini@megaitaliamedia.it

Abstract. Knowing the fundamentals of workplace safety is not only
an important right for all categories of workers, but also a legal duty in
Italy. Workers have to attend workplace safety courses and, in order to
obtain a legally valid certification of the training received, they have to
pass a written exam. This exam includes open-ended questions whose
answers (provided by the students) are evaluated by human teachers. In
the last few years, workplace safety courses have often been attended
online via e-learning platforms. This allows the companies offering this
kind of service to collect thousands of questions and answers regarding
workplace safety that are written in Italian. In this paper, we propose
an automatic scoring system for open-ended questions to assist a human
teacher in the task of evaluating the student answers. The system is
based on deep learning techniques exploiting the available textual data
about questions and answers. In particular, we put forward three different
approaches based on BERT, and we evaluate the necessary operations
in order to create an effective tool.

1 Introduction

Workplace safety courses train millions of Italian workers on very important matters such as basic skills in risk assessment, possible hazards, personal protective equipment and many other subjects which deeply concern their safety in their jobs. Under the Italian law, these courses are mandatory with several degrees of specificity. After an introductory course, typically one or two more specific courses are required depending on the type of job. These additional courses are usually related to the particular activities performed by the person, which could involve electrical equipment, chemical agents, heavy loads and other possible sources of risk. Given that these courses are mandatory, after attending one course, people have to take a final exam and receive an evaluation by a human teacher. Depending on the course, these exams can be multiple choice tests or contain open-ended questions. However, while multiple choice tests can be easily

A. Dovier et al. (Eds.): AIxIA 2022, LNAI 13796, pp. 457–471, 2023.
https://doi.org/10.1007/978-3-031-27181-6_32

checked and scored by a software, open ended questions require a considerable effort by the evaluator, which has to read, understand and score what has been written by the students. In the last few years (with an increase also due to the spread of the COVID-19 pandemic [24]), a large number of these courses have been taken online. The Italian company *MegaItaliaMedia* offers workplace safety courses providing an e-learning platform into which the students can watch the lessons and take their exams. Such exams are then scored by the course teachers, who are employees of the company.

Collecting these data and exploiting machine learning techniques can contribute to the reduction of the amount of this tedious and repetitive work. In fact, deep learning techniques such as word embedding and LSTM Neural Networks have proved very effective in scoring systems [8,13] and in other text applications even in very specific domains [15,23]. Moreover, new language models based on Transformer [21] like BERT [5], have determined a new state-of-the-art in Natural Language Processing (NLP) tasks like machine translation, text classification and sentiment analysis. For these reasons, we have exploited a pre-trained BERT model for creating a scoring system that can be applied to the exams in our application context. The most common approach for solving this kind of tasks is to feed a deep learning model with both the user's answer and a predefined reference. The score is usually based on the semantic similarity between the two sentences, which is calculated with typical distance metrics such as the cosine similarity. However, some recent studies show that BERT is not particularly effective with this kind of approach [6,17,22]. Therefore, instead of computing a score based on semantic similarity, we treat this problem as a classification task. More specifically, given that the questions are evaluated using scores from 1 to 100, we want to recognise if the answer deserves more or less than 80 points. We chose this threshold because if the answers deserve more than 80, it is obviously very good and it can be easily checked by a human without a thorough reading, with an important time saving. Instead, for the remaining answers the teachers should evaluate more carefully if all the important information is present.

Adapting a pre-trained language model to a scoring system is not a trivial operation and can be done in several ways. Thus, we designed and implemented three different models that differ mainly from the text they received in input. The Double Model is quite similar to the standard approach, receiving both the student's answer and a predefined, correct answer. However, we have also created a baseline (the Single Model) which receives in input only the student's answer. Since we have a limited amount of questions with respect to the amount of answers, this model could learn some common characteristics from the correct answers even without any reference. Finally, the Concept Model follows a completely different approach. Instead of simply predicting if the answer is sufficiently good, a BERT model is used for checking if the answer contains several specific concepts. If the answer contains at least 80% of the concepts required, the score will be higher than 80.

The realisation of such models requires also solving some practical issues like adapting a generic model like BERT (which is usually trained on newspaper articles and documents from Wikipedia) in our specific context and its technical lexicon. Moreover, a fine-tuning process is needed in order to create a classifier which can provide the scores. However, while our application is quite specific, the techniques we propose and analyse are general and could be easily adapted for other scoring systems in completely different domains.

The rest of the paper is organized as follows. In Sect. 2, we provide the background and an overview of the state-of-the-art and the related works. In Sect. 3, we describe our BERT-based scoring system, which is evaluated and discussed in Sect. 4. Finally, in Sect. 5 we propose some conclusions and future developments.

2 Background and Related Work

2.1 BERT

BERT (Bidirectional Encoder Representations from Transformer) [5] is an architecture based on Transformer [21] composed by several encoding layers which progressively analyse a sequence of tokens (i.e. words or parts of a word) in order to capture their meaning.

Each layer applies in parallel multiple self-attention mechanisms, called *heads*. Considering a sequence of tokens S of length N, this mechanism produces a matrix $A_{i,j} \in \mathbb{R}^{N \times N}$, into which i is the number of the encoding layer and j is the head number. For each token $w \in S$, the vector $a_w \in A_{i,j}$ contains the attention weights that represent how much w is related to the other tokens in S.

In order to calculate these weights, in each head the input representation of the token sequence $X \in \mathbb{R}^{N \times d}$ is projected into three new representations called key (K), query (Q) and value (V) with three matrices W_k, W_q and W_v:

$$K = X \times W_k, \ Q = X \times W_q, \ V = X \times W_v$$

Then, the attention weights are calculated using the softmax function on the scaled dot-product between Q and K. The new token representation Z is calculated by multiplying the attention weights for V.

$$A = softmax\left(\frac{Q \times K^{\mathsf{T}}}{\sqrt{d}}\right)$$
$$Z = A \times V$$

into which d is the length of the input representation of each token. Given that in each encoding layer there are multiple heads, in order to create a single representation provided by the *multi-head attention mechanism* the result of each head is concatenated and then passed to a feed-forward layer.

As described in [21], the multi-head attention mechanism is followed by a residual connection which adds the input representation with the one calculated by the multi-head attention. Next, the result is fed to a feed-forward layer and another residual connection. The output of the encoding layer is also the input of the next encoder.

Exploiting a large collection of documents, BERT is trained for two tasks: *masked language modeling*, into which BERT learns to predict a percentage (usually 15%) of tokens from context, and *next sentence prediction*. In this task, given a sequence of two sentences, the model has to distinguish if the second sentence reasonably follows the first one or it is randomly chosen from the corpus. For this second task two special tokens are introduced: at the beginning of the sentence, the token [CLS] represents the whole sequence and it is used by a feed-forward layer to perform the next sentence prediction task, and [SEP] which marks the separation of the two sentences. Learning these two tasks allows BERT to create a meaningful representation of each token and also how to summarise the most important information in a sentence. Once BERT is trained, it can be adapted using smaller datasets for specific NLP tasks like Named Entity Recognition, text classification, sentiment analysis, etc.

2.2 Related Work

In the past few years, several approaches and frameworks have been developed to solve scoring and graduation tasks. The main branches of this problem are two: assessing the quality of a long essay [9], and scoring the correctness of a short answer like in our application [7]. One of the first scoring systems based on machine learning is presented in [10]. They use Support Vector Machines fed with thirty hand-crafted features related to the syntax of the answers, their dependency graphs and a set of knowledge based semantic similarity measures calculated on the Bag of Words representation of the answers.

The authors of [14] compared different word overlapping methods for measuring the similarity between the reference and student's answer. They showed that overlapping algorithms cannot overcome the semantic similarity problem. This problem arises when the two sentences express the same meaning using different words and with these algorithms the two sentences obtain a low similarity score. Suzen *et al.* [19] developed a model that deals with automatic scoring for short answers through unsupervised and supervised approaches based simply on the words. They proposed a clustering method based on the vocabulary used in the answers and a mathematical supervised model based on the Hamming distance between the reference and student's answer. In [8], the authors tried different word embedding models and paragraph embedding algorithms for calculating a vectorial representation of the answers. Then, these vectors were used to calculate the student's answer score through the cosine similarity. An interesting approach is presented in [13]. In this work, a LSTM-based model takes in input the embedded representation of the answer and some other properties, such as the number of words contained in the answer, as additional features. Then, the score is computed using a feed-forward fully connected layer.

The introduction of Transformer [21] and in particular BERT [5] has radically changed the state-of-the-art for NLP tasks. These models have outperformed the older technologies, like RNN and LSTM, in many NLP tasks. Although these models are trained with generic documents, they can be easily adapted to more particular domains by adding domain-related texts in the training phase and/or with a thorough fine-tuning. For instance, Sung et al. [18] adapted BERT in four specific domains using both these techniques.

Another problem that arises using BERT for short answer grading is when the student provides an answer with words different from the reference answer, but with the same meaning. In the last few years the ability of BERT to understand semantics has been studied in several works [6,11,17]. Reimers et al. [17] proposed a new architecture, Sentence-BERT (SBERT), which uses Siamese and triplet network structures with a pooling layer on top of BERT to calculate semantically meaningful sentence embeddings. Another solution, proposed in [11], enriches BERT with explicit contextual semantic information. They support BERT with a role labeler to annotate the input sentences with a variety of semantic role labels. They demonstrated that explicit contextual semantics can be effectively integrated with vectorial representations derived from a pre-trained language model and have better performance.

While there are several applications of Natural Language Processing for the Italian language [2,4,12,16], at the best of our knowledge this is the first scoring system for open answers written in Italian.

3   A BERT-Based Scoring System

3.1   Dataset and Task Description

In this section we present the data used to train and to evaluate our model. The data were provided to us by *MegaItaliaMedia* and consist of a set of tests taken by the students of their workplace safety courses. These tests are composed by several questions (usually 5), and for each of these questions, we have the reference answer, which is written by a course teacher, and the answers provided by each student. From March 2020, some evaluators started rating the student's answers with a score from 1 to 100. We didn't notice any significant disparities within the scores given by different evaluators. However, in the presence of particularly complex questions or courses, it could be useful to conduct an inter-annotator agreement in order to ensure an uniform yardstick. During this period, we collected 4417 rated answers, belonging to 102 questions. In order to replicate real-world conditions, no pre-processing operations (such as removing typos or special characters) have been performed.

Analyzing the data we noticed that the 75% of the answers are composed by one or two sentences. However, analyzing the answers length in terms of number of words we saw some differences: 75% of the answers are made up by less than 77 words, but a third of these answers contain fewer than 24 words. This discrepancy is due to how different users respond to questions: some users respond briefly by doing as little as possible to obtain a sufficient mark, while other users made a considerable effort to make sure they will pass the test. Another problem we found was the imbalance of the scores. The first quartile

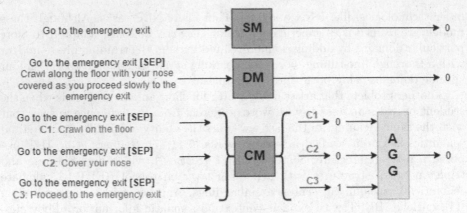

Fig. 1. Graphical representation of the Single Model (SM), the Double Model (DM) and the Concept Model (CM). All three models take as input the answer provided by the user (in black). In addition, the second model takes as input the reference answer (in blue), while the third model also takes as input some short sentences representing the concepts that the answer should include (in red). The first two models provide a prediction that informs whether the predicted score for the answer is greater than 80 (label 1) or less (label 0). The third model indicates whether the user's answer contains the single concept (label 1) or not (label 0). Then, the predictions are aggregated (AGG block) to provide the same prediction as the first two models. (Color figure online)

of the score distribution is equal to 80, very distant from the expected value of 25 that a normal distribution would have. Also the third quartile is very high, equal to 100, meaning that at least 25% of the answers obtain the maximum score. Finally, even the mean of the distribution, equal to 86.5, is leaning toward a higher value. This imbalance is due to the nature of the test and how it is administered. In fact, workplace safety courses are mandatory and users are very motivated to pass this test in order to maintain their job. Finally, it is noteworthy that there is no correlation between the score of the answers and their length.

Our rated answers are used for creating an automatic scoring system. In particular, we structure the problem as a classification task into which the model has to establish if an answer is correct. For each answer, we assign label 1 if the score is greater than 80 and 0 otherwise. This value represents the correction threshold: if the score exceeds this value, more likely the answer is correct and the human teacher will only have to provide a confirmation, otherwise a more accurate human evaluation is needed.

3.2 Approaches Proposed

In order to perform our classification task, we follow three different approaches: the **Single Model**, the **Double Model**, and the **Concept Model**. Each of these models need a purposely made dataset based on the answers rated provided to us by the company. A graphical representation of these models is available in Fig. 1.

First, we created a simple baseline model. All our answers (more than 4,000) respond only to 102 questions and therefore we have only 102 unique reference answers. Therefore, we want to check if BERT is able to detect some common characteristics in the answers to the same question, even without any reference. Moreover, given that the 102 questions have only one reference answer each, we wanted to check if seeing so much equivalent data improves the learning process or not. We consider this model as a baseline created just for comparison purposes: in fact, not passing the question or the reference answer as an input is a serious limit of the Single Model.

In the second approach, like in [8,19] we evaluate the correctness of the user's answer also considering the reference answer. Therefore, each instance of the dataset used for training the Double Model is made by a pair of sentences: the user's answer and the correct, reference answer provided by the company. Both these models have the goal to predict if the score is higher than 80 or not.

A possible issue of the previous two models can be the variety of the answers. In fact, several different words and phrases can be used to express the same meaning. By comparing the answers which belong to the same question and which obtained the maximum score, we noticed how these differ from the others. On average, high-scoring answers to the same question only share 40.58% of the words. Typically, the words shared contained in the answers are domain-specific words. Instead, words like conjunctions, adjectives and adverbs can be really different from an answer to another and these discrepancies could harm the classification process. Thus, we asked the company domain expert to extract the *key concepts* from the reference answers. With the term "concept" we do not intend a single keyword, but a small and simple grammatically correct sentence that expresses relevant information that an user's answer must contain in order to receive a positive evaluation. Therefore, the **Concept Model** is similar to the Double Model. However, the reference is not the entire answer but a short sentence representing a single concept. The goal of this model is to identify if the concept is explained correctly in the answer (label 1) or not (label 0). Given that a question in our tests presents more than one concept (typically two or three), therefore an answer, in order to be evaluated, has to be processed multiple times by the Concept Model, one for each concept. Please note that this model is trained only once for all the concepts, there are not several models each one dedicated to a specific concept. Once all concepts have been analyzed, the aggregation function (AGG block in Fig. 1) computes the predicted value of the answer. If at least 80% of the concepts are present, the value predicted of the entire answer is 1 (i.e. the score is higher than 80, like in the other two models), 0 otherwise. While this threshold has specifically set for our application, different aggregation functions (for instance, the presence of all the concepts or weighting

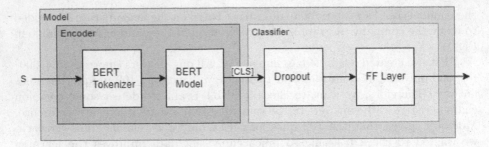

Fig. 2. The basic architecture of our models. The raw text is tokenized and then processed by a pre-trained BERT model. The resulting [CLS] vector is fed to a classifier made by a dropout layer and a feed-forward layer which provides the prediction.

differently each concept on the basis of its importance) could be implemented in other contexts, such as penalising very long answers with a lot of irrelevant information.

3.3 BERT-Based Implementation

All three models, as shown in Fig. 2, are made by two main parts: the BERT-based encoder and the classifier.

Starting from raw text, as explained in Sect. 2.1, the BERT-based Encoder produces a meaningful representation of the input sentence (or sentences). The model used in this encoding process is a customized version of a pre-trained BERT model for the Italian language[1] and it is made by two components: the tokenizer, which divides the sentence into single tokens (words or parts of a word), and the Model, which encodes the text in a vectorial representation.

Given that these models are trained with a generic corpus, in the customization process we add the most important words belonging to the workplace safety lexicon to the model vocabulary, such as *isolante* (insulating), *tecnostress* or *infortunato* (injured). Without this operation, these very important words would be divided into two or more tokens by the pre-trained tokenizer (for instance, *isolante* would be divided into *isola* and *##nte*) which are less meaningful to our context [20]. In order to identify and add the most important domain specific terms, we remove numbers, dates and stop words from our corpus and we tokenize these cleaned texts in single words using the NLTK tokenizer for the Italian language [3]. Next, if a word appears more than 50 times in our corpus and it is not present in the BERT vocabulary, we add it.

The result of the tokenization process is then fed to BERT. In particular, we are interested in the embedded representation of the special token [CLS], which represents the content of the entire sequence of tokens and it is commonly used in text classification tasks. Thus, the vector representation of [CLS] is the input of the second component of our BERT-based models. This component is made by

---

[1] https://huggingface.co/dbmdz/bert-base-italian-uncased.

Table 1. Dataset description in terms of total number of instances (second column), number of instances in the majority class (third column) and in the minority class (fourth column). In the fifth column we show the percentage of instances in the minority class.

Single/Double	Instances	Score >80	Score ≤80	%Score ≤80
Fine-tuning	3294	2366	928	28.17%
Validation	414	286	128	30.58%
Testing	411	285	126	30.66%
Concepts	Instances	Concept present	Concept absent	%Concept absent
Fine-tuning	8453	6091	2362	27.94%
Validation	1065	737	328	30.80%
Testing	1024	723	319	30.61%

a dropout layer and by a fully-connected layer. Given that both recognise if the answer deserves a score greater than 80 or not and the concept identification are binary tasks, for all the three models the fully-connected layer is made by a single neuron with sigmoid activation function which provides the final prediction.

In order to perform the binary scoring task, we train the classifier component and fine-tune the pre-trained encoder using our rated answers. Each model has been fine-tuned, validated and tested with the corresponding dataset. Each dataset is divided into three parts: 80% for fine-tuning, 10% for validation and 10% for testing. The numbers of instances used to train and evaluate our models are presented in Table 1. Please note that the Single Model and the Double Model are trained with the same answers. However, as explained in Sect. 3.2, the Double Model also takes in input the reference answers.

In our fine-tuning procedure, we used binary cross-entropy as the loss function, Adam as the optimizer and we exploited a linear scheduler with a warm-up for the learning rate.

4 Experimental Results

In this section we present the results achieved by the three models proposed. In order to find the best way to create an automatic correction system, we try and test several different configurations. Our results are evaluated in terms of F1-Score. This metric can be computed for both classes in our binary task and, from now on, we will refer using 1-F1 to the F1-score calculated on the data with label 1, which are the answers whose scoring higher than 80. The F1-Score for the other class, composed by all the other answers (with label 0), will be referred as 0-F1. Although our approach is based on BERT, in the past we have also tried several types of LSTM-based models using pre-trained word embeddings. Unfortunately, their results were not satisfactory and much lower with respect to BERT.

Table 2. Best set of hyper-parameters for each model. Max. Len. stands for the maximum length of the answer; LR stands for learning rate; WD for weight decay; WS are the warm-up steps of the learning rate scheduler.

Model	Max. Len	Dropout	Batch size	LR	WD	WS
Single model	64	0.42	8	2.6e–4	4.3e–4	22
Double model	160	0.47	8	1.9e–4	1.2e–5	16
Concept model	96	0.39	16	4.1e–4	1.4e–4	18

4.1 Training Configurations

We tried the uncased model of BERT for the Italian language, in both versions: the standard, which is trained using a corpus made by 13 GB of documents, and the XXL version which uses 81 GB of data. Both these versions come pre-trained and their hyper-parameters (such as the number of layers and heads) cannot be changed. However, the configuration of the learning process (which includes choosing the learning rate, the batch size, etc.) can strongly influence the predictive results. In order to find the best values of these hyper-parameters, we performed a hyper-parameter search using the Bayesian-optimisation approach provided by the Optuna framework [1]. For each model we run 100 iterations over 10 epochs and keep the best set of hyper-parameters which maximizes 0-F1 labelled data on the validation set. This choice was made because during the preliminary tests we found that the model predicted the 1 labelled class data quite well, but struggled on the data with class 0. In the same preliminary tests, we have verified that this optimisation does not have a negative impact on the performance in terms of 1-F1.

For each model, the best set of hyper-parameters is shown in Table 2. Although there are no important differences among the models, we can see that the Concept Model obtains the best performance with a higher batch size with respect to the other two models (16 instead of 8). This could be due to the fact that recognizing more than 100 different concepts requires a higher generalization capability. Another important aspect we found is that all the three models have better performance with the standard version of BERT compared to the XXL version, despite the latter being trained over a much larger corpus.

For all the models proposed, we tested two different ways to adapt the pre-trained model with the goal of performing our scoring task, which are the Freezing Fine Tuning (FFT) and the Complete Fine Tuning (CFT). In FFT, we train only the classifier, "freezing" the pre-trained weights of BERT which are not updated in the fine-tuning process. Instead, in CFT we perform a complete fine-tuning that also modifies the pre-trained weights.

In Fig. 3 we include a comparison among these three configurations of our models, in terms of 0-F1 (on the left) and 1-F1 (on the right). In terms of 1-F1, we can see that a fine-tuning (in both the frozen version and the complete one) is necessary to have acceptable performances. In terms of 0-F1 the situation changes drastically. In fact, freezing the BERT weights leads to a deterioration

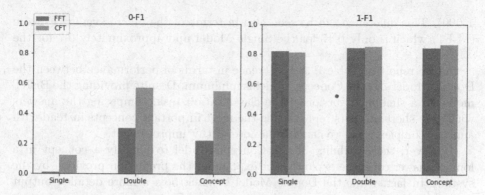

Fig. 3. Predictive performance of our three models in terms of 1-F1 and 0-F1 with training only the classifier without fine-tuning the pre-trained weights of BERT (FFT, in blue) and performing a complete fine tuning (CFT, in orange). (Color figure online)

Table 3. Results of our three models, with Complete Fine-Tuning, in terms of F1-Score for the minority class (0-F1), the majority class (1-F1), the macro-average (M-F1) and the weighted average (W-F1).

Model	0-F1	1-F1	M-F1	W-F1
Single model	0.12	0.81	0.47	0.60
Double model	**0.57**	0.85	**0.71**	0.76
Concept model	0.55	**0.86**	0.70	**0.77**

of the performance in all three models. For instance, for the Double Model and the Concept Models the 0-F1 value does not exceed 0.3.

As expected, the complete fine-tuning process improves the results in terms of the F1-Score of both classes, especially for the 0-F1 of the Double Model and the Concept Model. As we have seen previously, the Single Model (even in this configuration) is not able to identify answers with scores lower than 80.

4.2 Approaches Comparison

An overview of the comparison among the best configurations of our approaches is available in Table 3. The performance on the answers with a score higher than 80 is very good for all three models, with the Concept Model obtaining the best results in terms of F-Score (0.86 of 1-F1). However, in terms of 0-F1 there are some major differences. In fact, the Single Model performs much worse (0.12) with respect to the other two models (0.55 for the Concept Model and 0.57 for the Double Model). As expected, this demonstrates the usefulness of providing a correct reference (the entire answer for the Double Model or a set of concepts in the Concept Model) in the context of the scoring system, even if the number of questions (only 102) is much lower with respect to the answers (more than

4, 000). This difference can be seen also in terms of the macro-average F-Score (M-F1) which is only 0.47 for the Single Model and approximately 0.7 for the other two.

As we report in Table 3, the difference in terms of performance between the Double Model and the Concept Model is minimum. Despite providing the BERT model of a simplified version of the classification task, comparing the answers with only short snippets representing the most important concepts instead with another complex text, we can't see a noteworthy improvement.

However, the capability of the Concept Model to identify a concept in a longer answer could be exploited for explaining the prediction provided by the system. In fact, while the Double Model is black box, a more detailed output including which concepts are present or not, could better inform the evaluators about how final score was obtained. A possible drawback of this approach is that extracting the most important concepts required in an answer is an expensive annotation process which can be done only by domain experts such as our evaluators. Therefore, this could limit the scalability of the approach in complicated contexts with many possible concepts in different types of questions.

5   Conclusion and Future Work

We have presented an automatic scoring system for the Italian language. Our corpus is composed by more than 4, 000 open answers written by people attending a workplace safety course and scored by human evaluators.

We exploited a pre-trained BERT model and customized it with pre-processing and fine-tuning techniques in order to predict if the answers should receive a score higher than 80 (over a total of 100 points) or not. We tried several approaches, including one that recognizes if some specific concepts, represented a short sentence, are contained in the answer and then evaluates the overall score of the sentence with an aggregation function.

Our system is effective and obtains a good predictive performance in this evaluation and, in particular, our Concept Model reaches 0.77 of the weighted F1-Score. However, there are some issues for the minority class, which is made by the answers with lower scores. This may be due to class imbalance, the low quantity of training instances and the overall difficulties of BERT in capturing complex semantics [17]. We are currently studying with *MegaItaliaMedia* a real-world implementation of our system. This would allow to evaluate the performance of our models in a more complex environment but also to collect more data which could improve our predictive performance.

As future work, a further study of the limits of our system could help us also to identify specific cases into which the classifier is deceived by ambiguous answers, by the presence of negations or other issues. Moreover, we aim to convert our classification task in a regression task into which the model has to predict the score in a range from 1 to 100 (the same used by the company human corrector).

From a more general point of view, a scoring system is based on the capabilities of a neural language model to capture the semantics of text. Some new models, such as Sentence-BERT [17] or Semantics-Aware BERT [22], have shown some interesting improvements in this field and, as future work, we will try to adapt their techniques for the Italian language and evaluate them in our scoring task.

References

1. Akiba, T., Sano, S., Yanase, T., Ohta, T., Koyama, M.: Optuna: a next-generation hyperparameter optimization framework. In: Teredesai, A., Kumar, V., Li, Y., Rosales, R., Terzi, E., Karypis, G. (eds.) Proceedings of the 25th ACM SIGKDD International Conference on Knowledge Discovery & Data Mining, KDD 2019, Anchorage, AK, USA, 4–8 August 2019, pp. 2623–2631. ACM (2019)
2. Basile, V., Novielli, N., Croce, D., Barbieri, F., Nissim, M., Patti, V.: Sentiment polarity classification at EVALITA: lessons learned and open challenges. IEEE Trans. Affect. Comput. **12**(2), 466–478 (2021)
3. Bird, S., Klein, E., Loper, E.: Natural Language Processing with Python: Analyzing Text with the Natural Language Toolkit. O'Reilly Media Inc., Sebastopol (2009)
4. Croce, D., Zelenanska, A., Basili, R.: Neural learning for question answering in Italian. In: Ghidini, C., Magnini, B., Passerini, A., Traverso, P. (eds.) AI*IA 2018 - Advances in Artificial Intelligence, pp. 389–402. Springer International Publishing, Cham (2018). https://doi.org/10.1007/978-3-030-03840-3_29
5. Devlin, J., Chang, M., Lee, K., Toutanova, K.: BERT: pre-training of deep bidirectional transformers for language understanding. In: Burstein, J., Doran, C., Solorio, T. (eds.) Proceedings of the 2019 Conference of the North American Chapter of the Association for Computational Linguistics: Human Language Technologies, NAACL-HLT 2019, Minneapolis, MN, USA, 2–7 June 2019, vol. 1 (Long and Short Papers), pp. 4171–4186. Association for Computational Linguistics (2019)
6. Ethayarajh, K.: How contextual are contextualized word representations? comparing the geometry of BERT, ELMo, and GPT-2 embeddings. In: Inui, K., Jiang, J., Ng, V., Wan, X. (eds.) Proceedings of the 2019 Conference on Empirical Methods in Natural Language Processing and the 9th International Joint Conference on Natural Language Processing, EMNLP-IJCNLP 2019, Hong Kong, China, 3–7 November 2019, pp. 55–65. Association for Computational Linguistics (2019)
7. Haller, S., Aldea, A., Seifert, C., Strisciuglio, N.: Survey on automated short answer grading with deep learning: from word embeddings to transformers. CoRR abs /2204.03503 (2022)
8. Hassan, S., Fahmy, A.A., El-Ramly, M.: Automatic short answer scoring based on paragraph embeddings. Int. J. Adv. Comput. Sci. Appl. **9**(10), 397–402 (2018). https://doi.org/10.14569/IJACSA.2018.091048
9. Ke, Z., Ng, V.: Automated essay scoring: a survey of the state of the art. In: Kraus, S. (ed.) Proceedings of the 28th International Joint Conference on Artificial Intelligence, IJCAI 2019, Macao, China, 10–16 August 2019, pp. 6300–6308. ijcai.org (2019). https://doi.org/10.24963/ijcai.2019/879
10. Mohler, M., Bunescu, R.C., Mihalcea, R.: Learning to grade short answer questions using semantic similarity measures and dependency graph alignments. In: Lin, D., Matsumoto, Y., Mihalcea, R. (eds.) The 49th Annual Meeting of the Association for Computational Linguistics: Human Language Technologies, Proceedings of the Conference, 19–24 June 2011, Portland, Oregon, USA, pp. 752–762. The Association for Computer Linguistics (2011)

11. Peters, M.E., et al.: Deep contextualized word representations. In: Walker, M.A., Ji, H., Stent, A. (eds.) Proceedings of the 2018 Conference of the North American Chapter of the Association for Computational Linguistics: Human Language Technologies, NAACL-HLT 2018, New Orleans, Louisiana, USA, June 1–6 2018, vol.1 (Long Papers), pp. 2227–2237. Association for Computational Linguistics (2018)

12. Polignano, M., Basile, P., De Gemmis, M., Semeraro, G., Basile, V.: Alberto: Italian BERT language understanding model for NLP challenging tasks based on tweets. In: 6th Italian Conference on Computational Linguistics, CLiC-it 2019, vol. 2481, pp. 1–6. CEUR (2019)

13. Prabhudesai, A., Duong, T.N.B.: Automatic short answer grading using siamese bidirectional LSTM based regression. In: IEEE International Conference on Engineering, Technology and Education, TALE 2019, Yogyakarta, Indonesia, 10–13 December 2019, pp. 1–6. IEEE (2019)

14. Pribadi, F.S., Adji, T.B., Permanasari, A.E., Mulwinda, A., Utomo, A.B.: Automatic short answer scoring using words overlapping methods. In: AIP Conference Proceedings, vol. 1818, no. 1 (2017)

15. Putelli, L., Gerevini, A.E., Lavelli, A., Maroldi, R., Serina, I.: Attention-based explanation in a deep learning model for classifying radiology reports. In: Tucker, A., Henriques Abreu, P., Cardoso, J., Pereira Rodrigues, P., Riaño, D. (eds.) AIME 2021. LNCS (LNAI), vol. 12721, pp. 367–372. Springer, Cham (2021). https://doi.org/10.1007/978-3-030-77211-6_42

16. Putelli, L., Gerevini, A.E., Lavelli, A., Olivato, M., Serina, I.: Deep learning for classification of radiology reports with a hierarchical schema. In: Cristani, M., Toro, C., Zanni-Merk, C., Howlett, R.J., Jain, L.C. (eds.) Knowledge-Based and Intelligent Information & Engineering Systems: Proceedings of the 24th International Conference KES-2020, Virtual Event, 16–18 September 2020. Procedia Computer Science, vol. 176, pp. 349–359. Elsevier (2020)

17. Reimers, N., Gurevych, I.: Sentence-bert: sentence embeddings using siamese BERT-Networks. In: Inui, K., Jiang, J., Ng, V., Wan, X. (eds.) Proceedings of the 2019 Conference on Empirical Methods in Natural Language Processing and the 9th International Joint Conference on Natural Language Processing, EMNLP-IJCNLP 2019, Hong Kong, China, 3–7 November 2019, pp. 3980–3990. Association for Computational Linguistics (2019)

18. Sung, C., Dhamecha, T.I., Saha, S., Ma, T., Reddy, V., Arora, R.: Pre-training BERT on domain resources for short answer grading. In: Inui, K., Jiang, J., Ng, V., Wan, X. (eds.) Proceedings of the 2019 Conference on Empirical Methods in Natural Language Processing and the 9th International Joint Conference on Natural Language Processing, EMNLP-IJCNLP 2019, Hong Kong, China, 3–7 November 2019, pp. 6070–6074. Association for Computational Linguistics (2019)

19. Suzen, N., Gorban, A.N., Levesley, J., Mirkes, E.M.: Automatic short answer grading and feedback using text mining methods. CoRR abs/1807.10543 (2018)

20. Tai, W., Kung, H.T., Dong, X., Comiter, M., Kuo, C.F.: exBERT: extending pre-trained models with domain-specific vocabulary under constrained training resources. In: Findings of the Association for Computational Linguistics: EMNLP 2020, pp. 1433–1439. Association for Computational Linguistics, Online (2020). https://doi.org/10.18653/v1/2020.findings-emnlp.129

21. Vaswani, A., et al.: Attention is all you need. In: Guyon, I., et al., (eds.) Advances in Neural Information Processing Systems 30: Annual Conference on Neural Information Processing Systems 2017, 4–9 December 2017, Long Beach, CA, USA, pp. 5998–6008 (2017)

22. Zhang, Z., Wu, Y., Zhao, H., Li, Z., Zhang, S., Zhou, X., Zhou, X.: Semantics-aware BERT for language understanding. In: The 34th AAAI Conference on Artificial Intelligence, AAAI 2020, The 32nd Innovative Applications of Artificial Intelligence Conference, IAAI 2020, The 10th AAAI Symposium on Educational Advances in Artificial Intelligence, EAAI 2020, New York, NY, USA, 7–12 February 2020, pp. 9628–9635. AAAI Press (2020)
23. Zubani, M., Sigalini, L., Serina, I., Gerevini, A.E.: Evaluating different natural language understanding services in a real business case for the italian language. Procedia Computer Science 176, 995–1004 (2020), knowledge-Based and Intelligent Information & Engineering Systems: Proceedings of the 24th International Conference KES2020
24. Zubani, M., Sigalini, L., Serina, I., Putelli, L., Gerevini, A.E., Chiari, M.: A performance comparison of different cloud-based natural language understanding services for an Italian e-learning platform. Future Internet 14(2), 62 (2022)

Embedding Contextual Information in Seq2seq Models for Grounded Semantic Role Labeling

Claudiu Daniel Hromei[1,2(✉)], Lorenzo Cristofori[1], Danilo Croce[1(✉)], and Roberto Basili[1(✉)]

[1] Department of Enterprise Engineering, University of Rome, Tor Vergata, Italy
{croce,basili}@info.uniroma2.it
[2] Università Campus Bio-Medico di Roma, Rome, Italy
claudiudaniel.hromei@unicampus.it

Abstract. Natural Language interactions between humans and robots are meant to be situated, in the sense that both the user and the robot can access and make reference to the shared environment. Contextual knowledge plays thus a key role in the solution of inherent ambiguities in interpretation tasks, such as Grounded Semantic Role Labeling (GSRL). Explicit representations for the context (i.e. the map description of the surroundings) are crucial and the possibility of injecting such information in the training stages of semantic interpreters is very appealing. In this paper, we propose to make a sequence-to-sequence model for GSRL, thus eliminating the traditional cascade of tasks and effectively linking real-world entities with their identifiers, that is sensitive to map information in form of linguistic descriptions. The corresponding generation process, based on BART, achieves results competitive with the state-of-the-art on the GSRL task.

Keywords: Grounded semantic role labeling · Human robot interaction · End to end sequence to sequence architectures · Robotics and perception

1 Introduction

Domestic robots are increasingly part of our daily experience, and Human-Robot Interaction (HRI) is becoming a concrete example of novel activities people are becoming aware of, as anticipated in [12]. Countless virtual assistants are being designed and used, both by large companies and individuals. Just think of Alexa, Google Assistant or Siri, which are more and more advanced and precise in natural language recognition so that users increasingly adopt them in home automation or information search tasks, or just for chatting and entertainment purposes.

In general, domestic robots are expected [10]: (i) to navigate and self-localize within an environment, (ii) to accurately recognize people and objects (through some vision capabilities), (iii) to properly manipulate physical items (Grasping) and (iv) to interact with human beings in meaningful fashion (Human-Robot Interaction). Each of these challenges involves a complex interplay among several capabilities (and so paradigms) crucial to the design of interactive robots. They are going to act interactively with

A. Dovier et al. (Eds.): AIxIA 2022, LNAI 13796, pp. 472–485, 2023.
https://doi.org/10.1007/978-3-031-27181-6_33

humans in everyday life, so processing human language is becoming a strict requirement. For naturally perceived robots, the expressiveness and flexibility of human languages are required in support of the ability of a robot to correctly interpret users' commands as well as their needs and expectations, consistent with the environment these commands are expressed in. A sentence like *"take the pen next to the monitor"* has different interpretations whether or not the pen is already placed next to the monitor: the pen should be *brought* next to the monitor, if it is not already there, while the speaker may be asking the robot to *take* it to him if it is already there, next to the monitor.

We foster here *Grounded language Understanding via Transformers (GrUT)*, a neural approach for the interpretation of robotic spoken commands[1] that is consistent with (i) the world (with all the entities therein), (ii) the robotic platform (with all its inner representations and capabilities), and (iii) the linguistic information derived from the user's utterance. Moreover, the main goal is to show and describe a sequence-to-sequence method that performs Grounded Semantic Role Labeling in an end-to-end manner, thus avoiding the traditional cascade of interpretation tasks to be solved and effectively linking arguments on the basis of the status and properties of the real-world.

In the remaining, in Sect. 2 the task of Semantic Role Labeling and the use of Transformers will be defined in terms of achievements in literature, Sect. 3 presents the proposed method, Sect. 4 reports the experimental evaluation with the results in Sect. 5, while Sect. 6 derives some conclusions.

2 Related Work

The full understanding of a human-generated utterance generally corresponds to the set of Semantic Role Labeling (SRL) tasks [19]: this consists in detecting all the expressed linguistic predicates (e.g., BRINGING vs TAKING evoked by the verb *to take*) and their corresponding semantic arguments (e.g., *"the pen"* or *"to the monitor"*). Since the seminal work of Gildea and Jurafsky [11], data-driven methods for SRL gained a lot of attention, up to several benchmarking campaigns [1,3,20]. As in [6,17,29], most of the approaches decompose the processing tasks in at least two steps: first, the target predicates are discovered and disambiguated; in a second step, for each predicate, the corresponding arguments are identified and classified with respect to their roles in the associated predicate. Often the latter only focuses on the semantic roles labeling, thus ignoring previous predicate identification and disambiguation steps.

This decomposition generally is still in use even after transformer-based models have been introduced in SRL since the seminal works of [25]: in [22,23] or [27] a pre-trained architecture, such as BERT [7], RoBERTa [16], BART [15] or T5 [21] are successfully applied, but always according to the above task decomposition. In [23] the authors show how BERT can be adapted to semantic role labeling without relying on syntactic features, while still obtaining state-of-the-art results. On the contrary, [22] shows the usefulness of incorporating dependency structures within the transformers, by exploiting a graph neural network stacked on BERT encodings: first a graph neural network is applied to the output of the transformers and then semantic structures are

---

[1] The code is available at https://github.com/crux82/grut.

imposed within the attention layers. Both approaches show results comparable with the state of the art. In [27] the two tasks of predicate disambiguation and argument labeling are modeled using RoBERTa with the PropBank corpus [18], showing how predicate disambiguation is helpful for the overall process.

The first approaches to propose an end-to-end architecture, which takes in input a plain text and applies T5 and BART to detect both predicates and arguments in a single step, are proposed in [2, 13], respectively. In a nutshell, T5 and BART receive in input a plain sentence while producing an artificial text, which allows deriving the complete set of predicates and roles. BART is used to identify the predicate by indicating to the GSRL model the token that evokes it, and similarly, the argument is identified by indicating its position within the sentence. The model was tested on CoNLL2012 [20].

In any case, all the above approaches only rely on linguistic evidences. In [28] Grounded Semantic Role Labeling (GSRL) is shown to promote correct interpretations in a specific environment that depend on the grounding of language symbols into the real world objects in the environment referred by the speaker. In the same work, a probabilistic model is proposed to make interpretations dependent on information extracted from the processing of images representing the environment. This idea is further stressed in [24] where the interpretation of commands for a domestic robot is dependent on the evidences the robot itself encodes in an explicit semantic map. It logically defines the environment, the contained objects as well as properties and relations that hold between them. Interestingly, texts are annotated according to the Frame Semantics theory [9], which [24] suggest can be used to be directly mapped toward primitives of robotic actions. However, [24] adopts the classical processing chain used in SRL. Moreover, their output still expresses just the linguistic level: while the interpretation depends on the associations between words and objects in the environment, the labeling only produces roles attached to words, not to real-world objects. As suggested in [24, 28], modern approaches to the interpretation of robotic spoken commands must be harmonized across several semantic dimensions, including at least: (i) *spatial awareness*, i.e. knowledge about the physical world in which the robot acts, (ii) *self-awareness*, that is the knowledge about its proper capabilities and limitations as a robotic platform, and (iii) *linguistic competence* needed to understand user's utterance and produce meaningful statements in response to stimuli or needs.

In this paper, we propose *GrUT* a sequence-to-sequence (seq2seq) approach for GSRL, sensitive to the map information in form of linguistic descriptions. The idea is: (i) to encode the information extracted from a map as in [24] and (ii) to provide a first end-to-end processing chain that takes in input a sentence and the description of a map and produces a predicative structure. In particular, the process is made end-to-end, thus eliminating the traditional cascade of tasks. To the best of our knowledge, this is the first end-to-end approach for SRL that is made dependent on the knowledge about the environment where the utterance is expressed: this thus extends recent works like [2, 13]. Results suggest that the straightforward application of a seq2seq model achieves state-of-the-art performances even with respect to far more complex processing chains based on handcrafted features.

3 Embedding Contextual Information in Seq2seq Models

Human Robotic Interaction assumes that the user and the robot can share information about the problem and the environment in which they operate. In [24], an explicit representation of the environment map is adopted. It provides a domain of interpretation for NL commands and enables the resolution of ambiguous references. In this work, we assume the use of linguistic descriptions of the map and apply a seq2seq approach to semantic interpretation according to a transformer-based approach. In line with [4], who demonstrates how to leverage the transformer to reason over language, we map descriptions in natural language and pair them directly to the user commands, as part of the structured input. The seq2seq process enables capturing the relationships between the referents in the user sentence and the entities of the map, by providing a logic form in output. As an example, the sentence:

$$\text{``}Take\ the\ pen\ next\ to\ the\ monitor\text{ ''} \tag{1}$$

has different interpretations depending on the status of the *pen* of the sentence PP:

$$[VP\ take\ [NP\ the\ pen\ [PP\ next\ to\ the\ monitor\ ]]] \tag{2}$$

$$[VP\ take\ [NP\ the\ pen]\ [PP\ next\ to\ the\ monitor\ ]] \tag{3}$$

Notice that the two interpretations strictly depend on the position of the pen in the environment. If the pen is *already* next to the monitor, so the command is to be intended as a request to bring it from that place to the speaker. On the contrary, if the pen is not next to the monitor, then the robot is requested to move it there. Notice that the two situations are described by two different frames (BRINGING vs TAKING) [9]. "Grounding" is defined as the process of establishing what shared information is necessary for successful communication. In our HRI scenario, a minimal set of shared information involves the physical properties of the objects populating the robot operating environment. Grounding a command thus consists in sharing the definition and type of the surrounding entities (e.g. "*pen*" is a kind of writing instrument), their spatial location (such as the proximity of the "*pen*" and the "*monitor*"), possible synonymous referring expressions (such as "*pen*" or "*marker*") and their properties, like the contain ability (which is false for the "*pen*", but true for objects such as a "*bottle*").

As in [24], *GrUT* makes use of a purpose-built world map describing the surrounding elements. It should be derivable from the perception of the physical robot. Surrounding elements can be added by a knowledge engineer according to ontological assumptions (e.g. entities, classes, properties and domains). However, they could be acquired through dialogue with the user, assumed to explain, name and demonstrate the objects. In both situations, we give for granted the body of knowledge related to the environment. The idea is to use it *during the interpretation* in order to meaningfully disambiguate competing interpretations and produce accurate *grounded logic forms*. The idea pursued in this work is that the compilation of the grounded logic form glf, expressing the interpretation of command c, should be seen as the rewriting $\mathcal{M}(c) = glf$. Notice that the command is in natural language so the rewriting is mapped into a translation task. However, the need for the map information makes the input to $\mathcal{M}$ the pair (sd, c) combining the map spatial description sd and the user command c so that

$\mathcal{M}(sd, c) = glf$ and glf is the grounded logic form for c. Our proposal in this paper is to design a linguistic description lsd corresponding to each map sd. In this way, the overall rewriting task corresponds to a plain translation, i.e. $\mathcal{M}(lsd, c) = glf$ whereas the pair (lsd, c) gives rise to a micro-story for the robot, whose direct interpretation is the suitable ambiguity-free grounded logic form glf.

3.1   Describing a Map in Natural Language

As already discussed, the description of the surroundings, referred to as 'the map' in *GrUT*, plays a major role in the prediction of the predicative form for the robot's command. Much of the previous work using transformer-based architectures approached knowledge injection in form of input graphs or synthetic descriptions both during pre-training and/or fine-tuning [8,14,26]. The idea behind this paper is to use a natural language description of the map and append it to the input sentence, as also suggested in [4] in tasks of analogical reasoning. In our setting, one entity is known through its (English) noun (possibly its most commonly used lexical reference, e.g. the word *pen*) as well as its conceptual type. The association with the environment (i.e. the grounding) is realized through its identifier (Existence Constraint, *EC*) that is linked to the position of the corresponding physical object in the environment. For example, the map to be paired with the command in (1) can give rise to the following description:

EC: "p1, also known as pen or marker, is an instance of the class PEN *and m1, also known as monitor, is an instance of the class* MONITOR*."*.

Moreover, if the pen $p1$ and the monitor $m1$ are close to each other in the environment, a further declaration of a Proximity Constraint (*PC*) acting over them will be added:

PC: "p1 is near m1"

Finally, for each selected entity, a description of whether the property of containing other objects is true (Containability Constraint, *CC*) will be added. For illustrative purposes, imagine the existence of a hypothetical cup $c1$:

CC: "c1 can contain other objects"

The entire description is a micro-story[2] useful for the SRL model to disambiguate between the different situations in (2) and (3). Notice that only when the spatial constraint *PC* is true the correct interpretation for the ambiguous situation (1) is driven by the syntax (2) and finally corresponds to the role labeled logical form:

$$\text{TAKING}(\text{THEME}(\textit{"the pen next to the monitor"})).$$

As the pen $p1$, referenced through the monitor, is close to $m1$, it is interpreted thus as the THEME of the TAKING predicate. It is worth noticing that the linguistic description of the map enables the use of highly accurate transformers (such as BART [15] and T5 [21]). These are pre-trained on large natural language corpora and may take advantage of linguistic features, relationships and cross-dependencies to properly carry out SRL on the overall textual examples made by the informative pairs in *GrUT*. The extraction algorithm acting over a map, given a command c is reported in Algorithm 1.

---

[2] All the constraints are appended to the input, each of which is divided by a "#" delimiter character.

Algorithm 1. *GrUT* compilation Algorithm

1: **procedure** CONSTRUCT_INPUT(*Sentence* $s = (w_1, ..., w_{|s|})$)
2:     *Entities* $\leftarrow \emptyset$
3:     **for** $i = 1, ..., |s|$ **do**
4:         *Entities* $\leftarrow$ *Entities* $\cup$ *get_candidate_entity*(w_i)

5:     $ec \leftarrow$ "" $\qquad\qquad\qquad\qquad\qquad\qquad\qquad\qquad$ ▷ Existence Constraints
6:     **for** $e \in$ *Entities* **do**
7:         $ec \leftarrow ec+$" # "$+get\_ref(e)+$" also known as "$+get\_lexical\_ref(e)+$
8:                           " is an instance of class "$+get\_class(e)$

9:     $cc \leftarrow$ "" $\qquad\qquad\qquad\qquad\qquad\qquad\qquad$ ▷ Containability Constraints
10:     **for** $e \in$ *Entities* **do**
11:         **if** *containability*(e) **then**
12:             $cc \leftarrow cc+$" # "$+get\_ref(e)+$" can contain other objects"

13:     $pc \leftarrow$ "" $\qquad\qquad\qquad\qquad\qquad\qquad\qquad\qquad$ ▷ Proximity Constraints
14:     **for** $e_1 \in$ *Entities* **do**
15:         **for** $e_2 \in$ *Entities* **do**
16:             **if** $e_1 \neq e_2 \wedge distance(e_1, e_2) < \tau$ **then**
17:                 $pc \leftarrow pc+$" # "$+get\_ref(e_1)+$" is near "$+get\_ref(e_2)$

18:         *Entities* $\leftarrow$ *Entities* $- \{e_1\}$
19:     **return** $s + ec + pc + cc$

3.2 Embedding Frame Semantics

As demonstrated in [4], it is possible to inject knowledge during the training of Transformer based models by adding it directly to the input. Similarly, since SRL is strongly rooted in linguistic theories, such as Frame Semantics, we propose to inject such knowledge by adding textual information about Frames and Lexical Units to the command itself. This would make all the potential frames related to any lexical unit in the command explicit: the resulting sentence enriches the input in order to allow the Transformer to learn properties and relations concerning frames and their potential roles. It is useful to prime the frame annotation in the output and solve possible underlying ambiguities.

For example, for the phrase "*take the book*", the following description will be added: "*take can evoke TAKING or BRINGING*"[3]. While for "*go along with me*" the resulting description would be: "*go along can evoke COTHEME*". Notice how the verb "*take*" evokes different Frames that can be disambiguated only according to the input command.

---

[3] The frames connected with a lexical unit, such as *take*, are only the ones in FrameNet that are needed in the domain knowledge base: $TAKING$ and $BRINGING$ are the only frames for *take* that are possible, i.e. defined, in the Huric dataset, dealing with the robotic command language.

4   Experimental Evaluation

The impact of the proposed approach on the semantic interpretation of user utterances has been evaluated in a house Service Robotics scenario. The evaluation is carried out using the Human-Robot Interaction Corpus 2.0 (HuRIC[4]). Its 656 English utterances are paired with interpretations relative to explicit logically described maps as discussed in [24]. Quantitative SRL measures can be thus carried out about different SRL aspects and the results obtained in every run are reported in terms of F-Measure (F1). We adopted a 10-fold cross-validation schema with 80/10/10 data split between training/validation/test.

We are interested at least in the Frame Prediction (FP) task that accounts for the correctly recognized frames in a command. Moreover, the end-to-end task is achieved when also Argument Identification and Classification (AIC) is accomplished. AIC aims to recognize the arguments of an evoked frame in the input command c, and link segments in c to individual arguments. In Service Robotics, this process allows to identify individual entities in the map and assign them a role in the frame. In the command with interpretation (3), i.e. BRINGING, AIC maps *the monitor* to the GOAL argument of the frame. Notice that this is different from the potential role SOURCE in a TAKING frame (interpretation (2)). In particular, the evaluation of the AIC task will be of two types: *Exact Match* (AIC-EM), in which it is required that all the participating words of the Argument are correctly associated with it; *Head Match* (AIC-HM), in which arguments are accepted only if the Argument's segment include the correct semantic head. For example, when the SRL of the phrase "*take the book*" is TAKING(THEME("*book*")) then in AIC-EM will receive a score of 0, as *book* instead of the entire correct span, that is "*the book*", is associated to the THEME argument. On the contrary, in AIC-HM it will be 1 as *book* corresponds to the argument's head. Notice that while previous approaches apply independent models to the FP and AIC independent tasks, in the *GrUT* approach we propose them as side effects of a single (monolithic) rewriting process. The resulting single transformer shares weights across the two tasks and it is fine-tuned against both of them, simultaneously. Notice that the solution of such two sub-tasks results in a full interpretation of the input commands of a real scenario.

4.1   Testing Different Types of Input

The input of the transformer consists of the user sentence and possibly various pieces of information, including the natural language description of the map as in Sect. 3.1, the description of the lexical units (LU Descriptions) present in the text, as in Sect. 3.2. The goal is to test the contribution on the output of these limited changes to the input and decide on the best configuration. All the models we trained are described below.

- $BART_{base}$: the linguistic command alone is given to the model
- $GrUT$: the linguistic map description is added to the user sentence
- $GrUT_{LU}$: in addition to $GrUT$, the descriptions of every frame and lexical unit (LU) triggered by the input are added to the command

---

[4] https://github.com/crux82/huric.

Table 1. Input and Output examples for every model we trained.

Model	Input	Output
$BART_{base}$	*"take the pen next to the monitor"*	TAKING(THEME(*"the pen"*))
$GrUT$	*"take the pen next to the monitor # p1, also known as pen or marker, is an instance of the class PEN and m1, also known as monitor, is an instance of the class MONITOR # p1 is near m1"*	TAKING(THEME(*"the pen"*))
$GrUT_{LU}$	*"take the pen next to the monitor # take can evoke TAKING or BRINGING # p1, also known as pen or marker, is an instance of the class PEN and m1, also known as monitor, is an instance of the class MONITOR # p1 is near m1"*	TAKING(THEME(*"the pen"*))

In Table 1, we report some examples for every model we trained, with the input and output. The $BART_{base}$ model will only exploit linguistic information to produce the SRL output, so it can be expected to be the simplest one. For example, for the sentence *"take the pen next to the monitor"*, the $BART_{base}$ model will have to choose between two frames (BRINGING and TAKING) with no prior knowledge other than the information derived from the training instances. The $GrUT_{LU}$ derives instead this information directly from the input and only proceeds to disambiguate it. Moreover, both models have to decide the role of the argument *"monitor"*, i.e. GOAL vs. SOURCE. This depends on how close the *"pen"* is to the *"monitor"* in the environment. In fact, if they are close in the map, then the correct role assignment is SOURCE, and GOAL would be considered as incorrect labeling. On the contrary, if they are far, the opposite is true. Notice that $GrUT$ and $GrUT_{LU}$ are aware of the map given the existential (*EC*) and proximity (*PC*) evidence compiled into the input text. Table 2 shows the values of the main parameters used to train the models, estimated by a grid search policy.

5 Results

The accuracy measures are reported in Table 3. We compared with Lu4R [24], reported here in the first row, as it is currently state of the art for SRL on this dataset. In general, all BART-based models are comparable with Lu4R on the FP task and work much better on the AIC task. Notice that FP is modeled in LU4R as an independent task, for which specific supervised learning is carried out. On the contrary, for the seq2seq models, FP is just a side effect. As we will see, errors in FP introduced by these last systems are not always undesirable. The second row refers to the results of the $BART_{base}$ model. Notice how a very high accuracy is achieved although it is trained just on the textual features of the command: the Transformer alone seems capable of capturing most of the relations and properties of the commands. In the third row, we report about the model *GrUT* here proposed, which is trained on commands and linguistic map descriptions introduced in 3.1: *GrUT* improves the performance of Lu4R on the end-to-end tasks,

Table 2. Summary of models parameters estimated with a grid search policy.

Param name	Value
Optimizer	AdamW
Learning rate	5e–5
Early_stopping_delta	1e–4
Early_stopping_metric	eval_loss
Batch_size	16
Gradient_accumulation_steps	2
Early_stopping_patience	3
Scheduler	linear_schedule_with_warmup
Warmup Ratio	0.1
Max_length	96
Epochs	50(max)

both on *AIC-Exact Match* and *AIC-Head Match* (+5% and +2% in error reduction, respectively). This confirms the initial hypothesis that map descriptions are crucial for the proper interpretation. In the last row, we report on $GrUT_{LU}$, trained on commands, map descriptions as well as Frame Semantics information, as defined in 3.2: $GrUT_{LU}$ shows slight improvements on the Frame Prediction task, while not impacting positively on the EM and HM measures of the end-to-end task.

Table 3. Comparative evaluation on the Frame Prediction FP, Argument Identification and Classification AIC tasks of the different SRL models: Exact Match (*EM*) and Head Match (*HM*) are the different metrics for AIC.

Model	FP	AIC-EM	AIC-HM
$LU4R$ [24]	**95.94%**	87.77%	93.11%
$BART_{base}$	91.29%	84.26%	91.24%
$GrUT$	93.28%	**88.41%**	**93.29%**
$GrUT_{LU}$	93.34%	86.61%	92.00%

Overall, the results show that an end-to-end approach to SRL is viable and its performances are still state-of-the-art. Although LU4R adopts the specific training of independent FP and AIC classifiers, performances can still be improved by the proposed seq2seq approach. Notice that LU4R corresponds to a cascade of three classification steps, as AIC is carried out through the composition of two stages: the boundary detection (as Argument Identification) and the argument classification (AC) steps. In $GrUT$ and $GrUT_{LU}$ these three independent inferences are the side effect of one monolithic rewriting process, also responsible for the logic form compilation. The quality of the AIC task of the $GrUT$ model establishes a new state-of-the-art.

The availability of the map description, as defined in Sect. 3.1, is always beneficial, as the $GrUT$ and $GrUT_{LU}$ outcomes are significant improvements of the base BART approach: an error reduction of 26% and 15%, respectively, is observed with respect to $BART_{base}$.

Finally, the frame and lexical unit evidence available in the $GrUT_{LU}$ approach is a strong improvement of the BART base model: from 91.29% to 93.34%, we observe an error reduction of 23.53%. A drop in accuracy for $GrUT_{LU}$ is instead observable in the FP and AIC task if compared with LU4R and in the AIC task only if compared with $GrUT$. It seems that descriptions of Lexical Units enrich the available text too much, so to provide somehow misleading information. Examples of such phenomena are cases when the model seems to depend too much on the LU descriptions. For instance, the correct SRL for the input *"go get my book from the shelf"* is:

BRINGING(THEME(*"my book"*), SOURCE(*"the shelf"*)).

Adding the Lexical Units Description to the input we get *"go can evoke MOTION and get can evoke BRINGING"* as the input text. Unfortunately, it results in a wrong SRL, i.e.:

MOTION(GOAL(*"the shelf"*)&BRINGING(THEME(*"my book"*))).

Overall, the different logical form does not impact the behaviour of the robot, as the planning implied by both forms is the same: first the robot has to move towards the shelf and then bring the book to the user. Notice that these cases penalize only the performance score of the $GrUT_{LU}$ model for both FP and AIC tasks. However, such lower performances (e.g. with respect to the simpler counterpart $GrUT$) do not hurt the overall semantic capabilities of the neural system.

The Role of the Map Descriptions. In order to study the impact of map descriptions and confirm they are crucial, we studied cases where spatial relationships between entities are responsible for the identification of the suitable frame.

A subset of 34 complex sentences has been selected, for which different interpretations were specifically depending on the spatial relations of the corresponding map. This small dataset can be used to compare $BART_{base}$ and $GrUT$, in order to asses the impact of Map Descriptions on the Semantic Role Labeling quality.

In Table 4, some of such sentences are reported. The first column contains the command, as transcribed from speech; "Map Description" contains the description compiled by Algorithm 1 and "Output" is the desired (gold) interpretation. This test set is suitable for evaluating the contribution of the proposed $GrUT$ approach. For example, in the sentence in the first row, the correct interpretation is TAKING (instead of alternatively BRINGING) just on the basis of the position ($near$) of entities $s5$ (*"phone"*), $s4$ (*"table"*) and $a1$ (*"tv"*). In the second sentence, *"table"* is the filler of the GOAL argument of PLACING instead of the fragment *"dining room"*. This is totally justified by the fact that the table $h6$ is far from the bottle $p2$: in fact, every non mentioned $near$ relationship is negated in the map description.

On these restricted 34 instance dataset, an improvement of about 12% in F1 (from 78% to 90%) is obtained by $GrUT$ with respect to the baseline $BART_{base}$ model. This

Table 4. Examples of sentences for which map descriptions are crucial to the correct identification of the evoked Frames and respective Arguments.

Sentence	Map description	Output
take the phone near the tv on the table	s5, also known as phone or cellphone, is an instance of class PHONE and a1, also known as television, is an instance of class TELEVISION and s4, also known as table, is an instance of class TABLE # <u>s5 is near a1</u> & <u>s5 is near s4</u> & <u>a1 is near s4</u>	TAKING(THEME("*the phone*"))
put the bottle on the table in the dining room	p2, also known as bottle or nursing bottle, is an instance of class BOTTLE and h6, also known as table, is an instance of class TABLE	PLACING(THEME("*the bottle*"), GOAL("*on the table*"))
please robot take the box on the table on the couch	t3, also known as box or crate, is an instance of class BOX and d1, also known as table, is an instance of class TABLE and i4, also known as couch or sofa, is an instance of class COUCH # <u>t3 is near d1</u>	BINGING(THEME("*the box*"), GOAL("*on the couch*"))

Table 5. Error analysis table: Input is *GrUT* model input, Target is the expected SRL in logical form (the so called *gold*) and Prediction is the model output.

Input	Target	Prediction
leave the book in the bedroom # n8, also known as book or booklet, is an instance of class BOOK and f9, also known as bedroom, is an instance of class BEDROOM	RELEASING(THEME("*the book*"), GOAL("*the bedroom*"))	PLACING(THEME("*the book*"), GOAL("*the bedroom*"))
put the bottle on the table in the studio # d3, also known as bottle or nursing bottle, is an instance of class BOTTLE and e5, also known as table, is an instance of class TABLE and s3, also known as studio, is an instance of class STUDIO # e5 is near s3 # d3 can contain other objects	PLACING(THEME("*the bottle*"), GOAL("*the table*"))	PLACING(THEME("*the bottle*"), GOAL("*the studio*"))
could you please move forward # t2, also known as robot or you, is an instance of class ROBOT	MOTION(THEME("*you*"), DIRECTION("*forward*"))	MOTION(THEME("*you*"), GOAL("*forward*"))

shows that the Transformer is able to successfully learn spatial constraints from distance relationships in the map.

Error Analysis. Even though the Transformers introduce some errors in the FP predictions, interpretations are acceptable and roughly equivalents, from the semantic standpoint, to the gold ones. We report some examples below where 3 main classes of errors are shown.

In *FP errors*, as the first row in Table 5, predicted frames can be wrong: notice how close meanings are usually produced preserving intended and useful senses. *Arguments errors*, such as in third row in Table 5, are characterized by wrong argument labels (e.g. GOAL instead of DIRECTION) assigned to the correct spans (i.e. *"forward"*). Notice how close is the whole predicted command to the gold standard command (i.e. the DIRECTION is the GOAL). Finally, *Span errors*, as in the second row, are cases when the model assigns the wrong span, e.g. *"the studio"*, instead of the correct one , e.g.*"the table"*, to a given argument type, i.e. GOAL. These are the most dangerous ones and should be avoided, although, usually, the logical structure is fully preserved.

6 Conclusions

In this paper, the *Grounded language Understanding via Transformers* (*GrUT*) model is introduced, as a novel approach to embedding Contextual Information in sequence to sequence neural models. It addresses the Semantic Role Labeling task in an end-to-end fashion, thus eliminating the need of the cascade of classification and labeling tasks, usually applied in HRIs. The output is a logical form of the command making frames and arguments explicit. In *GrUT* spatial and lexical semantic information needed for the correct interpretation of the command is made available as an extension of the textual input. The extension describes the map of the environment and frame semantics information, respectively. First, the semantic map of the environment is translated: it is a description of the operational context of the robot, expressing information about the existence and position of different entities present in the surroundings of the robot. The text also describes semantic properties (e.g. *containability*) as well as relative spatial positions, in terms of binary, e.g. *near*, predicates between objects. Second, lexical semantics information regarding the Frames evoked by potential lexical units in the command is also added to the command. It textually represents the FrameNet information specifically evoked by the input. The resulting text extends the robotic command and is useful to leverage the ability of large transformer models to capture semantics via the correlations across different text fragments. The models thus designed have been tested over annotated HRI datasets publicly available. The comparative analysis shows that improvements up to the 5% error reduction wrt existing state-of-the-art models over the same datasets can be obtained. Moreover, *GrUT* is also more effective than a direct application of BART (about 26% error reduction in argument recognition) establishing its significant superiority among seq2seq transformer-based approaches.

The large applicability of the method suggests that improvements in grounded SRL can be obtained on the application side. In the future, an investigation on the grounding capabilities made possible by the neural rewriting process supported by *GrUT* will be carried out. It will further explore the flexibility of the proposed seq2seq approach along the dimension of multilinguality. Moreover, the capability of directly compiling ground variables, as reference to entity in the map (e.g. $e1$), will be experimented, in order to foster the integration of semantic maps with complete logical forms. Finally, the applicability of *GrUT* in a more real scenario, i.e. involving the real Human Robot Interaction as in [5] will be investigated.

Acknowledgement. We would like to thank the "Istituto di Analisi dei Sistemi ed Informatica - Antonio Ruberti" (IASI) for supporting the experimentations through access to dedicated computing resources. Claudiu Daniel Hromei is a Ph.D. student enrolled in the National Ph.D. in Artificial Intelligence, XXXVII cycle, course on *Health and life sciences*, organized by the Università Campus Bio-Medico di Roma.

References

1. Baker, C., Ellsworth, M., Erk, K.: SemEval-2007 task 19: frame semantic structure extraction. In: Proceedings of the Fourth International Workshop on Semantic Evaluations (SemEval-2007), pp. 99–104. Association for Computational Linguistics, Prague (2007)
2. Blloshmi, R., Conia, S., Tripodi, R., Navigli, R.: Generating senses and roles: an end-to-end model for dependency- and span-based semantic role labeling. In: IJCAI (2021)
3. Carreras, X., Màrquez, L.: Introduction to the CoNLL-2005 shared task: semantic role labeling. In: Proceedings of the Ninth Conference on Computational Natural Language Learning (CoNLL-2005), pp. 152–164. Association for Computational Linguistics, Ann Arbor (2005)
4. Clark, P., Tafjord, O., Richardson, K.: Transformers as soft reasoners over language. arXiv preprint arXiv:2002.05867 (2020)
5. Cristofori, L., et al.: Heal9000: an intelligent rehabilitation robot. In: Lucas, P., Stella, F. (eds.) Proceedings of the Workshop on Towards Smarter Health Care: Can Artificial Intelligence Help? co-located with 20th International Conference of the Italian Association for Artificial Intelligence (AIxIA2021), Anywhere, November 29th, 2021. CEUR Workshop Proceedings, vol. 3060, pp. 29–41. CEUR-WS.org (2021)
6. Das, D., Chen, D., Martins, A.F.T., Schneider, N., Smith, N.A.: Frame-semantic parsing. Comput. Linguist. **40**(1), 9–56 (2014)
7. Devlin, J., Chang, M.W., Lee, K., Toutanova, K.: Bert: pre-training of deep bidirectional transformers for language understanding. arXiv preprint arXiv:1810.04805 (2018)
8. Fan, Z., et al.: An enhanced knowledge injection model for commonsense generation. arXiv preprint arXiv:2012.00366 (2020)
9. Fillmore, C.J.: Frames and the semantics of understanding. Quaderni di Semantica **6**(2), 222–254 (1985)
10. Foster, M.E.: Natural language generation for social robotics: opportunities and challenges. Phil. Trans. Roy. Soc. B: Biol. Sci. **374**(1771), 20180027 (2019)
11. Gildea, D., Jurafsky, D.: Automatic labeling of semantic roles. Comput. Linguist. **28**(3), 245–288 (2002)
12. Goodrich, M.A., Schultz, A.C.: Human-robot interaction: a survey. Found. Trends Hum.-Comput. Interact. **1**(3), 203–275 (2007)
13. Kalyanpur, A., et al.: Open-domain frame semantic parsing using transformers (2020)
14. Lauscher, A., Majewska, O., Ribeiro, L.F.R., Gurevych, I., Rozanov, N., Glavas, G.: Common sense or world knowledge? investigating adapter-based knowledge injection into pretrained transformers. CoRR abs/2005.11787 (2020)
15. Lewis, M., et al.: Bart: denoising sequence-to-sequence pre-training for natural language generation, translation, and comprehension. ArXiv abs/1910.13461 (2020)
16. Liu, Y., et al.: Roberta: a robustly optimized BERT pretraining approach. CoRR abs/1907.11692 (2019)
17. Marcheggiani, D., Titov, I.: Encoding sentences with graph convolutional networks for semantic role labeling. In: Proceedings of the 2017 Conference on Empirical Methods in Natural Language Processing, pp. 1506–1515. Association for Computational Linguistics, Copenhagen (2017)

18. Palmer, M., Gildea, D., Kingsbury, P.: The proposition bank: an annotated corpus of semantic roles. Comput. Linguist. **31**(1), 71–106 (2005)
19. Palmer, M., Gildea, D., Xue, N.: Semantic Role Labeling: Synthesis Lectures on Human Language Technologies. Morgan & Claypool Publishers (2010)
20. Pradhan, S., Moschitti, A., Xue, N., Uryupina, O., Zhang, Y.: Conll-2012 shared task: modeling multilingual unrestricted coreference in ontonotes. In: Joint Conference on EMNLP and CoNLL-Shared Task, pp. 1–40 (2012)
21. Raffel, C., et al.: Exploring the limits of transfer learning with a unified text-to-text transformer. ArXiv abs/1910.10683 (2020)
22. Sachan, D.S., Zhang, Y., Qi, P., Hamilton, W.: Do syntax trees help pre-trained transformers extract information? arXiv preprint arXiv:2008.09084 (2020)
23. Shi, P., Lin, J.: Simple bert models for relation extraction and semantic role labeling. arXiv preprint arXiv:1904.05255 (2019)
24. Vanzo, A., Croce, D., Bastianelli, E., Basili, R., Nardi, D.: Grounded language interpretation of robotic commands through structured learning. Artif. Intell. **278**, 103181 (2020)
25. Vaswani, A., et al.: Attention is all you need. In: Guyon, I., Luxburg, U.V., Bengio, S., Wallach, H., Fergus, R., Vishwanathan, S., Garnett, R. (eds.) Advances in Neural Information Processing Systems, vol. 30. Curran Associates, Inc. (2017)
26. Wahab, A., Sifa, R.: DIBERT: dependency injected bidirectional encoder representations from transformers. In: IEEE Symposium Series on Computational Intelligence, SSCI 2021, Orlando, FL, USA, 5–7 December 2021, pp. 1–8. IEEE (2021)
27. Wang, N., Li, J., Meng, Y., Sun, X., He, J.: An mrc framework for semantic role labeling. arXiv preprint arXiv:2109.06660 (2021)
28. Yang, S., Gao, Q., Liu, C., Xiong, C., Zhu, S.C., Chai, J.Y.: Grounded semantic role labeling. In: Proceedings of the 2016 Conference of the North American Chapter of the Association for Computational Linguistics: Human Language Technologies, pp. 149–159. Association for Computational Linguistics, San Diego (2016)
29. Zhou, J., Xu, W.: End-to-end learning of semantic role labeling using recurrent neural networks. In: Proceedings of the 53rd Annual Meeting of the Association for Computational Linguistics and the 7th International Joint Conference on Natural Language Processing, vol. 1: Long Papers, pp. 1127–1137. Association for Computational Linguistics, Beijing (2015)

Keynote talk

Adventures with Datalog: Walking the Thin Line Between Theory and Practice

Georg Gottlob[⊠]

Department of Computer Science, University of Oxford, Oxford, UK
georg.gottlob@cs.ox.ac.uk

Abstract. This keynote paper features a concise introduction to Datalog, which is followed by an overview of some theoretical results about the complexity and expressive power of a number of Datalog variants. This will be interleaved with a tale of four Datalog-related companies co-founded by the author: DLVSystem, Lixto, Wrapidity, and DeepReason.ai.

Keywords: Datalog · Complexity · Logic · Expressive power · Applications

Datalog. Datalog [2,7,22,23] is a rule-based logical query and programming language whose rules (in the basic version) syntactically coincide with universally quantified function-free Horn clauses. Datalog is a language tailored for relational databases and assumes an *extensional database (EDB)*, for example, an enterprise database, whose tables correspond to so-called EDB predicates, that are (usually) read-only for a Datalog program. From such an EDB, a Datalog program computes an *intensional database (IDB)* which consists of relational instances of the so-called EDB predicates in the program. For example, if *parent* is a binary EDB relation where *parent(X, Y)* expresses that X is a parent of Y, then the following Datalog program computes the IDB relation *ancestor*, which is the transitive closure of *parent*

$$\text{ancestor(X,Y) :- parent(X,Y);}$$
$$\text{ancestor(X,Z) :- parent(X,Y), ancestor(Y,Z).}$$

Syntactically, the program corresponds to a conjunction of its two rules, and each rule corresponds to a first-order sentence. For example, the second rule is a syntactic equivalent of the first-order sentence $\forall X \, \forall Y \, \forall Z \, ((parent(X, Y) \land ancestor(Y, Z) \rightarrow ancestor(X, Z)))$. However, semantically, Datalog transcends first-order logic as, for example, the transitive closure of a relation (rather than its transitivity) is not first-order definable.

In the context of Datalog, interpretations are identified with sets of ground atoms whose predicate symbols are EDB or IDB predicate symbols, and whose

A. Dovier et al. (Eds.): AIxIA 2022, LNAI 13796, pp. 489–500, 2023.
https://doi.org/10.1007/978-3-031-27181-6_34

arguments range over the finite set of data elements in the EDB and in the program. The standard semantics of Datalog singles out as unique "designated" model for a program P with a given EDB D, the unique minimal model of $P^* \wedge D^*$ where P^* denotes the syntactical logical equivalent of a Datalog program P, as explained above, and where D^* is the conjunction of all ground atoms in D. This can be formulated in second-order logic and in fixed-point logic. An equivalent way of defining the semantics of Datalog is via first-order entailment (well-known not to be first-order definable): Let P be an EDB predicate, then a ground fact γ of the form $P(t_1, \ldots, t_n)$ is in the designated model of P and EDB iff $P^* \wedge D^* \models \gamma$. The latter is also denoted by $(P, D) \models \gamma$.

An essential decision problem for Datalog is the *atom entailment problem (AEP)*, to determine, for a Datalog program P, a database D, and a ground atom γ, (also called "the goal") whether $P^* \wedge D^* \models \gamma$, equivalently written as $(P, D)) \models \gamma$. The AEP is easily seen to be decidable. For assessing the complexity of this problem, one suitably distinguishes according to Vardi [49] between the *combined complexity*, where P, D and γ are given as input, and the *data complexity*, P and γ are fixed while D is the input[1]. Measuring the data complexity has become the standard method for assessing the complexity of query languages. This makes much sense, as databases are usually much larger objects than programs and queries, and there are many applications where a same fixed query is executed over varying (and often growing) databases – think of the typical queries made by accounting department companies. We here focus mostly on data complexity. As already observed by Vardi, the combined complexity of a database language "is usually one exponential higher than the data complexity[2]" [49]. For a survey on the complexity of various versions of logic programming and Datalog, see [26].

Datalog has been extended by various features, some of which are discussed further below. One important feature is negation in rule bodies. Here a safety condition is imposed: each variables of a negated atom also needs to occur in a positive atom of the same rule body. The most restricted form of negation is *semipositive negation*, where only EDB-atoms may be negated. It follows from results by Vardi [49] that, over (linearly) ordered structures, semipositive Datalog programs "capture" polynomial time (PTIME). In particular, which means that (i) semipositive Datalog programs (i.e., Datalog Programs with semipositive negation) can be evaluated in PTIME, and (ii) every PTIME query over ordered structures can be expressed as a semipositive Datalog program (and actually as a query in the fragment of fixed-point logic corresponding to Datalog). A similar result was shown independently by Immerman [41], and more explicitly for the second-order Horn fragment corresponding to Datalog by Grädel [40]. Other types of negation that have been added to Datalog include, for example, the *stratified negation* [3] and the more powerful *well-founded negation* [48], which both preserve tractable reasoning and query answering and both compute a sin-

---

[1] As γ is of the size of a single database atom only, it may equally be part of the input, without any effect whatsoever on the complexity.

[2] Vardi actually made this statement for a related setting.

gle "designated" model ($=$ EDB $\cup$ IDB) consisting of ground facts defined to be "certain consequences" of a given EDB and program with semi-positive negation.

A yet more powerful semantics for negation based on *multiple* designated models is the well-known *stable models semantics (SMS)* [32]. Let I be an interpretation for P over an EDB D. Then I is a *stable model* of (P, D) if (1) I is a model of $P^* \wedge EDB^*$ and (2) I is the unique minimal model of the negation-free propositional Datalog program $GL(P_{ground}, I)$ jointly with D, where P_{ground} is the *ground instantiation* of P resulting from P by replacing each rule ρ of P by all rules arising from the replacement of ρ by a uniform replacement of the variables of ρ by domain elements occurring in EDB and P, and where $GL(P_{ground}, I)$ is the so-called *Gelfond-Lifschitz reduct* of P_{ground}. This reduct is obtained from P_{ground} by (a) eliminating all rules whose body is not satisfied in I, and by then eliminating all negative atoms from the remaining rules. Deciding whether (P, D) has a stable model is NP-complete, and deciding whether a ground fact γ is a *certain consequence* of (P, D), i.e., if γ is in *all* stable models of (P, D), is co-NP-complete in data complexity. For references and more details, see [26].

In the rest of this short survey we illustrate some theoretical results by the author and his co-workers on various other extensions and restrictions of Datalog that gave rise to software further developed by start-ups and used in various industries.

Disjunctive Datalog, DLV, and the DLVSystem Company. Disjunctive logic programming (see [43,45]) and, in particular, disjunctive Datalog, extend the basic formalism by the possibility of disjunctions in rule heads. This extension is useful for directly modelling many real-life situations. For example, in disjunctive Datalog, one may write a rule of the form
Employee(X) $\vee$ Consultant(X) :- collaborator(X), which means that each collaborator (e.g. of a given company) must be an employee or a consultant. The SMS has been extended to disjunctive logic programming [47], and its definition is similar to the above SMS definition for non-disjunctive clauses, but where in condition (2), the half-sentence "I is the unique minimal model of the negation-free propositional Datalog program" is replaced by "I is *a* minimal model of the negation-free disjunctive propositional Datalog program". Based on various complexity results on disjunctive logic programming [27–29], the expressive power of disjunctive Datalog under the SMS was investigated in [30], where among other results, the following was shown:

Theorem 1 ([30]). *The expressive power of disjunctive Datalog with stratified negation is characterised as follows:*

1. *Certain consequence under the SMS captures the complexity class Π_2^p. More precisely, every Boolean property π that can be evaluated in Π_2^p over finite structures (that is, databases) of a given signature σ can be translated into a program P and a ground fact γ such that over each database D of signature σ, γ is in all stable models of (P, D) iff π is true over D.*
2. *Stable-model existence captures the complexity class Σ_2^p. More precisely, every Boolean property π that can be evaluated in Σ_2^p over finite structures (that is,*

databases) of a given signature σ can be translated into an equivalent disjunctive Datalog program $Tr(\pi)$ such that for each database D having signature σ, $(Tr(\pi), D)$ has a stable model iff π is true over D. An analogous result holds for the problem of deciding if a given ground fact is contained in at least one stable model (brave reasoning) of a given disjunctive Datalog program.

These results gave insight into the types of algorithms best suited for reasoning in disjunctive Datalog under the SMS. Based on these initial insight, and on many further related results, a first version of the DLV disjunctive Datalog system [46] was implemented in the latte 1990s s at TU Vienna in an effort led by Nicola Leone. After Leone moved back to Italy in 2000, the DLV project was continued at the University of Calabria in Rende (Cosenza), where it is still ongoing. In 2005, the DLVSystem company[3] was founded by Leone and by several other DLV contributors. The company has since worked with many corporate customers and has very successfully solved important industrial problems in disparate areas such as workforce management, E-tourism, intelligent call routing (used by Telecom Italia), and E-medicine. For a brief survey, see [1].

Monadic Datalog over Trees, Web Data Extraction, and Lixto. Some relevant applications deal with finite structures, that correspond to trees. This is the case with *semi-structured* HTML or XML Web documents, whose dom-tree (parsetree) corresponds to unranked labelled trees, for example, trees over the signature $\tau_{ur} = \langle Dom^1, Root^1, Leaf^1, Child^2, Firstsibling^2, Nextsibling^2, Lastsibling^1, Label^1_1 \ldots, Label^1_k \rangle$, where the superscripts indicate the arity, and where the names of the relations are self-explanatory. The labels of the non-leaf nodes of an HTML dom-tree, for example, are standard HTML labels, and the leaves are labelled by letters of an alphanumeric alphabet, where a text string can be encoded as a chain of letter-labelled leaves connected via *Nextsibling*.

At TU Vienna, we investigated formalisms for Web data extraction (i.e., extracting specific and possibly compound relevant data records such as items and associated prices from websites) and XML querying. A first basic insight was that data extraction from tree-structured documents is a task, which can be essentially described by monadic second-order logic (MSO). Since MSO is not a practical language and has a high complexity, we looked for a simpler extraction language having the same expressive power. We identified monadic Datalog (where IDB predicates are restricted to be unary) as a good candidate, and analysed the complexity and expressive power of this language over trees [34–36]. Here, the "complexity of reasoning with monadic Datalog" refers to the complexity of the Atom Entailment Problem, and (in this case, equivalently) to the complexity of of computing the unique minimal model of (P, EDB), where P is a monadic Datalog program and D an EDB. The "expressive power" here designates the set of all decision problems π over finite structures over τ_{ur} that can be reduced to some monadic Datalog program P and ground fact γ such that for any database D over τ_{ur}, $(D^* \wedge P^*) \models \gamma$.

---

[3] https://www.dlvsystem.it/dlvsite/ retrieved 24 July 2022.

We obtained the following main results:

Theorem 2 ([35]). *Over signature* τ_{ur}, *reasoning with monadic Datalog has linear-time data complexity, and its combined complexity is* $O(size(P) \times size(D))$ *for program* P *and EDB* D.

Theorem 3 ([35]). *Over signature* τ_{ur}, *monadic Datalog is exactly as expressive as MSO and hence captures MSO.*

Similar results hold for monadic Datalog over structures of bounded treewidth [36].

Based on the above Theorems 2 and 3, at TU Vienna, we developed the *Lixto* system [9,33] for visual data extraction, in which our theoretical results are implemented in form of efficient concrete algorithms. This system allows a designer to develop a wrapper, that is, a data extraction program, by mainly visual and interactive operations performed on a sample document in a strongly supervised fashion. By successively clicking, unclicking and naming data fields, the rules of a wrapper, formulated as a logic program with extraction primitives are systematically generated, see [9] for details. The resulting wrapper is formulated in Elog [8], an extension of monadic Datalog. The Lixto sytem (originally presented at VLDB'01) was further developed by the Lixto spin-off company (www.lixto.com) and has been successfully used by the industry, especially in the domains of automotive supply, tourism, and business intelligence [10]. The Lixto company had about 20 employees and over 50 corporate customers, and was acquired in 2013 by McKinsey[4] where the software is now used and further developed as part of McKinsey's *Periscope* solution.

Datalog$^\pm$ and Fully Automated Web Data Extraction. The Lixto approach of supervised wrapper generation is well-suited for applications where data from one to several dozens websites need to be integrated. However, there are application domains, where data from several thousand websites is needed. It is impossible to manually generate and maintain wrappers for so many sites. The idea thus arose to create *knowledge-based* fully automated wrapper generators for areas such as real-estate or used cars, where the relevant information is spread over thousands of different websites. Towards this goal, we needed a powerful logical language for knowledge representation and reasoning (KRR). Such a language would be based on Datalog, but would also be able to perform *ontological reasoning tasks*, such as those featured by F-Logic Lite [20] or by the DL-Lite [21] or $\mathcal{EL}$ [4] families of description logics.

We observed that, while plain Datalog cannot express certain ontological reasoning tasks, such tasks can be expressed in *existential Datalog*, also referred to as "Datalog($\exists$)", that is, Datalog extended by the possibility of $\exists$-quantified variables in rule heads. For example the DL-Lite axiom *House* $\sqcap \neg IsolatedBuilding \sqsubseteq \exists Neighbour$ can be rephrased in existential Datalog with stratified negation as: $\exists y Neighbour(x,y) \text{:-} House(x) \wedge \neg IsolatedBuilding(x)$. Another reason for existential variables in rule heads is *name invention*. In automated web data extraction it is often necessary to combine multiple objects, to a single object. To name the new compound object, existential quantification can be used.

---

[4] https://mergr.com/mckinsey-acquires-lixto-software, accessed 25 July 2022.

The designated model of a Datalog($\exists$) program P with a database D may be infinite and can be obtained by taking D as starting interpretation and applying all rules as long as possible by a fair (breadth-first) algorithm called the (oblivious) Chase [18, 31, 42, 44]. Let I be an intermediately computed interpretation. For a rule *head:-body*, whenever $\theta(body) \subseteq I$ for a uniform variable-substitution θ, then $\theta^*(head)$ is added to I, where θ^* acts like θ on body-variables, and replaces each existentially quantified variable by a fresh Skolem constant (a.k.a. labelled null value). Each such rule is applied (or "fired") only once with a given substitution θ as above. The possibly infinite result is a universal model of $(P^* \cup D^*)$, see [31]. Existential Datalog rules are also known as *tuple-generating dependencies (TGDs)* which play an important role in database theory, and which have also been used for *data exchange* [31].

Unfortunately, for Datalog with existential quantification in rule heads, all relevant decision tasks, in particular, the Atom Entailment Problem (AEP), are undecidable, [11, 24]. An explicit undecidability proof for a very restricted case is given in [18].

From 2006 on, at Oxford, we have been investigating restricted versions of existential Datalog for which the AEP and the slightly more general Boolean conjunctive query answering problem are decidable. This has given raise to a the *Datalog*$^\pm$ family of languages, which contain one or more extensions of Datalog such as stratified negation, existential quantification in rule heads, and/or equality and/or the falsum "$\perp$" in rule heads, and, at the same time, syntactic restrictions, mostly on rule bodies, that guarantee decidability. The $+$ in the superscript in the term Datalog$^\pm$ symbolises the extension(s) and the "$-$" the restriction(s). In all these formalisms, it is no longer required that EDB relations cannot be changed by a program, thus, as with description logics, there is no longer any significant distinction between EDB and IDB relations. Two closely related Datalog$^\pm$ member formalisms are *guarded* and *weakly guarded* Datalog($\exists$). Guarded Datalog($\exists$) restricts existential Datalog by imposing the requirement that all rule bodies of a program contain a *guard*, that is, an atom whose arguments cover all variables of the rule body. Weakly guarded is similarly defined, but only the *harmful variables* need to be covered by the guard (in this case also called *weak guard*), which are those that occur only in *affected argument positions* of atoms. Affected positions are argument positions in a rule body that may potentially contain Skolem constants generated by the Chase (see [18] for details). Note that not all Datalog programs can be expressed in guarded Datalog($\exists$). On the other hand, weakly guarded Datalog($\exists$) contains plain Datalog, and is actually strictly more expressive (at least over arbitrary, non linearly ordered finite structures). Among several other results on (weak) guardedness, we proved the following:

Theorem 4 ([18, 19]). *The following complexity results hold:*

1. *For weakly guarded Datalog[$\exists$], the Atom Entailment Problem (AEP) and the problem of Boolean Conjunctive Query Answering (BCQA) are both 2-EXPTIME-complete in combined complexity and are both EXPTIME-*

*complete in data complexity (actually in both cases, when (i) the program
and the query are fixed, or when (ii) only the program is fixed).*

2. *For guarded Datalog[∃], the AEP is 2-EXPTIME-complete in combined complexity and polynomial in data complexity (in both cases, when (i) the program
and the goal atom γ are fixed, or when (ii) only the program is fixed).*

3. *For guarded Datalog[∃], the BCQA problem is in polynomial time when both
the program and the query Q are fixed, and is NP-complete when only the
program is fixed (and Q is thus part of the input).*

Each of the above formalisms can be extended by stratified negation without
augmenting the complexity [19,39]. For the expressive power, we could show the
following:

Theorem 5 ([39]). *Weakly guarded Datalog[∃] with stratified negation captures
EXPTIME.*

Note that instead of requiring that *all* body variables (harmful body variables) are covered by a guard (weak guard), one may just require that only those
variables be covered that also appear in the rule head. This gave rise to *frontier guarded (f.g.)* and *weakly frontier guarded (w.f.g.)* rules, respectively [5,6].
The expressive power of w.f.g. Datalog[∃] is equal to the one of weakly guarded
Datalog[∃] [39]. However, f.g. Datalog[∃] is slightly more expressive than guarded
Datalog[∃]; the difference is discussed in [38].

Based on the theoretical framework of Datalog$^\pm$, in the context of the
ERC Advanced Grant[5] "DIADEM: Domain-centric Intelligent Automated Data
Extraction Methodology" the DIADEM knowledge-based system for Web data
extraction was developed at Oxford University during the years 2010–2015. DIA-
DEM fully automatically navigates thousands of sites from a given application
domain ('vertical') and extracts the relevant data from that domain. A major
team effort was necessary to design and build such a system, and the Author was
happy to obtain significant funding from the ERC and other sources to be able to
build a very strong team of post-doctoral researchers and doctoral students. we
succeeded to design a system that extracts data with extremely high accuracy
from tens of thousands of websites in verticals such as real estate, used cars,
consumer electronics, restaurant locations, jobs, and so on. In order to transfer the new technology to the commercial world, we founded, jointly with the
University of Oxford, the *Wrapidity* spin-out in 2015. Wrapidity was acquired
in 2016 by Meltwater[6], a media intelligence corporation, where the DIADEM
technology has since been intensively used and further improved for extracting
massive amounts of news articles and company data from the Web.

Warded Datalog[∃] and Vadalog for Reasoning in Knowledge Graphs.
Guarded Datalog[∃] is tractable but its expressive power does not cover plain
Datalog. For example, a simple natural join $S = R \bowtie S$ between two binary rela-
tions R and S having respective schemata (A, B) and (B, C) can be expressed

---

[5] https://cordis.europa.eu/project/id/246858 accessed 28 July 2022.
[6] https://www.meltwater.com/en/about/press-releases/meltwater-acquires-oxford-
university-data-extraction-spinout-wrapidity accessed 28 July 2022.

in plain Datalog as $S(X, Y, Z) : -R(X, Y), S(Y, Z)$. This fundamental database operation cannot be expressed by guarded Datalog[∃], not even in case R and S are simple "input" data relations that do not contain Skolem terms and that are never changed by the Datalog[∃] program. Thus, while guarded Datalog[∃] is well-suited for ontological reasoning, it is not suited for performing standard database operations on input relations. Weakly guarded Datalog[∃] can do both. However reasoning with this language is EXPTIME complete in data complexity, which is not suited for dealing with Big Data and large knowledge graphs. We were thus looking for a Datalog$^\pm$ language whose logical core (i) can express DL-Lite, and similar languages and is thus suited for ontological reasoning, (ii) extends plain Datalog, and (iii) has tractable data complexity for relevant reasoning tasks such as AEP and BCQA.

In [17,37] the notion of *ward* and of *warded* Datalog$^\pm$ was defined. Briefly, a ward A is a rule body atom such that (i) A covers all *dangerous* variables, i.e. those body variables that occur only in affected positions and also occur in the head, and (ii) all variables shared between A and the rest of the rule body occur in at least one unaffected body position. A rule is warded if either it has a ward or its body is empty (which stands for "true"). A Datalog$^\pm$ program is warded if each of its rule is warded. Trivially, by this definition, warded Datalog[∃] contains plain Datalog as a sub-language because a plain Datalog rule contains no affected position, hence, each body atom of a plain Datalog rule is a ward. As a further sub-language of warded Datalog[∃], we considered *piecewise linear warded Datalog[∃]*, where, in addition to the wardedness condition, it is required that each rule body contains at most one atom whose predicate is mutually recursive with a predicate in the head. Among other results on warded Datalog[∃], we proved:

Theorem 6 ([17,37]). *The following complexity results hold for warded Datalog[∃]:*

1. *The Atom Entailment Problem (AEP) and the problem of Boolean Conjunctive Query Answering (BCQA) are both EXPTIME-complete in combined complexity.*
2. *The AEP is PTIME-complete in data complexity.*
3. *The BCQA problem is PTIME-complete when both the program and the query Q are fixed, and is NP-complete when only the program is fixed (and Q is thus part of the input).*
4. *When restricted to the subclass of piece-wise linear warded Datalog[∃], the above EXPTIME-complete problems are PSPACE complete, and the above PTIME-complete problems are NLOGSPACE complete. The case when only the program is fixed remains NP-complete.*

In the context of the project "VADA: Value Added Data Systems – Principles and Architecture"[7], we designed and implemented the VADALOG system [15–17] with efficient algorithms for reasoning over knowledge graphs— [12] and

---

[7] https://gow.epsrc.ukri.org/NGBOViewGrant.aspx?GrantRef=EP/M025268/1 accessed 20 July 2022.

various types of databases, especially relational and graph databases. The main language is Vadalog which extends warded Datalog[∃] by various useful features including stratified negation, database access primitives, APIs to machine learning packages and other external systems, and (monotonic) aggregate functions.

Different versions of the Vadalog system have been further maintained and used for many applications (see, e.g., [13,14,25] both in the context of the VADA academic research project at Oxford, and by the DeepReason.ai spin-out, which was founded in 2018.

After Meltwater acquired the Owler[8] company, in the context of a proof-of-concept project, DeepReason.ai was given a chance to apply Vadalog to the Owler knowledge graph, which is one of the world's largest repository containing data about companies and competitor relationships. We showed that by using rule-based knowledge, it is possible to significantly enrich and improve crowd-generated knowledge bases such as Owler, for example, by using rules for finding new competitor pairs from existing ones, for completing missing size and revenue data of companies, or for detecting "data smells", i.e., implausible data. Our results were convincing, to the point that Meltwater acquired DeepReason.ai in 2021[9].

Acknowledgment. Georg Gottlob is a Royal Society Research Professor and acknowledges support by the Royal Society in this role through the "RAISON DATA" project (Reference No. RP\R1\201074).

References

1. Adrian, W.T., et al.: The ASP system DLV: advancements and applications. KI-Künstliche Intelligenz **32**(2), 177–179 (2018)
2. Afrati, F., Papadimitriou, C., Papageorgiou, G., Roussou, A., Sagiv, Y., Ullman, J.D.: Convergence of sideways query evaluation. In: Proceedings of the Fifth ACM SIGACT-SIGMOD Symposium on Principles of Database Systems, pp. 24–30 (1985)
3. Apt, K.R., Blair, H.A., Walker, A.: Towards a theory of declarative knowledge. In: Foundations of Deductive Databases and Logic Programming, pp. 89–148. Elsevier (1988)
4. Baader, F., Brandt, S., Lutz, C.: Pushing the el envelope. In: IJCAI, vol. 5, pp. 364–369 (2005)
5. Baget, J.F., Leclère, M., Mugnier, M.L.: Walking the decidability line for rules with existential variables. KR **10**, 466–476 (2010)
6. Baget, J.F., Leclère, M., Mugnier, M.L., Salvat, E.: Extending decidable cases for rules with existential variables. In: Twenty-First International Joint Conference on Artificial Intelligence (2009)

---

[8] See www.owler.com and https://en.wikipedia.org/wiki/Owler, both accessed 29 July 2022.

[9] https://www.meltwater.com/en/about/press-releases/meltwater-acquires-deepreason-ai.

7. Bancilhon, F., Maier, D., Sagiv, Y., Ullman, J.D.: Magic sets and other strange ways to implement logic programs. In: Proceedings of the Fifth ACM SIGACT-SIGMOD Symposium on Principles of Database Systems, pp. 1–15 (1985)
8. Baumgartner, R., Flesca, S., Gottlob, G.: The Elog web extraction language. In: Nieuwenhuis, R., Voronkov, A. (eds.) LPAR 2001. LNCS (LNAI), vol. 2250, pp. 548–560. Springer, Heidelberg (2001). https://doi.org/10.1007/3-540-45653-8_38
9. Baumgartner, R., Flesca, S., Gottlob, G.: Visual web information extraction with lixto. In: VLDB - International Conference on Very Large Data Bases, pp. 119–128. Morgan Kaufmann (2001)
10. Baumgartner, R., Gottlob, G., Herzog, M.: Scalable web data extraction for online market intelligence. Proc. VLDB Endowment (PVLDB) **2**(2), 1512–1523 (2009)
11. Beeri, C., Vardi, M.Y.: The implication problem for data dependencies. In: Even, S., Kariv, O. (eds.) ICALP 1981. LNCS, vol. 115, pp. 73–85. Springer, Heidelberg (1981). https://doi.org/10.1007/3-540-10843-2_7
12. Bellomarini, L., Benedetto, D., Gottlob, G., Sallinger, E.: Vadalog: a modern architecture for automated reasoning with large knowledge graphs. Inf. Syst. **105**, 101528 (2020)
13. Bellomarini, L., Blasi, L., Laurendi, R., Sallinger, E.: Financial data exchange with statistical confidentiality: a reasoning-based approach. In: Velegrakis, Y., Zeinalipour-Yazti, D., Chrysanthis, P.K., Guerra, F. (eds.) Proceedings of the 24th International Conference on Extending Database Technology, EDBT 2021, Nicosia, Cyprus, 23–26 March 2021, pp. 558–569. OpenProceedings.org (2021). https://doi.org/10.5441/002/edbt.2021.66
14. Bellomarini, L., et al.: Data science with Vadalog: knowledge graphs with machine learning and reasoning in practice. Futur. Gener. Comput. Syst. **129**, 407–422 (2022)
15. Bellomarini, L., Gottlob, G., Pieris, A., Sallinger, E.: Swift logic for big data and knowledge graphs (invited paper). In: IJCAI - International Conference on Artificial Intelligence, pp. 2–10. ijcai.org (2017)
16. Bellomarini, L., Sallinger, E., Gottlob, G.: The Vadalog system: datalog-based reasoning for knowledge graphs. Proc. VLDB Endowment (PVLDB) **11**(9), 975–987 (2018)
17. Berger, G., Gottlob, G., Pieris, A., Sallinger, E.: The space-efficient core of Vadalog. In: PODS:ACM Symposium on Principles of Database Systems, pp. 270–284. ACM (2019)
18. Calì, A., Gottlob, G., Kifer, M.: Taming the infinite chase: query answering under expressive relational constraints. J. Artif. Intell. Res. (JAIR) **48**, 115–174 (2013)
19. Calì, A., Gottlob, G., Lukasiewicz, T.: A general datalog-based framework for tractable query answering over ontologies. J. Web Semant. **14**, 57–83 (2012)
20. Calì, A., Kifer, M.: Containment of conjunctive object meta-queries. In: Proceedings of VLDB, pp. 942–952. Citeseer (2006)
21. Calvanese, D., De Giacomo, G., Lembo, D., Lenzerini, M., Rosati, R.: Tractable reasoning and efficient query answering in description logics: the dl-lite family. J. Autom. Reason. **39**(3), 385–429 (2007). https://doi.org/10.1007/s10817-007-9078-x
22. Ceri, S., Gottlob, G., Tanca, L.: What you always wanted to know about datalog (and never dared to ask). IEEE Trans. Knowl. Data Eng. **1**(1), 146–166 (1989)
23. Ceri, S., Gottlob, G., Tanca, L.: Logic Programming and Databases (Surveys in Computer Science). Springer, Cham (1990)
24. Chandra, A.K., Lewis, H.R., Makowsky, J.A.: Embedded implicational dependencies and their inference problem. In: Proceedings of the Thirteenth Annual ACM Symposium on Theory of Computing, pp. 342–354 (1981)

25. Clearman, J., et al.: Feature engineering and explainability with Vadalog: a recommender systems application. In: Datalog, pp. 39–43 (2019)

26. Dantsin, E., Gottlob, T.E.G., Voronkov, A.: Complexity and expressive power of logic programming. ACM Comput. Surv. **33**(3), 374–425 (2001)

27. Eiter, T., Gottlob, G.: Complexity aspects of various semantics for disjunctive databases. In: PODS - ACM Symposium on Principles of Database Systems, pp. 158–167. ACM Press (1993)

28. Eiter, T., Gottlob, G.: Complexity results for disjunctive logic programming and application to nonmonotonic logics. In: ILPS - International Symposium on Logic Programming, pp. 266–278. MIT Press (1993)

29. Eiter, T., Gottlob, G.: On the computational cost of disjunctive logic programming: propositional case. Ann. Math. Artif. Intell. **15**(3–4), 289–323 (1995). https://doi.org/10.1007/BF01536399

30. Eiter, T., Gottlob, G., Mannila, H.: Disjunctive datalog. ACM Trans. Database Syst. (TODS) **22**(3), 364–418 (1997)

31. Fagin, R., Kolaitis, P.G., Miller, R.J., Popa, L.: Data exchange: semantics and query answering. Theoret. Comput. Sci. **336**(1), 89–124 (2005)

32. Gelfond, M., Lifschitz, V.: The stable model semantics for logic programming. In: Proceedings of ICLP/SLP, pp. 1070–1080 (1988)

33. Gottlob, G., Koch, C., Baumgartner, R., Herzog, M., Flesca, S.: The lixto data extraction project - back and forth between theory and practice (invited paper). In: PODS - ACM Symposium on Principles of Database Systems, pp. 1–12. ACM (2004)

34. Gottlob, G., Koch, C.: Monadic queries over tree-structured data. In: LICS - ACM/IEEE Symposium on Logic in Computer Science, pp. 189–202. IEEE Computer Society (2002)

35. Gottlob, G., Koch, C.: Monadic datalog and the expressive power of languages for web information extraction. J. ACM (JACM) **51**(1), 74–113 (2004)

36. Gottlob, G., Pichler, R., Wei, F.: Monadic datalog over finite structures of bounded treewidth. ACM Trans. Comput. Logic (TOCL) **12**(1), 1–48 (2010)

37. Gottlob, G., Pieris, A.: Beyond SPARQL under OWL 2 QL entailment regime: rules to the rescue. In: Twenty-Fourth International Joint Conference on Artificial Intelligence (2015)

38. Gottlob, G., Pieris, A., Simkus, M.: The impact of active domain predicates on guarded existential rules. Fundam. Informaticae **159**(1–2), 123–146 (2018). https://doi.org/10.3233/FI-2018-1660

39. Gottlob, G., Rudolph, S., Simkus, M.: Expressiveness of guarded existential rule languages. In: Hull, R., Grohe, M. (eds.) Proceedings of the 33rd ACM SIGMOD-SIGACT-SIGART Symposium on Principles of Database Systems, PODS 2014, Snowbird, UT, USA, 22–27 June 2014, pp. 27–38. ACM (2014). https://doi.org/10.1145/2594538.2594556

40. Grädel, E.: Capturing complexity classes by fragments of second-order logic. Theoret. Comput. Sci. **101**(1), 35–57 (1992)

41. Immerman, N.: Relational queries computable in polynomial time (extended abstract). In: Proceedings of STOC 1982, San Francisco, CA, USA, 5–7 May 1982, pp. 147–152. ACM (1982). https://doi.org/10.1145/800070.802187

42. Johnson, D.S., Klug, A.: Testing containment of conjunctive queries under functional and inclusion dependencies. J. Comput. Syst. Sci. **28**(1), 167–189 (1984)

43. Lobo, J., Minker, J., Rajasekar, A.: Foundations of Disjunctive Logic Programming. MIT press, Cambridge (1992)

44. Maier, D., Mendelzon, A.O., Sagiv, Y.: Testing implications of data dependencies. ACM Trans. Database Syst. (TODS) **4**(4), 455–469 (1979)
45. Minker, J., Seipel, D.: Disjunctive logic programming: a survey and assessment. In: Kakas, A.C., Sadri, F. (eds.) Computational Logic: Logic Programming and Beyond. LNCS (LNAI), vol. 2407, pp. 472–511. Springer, Heidelberg (2002). https://doi.org/10.1007/3-540-45628-7_18
46. Leone, N., et al.: The DLV system for knowledge representation and reasoning. ACM Trans. Comput. Logic (TOCL) **7**(3), 499–562 (2006)
47. Przymusinski, T.C.: Stable semantics for disjunctive programs. N. Gener. Comput. **9**(3), 401–424 (1991). https://doi.org/10.1007/BF03037171
48. Van Gelder, A., Ross, K.A., Schlipf, J.S.: The well-founded semantics for general logic programs. J. ACM (JACM) **38**(3), 619–649 (1991)
49. Vardi, M.Y.: The complexity of relational query languages. In: Proceedings of STOC, pp. 137–146 (1982)

Author Index

A. Dovier et al. (Eds.): AIxIA 2022, LNAI 13796, pp. 501–502, 2023.
https://doi.org/10.1007/978-3-031-27181-6

Printed in the United States
by Baker & Taylor Publisher Services